REVIEWS AND TESTIMONIALS

"Ever wish you had a residential code expert on staff when working with local building officials and inspectors? Now you can. "Everybody's Building Code" is your project reference. Its complete Table of Contents and Index make searching for relevant code sections quick and easy. Each chapter provides definitions of complex terminology and Best Practices. Clear and easy to use charts and tables are provided through out. Use this book for a few days and you'll wonder how you ever got along without it."

Paul Finley, Construction Manager
Habitat for Humanity of the Jacksonville Beaches

"Is your project up to code? Would you know if it wasn't? Well, get a copy of Everybody's Building Code, and you'll have a quick reference to hold yourself---and your contractors---accountable to the International Residential Building Code. The book uses straightforward language and plenty of illustrations to help you understand how to apply the building code to all of your home improvements."

Workbench Magazine Product Showcase
p. 90, December 2008

A thorough reference guide that explains code requirements for residential buildings, top to bottom. Barker, licensed contractor and president of a building inspection and consulting firm, has compiled complete summary and explanation of the international residential code, or IRC. This book is not a how-to manual for residential construction, though Barker does provide brief tips on locating a qualified contractor. Designed to supplement the IRC as an easy reference for contractors, inspectors and real estate agents, the book examines each aspect of the IRC in clear detail. Barker ably addresses each topic and provides a glossary, photographs, tables and labeled diagrams to supplement the material. The guide covers the requirements for a residential building from bottom to top, including material requirements for a foundation; interior and exterior wall construction; roof and ceiling requirements; energy efficiency; and plumbing and electrical. Drawing on his experience in the building trades, Barker stresses topics that he considers to be of great importance, such as flashing. Additional topics such as radon, broadband wiring and manufactured homes appear in the appendix. Designed to allow quick reference, this manual includes a table of contents that is a complete outline of the chapters and subsections, as well as an index and a global glossary that defines building materials and parts from baluster to rabbet as a supplement to the topic glossaries. The writing is straightforward and concise without embellishment; instructions are precise and the reader is referred to the local code when necessary. Barker provides example calculations for many operations to ease the transfer of information from words to practicality. An easy-to-follow, complete reference recommended for anyone involved in the construction or remodeling of residential buildings.

Kirkus Discoveries

"Our society has many outstanding home inspectors, but few who are talented and generous enough to write articles that add to the body of knowledge for their fellow inspectors. Bruce Barker is a much appreciated member of this select group. His well-crafted articles have been a welcomed addition to ASHI's publications for years."

**Sandy Bourseau, Director of Communications,
American Society of Home Inspectors**

"If you want to do it yourself, you want to do it right. You don't want a code violation to cause you a problem when you're trying to resell, and you certainly don't want to make a mistake that will result in something unsafe or dangerous. So, how do you find out what is right?

In my experience, there are two problems with most building codes. Finding the relevant rules using the code's limited table of contents and skimpy index is one problem. Understanding the rules in the maze of tables, footnotes, and legalese is the other problem. This author has solved both problems. Between the table of contents and the index, it is relatively easy to find what you need. Once you've found the right section, the clear writing, the liberal use of examples, and numerous pictures and illustrations help you understand the code.

After looking up a little about the author's experience, I decided that this book belonged in my collection. He has the experience, and he explains the material clearly. Now I have a reference that I can use in two ways: 1) when I need to find out about a provision in the code, I use the table of contents to find the relevant section. 2) when I need to work on something specific, electrical, for instance, I use the index to guide me to the right place."

Harris Mateides, Homeowner

EVERYBODY'S BUILDING CODE

EVERYBODY'S BUILDING CODE

BRUCE A. BARKER

Everybody's Building Code

Copyright © 2010 by Dream Home Consultants, LLC. All rights reserved. No part of this book may be reproduced or retransmitted in any form or by any means without the written permission of the author.

Published by Wheatmark®
610 East Delano Street, Suite 104, Tucson, Arizona 85705 U. S. A.
(888) 934-0888 ext. 3
www.wheatmark.com

Publisher's Cataloging-in-Publication Data
Bruce A. Barker
  Everybody's building code / Bruce A. Barker

  Includes bibliographical references and index.
  ISBN: 978-1-60494-310-8

1. Housing—Standards--Popular works. 2. Building laws--Popular works. 3. Dwellings--Design and construction--Standards--Popular works. I. Title.

TH4815.5 .B37 2009
690/.837/0218   2009929262

rev201101

Bruce A. Barker is a building inspector, consultant, and contractor in Phoenix, Arizona. He has over twenty-three years experience in residential construction.

DISCLAIMER OF LIABILITY

Every effort has been made to ensure the accuracy of the material contained in this book. The author and publisher assume no liability whatsoever for any loss or damages caused by the use or interpretation of the material in this book. The author and publisher fully disclaim liability to any and all parties for any and all losses or damages including, but not limited to, losses or damages caused by deficiencies, errors, or omissions contained in this book and regardless of whether such deficiencies, errors, or omissions result from negligence, accident, or any other cause or theory. The author and publisher recommend that the reader consult the local building official and qualified professionals before and during all construction projects.

Acknowledgements

SOURCE MATERIAL

International Residential Code® 2009
International Code Council®, Inc

National Electrical Code® 2005
National Fire Protection Association

Dictionary of Architecture and Construction, Fourth Edition
Cyril M. Harris

PRODUCTION

Patricia Barker

BOOK DESIGN

Lori Sellstrom

ILLUSTRATIONS

Preliminary drawings by Shon Quannie, Designer, 4X Studio

Final drawings by Bruce A. Barker

Ejector Pump Diagram
Courtesy of Little Giant Pump Company Division of Franklin Electric

PHOTOGRAPHS

Bruce A. Barker

Furnace and Heater Photographs
Courtesy of Louisville Tin & Stove Co., Inc. (Cozy Heaters)

Contents

ACKNOWLEDGEMENTS viii

PREFACE li

PREFACE FOR HOME INSPECTORS lii

INTRODUCTION TO BUILDING CODES liii

The International Residential Code®
State and Local Building Codes
Local Code Amendments
Other Building Codes
Building Departments
Working with Government Building Inspectors
Working with Private Building Inspectors
Zoning Ordinances
Selecting a Qualified Contractor

CHAPTER 1: BUILDING PERMITS AND CODE ADMINISTRATION 1

BUILDINGS GOVERNED BY THE IRC (R101.2) 1

MANUFACTURER'S INSTRUCTIONS (R102.4) 1

Priority of Manufacturer's Instructions
Manufacturer's Instructions Discussion

BUILDING PERMITS (R105) 2

Local Regulations and Customs for Building Permits
When a Building Permit May be Required
When a Building Permit May Not be Required
Building Permit for Routine Maintenance
Building Permit Expiration
Building Permit Discussion

INSPECTIONS (R109) 4

Inspection General Requirements
Footing Inspections
Foundation Wall Inspections
Foundation Slab Inspections
Plumbing, HVAC, and Electrical Rough-in Inspections
Framing Inspection
Final Inspection
Other Inspections

CERTIFICATE OF OCCUPANCY (R110) 5

Certificate of Occupancy Required
Waiver of Code Violations

CHAPTER 2: DEFINITIONS ... 6

CHAPTER 3: BUILDING DESIGN AND SAFETY ... 12

SEISMIC AND WIND DESIGN AREAS (R301) ... 12
Seismic Design Areas
High Wind Design Areas
Wind Exposure Categories

DEFLECTION (BENDING) OF STRUCTURAL COMPONENTS (R301.7) ... 13
Limitations of the Material in this Section
Deflection and Loads Definitions
Deflection Under Live Load
Deflection Discussion

FIRE SEPARATION BETWEEN BUILDINGS (R302.1) ... 14
Fire Separation Distance Definition
Exterior Walls Near Fire Separation Line
Exterior Projections Near Fire Separation Line
Penetrations in Fire-Resistive Walls
Fire Separation Requirements Exceptions
Fire Separation Discussion

TOWNHOUSES (R302.2) ... 17
Townhouse Construction
Parapet Wall Construction

TWO-FAMILY DWELLINGS (R302.3) ... 18
Fire Separation of Two-Family Dwelling Units in One Building

PENETRATIONS IN FIRE-RESISTIVE WALLS AND CEILINGS (R302.4) ... 19
Summary of Penetration Requirements

FIRE SEPARATION BETWEEN GARAGE AND HOME (R302.5 AND R302.6) ... 19
Fire Separation Doors from Garage into Home
Fire Separation Walls and Ceilings Between Attached Garage and Home
HVAC Ducts in a Garage
Garage and Carport Floors (R309)
Fire Separation Between Detached Garage and Home (R302.6)

FIREBLOCKING (R302.11) ... 21
Fireblocking Definition
Where Fireblocking is Required
Fireblocking Materials and Installation

DRAFTSTOPPING (R302.12) ... 23
Draftstopping Definition
Where Draftstopping is Required
Draftstopping Materials and Installation

INSULATION CLEARANCE TO HEAT-PRODUCING DEVICES (R302.13) ... 24

Insulation Clearance Requirements
Insulation Clearance Discussion

HABITABLE ROOMS LIGHT AND VENTILATION (R303) 24
Habitable Rooms Definition
Habitable Rooms Light and Ventilation

BATHROOM LIGHT AND VENTILATION (R303.3) 25
Bathroom Light and Ventilation
Bathroom Ventilation Best Practice

OUTDOOR AIR INTAKE AND EXHAUST OPENINGS (R303.4) 26
Outdoor Air Intake Openings
Outdoor Exhaust Openings
Intake and Exhaust Opening Screens
Outdoor Air Intake Discussion

STAIRWAY LIGHTING (R303.6) 28
Interior Stairway Light Locations
Exterior Stairway Light Locations
Stairway Light Switching

ROOM SIZE AND CEILING HEIGHT REQUIREMENTS (R304 and R305) 29
Habitable Rooms Dimensions (R304)
Ceiling Height (R305.1)
Ceiling Height in Basements (R305.1.1)
Sloped Ceilings in Habitable Rooms (R305.1)
Sloped Ceilings in Bathrooms (R305.1)

PLUMBING FIXTURE MINIMUM CLEARANCES AND REQUIREMENTS (R306, 307) 30
Required Plumbing Fixtures (R306)
Bathroom Plumbing Fixture Clearances to Obstructions (R307 and P2705)
Shower Wall Coverings (R307)

SAFETY GLAZING (R308) 31
Safety Glazing Labeling
Safety Glazing in Doors
Safety Glazing Near Doors
Safety Glazing in Large Windows and Doors
Safety Glazing Near Bathing and Swimming Areas
Safety Glazing Near Stairs
Mounted Glazing Exception
Glass Block Exception

SKYLIGHTS AND SLOPED GLAZING (R308.6) 38
Sloped Glazing Definition
Sloped Glazing Materials
Sloped Glass Retaining Screens
Skylight Curbs

Glazing in Greenhouses

EMERGENCY ESCAPE OPENINGS (R310 and R311) 39
Escape Opening Locations and General Requirements
Escape Opening Size
Escape Opening Obstructions
Window Wells for Below Grade Escape Openings
Escape Openings Discussion

EXTERIOR DOORS (R311.1 – R311.3) 41
Egress Door Definition
Egress Door Requirements
Exterior Door Landing Requirements

HALLWAYS (R311.6) 43
Hallway Dimensions

STAIRWAYS (R311.7) 43
Stairway Definitions
Width
Headroom Height
Riser Height
Tread Depth
Tread Nosing
Tread Slope
Landings
Winder Stair Treads
Spiral Stairs
Stairway Live Loads (R301.5)

HANDRAILS (R311.7.7) 48
Location
Height
Continuity
Shape
Handrail Live Loads (R301.5)
Handrail Best Practice

RAMPS (R311.8) 49
Ramp Definition
Slope
Landings
Handrail Requirements

GUARDS (R312) 50
Guards Definition
Location
Height
Continuity

Openings
Guard Live Loads (R301.5)

FIRE SPRINKLER SYSTEMS (R313) 52

SMOKE AND CARBON MONOXIDE ALARMS (R314 and R315) 52
Smoke Alarm Required Locations
Smoke Alarm Locations Not Required
Smoke Alarm Power Source
Smoke Alarm Installation
Smoke Alarm Update when Remodeling
Carbon Monoxide Alarm Requirements
Alarms Discussion
Alarms Best Practice

FOAM PLASTIC INSULATION AND TRIM (R316) 55
Foam Plastic Products Definition
Foam Plastic Burning Limitations
Foam Plastic Separation from Building
Foam Plastic Separation from Building Exceptions
Foam Plastic Sheet Insulation as Foundation Insulation (R321.5)

WOOD ON CONCRETE AND MASONRY, WOOD IN THE GROUND, WOOD EXPOSED TO THE WEATHER (R317). 56
Treated and Decay Resistant Wood Definitions
Wood Decay Protection General Requirements
Wood in Contact with the Ground
Joists, Trusses, and Beams in Crawl Spaces
Sills and Sleepers on Concrete and Masonry
Beams and Girders in Concrete and Masonry Wall Pockets
Exterior Wood Siding, Sheathing, and Framing Near the Ground
Wood Attached to Concrete and Masonry Basement Walls
Wood Posts Encased in Concrete
Wood Posts Not Encased in Concrete
Exterior Decks and Balconies
Fasteners for Treated Wood
Treated Wood Cuts, Notches, and Holes (R317.1.1)
Exposed Glued-Laminated Timbers
Wood Decay Protection Best Practice

TERMITE PROTECTION (R318). 60

SITE ADDRESS (R319) 60

ACCESSIBILITY (R320) 60

FLOOD-RESISTANT CONSTRUCTION (R322) 60

CHAPTER 4: FOUNDATION CONSTRUCTION 61

EXTERIOR SURFACE DRAINAGE AND GUTTERS (R401.3 and R801.3) 61
Drainage Near Home (R401.3)
Gutters (R801.3)
Water Control Discussion
Water Control Best Practice

CONCRETE STRENGTH (R402.2). 62
Concrete in Foundation Walls and Footings Not Exposed to Weather
Concrete in Basement Slabs and Interior Slabs-on-Grade (Not Garage Floors)
Concrete in Foundation Walls, Exterior Walls, and Other Vertical Concrete Exposed to Weather
Concrete in Porches, Garage and Carport Floors, and Other Horizontal Concrete Exposed to Weather
Concrete Installation Best Practice

FOOTINGS (R403) 63
Soil Load Bearing Capacities (R401.1)
Footing Width
Footing Thickness and Slope
Foundation Anchors
Building Setbacks from Slopes General Requirements
Building Setback from Ascending Slopes
Building Setback from Descending Slopes
Level Site Foundation Height Above Street
Footing and Anchorage Requirements in Seismic and High Wind Areas

FOUNDATION AND RETAINING WALLS (R404.5). 68
Limitations of the Material in this Section
Retaining Walls
Retaining Walls Best Practice

FOUNDATION DRAINS AND DAMPPROOFING (R405 AND R406). 68
Dampproofing and Waterproofing Definitions
Foundation Drains (Footing Drains)
Dampproofing Masonry and Concrete Foundation Walls
Waterproofing Masonry and Concrete Foundation Walls
Waterproofing Discussion
Waterproofing Best Practice

CRAWL SPACES (R408) 70
Crawl Space Ventilated to Exterior
Unventilated Crawl Space
Crawl Space Access
Crawl Space Cleaning
Crawl Space Water Drainage
Crawl Space Discussion

Crawl Space Best Practice

CHAPTER 5: FLOOR CONSTRUCTION..73

APPLICATION OF THE MATERIAL IN THIS CHAPTER....................73

DECKS (R502.2.2)..73
Deck Attachment to the Building General Requirements
Deck Attachment to the Building
Deck Attachment Using Screws or Bolts

WOOD FLOOR JOIST SPANS (R502.3)..76
Floor Joist Span Tables

WOOD HEADER AND GIRDER SPANS (R502.5).............................79
Header and Girder Definitions
Header and Girder Spans

WOOD FLOOR FRAMING (R502)..80
Cantilever Definitions
Cantilevered Floor Joist (R502.3.3)
Floor Joists Under Load-Bearing Walls (R502.4)
Header, Girder, and Floor Joist Bearing on Supports (R502.6)
Floor Joist Lap at Supports (R502.6.1)
Floor Joist Attachment to Beams (R502.6.2)
Floor Joist Blocking (R502.7)
Floor Joist Bridging (R502.7.1)

WOOD FLOOR JOIST AND TRUSS BORING AND NOTCHING (R502.8).............88
Boring and Notching Definitions
Wood Floor Joist Notching
Wood Floor Joist Boring
Wood I-Beam Floor Truss Notching and Boring
Wood Web Floor Truss Notching and Boring
Engineered Wood Notching and Boring
Joist and Truss Notching and Boring Best Practice

FLOOR JOIST OPENINGS (R502.10)..90
Floor Joist Opening Description
Openings Not More than (≤) Four Feet Wide
Openings More than (>) Four Feet Wide

WOOD STRUCTURAL PANEL SHEATHING (R503.2)........................91
Limitations of the Material in this Section
Wood Structural Panel Definitions
Wood Structural Panel Installation Requirements
Wood Structural Panels Used as Roof Sheathing
Wood Structural Panels Used as Combination Subflooring
Wood Structural Panel Installation Best Practice

CONCRETE SLAB-ON-GRADE FLOORS (R506) 94

Concrete Thickness and Strength
Site Preparation

CHAPTER 6: WALL CONSTRUCTION 95

VAPOR RETARDERS (R601.3) 95

WOOD NAILING SCHEDULE (R602.3) 95

Limitations of the Material in this Section
Wood Nailing Definitions
Wood Nailing General Installation Requirements
Wood Nailing to Framing Materials
Nailing Discussion
Nailing Best Practice

WALL HEIGHT AND STUD SPACING (R602.3.1) 99

Limitations of the Material in this Section
Wood Grades Used in Wall Construction
Stud Size and Spacing for Load-Bearing Walls Not More than (≤) Ten Feet Tall
Stud Size and Spacing for Non-Load-Bearing Walls
Lumber Size and Spacing for Walls More than (>) Ten Feet Tall
Lumber Size and Spacing for Interior Non-Load-Bearing Walls

SILL, SOLE, AND TOP PLATES (R602.3.2 AND R602.3.4) 103

Top Plate Construction
Bottom Plate Construction

WOOD STUD AND PLATE BORING AND NOTCHING (R602.6) 103

Boring and Notching Definitions
Wood Stud Notching
Wood Stud Boring
Wood Top Plate Notching
Wall Construction Best Practice

CRIPPLE WALLS (R602.9) 105

Cripple Wall Definition
Cripple Wall Requirements

WALL BRACING (R602.10) 106

Limitations of the Material in this Section
Wall Brace and Braced Wall Definitions
Wall Bracing Method Selection Criteria
Wall Bracing General Installation Requirements
Let-in Wall Bracing
Wood Structural Panel Wall Bracing
Hardboard Panel Siding Wall Bracing
Garage Door Header Wall Bracing
Large Window and Door Header Wall Bracing

Wall Bracing Discussion

MASONRY WALLS ABOVE GRADE (R606, R607, R608) 115
Limitations of the Material in this Section
Block Wall Thickness (R606.2.1)
Block Wall Thickness Change (R606.2.3)
Block Parapet Walls (R606.2.4)
Block Wall (Masonry) Support (R606.4)
Block Piers (R606.6)
Block Wall Chases (R606.7)
Block Wall Lateral Support Type and Spacing (R606.9)
Block Wall Horizontal Support Installation (R606.9.1)
Block Wall Vertical Support Installation (R606.9.2)
Block Wall Openings (R606.10)
Block Wall Reinforcing Materials Protection (R606.13)
Block Wall Mortar (R607.1)
Block Wall Mortar Joints (R607.2)
Block Wall Ties (R607.3)
Bonding Multiple Wythes with Wall Ties (R608.1.2.1)
Bonding Multiple Wythes with Adjustable Wall Ties (R608.1.2.2)
Bonding Multiple Wythes with a Stone Veneer Wythe (R608.1.3.2)

GLASS BLOCK WALLS (R610). 120
Glass Block Size
Exterior Glass Block Wall Size
Interior Glass Block Wall Size
Glass Block Wall Structural Support
Glass Block Wall Anchors and Restraints
Glass Block Wall Horizontal Reinforcement
Glass Block Wall Expansion Joints
Glass Block Wall Sills
Glass Block Mortar Joints

WINDOW AND GLASS DOOR INSTALLATION (R613). 122
Flashing and Installation General Requirements
Windows Six Feet Above Adjacent Surface
Attaching Windows and Glass Doors to the Structure

CHAPTER 7: INTERIOR AND EXTERIOR WALL COVERING 124

DRYWALL (GYPSUM BOARD) INTERIOR APPLICATION (R702.3 AND R702.4) 124
Limitations of the Material in this Section
Drywall Application General Requirements
Drywall Floating Interior Angles
Drywall Adhesive Application to Wood Framing
Drywall Application to Ceilings with Sixteen Inches on Center Framing
Drywall Application to Ceilings with Twenty-four Inches
on Center Framing

Drywall Application to Walls with Sixteen Inches on Center Framing
Drywall Application to Walls with Twenty-four Inches
on Center Framing
Drywall Application to Ceilings with Twenty-four Inches
on Center Framing Using 5/8 inch Drywall
Drywall Around Tubs and Showers
Drywall Application Discussion
Drywall Application Best Practice

EXTERIOR WALL COVERINGS (R703) 128

Water-Resistive Barrier General Installation Requirements
Hardboard Panel Siding Installation
Plywood and Wood Structural Panel Siding Installation
Fiber Cement Panel Siding Installation
Wood Structural Panel Lap Siding Installation
Hardboard Lap Siding Installation
Fiber Cement Lap Siding Installation
Aluminum and Vinyl Siding Installation
Moisture Barrier and Vapor Retarder Discussion

STUCCO APPLICATION (R703.6) 132

Limitations of the Material in this Section
Water-Resistive Barrier General Installation Requirements
Lath and Paper Installation
Weep Screed Materials and Installation
Artificial Stone Veneer Installation
Stucco Curing
Stucco Water Penetration Discussion
Stucco Installation Best Practice

MASONRY (BRICK) AND STONE VENEER (R703.7) 134

Water-Resistive Barrier General Installation Requirements
Flashing for Masonry and Stone Veneer Locations and Installation
Weep Holes at Flashing
Air Space Between Masonry and Stone Veneer and Sheathing
Wall Anchors (Ties) for Masonry and Stone Veneer
Masonry and Stone Veneer Height Limits
Masonry and Stone Veneer Support by Framing General Requirements
Masonry and Stone Veneer Support by Steel Angle
Masonry and Stone Veneer Support by Roof Framing
Masonry and Stone Veneer Support Over Openings (Lintels)
Brick and Stone Veneer Installation Discussion

FLASHING (R703.8) 139

Flashing General Requirements
Flashing Required Locations
Flashing Discussion

Flashing Best Practice

CHAPTER 8: ROOF AND CEILING CONSTRUCTION 143

GUTTERS (R801.3) 143
When Gutters are Required
Gutters Best Practice

CEILING JOIST AND RAFTER FRAMING DETAILS (R802.3) 143
Ridge, Valley, and Hip Rafter Framing
Purlins (802.5.1)
Ceiling Joist Nailing to Rafter
Ceiling Joist Nailing to Rafter Exceptions
Collar Ties
Rafter and Ceiling Joist Bearing on Support
Rafter and Ceiling Joist Bridging and Lateral Support

CEILING JOIST AND RAFTER SPANS (R802.4 AND R802.5) 148
Ceiling Joist and Rafter Span Definitions
Ceiling Joist and Rafter Deflection
Ceiling Joist and Rafter Span Tables
Rafter Span Measurement and Adjustment for Ceiling Joist Location

CEILING JOIST AND RAFTER BORING AND NOTCHING (R802.7) 159
Boring and Notching Definition
Ceiling Joist and Rafter Notching
Ceiling Joist and Rafter Boring
I-Beam Ceiling Joist and Rafter Notching and Boring
Roof Truss Notching and Boring
Engineered Wood Notching and Boring

CEILING JOIST AND RAFTER OPENINGS (R802.9) 160
Joist and Rafter Openings Description
Openings Not More than (≤) Four Feet Wide
Openings More than (>) Four Feet Wide

WOOD TRUSS INSTALLATION AND BRACING (R802.10) 161
Truss Design and Bracing Written Specifications Requirements
Truss Installation Tolerance Recommendations
Truss Permanent Bracing Recommendations
Connection Between Roof Trusses and Walls
Alteration and Repair of Trusses
Truss Discussion

ATTIC VENTILATION (R806) 164
Attic Ventilation Requirements
Attic Ventilation Openings Area
Conditioned Attic Assemblies
Attic Ventilation Discussion

Attic Ventilation Best Practice
Attic Ventilation Examples

ATTIC ACCESS (R807) 167
Attic Access Requirements
Attic Access Best Practice

CHAPTER 9: ROOF COVERINGS AND FLASHING 169

ROOF FLASHING AND DRAINAGE (R903) 169
Roof Flashing Locations and Materials
Parapet Wall Coping
Enclosed Roof Drainage Methods and Installation
Crickets at Chimneys
Roof Flashing and Drainage Discussion

ASPHALT (FIBERGLASS) SHINGLE ROOF COVERING MATERIALS AND INSTALLATION (R905.2) 170
Shingle Roof Covering Description
Roof Slope Restriction
Roof Deck Type Restriction
Underlayment Specifications
Underlayment Application for Roof Slopes 4/12 and Greater
Underlayment Application for Roof Slopes Between 2/12 and 4/12
Underlayment Application in 110+ MPH Wind Areas
Underlayment Application in Ice Dam Areas
Closed-Cut Valley Flashing
Open Valley Flashing
Sidewall and Penetration Flashing
Fastener Type and Quantity in Standard Conditions
Fastener Type and Quantity in Special Conditions
Staples as Shingle Fasteners

CONCRETE AND CLAY TILE ROOF COVERING MATERIALS AND INSTALLATION (R905.3) 174
Tile Roof Covering Description
Roof Slope Restriction
Roof Deck Type Restriction
Underlayment Specifications
Underlayment Application for Roof Slopes 4/12 and Greater
Underlayment Application for Roof Slopes Between 2 ½/12 and 4/12
Underlayment Application in 110+ MPH Wind Areas
Batten Installation (Industry Recommendation)
Valley Flashing
Sidewall and Penetration Flashing
Fastener Type
Perimeter Tile Nailing
Field Tile Nailing in Standard Conditions
Field Tile Nailing in Special Conditions

Tile Roof Covering Best Practice

METAL SHINGLE ROOF COVERING MATERIALS AND INSTALLATION (R905.4) 178
Metal Shingle Roof Covering Description
Roof Slope Restriction
Roof Deck Type Restriction
Underlayment Specifications
Underlayment Application in Ice Dam Areas
Metal Shingle Installation
Valley Flashing

MINERAL-SURFACED ROLL ROOF COVERING MATERIALS AND INSTALLATION (R905.5) 179
Mineral-Surfaced Roll Roof Covering Description
Roof Slope Restriction
Roof Deck Type Restriction
Underlayment Application in Ice Dam Areas
Roll Roof Covering Installation

SLATE AND SLATE TYPE SHINGLE ROOF COVERING MATERIALS AND INSTALLATION (R905.6) 180
Slate and Slate Type Shingle Roof Covering Description
Roof Slope Restriction
Roof Deck Type Restriction
Underlayment Application
Underlayment Application in Ice Dam Areas
Slate Roof Covering Installation
Valley Flashing Material
Sidewall and Penetration Flashing
Slate Roof Covering Best Practice

WOOD SHINGLE ROOF COVERING MATERIALS AND INSTALLATION (R905.7) 182
Wood Shingle Roof Covering Description
Application of the Material in this Section
Roof Slope Restriction
Roof Deck Type Restriction
Underlayment Application
Underlayment Application in Ice Dam Areas
Wood Shingle Installation
Wood Shingle Exposure
Valley Flashing Material
Sidewall and Penetration Flashing
Wood Shingle Roof Covering Best Practice

WOOD SHAKE ROOF COVERING MATERIALS AND INSTALLATION (R905.8) 185
Wood Shake Roof Covering Description
Application of the Material in this Section
Roof Slope Restriction
Roof Deck Type Restriction

Underlayment Application
Underlayment Application in Ice Dam Areas
Interlayment Material and Installation
Wood Shake Installation
Wood Shake Exposure
Valley Flashing Material
Sidewall and Penetration Flashing
Wood Shake Roof Covering Best Practice

LOW SLOPE (FLAT) ROOF COVERING MATERIALS AND INSTALLATION (R905.9 AND 11-15)........... 187

Low Slope Roof Covering Description
Low Slope Roof Types
Minimum Roof Slope
Low Slope Roof Covering Installation

METAL PANEL ROOF COVERING MATERIALS AND INSTALLATION (R905.10) 188

Metal Panel Roof Covering Description
Roof Slope Restriction
Roof Deck Type Restriction
Underlayment Application
Fastener Types

REPAIR AND REPLACEMENT OF ROOF COVERINGS (R907).................. 189

Definition of Repair versus Replacement of Roof Coverings
Permit Requirements
Structural Loads Imposed by New Roof Covering Material
Installing Additional Layers Over Existing Roof Covering Material
Wood Roof Concealed Spaces
Reuse of Materials and Flashing
Roof Covering Repair and Replacement Best Practice

CHAPTER 10: FIREPLACES AND CHIMNEYS............ 191

MASONRY FIREPLACES (R1001).................. 191

Components Governed by this Chapter
Masonry Fireplace Parts Definitions
Masonry Firebox Construction
Masonry Hearth Construction
Masonry Hearth Extension Construction
Lintels
Masonry Fireplace Throat Construction
Masonry Fireplace Damper Location and Installation
Masonry Fireplace Smoke Chamber Construction
Masonry Fireplace Clearances to Combustible Materials
Masonry Fireplace Mantels and Trim
Masonry Fireplace Fireblocking
Masonry Fireplace Foundation

MASONRY CHIMNEYS (R1003) 196
Chimney Definition
Chimney Termination Height
Chimney Crickets
Spark Arrestors
Masonry Chimney Clearances to Combustible Materials
Masonry Chimney Clearances to Combustible Materials Exceptions
Masonry Chimney Fireblocking
Masonry Chimney Flue Liners
Fireclay Flue Liner Installation
Masonry Chimney Flue Sizes
Masonry Chimneys with Multiple Flues
Masonry Chimney Changes in Size and Shape
Masonry Chimney Wall Thickness
Masonry Chimney Cleanout Openings
Masonry Chimney Foundation
Masonry Chimney Additional Structural Loads
Fuel-Burning Appliance Connection to Masonry Chimneys
Masonry Chimney Seismic Reinforcing

FIREPLACE COMBUSTION AIR (R1006) 204
Combustion Air Required
Masonry Fireplace Combustion Air
Factory-Built Fireplace Combustion Air

FACTORY-BUILT FIREPLACES AND CHIMNEYS (R1004, R1005, G2430, G2432 AND, G2433) 205
Factory-Built Fireplace and Chimney Discussion
Factory-Built Fireplace and Chimney Installation
Decorative Chimney Covers
Structural Support for Factory-Built Fireplaces
Gas Logs and Gas Log Lighters (G2432 and G2433)

CHAPTER 11: ENERGY EFFICIENCY 206

LIMITATIONS OF THE MATERIAL IN THIS CHAPTER 206

BUILDINGS GOVERNED BY IRC ENERGY EFFICIENCY REQUIREMENTS 206

INSULATION INSTALLATION GENERAL REQUIREMENTS 206

ENERGY EFFICIENCY DEFINITIONS 207

INSULATION AND FENESTRATION REQUIREMENTS (N1102) 209
Insulation and Fenestration Requirements Table
Fenestration U-factor and SHGC Requirements
Replacement Window Efficiency Requirements
Ceiling Insulation Requirements
Exterior (Wood-Framed) Walls Insulation Requirements

Steel-Framed Wall Insulation Requirements
Mass Wall Insulation Requirements
Floor Insulation Requirements
Basement Wall Insulation Requirements
Slab-on-grade Floor Insulation Requirements
Crawl Space Foundation Insulation Requirements
Blown and Sprayed Insulation Installation Requirements
Sealing Openings in the Thermal Envelope
Access Doors and Openings
Recessed Light Types and Installation
Vapor Retarders
Duct Insulation and Sealing
Thermostats
Pipe Insulation
Hot Water Circulating Systems
Air Intake and Exhaust Systems
Fireplaces
Swimming Pools
Light Bulbs
Energy Efficiency Best Practice

CHAPTER 12: MECHANICAL SYSTEMS CHANGES AND MAINTENANCE 217

MECHANICAL SYSTEMS CHANGES AND MAINTENANCE (M1201 AND M1202) 217
Mechanical Systems Governed by the IRC
Updates and Changes to HVAC Systems
Grandfathering Existing HVAC Systems
Maintenance of Existing HVAC Systems Required

CHAPTER 13: MECHANICAL SYSTEMS GENERAL REQUIREMENTS 218

ACCESS TO MECHANICAL APPLIANCES (M1305) 218
Access Requirements for Mechanical Appliances
Access to Appliances Installed in Compartments, Closets, and Alcoves
Access to Appliances in Rooms where the Appliance
is Not Accessible from the Service Opening
Access to Appliances in Attics
Access to Appliances in Crawl Spaces

OIL AND SOLID-FUEL APPLIANCE CLEARANCE REDUCTION TO COMBUSTIBLE MATERIALS
  (M1306) 220
Appliances Governed by these Code Provisions
Clearance to Combustible Materials Definition and Discussion
Clearance Reduction Device Requirements
Clearance Reduction for Solid Fuel-Burning Appliances
Clearance Reduction Device Example

APPLIANCE INSTALLATION, ANCHORAGE, ELEVATION, AND PROTECTION 222

Appliances Governed by these Code Provisions
Flood-Resistant Installation (M1301.1.1)
Appliance Installation by Manufacturer's Instructions (M1307.1)
Seismic Anchorage of Water Heaters (M1307.2)
Elevation of Appliances in Garages (M1307.3 and G2408.2)
Protection of Appliances from Vehicle Impact (M1307.3.1)
Elevation of Outdoor HVAC Equipment Above Grade (M1308.3 and M1403.2)
Avoiding Fuel Pipe Strain (G2408.6)

CHAPTER 14: HEATING AND COOLING EQUIPMENT ... 226

HVAC EQUIPMENT GENERAL INSTALLATION REQUIREMENTS (M1401) ... 226
Equipment Installation by Manufacturer's Instructions
Equipment Sizing
Duct Design (M1601.1)

ELECTRIC RADIANT HEATING SYSTEMS INSTALLATION REQUIREMENTS (M1406) ... 226
Electric Radiant Heating Description
Installation Requirements

ELECTRIC HEATING ELEMENTS INSTALLED IN HVAC DUCTS, HEAT PUMPS, AND AIR CONDITIONERS (M1407) ... 227
Electric Heating Element Description
Installation Requirements
Clearance to Combustible Materials

VENTED FLOOR FURNACES (M1408 AND G2437) ... 227
Vented Floor Furnace Description
Installation Requirements
Crawl Space Installations
Upper Floor Installations (G2437.6)
Clearance to Combustible Materials
Service Access

VENTED WALL FURNACES (M1409 AND G2436) ... 229
Vented Wall Furnace Description
Installation Requirements
Clearance to Combustible Materials
Service Access

VENTED ROOM HEATERS (M1410) ... 230
Vented Room Heater Description
Installation Requirements
Clearance to Combustible Materials

AIR CONDITIONING CONDENSATE DISPOSAL (M1411) ... 231
Condensate Description
Condensate Disposal Location Requirements
Condensate Discharge Pipe Requirements

Condensate Auxiliary (Backup) System Requirements
Condensate Auxiliary Drain Pan with Discharge Pipe
Condensate Auxiliary Drain Pan with Water Level Cutoff Switch
Condensate Auxiliary Discharge Pipe Attached to Evaporator Coil
Water Level Cutoff Switch
Water Level Cutoff Switch for Downflow Air Conditioners
Auxiliary Drain Pan Separation from Appliances
Condensate Auxiliary (Backup) System Requirements for Category IV Appliances
Condensate Disposal Best Practice

COOLANT ACCESS CAPS (M1411.6) 234

EVAPORATIVE COOLING EQUIPMENT INSTALLATION REQUIREMENTS (M1413) 234
Evaporative Cooling Equipment Description
Installation Requirements
Water Supply Protection

CHAPTER 15: KITCHEN AND CLOTHES DRYER EXHAUST SYSTEMS 235

VENTILATION FAN DISCHARGE LOCATION 235

CLOTHES DRYER EXHAUST SYSTEMS (M1502 AND G2439) 235
Installation Requirements
Duct Construction
Duct Length
Duct Termination
Transition Duct
Clothes Dryer Makeup Air (G2439.4)
Clothes Dryer Installation Discussion

KITCHEN RANGE HOODS AND EXHAUST SYSTEMS (M1503) 238
Installation Requirements
Above Ground Exhaust Duct Construction
Downdraft Exhaust Duct Construction in Concrete
Exhaust Duct Termination
Exhaust Fan Rates
Domestic Open-top Broiler Hoods
Range Hood Best Practice

CHAPTER 16: HVAC DUCT SYSTEMS 240

FLEXIBLE DUCT INSTALLATION (M1601.3) 240
General Installation Requirements
Duct Support
Duct Bends
Duct Connections and Splices
Flexible Duct Installation Discussion

FRAMING CAVITY RETURN DUCTS (M1601.1.1) 244
Return Ducts in Framing Cavities Installation Requirements

UNDERGROUND DUCTS (M1601.1.2) 245
Ducts Installed Underground or in Concrete
Underground Duct Installation Best Practice

CRAWL SPACE USED AS HVAC SUPPLY PLENUM (M1601.5) 245
Crawl Space Prohibited as HVAC Supply Plenum

OUTDOOR AND RETURN AIR LOCATION AND INSTALLATION (M1403, M1602 AND G2442) 246
Appliances Governed by these Code Provisions
Return Air General Installation Requirements (M1602.1)
Prohibited Sources of Return Air (M1602.2)
Prohibited Sources of Outdoor Air (M1602.2)
Return Air Drawn from Rooms with Fuel-Burning Appliances (M1602.2 and G2442.8)
Minimum Furnace Duct Size (G2442.2)
Minimum Heat Pump Return Duct Size (M1403)

CHAPTER 17: COMBUSTION AIR 248
This Chapter is effectively deleted in IRC 2009

CHAPTER 18: CHIMNEYS AND VENTS FOR LIQUID AND SOLID-FUEL APPLIANCES 249

APPLIANCES GOVERNED BY THIS CHAPTER 249

CHIMNEYS AND VENTS FOR LIQUID AND SOLID-FUEL APPLIANCES GENERAL REQUIREMENTS (M1801) 249
Use of Flue Space Around Flue Liner Systems (M1801.4)
Connecting Negative and Positive Pressure Draft Systems (M1801.5)
Running Vents in HVAC Ducts (M1801.8)
Sealing Unused Openings (M1801.10)
Common Vent Connected to Multiple Appliances (M1801.11)
Flues for Multiple Solid-Fuel Appliances (M1801.12)
Vents for Appliances Using Different Fuels (M1801.12)

ADDING OR REMOVING LIQUID AND SOILD-FUEL APPLIANCES FROM CHIMNEYS AND VENTS (M1801.3) 250
Description of Potential Problems when Adding or Removing
 Fuel-Burning Appliances
Recalculate Size of Chimneys and Vents when Adding or Removing Appliances
Cleaning and Inspection of Chimneys and Vents
 when Adding or Removing Appliances
Chimney Cleanouts

DRAFT HOODS, DRAFT REGULATORS, AND DAMPERS FOR LIQUID AND SOLID-FUEL APPLIANCES (M1802) 251
Draft Hood Location
Dampers
Draft Regulators

CONNECTION OF VENT CONNECTORS TO CHIMNEYS FOR LIQUID AND SOLID-FUEL APPLIANCES (M1803 AND 1805) 252

Vent Connector Definition
Liquid and Solid-Fuel Vent Connector Material
Liquid and Solid-Fuel Vent Connector Installation
Liquid and Solid-Fuel Vent Connector Through Walls and Ceilings
Liquid and Solid-Fuel Vent Connector Length
Liquid and Solid-Fuel Vent Connector Clearance to Combustibles
Vent Connector Connection Through a Fireplace Firebox
Vent Connector Connection Directly to a Masonry Chimney (M1805.2)
Size of Chimney Flue Used as Appliance Vent (M1805.3)
Size of Chimney Flue for Solid-Fuel Appliance (M1805.3.1)

VENTS FOR LIQUID AND SOILD-FUEL APPLIANCES (M1804) 255

Appliances Governed by these Code Provisions
Liquid and Solid-Fuel Vent Types
Liquid and Solid-Fuel Vent Flashing and Shrouds
Liquid and Solid-Fuel Natural Draft Vent Height
Type L Vent Roof Termination Height
Liquid and Solid-Fuel Powered Vent System Termination
Liquid and Solid-Fuel Single Appliance Vent Size

CHAPTER 19: SPECIAL FUEL-BURNING EQUIPMENT 257

KITCHEN COOKING EQUIPMENT (M1901 and G2447) 257

Range and Cooktop Clearance to Combustible Material

SAUNA HEATERS (M1902 AND G2440) 257

Sauna Heater Installation Requirements

CHAPTER 20: BOILERS AND WATER HEATERS 258

HOT WATER AND STEAM BOILERS (M2001 AND G2452) 258

Labeling and Instructions Requirements
Shutoff Valves
Gauges
Pressure Relief Valve
Low Water Cutoff
Hot Water Boiler Expansion Tanks (Non-pressurized)
Hot Water Boiler Expansion Tanks (Pressurized)
Hot Water Boiler Expansion Tank Capacity

WATER HEATER INSTALLATION AND ACCESS (M2005) 260

Water Heater General Installation Requirements
Water Heater Prohibited Locations

POOL HEATER INSTALLATION (M2006) 260

Pool Heater General Installation Requirements
Pool Heater Relief Valves

Pool Heater Bypass Valve

CHAPTER 21: HYDRONIC PIPING 261

HYDRONIC PIPING SYSTEMS (M2101) 261
Hyronic Piping System Discussion
Limitations of the Material in this Section
Hydronic Piping System Materials
Hydronic Piping System Installation
Protection of Potable Water

CHAPTER 22: OIL PIPING AND STORAGE SYSTEMS 262

OIL PIPING AND STORAGE SYSTEMS (M2201) 262
Oil Storage Tanks Above Ground
Oil Storage Tanks Below Ground
Oil Gauges
Oil Pipes and Connector Materials
Oil Pipe Fittings
Oil Fill Pipe
Oil Tank Vent Pipe
Oil Tank Connection Between Two Tanks
Oil Pumps and Valves
Oil Pressure

CHAPTER 23: SOLAR ENERGY SYSTEMS 265

SOLAR ENERGY SYSTEMS (M2301) 265
Solar Energy Systems Governed by this Chapter
Solar Energy Systems Installation Requirements

CHAPTER 24: FUEL GAS 266

GAS APPLIANCES AND GAS PIPING SYSTEMS GENERAL REQUIREMENTS (G2401, G2403-G2405) 266
Gas Types Governed by the IRC
Gas Appliance Listing and Labeling
Gas Appliance Replacement Parts
Gas Appliance Seismic and Weather Protection
Gas Appliance and Piping Effects on Building Structural Members
Condensate Auxiliary (Backup) System Requirements for Category IV Appliances

GAS APPLIANCES PROHIBITED LOCATIONS AND PROHIBITED COMBUSTION AIR SOURCES (G2406) 267
Gas Appliance Prohibited Installation Locations
Gas Appliance Prohibited Installation Locations Exceptions

COMBUSTION AIR FOR GAS APPLIANCES GENERAL REQUIREMENTS (G2407) 268
Combustion Air Description
Appliances Needing Combustion Air

Combustion Air Depletion by Other Systems
Combustion Air Opening Covers Area
Combustion Air Opening Louvers and Grilles
Combustion Air Duct Materials and Construction
Homes Built Using Air Tight Construction Techniques Description

COMBUSTION AIR FOR GAS APPLIANCES FROM INSIDE THE BUILDING (G2407.5) **270**

Combustion Air from the Room where the Appliance is Located (Standard Method)
Combustion Air from the Room where the Appliance is Located (Calculated Method)
Combustion Air from Other Rooms on the Same Floor Level
Combustion Air from Other Rooms on Different Floor Levels

COMBUSTION AIR FOR GAS APPLIANCES FROM OUTSIDE THE BUILDING (G2407.6) **273**

Combustion Air Openings Directly Outside or Ducts Run Vertically
Combustion Air Ducts Run Horizontally
Combustion Air One Permanent Opening

COMBUSTION AIR FOR GAS APPLIANCES FROM INSIDE AND OUTSIDE THE BUILDING (G2407.7) **275**

Combustion Air Combining Inside and Outside Sources
Combustion Air Indoor Volumes
Combustion Air Outside Opening Size
Combustion Air Outside Opening Size Reduction Equation

GAS APPLIANCE INSTALLATION (G2408) **277**

GAS APPLIANCE CLEARANCE REDUCTION TO COMBUSTIBLE MATERIALS (G2409) **277**

Appliances and Equipment Governed by these Code Provisions
Clearance to Combustible Materials Definition and Discussion
Clearance Reduction Device Requirements
Clearance Reduction for Appliances in Small Rooms
Clearance to Gas Appliance Supply Plenums and Supply Ducts
Clearance to Doors, Drawers, and Projections
Clearance Reduction Device Example

GAS PIPING SYSTEM GROUNDING AND BONDING (G2410 AND G2411) **279**

Gas Piping System Use as a Grounding Electrode
Gas Piping System Bonding

GAS PIPING GENERAL INSTALLATION, MODIFICATION, AND IDENTIFICATION (G2412) **280**

Gas Piping Governed by the IRC
Gas Provider Piping Located Inside the Home
Recalculation of Gas Pipe Size when Modifying Piping or Adding Gas Appliances
Gas Pipe Labeling

Multiple Gas Meters for One Building

GAS PIPE SIZING (G2413) 281

Limitations of the Material in this Section
Input Rating for Typical Gas Appliances
Gas Pipe Size Example 1
Gas Pipe Size Example 2

GAS PIPE MATERIALS (G2414). 284

Materials Permitted for Use as Gas Pipes in Buildings
Plastic Gas Pipe (G2415.14)
Used Gas Pipe and Materials
Defective Pipe and Materials
Corrosion Protection of Gas Pipe and Materials
Metallic Gas Pipe Threads

GAS PIPE INSTALLATION AND PROTECTION (G2415) 286

Gas Pipe Prohibited Installation Locations
Gas Pipe in Masonry and Concrete Walls
Gas Pipe in Solid Floors
Gas Pipe Fittings in Concealed Locations
Gas Pipe Run Underground Through Foundations
Gas Pipe Shield Plates in Wood Framing
Gas Pipe Installed Above Ground Outdoors
Gas Pipe Protection from Corrosion
Gas Pipe Burial Depth
Gas Pipe Burial in Trenches
Closure of Gas Outlets
Extension of Gas Pipes Beyond Walls, Ceilings, and Floors
Gas Outlet Location

GAS PIPE INSPECTION, TESTING, AND PURGING (G2417) 289

Limitations of the Material in this Section
When to Inspect and Test Gas Pipe
Gas Pressure Test Gases
Appliance Isolation from Gas Pipe Testing
Gas Test Gauges
Gas Test Pressure
Gas Test Duration
Gas Leak Testing
Purging of Air from Gas Pipes

GAS PIPE SUPPORT (G2418 AND G2424). 290

Gas Pipe Support Materials and Installation (G2418)
Gas Pipe Support Intervals (G2424)

DRIPS AND SEDIMENT TRAPS (G2419) 291

Drips (Drip Tees)

xxxii Everybody's Building Code

Sediment Traps

GAS SHUTOFF VALVES (G2420) 293
Gas Shutoff Valve Access for Appliances
Gas Shutoff Valves Location for Appliances
Gas Shutoff Valves for Buildings
Gas Shutoff Valves for MP Regulators
Gas Shutoff Valves in Fireplaces

GAS PRESSURE REGULATORS (G2421) 294
Gas Pressure Regulators General Requirements
Gas Pressure Regulators (MP Regulators)

GAS CONNECTIONS TO APPLIANCES (G2422) 295
Gas Connection to Appliances General Requirements
Manufactured Gas Connectors Best Practice

VENTS FOR GAS APPLIANCES GENERAL
REQUIREMENTS (G2425, G2426, G2427). 296
Appliances and Equipment Governed by these Code Provisions
Manufacturer's Installation Instructions (G2426.5, G2426.6, and Other Sections)
Unused Vent and Chimney Openings (G2425.5)
Positive Pressure Gas Vent Systems Use Restrictions (G2425.6)
Gas Vent Entry into Fireplace Flue (G2425.7)
Gas Appliances for which Vents are Not Required (G2425.8)
Vents and Chimneys with Power Exhausters (G2425.10)
Flue Lining Systems (G2425.12, 13, 14)
Gas Vent Insulation Shields (G2426.4)
Gas Vent Protection Against Damage (G2426.7)
Gas Vent Labeling in Cold Climates (G2427.6.10)
Gas Vents Run Along Exterior Walls (G2427.6.7)

ADDING OR REMOVING GAS APPLIANCES FROM CHIMNEYS
AND VENTS (G2425.15) 299
Appliances and Equipment Governed by these Code Provisions
Description of Potential Problems
when Adding or Removing Fuel-Burning Appliances
Recalculate Chimney or Vent Size when Adding Gas Appliances
Cleaning and Inspection of Chimneys and Vents
Chimney Cleanout Openings

VENTING GAS APPLIANCES USING A MASONRY CHIMNEY (G2427.5) 300
Masonry Chimney Used for Gas Appliance Venting General Requirements
Masonry Chimney Termination Height
Masonry Chimney Flue Size for Gas Appliance Venting
Gas Venting with Solid-Fuel Appliances
Common Venting of Gas and Oil Appliances
Venting Dual Fuel Appliances

Use of Flue Space Around Flue Liner Systems

GAS VENT ROOF TERMINATION (G2427.6). 302
Gas Vent Roof Flashing and Cap
Gas Vent Height Above the Roof
Gas Vent Height Above Appliance
Decorative Shrouds for Gas Vents

SINGLE WALL VENTS FOR GAS APPLIANCES (G2427.7) 304
Single Wall Gas Vent Description
Single Wall Gas Vent Use Restrictions
Single Wall Gas Vent Roof Flashing and Termination
Single Wall Gas Vent Clearance to Combustible Material
Single Wall Gas Vent Size and Shape
Single Wall Gas Vent Support

VENT TERMINATION FOR MECHANICAL DRAFT AND DIRECT
VENT APPLIANCES (G2427.8). 306
Direct Vent and Mechanical Draft Appliance Definitions
Appliances and Equipment Governed by these Code Provisions
Mechanical Draft Vent Termination Locations
Direct Vent Appliance Vent Termination Locations
Condensate Disposal from Through-the-wall Vent Terminations

VENT CONNECTORS FOR CATEGORY I GAS APPLIANCES (G2427.10). 308
Vent Connector Definition
Vent Connectors in Unconditioned Space
Vent Connector Joints
Vent Connector Slope
Vent Connector Length
Vent Connector Support and Inspection
Vent Connector Size for Single Gas Appliance
Vent Connector Size for Single Gas Appliances with
Multiple Draft Hoods
Vent Connector Size for Multiple Appliances with a Common Vent
Vent Connector Size for Multiple Appliances with a Common Connector
Vent Connector Size Increase
Different Size Vent Connectors Connecting to a Common Vent
Vent Connector Connection to a Chimney
Vent Connector Passage Through Floors, Ceilings, or Walls
Single Wall Vent Connector Passage Through Combustible Exterior Wall

GAS VENT DRAFT HOODS AND DAMPERS (G2427.12,
G2427.13, G2427.14) 312
Draft Hoods (G2427.12)
Draft Control Devices (G2427.12)
Manual Vent Dampers (G2427.13)

GAS VENT SIZE TABLES DEFINITIONS (G2428.1) 312
Definitions of Terms Used to Calculate Gas Vent Size

TYPE B GAS VENT SIZE FOR ONE APPLIANCE GENERAL INSTALLATION REQUIREMENTS AND EXAMPLES (G2428.2) 315
Application of these Tables
Vent Obstructions
Vent Size from Tables Smaller than Draft Hood Size
Vent Connector Laterals (Elbows)
Appliance Btu/hour Input Reduction for High Altitude Installation
Appliance with Multiple Input Rates
Corrugated Chimney Liner System Sizing
Vent Connector Size Smaller than Vent
Chimneys and Vents Exposed to Outdoors
Vent Connector Size Larger than Flue Collar
Use of Different Vent and Connector Materials
Table Interpolation and Extrapolation
Table Interpolation Formulae

TYPE B GAS VENT SIZE TABLE FOR ONE APPLIANCE USING TYPE B VENT CONNECTOR (G2428.2-1) 320

TYPE B GAS VENT SIZE TABLE FOR ONE APPLIANCE USING SINGLE WALL VENT CONNECTOR (G2428.2-2) 321

TYPE B GAS VENT SIZE FOR MULTIPLE APPLIANCES GENERAL INSTALLATION REQUIREMENTS AND EXAMPLES (G2428.3) 323
Application of these Tables
Vent Obstructions
Vent Connector Length Limit
Long Length Vent Connectors
Common Vent Offset Length
Common Vent Offsets (Elbows)
Vent Connector Laterals (Elbows)
Common (Vertical) Vent Maximum Size
Common (Vertical) Vent Minimum Size
Vent Connector Size Larger than Flue Collar
Vent Size from Tables Smaller than Appliance Outlet Size
Appliance Btu/h Input Reduction for High Altitude Installation
Appliance with Multiple Input Rates
Corrugated Chimney Liner System Sizing
Chimneys and Vents Exposed to Outdoors
Vent Connector Manifold
Use of Different Vent and Connector Materials
Table Interpolation and Extrapolation

TYPE B GAS VENT SIZE TABLE FOR MULTIPLE APPLIANCES USING TYPE B VENT CONNECTOR (G2428.3-1) 330

TYPE B GAS VENT SIZE TABLE FOR MULTIPLE APPLIANCES USING SINGLE WALL VENT CONNECTOR (G2428.3-2) 333

MASONRY CHIMNEY SIZE TABLE WHEN CHIMNEY USED AS VENT FOR GAS APPLIANCES USING TYPE B VENT CONNECTOR (G2428.3-3) 336

MASONRY CHIMNEY SIZE TABLE WHEN CHIMNEY USED AS VENT FOR GAS APPLIANCES USING SINGLE WALL VENT CONNECTOR (G2428.3-4) 339

UNVENTED GAS ROOM HEATERS (G2445) 342

Unvented Room Heater Description
General Installation Requirements
Unvented Gas Room Heater Prohibited Locations
Unvented Log Heaters

GAS COOKING APPLIANCES (G2447) 344

Appliances and Equipment Governed by these Code Provisions
Commercial Cooking Appliances
Gas Ranges on Combustible Floors
Gas Cooking Appliance Clearance Above Cooktop

GAS LIGHTING (G2450) 344

Gas Lighting General Installation Requirements
Gaslight Pressure Regulator

CHAPTER 25: PLUMBING ADMINISTRATION 346

PLUMBING SYSTEMS CHANGES, INSPECTION, TESTING, AND MAINTENANCE (P2502 AND P2503) 346

Updates and Changes to Plumbing Systems
Using Existing Building Sewers
Plumbing System Inspection Notice to Inspector
Plumbing System Inspection Materials and Procedures
Backflow Prevention Devices Inspection and Testing
Test Gauges

CHAPTER 26: GENERAL PLUMBING INSTALLATION REQUIREMENTS 348

PLUMBING PIPE GENERAL INSTALLATION REQUIREMENTS 348

Connection of Drainage Pipes and Fixtures to Sewer Systems (P2602.1)
Flood-Resistant Installation (P2602.2)
Plumbing Pipe Protection Against Punctures (P2603.2.1)
Plumbing Pipe Protection Against Corrosion (P2603.3)
Plumbing Pipe Protection Against Breaking (P2603.4 and P2603.5)
Plumbing Pipe Protection Against Freezing (P2603.6)
Plumbing Pipe Trenching and Backfilling (P2604)
Trenches Parallel to Footings (P2604.4)
Plumbing Pipe Support (P2605)
Plumbing Pipe Roof and Wall Penetrations (P2606)

CHAPTER 27: PLUMBING FIXTURES 353

DEFINITIONS OF TERMS USED IN PLUMBING SYSTEMS. 353

PLUMBING FIXTURES GENERAL INSTALLATION REQUIREMENTS. 357

Plumbing Fixtures Specifications (P2701.1)
Strainers for Plumbing Fixtures (P2702.1)
Tail Pieces (P2703)
Slip Joints (P2704)
Fixture Installation (P2705)
Waste Receptor General Requirements (P2706.1 and 2706.3)
Standpipes (P2706.2)
Laundry Tray Connection to Standpipe (P2706.2.1)
Disposal and Dishwasher Directional Fittings (P2707.1)
Toilets (Water Closets) (P2712)
Plumbing Fixture Outlet Size
Bathtub Temperature Control Valve (P2713.3)
Dishwashing Machine Installation (P2717)
Clothes Washing Machine Installation (P2718)
Floor Drain Installation (P2719)
Whirlpool Tub Installation (P2720)
Bidet Installation (P2721)
Water Faucet and Valve Installation (P2722)

SHOWERS (P2708 AND P2709) 362

Shower Size (P2708.1)
Water Supply Riser (P2708.2)
Shower Temperature Control Valve (P2708.3)
Shower Receptor Construction (P2709.1)
Site-Built Shower Receptor Linings (P2709.3)

CHAPTER 28: WATER HEATERS 366

WATER HEATER DRIP PANS AND RELIEF VALVES. 366

Water Heater Drip Pan Requirements (P2801.5)
Water Heater Drip Pan Discharge Pipe (P2801.5)
Water Heater Relief Valves (P2803)
Water Heater Relief Valve Discharge Pipe (P2803.6.1)
Water Heater Relief Valve Discussion

CHAPTER 29: WATER SUPPLY SYSTEM INSTALLATION REQUIREMENTS. 369

BACKFLOW PROTECTION OF WATER SUPPLY (P2902). 369

Backflow and Cross-Connections Discussion

BACKFLOW PROTECTION BY AIR GAPS (P2902.3.1) 370

Air Gap Definition
Air Gap Required Locations
Air Gap Distance Measurement

Air Gap Minimum Distances

BACKFLOW PROTECTION USING BACKFLOW
   PREVENTION DEVICES (P2902.3 - P2902.6) 372

Backflow Protection Device General Installation Requirements
Backflow Protection of Toilet Fill Valves
Backflow Protection of Hose Bibbs
Backflow Protection of Boilers
Backflow Protection of Irrigation Systems
Backflow Protection of Automatic Fire Sprinkler Systems

WATER SUPPLY GENERAL REQUIREMENTS (P2903) 374

Drinking Water Required (P2901)
Minimum Water Pressure (P2903.3)
Maximum Water Pressure (P2903.3.1)
Thermal Expansion Devices (P2903.4)
Water-Hammer Arrestors (P2903.5)
Minimum Flow Rate at Fixtures (P2903.1)
Maximum Flow Rate at Fixtures (P2903.2)

WATER SUPPLY PIPE SIZE (P2903.7) 377

Limitations of the Material in this Section
Water Supply Fixture Units Description
Water Supply Pipe Size Table
Water Supply Pipe Size Example

WATER SUPPLY VALVES (P2903.9) 381

Water Supply Service Cutoff Valve
Water Heater Cutoff Valve
Fixture Cutoff Valve (Angle Stop)
Valves and Outlets Installed Below Ground
Hose Bibb Cutoff Valve (P2903.10)

FIRE SPRINKLER SYSTEM GENERAL REQUIREMENTS (P2904) 382

Limitations of the Material in this Section
Sprinkler System General Installation Requirements
Sprinkler System Heads Required Locations
Sprinkler System Head Type Required Locations
Sprinkler Head Coverage Area and Obstructions

WATER SERVICE AND DISTRIBUITON PIPE GENERAL INSTALLATION
   REQUIREMENTS (P2905) 383

Water Pipe Installed in Contaminated or Corrosive Ground
Water Service Pipe Materials
Water Service Pipe Installation
Water Distribution Pipe Materials
Plastic Pipe Joints
Soldered Pipe Joints

Joints in and Under Concrete
Joints Between Different Pipe Materials Within Buildings
Bending Copper Tubing (P2906.1)

REVERSE OSMOSIS WATER TREATMENT UNITS (P2908.2) 386

Air Gap for Waste Discharge

CHAPTER 30: SANITARY DRAINAGE SYSTEM INSTALLATION REQUIREMENTS 387

DRAINAGE AND SEWER PIPE MATERIALS, FITTINGS, AND JOINTS 387

Drainage and Sewer Pipe Materials (P3002.1 and P3002.2)
Drainage and Sewer Pipe Fittings General Requirements (P3002.3)
Drainage and Sewer Pipe Prohibited Joints and Connections (P3003.2)
ABS Plastic Pipe Joints (P3003.3)
Cast-Iron Hub and Spigot Joints (P3003.6)
Cast-Iron Hubless Pipe Joints (P3003.6)
Copper and Brass Pipe and Copper Tubing Joints (P3003.5, P3003.10, and P3003.11)
Steel Pipe Joints (P3003.12)
PVC Plastic Pipe Joints (P3003.14)
Joints Between Different Types of Pipe (P3003.18)
Toilet (Closet) Flange Joints (P3003.19)
Drainage and Sewer Pipe Slope (P3005.3)
Drainage and Sewer Pipe Offset Size (P3006)

DRAINAGE AND SEWER PIPE SIZE (P3005.4) 390

Limitations of the Material in this Section
Drainage Fixture Units Description (P3004.1)
Drainage Pipe Size Table
Sewer Pipe Size Table
Drainage and Sewer Pipe Size Calculation Method
Drainage and Sewer Pipe Size Calculation Example

DRAINAGE AND SEWER PIPE FITTINGS DEFINITIONS (P3005.1) 395

Drainage and Sewer Pipe Fittings Discussion
Drainage and Sewer Pipe Fittings Definitions

DRAINAGE AND SEWER PIPE FITTINGS INSTALLATION (P3005.1) 400

Drainage and Sewer Pipe Fittings for Changing Direction of Flow
Drainage and Sewer Pipe Fittings Changing from Horizontal to Vertical Using Multiple Fittings
Quarter Bends with Heel or Side-Inlet
Water Closet Connection Between Closet Flange and Pipe
Drainage and Sewer Pipe Dead Ends
Drainage and Sewer Pipe Sizing for Future Fixtures
Drainage and Sewer Pipe Reduction in Size

DRAINAGE AND SEWER PIPE CLEANOUTS (P3005.2) 403

Cleanout Locations and Spacing

Cleanout Substitutes
Cleanout Size
Cleanout Accessibility
Cleanout Plugs
Cleanout Direction
Cleanout Fixture Connections

SEWAGE PUMPS AND EJECTORS (P3007) 406
Sewage Pump and Ejector Installation
Sewage Pump and Ejector Specifications
Macerating Toilets Installation

BACKWATER VALVES (P3008) 409
Backwater Valves

CHAPTER 31: PLUMBING VENTS 410

PLUMBING VENTS GENERAL INSTALLATION REQUIREMENTS 410
Plumbing Vents Required (P3101 and P3102)
Flood Resistance (P3101)
Vent Slope and Support (P3104)
Vent Connection to Horizontal Drainage Pipes (P3104)
Vent Connection Height Minimums (P3104)
Vent Rough-in for Future Fixtures (P3104)

VENT EXTERIOR TERMINATIONS (P3103) 412
Vent Height Above Roof
Vent Freezing and Frost Closure Protection
Vent Flashing
Vent Prohibited Uses
Vent Exterior Termination Locations

FIXTURE DRAINS (P3105) 414
Vent Distance from Trap
Fixture Drain Slope
Crown Venting

INDIVIDUAL VENTS (P3106) 416

COMMON VENTS (P3107) 417

WET VENTS (P3108) 418

WASTE STACK VENTS (P3109) 421

CIRCUIT VENTS (P3110) 422

COMBINATION WASTE AND VENT (P3111) 423

ISLAND FIXTURE VENTS (P3112) 425

VENT PIPE SIZE (P3113) 427

Vent Pipe Size
Vent Pipe Developed Length
Branch Vent Size with Multiple Connected Vents
Sewage Pump and Ejector Vents

AIR ADMITTANCE VALVES (P3114) 428
General Installation Requirements and Approved Uses
Installation Location Requirements
Outside Vent Required

CHAPTER 32: TRAPS 430

FIXTURE TRAPS (P3201) 430
Trap Size
Trap Design
Trap Seal
Trap Installation
Prohibited Traps
Traps Serving Multiple Fixture Drain Outlets

CHAPTER 33: STORM WATER DRAINAGE 433

UNDERGROUND STORM WATER DRAINS 433
Underground Drain Materials and Installation Requirements

SUMP PITS AND PUMPS 433
Sump Pit and Sump Pump Requirements

CHAPTER 34: ELECTRICAL SYSTEM GENERAL REQUIREMENTS 434

ELECTRICAL SYSTEM GENERAL INSTALLATION
REQUIREMENTS (E3401 - E3404) 434
Electrical Systems Governed by the IRC
Updates and Changes to Electrical Systems
Changes to Building Structural Members
Penetrations of Firestops and Draftstops
Electrical Component Listing, Labeling, and Installation
Panelboard Cabinet Selection
Electrical Component Protection During Construction
Damaged Electrical Components
Openings in Boxes and Enclosures
Identification of Circuit Breakers and Fuses
Electrical Component Attachment
Electrical Component Protection Against Damage and Accidental Contact

ELECTRICAL EQUIPMENT ACCESS AND CLEARANCES (E3405) 436
Clearances Around Electrical Panel Enclosures and Energized Equipment
Clear Space Above and Below Electrical Panel Enclosures
Electrical Panel Prohibited Locations and Access
Electrical Panel Lighting

WIRE SPLICES AND GENERAL WIRE INSTALLATION REQUIREMENTS (E3406 AND E3407) 438

Wire Splices
Splicing Aluminum and Copper Wires
Length of Wires in Boxes
Connecting Wires to Terminals
Wire Color Codes
Wires Installed in Conduit
Wires Run in Parallel
Neutral and Equipment Grounding Wire Continuity
Wires Serving the Same Circuit
Terminal Identification Markings

CHAPTER 35: DEFINITIONS OF TERMS USED IN ELECTRICAL SYSTEMS 441

CHAPTER 36: ELECTRICAL SERVICES 448

ELECTRICAL SERVICES GENERAL REQUIREMENTS (E3601) 448

One Electrical Service Per Dwelling Unit
Electrical Service Run Through Building Interiors
Electrical Service Entrance Wires Commingled with Other Wires
Electrical Main Disconnecting (Service) Equipment

ELECTRICAL SERVICE LOAD CALCULATION (E3602) 449

Limitations of the Material in this Section
Electrical Service Minimum Size
Service Load Formula
Service Load Calculation Example

ELECTRICAL SERVICE, FEEDER, AND GROUNDING ELECTRODE WIRE SIZE (E3603) 453

Service, Feeder, and Grounding Electrode Wire Size
Feeder Wire Size for Accessory Structures
Grounding Electrode Wire Protection
Service Entrance Wire Overcurrent Protection
Service Wire Entrance Overcurrent Protection
-Multiple Fuses or Circuit Breakers
Wire and Circuit Ampacity Discussion

SERVICE DROP CLEARANCES AND INSTALLATION (E3604) 455

Service Drop Clearances to Decks and Openings
Service Drop Clearance Above Roofs
Service Drop Clearance Above Ground
Service Drop Attachment and Support

SERVICE ENTRANCE WIRE AND MAST INSTALLATION (E3605) 458

Service Entrance Wire Insulation
Service Entrance Cable Protection Against Damage

Service Entrance Wire Splices
Service Mast Installation

SERVICE GROUNDING GENERAL REQUIREMENTS (E3607) 459

Service Grounding
Service Grounding at Two Buildings Using Four Wire Feeder
Service Grounding at Two Buildings Using Three Wire Feeder
Grounding Discussion

GROUNDING ELECTRODES (E3608) 463

Connect (Bond) all Grounding Electrodes
Metal Underground Water Pipe Electrodes
Concrete Encased Electrodes
Ground Ring Electrodes
Rod and Pipe Electrode Materials
Grounding Electrode Installation
Metal Underground Gas Pipe Electrode

BONDING (E3609) 465

Bonding Metal Service Components
Bonding Connections for Cable TV and Other Systems
Bonding Jumper Size
Metal Water Pipe Bonding
Metal Gas and Other Pipe Bonding

GROUNDING ELECTRODE WIRES (E3610 AND E3611) 467

Aluminum Grounding Electrode Wires
Connecting Grounding Electrode Wires to the Electrode
Connections Around Equipment and Insulated Fittings

CHAPTER 37: BRANCH CIRCUIT AND FEEDER REQUIREMENTS 469

MULTIWIRE BRANCH CIRCUITS (E3701.5) 469

Multiwire Branch Circuit Definition
Multiwire Branch Circuit Requirements

BRANCH CIRCUIT VOLTAGE AND AMERAGE RATINGS (E3702) 470

Multiple Outlet Branch Circuit Amperage and Voltage Rating Limits
Multiple Outlet Branch Circuit Load Limits
Thirty Amp Branch Circuit Load Limits
Single-Motor Branch Circuit Wire Size
Combination Motor and Other Load / Branch Circuit Wire Size
Fluorescent Light Circuit Loads
Cooking Appliance Circuit Loads
Water Heating and Space Heating Branch Circuit Loads
Air Conditioning and Heat Pump Condenser Branch Circuit Size
Room Air Conditioner Branch Circuits

BRANCH CIRCUITS REQUIRED (E3703) 474

Central Heating Branch Circuit
Kitchen Receptacle Branch Circuit
Laundry Receptacle Branch Circuit
Bathroom Receptacle Branch Circuit
General Lighting Branch Circuits
Receptacle Quantity Limitation on Branch Circuit Discussion

FEEDER LOAD CALCULATION (E3704) 475

Limitations of the Material in this Section
Feeder Load Formula
Feeder Load Calculation Example
Feeder and Service Neutral (Grounded) Wire Load Calculation
Feeder and Service Neutral Load Calculation Example

WIRE SIZING AND OVERCURRENT PROTECTION (E3705) 481

NM Cable (Romex®) Ampacity and Overcurrent Protection
Wire Ampacity and Overcurrent Protection
Wire and Circuit Ampacity Discussion
Ampacity Reduction for High Temperature
Ampacity Reduction for Proximity
Ampacity Reduction Discussion
Electrical Device Limit on Circuit Ampacity
Overcurrent Protection

PANELBOARD PROTECTION AND RATING (E3706) 487

CHAPTER 38: WIRING METHODS 488

WIRING METHODS DEFINITION 488

KNOB-AND-TUBE WIRING 488

WIRING METHODS AND ALLOWED USES (E3801) 489

Wiring Methods Currently Allowed
Circuit Wires in Same Raceway
Wiring Method Allowed Uses

ABOVE GROUND WIRING INSTALLATION (E3802) 490

NM and UF Cable Installation
Conduit and Tubing Installation
Wiring Support Requirements
Wiring Protection in Attics
Wiring in Unfinished Basement Ceiling Joists
Bends in Cables and Conduit
Wiring Exposed to Direct Sunlight
Raceways and Cables Exposed to Different Temperatures

BELOW GROUND WIRING INSTALLATION (E3803) 495

Below Ground Wiring Burial Depth
Protection where Wires Emerge from Ground

Below Ground Splices and Taps
Raceway Seals

CHAPTER 39: RECEPTACLE, LIGHT, AND WIRING INSTALLATION 497

RECEPTACLE INSTALLATION (E3901) 497

Interior Receptacle General Installation Requirements
Interior Receptacle Height
Interior Receptacle Spacing
Interior Receptacle Spacing Discussion
Kitchen Receptacles General Installation Requirements
Kitchen Countertop Receptacle Spacing
Kitchen Island and Peninsula Receptacles Without a Sink or Cooking Appliance
Kitchen Island Receptacles with a Sink or Cooking Appliance
Appliance Receptacles
Bathroom Sink Receptacles
Exterior Receptacles
Laundry Receptacles
Basement Receptacles
Garage Receptacles
Hallway Receptacles
HVAC Service Receptacles

GROUND-FAULT AND ARC-FAULT PROTECTION REQUIRED
LOCATIONS (E3902) 502

Bathroom Receptacles
Garage and Accessory Building Receptacles
Exterior Receptacles
Crawl Space Receptacles
Basement Receptacles
Kitchen Countertop Receptacles
Laundry, Utility, and Bar Sink Receptacles
Boathouse Receptacles
Spas, Tubs, and Other Circuits Requiring Ground-Fault Protection
Arc-Fault Circuit Interrupters
Arc-Fault Circuit Interrupters Discussion

LIGHT FIXTURE REQUIRED LOCATIONS (E3903) 504

Lights Required in Habitable Rooms
Lights Required in Other Interior Spaces
Lights Required at Exterior Doors
Lights Required in Attics, Crawl Spaces, and Basements

CONDUIT, TUBING, AND CABLE INSTALLATION (E3904) 505

Conduit and Tubing Installation
Conduit and Tubing Wire Capacity
Wires in Stud Cavities used as HVAC Ducts

JUNCTION BOXES AND DEVICE BOXES (E3905 AND E3906). 506
Wire Splices and Terminations
Nonmetallic Box Installation
Light Fixture Box Installation
Floor Box Type
Ceiling Fan Boxes
Box Contents Limitations
Box Contents Limitations Example
Box Opening Covers
Box Installation Tolerances
Box Support in Walls, Ceilings, and Floors
Box Support by Raceways
Combustible Material Under Fixture Canopy

CABINETS AND PANELBOARDS (E3907) 510
Panelboard and Switch Cabinets as Junction Boxes
Panelboard Cabinets in Damp and Wet Locations
Panelboard Cabinet Installation Tolerances
Panelboard Cabinet Opening Covers
Cables Secured to Cabinet

EQUIPMENT GROUNDING (E3908). 511
When Equipment Grounding is Required
Grounding to Neutral Wires (Bootleg Grounds)
Grounding with Flexible Metal Conduit
Equipment Grounding Wire Size
Equipment Grounding Wires Installation in Boxes
Grounding Receptacles to Metal Boxes
Paint on Grounding Connections

FLEXIBLE CORDS (E3909) 513
Flexible Cord Permitted Uses

CHAPTER 40: FINAL INSTALLATION OF SWITCHES, RECEPTACLES, AND LIGHTS. 514

SWITCH INSTALLATION (E4001). 514
Switch Current Load Limitations
Switches Connected to Aluminum Wire
Switch and Circuit Breaker Orientation
Switch and Circuit Breaker Height
Timer Switches
Grounding of Switches, Boxes, and Faceplates
Switches and Circuit Breakers in Wet Locations
Switching Neutral (Grounded) Wires
Switch Mounting in Boxes
Switch Faceplate Installation

RECEPTACLE INSTALLATION (E4002) 516
Receptacle Current Rating
Receptacle Grounding Type Use
Receptacles Connected to Aluminum Wire
Receptacle Mounting in Boxes
Receptacle Mounting on Box Covers
Receptacle Faceplate Installation
Receptacles in Damp Locations
Receptacles in Wet Locations
Receptacles Greater than Twenty Amps in Wet Locations
Receptacles in Tubs and Showers
Receptacle Terminal Physical Contact

LIGHT FIXTURE INSTALLATION (E4003 AND E4004) 518
Light Fixture Definition
Light Fixture Support
Protection of Energized Light Fixture Parts
Receptacle Inserts for Lamp Holders
Recessed Lights Type and Installation
High Density Discharge Lights
Lights in Wet and Damp Locations
Ceiling Fans and Lights Near Tubs and Showers
Light Fixtures Installed on Low-density Cellulose Fiberboard
Light Fixtures Near Combustible Material
Light Fixture Wiring

CLOTHES CLOSET LIGHT INSTALLATION (E4003.11) 521
Closet Storage Area Definition
Light Fixture Clearances in Clothes Closets

TRACK LIGHTS (E4005) 523
Track Light Installation
Track Light Prohibited Locations

CHAPTER 41: APPLIANCE INSTALLATION 524

APPLIANCE DEFINITION 524

APPLIANCE INSTALLATION (E4101) 524
Appliance Installation Using Flexible Cords
Appliance Disconnecting Means
Ceiling Fan Support

CHAPTER 42: ELECTRICAL REQUIREMENTS FOR POOLS, SPAS, WHIRLPOOL TUBS, FOUNTAINS 525

APPLICATION OF THE MATERIAL IN THIS CHAPTER 525

SWIMMING POOL AND SPA DEFINITIONS (E4201) 525

SWIMMING POOL AND SPA WIRING METHODS (E4202) 526
Swimming Pool and Spa Common Wiring Methods
Flexible Cord Uses and Limitations Near Swimming Pools and Spas

RECEPTACLES AND SWITCHES NEAR SWIMMING POOLS
    AND SPAS (E4203.1 – E4203.3) 527
Measuring Distance Between Receptacles and Pools and Spas
Receptacles Near Swimming Pools and Outdoor Spas and Hot Tubs
Receptacles Near Indoor Spas and Hot Tubs
Switches Near Swimming Pools and Spas
Electrical Disconnecting Means Near Swimming Pools and Spas

LIGHTS AND FANS NEAR SWIMMING POOLS AND SPAS (E4203.4). 528
Outdoor Pools, Spas, and Hot Tubs – New Lights and Fans
Indoor Pools, Spas, and Hot Tubs – New Lights and Fans
Pools and Outdoor Spas, and Hot Tubs – Existing Lights
Pools, Spas, and Hot Tubs – Lights Between Five and Ten Feet from Water's Edge
Communication, Telephone, and Other Outlets Clearances (E4203.5)
Overhead Wire Clearances (E4203.6)
Underground Wire Clearances (E4203.7)

BONDING OF METAL NEAR SWIMMING POOLS AND SPAS (E4204) 533
Metal Parts Requiring Bonding - all Pools and Outdoor Spas and Hot Tubs
Metal Parts Requiring Bonding - Indoor Spas and Hot Tubs
Bonding Method
Bonding Discussion

GROUNDING OF METAL NEAR SWIMMING POOLS AND SPAS (E4205) 534
Equipment Required to be Grounded
Grounding Underwater Lights
Grounding Nonmetallic Conduit Serving Underwater Lights
Grounding Underwater Lights Supplied by Flexible Cords
Grounding Motors
Grounding Panelboards

INSTALLATION REQUIREMENTS FOR UNDERWATER LIGHTS, JUNCTION BOXES,
    AND OTHER EQUIPMENT NEAR POOLS AND SPAS (E4206). 536
Mixing GFCI Protected and Non-GFCI Protected Wires
Underwater Light GFCI Protection
Underwater Light Depth
Wet-Niche Light Servicing
Underwater Light Junction Boxes
Underwater Light Device Boxes
Strain Relief for Flexible Cords
Underwater Speakers
Pool Cover Motors
Electric Pool Area Heaters
Storable Swimming Pool Pumps and Lights (E4207)

Spa and Hot Tub GFCI Protection (E4208)
Whirlpool Bathtubs (E4209)

CHAPTER 43: LOW VOLTAGE CIRCUITS 539

Application of the Material in this Chapter 539
Low Voltage Power Sources
Low Voltage Wiring Methods
Low Voltage and Electric Power Wire Separation
Low Voltage Wire Installation and Support

APPENDIX E: MANUFACTURED HOMES. 541
Manufactured Home Definition
Application of the Material in this Appendix
Manufactured Home Use
Manufactured Home Foundations
Manufactured Home Footings and Piers (E600)
Manufactured Home Anchors and Tie-Down Hardware
Manufactured Home Accessory Structures
Manufactured Home Crawl Spaces

APPENDIX A: RADON CONTROL 543
Radon Definition
Application of the Material in this Appendix
Radon Control General Discussion
Radon Control Measures Under Concrete Slabs in Slab and Basement Foundations
Sealing Penetrations of Slab and Basement Foundations
Sealing Foundation Walls
Sealing HVAC Equipment and Ducts in Crawl Spaces
Sealing Crawl Space Openings to Living Areas
Crawl Space Ventilation System
Concrete Slab Ventilation System
Ventilation of Different Foundation Areas
Ventilation Pipe Requirements

APPENDIX G: SWIMMING POOL AND SPA BARRIERS
AND ACCESS CONTROL 547
Application of the Material in this Appendix
Swimming Pool Definition – Barrier and Access Control
Outdoor Swimming Pool Barriers
Gates in Pool Barriers
House Door Barriers
House Barriers Best Practice
Above Ground Pool Barrier
Indoor Swimming Pool Barriers
Spa and Hot Tub Barrier Exception
Entrapment Protection
Entrapment Protection Best Practice

SATELLITE DISHES AND TELEVISION AND RADIO ANTENNAS (NEC ARTICLE 810) 550

Source of this Material
Application of the Material in this Article
Antenna Wire and Coaxial Cable Description
Antenna Prohibited Installation Locations
Antenna Wire and Cable Clearance to Electric Power Wires
Lightning Arrestors
Grounding Antennas, Masts, Wires, and Cables
Grounding Wire Connection to the Grounding Point

CABLE TELEVISION SYSTEM WIRING – RESIDENTIAL (NEC ARTICLE 820) 554

Source of this Material
Application of the Material in this Article
Coaxial Cable Description
Television Cable Clearance to Electric Power Wires
Overhead Television Cable Clearance Above Roofs
Grounding Television Cables
Grounding Wire Connection to the Grounding Point
Television Cable and Electric Power Wire Separation
Television Cable Separation from Low Voltage and Communication Wires
Television Cable Installation and Support

BROADBAND COMMUNICATION WIRING – RESIDENTIAL (NEC ARTICLE 830) 558

Source of this Material
Application of the Material in this Article
Broadband Cable Description
Low and Medium Power Broadband System Definition
Overhead Broadband Cable Clearance to Electric Power Wires
Overhead Broadband Cable Clearance Above Ground
Overhead Broadband Cable Clearance Above Roofs
Broadband Cable Burial Depth
Grounding Broadband Cables
Grounding Wire Connection to the Grounding Point
Broadband Cable and Electric Power Wire Separation
Low Power Broadband Separation from Low Voltage and Communication Wires
Medium Power Broadband Separation from Low Voltage and Communication Wires
Broadband Cable Installation and Support

SOLAR PHOTOVOLTAIC SYSTEMS (NEC ARTICLE 690) 562

Source of this Material
Limitations of the Material in this Chapter
Photovoltaic System Types
Common Photovoltaic System Components
Photovoltaic Component Grounding and Bonding

Photovoltaic Wire Protection
Photovoltaic Disconnecting Equipment
Photovoltaic Batteries

INDEX **568**

Preface

Building codes are adopted by governments to preserve your family's physical and fiscal health and safety. If you are someone who likes to do-it-yourself, a homeowner acting as your own contractor, a contractor, a home inspector, a real estate agent, or anyone else who wants to protect themselves, their family, and their customers by using the International Residential Code® (IRC) 2009, then this is your building code book. This book makes the IRC more accessible and easier to understand so you can use the IRC without becoming a code expert.

This book does not replace the IRC. It contains selected IRC provisions and omits others. While every effort has been made to accurately present the IRC with easy to understand language, pictures, and diagrams, this book is not the IRC. In a dispute, the wording in the IRC, as interpreted by the local building official, is the final authority on what IRC provisions mean.

This book does not replace "how to do it" books. If, for example, you wish to replace a water heater, learn the steps for doing so in a "how to do it" book. Use this book to learn if your work complies with IRC 2009 provisions. You should review the IRC provisions in this book before you do the work to avoid changing completed work that does not comply with the IRC.

If you need a more detailed and professional understanding of the IRC, I urge you to acquire the IRC Commentary. This large two-volume work contains all IRC provisions accompanied by lengthy explanations and illustrations. It is a valuable resource and is well worth the cost.

Finding all relevant IRC provisions is often a challenge. This book gives you two options for finding the provisions you need. You may use the extensive index at the back of this book to find code provisions relating to a word such as switch, stud, or shingle. You may also use the Table of Contents to find code provisions relating to a topic such as receptacle installation. Be careful when using the Table of Contents because code provisions about a topic may appear in more than one place. Looking for similar topics in related areas is often a good idea to be certain you have found all relevant code provisions.

The Table of Contents is almost a book in itself. It lists every IRC provision discussed in this book, along with additional explanation and discussion material. Once you are familiar with the material in the Table of Contents, you will know if the IRC addresses a topic and, if so, where to find it. By using both options, you should find the IRC provisions that will help you safeguard those who rely on you to keep their home safe.

Preface for Home Inspectors

It is an article of faith among home inspectors that we do not perform building code compliance inspections. This is as it should be. On any given day, we could inspect anything from the footings for a new home to a home built in the 18th century. Some of us practice in areas where building code enforcement has been active for many years and others of us practice in areas where code enforcement is still lax or does not exist. Some of us practice in multiple cities and even in multiple states. Each city and state usually has a different building code and almost always has different local amendments and interpretations of their local building code. For these reasons and others, it is impractical for us to determine what, if any, building codes were in effect when a home was built or remodeled and it is impossible for us to know how the code was interpreted and enforced at that time.

Building codes are government regulations similar to traffic laws, zoning ordinances and countless other government imposed rules that control how people function in a complex modern society. Government regulations need a government representative to interpret and enforce them. Just as one person cannot issue a ticket to another person for violating a traffic law, we cannot "red tag" or otherwise issue a legally binding opinion that a certain construction practice is a building code violation. Only the authorized building official from the Authority Having Jurisdiction (AHJ) may interpret the meaning and intent of the building code and issue a legally binding order about code violations.

This, too, is as it should be. If our code interpretations had the force of law, chaos would ensue. We would issue conflicting opinions about what is and what is not a code violation. It is difficult enough to get a consistent interpretation of code provisions from different representatives of the local AHJ. For this reason, home inspectors who are knowledgeable about building codes must be content to act in an advisory capacity regarding possible code violations.

Why, then, should home inspectors understand basic code provisions if we cannot and should not perform code compliance inspections? Just because we cannot issue binding code interpretations does not mean that we should be ignorant of code provisions. We can and should use whatever knowledge of building codes that we have to identify important health and safety issues. Home inspectors who have a good understanding of basic code provisions can perform a valuable client service by helping to identify possible code issues that may have been missed by overworked code enforcement officials.

Introduction to Building Codes

THE INTERNATIONAL RESIDENTIAL CODE®

The International Residential Code® (IRC) is one of an extensive collection of model building codes published by the International Code Council (ICC). A model building code is a recommended building code developed by a national organization that specializes in writing building codes. When adopted by a government, the IRC regulates the construction, renovation, maintenance, and repair of buildings used as homes. The IRC, by itself, has no formal legal status. It must first be adopted by a government agency before it has any legal status in a local area.

STATE AND LOCAL BUILDING CODES

Almost all areas of the United States have adopted some version of a building code. Some states, such as California, Florida, and New York, have a state building code. Some large cities, such as Chicago and New York City, have a city building code. Many of these state and local building codes are based on the model codes from the ICC.

Smaller cities and counties often use ICC model codes, such as the IRC. Some rural areas may not have adopted a building code, but this is becoming a rare situation. If you do any work that is regulated by the local building code, you are responsible for knowing, or for hiring someone who knows, the applicable building code where the building is located. Ignorance of the code is no excuse.

LOCAL CODE AMENDMENTS

Most building departments that use the IRC adopt local changes to the IRC. Many of these changes are minor and help to adapt the IRC to local conditions and needs. Some of these changes can significantly alter IRC provisions. The building department should publish, in writing, any changes adopted by the local government. You are responsible for knowing and complying with all local changes. Ask the building official if there are any local code changes.

OTHER BUILDING CODES

The IRC is not the only building code. Other commonly used building codes include The International Building Code® (IBC), The International Mechanical Code® (IMC), The International Plumbing Code® (IPC), The Uniform Plumbing Code® (UPC), The International Fuel Gas Code® (IFG), The National Electrical Code® (NEC), and The International Energy Conservation Code® (IECC). Each of these building codes regulates a different aspect of building construction.

The IBC regulates the structural aspects of all buildings, although it is not commonly applied to most residential buildings. The IBC usually applies to commercial, industrial, and multi-family buildings such as apartments. The IRC references the IBC and the IECC when a part of a residential building is more complex than is addressed by the IRC.

Each major system in a building has its own code. The IMC regulates heating, ventilation, and air conditioning systems; the IPC regulates plumbing systems; and the IFG regulates gas piping and gas equipment. These codes usually apply to commercial-type buildings. The UPC is a separate code, published by another code writing organization, that also regulates plumbing systems. It may replace the IRC plumbing chapters in areas that adopt the UPC. The NEC regulates electrical systems. The IRC contains an adapted version of the NEC in the IRC electrical chapters. When the IRC does not address an electrical situation in a home, the NEC usually applies.

The IECC regulates energy-related aspects of all buildings. These aspects include: insulation, air infiltration, and window and door energy efficiency. The IRC contains a simplified subset of the IECC in IRC Chapter Eleven.

You should know which codes apply to your construction project. Ask your local building official which codes apply in your area.

BUILDING DEPARTMENTS

A local building department enforces the building code in its jurisdiction. The technical term often used to describe this department is the Authority Having Jurisdiction (AHJ). The term used to describe the person responsible for enforcing the code is the Building Official or Chief Building Official. The public name for the local building department varies by jurisdiction. Many building departments will have the terms "building" or "safety" somewhere in the name. In some larger jurisdictions, the building department may be a division of a larger agency that is also responsible for land planning, zoning, and development. Some building department names may not sound like they have anything at all to do with building code enforcement. If you do any work that requires a building permit, you are responsible for finding and contacting the building department. Work done without a permit can have serious legal and financial consequences.

WORKING WITH GOVERNMENT BUILDING INSPECTORS

The building official is the king of his building jurisdiction. Don't mess with the king. He can make your life very difficult. If you must disagree with him, do so respectfully and with facts that support your position. The building official has the right to interpret any code provision. While he does not have the right to waive code provisions or to require more than the code requires, interpretations can sometimes have that effect. Even if his interpretation seems unreasonable, eventually it will probably prevail. In almost all cases, you should just smile and do what he tells you.

Most building officials and inspectors are honest, hard working people who want to ensure that your project complies with local codes. They can be a valuable resource. Take advantage of that resource. Ask questions and work with them. Most will, in turn, work with you.

WORKING WITH PRIVATE BUILDING INSPECTORS

Time is not the friend of government building inspectors. From an eight hour day, they must subtract doing paperwork, discussing inspections with stakeholders, traveling between inspections, and performing other duties. Divide the remaining time by twenty to thirty inspections per day, or more, and they may have only a few minutes to perform each inspection. It's a credit to government inspectors that they find many major code violations. Most will admit, however, that they cannot find all code violations. They will also admit that they are not even looking for issues that are not code violations, but that can have a significant impact on the cost to operate and maintain the home.

Private building inspectors fill this quality control gap for many people. People building homes and people performing major remodeling projects hire and pay for a private inspector who helps the government inspector and the contractor provide quality construction. A private inspector can perform a far more thorough inspection than a government inspector because a private inspector can invest more time on each inspection. In addition, a private inspector usually inspects areas such as attics and roofs where government inspectors rarely go.

When building a new home or during a major remodeling project, a private inspector is often most useful at two critical points. The most critical point is just before insulation and drywall is installed. This inspection is sometimes called the pre-drywall inspection and is the most important inspection a home will ever have. At this time, an inspector can see many important components that will be covered by finish materials and, in most cases, will never visible again. The other critical point is at the end of construction. At this time, an inspector can see and test important systems in the home.

Private inspectors are increasingly common on construction sites. While some contractors welcome private inspectors, many do not. Even if you decide not to engage a private inspector, is wise to discuss the option with the contractor before signing a contract and it is wise to agree, in writing, how the contractor will work with the private inspector during construction.

ZONING ORDINANCES

Many areas, particularly the more densely populated ones, have land use and zoning ordinances that also control what you can build on your property. You are responsible for knowing and complying with them. In larger jurisdictions, the planning and zoning department may be separate from the building inspection department and sometimes one does not know what the other is doing. It is possible that the building inspection department might issue a permit that would create a zoning violation. Projects that might run afoul of zoning ordinances include new, free-standing buildings, basement remodels that add a bedroom, bathroom, and kitchen, and any project that adds an additional full kitchen on property zoned for single family use.

SELECTING A QUALIFIED CONTRACTOR

Successful construction projects that comply with the local building code have several important elements. Careful initial planning is important. Detailed written project specifications and a budget are important. Regular comparison of work performed to specifications and to the budget is important. No element, though, is more important to success than selecting a qualified contractor who is familiar with the local building code. But how do you find a qualified contractor and how do you determine if the contractor is indeed qualified?

The best source of qualified contractors is, of course, family, friends, coworkers, and neighbors. If a contractor has satisfied someone you know, there is a chance (and only a chance) that it may satisfy you as well. Another good source is a trade group, such as the National Association of Home Builders. Contractors who have the financial and other resources to maintain membership in a trade group may be more stable and qualified than other contractors. The source of last resort is advertising. You should not always go to the largest or fanciest display ads first. Some of the best contractors only have a one line listing in the phone book.

How do you determine if a contractor might be qualified? Start with the usual questions. How many years experience do you have doing similar work? How long have you been in business locally? Have you done similar work nearby that I can see? Can you give me at least three references, one of which had the work completed at least two years ago? The two years reference helps you determine the quality of warranty follow-up and helps you determine how well the work holds up over time. Do you have a contractor license covering the work you might do for me? Do you have a business license? A contractor license and a business license are different. Do you carry workman's compensation and general liability insurance? Do you take continuing education courses? Are you familiar with the local building code? Answers to these questions will often separate stable and qualified contractors from other contractors.

In states that license contractors (this includes most states) you should always verify the status of the contractor license and the business license with the licensing authority. Determine if the licenses are in good standing. Determine if the license holder will actually perform, or at least supervise, the work. Determine if complaints or disciplinary actions are pending against the license holder. Complaints or disciplinary actions are not automatic disqualifications. They are; however, red flags that mean you need to ask more questions.

In addition to verifying the contractor's license status, you should determine that the work the contractor might perform is within the scope of the license. For example, a landscaping contractor's license may allow the holder to install wood fences, but not fences made from concrete blocks. The license may allow the holder to build steps up to a specified height (such as three steps), but not more. The license may allow the holder to tap into existing plumbing and electrical systems only as required to install exterior irrigation systems. Work performed by a contractor that is outside the scope of his license is, in effect, unlicensed work. Such work carries increased risks and may not be covered by any existing consumer protection laws.

Before interviewing contractors you should determine if the work requires a building permit from the local building department. Refer to Chapter One in this book for more information about building permits. If a permit is required, ask the contractor if he intends to obtain a permit. If the contractor does not wish to obtain a permit, or suggests that you obtain the permit in your name, this is a red flag. Contractors who do not wish to obtain a permit in their own name may have problems with the local building department. You may wish to ask the local building department if they are aware of problems with the contractor. There are sometimes valid reasons why a contractor may not want to obtain a permit in its own name, but it should be able to provide a clear and convincing explanation about why not.

BUILDING PERMITS AND CODE ADMINISTRATION

BUILDINGS GOVERNED BY THE IRC (R101.2)

Apply the IRC to buildings containing one or two individual residential dwelling units in one building. Duplex is a common term for one building containing two individual dwelling units.

Apply the IRC to townhouses. A townhouse contains at least (≥) 3 individual dwelling units in one building.

Apply the IRC to residential buildings with not more than (≤) 3 stories above grade. Whether a basement is a story above grade depends on a complex set of rules. Basements with walls that are completely or mostly covered by dirt are not a story above grade. Example: a basement with one wall completely covered by dirt and two walls more than fifty percent covered by dirt is not a story above grade. Example: a basement with the rear wall not covered by dirt and two side walls that are less than fifty percent covered by dirt may be a story above grade. Refer to the definitions in IRC Chapter 2 and consult the local building official if there is a question about whether a basement is a story above grade.

Do not apply the IRC to buildings used for business, office, commercial, or industrial purposes. This is true even if the building was once used as a residence. You may apply the IRC to an office in the home if the office is incidental to the residential use of the building. Refer to the International Building Code (IBC) for code provisions governing buildings not governed by the IRC.

MANUFACTURER'S INSTRUCTIONS (R102.4)

Priority of Manufacturer's Instructions

1. Install components, equipment, and appliances according to the terms of their listing, including the manufacturer's instructions. If there is a difference between IRC provisions and the manufacturer's instructions, use the manufacturer's instructions unless the IRC specifies otherwise. <u>Manufacturer's instructions are an enforceable extension of the IRC</u>.

Manufacturer's Instructions Discussion

The priority of manufacturer's instructions is an important IRC provision. It is repeated many times in the IRC and in the Commentary.

Independent organizations test many components used to build homes. This includes almost all manufactured components. The tests are conducted under defined conditions that include using the manufacturer's instructions to install the component. The testing organization certifies that the component is safe when installed and used according to manufacturer's instructions. The testing organization places the certified components on a list maintained by the testing organization. This process is called listing and the components are referred to in the IRC as listed.

The IRC cannot anticipate every possible building component and every possible way the component could be installed. As such, the IRC relies on the manufacturer's instructions to specify how components should be installed.

When a difference between the IRC and the manufacturer's instructions occurs, the IRC assumes that the manufacturer is in a better position to know its product and how it should be installed in a given situation. This is why the IRC usually defers to the manufacturer's instructions.

BUILDING PERMITS (R105)

Local Regulations and Customs for Building Permits

1. Contact the building official to determine which construction activities require a building permit and to determine the documents and procedures required to obtain a permit. The building official may not enforce some building permit requirements contained in the IRC and may add additional building permit requirements not contained in the IRC.
2. Wait until the required permit is issued before beginning work. Beginning work before the permit is issued will often result in fines and the building official could require removal of the work.
3. Comply with the applicable building code where the building is located. The applicable building code is usually the code in force when the permit is issued. If you do not obtain a building permit, comply with the building code in force when the work is performed. The building code applies whether or not you obtain a building permit. This is important. <u>Lack of a building permit does not relieve the building owner or the contractor of responsibility for code compliance.</u>

When a Building Permit May be Required

1. You often need a building permit for:
   a) construction of new buildings,
   b) additions and structural modifications to existing buildings,
   c) structural repairs to existing buildings,
   d) replacement of or major repairs to building components such as roof coverings and exterior wall coverings,
   e) movement and demolition of existing buildings,
   f) changes to building occupancy.
      A change to building occupancy means changing how the building is used. Example: using a single family home as a place of business is a change in occupancy that may require a building permit and may require a zoning change or zoning waiver.

2. You often need a building permit for additions to, major changes to, and/or replacement of electrical, plumbing, gas, and HVAC components.

When a Building Permit May Not be Required

1. You may not need a building permit for:
   a) one-story detached accessory structures (such as storage sheds and playhouses) with a floor area not more than (≤) 200 square feet,
   b) fences not more than (≤) 6 feet tall,
   c) retaining walls not more than (≤) 4 feet tall measured from the bottom of the footing to the top of the wall and not supporting a surcharge (a vertical load in addition to and/or above the retained ground),
   d) driveways and sidewalks,
   e) painting, papering, floor covering installation, cabinet and countertop installation, and similar finish work,
   f) installation of portable plug-and-cord connected decorative lights and similar plug-and-cord connected electrical equipment,
   g) replacement of fuses and circuit breakers,
   h) low voltage lights and other electrical wires and equipment operating at less than (<) 25 volts and not more than (≤) 50 watts,
   i) installation of portable gas heating, cooking and clothes drying equipment,
   j) installation of portable HVAC equipment (such as window air conditioners),
   k) clearing of plumbing stoppages and repair of plumbing leaks and removal and reinstallation of toilets if the repairs do not involve replacement or rearrangement of valves, pipes or fixtures,
   l) decks that are not more than (≤) 30 inches above ground, and are not more than (≤) 200 square feet in area, and are not attached to the building, and do not serve the required egress door.

Building Permit for Routine Maintenance

1. You usually do not need a building permit for routine maintenance of existing buildings, fixtures, and equipment if the building structure is not affected and if the nature and use of the electrical, plumbing, gas or HVAC system is not changed.

Building Permit Expiration

1. Verify building permit expiration rules with the local building official. A building permit may expire if more than 180 days lapse without an inspection or without some other evidence of work on the project.

Building Permit Discussion

Work performed without a building permit and inspections is one of the most common sources of problems found during home inspections. Brother-in-law installed water heaters, homeowner installed electrical work, projects by unlicensed contractors, and similar work performed without building permits and inspections is often unsafe and often costs the homeowner more to remove and replace the improper work.

While rarely enforced, the building official can require that work performed without a building permit be removed or at least uncovered so that an inspection for code compliance can be performed.

INSPECTIONS (R109)

Inspection General Requirements

1. Contact the building official to determine the required inspections for a construction project. Each jurisdiction has its own rules for inspections. These rules include: which inspections it performs, what work must be complete before requesting the inspection, how and when to schedule the inspection, and how it handles inspections of work that fails inspection. The following descriptions list the work that is often completed before scheduling the inspection.

Footing Inspections

1. Install, square, and level forms.
2. Dig footing and pier trenches according to the width and depth requirements from Chapter 4.
3. Install any required reinforcing bars.

Foundation Wall Inspections

1. Install, square, straighten, plumb, and secure wall forms.
2. Install any required reinforcing bars.

Foundation Slab Inspections

1. Install, square, straighten, and level forms.
2. Dig any footing, thickened slab, and pier trenches according to the width and depth requirements from Chapter 4.
3. Install any plumbing, electrical, and Radon control pipes and conduit that will be in or under the foundation slab. These components often require a separate inspection.
4. Install and compact any required sand or gravel.
5. Install any required reinforcing bar, crack control wire, and vapor retarder.

Plumbing, HVAC, and Electrical Rough-in Inspections

1. Install plumbing water supply and drain pipes in the building. Note that building sewer and building water supply pipes often require a separate inspection. Install fixtures such as tubs and showers that may be difficult to install after the home is complete.
2. Install HVAC ducts, pipes, and thermostat wires. Install appliances such as furnaces and air handlers that may be difficult to install after the home is complete.
3. Install electrical service panel and subpanel cabinets, and boxes for switches, receptacles, and fixtures, and all electrical cables.

4. Note that some jurisdictions conduct a separate inspection for each trade, some jurisdictions conduct one inspection when all trades work is complete, and some jurisdictions conduct trade inspections during the framing inspection.

Framing Inspection

1. Install all interior and exterior walls, floor joists and subflooring, ceiling joists and rafters, and roof sheathing. Install all required bracing, firestops, and draftstops.
2. Note that some jurisdictions may require installation of other components such as moisture barriers, and roofing felt before calling for a framing inspection.

Final Inspection

1. Install all plumbing, HVAC, and electrical fixtures, equipment, and appliances. Install all required safety components such as stair hand rails and guards, safety glazing, and smoke alarms.
2. Note that jurisdictions have different rules about whether you must install finish components, such as floor coverings, before the final inspection. Jurisdictions also differ on whether tasks such as final grading and landscaping must be installed.

Other Inspections

1. Check with the building official to determine if other inspections are required. Other required inspection may include flood plain and elevation, roof coverings, insulation and energy efficiency, interior drywall, and exterior wall coverings such as stucco and masonry.

CERTIFICATE OF OCCUPANCY (R110)

Certificate of Occupancy Required

1. Do not move into or occupy a building until after the building official issues a certificate of occupancy.
2. Do not change the use of a building without a new certificate of occupancy. Example: do not use a building as an office if the building once was a home without receiving a new certificate of occupancy. The new certificate of occupancy may require changes to the building that reflect its new commercial use.
3. You are not required to obtain a certificate of occupancy for accessory structures.

Waiver of Code Violations

1. Do not assume that passing an inspection or receiving a certificate of occupancy is a waiver of any code violations. The building owner and contractor are responsible for any code violations regardless of whether the building has passed inspections.

2
DEFINITIONS

Accessory structure An accessory structure is another building on the same lot, the use of which is incidental to the main building. Examples of accessory structures are detached garages, storage sheds, and guest houses. An accessory structure must be not more than (≤) 3,000 square feet in floor area and not more than (≤) 2 stories tall.

Air-entrained concrete Air-entrained concrete is concrete that contains air bubbles. It is used in severe weathering environments to reduce wear caused by freeze and thaw cycles and wear caused by chemical deicers. It also improves the concrete's workability during pouring and finishing.

Air intake opening (gravity) A gravity air intake opening is any opening that allows air to flow into the home through natural means. Operable windows and doors are the most common examples. Less common examples include combustion air openings, makeup and ventilation air openings, and soffit vent openings.

Air intake opening (mechanical) A mechanical air intake opening is one that draws air into the home using a fan, blower, or other powered means. A common example is an outside air intake duct connected to the return boot of a forced-air HVAC system. These ducts are being installed in some new homes to mix outdoor air with the return air to increase air changes per hour in the home and to improve indoor air quality.

Attic, habitable A habitable attic is a habitable space located directly under the roof. Habitable attics have no exterior walls. Interior walls, if any, are knee walls between the rafters above and the floor below. An example of a habitable attic is an attic area that is accessible by permanent stairs. A habitable attic is not considered a story so it does not add to the number of stories above grade and it does not place additional load requirements on the supporting framing. A habitable attic is designed as a sleeping area for determining floor joist spans. A habitable attic must have the minimum floor space (70 square feet) and minimum ceiling height as required in Sections R304 and R305.

Balloon framing Balloon framing is a building system where walls extend from the foundation to the ceiling joists. Intermediate floor joists are attached to the walls and are often supported by a ledger. Balloon framing is rare in modern residential construction.

Baluster A baluster (also called a picket) is a vertical piece found in guard rails and handrails that supports the rail and provides protection against occupants falling through or being caught between the balusters.

Batten (1) A batten is a vertical wood strip applied at the seam between two pieces of vertical siding, such as 4x8 panel siding. When used with siding material, such as 1x6 vertical boards, the siding is called board and batten.

(2) A batten is a wood strip, usually a 1x2, applied on a roof to help secure roof coverings such as tile and slate.

(3) A batten is a wood strip applied to framing or to masonry as a place to attach drywall or lathing for plaster. In this application it is often called a furring strip.

Blocking Blocking usually consists of pieces of wood that are used to connect, reinforce, or fill spaces between studs, joists, and rafters. Blocking may be installed at the ends of floor joists to help keep the joists from twisting and to provide support for wall systems above. Blocking may be installed between studs, joists, and rafters to provide support for wood structural panels such as plywood. Blocking is sometimes installed between studs that have been bored or notched to help distribute the load between the studs and to help keep them from twisting.

Braced wall line A braced wall line (also called a shear wall) is a wall that is secured and braced to resist movement (racking) during high winds and seismic events. Bracing usually consists of wood panels, metal straps, or drywall installed as described in Chapter 6.

Bridging Bridging is sometimes installed near the center of floor joists to help hold the joists in place and to help keep them from twisting. Bridging is usually 1x4 wood installed in an X pattern, or wood blocks that are the same depth as the joist, or metal bridging brackets. Bridging is required only on larger joists (deeper than 2x12), but is often installed on other depth floor joists.

Buttress A buttress is a vertical column of masonry that helps a wall resist horizontal (lateral) loads.

Carport A carport is a space for parking motor vehicles that is open to the outdoors on at least (≥) two sides. Garages and carports may be attached to or detached from the dwelling. Garage fire separation requirements do not apply to carports.

Chimney A chimney is a generally vertical, non-combustible structure that contains at least one flue and exhausts combustion products to the outdoors. A chimney may be constructed using masonry or it may be a factory-built system using a metal flue. Chimneys are usually built for use with solid-fuel-burning fireplaces, but may serve as vents for other fuel-burning devices such as gas or oil-burning equipment.

A properly sized chimney may serve as a vent for gas and oil-burning equipment, but chimneys and vents are constructed differently. The rules that apply to chimneys do not always apply to vents. Refer to Chapter 18 for oil-burning equipment vents and Chapter 24 for gas-burning equipment vents.

Coping Coping is a cap on top of a wall, chimney, or similar exterior structure that protects the structure from water. Coping is usually sloped to drain water.

Draft inducer A draft inducer is a device that pulls combustion products by suction through a vent or through an appliance. A vent draft inducer will usually be located near the vent termination. An appliance draft inducer will usually be located near the final exhaust point of the appliance combustion chamber. Most modern medium efficiency gas furnaces are induced draft appliances.

Exposure Exposure is the amount of material visible when installed. The term is used in roof coverings to describe how much of a shingle is visible below the head lap of the shingle course above. See Head lap.

Flashing Flashing is a material that does not allow water to pass and is placed at joints and openings to prevent water entry into a building. Flashing may be sheet metal, rubber, plastic, or roll roofing material. Caulk, roofing tar, and mastic are sealants, and are not flashing.

Footing (spread) A spread footing is a rectangular concrete base that usually supports basement and crawl space foundation walls. It is usually installed first, then foundation walls are installed on the footing in a separate process. Contrast with a monolithic slab footing in which the footing and concrete foundation slab are poured in one process.

Garage A garage is a space for parking motor vehicles that is completely closed to the outdoors on three or more sides. A space with three solid walls and an opening without a vehicle door is a garage.

Glazing Glazing is the transparent or translucent material in a window, door, or skylight. Glazing is usually glass and also includes glass substitutes such as plastic and glass or plastic block.

Head lap Head lap is the distance one piece of material covers another piece of material. The term is used in roof coverings to describe how far an upper layer of material covers a lower piece of material. See Exposure.

Jalousie (doors and windows) A jalousie door or window contains several horizontal overlapping glass panes that are opened and closed by one or more controls. The bottom of the pane swings toward the exterior and the top swings toward the interior. Jalousie doors and windows are most often found in older homes in the Deep South.

Labeled Labeled equipment and components have the seal of an approved testing agency affixed to the equipment or components attesting to the fact that they comply with an approved standard when installed according to manufacturer's instructions. The term labeled is often used with the term listed.

Ledger (1) A ledger (also called a ribbon strip) is a horizontal support for floor joists that is attached near the bottom of a beam so that the tops of the floor joists are flush with the top of the beam. Ledgers attached to wood beams used in residential framing are often 2x2 inches wood strips. Ledgers may also be attached to wall studs to support floor or ceiling joists that intersect perpendicular to the wall.

(2) A ledger is a horizontal support for deck and balcony floor joists that is attached to the house wall using bolts or lag screws.

Listed (Listing) Independent testing agencies maintain lists of equipment and components used in the construction industry. The testing agency confirms that the equipment and components comply with an approved standard when installed according to manufacturer's instructions. The term listed is often used with the term labeled. Listing and labeling are often required by the IRC for manufactured equipment and components.

Monolithic (slab) A monolithic slab is a type of residential foundation in which the footing and the foundation slab are poured in one continuous process.

Parapet wall A parapet wall is a wall that extends above a roof. Parapet walls are common on homes with low slope (flat) roofs and they are required between townhomes.

Pier A pier is a column that supports a concentrated vertical load. Piers are often used in residential construction to support beams and girders in crawl space foundations. Piers are often constructed with concrete blocks that rest on footings called pier pads.

Pilaster A pilaster is a column or pier that supports a concentrated vertical load. A pilaster may be on the interior or exterior of a building and may be taller and more decorative than a pier.

Platform framing Platform framing is a building system where walls are one story high and built upon a floor system below. The floor system is the platform upon which the next story is supported and the platforms are stacked one upon another until the ceiling and roof system. Platform framing is the most common framing system in modern residential construction.

Purlin A purlin is a piece of lumber applied horizontally across rafters to support the rafters and allow them to span a greater distance than they would without the purlin. The purlin is supported by posts attached to a load-bearing wall.

PSI PSI is an abbreviation for pounds per square inch. This is the pressure one material (usually a gas or liquid) exerts against another. Example: the pressure of the atmosphere at sea level is about 14.7 pounds per square inch.

PSIG PSIG is an abbreviation for pounds per square inch as measured by a gauge.

Rabbet A rabbet is a groove or channel cut into material that is intended to receive another piece of rabbeted material. Two pieces of rabbeted material overlap to form a tight and water-resistive joint. A rabbet joint is normally used in interior and exterior trim work and in exterior siding. When used in exterior siding, the term shiplap is often used.

Retaining Wall A retaining wall is a structure that separates and holds back ground at a higher level from ground at a lower level. Retaining walls are not part of the structural support for a building. They are primarily used for landscaping and to adjust the level of sloped lots for easier building construction.

Roof Span The roof span is the overall distance between supports for a roof system. Example: the span of a gable roof is the base of the triangle formed by each half of the gable roof. See also Span.

Shiplap See Rabbet.

Sill (sill plate) A sill plate is a horizontal piece of wood that is supported directly on the foundation and is the bottom part of a wood-framed exterior wall. Sill plates are almost always made with treated lumber.

Sleeper Sleepers are horizontal pieces of wood laid on concrete that provide a nailing surface for flooring. Sleepers are sometimes used to separate hardwood flooring from the moisture that can migrate through concrete.

Soleplate A soleplate is a horizontal piece of wood that is the bottom part of a wood-framed wall other than an exterior wall on the foundation.

Span The span is the unsupported distance between framing members. Example: the span of a 120 inches long floor joist with 1 ½ inches bearing on each end support is 117 inches. Example: the span of a sheet of subfloor between joists spaced 16 inches on center is 14 ½ inches. See also Roof span.

Spark Arrestor A spark arrestor is a metal screen installed at the outside termination of a chimney. A spark arrestor is often installed with a rain cap. A spark arrestor helps prevent hot embers from escaping and starting a fire. A rain cap helps keep water from entering a chimney. Water can damage chimney materials. Spark arrestors and rain caps are recommended on all chimneys, but are not required by the IRC.

Stud, jack A jack stud is a vertical support member in a wall that runs between the bottom of a header and the wall bottom plate and helps support the header.

Stud, king A king stud is a vertical support member in a wall that runs beside a header between the wall top and bottom plates and helps support the header.

Surcharge A surcharge on a retaining wall is a vertical load in addition to the retained earth. The load is usually additional earth above the top of the retaining wall, but the load could be imposed by a nearby structure such as a swimming pool or a building.

Swale A swale is a ditch or depression intended to drain storm water runoff from a residential lot to the street or other storm water collection area.

Townhouse - definition A townhouse contains three or more attached dwelling units in one building. A townhouse must: (a) be continuous from the foundation to the roof (not one dwelling unit on top of another), and (b) have at least (≥) two sides exposed to a yard or public way, and (c) have an independent door to the outside for each unit.

```
        2   1  1   2
        ┌───┬┐┌┬───┐
      2 │HOME 1│ 3 │HOME 3│ 2
        │   3  │   3  │
        ├──────┼──────┤
      2 │HOME 2│ 3 │HOME 4│ 2
        └───┴┘└┴───┘
        2   1  1   2
```

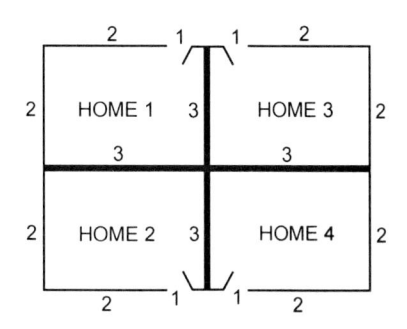

1 DOOR OPENS TO OUTSIDE
2 TWO SIDES EXPOSED TO OUTSIDE
3 STRUCTURALLY INDEPENDENT 1-HOUR
  FIREWALL ON BOTH SIDES OR
  COMMON 2-HOUR FIREWALL

Townhouse – Plan View (R200-0)
Figure 2-1

Underlayment (1) Underlayment is a smooth material laid on the subfloor that serves as a base for a finish flooring material such as vinyl or linoleum. In modern homes, the underlayment is often plywood or particleboard.

(2) Underlayment is a waterproof material placed under roof coverings including fiberglass shingles and tile. It is usually either 15 or 30 pound (per 100 square feet) roofing felt.

Valley (open) An open roof valley is one where the valley lining material is exposed and the roof covering material is cut away from the valley centerline.

Valley (closed) A closed roof valley is one where the roof covering material is installed through the valley and up the opposite side of the valley.

Valley (closed-cut) A closed-cut valley is a type of closed valley where roof covering material is installed through the valley on one side and where the roof covering material from the other side of the valley is cut along the valley center line.

Valley (woven or laced) A woven valley (also called a laced valley) is a type of closed valley where the roof covering material from one side of the valley is installed under the roof covering material from the other side of the valley giving the valley a woven appearance.

Vent (dry) A dry vent is a plumbing vent that is not intended for soil or waste water flow.

Wythe A wythe (also spelled withe) describes a masonry wall one masonry unit thick. A brick wall that is one brick wide is said to be one wythe of brick.

3
BUILDING DESIGN AND SAFETY

SEISMIC AND WIND DESIGN AREAS (R301)

Seismic Design Areas

1. Provide increased strength and structural integrity for foundations, walls, roofs, gas pipes and appliances, and other components in seismic design areas. Refer to the IRC and consult a qualified engineer or other qualified professional when building in seismic design areas.
2. Verify the seismic design category with the local building official. The following areas may be in seismic design areas: large parts of Alaska, California, Hawaii, Nevada, Oregon, and Washington State, small parts of Arizona, Colorado, Idaho, Montana, New Mexico, New York, and Utah, the area near Memphis, Tennessee, and the area near Charleston, South Carolina.

High Wind Design Areas

1. Provide increased strength and structural integrity for foundations, walls, roofs, windows and other components in high wind design areas. Refer to the IRC and consult a qualified engineer or other qualified professional when building in high wind design areas.
2. Verify the wind design category with the local building official. The following areas may be in high wind design areas: much of Florida, and Hawaii, the areas within about 100 miles of the coastlines of Alabama, Alaska, Georgia, Louisiana, Mississippi, North and South Carolina, Texas, and Virginia, the areas within about 50 miles of the coastlines of Connecticut, Delaware, Maine, Maryland, Massachusetts, New Jersey, New Hampshire, and New York. Several "Special Wind Areas" exist in scattered areas of the country. These areas are mostly in mountainous areas and are mostly in the West.

Wind Exposure Categories

The potential damage caused by wind can increase or decrease depending on what surrounds a home. Homes in urban and suburban areas are protected by other homes and sometimes by trees and surrounding hills. Homes in isolated and flat rural areas and homes on large bodies of water have little or no protection and are more vulnerable to wind damage.

The IRC contains four wind exposure categories. Category A applies to dense urban cores with many large buildings. This category rarely applies to homes. Category B applies to most urban and suburban homes and is the assumed wind exposure category. Category C applies to isolated and flat rural areas with few homes or other obstructions. Category D applies to homes directly on large bodies of water.

DEFLECTION (BENDING) OF STRUCTURAL COMPONENTS (R301.7)

Limitations of the Material in this Section

Most readers should not deal with bending of structural components such as floors, walls, ceilings, and roofs. Leave this to qualified engineers and contractors. Because "spongy" floors and rattling walls are common complaints, this section explains some basic concepts involved in deflection and helps you understand when deflection may be excessive.

Deflection and Loads Definitions

Deflection Deflection is when a component of a building bends under a load. The component can be a single component, such as a floor joist, or it can be a system, such as a floor or a wall. Deflection causes a component to compress on one side (compression) and expand on the other side (tension).

Load A load is a force (weight) placed on a component of a building. Example: a building's foundation carries the load of the entire building. The dead load is the weight of the construction materials, such as drywall, shingles, siding, and floor coverings, and the weight of fixed equipment, such as a water heater. The live load is the weight of people and furnishings that occupy a building. A point load is a load in a small area. The heel of a woman's high heel shoe is an example of a point load. Environmental loads include wind, snow, and forces created during earthquakes.

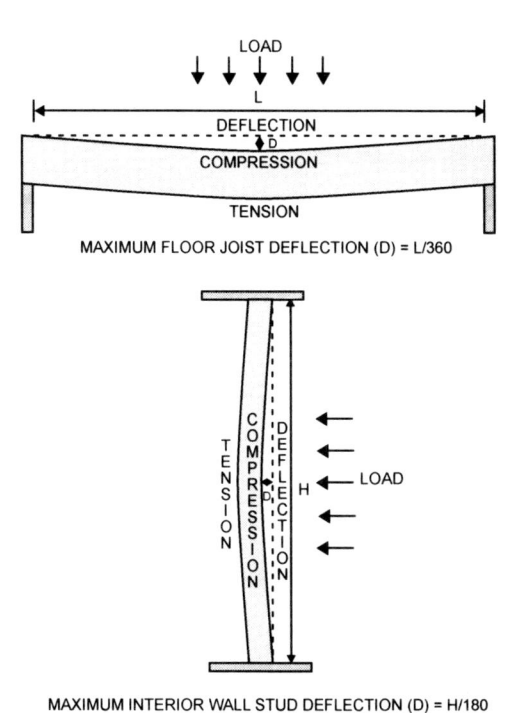

Deflection of Structural Components (R301.7-0)
Figure 3-1

Deflection Under Live Load

1. Install structural components, such as joists, studs, and rafters, so that they will not bend more than the amount shown in Table R301.7 under an <u>evenly distributed</u> live load. L is the unsupported length of the component in inches. H is the unsupported height of the component in inches. Example: for a bedroom floor, the IRC assumes that a live load of at least (≥) 30 pounds of people, floor coverings, and furnishing will be placed over each square foot of the floor area. Example: the maximum deflection of bedroom floor joists with the length between supports of 180 inches would be 180/360, or ½ inch.

TABLE R301.7
Deflection of Selected Structural Components Under Live Load

structural component	maximum deflection
rafters with greater than (>) 3/12 slope and no attached ceiling finish	L/180
interior walls	H/180
floors and plastered ceilings	L/360
exterior walls with plaster or stucco finish	H/360
other structural members	L/240
exterior stucco or plaster walls	H/360

Deflection Discussion

Walking on a floor or closing a door hard is not the evenly distributed live load assumed in the deflection table. In addition, the load caused by an adult walking on a floor or by a door being closed hard may be greater than the design live load at the point where the load is applied. Thus, a floor that feels "spongy" or a wall that shakes may not exceed the maximum deflection allowed by the IRC. If a "spongy" floor or a shaky wall is not causing other problems, such as cracking drywall or plaster, then it is probably not exceeding the maximum allowed deflection.

Note that the maximum deflection allowed by the IRC does not apply to floor coverings such as tile. Refer to manufacturer's design and installation instructions when installing stiff finish materials. The manufacturer may require a maximum deflection less than that required by the IRC.

FIRE SEPARATION BETWEEN BUILDINGS (R302.1)

Fire Separation Distance Definition

Fire separation distance The fire separation distance is the horizontal distance between the home's exterior wall (the face of the building) and a fire separation line. The fire separation distance is measured between the fire separation line and the exterior wall <u>at a right angle to the exterior wall</u>. The fire separation line is usually the property line between lots. In urban settings where buildings are close together and close to streets and sidewalks, the fire separation distance may also be measured to the centerline of a street, alley, or public sidewalk as determined by the local building official. For two-family dwellings and townhouses, the fire separation line is an imaginary line between dwellings. When two or more dwellings are attached, the fire separation distance is zero.

Exterior Walls Near Fire Separation Line

1. Build at least (≥) a 1 hour fire-resistive exterior wall if a home's exterior wall is less than (<) 5 feet from the fire separation line. The IRC does not describe how to build a fire-resistive wall. Type X gypsum board ⅝ inch thick applied horizontally to both sides of 2x4 studs spaced 16 inches on center, and with the stud cavity filled with 3 ½ inch thick mineral wool insulation is usually accepted as a 1 hour fire-resistive wall. The same wall built with 2x6 studs is usually accepted as a 1 hour fire-resistive wall without the mineral wool insulation. Refer to the publication *Fire Rated Wood Floor and Wall Assemblies* that is currently available at http://www.awc.org/Codes/dcaindex.html for more information.

Exterior Projections Near Fire Separation Line

1. Do not extend combustible projections, such as wood soffit, eaves, fascia, and rafter tails, closer than (<) 2 feet to the fire separation line.
2. Build at least (≥) a 1 hour fire-resistive assembly on the underside of projections between (≥) 2 feet and (<) 5 feet from the fire separation line.

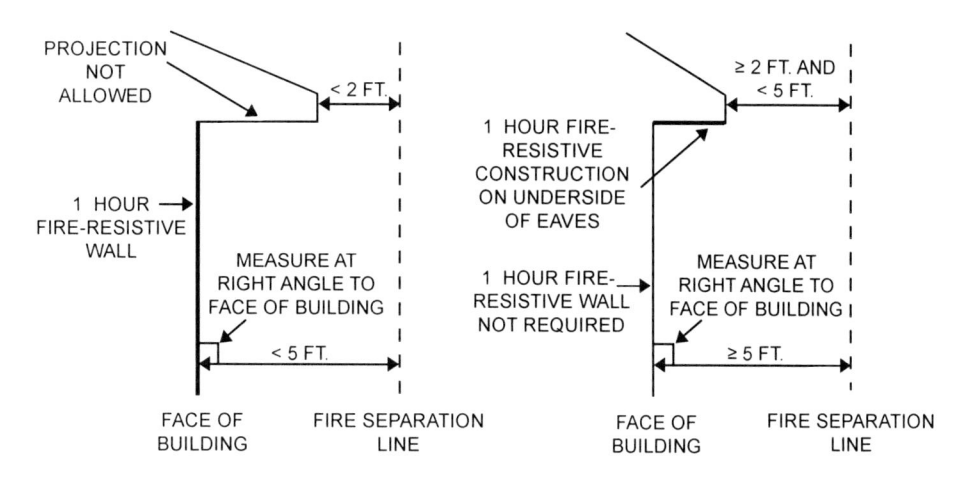

Exterior Wall and Projection Separation from Fire Separation Line (R302.1-1)
Figure 3-2

Penetrations in Fire-Resistive Walls

1. Do not place openings (such as windows, doors, and exhaust terminations) in fire-resistive walls that are less than (<) 3 feet from the fire separation line.
2. You may place openings in fire-resistive walls that are at least (≥) 3 feet and not more than (≤) 5 feet from the fire separation line if the total area of the openings is not more than (≤) twenty-five percent of the wall area.
3. Refer to Section R302.4 in this book and to the IRC Commentary for more information about fire-resistive wall penetration provisions and exceptions.

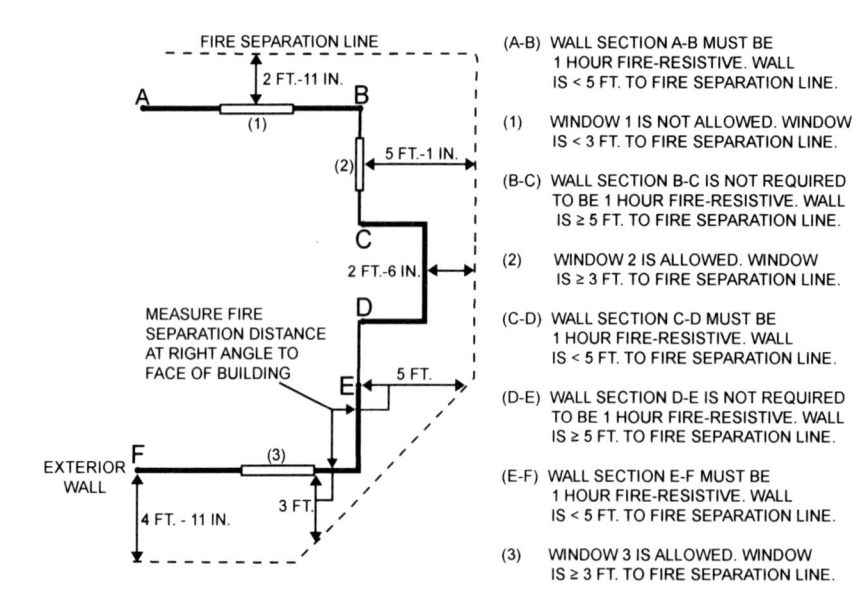

Exterior Wall Openings Separation from Fire Separation Line (R302.1-2)
Figure 3-3

Fire Separation Requirements Exceptions

1. You are not required to build fire-resistive walls for detached tool and storage sheds and similar structures that do not require a permit for construction. Do not build projections from these accessory structures that extend over the property line.
2. You are not required to build fire-resistive walls for exterior walls that are within the fire separation distance and that are perpendicular to the fire separation line. Example: a rectangular shaped home's rear wall is 3 feet from its fire separation line. The side walls are more than 5 feet from their fire separation lines. The rear wall must be a 1 hour fire-resistive wall on both sides of the wall. The side walls are not required to be fire-resistive at any point, including points that are within 5 feet from the rear fire separation line.
3. You are not required to build fire-resistive walls for dwellings and accessory structures located on the same lot.
4. Do not build eave projections that extend more than (>) 4 inches from the wall of detached garages that are within (≤) 2 feet of the property line.
5. You may install foundation vents required by the IRC in fire-resistive walls.

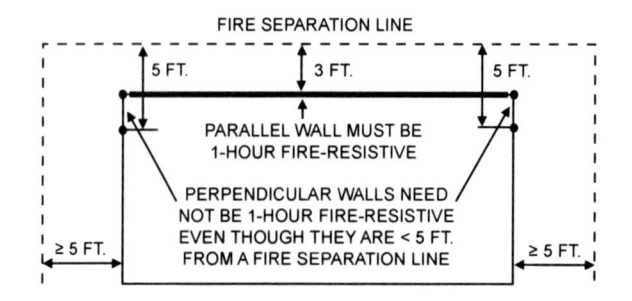

Fire Separation of Perpendicular Walls (R302.1-3)
Figure 3-4

Fire Separation Discussion

When buildings are close to each other, a fire in one can spread to another. This IRC provision helps keep one fire from consuming multiple buildings. It does not matter if another building currently exists close to the fire separation line. The IRC assumes that the owner of one building has no control over adjacent property; therefore, the fire separation distance measurement is from the fire separation line, not from another building on another lot.

TOWNHOUSES (R302.2)

Townhouse Construction

1. Build townhouses as structurally independent buildings. The foundation and a 2 hour fire-resistive common wall need not be structurally independent.
2. Build townhouse common walls with a total fire-resistive rating of at least (≥) 2 hours. You may build two structurally independent 1 hour walls or one common 2 hour wall.
3. Build townhouse common walls continuous from foundation to the underside of the roof sheathing. The IRC does not describe how to build fire-resistive walls. Type X gypsum wallboard ⅝ inch thick applied horizontally to both sides of 2x4 studs spaced 16 inches on center, and with the stud cavity filled with 3 ½ inch thick mineral wool insulation is usually accepted as a 1 hour fire-resistive wall. The same wall built with 2x6 studs is usually accepted as a 1 hour fire-resistive wall without the mineral wool insulation. Refer to the publication *Fire Rated Wood Floor and Wall Assemblies* that is currently available at http://www.awc.org/Codes/dcaindex.html for more information.
4. Refer to the IRC Commentary for more information about townhouse construction requirements and exceptions.

Parapet Wall Construction

1. Build parapet walls with the same 2 hour total fire resistance as the common wall below.
2. Build parapet walls that extend the common wall at least (≥) 30 inches above the roof deck, if the roof decks are at the same height.
3. Build parapet walls that extend the common wall at least (≥) 30 inches above the lower roof deck, if the upper roof deck is less than (<) 30 inches above the lower roof deck.
4. You do not need parapet walls if the upper roof deck is more than (>) 30 inches above the lower roof deck.
5. You do not need parapet walls if: (a) the roof deck is built using non-combustible material, or if (b) the roof deck is built using fire-retardant treaded wood for 4 feet on both sides of the common wall, or if (c) the roof deck is protected by ⅝ inch gypsum board for 4 feet on both sides of the common wall.
6. Refer to the IRC Commentary for more information about parapet wall construction requirements and exceptions.

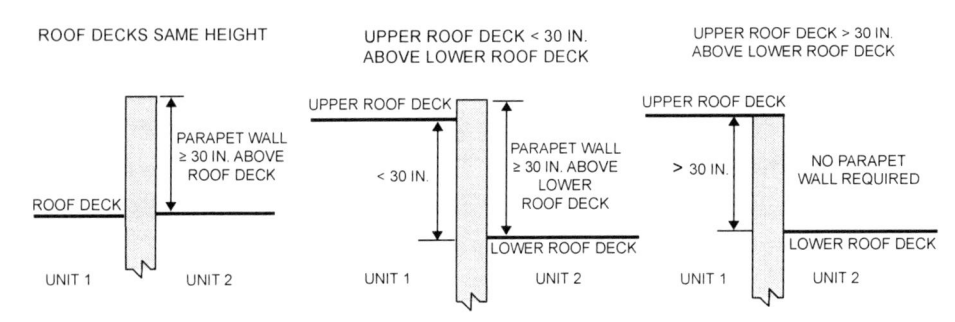

Parapet Wall Height (R302.2-0)
Figure 3-5

TWO-FAMILY DWELLINGS (R302.3)

Fire Separation of Two Dwelling Units in One Building

1. Separate two-family dwelling units that are built side-by-side in one building by building at least (≥) a 1 hour fire-resistive common wall between the dwellings. Build the common wall continuous between the foundation and the underside of the roof sheathing. Make the common wall tight against the foundation and the roof sheathing.

2. You may, as an alternative, eliminate the fire-resistive common wall only in the attic if you install:

   a) ⅝ inch Type X drywall on the ceiling between both dwellings and the attic, and

   b) ½ inch drywall on the interior walls supporting the Type X drywall ceilings, and

   c) a draft stop as described in R302.12 above and along the wall between the dwelling units.

3. Separate two-family dwelling units that are built one on top of the other in one building by installing at least (≥) a 1 hour fire-resistive common floor/ceiling between the dwellings. Build the common floor/ceiling continuous between the exterior walls. Make the common floor/ceiling tight against the exterior walls. Make walls supporting a fire-resistive common floor/ceiling 1 hour fire-resistive walls.

4. You may use a ½ hour fire-resistive wall or floor/ceiling if an automatic sprinkler system is installed in the entire building.

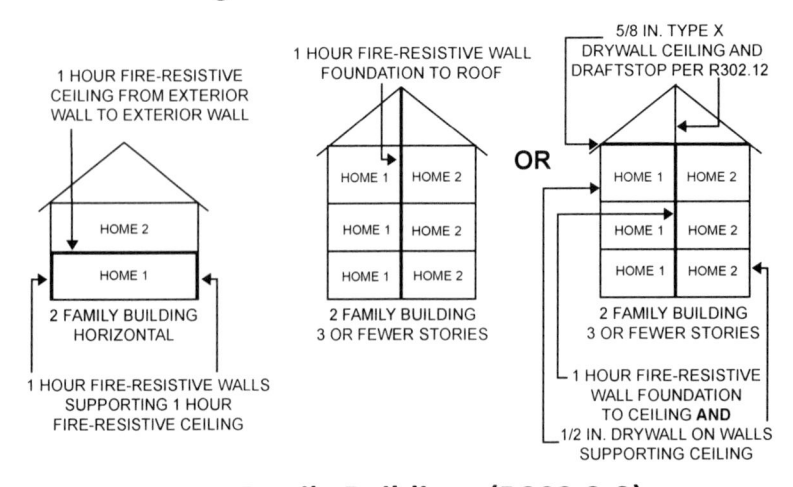

Two-Family Buildings (R302.3-0)
Figure 3-6

3 : Building Design and Safety

PENETRATIONS IN FIRE-RESISTIVE WALLS AND CEILINGS (R302.4)

Summary of Penetration Requirements

1. Refer to the IRC Commentary for more information about fire-resistive wall and ceiling penetration requirements and exceptions. Most readers of this should not deal with this complex subject. The following is a summary of the basic provisions.
2. Do not place openings, such as windows, doors, and exhaust terminations, in fire-resistive walls and ceilings.
3. Do not install plumbing and HVAC components (including ducts and vents) inside the cavity of 2 hour common fire-resistive walls. You may install properly protected electrical boxes inside this cavity.
4. You may install steel electrical outlet boxes in fire-resistive walls if the outlet boxes on opposite sides of the wall are:
   a) separated horizontally by at least (≥) 24 inches, or
   b) protected by solid fire blocking, or
   c) protected by listed putty pads, or
   d) protected by other approved means.

   Each outlet box opening size must be not more than (≤) 16 square inches and the total area of all boxes in the wall must be not more than (≤) 100 square inches in 100 square feet.
5. You may penetrate one or both membranes (sides) of a fire-resistive wall or ceiling if both the penetration and the material filling the space around the penetration are designed and tested as a fire-resistive system. This means that both the penetration itself (e. g., the pipe) and the material filling the space around the penetration must be tested together as a fire-resistive system and installed as tested.

FIRE SEPARATION BETWEEN GARAGE AND HOME (R302.5 AND R302.6)

Fire Separation Doors from Garage into Home

1. Do not open doors from a garage directly into a bedroom.
2. Use at least (≥) a 20 minute fire-rated door, solid wood door, or door made of solid or honeycomb core steel for doors between an attached garage and the home. Use doors that are at least (≥) 1 ⅜ inches thick.
3. Do not install pet doors or other openings in doors or walls from a garage into the home unless the pet door or opening is listed to maintain fire separation.
4. Note that some jurisdictions, particularly in the West, require self-closing hinges on doors between a garage and the home.

Fire Separation Walls and Ceilings Between Attached Garage and Home

1. Install at least (≥) ½ inch gypsum drywall on attached garage walls that separate the home from the garage.
2. Install at least (≥) ½ inch gypsum drywall on attached garage ceilings.
3. Install at least (≥) ⅝ inch type X gypsum drywall on garage ceilings under habitable rooms.

4. Install at least (≥) ½ inch gypsum drywall on garage walls that provide structural support under habitable rooms.
5. Maintain the same fire separation for drywall penetrations, such as attic scuttle holes, pull-down attic stairs, gas vents, and plumbing pipes, as provide by the gypsum drywall. Most pull-down attic stairs interrupt the ceiling fire separation because the panel to which the stairs are attached is thin plywood.
6. Seal penetrations between the garage and the home, such as pipes and ducts, with materials that resist the free flow of fire and smoke. Such materials include fire-resistant caulk.

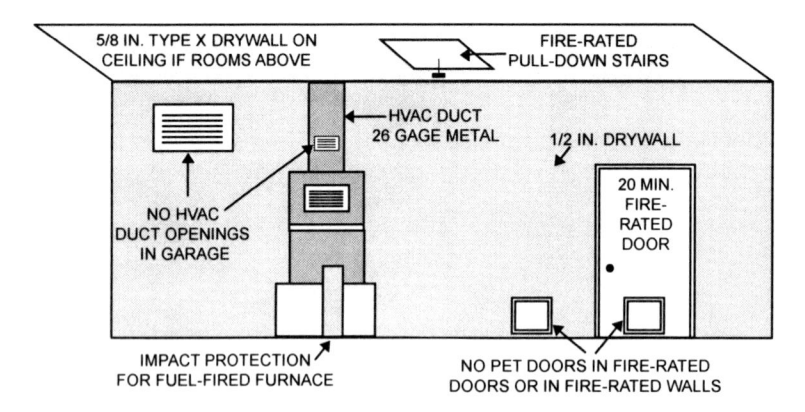

Fire Separation Between Garage and Home (R302.5-0)
Figure 3-7

HVAC Ducts in a Garage

1. Use at least (≥) 26 gage sheet steel or other approved material to construct HVAC ducts that are installed in a garage and ducts that pass through garage walls and ceilings.
2. Do not install HVAC supply or return air openings in the garage. This restriction does not apply to an independent HVAC system that serves only the garage.
3. Do not use flexible HVAC duct or duct board to penetrate garage walls and ceilings. Flexible ducts and duct board may attach to steel ducts after the steel ducts penetrate the garage firewall.

Garage and Carport Floors (R309)

1. Construct garage and carport floors using approved noncombustible material, usually concrete.
2. Slope garage and carport floors toward the vehicle entry opening.
3. You may use asphalt floors for ground level carports.

Fire Separation Between Detached Garage and Home (R302.6)

1. Install at least (≥) ½ inch gypsum drywall on the interior wall of a detached garage that is less than (<) 3 feet from a home on the same lot. This applies to the garage wall that is parallel to the home, not to any garage walls that are perpendicular to the home.
2. Install at least (≥) a 20 minute fire-rated door, solid wood door, or door made of solid or

honeycomb core steel in any doors in the wall that is parallel to the home. Use at least (≥) 1 ⅜ inches thick doors for fire separation doors.
3. Do not install windows or other openings in the wall that is parallel to the home.

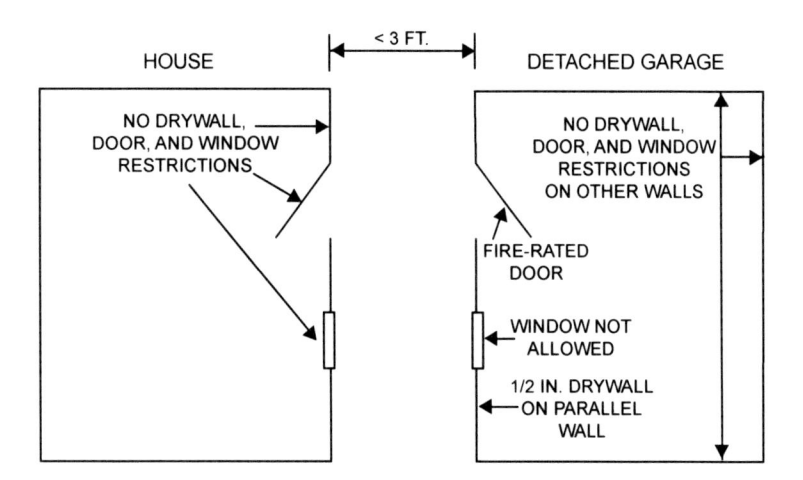

Fire Separation Between Detached Garage and Home (R302.6-0)
Figure 3-8

FIREBLOCKING (R302.11)

Fireblocking Definition

Fireblocking Fireblocking (also called firestopping) limits the spread of fires between stories in concealed vertical wood-framed walls. Concealed openings in wood-framed walls can act like a chimney providing fire an easy and rapid path between stories. Lack of fireblocking increases the chance of property damage and loss of life during a fire.

Do not confuse fireblocking with draftstopping. Draftstopping limits the horizontal spread of fires in floor/ceiling assemblies. Fireblocking limits the vertical spread of fires between stories.

Where Fireblocking is Required

1. Install fireblocking in any concealed wall space if an opening exists that allows fire to spread from one story to another or from a lower story into the attic. Examples of such openings include: openings for plumbing pipes, openings for electrical wires and conduit, HVAC duct chases between stories, laundry chutes, and openings at the tops of framed columns, niches, and arches.
2. Install fireblocking in concealed wall spaces at every ceiling and floor level. An intact top and bottom plate usually provides fireblocking in platform framing.
3. Install fireblocking where concealed vertical and horizontal wall spaces intersect. Examples of concealed horizontal spaces include soffits for kitchen cabinets and recessed vanity lights, and drop ceilings.
4. Install fireblocking between stair stringers at the top and bottom of each <u>flight of stairs.</u>
5. Install fireblocking around chimneys and flues where they intersect framing at floor and ceiling levels.
6. Install fireblocking in concealed wall spaces if the concealed space is open for more than (>)

10 feet horizontally. A long concealed horizontal wall space is rare in residential construction. Examples of framing that could produce a concealed horizontal wall space include some methods of framing large arched openings between rooms, and walls built using two rows of staggered studs.

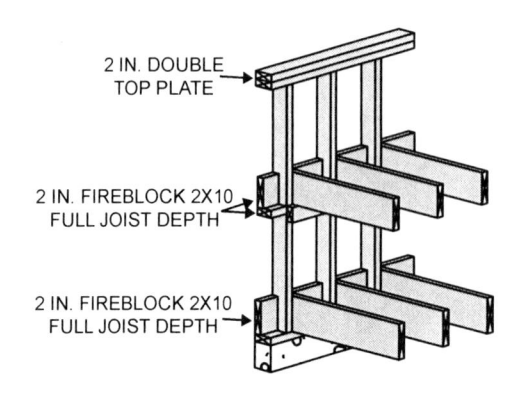

Fireblocking Balloon Framing (R302.11-1)
Figure 3-9

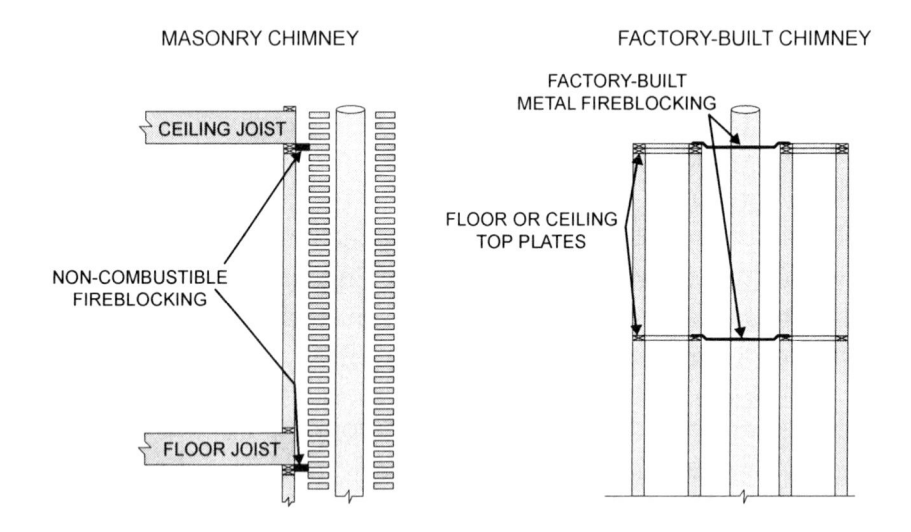

Fireblocking Chimneys (R302.11-2)
Figure 3-10

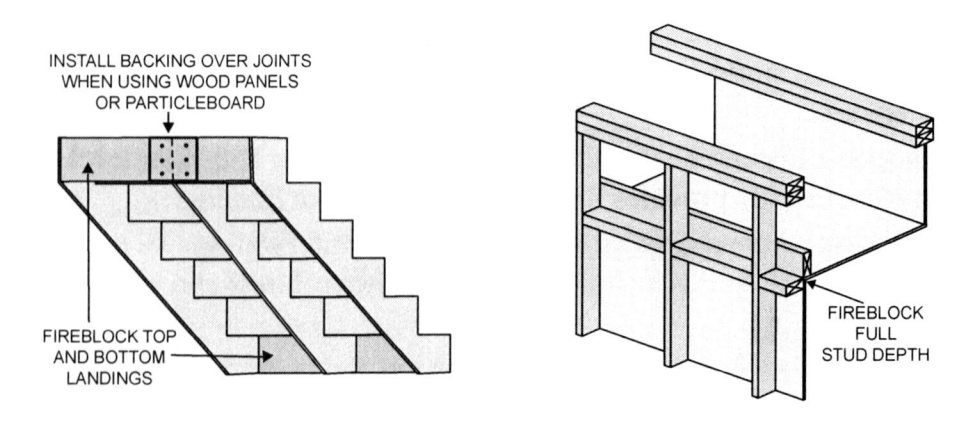

Fireblocking Stairs, Soffits, and Drop Ceilings (R302.11-3)
Figure 3-11

Fireblocking Materials and Installation

1. You may use any of the following fireblocking materials:
   a) 2 inch thick lumber (example: a 2x4), or
   b) 2 pieces of 1 inch thick lumber with staggered joints (example: two 1x4), or
   c) at least (≥) 23/32-inch thick wood structural panels, or
   d) at least (≥) ¾ inch thick particleboard, or
   e) at least (≥) ½ inch thick gypsum board, or
   f) at least (≥) ¼ inch thick cement-based millboard, or
   g) unfaced batts or blankets of mineral wool or fiberglass insulation if it is secured in place.
2. Install backing at any joints in fireblocking material when using wood structural panels or particleboard. Use the same fireblocking material for the backing Example: if a joint exists in OSB fireblocking material, place another piece of the same OSB material over the joint. The IRC does not state how far to extend the backing.
3. Do not use loose fill insulation as a fireblocking material unless it is specifically tested and approved for the intended location and installation method.
4. Repair fireblocking that is damaged or penetrated by pipes, ducts, or other materials.

DRAFTSTOPPING (R302.12)

Draftstopping Definition

Draftstopping Draftstopping helps limit the spread of fires in floor framing and in floor/ceiling assemblies. It is most often required when using open web floor trusses and when a ceiling is suspended under a floor. Do not confuse draftstopping with fireblocking. Fireblocking occurs in wall assemblies.

Where Draftstopping is Required

1. Install draftstopping when useable space exists both above and below the floor/ceiling assembly and when the open area within the concealed floor/ceiling assembly exceeds (>) 1,000 square feet.

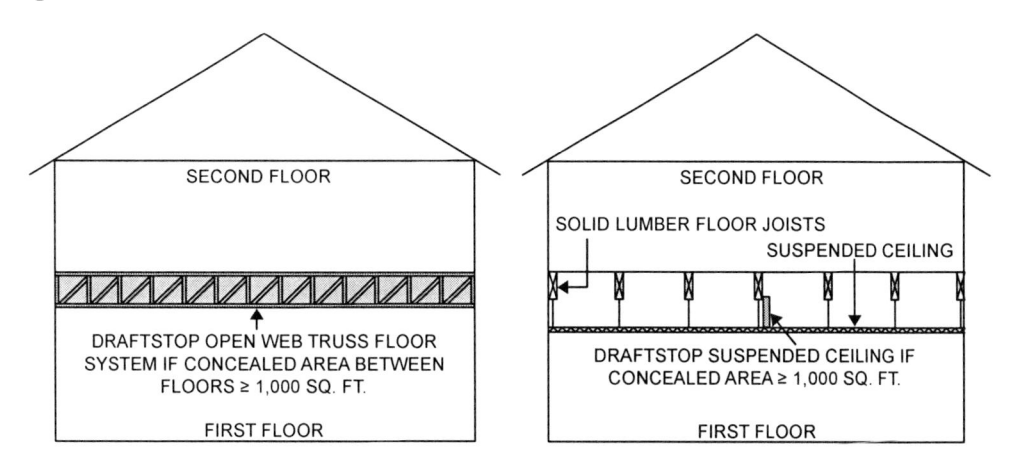

Draftstopping Required Locations (R302.12-1)
Figure 3-12

Draftstopping Materials and Installation

1. Use at least (≥) ½ inch gypsum board, ⅜ inch wood structural panels (plywood or OSB), or other approved material.
2. Divide the space to be draftstopped into approximately equal areas.
3. Install the draftstopping material parallel with the framing.
4. Repair draftstopping that is damaged or penetrated by pipes, ducts, or other materials.

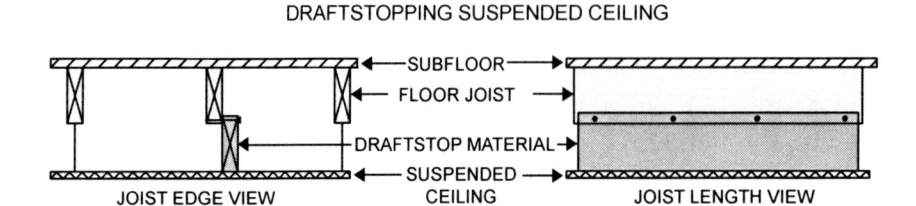

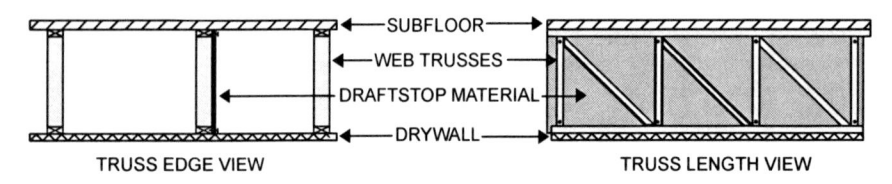

Draftstopping Installation (R302.12-2)
Figure 3-13

INSULATION CLEARANCE TO HEAT-PRODUCING DEVICES (R302.13)

Insulation Clearance Requirements

1. Provide at least (≥) 3 inches clearance between combustible insulation and heat-producing devices such as recessed lighting fixtures and fan motors. Most insulation used in modern homes is considered combustible.
2. You may reduce the 3 inch clearance requirement if the device is listed for a lesser clearance and is installed according to manufacturer's instructions.

Insulation Clearance Discussion

While insulation is unlikely to burn, most insulation is considered combustible for purposes of clearance requirements. Even if the insulation does not burn, devices not intended for insulation contact can overheat when in contact with insulation. At best, the device may simply fail. At worst, the device may become hot enough to ignite other nearby combustible material.

HABITABLE ROOMS LIGHT AND VENTILATION (R303)

Habitable Rooms Definition

Habitable rooms Habitable rooms (also called habitable spaces) are living, sleeping, eating, and cooking rooms. Bathrooms, toilet rooms, closets, hallways, storage and utility rooms are not habitable rooms. Habitable rooms have special size, ceiling height, heating, lighting, and ventilation, requirements. Rooms that are not considered habitable do not have those requirements.

Habitable Rooms Light and Ventilation

1. Provide outdoor light to habitable rooms using windows or doors containing glazing. Provide a total glazing area of at least (≥) 8 percent of the room's floor area. Open the glazing directly on to a street, public alley, or on to a yard or court located on the same lot.
2. Provide outdoor ventilation openings to habitable rooms equal to at least (≥) 4 percent of the room's floor area. Ventilation openings may be doors, windows, or other openings.
3. You may use central heating and electric lighting to replace glazing and ventilation openings. This means that natural light and ventilation are rarely required in modern residential construction.
4. Provide all bedrooms with emergency escape openings. Refer to Section R310.
5. Provide central heat to all habitable rooms to maintain at least 68° F where the winter design temperature is below 60° F. Measure heat at 3 feet above the floor and at least (≥) 2 feet from exterior walls.
6. Do not use portable space heaters to satisfy the minimum heating requirement.
7. You need not provide central cooling for habitable rooms

BATHROOM LIGHT AND VENTILATION (R303.3)

Bathroom Light and Ventilation

1. Provide outdoor light and ventilation to bathrooms, toilet rooms, and similar areas using windows or doors containing glazing. Provide a total glazing area of at least (≥) 3 square feet with at least (≥) 1 ½ square feet operable. Open the glazing directly on to a street, public alley, or on to a yard or court located on the same lot.
2. You may replace the glazing with artificial light and exhaust ventilation. Provide exhaust ventilation of at least (≥) 20 cubic feet per minute continuous ventilation or at least (≥) 50 cubic feet per minute for a switched ventilation fan.
3. Discharge bathroom and toilet room ventilation fan exhaust directly outdoors. Discharging a ventilation fan exhaust duct into or toward an attic, soffit, or crawl space vent does not comply with this provision. The duct must discharge directly outdoors (M1501.1).
4. Do not recirculate air from bathrooms within a residence or into another residence (M1506.2).
5. Provide an automatic or gravity operated damper for exhaust systems that will close the damper when the system is not operating (N1103.5).

Bathroom Ventilation Best Practice

Provide bathroom exhaust fans in all bathrooms, even those with operable windows.. Bathroom exhaust fans improve air quality and help maintain proper moisture levels in the home. Excess moisture can migrate into wall and floor cavities and into the attic. This moisture can damage materials and provide moisture for fungal growth.

OUTDOOR AIR INTAKE AND EXHAUST OPENINGS (R303.4)

Outdoor Air Intake Openings

1. Provide at least (≥) 10 feet horizontal separation between all outdoor air intake openings and gas and oil vents, chimneys, plumbing vents, streets, alleys, and similar contaminant sources. Gravity outdoor air intake openings include: (a) openings for makeup air and combustion air, and (b) attic soffit vents, and (c) windows, doors, and similar openings. Mechanical outdoor air intake openings include air intakes connected to furnaces and air handlers and powered air exchange ventilation systems.

2. You may locate outdoor air intake openings closer than (<) 10 feet horizontally from a contaminant source <u>if the outdoor air intake opening is at least (≥) 2 feet below the contaminant source</u>. Exhaust from household toilet rooms, bathrooms, and kitchens is not considered a contaminant source in this Section.

3. Note that Sections M1602.2 and G2442.5 require that an outdoor air intake opening connected to a forced-air heating or cooling system must be at least (≥) 10 feet horizontally or at least (≥) 3 feet below the contaminant source. Exhaust from toilet rooms, bathrooms, and kitchens is considered a contaminant source by these sections.

4. Measure the 10 feet horizontal distance to the center of streets and alleys.

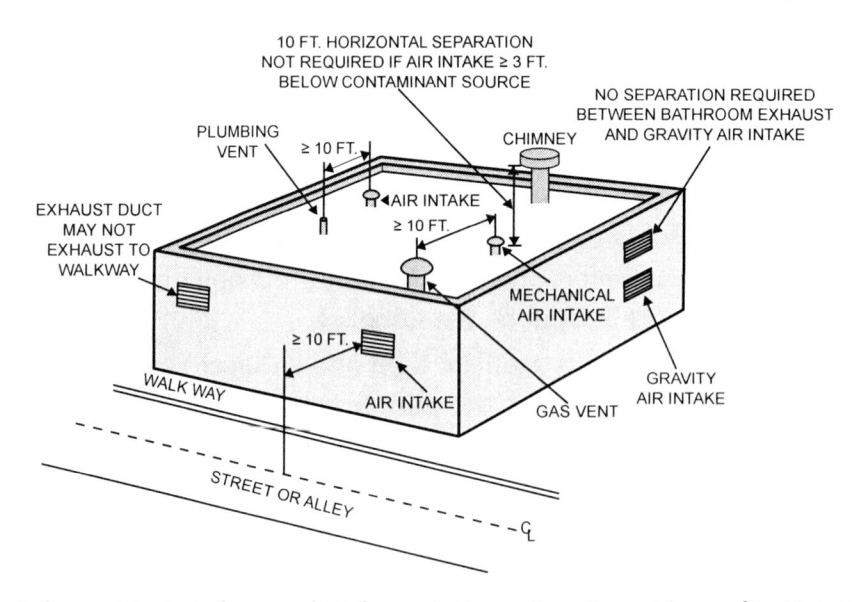

Outdoor Air Intake and Exhaust Opening Locations (R303.4-0)
Figure 3-14

3 : Building Design and Safety 27

TABLE R303.4
Outdoor Air Intake Openings Separation from Vents, Chimneys, and Exhaust Openings

components requiring separation	separation distance	exceptions to separation distance	IRC 2009 reference
Type B gas vents and gravity air intake openings	≥ 10 Ft. horizontal	OK if vent ≥ 2 Ft. above intake opening	R303.4
Type B gas vents and mechanical air intake openings	≥ 10 Ft. horizontal	OK if vent ≥ 3 Ft. above intake opening connected to HVAC system	M1602.2 and G2442.5
Type L oil vents and gravity air intake openings	≥ 10 Ft. horizontal	OK if vent ≥ 2 Ft. above intake opening	R303.4
Type L oil vents and mechanical air intake openings	≥ 10 Ft. horizontal	OK if vent ≥ 3 Ft. above intake opening connected to HVAC system	M1602.2
Chimneys and gravity air intake openings	≥ 10 Ft. horizontal	OK if chimney ≥ 2 Ft. above intake opening	R303.4
Chimneys and mechanical air intake openings	≥ 10 Ft. horizontal	OK if chimney ≥ 3 Ft. above intake opening connected to HVAC system	M1602.2 and G2442.5
Plumbing vents and gravity and mechanical air intake openings	≥ 10 Ft. horizontal	OK if vent ≥ 2 Ft. above intake opening	P3103 and R303.4
Exhaust ducts and gravity air intake openings	none required	none	R303.4
Exhaust ducts and mechanical air intake openings	≥ 10 Ft. horizontal	OK if exhaust duct ≥ 3 Ft. above intake opening connected to HVAC system	M1602.2 and G2442.5

Outdoor Exhaust Openings

1. Do not discharge outdoor exhaust openings, such as from bathroom and kitchen exhaust fans, on to a walkway.
2. Refer to Sections M1502 and G2439 for clothes dryer exhaust opening provisions.

Intake and Exhaust Opening Screens

1. Protect outdoor air intake and exhaust openings with a corrosion-resistant screen having openings at least (≥) ¼ and not more than (≤) ½ inch or by louvers, dampers or similar means. This does not include clothes dryer exhaust openings. Do not cover clothes dryer exhaust openings with a screen.
2. Protect outdoor openings against local weather conditions such as from rain and snow infiltration and from blockage by snow accumulation.

Outdoor Air Intake Discussion

Outdoor air intake openings must be far enough away from contaminant sources so that the contaminated air is not drawn back into the building. Contaminated air that is drawn back into the home will reduce indoor air quality and could affect occupant health and safety. Separating outdoor air intake openings and contaminant sources is particularly important in tightly sealed homes that depend on controlled introduction of outdoor air to maintain the required air changes per hour.

STAIRWAY LIGHTING (R303.6)

Interior Stairway Light Locations

1. Locate a light fixture near each stairway landing, including the top, bottom, and any intermediate landings. You may locate a light fixture near each stairway flight instead of near each landing. The light must be capable of illuminating treads and landings to at least ($\geq$) 1 foot-candle.

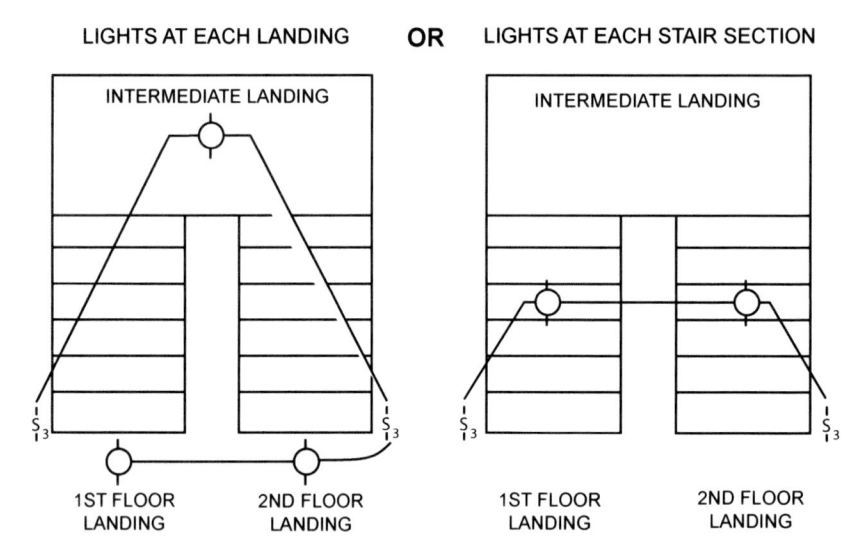

Interior Stairway Lighting (R303.6-1)
Figure 3-15

Exterior Stairway Light Locations

1. Locate a light fixture near the top landing for stairs providing access to doors above grade level.
2. Locate a light fixture near the bottom landing for stairs providing access to doors below grade level.
3. Use stairway lights capable of illuminating treads and landings to at least ($\geq$) 1 foot-candle.

Stairway Light Switching

1. Locate a switch for interior stairway lights at the top and bottom of interior stairs with at least ($\geq$) 6 risers. Only one switch is required for interior stairs with fewer than (<) 6 risers.
2. Locate the switch inside the dwelling for exterior stairs.
3. Locate stair switches so they can be used without climbing any steps.
4. You are not required to install switches if lights are on continuously or are automatically controlled (e. g., motion sensors).

ROOM SIZE AND CEILING HEIGHT REQUIREMENTS (R304 AND R305)

Habitable Rooms Dimensions (R304)

1. Provide every home with at least (≥) one habitable room that has an area of at least (≥) 120 square feet.
2. Provide every habitable room with an area of at least (≥) 70 square feet.
3. Provide every habitable room with a horizontal dimension of at least (≥) 7 feet. You may make kitchens smaller than 70 square feet and smaller than 7 feet minimum dimension.

Ceiling Height (R305.1)

1. Provide a finished ceiling height of at least (≥) 7 feet in habitable rooms, hallways, bathrooms, toilet rooms, laundry rooms. This applies to all areas in the home, including basements. Measure ceiling height from the finished floor to the lowest projection from the ceiling. Projections from the ceiling usually include beams, joists, and HVAC ducts. Projections usually do not include light fixtures and ceiling fans.

Ceiling Height in Basements (R305.1.1)

1. Provide a finished ceiling height of at least (≥) 80 inches in the parts of basements <u>without</u> habitable rooms, bathrooms, toilet rooms, laundry rooms, and hallways to these areas.
2. You may install beams, girders and ducts that are at least (≥) 76 inches above the finished floor in the parts of basements <u>without</u> habitable rooms, bathrooms, toilet rooms, laundry rooms and hallways to these areas.
3. Use basements without habitable rooms, bathrooms, toilet rooms, and laundry rooms only for mechanical equipment and for storage.

Sloped Ceilings in Habitable Rooms (R305.1)

1. Provide a finished ceiling height of at least (≥) 84 inches for at least (≥) 50 percent of a habitable room's required floor area in rooms with sloped ceilings. This means that every habitable room must have at least (≥) 35 square feet of space with a ceiling that is at least (≥) 84 inches tall. Refer to the definition of and to the required dimensions of a habitable room.
2. Do not count the floor area under a ceiling height less than (<) 5 feet tall toward a habitable room's required floor area.

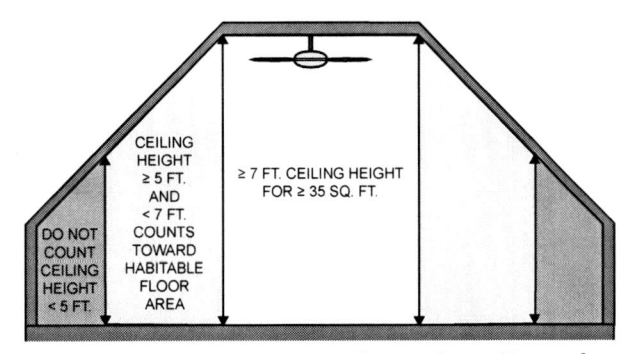

Ceiling Height in Rooms with Sloped Ceilings (R305.1-0)
Figure 3-16

Sloped Ceilings in Bathrooms (R305.1)

1. Provide at least (≥) 80 inches finished ceiling height above sinks, toilets, bidets, and similar fixtures. Provide the required ceiling height <u>at the center of the clearance area in front of the fixture</u>. You may reduce the ceiling height above the center of the fixture to at least (≥) 5 feet.
2. Provide at least (≥) 80 inches finished ceiling height in showers and in tubs with showerheads for all of the required floor area under the showerhead.

PLUMBING FIXTURE MINIMUM CLEARANCES AND REQUIREMENTS (R306 AND 307)

Required Plumbing Fixtures (R306)

1. Provide every home with at least (≥) one toilet, and one bathroom sink, and one tub or shower, and one kitchen sink.
2. Provide hot and cold water to kitchen and bathroom sinks, tubs, showers, bidets, laundry sinks, and washing machine connections.
3. Connect all plumbing drain fixtures to a sanitary sewer or a private sewage system.

Bathroom Plumbing Fixture Clearances to Obstructions (R307 and P2705)

1. Provide toilets, bidets, bathroom sinks, and tubs and showers with the minimum clearances shown in the illustration.

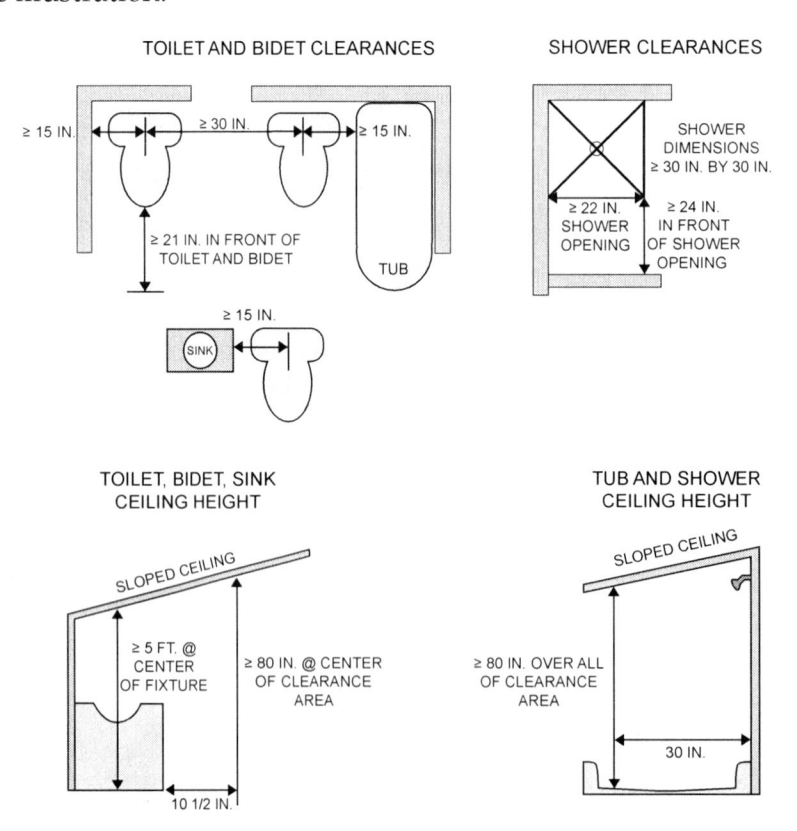

Bathroom Plumbing Fixture Minimum Clearance to Obstructions (R307-0)
Figure 3-17

Shower Wall Coverings (R307)

1. Provide showers and tubs with showerheads with non-absorbent wall covering material such as tile, cultured marble, or fiberglass. Extend the non-absorbent surface to at least 6 feet above the floor.

SAFETY GLAZING (R308)

Safety Glazing Labeling

1. Label <u>every</u> pane of glazing in a hazardous location with a permanent marking that identifies the type and thickness of glazing and the safety glazing standard with which it complies. This includes inside, outside, and any middle panes in a multiple-pane window. The glazing manufacturer usually etches this label into a corner of the glazing.
2. Label at least one pane in a multi-pane window or door if the panes are not more than ($\leq$) one square foot. Provide the label in previous sentence number one. Label the other panes with "16 CFR 1201." This situation usually applies to divided-light doors and windows with individual glass panes.

Safety Glazing in Doors

1. Install safety glazing if the following doors contain glazing:
   a) framed swinging doors (except jalousies), and
   b) sliding and bifold doors (such as mirrored closet doors and sliding glass patio doors), and
   c) storm doors, and
   d) doors for tubs, showers whirlpools, saunas, and similar areas, and
   e) unframed swinging doors.
2. You are not required to install safety glazing in framed swinging doors with decorative glazing, such as stained and cut glass.
3. You are not required to install safety glazing in doors if the glazing is protected by bars that will not pass a 3 inches diameter sphere.

Safety Glazing Near Doors

1. Install safety glazing in windows that are near doors if:
   a) the closest vertical edge of the <u>glazing</u> is within ($\leq$) 24 inches from both the lock side and hinge side of the door, and if
   b) the closest horizontal edge of the <u>glazing</u> is less than (<) 60 inches above a walking surface. Measure from the door jamb to the window frame or other glazing support.
2. You are not required to install safety glazing in a window that is perpendicular to the lock side of a door, even if the glazing is within ($\leq$) 24 inches from the door.
3. You are not required to install safety glazing in decorative glazing, such as stained and cut glass.
4. You are not required to install safety glazing if a wall or permanent barrier is between the door and glazing. <u>Use both inside and outside walking surfaces, to determine if safety glazing is required</u>. Example: a wall exists between a door and a window at the inside walking surface,

but not at the outside walking surface. Safety glazing is required in this example because the window is not more than (≤) 24 inches from the outside walking surface.

5. You are not required to install safety glazing in an opening next to a closet or storage area door if the closet or storage area is not more than (≤) 3 feet deep.
6. You are not required to install safety glazing next to the fixed panel of a patio door, including sliding glass doors and hinged double doors with one fixed panel.

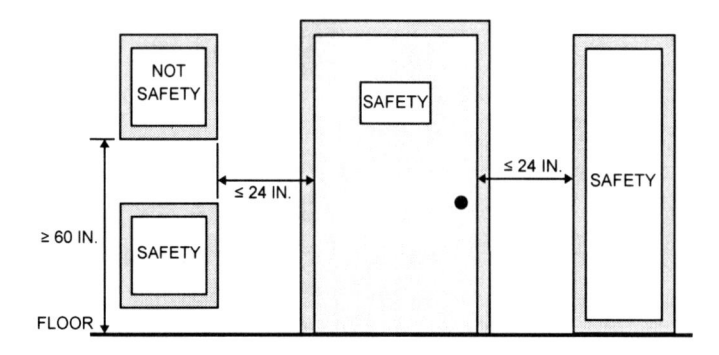

Measuring Hazardous Locations Near Doors (R308-1)
Figure 3-18

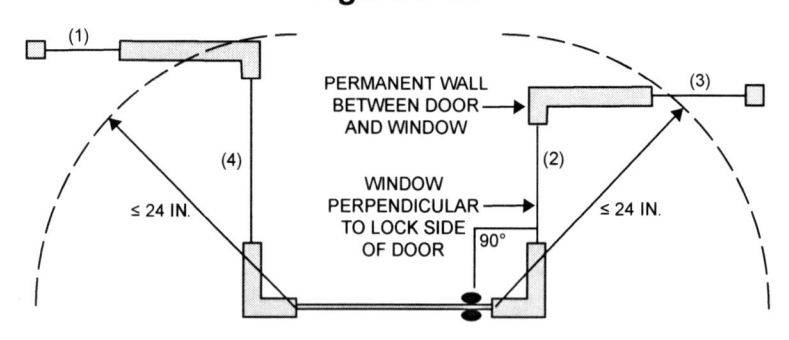

Safety Glazing Requirements Near Doors (R308-2)
Figure 3-19

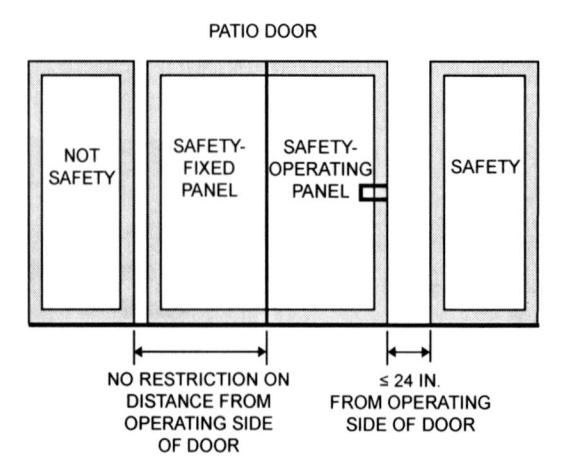

Safety Glazing in Sliding Glass Doors (R308-3)
Figure 3-20

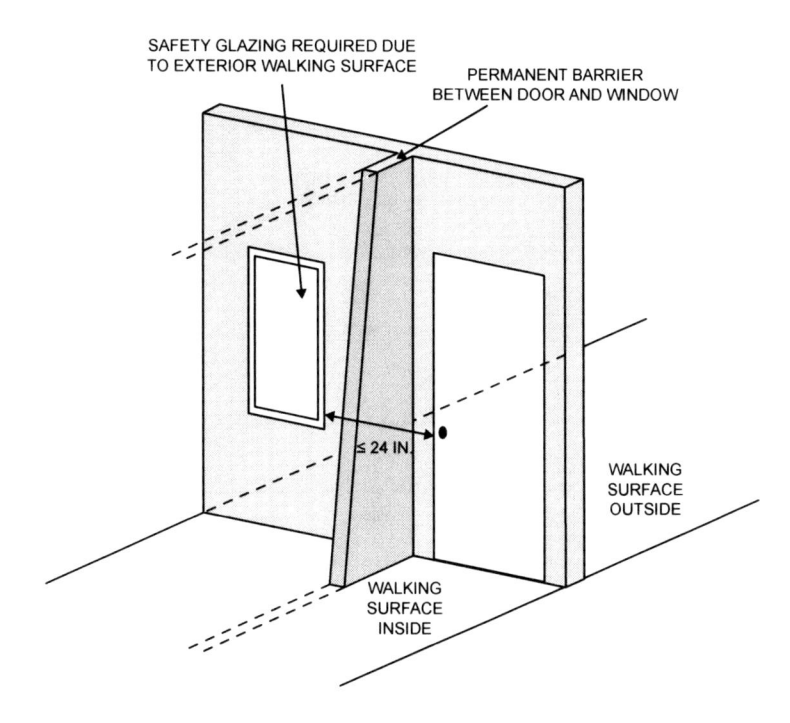

Safety Glazing at Interior and Exterior Walking Surfaces (R308-4)
Figure 3-21

Safety Glazing in Large Windows and Doors

1. Install safety glazing in large windows and doors if <u>all</u> of the following conditions are true:
   a) individual panes are more than (>) 9 square feet, and if
   b) the bottom edge of the <u>glazing</u> is less than (<) 18 inches above an adjacent walking surface, and if
   c) the top edge of the <u>glazing</u> is more than (>) 36 inches above an adjacent walking surface, and if
   d) a walking surface is within (≤) 3 feet horizontally of the <u>glazing</u>.
2. You are not required to install safety glazing in the exterior pane of an insulated glazing assembly if the bottom edge of the exterior pane is at least (≥) 25 feet above grade or above any walking surface adjacent to the glazing.
3. You are not required to install safety glazing in decorative glazing, such as stained and cut glass.
4. You are not required to install safety glazing if the glazing is protected by a bar that complies with all of the following: (a) bar is at least (≥) 1 ½ inches high, and (b) bar is installed at least (≥) 34 inches and not more than (≤) 38 inches above any walking surface on each accessible side of the glazing, and (c) bar is capable of bearing at least (≥) 50 pounds per lineal foot load without touching the glazing.
5. Do not apply the bar protection exception near doors and near bathing and swimming areas.

34 Everybody's Building Code

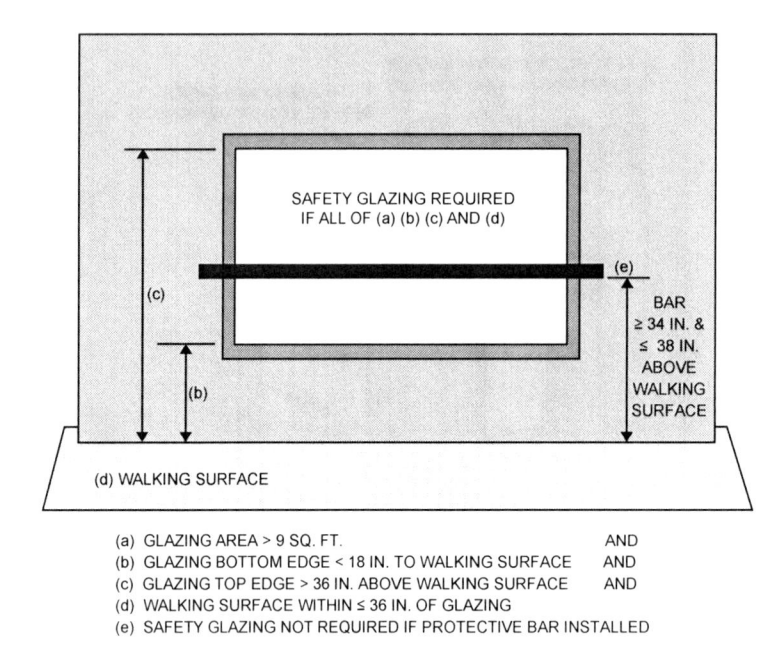

```
(a) GLAZING AREA > 9 SQ. FT.                              AND
(b) GLAZING BOTTOM EDGE < 18 IN. TO WALKING SURFACE       AND
(c) GLAZING TOP EDGE > 36 IN. ABOVE WALKING SURFACE       AND
(d) WALKING SURFACE WITHIN ≤ 36 IN. OF GLAZING
(e) SAFETY GLAZING NOT REQUIRED IF PROTECTIVE BAR INSTALLED
```

Safety Glazing in Large Windows and Doors (R308-5)
Figure 3-22

Safety Glazing Near Bathing and Swimming Areas

1. Install safety glazing in walls and enclosures around tubs, showers, whirlpool tubs, saunas, and similar areas if the bottom edge of the glazing is less than (<) 60 inches above a walking surface.

2. Install safety glazing in walls and fences around pools, hot tubs, and spas if: (a) the bottom edge of the glazing is less than (<) 60 inches above a walking surface, and if (b) the glazing is less than (<) 60 inches horizontally to the water's edge.

WINDOWS AND DOORS IN TUB/SHOWER

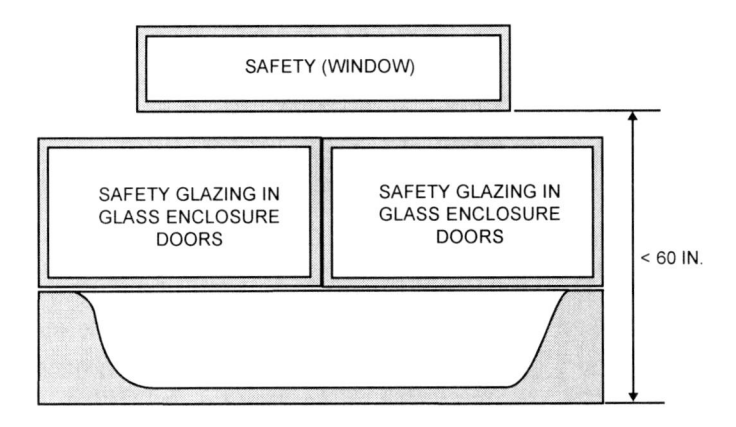

WINDOWS IN WALLS NEAR SWIMMING POOL

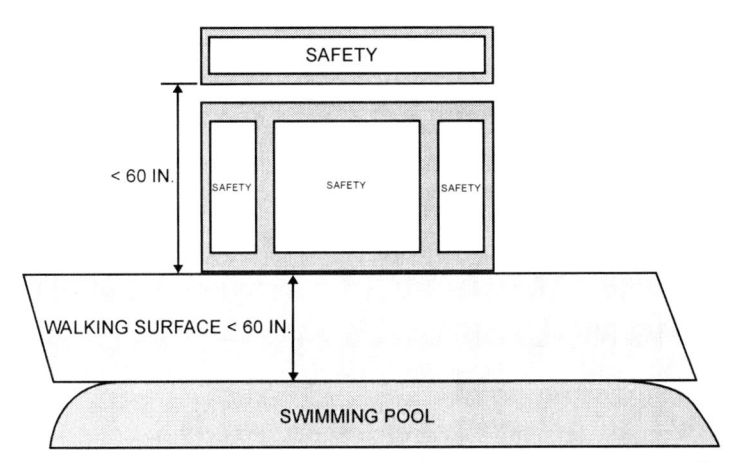

Safety Glazing Near Bathing and Swimming Areas (R308-6)
Figure 3-23

Safety Glazing Near Stairs

1. Install safety glazing in all guards and railings that contain glazing.
2. Install safety glazing in windows adjacent to stairs, landings, and ramps if:
    a) the bottom edge of the glazing is less than (<) 60 inches above an adjacent walking surface, and if
    b) the glazing is within (≤) 36 inches horizontally from a walking surface, and if
    c) the area below the window is not a solid wall or panel, and if
    d) no rail is installed adjacent to the window (see the rail exception in number 6 below). The situation described here could occur when two windows are placed one above the other.
3. Install safety glazing in windows adjacent to stairs, landings and ramps if:
    a) the bottom edge of the glazing is less than (<) 36 inches above an adjacent walking surface, and if
    b) the glazing is within (≤) 36 inches horizontally from a walking surface, and if
    c) there is a wall or other solid barrier under the window, and if
    d) no rail is installed adjacent to the window (see the rail exception in number 6 below).

4. Install safety glazing within (≤) 60 inches horizontally <u>from the bottom tread of a stairway</u>, measured in any direction if:
   a) the bottom edge of the <u>glazing</u> is less than (<) 60 inches above the nose of the tread, and if
   b) the <u>glazing</u> is within (≤) 36 inches horizontally from a walking surface, and if
   c) the area below the window is not a solid wall or panel, and if
   d) no rail is installed adjacent to the window (see the rail exception in number 6 below). The situation described here could occur when two windows are placed one above the other.
5. Install safety glazing within (≤) 60 inches of the bottom tread of a stairway, measured in any direction if: (a) the bottom edge of the <u>glazing</u> is less than (<) 36 inches above an adjacent walking surface, and if (b) the <u>glazing</u> is within (≤) 36 inches horizontally from a walking surface, and if (c) there is a wall or other solid barrier under the window.
6. You are not required to install safety glazing in windows adjacent to stairs, landings, and ramps if you install a rail adjacent to the windows. Install a rail that:
   a) is at least (≥) 1 ½ inches high (measured diagonally), and that
   b) will not touch the window when 50 pounds of horizontal force is applied, and that
   c) is at least (≥) 34 inches and not more than (≤) 38 inches above the walking surface. This is similar to the bar exception for large windows discussed earlier.
7. You are not required to install safety glazing in windows adjacent to stairs, landings, and ramps and within (≤) 60 inches of the bottom tread of a stairway if both of the following are true: (a) a rail or guard that conforms to IRC requirements is installed between the window and stairs, landing, ramp, and if (b) the <u>glazing</u> is more than (>) 18 inches horizontally from the rail or guard.

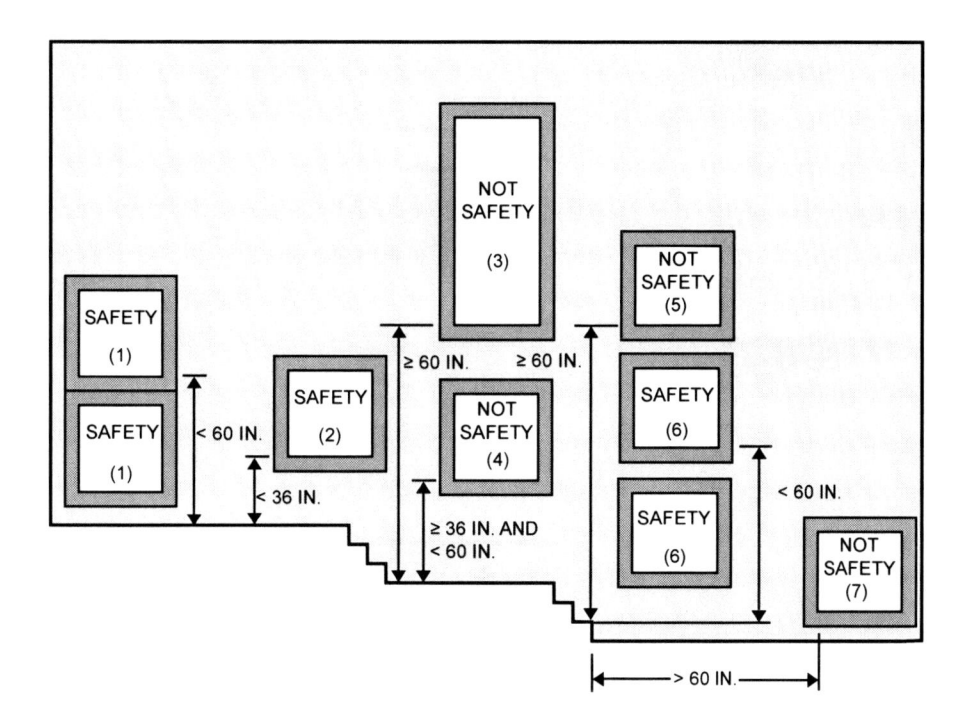

(1) BOTTOM OF GLAZING < 60 IN. ABOVE AND ≤ 36 IN. HORIZONTALLY FROM WALKING SURFACE AND AREA BELOW WINDOW IS NOT A SOLID WALL

(2) BOTTOM OF GLAZING < 36 IN. ABOVE AND ≤ 36 IN. HORIZONTALLY FROM WALKING SURFACE AND AREA BELOW WINDOW IS A SOLID WALL

(3) BOTTOM OF GLAZING ≥ 60 IN. ABOVE WALKING SURFACE

(4) BOTTOM OF GLAZING ≥ 36 IN. AND < 60 IN. ABOVE AND ≤ 36 IN. HORIZONTALLY FROM WALKING SURFACE AND AREA BELOW WINDOW IS A SOLID WALL

(5) BOTTOM OF GLAZING ≥ 60 IN. ABOVE NOSE OF BOTTOM TREAD

(6) BOTTOM OF GLAZING < 60 IN. ABOVE AND ≤ 60 IN. HORIZONTALLY FROM THE NOSE OF THE BOTTOM TREAD AND THE AREA BELOW THE WINDOW IS NOT A SOLID WALL

(7) VERTICAL EDGE OF GLAZING > 60 IN. HORIZONTALLY FROM NOSE OF BOTTOM TREAD

Safety Glazing Near Stairs (R308-7)
Figure 3-24

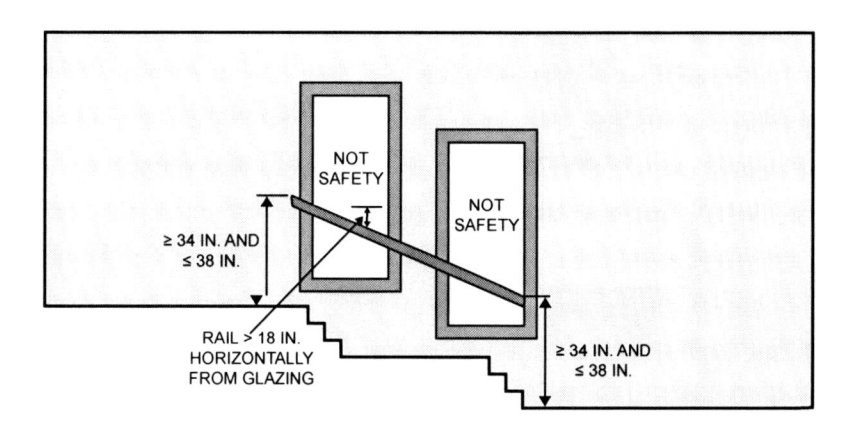

Rail Exception to Safety Glazing Near Stairs (R308-8)
Figure 3-25

Mounted Glazing Exception

1. You are not required to install safety glazing in mirrors and glass panels hung or mounted on a solid surface that provides continuous rear support.

Glass Block Exception

1. You are not required to install safety glazing in glass blocks that comply with IRC Section R610.

SKYLIGHTS AND SLOPED GLAZING (R308.6)

Sloped Glazing Definition

Sloped glazing, including skylights, is any glazing material installed with a slope of at least (≥) 15 degrees from vertical.

Sloped Glazing Materials

1. Use any of these materials for sloped glazing: (a) laminated glass (restrictions apply, see IRC Section R308), fully tempered glass, heat-strengthened glass, wired glass, or approved rigid plastics.

Sloped Glass Retaining Screens

1. Install a retaining screen under sloped glass, unless an exception applies. Install the screen so that it will support at least (≥) twice the weight of the glass and has mesh openings not more than (≤) 1 inch by 1 inch.
2. You are not required to install a retaining screen under fully tempered sloped glass if: (a) the glass area is not more than (≤) 16 square feet, and if (b) the highest point of the glass is not more than (≤) 12 feet above an accessible area, and if (c) the glass is not more than (≤) 3/16 inch thick.
3. You are not required to install a retaining screen under fully tempered glass if: (a) the glass area is more than (>) 16 square feet, and if (b) the slope is not more than (≤) 30 degrees from vertical, and if (c) the highest point of the glass is not more than (≤) 10 feet above an accessible area.

Skylight Curbs

1. Install a curb at least (≥) 4 inches above the roof surface when installing a skylight on a roof with a slope less than (<) 3 inches rise in 12 inches run.

Glazing in Greenhouses

1. You may install any type of glazing in a greenhouse. The glazing does not have to be one of the approved sloped glazing materials.

EMERGENCY ESCAPE OPENINGS (R310 AND R311)

Escape Opening Locations and General Requirements

1. Provide at least (≥) one escape opening in every bedroom including bedrooms above, at, and below ground level. This escape opening is not required if the building is equipped with an automatic fire sprinkler system.
2. Provide at least (≥) one escape opening in basements. You are not required to provide a basement escape opening if: (a) the basement area is not more than (≤) 200 square feet, and if (b) the basement is used only to house mechanical equipment. You are not required to provide additional escape openings in basements that have bedroom escape openings, but each basement bedroom must have an escape opening.
3. Open all escape openings directly on to an area that leads directly to a public way. This means that escape openings cannot open on to an enclosed courtyard or on to a similar area that does not lead directly and without obstruction to an area that is accessible by the public.
4. You may open an escape opening under a deck or porch if: (a) the escape opening can be opened to the full required dimensions, and if (b) the space under the deck or porch is at least (≥) 36 inches high.
5. Note that an escape opening may be required when converting a previously unfinished basement into finished space, especially if the finished space is a bedroom. Verify requirements with the local building official.

Escape Opening Size

1. Provide escape openings with a clear opening area of at least (≥) 5.7 square feet. This includes escape openings above and below grade level. You may reduce an escape opening at grade level to at least (≥) 5.0 square feet.
2. Provide each escape opening with a clear opening at least (≥) 24 inches high and at least (≥) 20 inches wide.
3. Locate the <u>sill</u> of each escape opening not more than (≤) 44 inches above the finished floor.
4. Measure escape opening height and width using the clear opening area. Clear opening area does not include obstructions such as window frames.

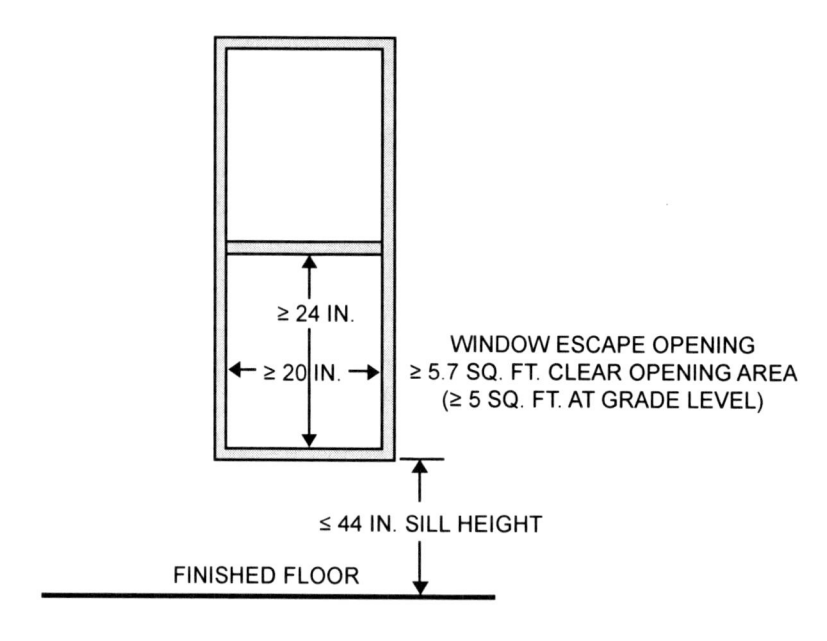

Escape Opening Size (R310-1)
Figure 3-26

Escape Opening Obstructions

1. Do not cover or obstruct escape openings with locks, bars, screens, or similar devices unless they can be operated from the inside without tools, keys, lock combinations, and special knowledge, and can be operated with the same force required to open the escape opening.

Window Wells for Below Grade Escape Openings

1. Provide all below grade escape openings with a window well.
2. Provide each window well with at least (≥) 9 square feet clear opening area and a depth and width of at least (≥) 36 inches in each direction.
3. Install a permanent ladder if the window well bottom is more than (>) 44 inches below grade. Ladder rung specifications include: (a) rung width at least (≥) 12 inches, and (b) rung projection at least (≥) 3 inches from the window well wall, and (c) rung vertical spacing not more than (≤) 18 inches apart, and (d) ladder may encroach not more than (≤) 6 inches into minimum window well width or depth dimension.

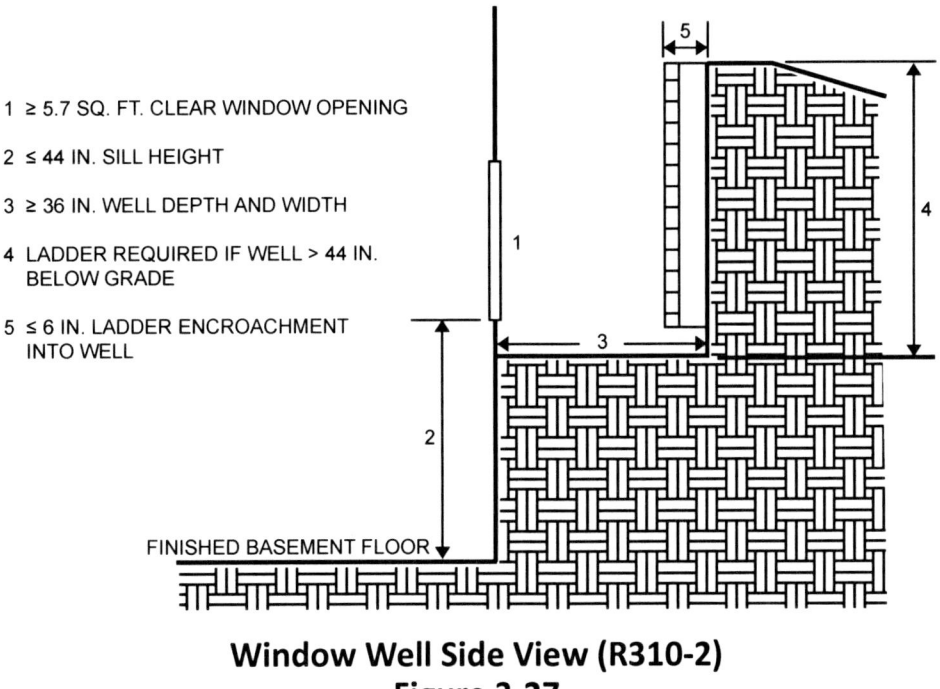

1 ≥ 5.7 SQ. FT. CLEAR WINDOW OPENING

2 ≤ 44 IN. SILL HEIGHT

3 ≥ 36 IN. WELL DEPTH AND WIDTH

4 LADDER REQUIRED IF WELL > 44 IN. BELOW GRADE

5 ≤ 6 IN. LADDER ENCROACHMENT INTO WELL

Window Well Side View (R310-2)
Figure 3-27

Escape Openings Discussion

Entry of rescue personnel and escape of occupants may be required during an emergency. The minimum opening sizes are intended to allow rescue personnel carrying full equipment to enter the building.

EXTERIOR DOORS (R311.1 – R311.3)

Egress Door Definition

Egress door The egress door is a door to the outside that meets all egress door requirements. Every dwelling must have at least one egress door. The egress door is usually the front door. Other exterior doors need not comply with the egress door requirements.

Egress Door Requirements

1. Provide at least (≥) one egress door that: (a) is accessible from all areas of the home, and (b) allows people to go directly outside without traveling through the garage.
2. Install a side-hinged egress door that is at least (≥) 36 inches wide and 80 inches high.
3. Provide a landing on the interior and exterior sides of the egress door. Build each landing at least (≥) as wide as the egress door. Example: if the egress door is 36 inches wide, then build each landing at least (≥) 36 inches wide. Build each landing at least (≥) 36 inches deep, measured in the direction of travel.
4. Build the interior and exterior landings not more than (≤) 1 ½ inches below the top of the threshold.
5. You may build the exterior landing not more than (≤) 7 ¾ inches below the top of the threshold, if the egress door does not swing over the landing. You may build the exterior landing

with not more than a (≤) 2% slope away from the door. You may have a storm door or a screen door swing over any landing.

6. Provide a ramp or a stairway to any egress door that is not at grade level.
7. Do not install a double cylinder dead bolt lock or any other lock or device that requires use of a key, tool, or any special knowledge or effort to open the egress door. This includes screen and security doors. This requirement does not apply to other exterior doors.

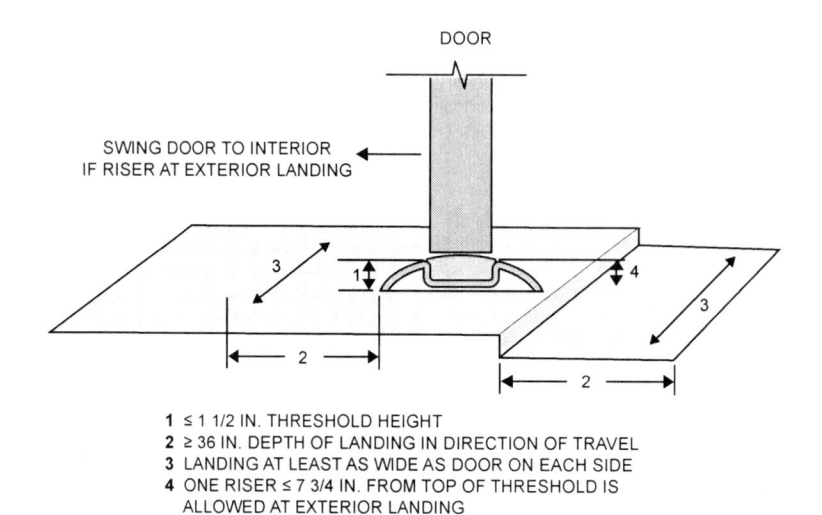

1 ≤ 1 1/2 IN. THRESHOLD HEIGHT
2 ≥ 36 IN. DEPTH OF LANDING IN DIRECTION OF TRAVEL
3 LANDING AT LEAST AS WIDE AS DOOR ON EACH SIDE
4 ONE RISER ≤ 7 3/4 IN. FROM TOP OF THRESHOLD IS ALLOWED AT EXTERIOR LANDING

Egress Door Requirements (R311.2-0)
Figure 3-28

Exterior Door Landing Requirements

1. Provide a landing on the interior and exterior sides of exterior doors.
2. Build each landing at least (≥) as wide as the door served. Example: if the door is 36 inches wide, then build each landing at least (≥) 36 inches wide.
3. Build each landing at least (≥) 36 inches deep, measured in the direction of travel.
4. Build each landing not more than (≤) 1 ½ inches below the top of the threshold.
5. You may build the exterior landing with not more than a (≤) 2 percent slope away from the door.
6. You are not required to build a landing on exterior side of a door if: (a) a stairway of not more than (≤) two risers is on the exterior side, and if (b) the exterior door does not swing over the stairway.
7. You may build an exterior landing not more than (≤) 7 ¾ inches below the top of the door threshold, if the exterior door does not swing over the landing.
8. Provide a ramp or a stairway to any exterior door that is not at grade level.
9. You may have a storm door or a screen door swing over any stairway and landing.
10. You are not required to build a landing on the exterior side of a door the opens to a narrow above grade balcony or to a similar structure.

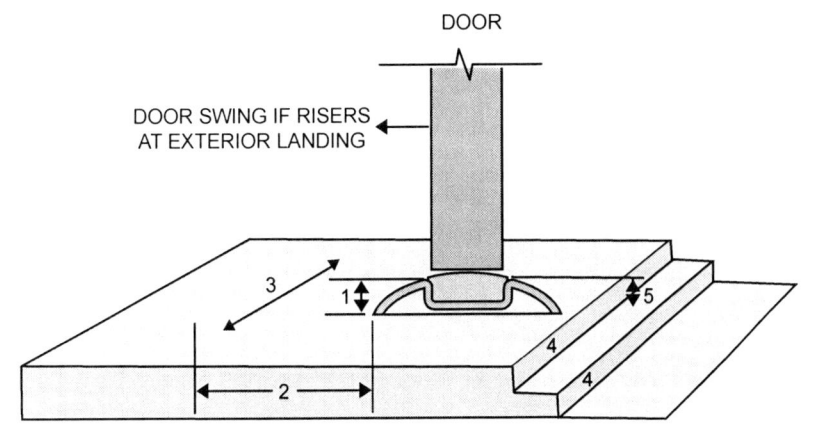

1 LANDING ≤ 1 1/2 IN. BELOW TOP OF THRESHOLD

2 LANDING ≥ 36 IN. DEEP IN DIRECTION OF TRAVEL

3 LANDING ≥ WIDTH OF DOOR

4 ONE OR TWO RISERS ALLOWED ON EXTERIOR SIDE OF DOOR IF DOOR DOES NOT SWING OVER STEPS

5 LANDING OR FIRST TREAD ≤ 7 3/4 IN. BELOW TOP OF THRESHOLD

Exterior Door Landing Requirements (R311.3-0)
Figure 3-29

HALLWAYS (R311.6)

Hallway Dimensions

1. Build each hallway with a minimum finished width of at least (≥) 36 inches.
2. Build each hallway with a finished ceiling height of at least (≥) 7 feet measured to the lowest projection from the ceiling. Note the ceiling projection exceptions for beams and for basements contained in Section R305.

STAIRWAYS (R311.7)

Stairway Definitions

Landing A landing is a flat surface at the top and bottom of a stairway. Landings may also occur at points within a stairway. A landing must be at least (≥) as wide as the stairway and at least (≥) 36 inches deep.

Nosing A tread nose (nosing) is the part of a tread that projects beyond a solid (closed) riser below.

Riser (stairway) A riser is the vertical part of a stairway. A closed riser has solid material between adjacent treads. An open riser has no material (except for any required guards) between adjacent treads.

Stairway (flight of stairs) A flight of stairs is a series of risers and treads that is not interrupted by a landing. A flight of stairs includes the landings at the top and bottom of the flight. A stairway with only a top and bottom landing has one flight of stairs. A stairway with a landing in the middle has two flights of stairs.

Tread A tread is the horizontal part of a stairway. A tread is sometimes called the step.

Winder (tread) A winder is a tread with one end wider than the other. Winders are often used at intermediate landings to change a stairway's direction.

Width

1. Provide a finished stairway width of at least (≥) 36 inches above handrail to the minimum headroom height.
2. Provide a finished stairway width of at least (≥) 31 ½ inches at and below the handrail for stairs with one handrail, and at least (≥) 27 inches at and below both handrails for stairs with two handrails.

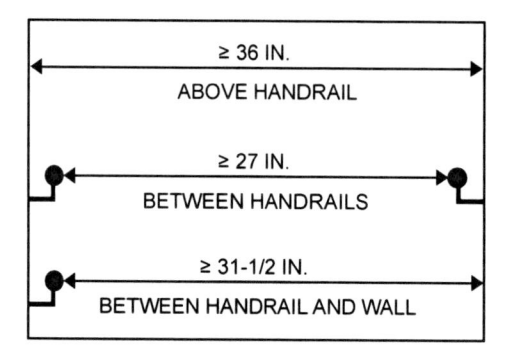

Stairway Width Clearances (R311.7-1)
Figure 3-30

Headroom Height

1. Provide a finished stairway headroom height of at least (≥) 80 inches measured vertically from a sloped plane connecting the tread nosing or from the finished floor of a landing. Projections from the ceiling are permitted above the minimum finished headroom height.
2. You may allow a floor opening above a flight of stairs to project not more than (≤) 4 ¾ inches into one side of the required headroom.

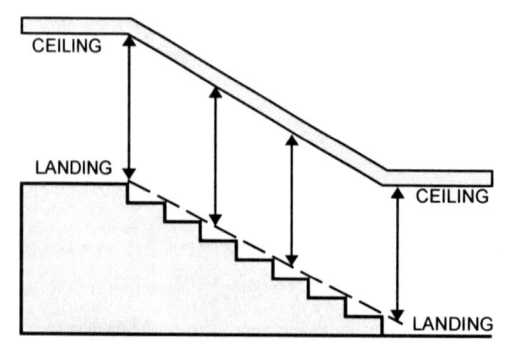

Stairway Headroom Clearances (R311.7-2)
Figure 3-31

Riser Height

1. Provide a finished riser height of not more than (≤) 7 ¾ inches. Measure riser height vertically from leading edges of adjacent treads. The IRC does not mandate a minimum riser height.
2. Do not exceed (≤) ⅜ inch finished riser height difference between any two risers in a flight of stairs.
3. Do not allow open risers to pass a 4 inch sphere. This includes interior stairs and exterior stairs, such as stairs for decks and balconies.
4. Beware of height differences caused by changes in floor covering materials. This often occurs at the top and bottom and landings. Stair stringers should be cut so that the finished risers comply with riser height and height difference requirements at treads and landings with different floor covering materials.

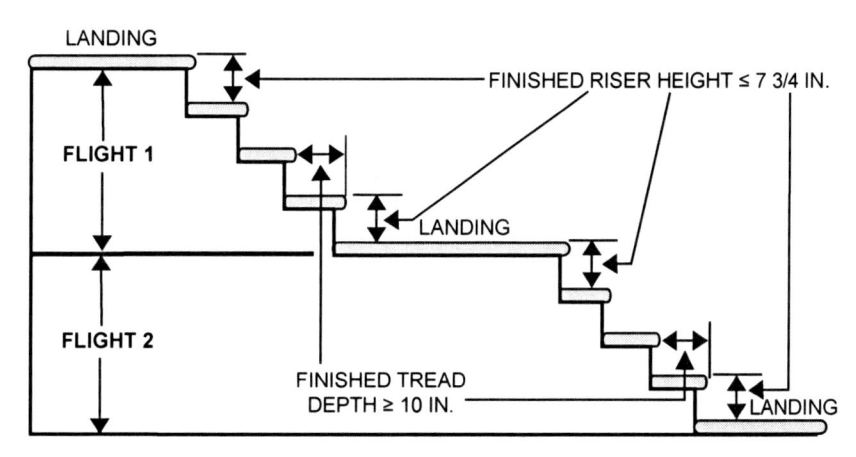

Riser and Tread Dimensions (R311.7-3)
Figure 3-32

Tread Depth

1. Provide a finished tread depth of at least (≥) 10 inches. Measure tread depth horizontally from the leading edges of adjacent treads.
2. Do not exceed (≤) ⅜ inch finished tread depth difference between any two treads in a flight of stairs. This does not apply to consistently shaped winder treads contained within the same flight of stairs.

Tread Nosing

1. Provide a finished tread nosing depth of at least (≥) ¾ inch and not more than (≤) 1 ¼ inches for stairs with solid risers. You are not required to provide tread nosing if treads are at least (≥) 11 inches deep.
2. Do not exceed (≤) ⅜ inch finished tread nosing depth difference between any two treads for all treads between two stories, including at floors and landings. Note that this differs from

the tread and riser maximum difference. The tread and riser differences are for a flight of stairs and the nosing depth difference is for all treads between two stories.

3. Do not exceed (≤) 9/16-inch for the curvature radius of a tread nosing and do not exceed (≤) ½ inch for the bevel of a tread nosing.

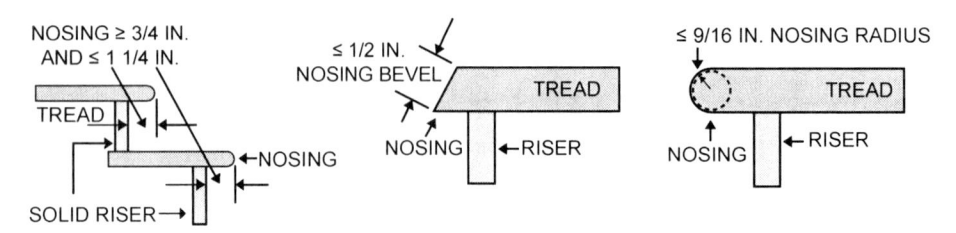

Tread Nosing Dimensions (R311.7-4)
Figure 3-33

Tread Slope

1. Slope treads and landings not more than (≤) 2 percent from horizontal in any direction.

Landings

1. Provide a landing or floor at the top and bottom of stairs.
2. Make the landing width at least (≥) as wide as the stairway. Example: if the stairway is 36 inch wide, build the landing at least (≥) a 36 inch wide.
3. Make the landing depth at least (≥) 36 inches, measured in the direction of travel.
4. You are not required to provide a landing or floor at top of interior stairs, including stairs in an attached garage, unless a door swings over stairs. This means you may terminate a flight of stairs directly into a door if the door swings away from the stairs.
5. Do not exceed (≤) 12 feet vertical rise of a flight of stairs without providing a landing. Example: do not install more than nineteen 7 ⅝ inch high risers without an intermediate landing.
6. Refer to Section R310.4 for provisions regarding landings at doors.

Winder Stair Treads

1. Provide a finished winder tread depth of at least (≥) 10 inches measured at 12 inches from the tread's narrow side.
2. Provide a finished winder tread depth of at least (≥) 6 inches at any point on a winder tread.

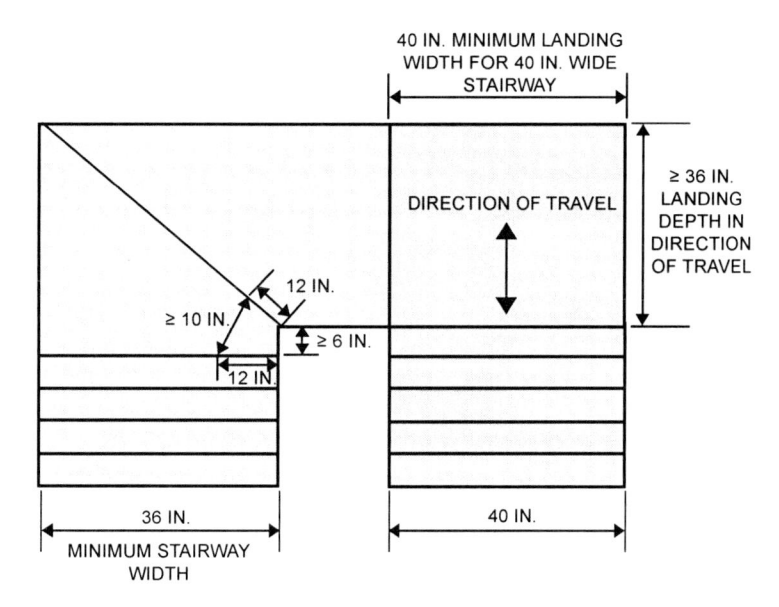

Stairway Landings and Winder Treads (R311.7-5)
Figure 3-34

Winder Stairway (PR311.7-0)
Figure 3-35

Spiral Stairs

1. Build a spiral stairway with:
   a) a finished width below the handrail of at least (≥) 26 inches, and
   b) a finished headroom height of at least (≥) 6 feet 6 inches, and
   c) a finished riser height of not more than (≤) 9 ½ inches, and
   d) a finished tread depth of at least (≥) 7 ½ inches measured at 12 inches from the tread's narrow point, and
   e) each tread being identical.

2. Comply with all other stairway requirements, such as handrails and guards, when building spiral stairways.

Stairway Live Loads (R301.5)

1. Install stair treads to bear a uniform distributed live load of at least (≥) 40 pounds per square foot or a 300 pound concentrated load over 4 square inches, whichever produces the greater stress.

HANDRAILS (R311.7.7)

Location

1. Provide a handrail on at least (≥) one side of every continuous flight of stairs with four or more risers.

Height

1. Install the handrail at least (≥) 34 inches and not more than (≤) 38 inches above the treads measured vertically from a sloped plane connecting the tread nosing or from the finished floor of a ramp.
2. You may exceed the 38 inch maximum height where a handrail connects with a guard to provide a continuous structure. Example: a handrail connects to a guard at an intermediate stairway landing. The handrail height at the beginning and ending of the intermediate landing guard may exceed 38 inches high.

Continuity

1. Run the handrail continuously from at least a point directly above the top riser of the flight of stairs to at least a point directly above the lowest riser of the flight.
2. Provide all handrails with a return or terminate them in a newel post, volute, starting easing, or starting newel.
3. Project handrails at least (≥) 1 ½ inches and not more than (≤) 4 ½ inches from any adjacent wall.
4. You may interrupt a handrail by a newel post at a turn.

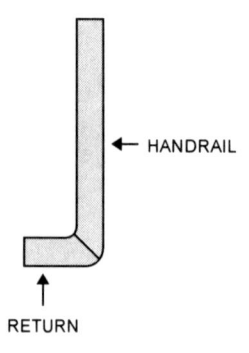

Handrail with Return (R311.7.7-1)
Figure 3-36

Shape

1. Use material with an outside diameter of at least (≥) 1 ¼ inches and not more than (≤) 2 inches for Type 1 circular handrails.
2. Use material with a perimeter dimension at least (≥) 4 inches and not more than (≤) 6 ¼ inches and a cross section dimension of not more than (≤) 2 ¼ inches for Type 1 non-circular handrails.
3. Provide Type 2 handrails that have a perimeter dimension greater than (>) 6 ¼ inches with a graspable finger recess on both sides of the profile. Refer to the illustration for profile and finger recess dimensions.
4. Apply handrail shape requirements to interior and to exterior stairways, including stairways for decks and balconies.

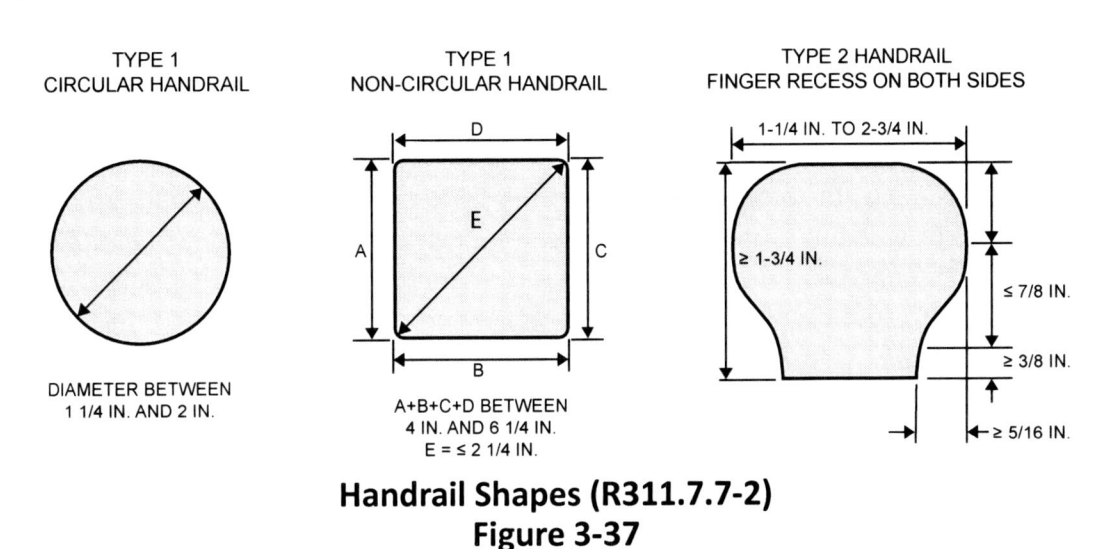

Handrail Shapes (R311.7.7-2)
Figure 3-37

Handrails Live Loads (R301.5)

1. Install handrails so they will resist a uniform distributed force of at least (≥) 200 pounds per square foot applied in any direction at any point along the top.

Handrail Beat Practice

Provide handrails on all stairways with two or more risers. Provide handrails at intermediate landings. This will help people with reduced mobility use stairs safely.

RAMPS (R311.8)

Ramp Definition

Ramp A ramp is a continuous sloped walking surface with a slope greater than (>) 1 vertical unit in 20 horizontal units and not more than (≤) the maximum permitted slope of 1 vertical unit in 12 horizontal units.

Slope

1. Build ramps with a slope of not more than (≤) 1 vertical unit in 12 horizontal units (8.3%).

You may build a ramp with a slope of not more than (≤) 1 vertical unit in 8 horizontal units (12.5%) if site constraints make building a shallower slope ramp infeasible.

Landings

1. Provide landings: (a) at the top and bottom of the ramp, and (b) where doors open on to the ramp, and (c) where the ramp changes direction.
2. Provide a ramp landing at least (≥) 3 feet by 3 feet.

Handrail Requirements

1. Install handrails on at least (≥) one side of all ramps with a slope more than (>) 1 vertical unit in 12 horizontal units.
2. Install handrails that conform to stairway handrail requirements of Section R311.5.6.

GUARDS (R312)

Guards Definition

Guard A guard is a barrier that protects occupants from falling from a raised surface such as a stairway, deck, or balcony. Guards are often call guardrails when the guard also serves as a handrail; however, guards need not be an open rail. A guard may be a partial height solid wall, a partial height wall containing safety glazing, or any other structure that complies with IRC requirements.

Location

1. Provide a guard at raised floor surfaces more than (>) 30 inches above adjacent an interior or exterior surface. Areas that require guards include porches, balconies, decks, hallways, screened enclosures, ramps, and the open sides of stairs with a total rise of more than (>) 30 inches.

Height

1. Provide guards at least (≥) 36 inches tall at raised surfaces other than the open sides of stairs.
2. Provide guards at least (≥) 34 inches high on the open sides of stairs. Measure the guards vertically from the nosing of the treads.
3. Limit the height of guards that are also handrails to not more than (≤) 38 inches. The IRC does not limit guard height other than for handrails.

Continuity

1. Provide continuous guards for open sides of the entire flight of stairs, even if some of the flight is less than (<) 30 inches above an adjacent surface.
2. You need not provide a guard if the entire flight of stairs is less than (<) 30 inches above an adjacent surface. This applies even if a lower flight of stairs connects with an upper flight of stairs at a landing. Example: a landing occurs before the last 3 risers of a stairway. The last 3 risers are a separate flight of stairs and do not require a guard or a handrail.

Stair Guards (R312-1)
Figure 3-38

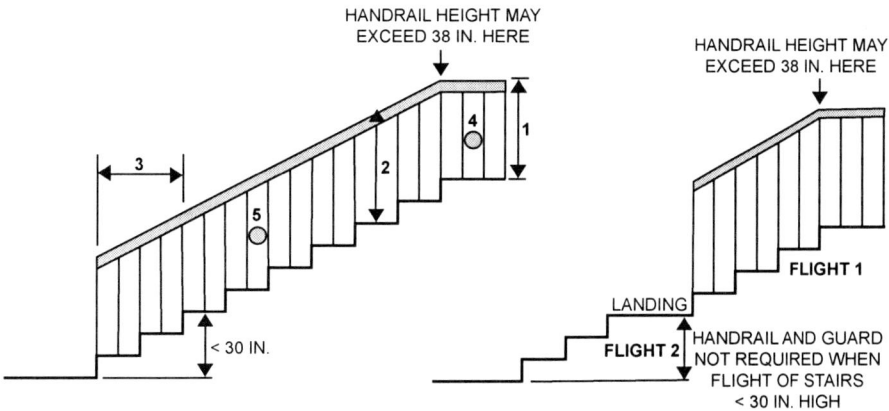

1 GUARD HEIGHT ≥ 36 IN.
2 STAIR GUARD HEIGHT ≥ 34 IN. AND ≤ 38 IN.
3 STAIR GUARD MUST CONTINUE FOR STAIRS LESS THAN 30 IN. ABOVE FLOOR BECAUSE STAIRS ARE ONE FLIGHT WITH NO LANDING
4 GUARD OPENING MUST NOT PASS 4 IN. DIAMETER SPHERE
5 STAIR GUARD OPENING MUST NOT PASS 4 3/8 DIAMETER SPHERE

Openings

1. Do not allow openings in guards to pass a 4 inch diameter sphere.
2. Do not allow <u>stair guard</u> openings, such as balusters, to pass a 4 ⅜ inch diameter sphere.
3. Do not allow openings under stair guards formed by a riser, tread, and the guard's bottom rail to pass a 6 inch diameter sphere.

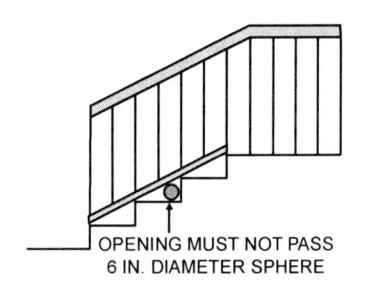

Intersection of Guard Bottom Rail with Stair Tread and Riser (R312-2)
Figure 3-39

Guards Live Loads (R301.5)

1. Install guards so they will resist a uniform distributed force of at least 200 pounds per square foot applied in any direction at any point along the top.
2. Install guard fill-in components, such as balusters, so they will resist a horizontally applied uniform distributed force of at least (≥) 50 pounds per square foot.

FIRE SPRINKLER SYSTEMS (R313)

1. Install an approved automatic fire sprinkler system in new one and two-family homes according to NFPA 13D or IRC Section P2904. This section is not effective until 1 January 2011. Note that adoption of this provision may vary by jurisdiction. Verify local adoption with the local building official.
2. Install an approved automatic fire sprinkler system in new townhouses according to NFPA 13D or IRC Section P2904. This section does not have a delayed adoption date.
3. Refer to Section P2904 and to the IRC for details about installing sprinkler systems.

SMOKE AND CARBON MONOXIDE ALARMS (R314 AND R315)

Smoke Alarm Required Locations

1. Locate a smoke alarm: (a) in every bedroom, and (b) outside all bedroom areas in the immediate vicinity (usually about 10 feet) of all bedrooms, and (c) on every level in the home, including basements.
2. You may substitute a security system that includes smoke alarms if it provides the same protection as hard-wired smoke alarms. The security system smoke alarms must: (a) comply with the National Fire Protection Association (NFPA) 72 standard, and (b) must be a permanent fixture in the home. Security system smoke alarms installed as a substitute system cannot be leased. They must be a permanent part of the home.

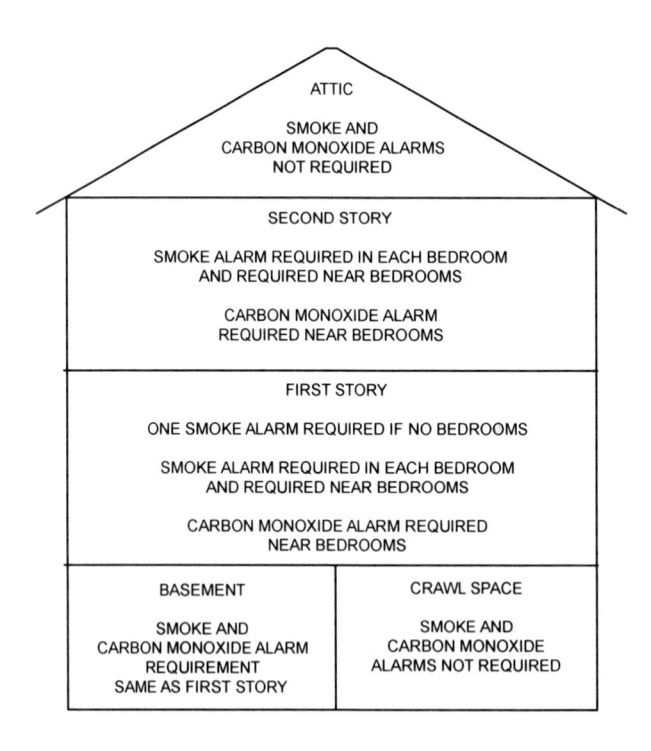

Alarm Location Requirements in Two Story Home (R314-1)
Figure 3-40

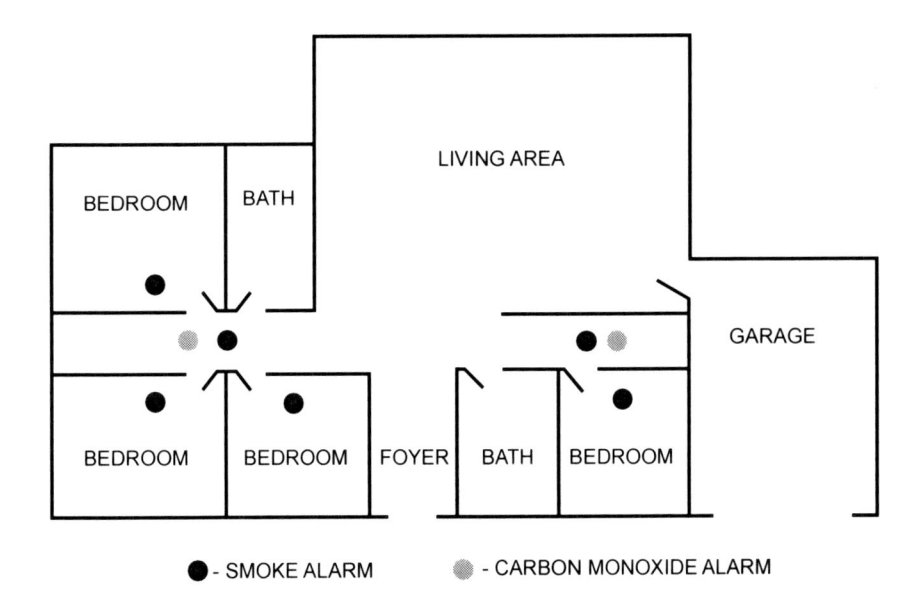

Alarm Location General Requirements (R314-2)
Figure 3-41

Smoke Alarm Locations Not Required

1. You are not required to locate smoke alarms:
   a) in crawl spaces and in uninhabitable attics, and
   b) on the middle level of split-level homes if smoke alarms are installed on the upper level, and if the middle level is less than one story below upper level, and if there is no door between levels. Note that some jurisdictions require smoke alarms on all levels of a split-level home.
2. Verify smoke alarm location requirements with the local building official.

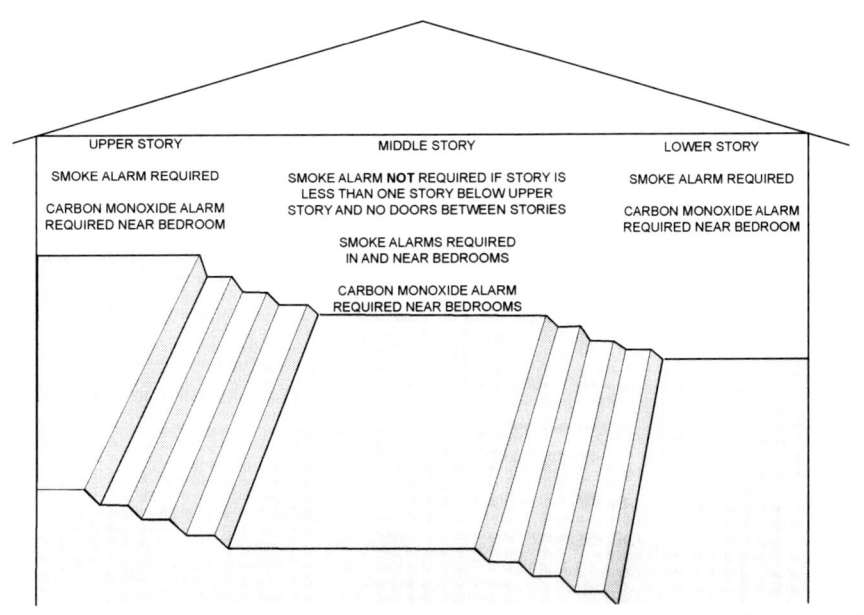

Alarm Location Requirements in Split Level Home (R314-3)
Figure 3-42

Smoke Alarm Power Source

1. Install smoke alarms that take primary power from the building electrical wiring and that have a battery backup.
2. Connect all smoke alarms together so one alarm activates all alarms (interconnection).
3. Provide arc-fault circuit interrupt protection for the smoke alarm primary power.

Smoke Alarm Installation

1. Install smoke alarms according to manufacturer's instructions. This often includes locating the smoke alarm on the ceiling or on a wall not more than (≤) 12 inches from the ceiling.

Smoke Alarm Update when Remodeling

1. Update the entire smoke alarm system to current code requirements (including interconnection and hard-wiring) when building alterations or additions require a permit or when bedrooms are added. This update requirement does not apply to:
    a) exterior work such as roofing, siding, window, and door repair and replacement, and
    b) installation of or repairs to plumbing and HVAC systems, and
    c) situations where installing electrical wires would require removal of finish materials that would not otherwise have been removed. This means that you do not have to hard-wire smoke alarms during remodeling if you must damage wall coverings to install the wires.
2. Verify requirements and exceptions with the local building official. Interpretation and enforcement of this provision varies between jurisdictions.

Carbon Monoxide Alarm Requirements

1. Install carbon monoxide alarms in homes equipped with fuel-fired equipment, such as gas and oil-fired furnaces, and in homes with attached garages. The alarms must comply with UL2034.
2. Install an alarm outside of bedroom areas in the immediate vicinity (usually about 10 feet) of all bedrooms. Connection of carbon monoxide alarms to each other is not required.
3. Install carbon monoxide alarms in existing homes when building alterations or additions require a permit or when bedrooms are added.
4. Install carbon monoxide alarms according to manufacturer's instructions.

Alarms Discussion

Smoke and carbon monoxide alarms are one of the least expensive life safety components in the home. They can alert occupants to smoke from fires and allow time to escape. These alarms have proven so effective that the IRC contains a unique provision mandating the updating of homes to current alarm requirements when major remodeling occurs.

Alarms Best Practice

Replace smoke and carbon monoxide alarms after about 10 years or as recommended by the alarm manufacturer. Do not rely only on the alarm test button. The button tests the alarm sounding mechanism, not the sensor that detects the smoke or carbon monoxide.

FOAM PLASTIC INSULATION AND TRIM (R316)

Foam Plastic Products Definition

Foam plastic Foam plastic products addressed in this section include: (a) extruded polystyrene sheet insulation from manufacturers such as Dow® and Owens Corning®, and (b) spray-applied polyisocyanurate foam products such as Great Stuff® and spray-applied foam insulation that is now available for insulating wall cavities and for insulating around rafters in semi-conditioned attics, and (c) flexible interior trim moldings such as crown and base moldings.

Foam Plastic Burning Limitations

1. Use foam plastic products with a flame spread index of not more than (≤) 75 and a smoke-developed index of not more than (≤) 450. This information should be on the product packaging and on individual pieces of sheet insulation.

Foam Plastic Separation from Building

1. Separate foam plastic from the building's interior using at least (≥) ½ inch drywall secured with screws, nails or approved mechanical fasteners. You may use other approved material if it provides the same or better fire protection. Note that several exceptions to this provision exist. Building interiors include attics, crawl spaces, and attached garages.
2. Verify requirements for foam plastic separation with the local building official.

Foam Plastic Separation from Building Exceptions

1. You are not required to cover foam plastic with ½ inch drywall when the foam plastic is used:
   a) inside the cells of concrete blocks or attached to masonry or concrete if the foam plastic is separated from the interior of the building by at least (≥) 1 inch of masonry or concrete;
   b) on the exterior side of a roof assembly if the foam plastic is: (a) installed according to manufacturer's instructions, and if (b) installed over at least (≥) 15/32 inch thick wood structural panels that are bonded to the roof supports with exterior glue and has edges supported by blocking and is attached as required by Section R803;
   c) in the interior of an attic or crawl space if: (a) the attic or crawl space is entered only for repair and maintenance and if (b) the plastic is covered with one of several materials including ¼ inch wood structural panels and ⅜ inch drywall;
   d) in foam-filled exterior doors and garage doors;
   e) as a foam backer board and in re-siding applications under specified conditions, see the IRC for additional information;
   f) as decorative interior trim molding under specified conditions including: (a) trim thickness not more than (≤) ½ inch, and (b) trim width not more than (≤) 8 inches;
   g) to seal sill plates and headers if the foam plastic thickness is not more than (≤) 3 ½ inches
   h) in a system where the foam plastic is tested in a specific type of installation by an inde-

pendent testing service such as the ICC Evaluation Service. The testing must include the foam plastic material, the materials to which it is attached, and the fasteners used to attach the foam plastic.

Foam Plastic Sheet Insulation as Foundation Insulation (R321.5)

1. Do not install foam plastic sheet insulation on the exterior face of foundation walls and under foundations in very heavy termite areas.
2. Maintain at least (≥) 6 inches between exposed ground and foam plastic sheet insulation installed above grade.
3. You may install foam plastic sheet insulation on or under foundation walls if the home is constructed entirely with non-combustible and/or treated wood construction materials, or if the insulation and structure are protected from termite damage. You may install foam sheet plastic insulation on the interior of basement walls.

WOOD ON CONCRETE AND MASONRY, WOOD IN THE GROUND, WOOD EXPOSED TO THE WEATHER (R317)

Treated and Decay Resistant Wood Definitions

Treated wood Treated wood (also called pressure treated) is wood into which chemicals have been forced under pressure. The chemicals help the wood resist insects and decay. The wood is often Southern Pine. Note that the cut ends, holes, and notches in treated wood are not insect and decay resistant. Cuts, holes, and notches must be field treated to restore resistance. Note that smaller dimensions of treated wood (such as 2x4) may not be suitable for direct ground contact. Verify ground contact rating of treated wood with the wood supplier.

Decay-resistant wood Decay-resistant wood comes from the heart (interior) of trees that produce wood naturally resistant to insects and decay. Such wood includes cedar and redwood.

Wood Decay Protection General Requirements

1. Use only treated or decay-resistant wood and wood-based products (such as plywood) if it is in contact with ground or is exposed to weather, except where the IRC defines the decay probability as being none to slight, or where the IRC provides another exception. Areas of the United States with none to slight decay probability include most of the area from central Texas west to, but not including, the west coast. Also included are areas along the Canadian border. In practice, most areas of the country use treated wood and wood-based products in decay prone areas of the building, such as sill plates, and wood exposed to the weather. Verify local requirements with the building official.

Wood in Contact with the Ground

1. Use only <u>treated wood suitable for ground contact</u> (not decay resistant wood) if the wood is in direct contact with the ground and if the building is permanent and intended for occupancy by people. Example: this provision would not apply to detached storage sheds. Smaller dimensions of treated wood, such as 2x4, may not be suitable for ground contact.

Joists, Trusses, and Beams in Crawl Spaces

1. Place floor joists and trusses that are not made from treated or decay-resistant wood at least (≥) 18 inches above exposed ground.
2. Place beams, girders, and supporting posts that are not made from treated or decay-resistant wood at least (≥) 12 inches above exposed ground.
3. Apply these provisions to crawl spaces and similar areas inside the foundation walls.

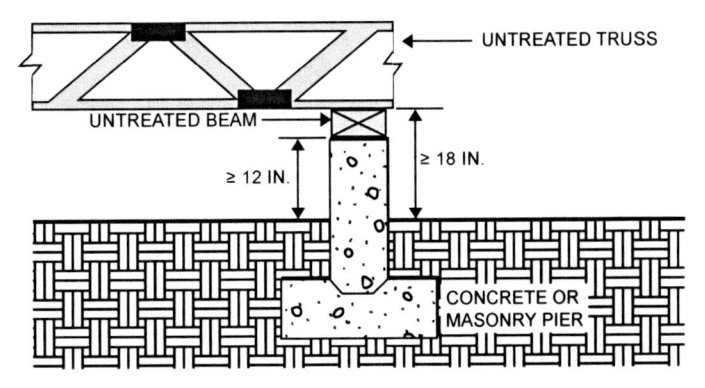

Joists, Trusses, and Beams in Crawl Spaces (R317-1)
Figure 3-43

Sills and Sleepers on Concrete and Masonry

1. Use treated or decay-resistant wood for framing members <u>that are in contact with concrete and masonry exterior foundation walls</u> if the framing members are less than (<) 8 inches from exposed ground.
2. Use treated or decay-resistant wood for sill plates, soleplates, and sleepers resting on concrete and masonry slabs and stem walls, if the slab or stem wall does not rest on a moisture barrier such as plastic sheeting.

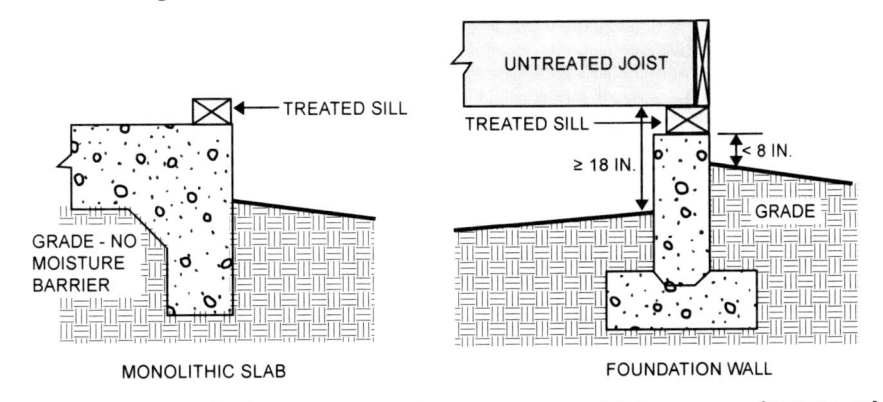

Sill Plates and Sleepers on Concrete and Masonry (R317-2)
Figure 3-44

Beams and Girders in Concrete and Masonry Wall Pockets

1. Provide an air space at least (≥) ½ inch on the sides, top, and rear of beams or girders that enter a concrete or masonry wall beam pocket, or use treated or decay-resistant wood for the beams and girders.

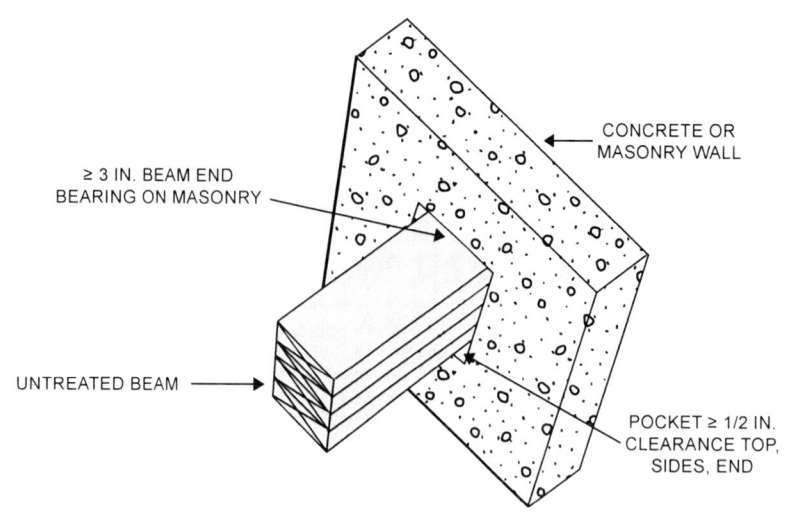

Beams and Girders in Concrete and Masonry Wall Pockets (R317-3)
Figure 3-45

Exterior Wood Siding, Sheathing, and Framing Near the Ground

1. Place wood siding, sheathing and framing members that are not made from treated or decay-resistant wood at least (≥) 6 inches above the ground and at least (≥) 2 inches above horizontal concrete steps and slabs that are exposed to weather. This means that all wood, including wall studs and sill plates, must have the required clearances to ground and concrete or the wood must be treated or decay-resistant. It does not matter if the wood is covered with other material, such as stucco or brick, because other materials can admit moisture that over time can cause decay in untreated wood.

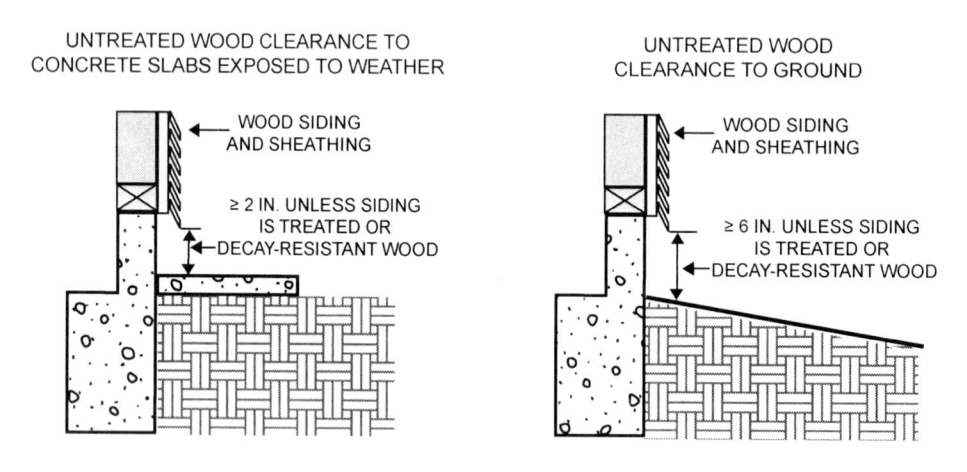

Exterior Wood Siding, Sheathing, and Framing Near the Ground (R317-4)
Figure 3-46

Wood Attached to Concrete and Masonry Basement Walls

1. Use treated or decay-resistant wood attached to the interior side of exterior below grade walls unless the wood is separated from the concrete or masonry by an approved vapor retarder.

Wood Posts Encased in Concrete

1. Use only <u>treated wood suitable for ground contact</u> (not decay resistant wood) for posts, columns, and poles encased in concrete that is in direct contact with the ground.
2. Use only <u>treated wood suitable for ground contact</u> (not decay resistant wood) for posts, columns, and poles encased in concrete and exposed to weather. Note that cut treated wood is not treated at the cut. Do not encase cut treated wood in concrete or expose it to weather without field-treating the cut end with approved material.
3. Apply these restrictions only to posts, columns, and poles supporting permanent structures. Smaller dimensions of treated wood, such as 2x4, may not be suitable for ground contact.

Wood Posts Not Encased in Concrete

1. Use treated or decay-resistant wood posts, columns, and poles that support permanent structures if the posts, columns, and poles are not encased in concrete. Note that cut treated wood is not treated at the cut. Do not expose the cut end to weather without field-treating the cut end with approved material.
2. You may use untreated wood if the concrete on which the wood rests is separated from the ground by a moisture barrier and if the post is above the ground by the required distance.

Exterior Decks and Balconies

1. Use treated or decay-resistant wood as structural supports for exterior structures such as decks, balconies, and porches if: (a) the structures are exposed to the weather, and if (b) a roof does not protect the structures, and if (c) required by the local building official.
2. Verify requirements with the local building official.

Fasteners for Treated Wood

1. Use hot-dipped galvanized steel or other approved corrosion-resistant fasteners with treated wood. One-half inch and larger steel bolts are exempt from this requirement. Note that some fasteners are not compatible with some chemicals used to treat wood. The chemicals can cause the fasteners to deteriorate faster than normal. Use manufacturer's instructions for both the fastener and the treated wood to determine if the fasteners and the wood are compatible.

Treated Wood Cuts, Notches, and Holes (R317.1.1)

1. Apply an approved preservative to cuts, holes, and notches in treated wood. Cuts, holes, and notches remove the thin treated exterior layer of treated wood and must be field-treated to restore the protection to the cut or drilled area.

Exposed Glued-Laminated Timbers

1. Use glued-laminated timbers that are made from decay-resistant or treated wood if: (a) the timbers provide structural support for the building, and if (b) the timbers are exposed to the weather and are not protected by the roof, eaves, or similar structure. Only the parts of the timber exposed to the weather must be made from decay-resistant or treated wood.

Wood Decay Protection Best Practice

1. Place a moisture barrier under beams and girders in concrete and masonry pockets to avoid wicking of moisture from the masonry into the beam or girder.

TERMITE PROTECTION (R318)

1. Provide protection against termite damage in areas subject to termites. These areas include almost all of the continental United States. You may use any approved protection method including: (a) chemical treatment, or (b) termite baiting systems, or (c) treated or naturally termite-resistant wood, or (d) physical barriers, or (e) steel framing materials.
2. Reapply chemical termite treatment to areas that are disturbed after the original chemical treatment. Example: reapply chemical termite treatment when the foundation concrete slab is broken to move improperly placed electrical and plumbing rough-ins.
3. Refer to IRC Appendix R for special requirements in areas subject to Formosan termites. These areas are currently in parts of Texas and the Southeast.

SITE ADDRESS (R319)

1. Install approved building address numbers and/or letters that are clearly legible from the road fronting the property. This is so emergency responders can quickly locate the property. Make the letters and/or numbers Arabic type that are at least (≥) 4 inches tall and at least ½ inch wide. Make the letters and/or numbers contrast with the background.

ACCESSIBILITY (R320)

1. Provide disability accessibility features as required by the International Building Code for Group R-3 occupancy when at least (≥) 4 dwelling or sleeping units are located in one building. This means that one and two-family homes and townhomes with fewer than (<) four units in one building need not have disability accessibility features.

FLOOD-RESISTANT CONSTRUCTION (R322)

1. Use flood-resistant construction in designated flood hazard areas. Verify with the local building official if the area is in a flood hazard area. Flood-resistant construction involves elevating the lowest floor level of the structure above the flood level, installing mechanical, electrical, and plumbing components above the flood level, and reinforcing the foundation to withstand forces from water and wave action. Refer to the IRC for more information about flood-resistant construction requirements.

4

FOUNDATION CONSTRUCTION

EXTERIOR SURFACE DRAINAGE AND GUTTERS (R401.3 AND R801.3)

Drainage Near Home (R401.3)

1. Direct surface water away from the foundation to a storm sewer or other approved collection point.
2. Provide at least (≥) 6 inches of fall away from foundation walls and foundation slabs within the first 10 feet from the foundation (5% slope).
3. Provide alternate drainage means, such as swales or underground (French) drains if tight lot lines or physical barriers prevent having 6 inches of fall within the first 10 feet.
4. Slope impervious surfaces, such as concrete and asphalt, at least (≥) 2% away from the building.

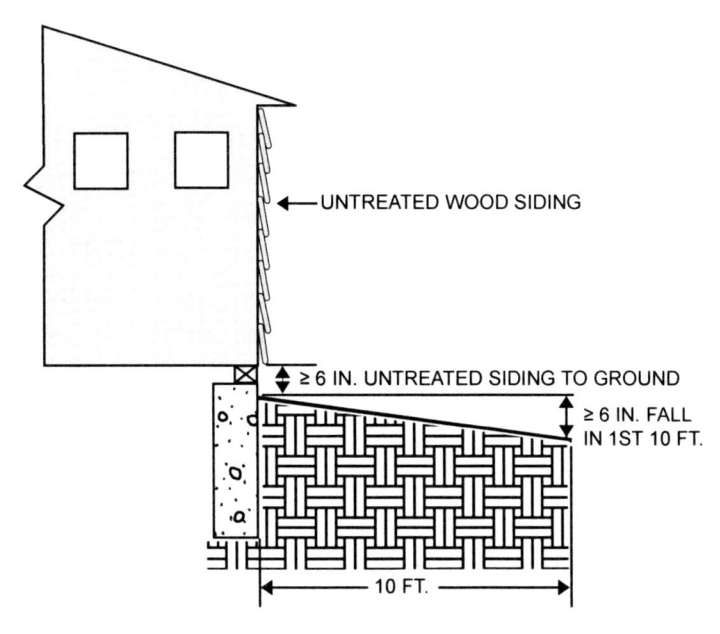

Drainage Near Home (R401.3-0)
Figure 4-1

Gutters (R801.3)

1. Provide gutters or other means to control roof runoff in areas with expansive or collapsible soil. Discharge the gutter water at least (≥) 5 feet away from the foundation or into an approve drainage system.

Water Control Discussion

Water control at the foundation is one of the most important ways to protect the home. Improper foundation water control can cause wet basements and crawl spaces. Wet foundations provide an environment for fungal growth. Improper foundation water control can cause significant foundation damage in areas with expansive or collapsible soils and in areas subject to frost heaving. Improper foundation water control can leave damp soil around the foundation and provide an attractive environment for termites.

Water Control Best Practice

Install a full system of gutters and downspouts on all homes. Provide splash blocks or other means at downspouts to divert the water at least 5 feet away from the foundation. If feasible, collect rain water for irrigation use.

CONCRETE STRENGTH (R402.2)

Concrete in Foundation Walls and Footings Not Exposed to Weather

1. Use at least (≥) 2,500 psi concrete in all weathering potential environments.
2. Use air-entrained concrete ((≥) 5% and (≤) 7% total air content) in severe weathering potential environments if the concrete may be subject to freezing and thawing during construction.

Concrete in Basement Slabs and Interior Slabs-on-Grade (Not Garage Floors)

1. Use at least (≥) 2,500 psi concrete in all weathering potential environments.
2. Use air-entrained concrete ((≥) 5% and (≤) 7% total air content) in severe weathering potential environments if the concrete may be subject to freezing and thawing during construction.

Concrete in Foundation Walls, Exterior Walls, and Other Vertical Concrete Exposed to Weather

1. Use at least (≥) 2,500 psi concrete in negligible weathering potential environments.
2. Use at least (≥) 3,000 psi air-entrained concrete ((≥) 5% and (≤) 7% total air content) in moderate and severe weathering potential environments.

Concrete in Porches, Garage and Carport Floors, and Other Horizontal Concrete Exposed to Weather

1. Use at least (≥) 2,500 psi concrete in negligible weathering potential environments.
2. Use at least (≥) 3,000 psi air-entrained concrete ((≥) 5% and (≤) 7% total air content) in moderate weathering potential environments.
3. Use at least (≥) 3,500 psi air-entrained concrete ((≥) 5% and (≤) 7% total air content) in severe weathering potential environments.
4. You may use at least (≥) 4,000 psi concrete air-entrained concrete with at least (≥) 3% total air content in steel-toweled garage floors in moderate and severe weathering potential environments.

Concrete Installation Best Practice

Order a concrete mix that is at least 500 psi greater than the minimum required. By the time the concrete is deposited and finished, you'll be lucky if the concrete actually satisfies minimum requirements. Use crack control material such as 6x6x10 wire mesh in all basement, garage and carport, and porch slabs. It won't stop all cracks, but it usually helps reduce their number and severity. Use plenty of reinforcing bars in footings, basement walls, and all slabs poured over compacted fill. It's the cheapest insurance against foundation problems that you can buy.

FOOTINGS (R403)

Soil Load Bearing Capacities (R401.4)

1. Place footings on undisturbed soil of known bearing capacity or on fill approved by an engineer.
2. Have a geotechnical engineer evaluate the soil in areas known to have expansive or other unfavorable soils or if the soil bearing capacity is unknown. Beware of clay soils. Some clay soils can be unstable and cause serious foundation problems.
3. Use the following table to estimate soil bearing capacity if the soil type is known and if the local building official approves.

TABLE R401.4
Soil Load Bearing Capacities

soil type	presumed soil bearing capacity
bedrock (e. g. granite)	12000 psf
sedimentary type rock	4000 psf
gravel & sandy gravel	3000 psf
sand, silty sand, clayey sand, silty gravel, clayey gravel	2000 psf
clay, sandy clay, silty clay, clayey slit, slit, sandy silt	1500 psf

Footing Width

1. Use the following tables to determine the minimum footing width required to support load-bearing walls. You may also use material found in The American Concrete Institute document ACI 332, currently available for purchase at http://www.concrete.org/bookstorenet.
2. Refer to the IRC for special footing and footing reinforcement requirements in seismic design areas.

TABLE R403-1
Minimum Footing Width for Light Frame Wall Construction

	1500 psi bearing soil	2000 psi bearing soil	3000 psi bearing soil
1-story home	12 inches	12 inches	12 inches
2-story home	15 inches	12 inches	12 inches
3-story home	23 inches	17 inches	12 inches

TABLE R403-2
Minimum Footing Width for Light Frame Wall Construction with Four Inch Brick Veneer or for Eight Inch Hollow Masonry Walls

	1500 psi bearing soil	2000 psi bearing soil	3000 psi bearing soil
1-story home	12 inches	12 inches	12 inches
2-story home	21 inches	16 inches	12 inches
3-story home	23 inches	17 inches	12 inches

TABLE R403-3
Minimum Footing Width for Eight Inch Solid or Fully Grouted Masonry Walls

	1500 psi bearing soil	2000 psi bearing soil	3000 psi bearing soil
1-story home	16 inches	12 inches	12 inches
2-story home	29 inches	21 inches	14 inches
3-story home	42 inches	32 inches	21 inches

Footing Thickness and Slope

1. Make spread footings at least (≥) 6 inch thick.
2. Project spread footings at least (≥) 2 inches beyond the framing or foundation wall. Do not project the footing beyond the framing or foundation wall more than (>) the thickness of the footing. Example: if the footing is 6 inches thick, then the edge of the footing should be not more than (≤) 6 inches beyond the edge of the framing or foundation wall.
3. Locate the bottom of footings at least (≥) 12 inches below finish grade or below the local frost line, whichever is deeper. This does not apply to light-frame-constructed accessory buildings with an area of not more than (≤) 600 square feet and an eave height of not more than (≤) 10-feet and this does not apply to decks not supported by the home.
4. Do not place footings on frozen ground unless the frozen condition is permanent (permafrost).
5. Make the top surface of footings level.

6. You may slope the bottom of footings not more than (≤) 10 percent, without reducing the minimum thickness.
7. Make step footing thickness at least (≥) 6 inches. Make step footing height not more than (≤) the length of the footing above the step.
8. You are not required to place steel reinforcing bars in footings in areas that are not subject to seismic risk. Placing steel reinforcing bars in footings and in other foundation concrete is often recommended as additional insurance against foundation problems.

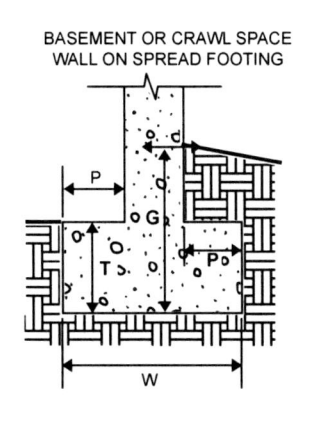

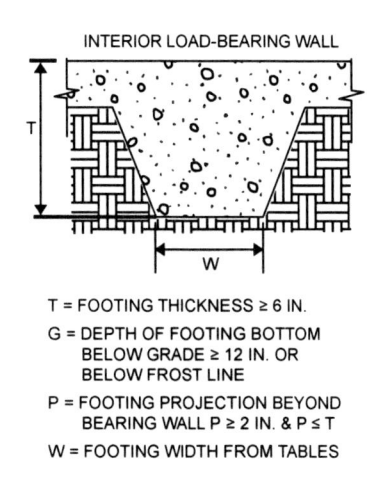

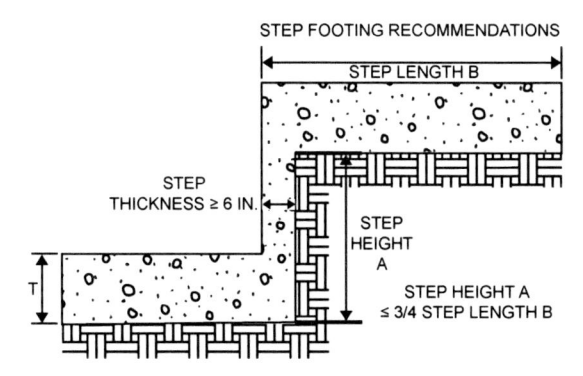

Footings (R403-1)
Figure 4-2

Foundation Anchors

1. Install at least (≥) ½ inch diameter bolts in exterior footings, stem walls, basement walls, monolithic slabs, and other places to which sill or sole plates for load-bearing and braced walls will be attached.
2. Install and tighten a nut and washer on each bolt. You may use standard cut round washers in other than seismic risk areas. Verify washer type with the local building official.
3. Locate the bolts at least (≥) 7 bolt diameters and not more than (≤) 12 inches from the ends of each plate and not more than (≤) every 6 feet on center in between.
4. Install at least (≥) two bolts per plate section. Refer to the IRC about exceptions for offset braced walls not more than (≤) 24 inches long.
5. Embed the bolts at least (≥) 7 inches into the foundation.
6. Use approved fasteners to anchor interior load-bearing wall sole plates.

7. You may substitute anchor straps for bolts if they provide equal anchorage. Straps are often installed not more than (≤) every 3 feet.
8. Refer to the IRC for special foundation anchor requirements in seismic design and high wind areas.

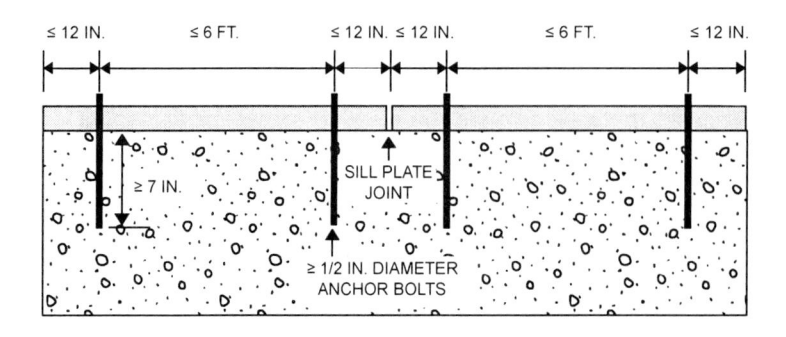

Foundation Anchors (R403-2)
Figure 4-3

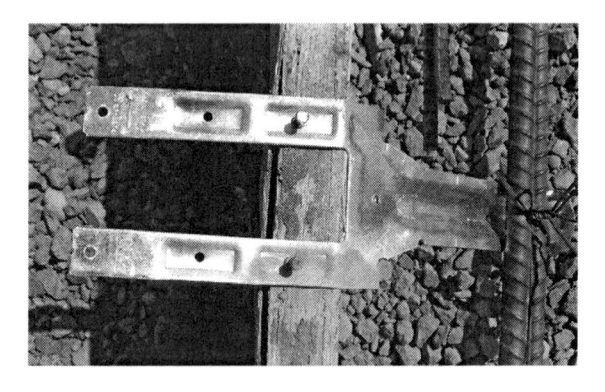

Anchor Strap (PR403-1)
Figure 4-4

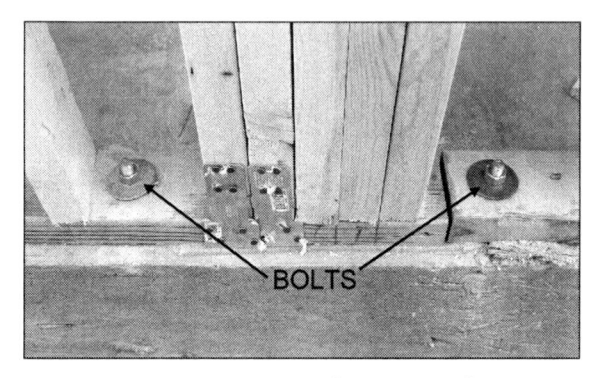

Anchor Bolts (PR403-2)
Figure 4-5

Building Setbacks from Slopes General Requirements

1. Apply the following building setback solutions to buildings located on or near ascending and descending slopes between 1 vertical unit in 3 horizontal units (33.3 percent slope) and 1 vertical unit in 1 horizontal unit (100 percent slope).
2. Refer to the IRC if the slope is steeper than 1 vertical unit in 1 horizontal unit.
3. The building official may approve an engineered solution that differs from the code solution.

Building Setback from Ascending Slopes

1. Locate the <u>face of the building</u> closest to the slope not closer to the bottom (toe) of the slope than the height of the slope divided by 2, or 15 feet, whichever is less.

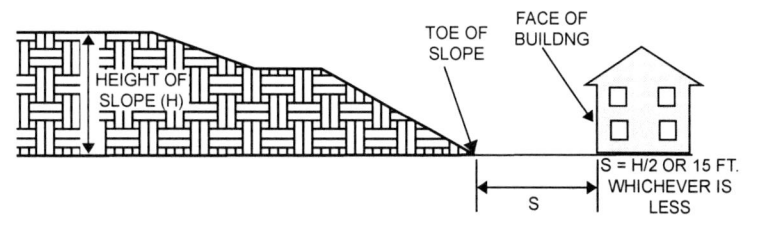

Building Setback from Ascending Slope (R403-3)
Figure 4-6

Building Setback from Descending Slopes

1. Locate the <u>face of the footing</u> closest to the slope not closer to the top of the slope than the height of the slope divided by 3, or 40 feet, whichever is less.

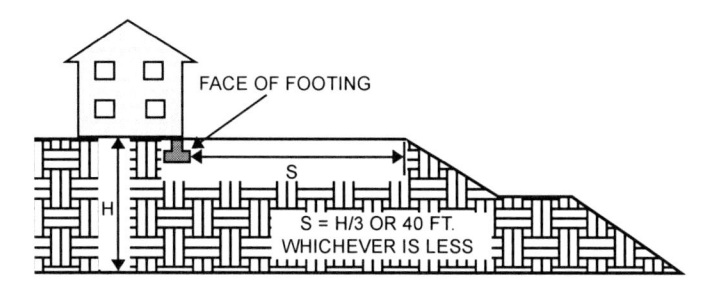

Building Setback from Descending Slope (R403-4)
Figure 4-7

Level Site Foundation Height Above Street

1. Place the top of the foundation at least (≥) 12 inches plus 2 percent of the distance from the foundation to the street gutter or to the inlet of an approved drainage device. This applies only to graded (level) building sites where drainage of storm water off of the site may be an issue.
2. The building official may approve alternate foundation heights.

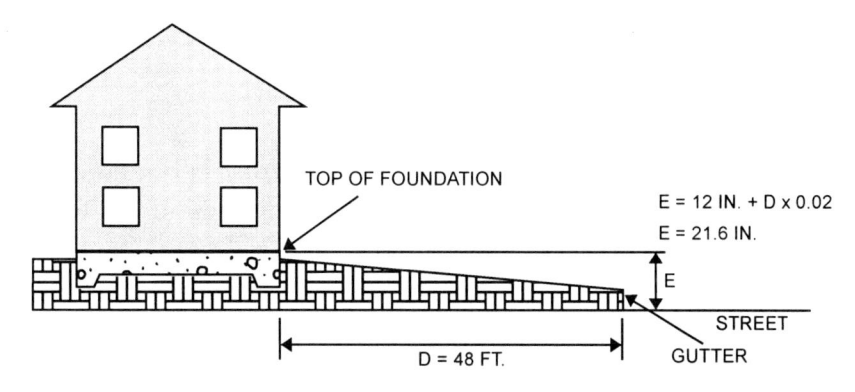

Level Site Foundation Height (R403-5)
Figure 4-8

Footing and Anchorage Requirements in Seismic and High Wind Areas

1. Refer to the IRC and to the local building official for additional footing and anchorage requirements in seismic design and high wind areas.

FOUNDATION AND RETAINING WALLS (R404.5)

Limitations of the Material in this Section

The IRC provides complex rules governing the design of and the lateral support of foundation walls. We do not recommend that readers of this book attempt to design or build foundation walls. Consult a qualified contractor or engineer regarding foundation walls. Refer to the IRC Commentary for more information about foundation wall construction.

Retaining Walls

1. Design and build retaining walls to resist problems such as overturning, sliding, and uplift when: (a) the wall retains more than (>) 24 inches of fill, and (b) the wall has no horizontal support at the top. Retaining walls more than (>) 48 inches tall and retaining walls that retain a surcharge may require design by a qualified contractor or engineer. Verify permit requirements for retaining walls with the building official.

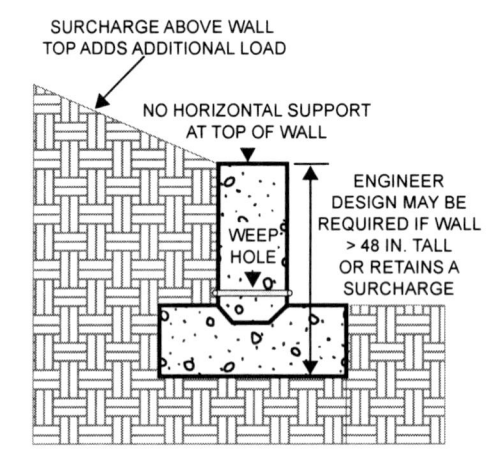

Retaining Wall with Surcharge Load (R404-1)
Figure 4-9

Retaining Walls Best Practice

Provide all retaining walls with some means to drain water from behind the wall. Walls without drainage often fail because of the water pressure that builds behind the wall. Retaining walls made from concrete and concrete blocks should have weep hole near the bottom of the wall. If the soil behind the wall is poorly drained, such as clay soils, separate the weep holes from the soil with gravel covered by a filter fabric. Otherwise, the weep holes may become clogged.

FOUNDATION DRAINS AND DAMPPROOFING (R405 AND R406)

Dampproofing and Waterproofing Definitions

Dampproofing Dampproofing inhibits the flow of water vapor and small quantities of liquid water under slight pressure through a foundation wall.

Waterproofing Waterproofing inhibits the flow of water vapor and larger quantities of liquid water under higher pressure through a foundation wall.

Foundation Drains (Footing Drains)

1. Install foundation drains around foundation walls with earth on one side and habitable or usable spaces on the other side. You may omit foundation drains when the foundation is constructed on naturally well-drained sandy soil and gravel.
2. Enclose perforated plastic pipe drains enclosed in a filter fabric (sock), and place the drains on at least (≥) 2 inches of gravel at the base of the footing, and cover the drains with at least (≥) 6 inches of gravel above the pipe.
3. Extend gravel only drains at least (≥) 12 inches from the base of the footing, and cover the footing with gravel to at least (≥) 6 inches above the top of the footing, and cover the gravel with an approved filter membrane.

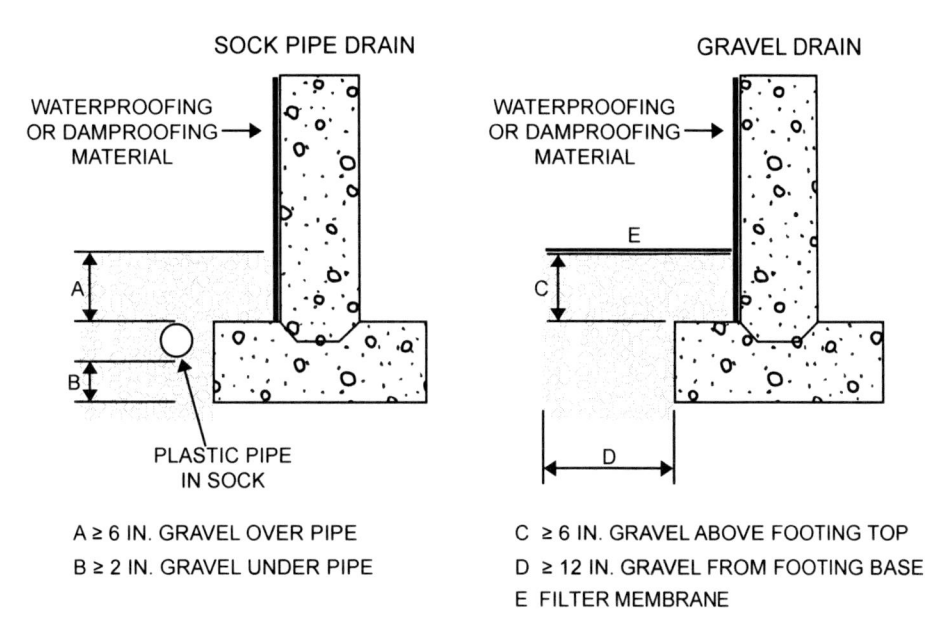

SOCK PIPE DRAIN
WATERPROOFING OR DAMPROOFING MATERIAL
A ≥ 6 IN. GRAVEL OVER PIPE
B ≥ 2 IN. GRAVEL UNDER PIPE
PLASTIC PIPE IN SOCK

GRAVEL DRAIN
WATERPROOFING OR DAMPROOFING MATERIAL
C ≥ 6 IN. GRAVEL ABOVE FOOTING TOP
D ≥ 12 IN. GRAVEL FROM FOOTING BASE
E FILTER MEMBRANE

Foundation Drains (R405-0)
Figure 4-10

Dampproofing Masonry and Concrete Foundation Walls

1. Dampproof foundation walls that have earth on one side and interior spaces and floors on the other side. Verify with the local building official if dampproofing applies to crawl space walls in your jurisdiction.
2. Use at least (≥) a ⅜ inch layer of Portland cement parging and an approved dampproofing compound to dampproof masonry walls. You do not need a parging coat if the dampproofing compound is approved for direct application to the masonry.
3. Use an approved dampproofing compound to dampproof concrete walls. Approved dampproofing compounds are usually an oil-based coating.
4. You may use any approved waterproofing material as a dampproofing material if you apply the material according to manufacturer's instructions.
5. Extend dampproofing from the top of the footing to the finished grade level.

Waterproofing Masonry and Concrete Foundation Walls

1. Waterproof foundation walls that have earth on one side and interior spaces and floors on the other side when a high water table or other conditions exist that might subject the foundation to liquid water under pressure.
2. Use an approved waterproofing material, such as 6 mil polyethylene or 6 mil polyvinyl chloride sheeting, or an approved commercially available waterproofing system to waterproof masonry and concrete walls.
3. Lap and seal joints in the waterproofing material with a sealant compatible with the waterproofing material.
4. Extend waterproofing from the top of the footing to the finished grade level.

Waterproofing Discussion

Moisture problems in below grade walls are extremely difficult to repair from the inside and extremely expensive to repair from the outside once the foundation is backfilled and landscaping is installed. Properly applied waterproofing or dampproofing and foundation drains are inexpensive insurance against future foundation and basement water problems. Installing gutters, downspouts, and downspout extensions is another way to reduce foundation and basement water problems.

Waterproofing Best Practice

Dampproofing can degrade over time if exposed to excessive moisture. Waterproof foundations if a finished basement is likely. Provide adequate grading away from the foundation and install gutters on all homes.

CRAWL SPACES (R408)

Crawl Space Ventilated to Exterior

1. Provide at least (≥) one square foot of net free ventilation area for every 150 square feet of crawl space floor in a ventilated crawl space. You may reduce the net free ventilation area to at least (≥) one square foot for every 1,500 square feet of crawl space floor if you cover the floor with a vapor retarder such as 6-mil polyethylene.
2. Install covers such as screens or grates in the ventilation openings. Use screens, grates, grills, or plates with openings at least (≥) ⅛ inch and not more than (≤) ¼ inch.
3. Subtract the space used by opening covers from the net free ventilation area of a ventilation opening. Example: a one square foot opening may be reduced to an effective 2/3 square foot opening when covered by a cast iron grill or grate. The cover manufacturer's instructions should indicate the cover's opening reduction amount.
4. Locate a ventilation opening not more than (≤) 3 feet from every corner of the crawl space wall.

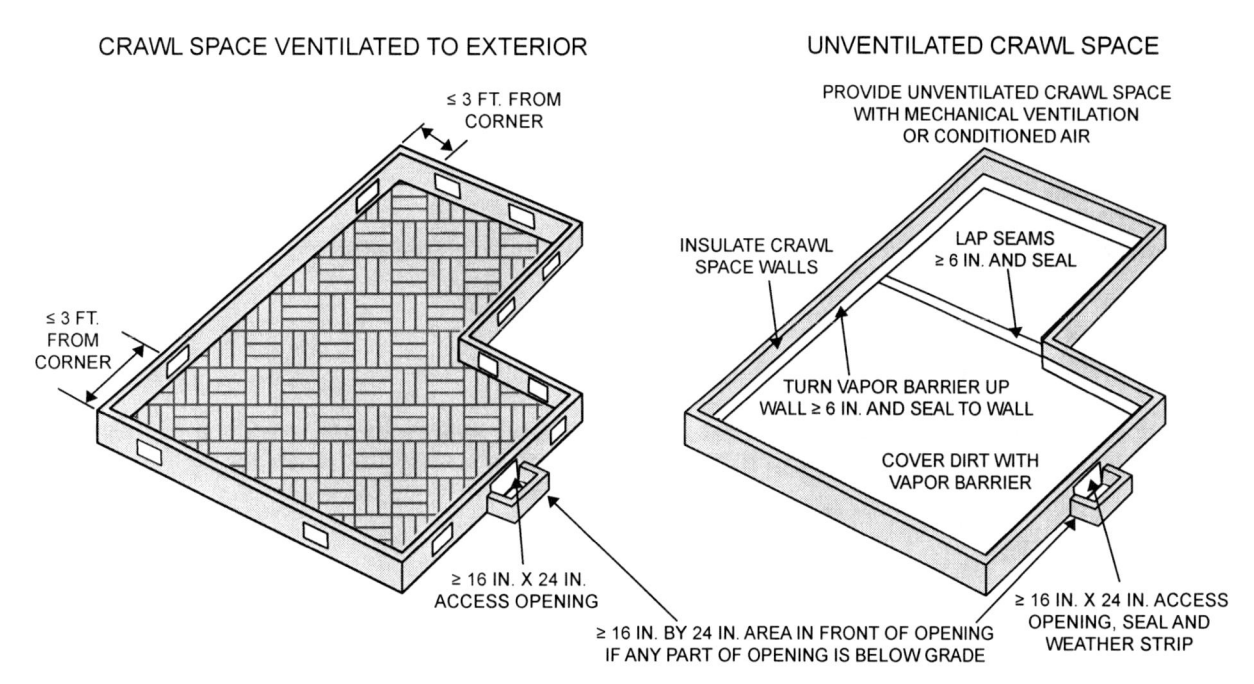

Ventilated and Unventilated Crawl Spaces (R408-0)
Figure 4-11

Unventilated Crawl Space

1. You may eliminate crawl space ventilation openings by insulating the crawl space as required in Chapter 11 and by installing the following moisture control and ventilation components:
   a) cover all exposed dirt in the crawl space floor with an approved vapor retarder, such as 6 mil polyethylene sheeting, and
   b) lap all vapor retarder seams by at least (≥) 6 inches and seal or tape the seams, and
   c) extend the vapor retarder at least (≥) 6 inches up the crawl space wall and attach and seal the vapor retarder to the wall; and
   d) provide one of the following ventilation methods:
      a) continuous mechanical exhaust ventilation, or
      b) a conditioned air supply at a rate of at least (≥) 1 cubic foot per minute for every 50 cubic feet of crawl space floor area and provide a return air opening to the common area of the building interior.

Crawl Space Access

1. Provide access to the crawl space for inspection and maintenance. You may provide access through an opening in the floor at least (≥) 18 inches by 24 inches or you may provide access through an opening in the crawl space wall at least (≥) 16 inches by 24 inches. Provide a well at least (≥) 16 inches by 24 inches in front of the crawl space entrance if any part of the opening is below grade. Locate the bottom of the well below the bottom of the access opening.
2. Do not locate a crawl space wall access opening under a door to the dwelling.
3. Provide a crawl space access opening at least (≥) 22 inches by 30 inches, or large enough

to remove the largest appliance, if appliances such as water heaters or furnaces are in the crawl space. Refer to Chapter 13 for additional requirements when the crawl space contains mechanical appliances.

Crawl Space Cleaning

1. Remove all wood debris from the crawl space including tree stumps and branches, form boards, and construction debris.

Crawl Space Water Drainage

1. Refer to the IRC for requirements that apply to crawl spaces in areas with a high ground water table and in areas subject to flooding.

Crawl Space Discussion

Disagreement exists about ventilating crawl spaces, particularly in humid climates; however, some means of controlling crawl space moisture is necessary to reduce wood deterioration and fungal growth. Instead of ventilating a crawl space, consider the best practice of building an unventilated crawl space.

All crawl spaces need maintenance and inspection. Providing convenient access means that small problems may be discovered early before they become big problems. Convenient access includes leaving enough space between beams and floor joists and the crawl space floor to access all areas of the crawl space. Eighteen inches is the minimum clearance between untreated floor joists and the crawl space floor and twelve inches is the minimum clearance between untreated beams and the crawl space floor. More clearance is better. Clean all unnecessary wood from the crawl space. Wood left in crawl spaces may attract termites.

Crawl Space Best Practice

Avoid building crawl spaces, if possible. Basements may not cost much more and they provide potentially useful storage and living space at a low cost per square foot. If a crawl space is unavoidable, use the approved method for eliminating crawl space ventilation.

5

FLOOR CONSTRUCTION

APPLICATION OF THE MATERIAL IN THIS CHAPTER

Unless otherwise stated, this chapter applies to floor systems framed using nominal 2 inch wide dimension lumber, such as 2 x 10 southern pine.

DECKS (R502.2.2)

Deck Attachment to the Building General Requirements

1. Design decks to resist both vertical and horizontal (lateral) loads where the deck is attached to the building.
2. Install at least (≥) 2 hold down devices connected to building floor joists to resist horizontal (lateral) loads. Refer to Figure R502.2.2-1.
3. Install straps or other devices to resist uplift forces if the deck is attached to the building and if the deck has floor joists that extend beyond a support beam (cantilevered framing). This includes connections at the ledger and at support points such as beams.
4. Leave attachment methods and materials exposed for inspection before applying finish materials.
5. Do not use nails to attach a deck ledger to the building.
6. Refer to the American Wood Council booklet: *Prescriptive Residential Wood Deck Construction Guide* available at http://ww.awc.org for detailed information about wood deck design and construction.

Deck Attachment to the Building

1. Install at least (≥) a 2x8 inch pressure treated Southern Pine or Hem Fir deck ledger board.
2. Secure the deck ledger board to a 2 inch (nominal thickness) Spruce Pine Fir band joist <u>or</u> to at least (≥) a 1 inch thick engineered wood band joist <u>or</u> to at least (≥) a 1 inch thick by 9 ½ inch Douglas Fir laminated veneer lumber rim board. The band joist or rim board must bear on the foundation. Do not attach a deck to the band joist or rim board of a cantilevered floor, such as a chimney or a bay window. Do not attach a deck through wall covering materials such as siding and brick.
3. You may use alternate attachment methods and materials designed by an engineer to attach the deck ledger board to the band joist or rim board.
4. You may make a deck entirely self-supporting as an alternative to attaching the deck to the building.

Deck Attachment Using Screws or Bolts

1. Install at least (≥) ½ inch hot-dipped galvanized or stainless steel lag screws or bolts as specified in Table R502.2.2. Install the screws or bolts at least (≥) 2 inches from the top and bottom of the ledger board and between 2 inches and 5 inches from each end. Stagger the screws or bolts vertically along the length of the ledger board.
2. Make the distance between the ledger board and the building sheathing not more than (≤) ½ inch.
3. Make the distance between the interior face of the ledger board and the exterior face of the band board not more than (≤) 1 inch.
4. Use lag screws that are long enough to penetrate the band or rim board.
5. Flash the ledger board to keep water away from the ledger and band boards.
6. Design connections to engineered rim boards (such as those commonly used with floor trusses) using accepted engineering practices.

TABLE R502.2.2
Deck Attachment Using Screws or Bolts
50 psf Design Load
On Center Fastener Spacing

joist span	≤ 6'	> 6' & ≤ 8'	> 8' & ≤ 10'	> 10' & ≤ 12'	> 12' & ≤ 14'	> 14' & ≤ 16'	> 16' & ≤ 18'
connector							
½ inch lag screw with ≤ 15/35 inch sheathing	30 in.	23 in.	18 in.	15 in.	13 in.	11 in.	10 in.
½ inch lag bolt with ≤ 15/32 inch sheathing	36 in.	36 in.	34 in.	29 in.	24 in.	21 in.	19 in.
½ inch lag bolt with ≤ 15/35 inch sheathing and ≤ ½ inch stacked washers	36 in.	36 in.	29 in.	24 in.	21 in.	18 in.	16 in.

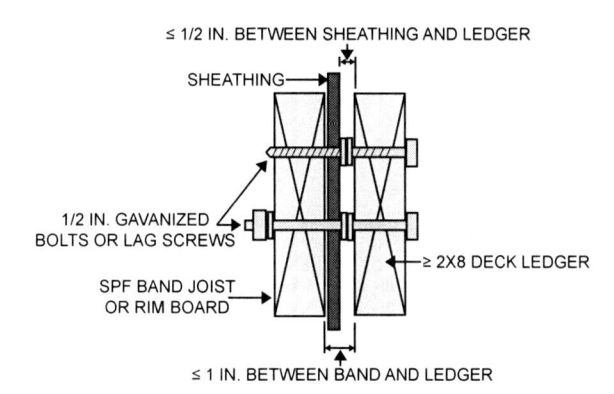

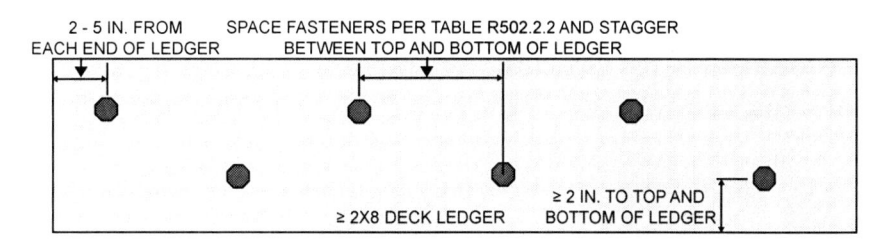

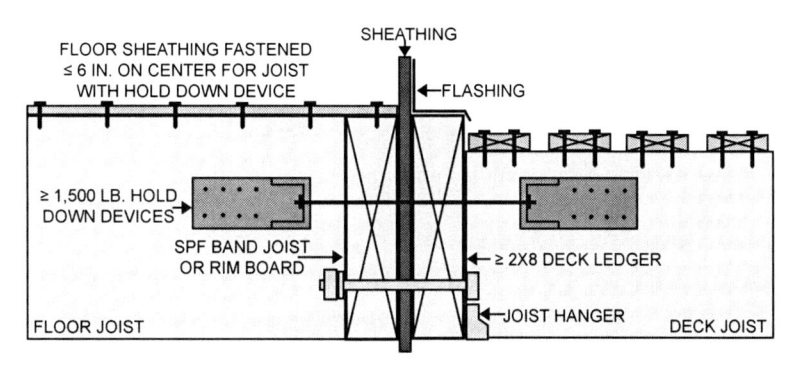

Deck Attachment to Building (R502.2-1)
Figure 5-1

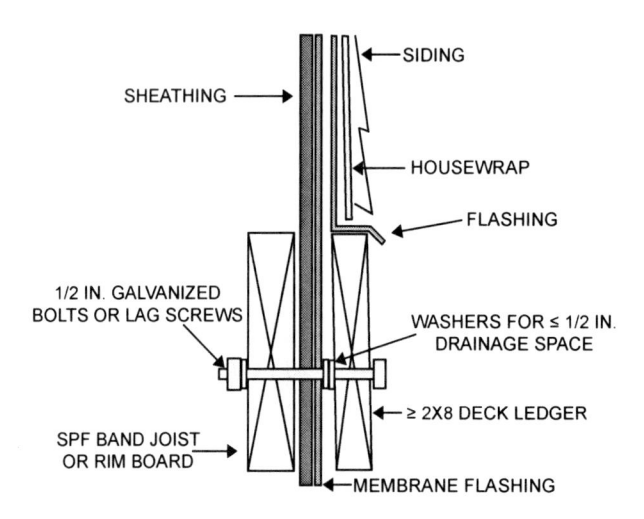

Deck Flashing (R502.2.2-2)
Figure 5-2

WOOD FLOOR JOIST SPANS (R502.3)

Floor Joist Span Tables

1. Use 30 psf live load and 10 psf dead load for joists under bedrooms and in attics with access by permanent stairs, in most cases. Permanent stairs do not include pull-down folding attic ladders.
2. Use 40 psf live load and 10 psf dead load for joists under living areas, other than bedrooms, and under decks, and balconies, in most cases.
3. Use L/360 deflection for all floor joists.
4. Refer to the IRC or to the AF&PA Span Tables for Joists and Rafters to find joist spans not contained in the following tables.
5. Apply the following tables to floor systems framed with nominal 2 inch wide dimension lumber such as 2x10. An engineer must design floor truss systems.

Examples:

Question: What grade and spacing of southern pine would you use to frame a floor under a bedroom with a clear (unsupported) span of 16 feet if you want to use the fewest number of joists?

Answer: Use the grade and spacing where the clear span distance in the tables equals or exceeds the required clear span. Number 2 grade southern pine 2x10 joists at 16 inches on center will span a maximum of 18 feet – 0 inches. Find this in the Table R502.3-2 Bedroom Floor Joist Spans at 16 Inches on Center.

Question: The overall distance between the outside of two 2x4 inches walls supporting a living area floor system is 16 feet. What grade and species of 2x10 floor joists at 16 inches on center will span this distance?

Answer: The clear (unsupported) span between the outside of 2x4 walls is 16 feet minus the 3 ½ inch width of each wall (16 feet − (2 x 3 ½ inches) = 15 feet − 5 inches). Use the grade and spacing where the clear span distance in the tables equals or exceeds the required clear span. In the Table R502.3-5 Living Area Floor Joist Spans at 16 Inches on Center, number 2 grade Douglas fir, southern pine, and spruce-pine-fir will all span 15 feet − 5 inches.

TABLE R502.3-1
Bedroom Floor Joist Spans at Twelve Inches on Center

species	grade	2x8 feet-inches	2x10 feet-inches	2x12 feet-inches
douglas fir	2	15-7	19-10	23-0
douglas fir	3	12-4	15-0	17-5
hem fir	2	14-6	18-6	22-6
hem fir	3	12-4	15-0	17-5
southern pine	2	15-7	19-10	24-2
southern pine	3	13-3	15-8	18-8
spruce-pine-fir	2	14-11	19-0	23-0
spruce-pine-fir	3	12-4	15-0	17-5

TABLE R502.3-2
Bedroom Floor Joist Spans at Sixteen Inches on Center

species	grade	2x8 feet-inches	2x10 feet-inches	2x12 feet-inches
douglas fir	2	14-1	17-2	19-11
douglas fir	3	10-8	13-0	15-1
hem fir	2	13-2	16-10	19-8
hem fir	3	10-8	13-0	15-1
southern pine	2	14-2	18-0	21-1
southern pine	3	11-6	13-7	16-2
spruce-pine-fir	2	13-6	17-2	19-11
spruce-pine-fir	3	10-8	13-0	15-1

TABLE R502.3-3
Bedroom Floor Joist Spans at Twenty-four Inches on Center

species	grade	2x8 feet-inches	2x10 feet-inches	2x12 feet-inches
douglas fir	2	11-6	14-1	16-3
douglas fir	3	8-8	10-7	12-4
hem fir	2	11-4	13-10	16-1
hem fir	3	8-8	10-7	12-4
southern pine	2	12-4	14-8	17-2
southern pine	3	9-5	11-1	13-2
spruce-pine-fir	2	11-6	14-1	16-3
spruce-pine-fir	3	8-8	10-7	12-4

TABLE R502.3-4
Living Area Floor Joist Spans at Twelve Inches on Center

species	grade	2x6 feet-inches	2x8 feet-inches	2x10 feet-inches	2x12 feet-inches
douglas fir	2	10-9	14-2	17-9	20-7
douglas fir	3	8-8	11-0	13-5	15-7
hem fir	2	10-0	13-2	16-10	20-4
hem fir	3	8-8	11-0	13-5	15-7
southern pine	2	10-9	14-2	18-0	21-9
southern pine	3	9-4	11-11	14-0	16-8
spruce-pine-fir	2	10-3	13-6	17-3	20-7
spruce-pine-fir	3	8-8	11-0	13-5	15-7

TABLE R502.3-5
Living Area Floor Joist Spans at Sixteen Inches on Center

species	grade	2x6 feet-inches	2x8 feet-inches	2x10 feet-inches	2x12 feet-inches
douglas fir	2	9-9	12-7	15-5	17-10
douglas fir	3	7-6	9-6	11-8	13-6
hem fir	2	9-1	12-0	15-2	17-7
hem fir	3	7-6	9-6	11-8	13-6
southern pine	2	9-9	12-10	16-1	18-10
southern pine	3	8-1	10-3	12-2	14-6
spruce-pine-fir	2	9-4	12-3	15-5	17-10
spruce-pine-fir	3	7-6	9-6	11-8	13-6

TABLE R502.3-6
Living Area Floor Joist Spans at Twenty-four Inches on Center

species	grade	2x6 feet-inches	2x8 feet-inches	2x10 feet-inches	2x12 feet-inches
douglas fir	2	8-1	10-3	12-7	14-7
douglas fir	3	6-10	8-8	10-7	12-4
hem fir	2	7-11	10-2	12-5	14-4
hem fir	3	6-2	7-9	9-6	11-0
southern pine	2	8-6	11-0	13-1	15-5
southern pine	3	6-7	8-5	9-11	11-10
spruce-pine-fir	2	8-1	10-3	12-7	14-7
spruce-pine-fir	3	6-2	7-9	9-6	11-0

WOOD HEADER AND GIRDER SPANS (R502.5)

Header and Girder Definitions

Header A header is a framing member that supports openings for windows, doors, and other openings. A wood header is often built on-site from nominal 2 inch lumber, although some headers may be engineered wood such as glue-laminated beams. Headers are supported on each side by studs called jacks.

Girder A girder is usually the principal supporting member in the center of a home. Girders may be built on-site, but many modern girders are glue-laminated or similar engineered wood. Many modern homes use engineered floor trusses and other means of supporting floor joists and do require center girders.

The terms girder and beam are effectively the same. A girder is a type of beam that, traditionally, is the center support beam for a house. A beam may be placed anywhere support is required.

Header and Girder Spans

1. Use Table R502.5 to determine clear unsupported spans for window and door headers built using #2 grade dimension lumber. Spans are in feet-inches.
2. Measure building width perpendicular to the roof ridge. You may interpolate to calculate span values for building widths not included in the table.
3. Use the number of jack studs indicated in the table on each side of the header. Example: use 2 jack studs on each side of a header (4 total jack studs) if the value in the jacks column is 2.

TABLE 502.5
Window and Door Header Spans
(feet-inches)

header supporting	lumber size	30 psf, 20 span	jacks	30 psf, 28 span	jacks	30 psf, 36 span	jacks	50 psf, 20 span	jacks	50 psf, 28 span	jacks	50 psf, 36 span	jacks	70 psf, 20 span	jacks	70 psf, 28 span	jacks	70 psf, 36 span	jacks
roof and ceiling	2-2x8	6-10	1	5-11	2	5-4	2	5-11	2	5-2	2	4-7	2	5-4	2	4-7	2	4-1	2
	2-2x10	8-5	2	7-3	2	6-6	2	7-3	2	6-3	2	5-7	2	6-6	2	5-7	2	5-0	2
	2-2x12	9-9	2	8-5	2	7-6	2	8-5	2	7-3	2	6-6	2	7-6	2	6-6	2	5-10	3
	3-2x10	10-6	1	9-1	2	8-2	2	9-1	2	7-10	2	7-0	2	8-2	2	7-0	2	6-4	2
roof and one floor	2-2x8	5-0	2	4-4	2	3-10	2	4-10	2	4-2	2	3-9	2	4-6	2	3-11	2	3-6	2
	2-2x10	6-1	2	5-3	2	4-8	2	5-11	2	5-1	2	4-7	3	5-6	2	4-9	2	4-3	3
	2-2x12	7-1	2	6-1	3	5-5	3	6-10	2	5-11	3	5-4	3	6-4	2	5-6	3	5-0	3
	3-2x10	7-7	2	6-7	2	5-11	2	7-5	2	6-5	2	5-9	2	6-10	2	6-0	2	5-4	2
roof and two floors	2-2x8	3-10	2	3-4	2	3-0	3	3-10	2	3-4	2	2-11	3	3-9	2	3-3	2	2-11	3
	2-2x10	4-9	2	4-1	3	3-8	3	4-8	2	4-0	3	3-7	3	4-7	3	4-0	3	3-6	3
	2-2x12	5-6	3	4-9	3	4-3	3	5-5	3	4-8	3	4-2	3	5-4	3	4-7	3	4-1	4
	3-2x10	5-11	2	5-1	2	4-7	3	5-10	2	5-0	2	4-6	3	5-9	2	4-11	2	4-5	3

WOOD FLOOR FRAMING (R502)

Cantilever Definitions

Backspan Backspan is the part of a cantilevered joist within the supporting wall.

Cantilever A cantilever is an extension of a floor joist beyond a supporting wall or beam. The distance that one may cantilever a floor joist depends on the width of the roof parallel to the cantilevered joists, the floor joist depth and spacing, and the design snow load. Most readers should not design floor joist cantilevers.

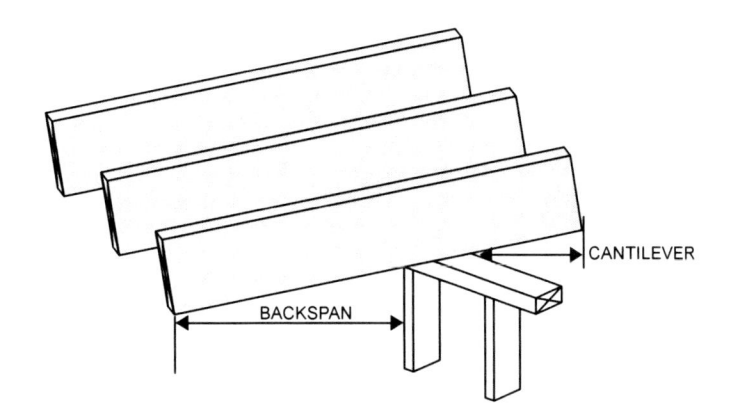

Floor Joist Cantilever and Backspan (R502.3.3-1)
Figure 5-3

Cantilevered Floor Joists (R502.3.3)

1. You may cantilever a floor joist not more than (≤) the depth of the joist. Example: you may cantilever a 2x10 floor joist not more than (≤) 10 inches. You may support one and two story light frame walls and a roof on these joist depth cantilevers.
2. You may cantilever solid lumber floor joists supporting one single story light frame wall and one roof according to Table R502.3.3-1. Column headings refer to ground snow load and the width of the roof supported by the cantilever.
3. Use #2 Douglas fir, southern pine, hem-fir, or spruce-pine-fir for cantilevered floor joists. Use a backspan ratio of at least (≥) 1 inch of cantilever to 3 inches of backspan. Install a full depth rim joist on the ends of the cantilevered joists and full depth blocking at the cantilever support wall.
4. You may cantilever solid lumber floor joists, supporting an exterior balcony according to Table R502.3.3-2. Column heading refers to ground snow load.
5. Use #2 Douglas fir, southern pine, hem-fir, or spruce-pine-fir for cantilevered floor joists. Use a backspan ratio of at least (≥) 1 inch of cantilever to 3 inches of backspan. Install a full depth rim joist on the ends of the cantilevered joists and full depth blocking at the cantilever support wall.
6. You may interpolate to calculate values for building widths and snow loads not contained in both tables.
7. Refer to the IRC for more cantilever distances.

TABLE R502.3.3-1
Cantilever Distance Supporting a Wall and a Roof

floor joist and spacing	≤20 psf 24 feet	≤20 psf 32 feet	≤20 psf 40 feet	30 psf 24 feet	30 psf 32 feet	30 psf 40 feet
2x8 @ 12" on center	20 in.	15 in.	no	18 in.	no	no
2x10 @ 16" on center	29 in.	21 in.	16 in.	26 in.	18 in.	no
2x10 @ 12" on center	36 in.	26 in.	20 in.	34 in.	22 in.	16 in.

TABLE R502.3.3-2
Cantilever Distance Supporting an Exterior Balcony

floor joist and spacing	≤30 psf
2x8 @ 12" on center	42 in.
2x8 @ 16" on center	36 in.
2x10 @ 12" on center	61 in.
2x10 @ 16" on center	53 in.
2x10 @ 24" on center	43 in.

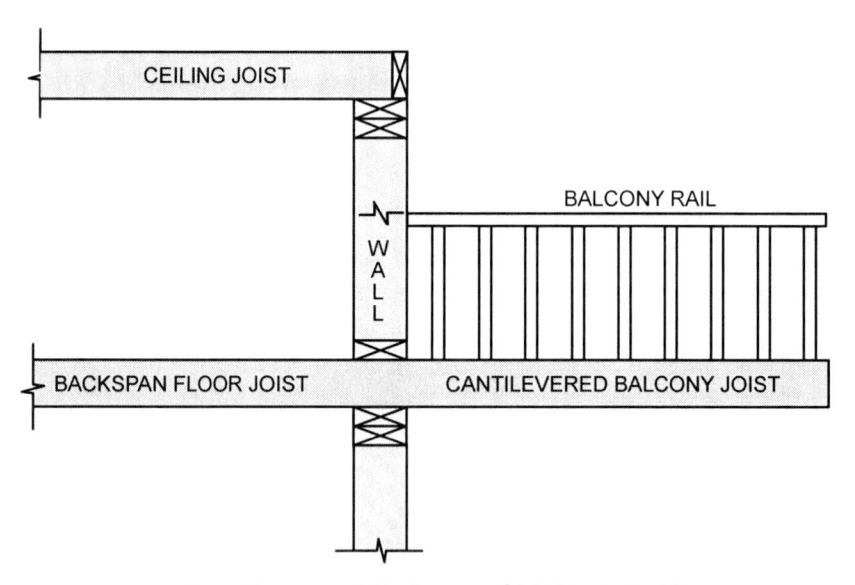

Cantilevered Balcony (R502.3.3-2)
Figure 5-4

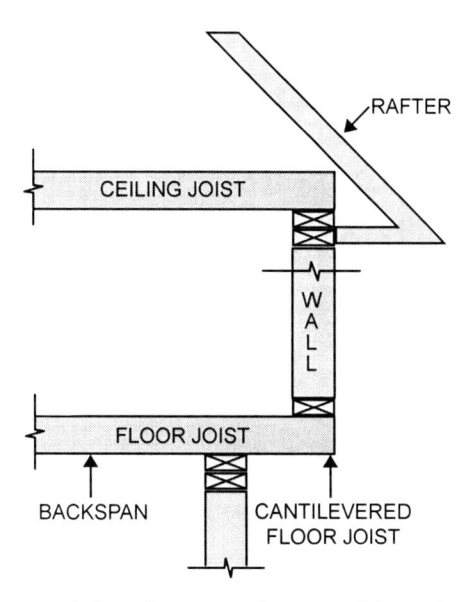

Cantilevered Floor Joist Supporting Wall and Roof (R502.3.3-3)
Figure 5-5

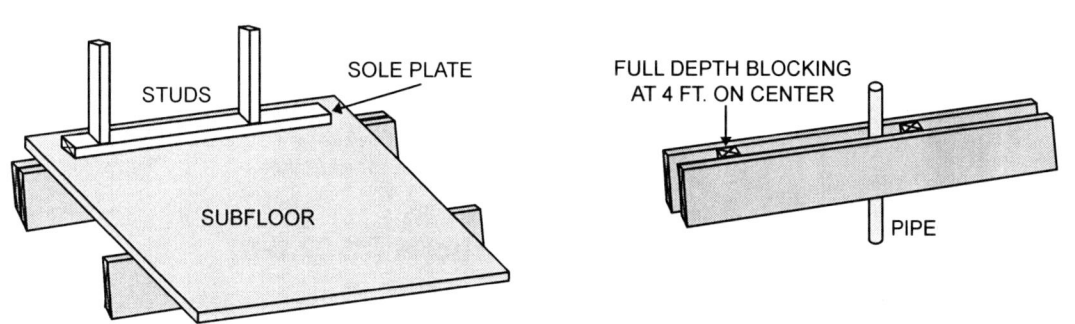

Floor Joists Under Load-Bearing Walls (R502.4)

1. Install additional floor joists under load-bearing walls that run parallel with the floor joists. Ensure that the number of joists is sufficient to support the load imposed by the wall and the loads supported by the wall. Parallel floor joists run the same direction as the wall being supported. Example: install at least (≥) 2 floor joists under a wall supporting a roof and at least (≥) 3 floor joists under a wall supporting a story above and a roof.

2. You may separate the additional joists under a load-bearing wall, if necessary, to fit pipes, vents, or ducts. Install solid 2 inch thick blocking at least (≥) every 4 feet along the full depth of the separated joists.

3. Place load-bearing walls that run perpendicular to the floor joists not more than (≤) one joist depth from the supporting wall or beam below unless the joists are sized to carry the load. Perpendicular joists run at a 90 degree angle to the wall being supported. Example: place a load-bearing wall that runs perpendicular to 2x10 floor joists not more than (≤) 10 inches from the supporting wall or beam below.

Floor Joists Under Load-Bearing Walls (R502.4-0)
Figure 5-6

Header, Girder, and Floor Joist Bearing on Supports (R502.6)

1. Place at least (≥) 1 ½ inches of a floor joist, header, girder, or beam on the supporting wood or metal wall. Supporting wood includes a sill plate bearing on a masonry or concrete wall.
2. Place at least 3 inches of a floor joist, header, girder, or beam on the supporting masonry or concrete wall. Comply with this requirement when the member bears directly on the masonry or concrete wall, not on a sill plate that bears on the wall. This requirement usually applies to beams and girders.
3. You may support floor joists on at least (≥) a 1x4 ledger if the ledger is attached to each stud and if the joist is attached to a stud.

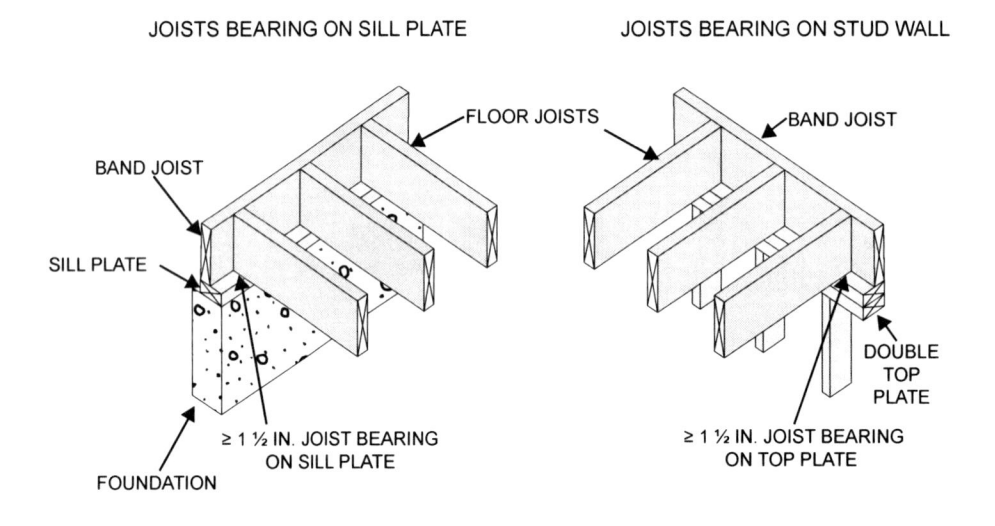

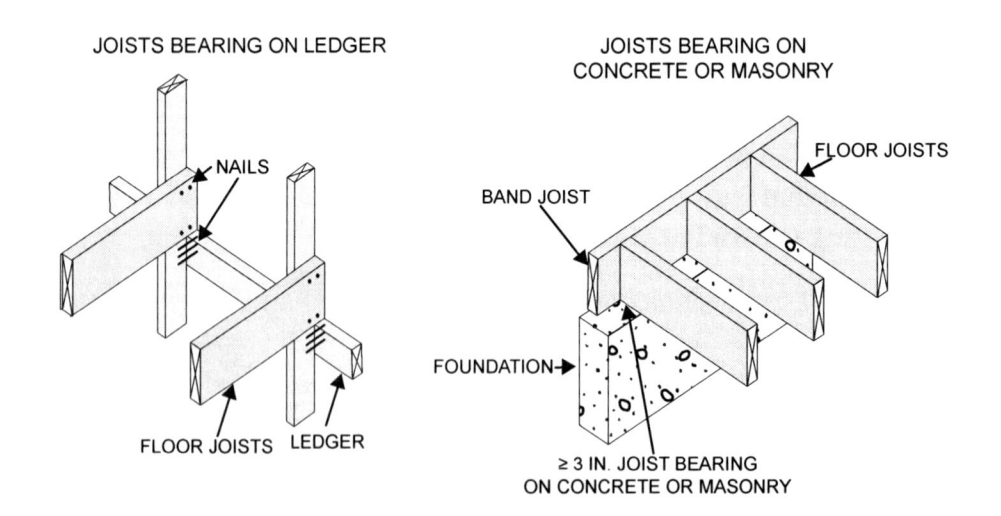

Floor Joists Bearing on Supports (R502.6-0)
Figure 5-7

Floor Joist Lap at Supports (R502.6.1)

1. Lap floor joists from opposite sides that meet over a bearing support at least (≥) 3 inches at the support and nail the joists at the lap using at least (≥) three 10d nails. You may substitute a wood or metal splice of equal or greater strength for the nailed lap.

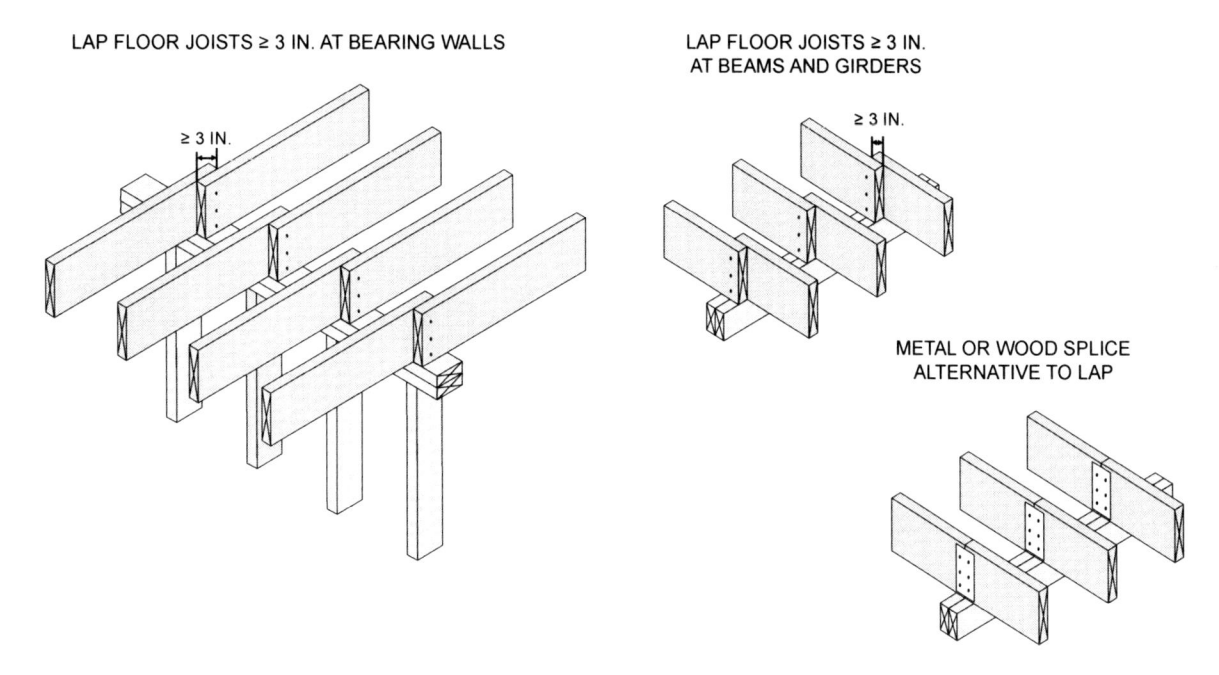

Floor Joist Lap at Supports (R502.6.1-0)
Figure 5-8

Floor Joist Attachment to Beams (R502.6.2)

1. Use an approved joist hanger or at least (≥) a 2x2 wood ledger to support floor joists that connect to a beam or girder.

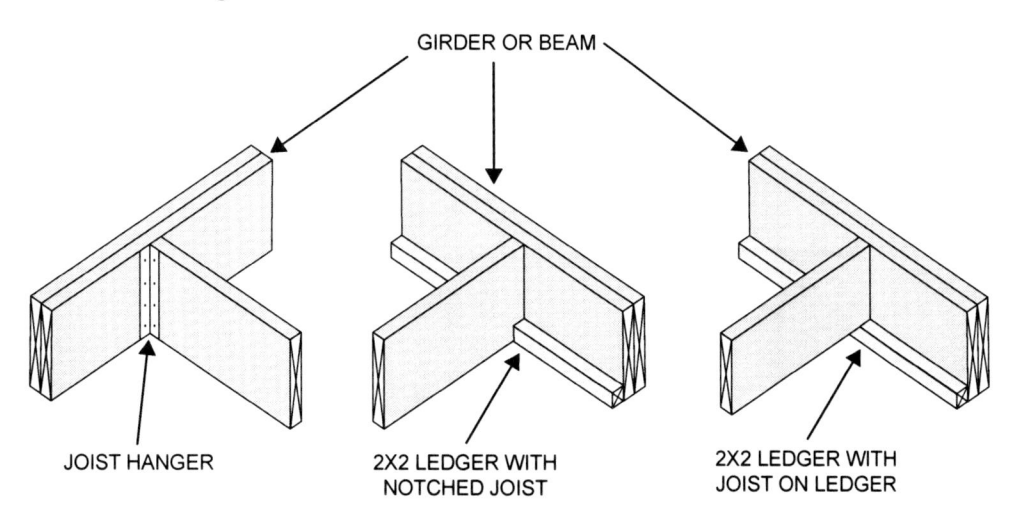

Floor Joist Attachment to Beams (R502.6.2-0)
Figure 5-9

Joist Hanger (PR502.6.2-0)
Figure 5-10

Floor Joist Blocking (R502.7)

1. Install full depth solid blocking at least (≥) 2 inches thick at both ends of floor joists, or attach the joists to a header, band or rim joist, or attach the joists to an adjoining stud. This helps reduce joist twisting.
2. Install blocking at all intermediate load-bearing supports in seismic design areas.

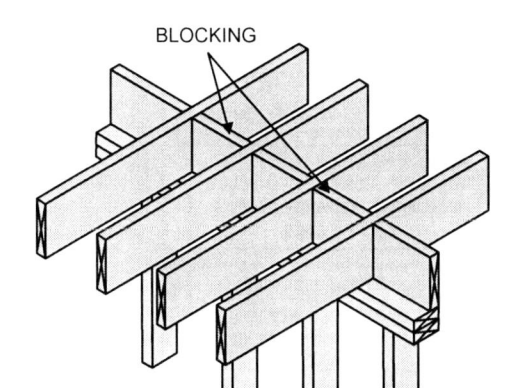

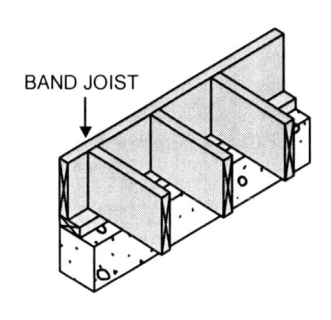

Floor Joist Blocking (R502.7-0)
Figure 5-11

Floor Joist Bridging (R502.7.1)

1. Install bridging not more than (≤) every 8 feet of floor joist length on floor joists deeper than (>) 2x12.
2. You may use solid full depth blocking, wood or metal diagonal bridging, or other means to provide required floor joist bridging. Some code officials require bridging on all floor joists regardless of what the code requires.

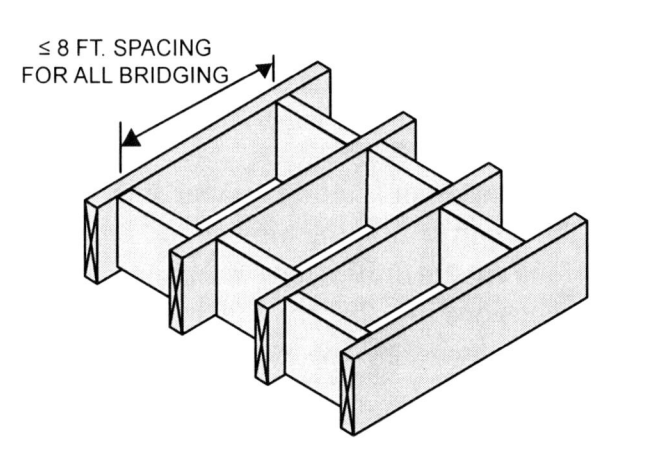

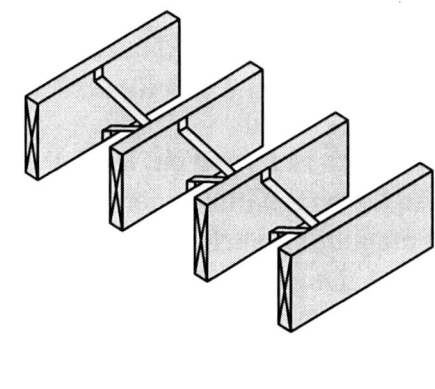

Floor Joist Bridging (R502.7.1-0)
Figure 5-12

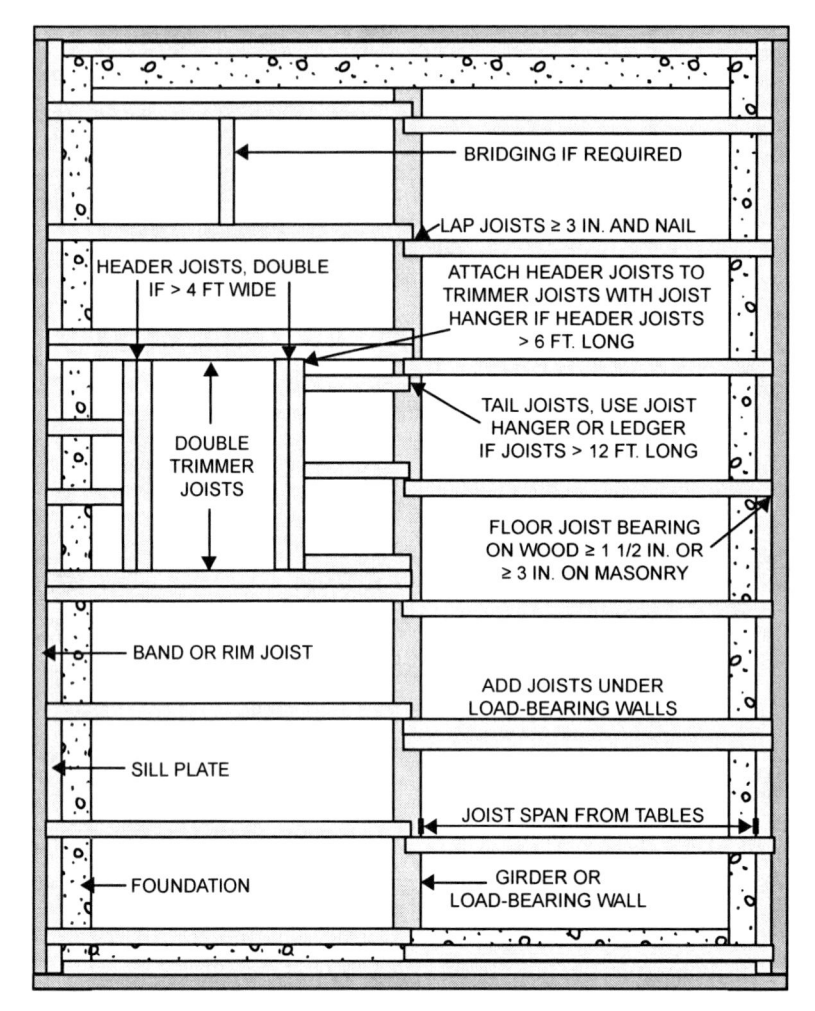

Floor Joist Framing Requirements Summary (R502-0)
Figure 5-13

WOOD FLOOR JOIST AND TRUSS BORING AND NOTCHING (R502.8)

Boring and Notching Definitions

Bore A bore is a hole drilled in a stud or joist. Use the actual dimensions to determine the depth of framing lumber and when calculating the maximum hole diameter.

Notch A notch is a piece cut from the smaller dimension of framing lumber such as a stud or joist. Use the actual dimensions to determine the depth of framing lumber and when calculating the maximum notch depth. Actual dimensions are the dimensions of framing lumber after finishing at the mill. Example: the nominal dimensions of a 2x6 are 2 inches by 6 inches and the actual dimensions, after finishing, are about 1 ½ inches by 5 ½ inches. Example: the actual depths of a 2x8 and a 2x10 are about 7 ¼ and 9 ¼ inches.

Wood Floor Joist Notching

1. You may notch solid lumber floor joists and beams <u>not deeper</u> than (≤) one-sixth of the depth of the member. You may notch the ends of the member not deeper than (≤) one-quarter of the depth of the member. Example: notch a 2x10 joist not deeper than (≤) 1 1/2 inches, except at the ends where you may notch not deeper than (≤) 2 5/16 inches.

2. You may notch solid lumber floor joists and beams <u>not longer</u> than (≤) one-third of the depth of the member. Example: notch the top or bottom of a 2x10 joist not longer than (≤) 3 1/16 inches.
3. You may notch solid lumber joists and beams only within the outer one-third of the span. Example: notch a 10 feet long joist only within 40 inches from each end.
4. You may notch the tension side (bottom) of solid lumber joists and beams more than (>) 4 inches thick only at the ends.
5. Use actual joist depths, not nominal joist depths. Example: use 9 1/4 inches for a 2x10 joist, not the nominal depth of 10 inches.

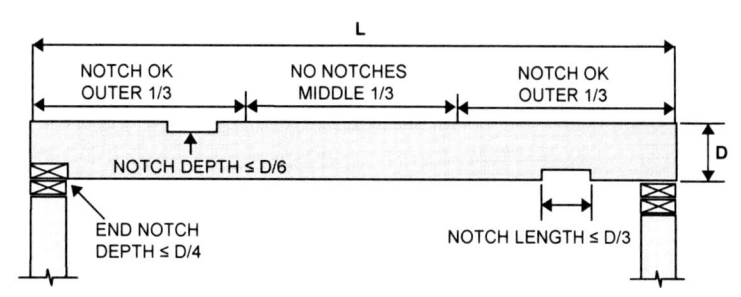

Floor Joist Notching (R502.8-1)
Figure 5-14

Wood Floor Joist Boring

1. You may drill holes in solid lumber floor joists and beams with a diameter not more than (≤) one-third of the depth of the member. Example: drill a hole with a diameter not more than (≤) 3 ⅛ inches in a 2x10 joist.
2. Locate holes at least (≥) 2 inches from the edge of the member and at least (≥) 2 inches from any other hole or notch.

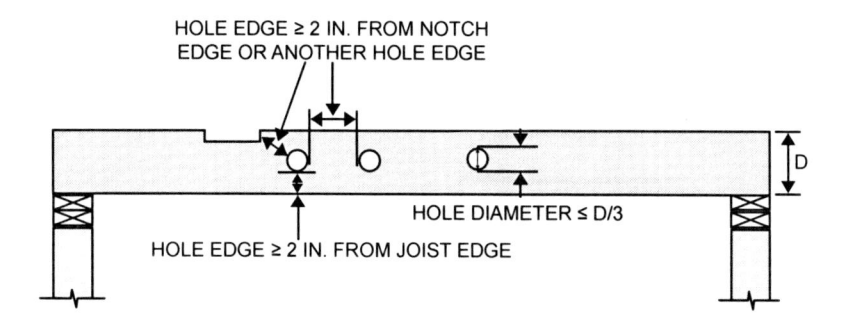

Floor Joist Hole Boring (R502.8-2)
Figure 5-15

Wood I-Beam Floor Truss Notching and Boring

1. Notch, bore, splice or alter wood I-Beam floor trusses only according to manufacturer's instructions. Altering the top and bottom flange is usually not allowed. Hole boring is usually allowed in the middle third of the span and is restricted near the truss ends.

Wood Web Floor Truss Notching and Boring

1. Do not notch, bore, cut, splice or alter wood web floor trusses unless specifically permitted in writing by the manufacturer or an engineer.

Engineered Wood Notching and Boring

1. Do not notch, bore, cut, splice or alter engineered wood members (such as laminated beams) unless specifically permitted in writing by the manufacturer or an engineer. Cutting the ends of engineered wood beams to length is usually permitted.

Joist and Truss Notching and Boring Best Practice

Consider where pipes, bathtubs, showers, toilets, and ducts will be located when designing the home and specify appropriate framing materials and spacing so that the fewest number of holes and notches will be necessary. Beware of notching and boring in the same area of a joist or beam and in the same vertical plane. Example: notches directly above and below each other could be interpreted as exceeding the one-sixth depth of member limit even if each individual notch does not exceed the limit.

FLOOR JOIST OPENINGS (R502.10)

Floor Joist Openings Description

Framed openings in floor joists are mostly used for stairways between floors and for chimneys. The header joists distribute the load of the tail joists to the trimmer joists.

Openings Not More than (≤) Four Feet Wide

1. Install double trimmer joists on both sides of header joists. You may use a single trimmer joist on both sides of the header joists if the header is not more than (≤) 3 feet from the trimmer bearing point.
2. You may use a single header joist if the header joist span is not more than (≤) 4 feet wide.
3. Install approved joist hangers or a 2x2 ledger strip to connect tail joists to header joists if the tail joists are more than (>) 12 feet long.

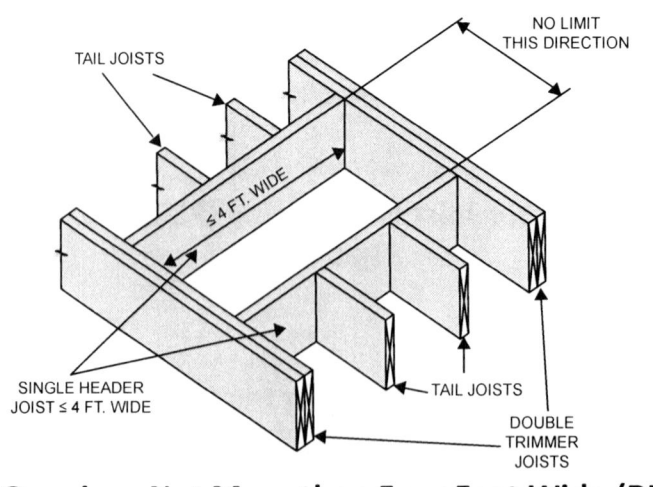

Floor Joist Openings Not More than Four Feet Wide (R502.10-1)
Figure 5-16

Openings More than (>) Four Feet Wide

1. Install double trimmer joists and double header joists if the header joist span is more than (>) 4 feet wide.
2. Install approved joist hangers to connect header joists to trimmer joists if the header joist span is more than (>) 6 feet wide.
3. Install approved joist hangers or a 2x2 ledger strip to connect tail joists to header joists if the tail joists are more than (>) 12 feet long.

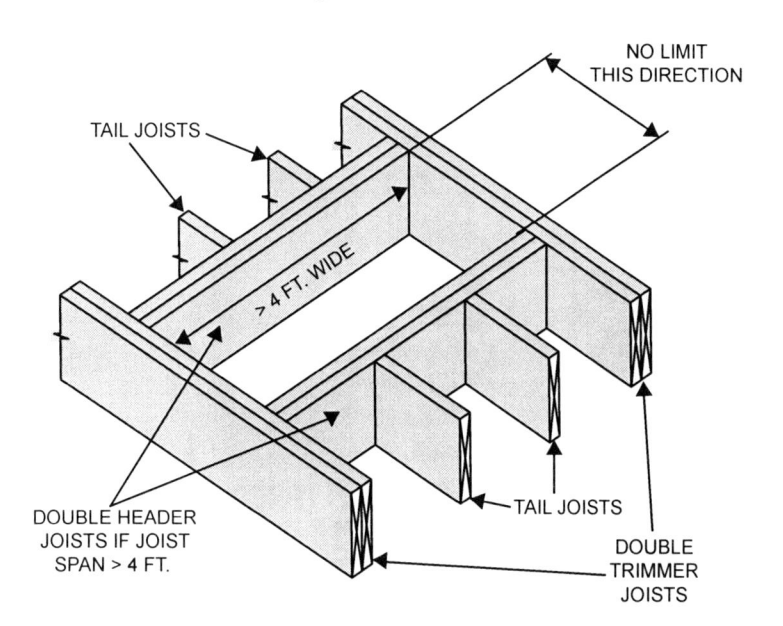

Floor Joist Openings More than Four Feet Wide (R502.10-2)
Figure 5-17

WOOD STRUCTURAL PANEL SHEATHING (R503.2)

Limitations of the Material in this Section

The IRC presents many combinations of materials and installation techniques for installing wood structural panels as sheathing on roofs and as subflooring and underlayment. This section includes common materials and installation techniques used in modern residential construction. Refer to the IRC for information about less common materials and installation techniques.

Wood Structural Panel Definitions

Combination subflooring Combination subflooring is one panel secured directly to floor joists that acts as both the subflooring and underlayment.

Edge supports Edge supports are approved materials that support structural panel ends or edges between rafters or joists. Edge supports include tongue-and-groove joints, panel edge clips, and wood blocking between rafters or joists. The IRC requires edge support for single panels used as a combination subfloor and underlayment and for some roof sheathing.

Panel span ratings Panel span ratings appear on the panel as two numbers separated by a slash. The first number is the maximum distance between rafters when the panel is used as roof sheathing. The second number is the maximum distance between floor joists when the panel is used as subflooring. The span is the unsupported distance between the framing members such as floor joists or roof rafters.

Sheathing Span Label (PR502.3-0)
Figure 5-18

Subfloor Subfloor is the panel secured directly to floor joists.

Underlayment (flooring) Underlayment is at least (≥) ¼ inch thick panel installed over the subfloor, usually as a smooth base for resilient floor coverings such as linoleum.

Wood structural panels Wood structural panels include plywood, oriented strand board (OSB), and composite panels. OSB is often used in modern residential construction as roof sheathing and as subflooring. Plywood is often used as subflooring and underlayment.

Wood Structural Panel Installation Requirements

1. Install wood floor sheathing panels:
   a) so that they continuously span at least two framing members, and
   b) with the long dimension perpendicular (90 degree angle) to supports, and
   c) that are at least (≥) 24 inches wide. Panels less than 24 inches wide can deflect or fail under load.

2. Support wood floor sheathing panel edges with solid blocking, tongue-and-groove edges, or other approved means. Underlayment or ¾ inch wood flooring can substitute for edge support in some cases.

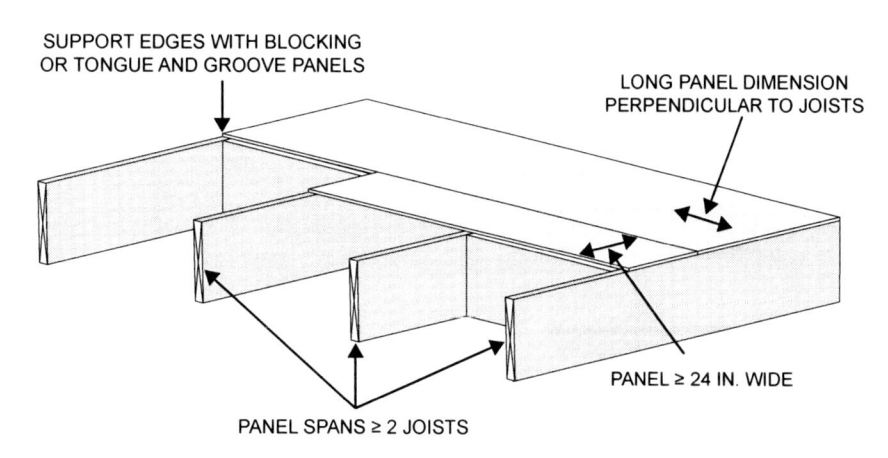

Wood Structural Panel Flooring Installation (R503.2-0)
Figure 5-19

Wood Structural Panels Used as Roof Sheathing

1. Use wood roof sheathing panels such as 24/16 rated panels (7/16 inch nominal thickness) and 32/16 rated panels (15/32 inch and ½ inch nominal thickness). Do not span a 24/16 rated panel more than (>) 24 inches between rafters when used as roof sheathing. Do not span a 32/16 rated panel more than (>) 32 inches between rafters <u>with edge support</u> or more than (>) 28 inches <u>without edge support</u> when used as roof sheathing.
2. You may use panels of other thicknesses as allowed by the IRC.
3. Install panels that are at least (≥) 24 inches wide. Panels less than 24 inches wide can deflect or fail under load.

Wood Structural Panels Used as Combination Subflooring

1. You may use wood floor sheathing panels (such as 23/32-inch and ¾ inch nominal thickness plywood or OSB and ¾ inch sanded plywood) as a combination subfloor and underlayment. Do not span these panels more than (>) 24 inches between floor joists. Use tongue-and-grove panels or install blocking at unsupported edges. Be aware that while these panels comply with the IRC, they may not comply with manufacturer's installation for some floor coverings such as tile.
2. You may use other, thicker, panels as a combination subfloor and underlayment. You may use two separate panels, one as a subfloor and one as an underlayment.

Wood Structural Panel Installation Best Practice

Wood structural panels can deflect and sag under load when installed at their IRC permitted span limits. This can allow cracks in rigid floor covering materials such as tile and marble. Be aware of manufacturer and industry installation guidelines when selecting, supporting, and installing wood structural panels under all floor coverings, particularly under tile.

CONCRETE SLAB-ON-GRADE FLOORS (R506)

Concrete Thickness and Strength

1. Make concrete slab-on-grade floors at least (≥) 3 ½ inches thick. This does not include extra thickness for footings and interior bearing walls.
2. Use at least (≥) 2,500 psi concrete for interior slab-on-grade floors. Refer to Chapter 4 for concrete strength of garage and exterior slabs.

Site Preparation

1. Pour concrete slab-on-grade floors over clean and undisturbed soil or use clean and properly compacted fill. Soil and fill should be free from vegetation.
2. You may use sand or gravel fill that is not more than (≤) 24 inches deep or you may use earth fill that is not more than (≤) 8 inches deep. Obtain building official or engineering approval for deeper fill depths.
3. Install at least (≥) 4 inches clean sand or gravel not more than (≤) 2 inches sieve size on top of any compacted fill or undisturbed ground.
4. Install a 6-mil polyethylene or similar approved vapor retarder on top of the sand or gravel base. You may omit the vapor retarder from detached garages, carports, unconditioned accessory buildings, driveways, patios, and similar concrete flatwork if the areas are unlikely to be enclosed and conditioned at a later date.
5. Provide supports for reinforcing bars and welded-wire mesh so that they will remain in place during concrete placement. Support is usually provided by plastic devices made so that the bars or wire will remain above the bottom of the concrete slab when the concrete is being poured.

Plastic Supports for Cables in a Post Tensioned Slab (PR506-0)
Figure 5-20

6

WALL CONSTRUCTION

VAPOR RETARDERS (R601.3)

1. Install a Class I or a Class II vapor retarder on the interior side of framed walls in climate zones Marine 4, 5, 6, 7, and 9. You may use a Class III vapor retarder in these zones using exceptions specified in the IRC. The Class III vapor retarder exceptions refer to ventilated exterior wall cladding (such as brick and vinyl siding) and high R-value insulated sheathing.
2. Class I vapor retarders include sheet polyethylene and unperforated aluminum foil. Class II vapor retarders include Kraft-faced fiberglass batt insulation. Class III vapor retarders include latex and enamel paint.

WOOD NAILING SCHEDULE (R602.3)

Limitations of the Material in this Section

The IRC describes many combinations of materials and fasteners used to attach wood structural members to other wood structural members. The discussion in this book section is limited to using nails to attach materials commonly used in new construction. Refer to the IRC for more information about other materials and fasteners.

Wood Nailing Definitions

Edge spacing Edge spacing means installing a nail every indicated number of inches around the perimeter of a wood structural panel. If blocking is required by the IRC, then edge spacing includes nailing the panel to the blocking.

End nailing An end nail is driven straight into the end of the member. An example of end nailing is attaching studs to sill plates through the sill plate before the sill plate is attached to the foundation or subfloor.

Face nailing A face nail is driven straight into the member, often into the long dimension of the member. Examples of face nailing include ceiling and floor joist laps over supports and attaching wood panels to studs and joists.

Intermediate spacing Intermediate spacing means installing a nail every indicated number of inches at studs or joists in the interior area of the wood structural panel.

O. C. O. C. means on center. Install nails every indicated number of inches.

Toe nailing A toe nail is driven at an angle through the edge of the member. Toe nailing usually occurs when one member is already attached in place, such as when a stud is toe nailed to a sill plate that is already attached.

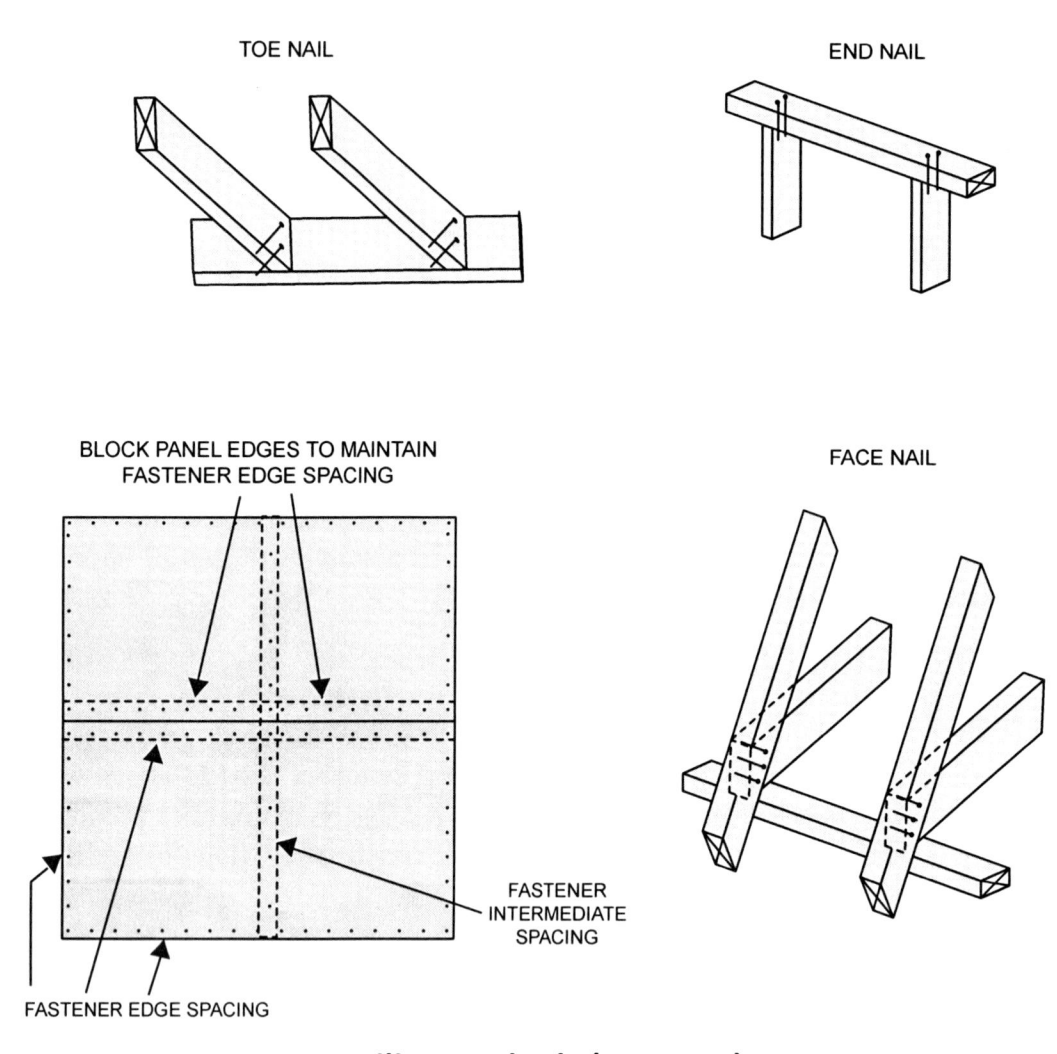

Nailing Methods (R602.3-0)
Figure 6-1

Wood Nailing General Installation Requirements

1. Use nails that are at least as thick and long as indicated in the following tables. Common and box nails are often thicker and longer than the hand-driven sinker nails and gun-driven nails commonly used in residential construction. Deformed shank nails are often called ring shank or screw shank nails. <u>You cannot directly substitute sinker and gun nails for the common, box, and deformed shank nails used in the IRC.</u> Substitution of sinker and gun nails should be based on engineering analysis.

Wood Nailing to Framing Materials

1. Use the following tables to determine the type of nail and nail spacing for attaching wood framing materials to other wood framing materials in other than high wind and seismic de-

sign areas. Refer to the IRC for fastener type, quantity and spacing in high wind and seismic design areas. High wind usually means 100 mph or more.

TABLE R602.3-1
**Nailing Requirements
When Fastening OSB and Plywood
Subfloor, Roof and Wall Sheathing to Framing**

panel thickness	nail type	edge spacing	intermediate spacing
5/16 - ½ inch	6d common (2" x 0.113") subfloor & wall 8d common (2 ½" x 0.131") roof	6 inches o.c.	12 inches o.c
19/32 – 1 inch	8d common (2 ½" x 0.131")	6 inches o.c.	12 inches o.c
1 1/8 – 1 ¼ inch	10d common (3" x 0.148") or 8d deformed (2 ½"x 0.120")	6 inches o.c.	12 inches o.c

TABLE R602.3-2
**Nailing Requirements
When Fastening OSB and Plywood One-piece Subfloor to Framing**

panel thickness	nail type	edge spacing	intermediate spacing
¾ inch & less	6d deformed (2" x 0.120") or 8d common (2 ½" x 0.131")	6 inches o.c.	12 inches o.c
7/8 - 1-inch	8d common (2 ½" x 0.131") or 8d deformed (2 ½"x 0.120")	6 inches o.c.	12 inches o.c
1 ⅛ - 1 ¼ inch	10d common (3" x 0.148") or 8d deformed (2 ½"x 0.120")	6 inches o.c.	12 inches o.c

TABLE R602.3-3
**Nailing Requirements
When Fastening Structural Lumber**

lumber description, nailing method	number-type of fasteners	fastener spacing
FLOOR NAILING		
joist to sill, girder, plate, toe nail	3-8d (2 ½" x 0.113")	--
rim joist to top plate, toe nail	8d (2 ½" x 0.113")	6 inches o.c.
ledger supporting joists	3-16d (3 ½" x 0.135")	under each joist
built-up beams, using 2 inches thick lumber	3-16d (3 ½" x 0.135")	nail each layer: staggered 32 inches o.c. at top and bottom and 2 nails at ends and at each splice

lumber description, nailing method	number-type of fasteners	fastener spacing
WALL NAILING		
sole plate to joist or blocking, face nail	16d (3 ½" x 0.135")	16 inches o.c.
sole plate to joist or blocking at braced wall panels, face nail	3-16d (3 ½" x 0.135")	16 inches o.c.
stud to sole plate, toe nail	3-8d (2 ½" x 0.113") or 2-16d (3 ½" x 0.135")	--
stud to top or sole plate, end nail	2-16d (3 ½" x 0.135")	--
double studs, face nail	10d (3" x .0128")	24 inches o.c.
double top plate, face nail	10d (3" x .0128")	24 inches o.c.
double top plate, minimum 24-inch offset of end joints, face nail in lap area	8-16d (3 ½" x 0.135")	--
built-up corner studs	10d (3" x .0128")	24 inches o.c.
top plates, laps at corners and intersections, face nail	2-10d (3" x .0128")	--
built-up headers: 2-piece with ½ inch spacer	16d (3 ½" x 0.135")	16 inches o.c. along each edge
header to stud, toe nail	10d (3" x .0128")	--
1 inch let-in brace to each stud and plate, face nail	2-8d (2 ½" x 0.113")	--
ROOF NAILING		
blocking between joists or rafters to top plate, toe nail	3-8d (2 ½" x 0.113")	--
ceiling joist to plate, toe nail	3-8d (2 ½" x 0.113")	--
ceiling joist, lap over partitions, face nail	3-10d (3" x .0128")	--
ceiling joist to parallel rafters, face nail	3-10d (3" x .0128")	--
collar tie to rafter and joist, face nail or 1 ¼ inches by 20 gage strap	3-10d (3" x .0128")	--
rafter to plate, toe nail	2-16d (3 ½" x 0.135")	--
rafters to ridge, valley or hip rafters, toe nail	4-16d (3 ½" x 0.135")	--
rafters to ridge, valley or hip rafters, face nail	3-16d (3 ½" x 0.135")	--

Nailing Discussion

Proper selection and installation of fasteners helps ensure structural integrity, particularly under stress conditions such as high winds and seismic events. Investigations after wind and seismic disasters find that failure to install proper fasteners is a major reason for structural failure.

Nailing Best Practice

To help prevent squeaks in wood floors, apply a continuous bead of construction adhesive to floor joists or trusses and use screws or deformed shank nails to secure subfloors.

WALL HEIGHT AND STUD SPACING (R602.3.1)

Limitations of the Material in this Section

The IRC presents many combinations of wall heights, lumber sizes, and spacing. The discussion in this book section includes wall heights and stud spacing commonly used in new construction. Refer to the IRC for more information about other wall height and stud spacing combinations. Refer to the IRC for wall height and stud spacing requirements in high wind, heavy snow load, and seismic design areas.

Wood Grades Used in Wall Construction

1. Use Number 3, standard, or stud grade wood for most load-bearing walls not more than (≤) 10 feet tall. Use Number 2 grade or better lumber for walls more than (>) ten feet tall.
2. You may use utility grade wood for non-load-bearing walls.
3. You may use utility grade wood for load-bearing exterior walls that support only a ceiling and a roof if the studs are spaced not more than (≤) 16 inches on center and the walls are not more than (≤) 8 feet tall.

Stud Size and Spacing for Load-Bearing Walls Not More than (≤) Ten Feet Tall

1. Use Table R602.3.1-1 to determine stud size and spacing when the unsupported vertical wall height of an exterior load-bearing wall is not more than (≤) ten feet tall. Measure vertical wall height between points of lateral support perpendicular to the studs. Vertical wall height is usually measured between the bottom of the sole or sill plate and the bottom of the floor or ceiling. Consult a qualified engineer before measuring unsupported vertical wall height between points other than at floor levels.

TABLE R602.3.1-1
Stud Size and Spacing for Exterior Load-Bearing Walls
Not More than (≤) Ten Feet Tall

stud size (inches)	column 1 maximum stud spacing supporting only one floor, or supporting a ceiling and roof with or without a habitable attic (inches)	column 2 maximum stud spacing supporting one floor and a ceiling and roof with or without a habitable attic (inches)	column 3 maximum stud spacing supporting two floors and a ceiling and roof with or without a habitable attic (inches)
2 x 4	24	16	not allowed
2 x 6	24	24	16

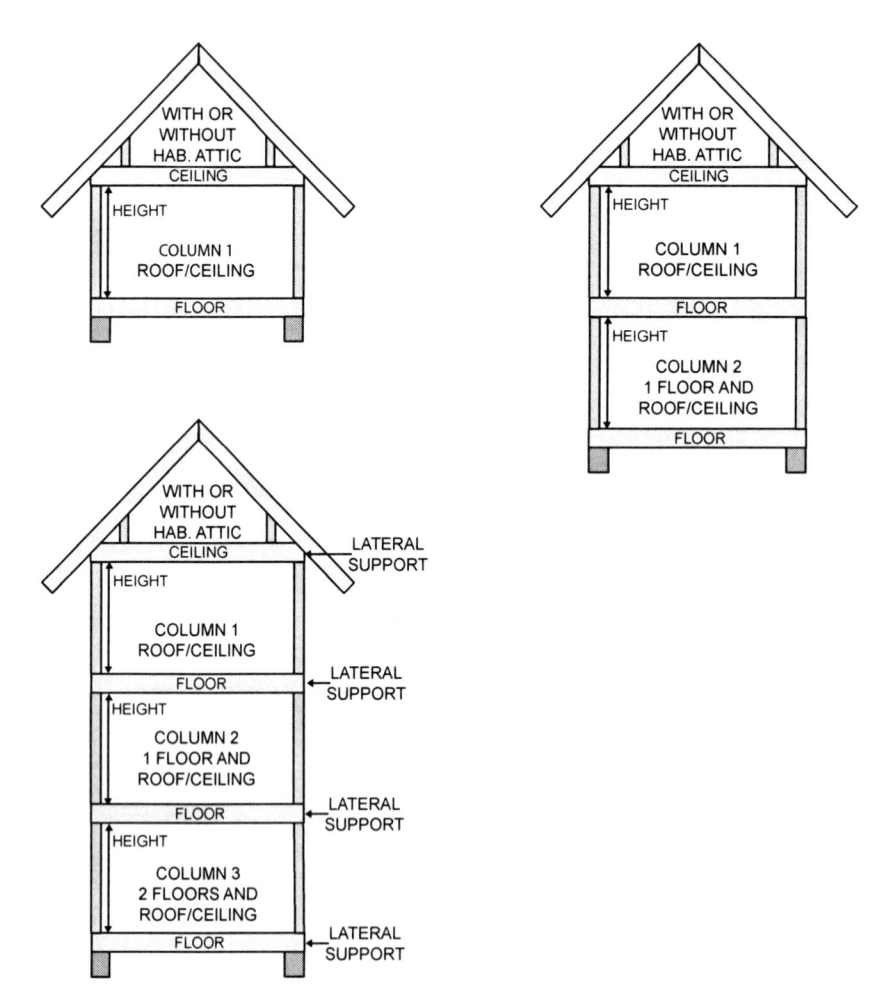

**Load-Bearing Walls Supporting
Different Numbers of Floors and Ceilings (R602.3.1-0)
Figure 6-2**

Stud Size and Spacing for Non-Load-Bearing Walls

1. Use Table R602.3.1-2 to determine stud size and spacing for non-load-bearing walls. Measure vertical wall height between points of lateral support perpendicular to the studs. Vertical wall height is usually measured between the bottom of the sole or sill plate and the bottom of the floor or ceiling. Consult a qualified engineer before measuring unsupported vertical wall height between points other than at floor levels.

TABLE R602.3.1-2
Stud Size and Spacing for Non-Load-Bearing Walls

stud size (inches)	maximum stud height (feet)	maximum stud spacing (inches)
2 x 4	14	24
2 x 6	20	24

Lumber Size and Spacing for Walls More than (>) Ten Feet Tall

1. Use Tables R602.3.1-3, -4, and -5 to determine stud size and spacing for an exterior load-bearing wall more than (>) ten feet tall. Measure vertical wall height between points of lateral support perpendicular to the studs. Vertical wall height is usually measured between the bottom of the sole or sill plate and the bottom of the floor or ceiling. Consult a qualified engineer before measuring unsupported vertical wall height between points other than at floor levels.

2. Do not use Tables R602.3.1-3, -4, and -5 if: (a) wind design speed exceeds (>) 100 MPH, or if (b) snow load exceeds (>) 25 psf, or if (c) unsupported floor or roof span supported by the wall exceeds (>) 12 feet, or if (d) eaves exceed (>) 2 feet wide, or if (e) exterior sheathing is not used. Consult a qualified engineer if you cannot use this table. The unsupported floor span is the distance between floor supports, such as a load-bearing wall or a beam. The unsupported roof span is the distance between rafter supports, such as a load-bearing wall or a purlin supported by a load-bearing wall.

3. Do not use utility, standard, stud, and #3 grade lumber when using these tables.

TABLE R602.3.1-3
Lumber Size and Spacing for Walls
More than (>) Ten Feet Tall Supporting only a Roof

wall height (feet)	on-center stud spacing 12 inches	on-center stud spacing 16 inches	on-center stud spacing 24 inches
over 10	2 x 4	2 x 4	2 x 4
12	2 x 4	2 x 4	2 x 6
14	2 x 6	2 x 6	2 x 6
16	2 x 6	2 x 6	2 x 6
18	2 x 6	2 x 6	design

TABLE R602.3.1-4
Lumber Size and Spacing for Walls
More than (>) Ten Feet Tall Supporting One Floor and a Roof

wall height (feet)	on-center stud spacing 12 inches	on-center stud spacing 16 inches	on-center stud spacing 24 inches
over 10	2 x 4	2 x 4	2 x 6
12	2 x 6	2 x 6	2 x 6
14	2 x 6	2 x 6	2 x 6
16	2 x 6	2 x 6	design
18	2 x 6	2 x 6	design

TABLE R602.3.1-5
Lumber Size and Spacing for Walls
More than (>) Ten Feet Tall Supporting Two Floors and a Roof

wall height (feet)	on-center stud spacing 12 inches	on-center stud spacing 16 inches	on-center stud spacing 24 inches
over 10	2 x 4	2 x 6	2 x 6
12	2 x 6	2 x 6	2 x 6
14	2 x 6	2 x 6	2 x 6
16	2 x 6	design	design
18	2 x 6	design	design

Lumber Size and Spacing for Interior Non-Load-Bearing Walls

1. You may use 2x3 studs spaced at 24 inches on center to build interior non-load-bearing walls, if the wall is not part of a braced wall line.
2. You may use 2x4 studs turned flat (wide dimension out) spaced not more than (≤) 16 inches on center to build interior non-load-bearing walls.
3. You may use a single top plate to cap interior non-load-bearing walls.

SILL, SOLE, AND TOP PLATES (R602.3.2 AND R602.3.4)

Top Plate Construction

1. Use at least (≥) two 2 inch (nominal) depth top plates that are at least (≥) as wide as the studs at the top of load-bearing walls. Example: use two 2x4 top plates on top of a 2x4 wall.
2. Offset joints where two pieces of top plate meet by at least (≥) 24 inches. You do not need to place a stud under a joint in a top plate unless the stud would be placed there for other reasons.
3. Lap one top plate from one wall over the top plate of an intersecting wall at the wall corners and at the intersection with load-bearing walls.
4. You may use a single top plate at the top of non-load-bearing walls.
5. You may use a single top plate on load-bearing walls if wall joints and corners and top plate end joints are secured with at least (≥) a 3 inch by 6 inch by 0.036-inch thick galvanized steel plate secured by at least (≥) six 8d nails on each side of the connection; and if the supported framing above (such as joists or rafters) is not more than (≤) 1-inch from the stud below. This exception is not commonly used.

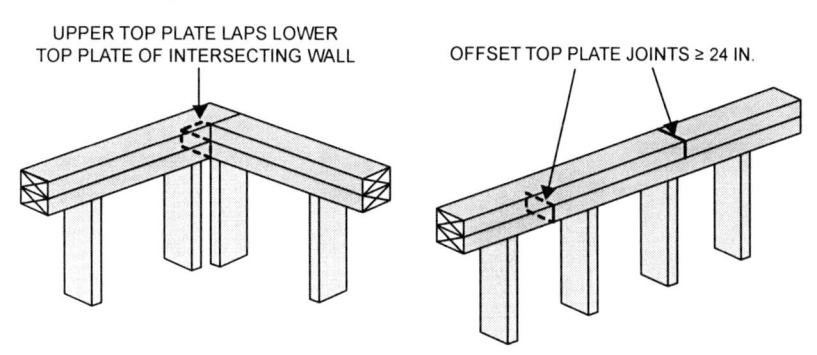

Top Plate Construction (R602.3.2-0)
Figure 6-3

Bottom Plate Construction

1. Use at least (≥) one 2 inch (nominal) depth bottom plate that is at least (≥) as wide as the studs.

WOOD STUD AND PLATE BORING AND NOTCHING (R602.6)

Boring and Notching Definitions

Bore A bore is a hole drilled in a stud or joist. Use the actual dimensions to determine the depth of framing lumber and when calculating the maximum hole diameter.

Notch A notch is a piece cut from the smaller dimension of framing lumber such as a stud or joist. Use the actual dimensions to determine the depth of framing lumber and when calculating the maximum notch depth. Actual dimensions are the dimensions of framing lumber after finishing at the mill. Example: the nominal dimensions of a 2x6 are 2 inches by 6 inches and the actual dimensions, after finishing, are about 1 ½ inches by 5 ½ inches.

Wood Stud Notching

1. Notch a load-bearing stud not more than (≤) 25 percent of its actual depth. Example: notch a 2x6 load-bearing stud not more than (≤) 1 ⅜ inches.
2. Notch a non-load-bearing stud not more than (≤) 40 percent of its actual depth. Example: notch a 2x6 non-load-bearing stud not more than (≤) 2 ¼ inches.

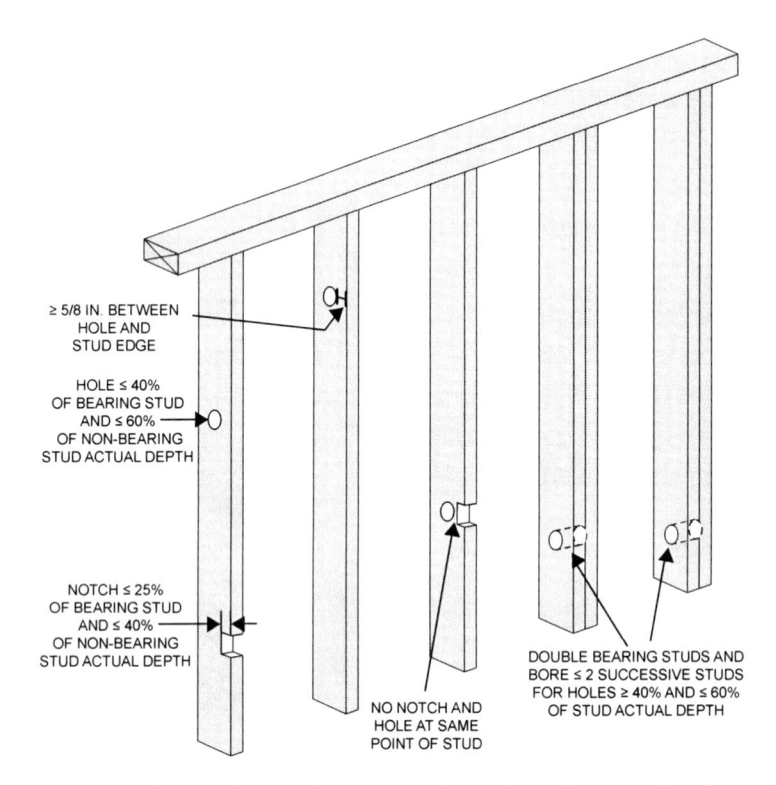

Wood Stud Notching and Boring (R602.6-1)
Figure 6-4

Wood Stud Boring

1. Bore a hole in a single load-bearing stud not more than (≤) 40 percent of its actual depth. Example: bore a 2x6 load-bearing stud not more than (≤) 2 ¼ inches diameter.
2. You may bore holes in load-bearing studs not more than (≤) 60 percent of their depth if you install a double stud and do not bore more than (≤) 2 successive studs.
3. Bore a hole in a non-load-bearing stud not more than (≤) 60 percent of its actual depth. Example: bore a 2x6 non-load-bearing stud not more than (≤) 3 ¼ inches diameter.
4. Leave at least (≥) ⅝ inch of undisturbed wood between the hole and the stud edge.
5. Do not place a hole and a notch in the same horizontal section of the stud.

Wood Top Plate Notching

1. Install one galvanized metal strap at least (≥) 0.054-inch thick and 1 ½ inches wide on a top plate if it is cut more than (>) 50 percent of its actual depth. These metal straps are sometimes called FHA straps. It is not necessary to install a strap on both top plates for purposes of this section. You may need to install nail guards to protect plumbing pipes and electrical wires.
2. Extend the strap at least (≥) 6 inches beyond each side of the cut opening. Secure the strap with at least (≥) eight 16d nails on each side of the strap.
3. Apply this requirement to top plates in exterior and interior load-bearing walls.
4. You do not need to install the strap if wood structural panel sheathing covers the entire side of the wall with the notched or cut top plates.

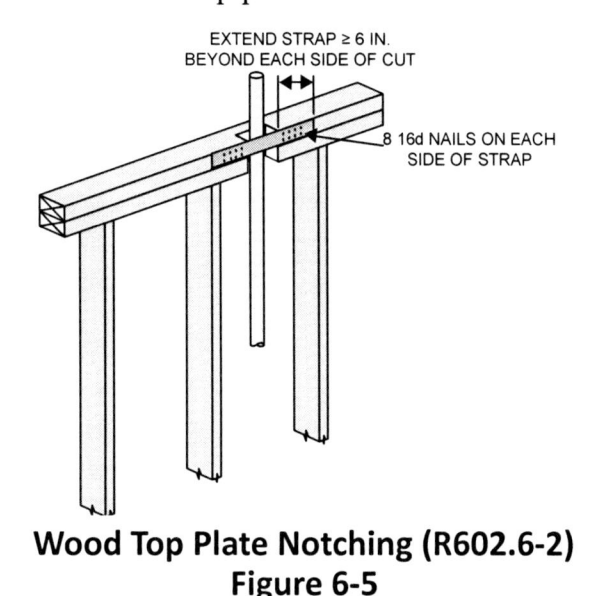

Wood Top Plate Notching (R602.6-2)
Figure 6-5

Wall Construction Best Practice

Consider where pipes, bathtubs, showers, toilets, and ducts will be located when designing the home and specify appropriate framing materials and spacing so that the fewest number of holes and notches will be necessary. Use appropriate size studs for walls in which DWV plumbing pipes will be run so that holes and notches should not exceed maximum percentages. Example: use 2x6 studs in walls where DWV plumbing pipes 2 inches or larger will be run.

CRIPPLE WALLS (R602.9)

Cripple Wall Definition

Cripple wall A cripple wall is a framed wall that is less than one story tall. Cripple walls often occur with basement foundations that are stepped down to follow finished grade, and they may occur in split-level homes.

Cripple Wall Requirements

1. Install cripple walls using studs that are at least (≥) the same width as the wall studs above.

2. Frame cripple walls more than (>) 4 feet tall as though they are full height walls. This means using the stud sizes and framing requirements specified in Section R602.3. Example: if full height wall studs on the same floor level as the cripple wall are 2x6, use 2x6 studs for the cripple wall.
3. Brace cripple walls as required for the wall above, except: (a) increase the required wall brace length by 1.15, and (b) decrease the distance between wall braces to 18 feet. Example: if the cripple wall is a 2 feet tall basement wall and the wall brace length for the first story wall above is 4 feet, brace at least (≥) 4.6 feet (4 x 1.15) of the cripple wall.
4. Install sheathing that covers at least (≥) one full side of a cripple wall less than (<) 14 inches tall. Fasten the sheathing to both the top and bottom plate.
5. Support cripple walls on a continuous foundation.
6. You may substitute solid blocking for a framed and sheathed cripple wall less than (<) 14 inches tall.
7. Anchor cripple walls to the foundation like other framed walls.
8. Refer to the IRC for additional bracing requirements in seismic design areas.

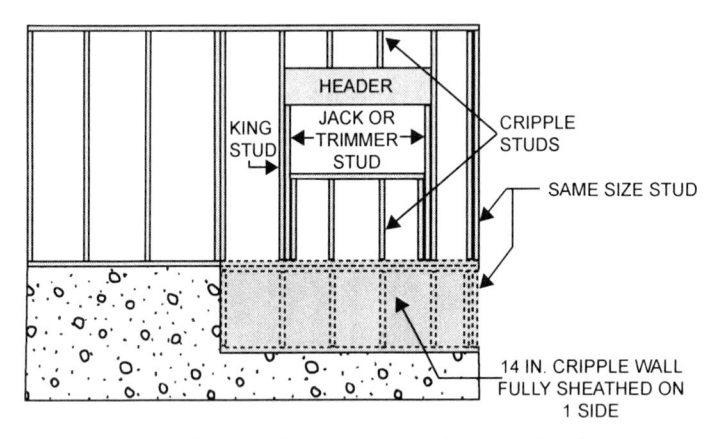

Cripple Wall Framing (R602.9-0)
Figure 6-6

WALL BRACING (R602.10)

Limitations of the Material in this Section

The IRC presents many methods and complex rules for wall bracing. Wall bracing is best left to qualified engineers and architects. This section discusses a few common wall bracing methods and some general rules about how to install them. Refer to the IRC and to qualified professionals for more information about wall bracing, particularly when dealing with wall bracing in high wind and seismic design areas, and when bracing walls in large and complex homes.

Wall Brace and Braced Wall Definitions

A braced wall (braced wall line) is an interior or an exterior wall that contains the required length of approved wall braces (braced wall panels). Most exterior walls and some interior walls are braced walls. A wood structural panel (such as OSB) is a common example of an approved wall brace. Be careful not to confuse the similar terms braced wall and wall brace. A braced wall begins and ends where one braced wall intersects perpendicular braced walls.

Wall Bracing Method Selection Criteria

1. Select an appropriate wall bracing method based on factors that include: (a) the mean roof height above grade ((≤) 30 feet), and (b) the height from the eaves to the roof ridge ((≤) 10 feet), and (c) the height of each story ((≤) 10 feet), and (d) the seismic design area (A and B), and (e) the wind speed design area ((≤) 90 mph.), and (f) and the wind exposure category (B), and (g) not more than (≤) two parallel braced walls connected to one perpendicular braced wall.
2. Wall bracing requirements may increase or decrease when factors (a)-(g) are outside the indicated ranges. The indicated ranges in factors (a)-(g) will accommodate most homes in most areas of the continental United States.
3. The wall bracing information in this section applies only to one and two-family homes, not to townhomes.
4. The wall bracing information in this section applies only when braced walls are straight and are parallel or perpendicular to each other. Refer to the IRC when bracing angled walls.

Wall Bracing General Installation Requirements

1. Install a wall brace at each end of a braced wall. Most exterior walls and some interior walls are braced walls.
2. Begin the wall brace not more than (≤) 12 ½ feet from each braced wall end. Begin the wall braces at each braced wall end so that the total distance of both wall braces from the ends of the braced wall is not more than (≤) 12 ½ feet. Example: the wall brace at one end of a braced wall begins 5 feet from the braced wall end and the wall brace at the other end of a braced wall begins 6 feet from the braced wall end. The sum of 5 feet and 6 feet is 11 feet. This is less than 12 ½ feet and is acceptable.
3. Install a wall brace at not less than (≤) 25 feet on center along a braced wall when the distance between braces exceeds (>) 25 feet.
4. Install wall bracing material that covers at least (≥) the length (in feet) of the braced wall specified in Table R602.10-1. Refer to the IRC when selection factors (a) through (g) are outside the ranges indicated in the previous section.
5. Fasten wall braces to framing and fasten framing (such as roof trusses and rafters) to braced walls according to the fastening schedules in Section R602.3 or according to the brace manufacturer's instructions. Refer to the IRC for additional fastening requirements when selection factors (a) through (g) are outside the ranges indicated in the previous section.
6. Install at least (≥) ½ inch drywall as required in Chapter 7 on the interior of braced walls. You may omit the drywall if you multiply the bracing percentage by 1.5.
7. You may use different wall bracing methods within the same braced wall and you may use different bracing methods on different stories. Example: you may use let-in bracing at one end of a braced wall and structural panel bracing on the other end. Use the highest required bracing length in the table when using different bracing methods in the same braced wall.
8. Install at least (≥) 48 inches of wall bracing in every braced wall regardless of the values in Table R602.10-1 and any allowed adjustments to those values.
9. Refer to the IRC when braced walls intersect with other braced walls at other than a 90° angle.

108 Everybody's Building Code

TABLE R602.10-1
Minimum Total Length of Braced Wall Required to be Braced Based on Selection Factors (a)-(g)

stories above braced wall	distance between braced walls (feet)	wood structural panels, hardboard siding panels (feet)	let-in brace (feet)
0	10	2.0	3.5
0	20	4.0	7.0
0	30	5.5	9.5
1	10	4.0	7.0
1	20	7.5	13.0
1	30	10.5	18.5
2	10	6.0	No
2	20	11.0	No
2	30	15.5	No

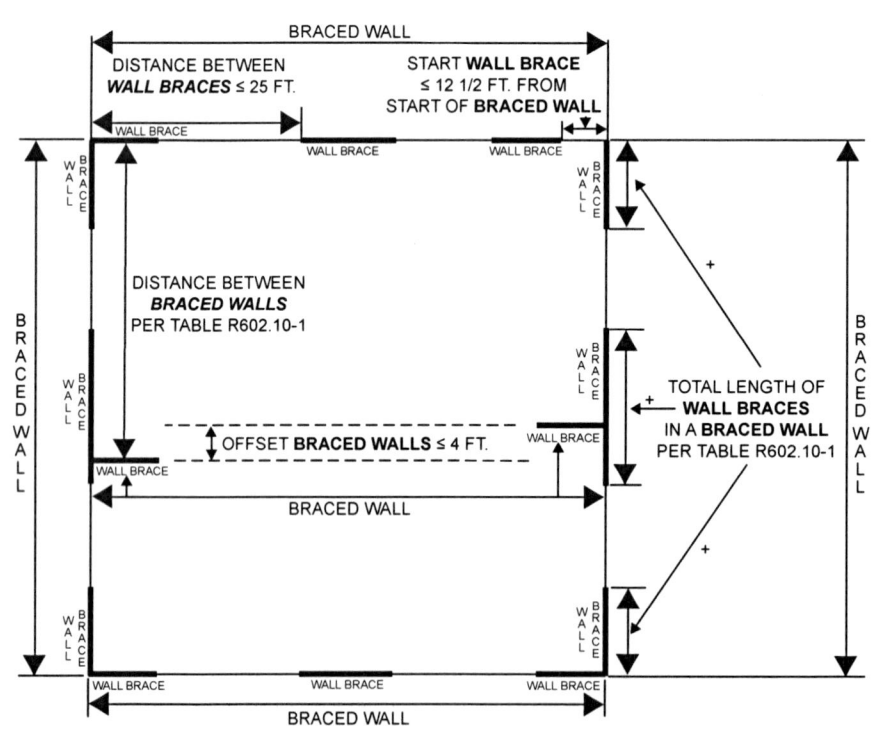

Braced Wall Line Length and Spacing (R602.10-1)
Figure 6-7

Let-in Wall Bracing

1. Install let-in wall bracing using a continuous wood 1x4, or an approved metal strap, cut into the studs diagonally from the top to the bottom plate at an angle at least (≥) 45 degrees and not more than (≤) 60 degrees from horizontal.
2. Secure wood 1x4 bracing to each stud using two 8d nails. Secure metal strap bracing according to the brace manufacturer's instructions.

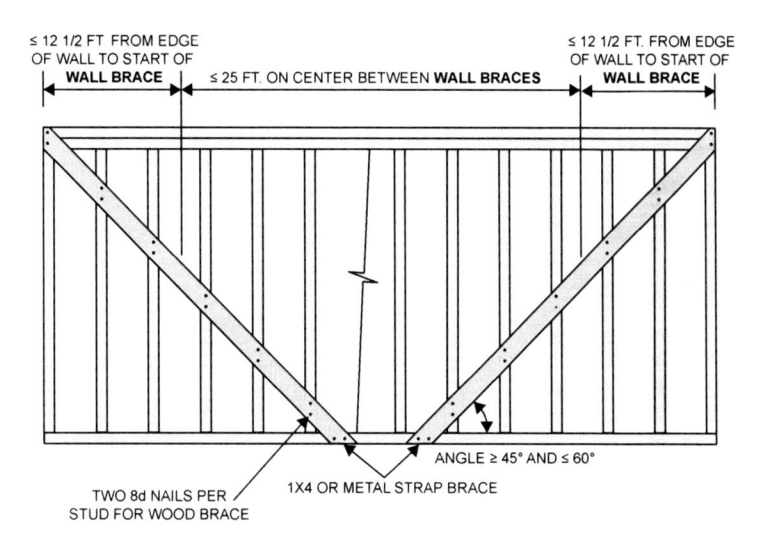

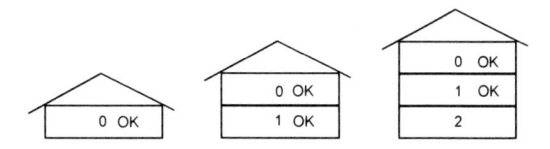

Wall Bracing – Let-in (R602.10-2)
Figure 6-8

Metal Strap Let-in Wall Brace (PR602.10-1)
Figure 6-9

Wood Structural Panel Wall Bracing

1. Install wood structural panel wall bracing using 4x8 or 4x9 panels at least (≥) 3/8 inch thick (span rating 24/0).
2. Install panels that are at least (≥) 48 inches wide and cover at least (≥) 3 stud bays for studs spaced 16 inches on center. You may install the panels horizontally or vertically.
3. Secure 3/8 inch thick wood structural panel bracing to studs using at least (≥) 6d common nails spaced not more than (≤) 6 inches on center at panel edges and 12 inches on center at intermediate supports. Secure 7/16 inch thick panels (span rating 24/16) using 8d common nails and using the same spacing previously described.
4. Install solid blocking where panel joints occur between studs to maintain fastener spacing. Use at least 1 ½ inches thick wood for blocking. The blocking is usually the same dimensions as the studs. Example: 2x6 blocking is normally used with 2x6 studs, although 2x4 blocking is acceptable.

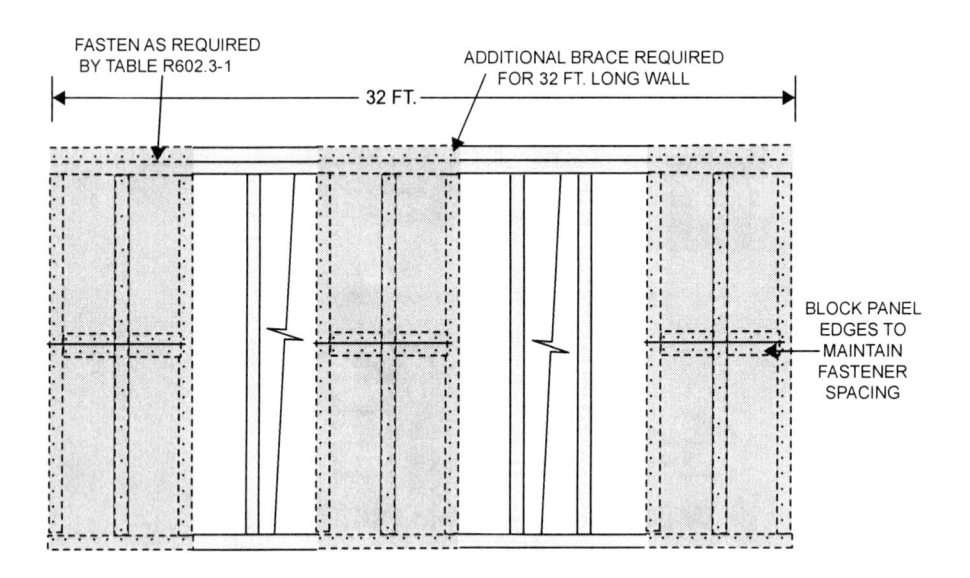

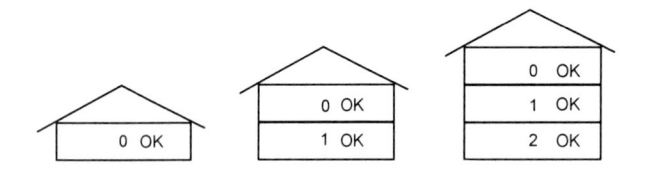

Wall Bracing – Wood Panels (R602.10-3)
Figure 6-10

Wood Panel Wall Brace (PR602.10-2)
Figure 6-11

Hardboard Panel Siding Wall Bracing

1. Install hardboard panel siding wall bracing using 4x8 or 4x9 siding panels at least (≥) 7/16 inch thick and at least (≥) 48 inches wide.
2. Secure hardboard panel siding to studs using nails with at least (≥) 0.092 inch diameter shank and at least (≥) 0.225 inch head. Space nails not more than (≤) 4 inches on center at panel edges and at not more than (≤) 8 inches on center at intermediate supports when hardboard panel siding is used as wall bracing.

Garage Door Header Wall Bracing

1. You may use the following method to build a wall brace for a garage door header that supports a roof or that supports one story and a roof. You may install this wall brace on one or both sides of the garage door. You may use approved engineered designs or commercially available products instead of this method. You may use alternate bracing methods described in the IRC.
2. Build the wall brace not more than (≤) 10 feet tall and at least (≥) 24 inches wide.
3. Install wood structural panel(s) at least (≥) 7/16 inch thick vertically (long dimension vertical) on one side of the wall brace. Extend the panel(s) to cover the header. Attach the panel(s) using at least (≥) 8d common nails spaced at 3 inches on center. Install double blocking at panel joints, if any, to maintain nail spacing. Locate any panel joints within 24 inches of the wall brace center.
4. Install at least (≥) a 3x11 ¼ inches glue laminated header or a site-built header made from at least two solid 2x12s. Extend the header to the outer (king) studs of the supporting walls. Make the header clear span at least (≥) 6 feet and not more than (≤) 18 feet.
5. Install a tie-down strap of at least (≥) 1,000 pound uplift capacity between the header and the studs nearest to the opening. Install the tie-down strap on the side of the wall brace that

is opposite the sheathing. Example: if the sheathing is on the outside, install the strap on the inside. Secure the strap to the studs and to the header according to the strap manufacturer's instructions.

6. Install at least (≥) two foundation anchor bolts at least (≥) ½ inch diameter in the wall brace bottom plate. Install the anchor bolts in the foundation according to Section R403. Install a 3/16 inch thick by 2 ½ inches square washer between the bottom plate and the nut of each bolt.

7. Support the braced wall on a continuous foundation under the entire wall brace.

8. Install a tie-down strap of at least (≥) 1,000 pound uplift capacity between the header and the studs on the side of the garage door opposite from the wall brace. This tie-down strap is required only if you install the garage door header wall brace on one side of the garage door. Install an additional tie-down strap between the studs and the foundation if the wall on the opposite side of the garage door wall brace is not a braced wall.

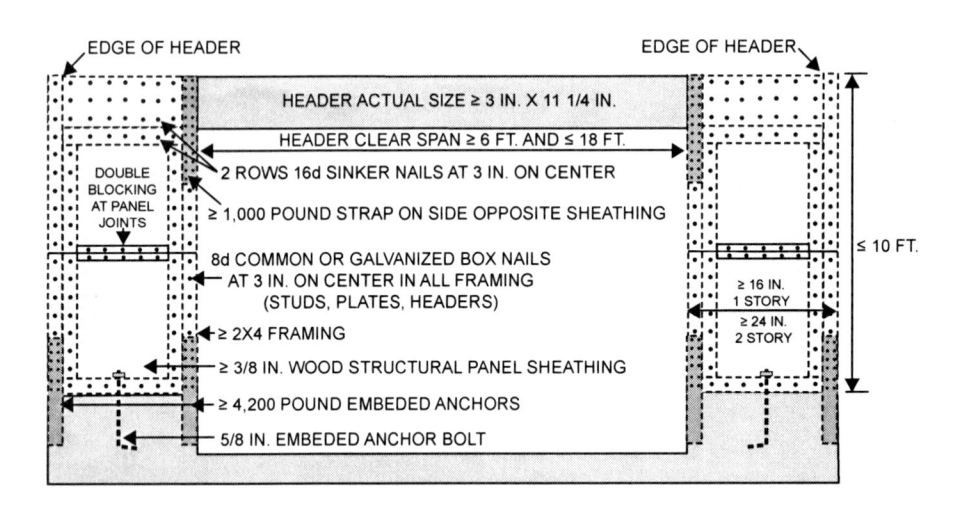

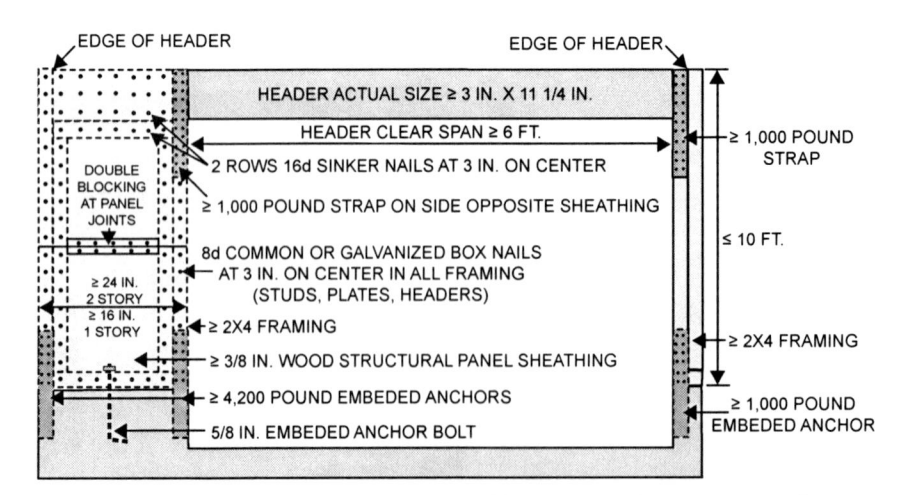

Garage Door Header Wall Bracing (R602.10-4)
Figure 6-12

Large Window and Door Header Wall Bracing

1. You may use the following method to build a wall brace adjacent to large window and door headers. Each wall brace built using this method equals 4 feet of wall bracing when calculating total wall bracing length required in Table R602.10-1. You may use approved engineered designs or commercially available products instead of this method. You may use alternate bracing methods described in the IRC.
2. Build the wall brace not more than (≤) 10 feet tall and at least (≥) 24 inches wide for a wall on the first story of a two story home and at least (≥) 16 inches wide for a wall on a one story home.
3. Install wood structural panel(s) at least (≥) 3/8 inch thick vertically (long dimension vertical) on one side of the wall brace. Extend the panel(s) to cover the header. Attach the panel(s) using at least (≥) 8d common nails spaced at 3 inches on center. Install double blocking at panel joints, if any, to maintain nail spacing. Nail any blocking using at least (≥) 3 16d sinker nails. Locate any panel joints within (≤) 24 inches of the wall brace center.
4. Install at least (≥) a 3x11 ¼ inches glue laminated header or a site-built header made from at least two solid 2x12s. Extend the header to the outer (king) studs of the supporting walls. Make the header clear span not more than (≤) 18 feet.
5. Install a tie-down strap with at least (≥) 1,000 pound uplift capacity between the header and the studs nearest to the opening. Install the tie-down strap on the side of the wall brace that is opposite the sheathing. Example: if the sheathing is on the outside, install the strap on the inside. Secure the strap to the studs and to the header according to the strap manufacturer's instructions.
6. Install at least (≥) 1 foundation anchor bolt that is at least (≥) 5/8 inch diameter in the wall brace bottom plate. Install the anchor bolt in the footing according to Section R403.
7. Install two tie-down devices with at least (≥) 4,200 capacity embedded into the foundation and attached to the studs according to the device manufacturer's instructions.
8. Support the wall brace directly on a continuous foundation, which is at least (≥) 12 inches by 12 inches, under the entire wall brace. Install at least (≥) one #4 reinforcing bar near the bottom and one near the top of the foundation.

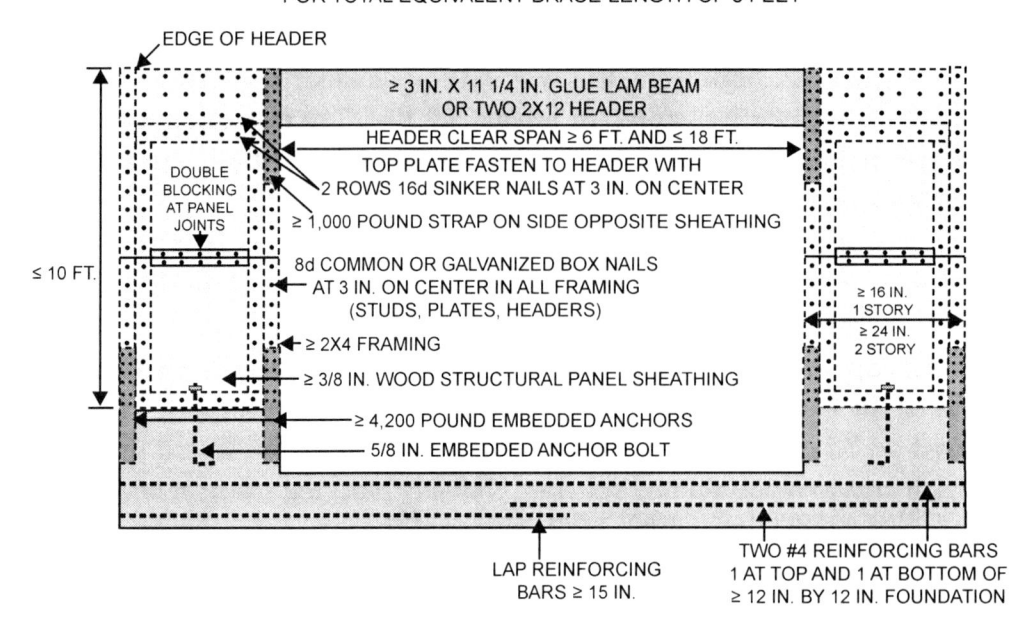

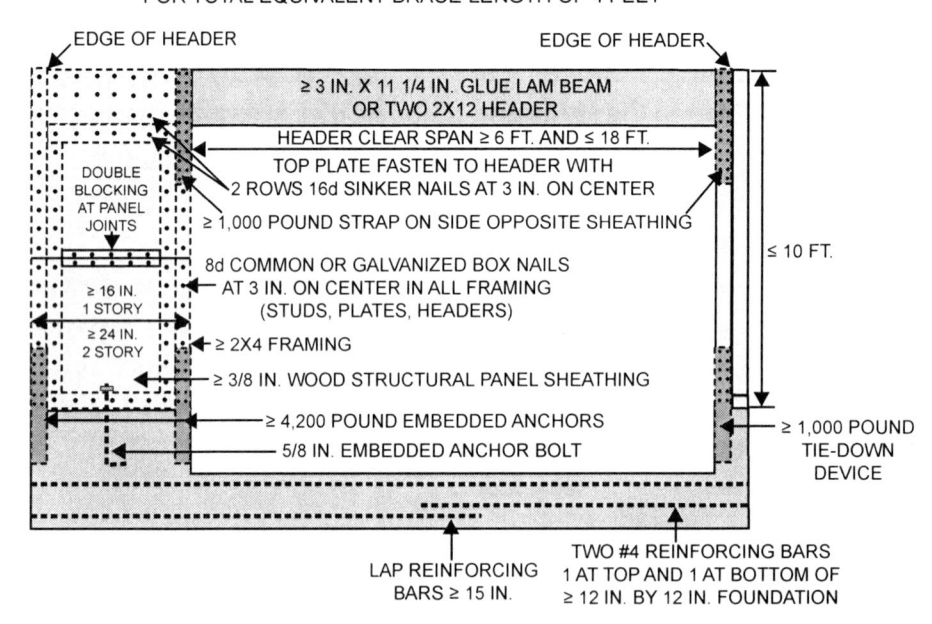

Large Window and Door Header Wall Bracing (R602.10-5)
Figure 6-13

Wall Bracing Discussion

Wall bracing helps the building resist movement during stress events such as high winds and seismic activity. This movement is called racking. During high wind events, roof framing and upper floors will be moved by the wind while the lower floors will remain more stable. During seismic events the lower floors will be moved while the upper floors will remain more stable. Without adequately braced walls that are secured to the foundation, this differential movement can tear a building apart.

MASONRY WALLS ABOVE GRADE (R606, R607, R608)

Limitations of the Material in this Section

These IRC sections present requirements for building above-grade walls using several types of masonry units. These sections also present requirements for anchoring joists and rafters to masonry walls. You may build masonry walls using single wythe (layer) or multiple wythe masonry units. Note that these IRC sections do not apply to basement, crawl space, or other foundation walls.

The most common masonry unit for building residential walls is the concrete masonry unit (CMU), also known as a concrete block or cinder block. Other units include structural brick (rare in modern residential construction), glass blocks, and insulated concrete forms. The material in this book section presents wall construction requirements for the following type of building: one-story, using vertical (not corbelled) concrete blocks, that may be faced with a brick or stone veneer, in areas not subject to seismic and high wind loads. Refer to the IRC for more information about building masonry walls, particularly when dealing with walls in high wind and seismic design areas.

Block Wall Thickness (R606.2.1)

1. Use solid or hollow blocks at least (≥) 8 inches thick for a load-bearing wall more than (>) 9 feet high.
2. You may use solid blocks at least (≥) 6 inches thick for load-bearing walls in one story dwellings and garages if the wall height is not more than (≤) 9 feet. You may extend a gable end wall not more than (≤) 6 feet at the gable peak above the wall height.

Block Wall Thickness Change (R606.2.3)

1. Use a course of solid blocks at the transition between a thinner course of hollow blocks above and a thicker course below.
2. You may use approved methods other than a solid course of blocks between thinner and thicker courses if the method adequately transmits the loads from the thinner course to the thicker course and to the foundation.

Block Parapet Walls (R606.2.4)

1. Use blocks at least (≥) 8 inches thick for unreinforced parapet walls. Build unreinforced solid block parapet walls not more than (≤) four times the block's thickness. Example: the top of an 8 inch thick unreinforced solid block parapet wall may not exceed (≤) 32 inches above the adjacent roof. Build unreinforced hollow block parapet walls not more than (≤) three times the block's thickness. Example: the top of an 8 inch thick unreinforced hollow block parapet wall may not exceed (≤) 24 inches above the adjacent roof.

Block Wall (Masonry) Support (R606.4)

1. Support at least (≥) 2/3 of the width of a masonry wythe on the supporting foundation wall,

lintel, or header. Example: a standard 8 x 8 x 16 block must have at least (≥) 5 3/8 inches on the support below.

Block Piers (R606.6)

1. Build a single, isolated <u>solid block</u> or mortar-filled hollow block pier that supports a beam or girder not more than (≤) ten times the block's least dimension. Fill hollow blocks solid with Type M or S mortar. Example: the top of an isolated 8x8x16 inch solid block pier may not be more than (≤) 80 inches (10x8 inches) above its footing.
2. Build an isolated <u>hollow block</u> pier that supports a beam or girder not more than (≤) four times the block's least dimension.
3. Install at least (≥) 4 inch thick solid cap block on hollow block piers. You may fill the top block course with concrete or mortar instead of using a cap block.

Block Wall Chases (R606.7)

1. Build a chase or a recess in block walls not deeper than (≤) one-third of the wall thickness and not more than (≤) 4 feet long for horizontal chases. Do not locate a chase or recess within a pier.
2. Provide at least (≥) 8 inches of masonry behind chases and recesses, and between adjacent chases and recesses, and between chases and recesses and the jambs for openings such as windows and doors.
3. Support blocks above chases and recesses more than (>) 12 inches wide with a noncombustible lintel.
4. Do not build chases and recesses in block walls that decrease the wall's required strength or fire resistance.

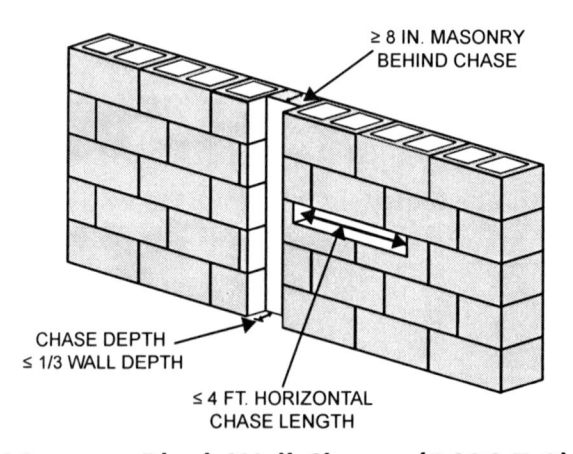

Masonry Block Wall Chases (R606.7-0)
Figure 6-14

Block Wall Lateral Support Type and Spacing (R606.9)

1. Provide lateral support to block walls that limits either the horizontal or vertical distance between supports. You may install both horizontal and vertical lateral supports. You may use intersecting walls, or pilasters, or buttresses to limit the unsupported horizontal dis-

tance or you may use floor or ceiling or roof structural framing members to limit the unsupported vertical distance.

2. Do not exceed the distances between vertical or horizontal lateral supports in the following table. Values in the table are the maximum ratio of block wall thickness to the distance between supports. Example: an 8 inch thick solid grouted concrete block wall may not exceed (≤) 8 inches times 20, or 160 inches between supports. The 160 inches may be between a floor and a ceiling (vertical supports) or between walls, pilasters, or buttresses (horizontal supports).

TABLE 606.9
Block Wall Support Spacing

wall construction	max. wall thickness to height or length ratio
load-bearing wall solid or solid grouted	20
load-bearing wall all others	18
non-load-bearing wall exterior	18
non-load-bearing wall interior	36

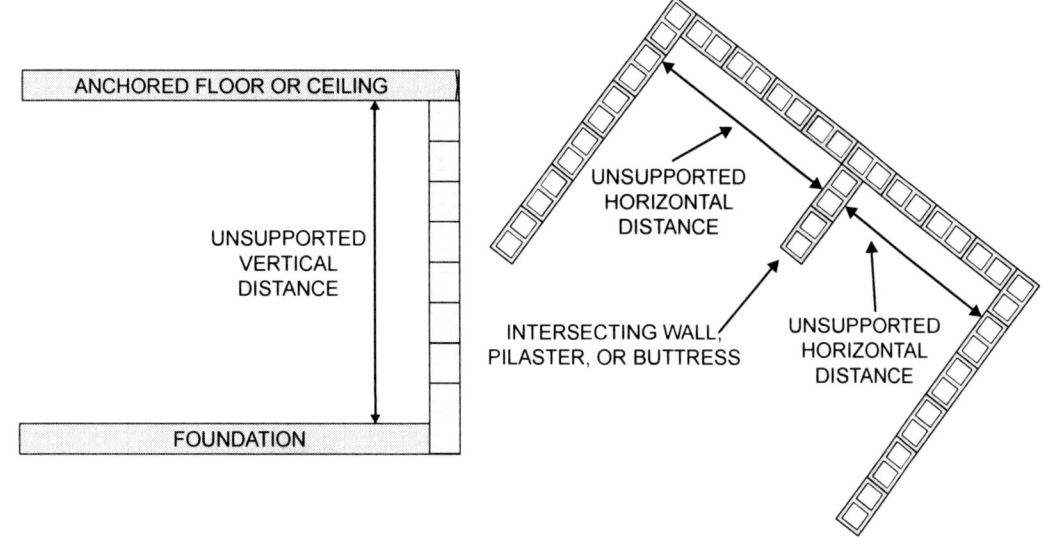

Masonry Block Wall Lateral Support (R606.9-0)
Figure 6-15

Block Wall Horizontal Support Installation (R606.9.1)

1. You may connect all supported block walls to their supporting block walls by overlapping at least (≥) 50 percent of the blocks in the supported walls with blocks in the supporting walls using an overlapping bond pattern. Install overlapping blocks so that at least (≥) 3 inches of block bears on the block below. This is a common support method in residential construction.

2. You may connect a supporting block wall to a supported interior non-load-bearing block wall by installing at least (≥) 9 gage joint reinforcement, or at least (≥) ¼ inch galvanized mesh hardware cloth, at not more than (≤) 16 inches vertical intervals.
3. You may connect a supporting block wall to a supported block walls, other than a interior non-load-bearing wall, by installing at least (≥) 9 gage joint reinforcement that extends at least (≥) 30 inches in each direction at not more than (≤) 8 inches vertical intervals.
4. You may use other approved materials to connect supporting block walls to supported block walls if the connection provides equivalent area of connection.

Block Wall Vertical Support Installation (606.9.2)

1. Anchor roof structures to block walls using metal strap anchors installed according to manufacturer's instructions, or using ½ inch bolts spaced not more than (≤) 6 inches on center, or using other approved anchors.
2. Embed roof anchors at least (≥) 16 inches into the block, or hook or weld the anchors to bond beam reinforcement located at least (≥) 6 inches below the top of the block wall.
3. Anchor floor systems to block walls using metal strap anchors installed according to manufacturer's instructions, or using at least (≥) ½ inch bolts spaced not greater than (≤) 6 inches on center, or using other approved anchors.

Block Wall Openings (R606.10)

1. Support openings in block walls using steel lintels, reinforced concrete or masonry lintels, or masonry arches. Use lintels designed to support the load from above.

Block Wall Reinforcing Materials Protection (R606.13)

1. Cover all horizontal and vertical reinforcing material completely in mortar or grout.
2. Provide at least (≥) 5/8 inch mortar coverage from exposed faces for all horizontal reinforcing material.
3. Provide at least (≥) one bar diameter, and at least (≥) ¾ inch, mortar or grout coverage for all other reinforcing material, except provide at least (≥) 2 inches mortar or grout coverage if the walls are exposed to weather or soil.

Block Wall Mortar (R607.1)

1. Use Type M, N, or S mortar for block walls in Seismic areas A, B, and C.

Block Wall Mortar Joints (R607.2)

1. Use a ⅜ inch thick bed (horizontal) and head (vertical) joint in block walls unless a different thickness is approved on the construction plans.
2. You may vary the thickness of the starter (first) course joint at the foundation between at least (≥) ¼ inch and not more than (≤) ¾ inch.
3. Do not exceed the joint thickness tolerances in Table R607.2.
4. Place blocks in mortar that has proper moisture content and is workable.

5. Place the blocks with sufficient pressure that mortar extrudes from the joints and produces a tight joint.
6. Fill all joints that are designed to receive mortar with a solid layer of mortar. For hollow core blocks, this means completely filling the areas between the face of the block and the inner core. Cross webs in the cells usually do not receive mortar unless the cells are to be filled with grout or mortar.

TABLE R607.2
Block Wall Mortar Joints

bed joint	⅜ inch min. ½ inch max.
head joint	¼ inch min. ¾ inch max.

Block Wall Ties (R607.3)

1. Embed all wall ties in solid mortar joints.
2. Embed wall ties at least (≥) ½ inch into the outer face of hollow core blocks.
3. Embed wall ties at least (≥) 1 ½ inches into solid blocks or filled core blocks.
4. Do not bend wall ties after being embedded in mortar. This will weaken the mortar around the wall tie and may allow the tie to come loose.

Bonding Multiple Wythes with Wall Ties (R608.1.2.1)

1. Apply this IRC section to bonding multiple wythe masonry using 3/16 inch wire wall ties embedded in horizontal mortar joints. Multiple wythe masonry construction is unusual in modern residential construction.
2. Provide at least (≥) one tie for not more than (≤) 4 ½ square feet of wall space. Stagger the ties horizontally in alternate courses. Space ties not more than (≤) 24 inches apart vertically and not more than (≤) 36 inches apart horizontally.
3. Provide additional ties not more than (≤) 12 inches from every wall opening. Space the ties not more than (≤) 36 inches apart.
4. Use rods or ties bent to a rectangular shape for hollow blocks with cells placed vertically.
5. Bend the ends of ties into hooks at least (≥) 2 inches long for other masonry walls.

Bonding Multiple Wythes with Adjustable Wall Ties (R608.1.2.2)

1. Apply this IRC section to bonding multiple wythe masonry using adjustable wall ties. Multiple wythe masonry construction is unusual in modern residential construction.
2. Provide at least (≥) one tie for not more than (≤) 2 2/3 square feet of wall space. Space ties not more than (≤) 24 inches apart either vertically or horizontally. Offset the bed (horizontal) joints between masonry wythes vertically not more than (≤) 1 ¼ inches. Place connecting parts of the ties not more than (≤) 1/16 inch apart.

Bonding Multiple Wythes with Stone Veneer Wythe (R608.1.3.2)

1. Place bonder units in rubble stone veneer spaced not more than (≤) 3 feet apart both vertically and horizontally if the stone is 24 inches or less thick.

GLASS BLOCK WALLS (R610)

Glass Block Size

1. Use standard size hollow or standard size solid glass blocks that are at least (≥) 3 7/8 inches thick.
2. Use thin hollow or thin solid glass blocks that are at least (≥) 3 inches thick for solid glass blocks and are at least (≥) 3 1/8 inches thick for hollow glass blocks.

Exterior Glass Block Wall Size

1. Limit the area of standard size glass block exterior walls to not more than (≤) the value in Table R610-1. Limit the width of these walls between structural supports to not more than (≤) 25 feet. Limit the height of these walls between structural supports to not more than (≤) 20 feet.
2. Limit the area of thin glass block exterior walls to not more than (≤) 85 square feet for design wind pressure of not more than (≤) 20 psi. Limit the width of these walls between structural supports to not more than (≤) 15 feet. Limit the height of these walls between structural supports to not more than (≤) 10 feet. Do not use thin glass blocks for exterior walls in areas where the wind design pressure is more than (>) 20 psi.

TABLE R610-1
Glass Block Exterior Wall Area Limits

wind design pressure (psf)	maximum wall area sq. ft.
10	230
20	144
30	110
40	80
50	67
60	57

Interior Glass Block Wall Size

1. Limit the area of standard size glass block interior walls to not more than (≤) 250 square feet. Limit the area of thin glass block walls to not more than (≤) 150 square feet.
2. Limit the width between structural supports of standard size and thin glass block interior walls to not more than (≤) 25 feet. Limit the height between structural supports of these walls to not more than (≤) 20 feet.

Glass Block Wall Structural Support

1. Support glass block walls using structural members, such as wood, that have a deflection ratio of at least (≥) 1/600.
2. Support glass block walls that are more than (>) one block wide and one block tall along the top and sides. Example: support a block wall consisting of 2 horizontal blocks and 5 vertical blocks along both sides and along the top. Use supports that will resist at least (≥) 200 pounds per linear foot, or the actual applied loads, whichever is greater. Use either panel anchors spaced not more than (≤) 16 inches on center or channel-type restraints. Use channel-type restraints when the block wall is either one block wide or one block tall.
3. You need not support glass block walls at the top that are 1 block wide.
4. You need not support glass block walls on the sides that are 1 block high.
5. Provide a beam, header, or lintel above a glass block wall within a load-bearing wall.

Glass Block Wall Anchors and Restraints

1. Install panel anchors not more than (≤) 16 inches on center along the tops and sides of glass block walls. Embed the anchors at least (≥) 12 inches into the block joint. Secure the anchor with two screws.
2. Place at least (≥) 1 inch of the glass block into a channel-type restraint. Use channel-type restraints that are oversized to allow for the expansion strip, sealant, and other materials.

Glass Block Wall Horizontal Reinforcement

1. Place reinforcing wire in glass block wall horizontal mortar joints. Run the reinforcing the entire length of the glass block wall. Do not extend the reinforcing wire across expansion joints.
2. Space reinforcing wire not more than (≤) 16 inches apart vertically.
3. Lap wire joints at least (≥) 6 inches.
4. Place reinforcing wire immediately above and below any openings in the glass block wall.
5. Use parallel or welded cross reinforcing wire that is at least (≥) size W1.7.

Glass Block Wall Expansion Joints

1. Install expansion joints at the top, sides, and at structural supports of glass block walls.
2. Make expansion joints at least (≥) 3/8 inch thick and thick enough to allow for movement of the supporting structure.
3. Leave expansion joints completely free of mortar and debris.
4. Fill expansion joints with resilient material made for use in glass block wall expansion joints.

Glass Block Wall Sills

1. Apply a water-base asphaltic emulsion coating to the glass block wall sill before laying the first layer of glass blocks.

Glass Block Mortar Joints

1. Use Type S or Type N mortar in mortar joints between glass blocks. Do not cut a depression (furrow) in the mortar joint.
2. Discard mortar not used within 1 ½ hours after initial mixing. Do not add water or otherwise disturb a mortar joint after it has set.
3. Fill joints between glass blocks completely with mortar.
4. Make top, bottom, and vertical mortar joints between glass blocks in a straight wall ¼ inch thick. Make vertical mortar joints between glass blocks in a curved wall at least (≥) 1/8 inch thick and not more than (≤) 5/8 inch thick. You may vary the thickness of bottom mortar joints between 3/16 inch thick and 5/8 inch thick. You may vary the thickness of top mortar joints between 1/8 inch thick and 5/8 inch thick.

WINDOW AND GLASS DOOR INSTALLATION (R613)

Flashing and Installation General Requirements

1. Install and flash windows according to the manufacturer's written installation instructions. The manufacturer must provide written installation instructions with each window. Manufacturers usually comply with this requirement by attaching a sticker on each window.

Windows Six Feet Above Adjacent Surface

1. Install operable windows so that the lowest edge of the window opening is at least (≥) 24 inches above the finished floor, if the lowest edge of the window opening is more than (>) 72 inches above finished grade or the surface below. This provision applies to all operable windows regardless of where they are located in the home. This provision does not apply to fixed windows and it does not apply if the window opening will not allow a 4 inches diameter sphere to pass through the opening.
2. You may install an operable window with an opening less than 24 inches above the finished floor if: (a) you install a device that limits the window opening size so that a 4 inches diameter sphere cannot pass through the window, or if (b) you install a fall protection device that complies with ASTM F2090. Opening size limit and fall protection devices attached to emergency escape windows must be removable as described in the emergency escape opening section.

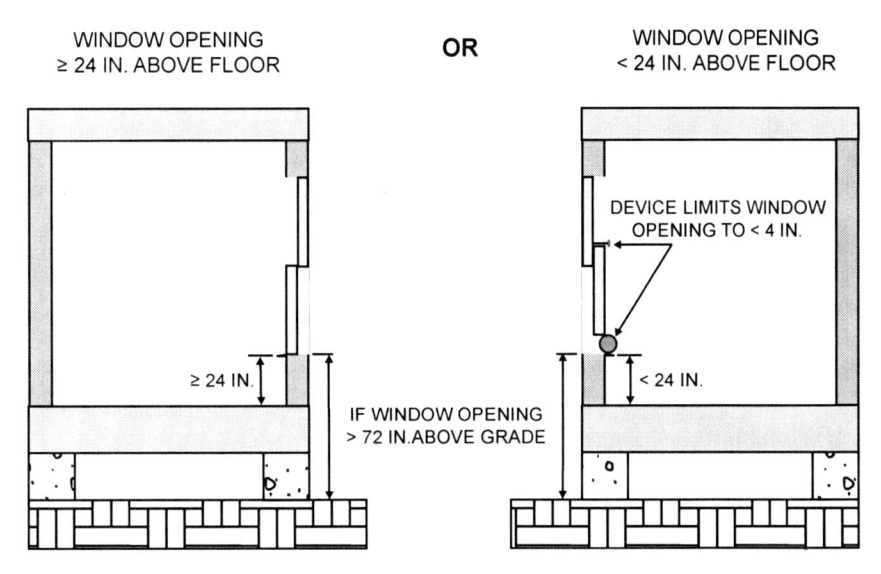

Installation of Windows Six Feet Above Adjacent Surface (R613-0)
Figure 6-16

Attaching Windows and Glass Doors to the Structure

1. Attach windows and glass doors to the structure according to manufacturer's instructions. Use the following if manufacturer's instructions are not available.
2. Attach wood shims or bucks that are at least (≥) 1 ½ inches thick directly to openings for windows and glass doors in masonry and concrete, then attach the window and glass door to the shims or bucks.
3. Attach windows and glass doors directly to masonry and concrete window and glass door openings, when using wood shims or bucks that are less than (<) 1 ½ inches thick.
4. Attach windows and glass doors directly to wood framing using common small thickness shims, when necessary.
5. You may use frame clips to attach windows and glass doors to concrete, masonry, and wood when allowed by manufacturer's installation instructions.
6. Use and install fasteners that adequately transfer the window and glass door loads to the structure.

7

INTERIOR AND EXTERIOR WALL COVERING

DRYWALL (GYPSUM BOARD) INTERIOR APPLICATION (R702.3 AND R702.4)

Limitations of the Material in this Section

The IRC Section and the Gypsum Association publication GA-216-04 present the methods for applying different thicknesses of drywall (gypsum board) to interior supports such as wood framing, metal framing, and masonry. The material in this section presents the more common methods of attaching drywall to wood framing. Refer to the IRC and GA-216-04 for more information about drywall application requirements. <u>All material in this section refers to ½ inch thick drywall unless otherwise indicated.</u>

Drywall Application General Requirements

1. Apply drywall to wood framing that is at least (≥) 2 inches nominal thickness. Example: a 2x4 is actually about 1 ½ inches thick with a 2 inches nominal thickness. You may use nominal 1x2 inch furring strips installed over solid backing (such as masonry) or installed on framing spaced at not more than (≤) 24 inches on center.
2. Attach nails or screws between at least (≥) ⅜ inch and not more than (≤) ½ inch from the edges of drywall.
3. Use Type W or S screws to attach drywall to wood framing. Use screws that penetrate the wood at least (≥) ⅝ inch.

Drywall Floating Interior Angles

1. Omit <u>ceiling and wall fasteners</u> where ceilings and walls meet in perpendicular (90 degree angle) corners. Do not omit ceiling fasteners when using Type X drywall in a fire-resistant ceiling application.
2. Omit the <u>corner fasteners</u> on the interior piece of drywall when walls meet in perpendicular (90 degree angle) corners.
3. Install blocking as necessary so that ceiling and wall fasteners are within the recommended spacing distance of the corner.

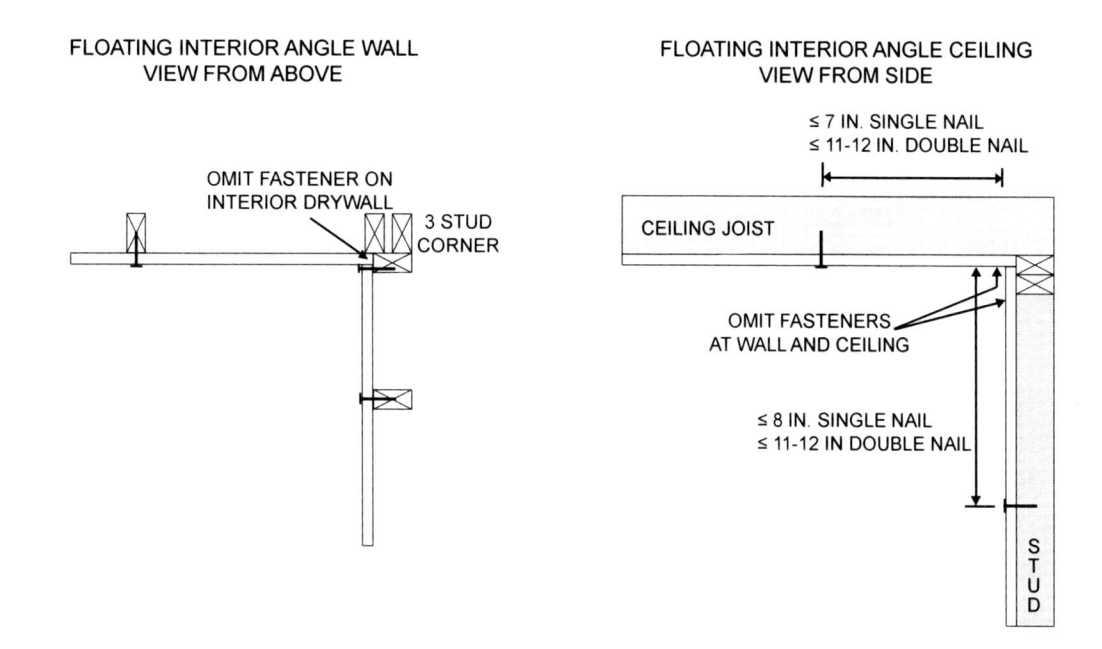

Drywall Interior Angle Fastening (R702.3-1)
Figure 7-1

Drywall Adhesive Application to Wood Framing

1. Apply at least (≥) a ⅜ inch diameter bead of adhesive to studs and joists, if using adhesive. Do not apply adhesive to top and bottom plates.
2. Apply two beads of adhesive at least (≥) ⅜ inch diameter near the edges of studs and joists where a drywall joint occurs, if using adhesive.

Drywall Application to Ceilings with Sixteen Inches on Center Framing

1. <u>Not using adhesive.</u> You may install: (a) one nail not more than (≤) 7 inches on center, or (b) one screw not more than (≤) 12 inches on center, or (c) two nails between 2 inches and 2 ½ inches apart with each two nail pair spaced not more than (≤) 12 inches on center.
2. <u>Using adhesive.</u> You may install nails or screws not more than (≤) 16 inches on center.
3. Apply drywall either perpendicular (long dimension horizontal) or parallel (long dimension vertical) to framing.
4. Use at least (≥) 0.086 inch diameter, 1 ⅝ inches long, 9/32 inch head gypsum board nails or other approved fasteners.

Drywall Application to Ceilings with Twenty-four Inches on Center Framing

1. <u>Not using adhesive.</u> You may install: (a) one nail not more than (≤) 7 inches on center, or (b) one screw not more than (≤) 12 inches on center, or (c) two nails at least (≥) 2 inches and not more than (≤) 2 ½ inches apart with each two nail pair spaced not more than (≤) 12 inches on center.
2. <u>Using adhesive.</u> You may install nails or screws not more than (≤) 16 inches on center.
3. Apply drywall perpendicular to framing (long dimension across framing members).

4. Use at least (≥) ⅝ inch drywall if ceiling will receive a water-based textured finish.
5. Use at least (≥) 0.086 inches diameter, 1 ⅝ inches long, 9/32 inch head gypsum board nails or other approved fasteners.

Drywall Application to Walls with Sixteen Inches on Center Framing

1. <u>Not using adhesive.</u> You may install: (a) one nail not more than (≤) 8 inches on center, or (b) one screw not more than (≤) 16 inches on center, or (c) two nails spaced at least (≥) 2 inches and not more than (≤) 2 ½ inches apart with each two nail pair spaced not more than (≤) 12 inches on center.
2. <u>Using adhesive.</u> You may install: (a) nails not more than (≤) 16 inches on center, or (b) screws not more than (≤) 24 inches on center.
3. Apply drywall either perpendicular (long dimension horizontal) or parallel (long dimension vertical) to framing.
4. Use at least (≥) 0.086 inch diameter, 1 ⅝ inches long, 9/32 inch head gypsum board nails or other approved fasteners.

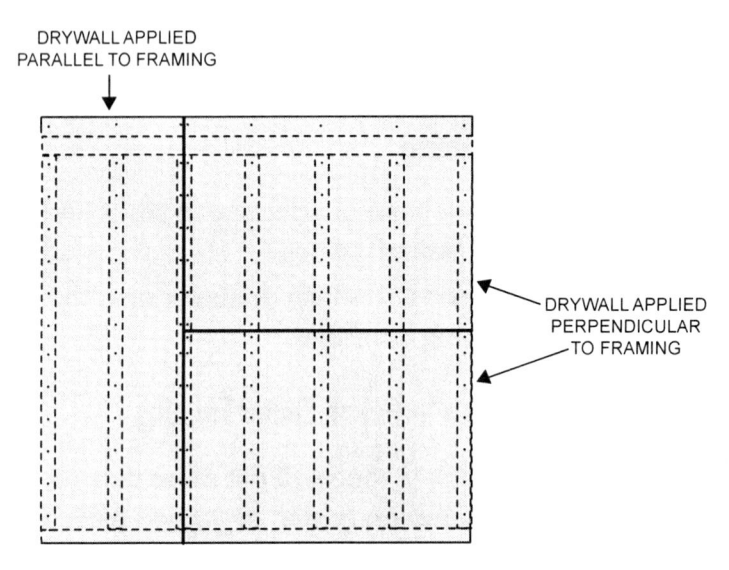

Drywall Orientation to Framing (R702.3-2)
Figure 7-2

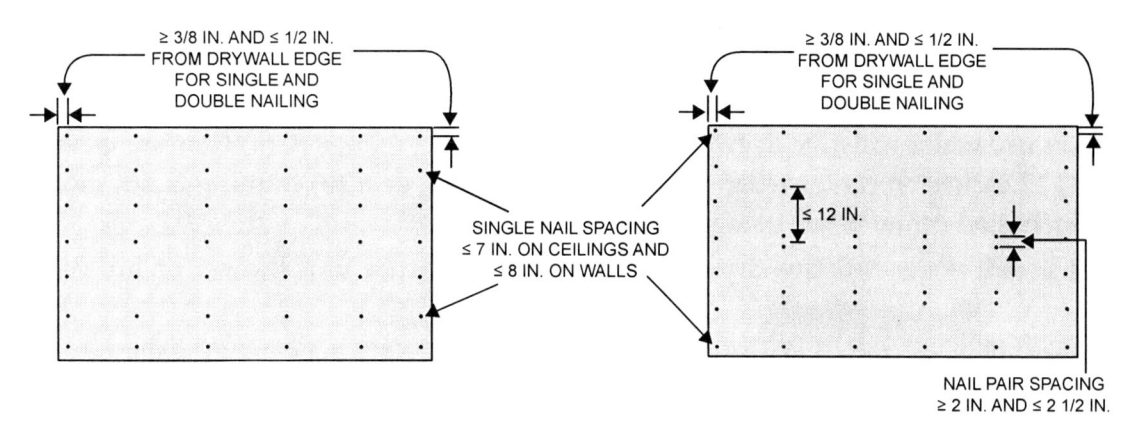

Single and Double Drywall Nailing (R702.3-3)
Figure 7-3

Drywall Application to Walls with Twenty-four Inches on Center Framing

1. <u>Not using adhesive.</u> You may install: (a) one nail not more than (≤) 8 inches on center, or (b) one screw not more than (≤) 12 inches on center, or (c) two nails spaced at least (≥) 2 inches and not more than (≤) 2 ½ inches apart with each two nail pair spaced not more than (≤) 12 inches on center.
2. <u>Using adhesive.</u> You may install: (a) nails not more than (≤) 16 inches on center, or (b) screws not more than (≤) 24 inches on center.
3. Apply drywall either perpendicular (long dimension horizontal) or parallel (long dimension vertical) to framing.
4. Use at least (≥) 0.086 inch diameter, 1 ⅝ inches long, 9/32 inch head gypsum board nails or other approved fasteners.

Drywall Application to Ceilings with Twenty-four Inches on Center Framing Using 5/8 Inch Drywall

1. <u>Not using adhesive.</u> You may install: (a) one nail not more than (≤) 7 inches on center, or (b) one screw not more than (≤) 12 inches on center, or (c) two nails spaced at least (≥) 2 inches and not more than (≤) 2 ½ inches apart with each two nail pair spaced not more than (≤) 12 inches on center.
2. <u>Using adhesive.</u> You may install: (a) nails not more than (≤) 12 inches on center, or (b) screws not more than (≤) 16 inches on center.
3. Apply drywall perpendicular to framing (long dimension across framing members).
4. Use at least (≥) 0.086 inch diameter, 1 7/8 inches long, 9/32 inch head gypsum board nails or other approved fasteners.
5. Use at least (≥) 1 7/8 inches, 6d coated nails or equivalent drywall screws not more than (≤) 6 inches on center when applying Type X drywall in a garage ceiling under habitable rooms and when not using adhesive.

Drywall Around Tubs and Showers

1. Do not use any type of drywall, including water-resistive drywall (sometimes called green

board), on walls around showers and tubs with showers that will receive tile, cultured marble, or plastic finished wall panels.

2. Use approved cement based tile backer board, or glass mat gypsum backer, or traditional mortar and lath as the backing on walls around showers and tubs with showers.
3. You may use water-resistive drywall on tub and shower <u>ceilings</u> if: (a) framing is not more than ($\leq$) 12 inches on center when using ½ inch drywall, or if (b) framing is not more than ($\leq$) 16 inches on center when using ⅝ inch drywall.
4. Do not install water-resistive drywall over a vapor retarder in a shower or tub compartment.
5. Do not install water-resistive drywall where it will be directly exposed to water or where it will be exposed to continuous high humidity (such as in a steam room).
6. Seal all drywall cuts as recommended by the drywall manufacturer. This includes cuts at ceiling and wall intersections.

Drywall Application Discussion

Many drywall finish problems, such as nail pops and cracks in corners, are the normal result of drying and settling of framing lumber. Some drywall problems are caused by improper application and finishing of the drywall. Proper application and finishing of drywall can reduce some, but not all, of the drywall problems in new construction.

Drywall Application Best Practice

Use drywall adhesive and screws when installing drywall on all ceilings. Consider using drywall adhesive and screws when installing drywall on walls. Drywall installed with adhesive and screws is much less likely to show fastener pops and cracks than drywall installed only with nails.

EXTERIOR WALL COVERINGS (R703)

Water-Resistive Barrier General Installation Requirements

1. Install at least ($\geq$) 1 layer of No. 15 asphalt felt over all exterior stud walls and wood sheathed walls, unless an exception applies. You may use other approved water-resistive materials, such as some house wraps and Grade D paper, instead of felt.
2. Install felt and other water-resistive materials beginning at the top of the wall and ending at an appropriate drainage point such as weep holes. Install felt horizontally. Lap horizontal joints at least ($\geq$) 2 inches. Lap vertical joints at least ($\geq$) 6 inches. Lap the upper layer over the lower layer in a shingle fashion. Install other approved water-resistive materials according to manufacturer's instructions. Install felt and other water-resistive materials that are free from holes, tears, and damage. See illustration R703.7-1.
3. Install flashing and other means to capture and drain any water that penetrates behind the exterior wall covering material. Such means may include weep holes, weep screeds, or other openings at the bottom of the wall covering material.
4. You need not install water-resistive materials: (a) over concrete and masonry walls that are built and flashed according to the requirements in Chapters 6 and 7, and (b) at detached accessory buildings.

Hardboard Panel Siding Installation

1. Install felt or other water-resistive materials behind hardboard panel siding.
2. Place vertical panel joints over studs unless the joints occur over wood (blocking) or over wood structural panel sheathing.
3. Weatherproof horizontal joints by: (a) lapping the joint at least (≥) 1 inch, or (b) using shiplap joints, or (c) installing Z-flashing over solid blocking, or over framing, or over wood structural panel sheathing.
4. Use galvanized nails with at least (≥) 0.092 inch shank diameter, and 0.225 inch head diameter and long enough to penetrate framing at least (≥) 1 ½ inches.
5. Space nails not more than (≤) 6 inches on center at panel edges and not more than (≤) 12 inches on center at intermediate supports.
6. Space nails not more than (≤) 4 inches on center at panel edges and not more than (≤) 8 inches on center at intermediate supports when using the panels as bracing in a shear wall.
7. Install hardboard panel siding with the long dimension vertical.

Plywood and Wood Structural Panel Siding Installation

1. Install felt or other approved water-resistive materials behind plywood and wood structural panel siding.
2. Place vertical joints over studs, wood (blocking), or wood structural panel sheathing. Use shiplap vertical joints or cover vertical joints with a batten.
3. Waterproof horizontal joints by: (a) lapping the joint at least (≥) 1 inch, or (b) using shiplap joints, or (c) installing Z-flashing over solid blocking, or over framing, or over wood structural panel sheathing.
4. Use galvanized nails: (a) at least (≥) 0.099 inch shank diameter and 2 inches long when attaching to wood, studs, or wood structural panel sheathing, or (b) at least (≥) .113 inch shank diameter when attaching to studs through foam sheathing. Use a nail that is long enough to penetrate framing at least (≥) 1 ½ inches.
5. Space nails not more than (≤) 6 inches on center at panel edges and not more than (≤) 12 inches on center at interior supports.
6. Be aware of the panel span rating printed on the plywood. Plywood ⅜ inch thick may not be installed parallel to the studs (long dimension vertical) on studs spaced more than 16 inches on center. Plywood ½ inch thick may not be installed parallel to studs spaced more than 24 inches on center.
7. Install plywood and wood structural panel siding with the long dimension vertical.

Fiber Cement Panel Siding Installation

1. Install felt or other water-resistive materials behind fiber cement panel siding.
2. Install panels with long dimension vertical and parallel to studs.
3. Place vertical joints over studs and seal with caulk or cover with battens.
4. Install Z-flashing in horizontal joints over solid blocking.
5. Use galvanized nails with: (a) at least (≥) 0.099 inch shank diameter and 0.250 inch head diameter when applying directly to studs, or (b) at least (≥) 0.102 inch shank diameter and

0.255 inch head diameter when applying to wood, wood structural panel sheathing, or through foam plastic sheathing. Use a nail that is long enough to penetrate framing at least (≥) 1 ½ inches.

6. Space nails not more than (≤) 6 inches on center at panel edges and not more than (≤) 12 inches on center at intermediate supports.

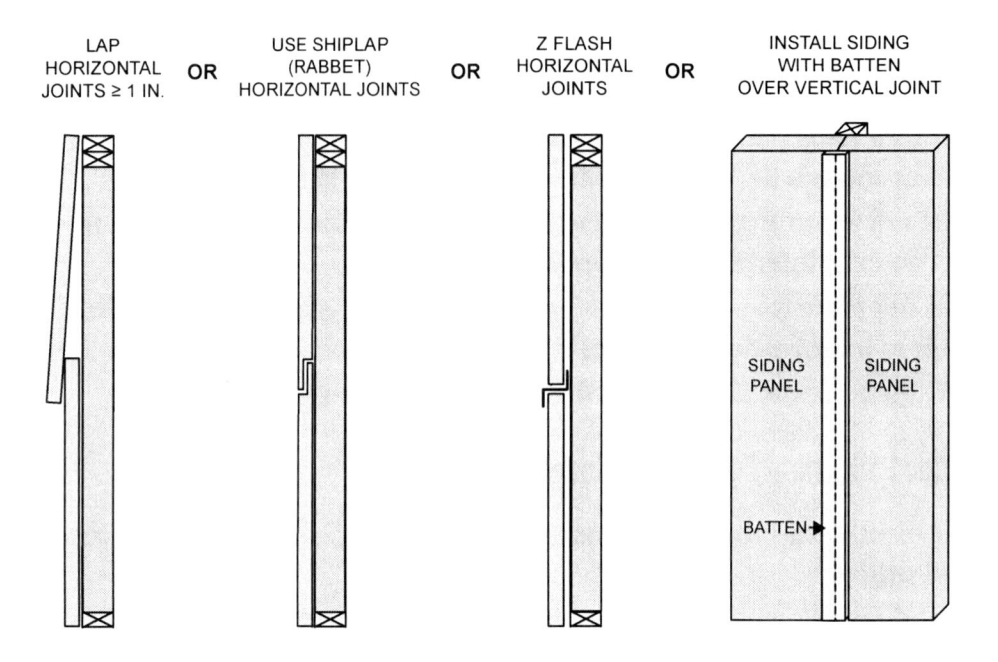

Panel Siding Joint Treatments (R703-1)
Figure 7-4

Wood Structural Panel Lap Siding Installation

1. Install felt or other water-resistive material behind wood structural panel lap siding.
2. Place vertical joints over studs and seal with caulk or cover with a joint cover. You may place staggered vertical joints anywhere if the siding is nailed into wood structural panel sheathing.
3. Waterproof horizontal joints by lapping the joint at least (≥) 1 inch. You may install horizontal lap siding according to manufacturer's instructions if the instructions differ from code requirements.
4. Use galvanized nails: (a) at least (≥) 0.099 inch shank diameter and 2 inches long when attaching to wood, studs, or wood structural panel sheathing, (b) at least (≥) .113 inch shank diameter when attaching to studs through foam sheathing. Use a nail that is long enough to penetrate framing at least (≥) 1 ½ inches.
5. Install nails every 8 inches along the bottom edge.

Hardboard Lap Siding Installation

1. Install felt or other water-resistive material behind hardboard lap siding.
2. Place vertical joints over studs and seal with caulk or cover with a joint cover.
3. Waterproof horizontal joints by lapping the joint at least (≥) 1 inch. You may install horizon-

tal lap siding according to manufacturer's instructions if the instructions differ from code requirements.

4. Use galvanized nails with at least (≥) 0.099 inch shank diameter, and 0.240 inch head diameter and long enough to penetrate framing at least (≥) 1 ½ inches.
5. Install 2 nails at every stud.

Fiber Cement Lap Siding Installation

1. Install felt or other water-resistive material behind fiber cement lap siding.
2. Install vertical siding joints by: (a) placing them over framing and sealing them with caulk, or (b) covering them with a joint cover, or (c) placing the vertical joint over a strip of flashing.
3. Lap horizontal siding courses at least (≥) 1 ¼ inches.
4. Use two 6d corrosion-resistant nails per stud, if face nailing.
5. Use one 6d galvanized box nail or one 1 ½ inches long, 11 gage galvanized roofing nail per stud, if concealed (blind) nailing directly to studs.

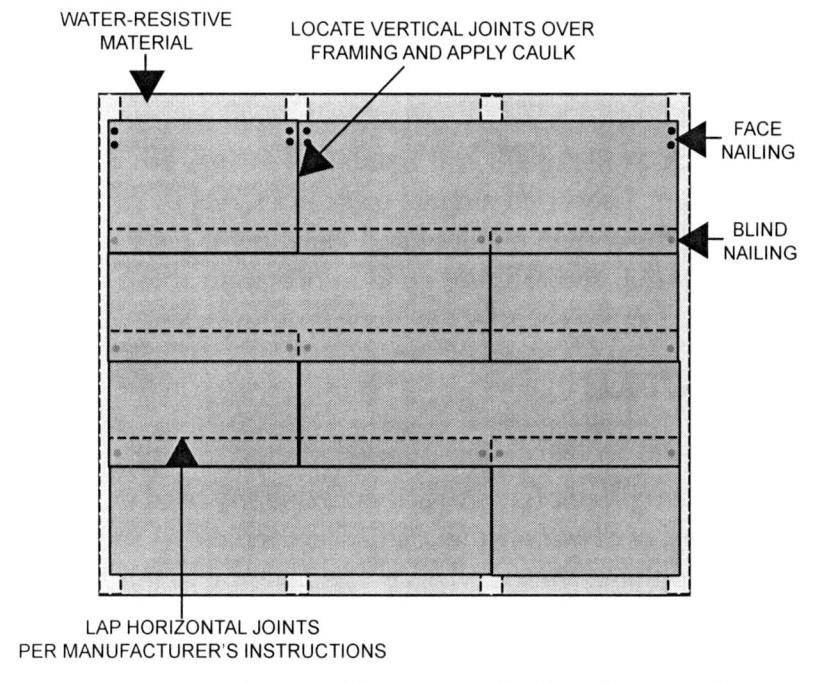

Horizontal Lap Siding Installation (R703-2)
Figure 7-5

Aluminum and Vinyl Siding Installation

1. Install vinyl and aluminum siding according to the manufacturer's instructions.
2. Install felt or other water-resistive material behind aluminum and vinyl siding.
3. Use J channels or other materials provided by the siding manufacturer around wall penetrations including windows, doors, plumbing pipes, exhaust ducts, and utilities.
4. Use aluminum nails to install aluminum siding. Use nails with at least (≥) 0.120 inch shank diameter and at least (≥) 1 ½ inches long when attaching to wood structural panel sheath-

ing or to foam plastic sheathing. Use nails long enough to penetrate studs at least (≥) 1 1/2-inches.

5. Use fasteners recommended by the siding manufacturer to install vinyl siding. The type of fastener will depend on the type of exterior wall sheathing (wood structural panels or foam plastic), the presence or absence of drywall on the interior wall, and the design wind pressure where the building is located.

6. You may use staples to attach vinyl siding. Use staples with between 3/8 and 1/2-inch crown and at least (≥) 16 gage. Use staples long enough to penetrate studs or wood structural panel sheathing at least (≥) ¾ inch, if approved by the siding manufacturer.

7. Install fasteners in every stud or as specified by the siding manufacturer.

8. Do not attach aluminum and vinyl siding directly to the studs. Attach siding to sheathing applied over studs.

Moisture Barrier and Vapor Retarder Discussion

The terms moisture barrier and vapor retarder are sometimes used to describe the same material. It is sometimes, but not always, true that one material is both a moisture barrier and a vapor retarder. A moisture barrier stops the flow of liquid water and a vapor retarder stops the flow of water vapor (moisture contained as a gas in the air). Polyethylene sheeting is both a water barrier and a Class I vapor retarder. No. 15 asphalt felt, Grade D paper, and some house wraps, such as Tyvek, are moisture barriers, but are not vapor retarders. Some types of asphalt saturated Kraft paper, such as fiberglass batt insulation facing, are a Class II vapor retarder but are not moisture barriers. Latex and enamel paint is a Class III vapor retarder, but is not a moisture barrier. Selecting the correct material and installing it correctly is critical to avoiding problems such as rot and mold. You can find good information about the proper selection and use of moisture barriers and vapor retarders at www.buildingscience.com.

STUCCO APPLICATION (R703.6)

Limitations of the Material in this Section

Traditional three-coat cement plaster (stucco) is less frequently used in many parts of the country because of the lower cost of newer synthetic stucco materials. As such, we will not deal with the rules for mixing and applying cement plaster. The material in this section addresses issues common to synthetic and traditional stucco.

Water-Resistive Barrier General Installation Requirements

1. Install at least (≥) 2 layers of 60 minute Grade D paper over wood sheathed walls that will receive an exterior stucco finish You may use other approved water-resistive material, such as some house wraps, that provides at least the same performance as 2 layers of 60 minute Grade D paper. Note that No. 15 felt and Grade D paper are not the same material and cannot be substituted for each other.

2. Install Grade D paper horizontally with horizontal joints lapped at least (≥) 2 inches and with the top layer lapped over the lower layer. Lap vertical joints at least (≥) 6 inches. Install other approved water-resistive material according to manufacturer's instructions. Install Grade D paper and other water-resistive materials beginning at the top of the wall and ending at an appropriate drainage point. See illustration R703.7-1.

3. Install flashing and other means to capture and drain any water that penetrates behind the exterior wall covering material. Such methods may include weep holes, weep screeds, or other openings at the bottom of the wall covering material.
4. You need not install water-resistive material: (a) over concrete and masonry walls that are built and flashed according to the requirements in Chapters 6 and 7, and (b) at detached accessory buildings.

Lath and Paper Installation

1. Use only corrosion-resistant lath.
2. Use at least (≥) 1 ½ inch long, 11 gage, 7/16 inch head nails or use 7/8 inch long, 16 gage, staples to secure the lath. Place nails or staples not more than (≤) 6 inches on center.
3. You may use other approved fasteners and spacing depending on the type of sheathing and lath used.

Weep Screed Materials and Installation

1. Install a corrosion-resistant metal or a plastic weep screed with at least a (≥) 3 ½ inches high vertical attachment flange at or below the sill plate line on exterior walls.
2. Place the weep screed at least (≥) 4 inches above the earth or 2 inches above paved surfaces.
3. Lap the water-resistive paper over the vertical attachment flange so that any water that penetrates the stucco will drain out the holes in the weep screed.
4. Do not cover the weep screed holes with stucco or other materials.

Artificial Stone Veneer Installation

1. Install a water-resistive barrier behind artificial stone veneer using the same procedures as for stucco.
2. Install artificial stone according to manufacturer's instructions.

Stucco Curing

1. Keep every stucco coat moist for at least (≥) 48 hours after application. This may be done by applying a light spray of water on the curing stucco. Keeping stucco moist helps avoid shrinkage cracking.
2. Apply a stucco finish coat at least (≥) 7 days after application of the previous coat.

Stucco Water Penetration Discussion

Moisture will penetrate behind stucco at some point during the building's life. There is no practical way to avoid it. Proper installation of a water-resistive barrier in combination with penetration (window and door) flashing and the weep screed provides a means to drain the water harmlessly away from the vulnerable wood framing.

Stucco Installation Best Practice

Consider using a ribbed stucco house wrap instead of Grade D paper or paper-backed lath. Stucco can adhere to a flat building paper and eliminate the drainage plane that allows the moisture to drain to the weep screed. Water that remains too long on the flat paper can degrade the paper and allow water to penetrate into the wall. Ribbed stucco house wrap provides grooves that let the moisture escape. Verify if local building official accepts house wrap instead of or in addition to other water-resistive barriers.

MASONRY (BRICK) AND STONE VENEER (R703.7)

Water-Resistive Barrier General Installation Requirements

1. Install a water-resistive barrier over all sheathing covered by masonry and stone veneer. This includes wood-based sheathing and foam plastic sheathing.

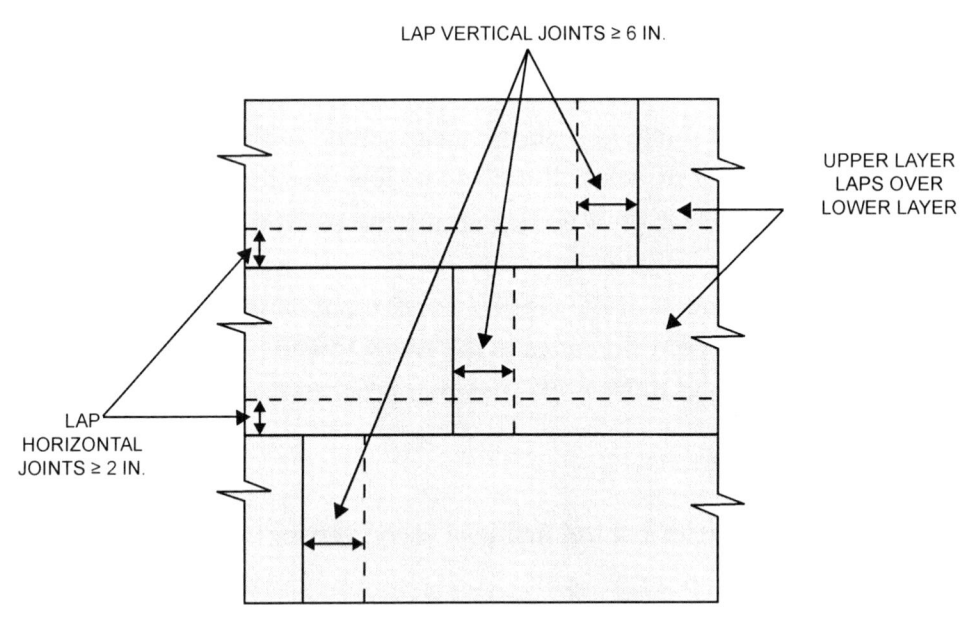

Water-Resistive Barrier Installation (R703.7-1)
Figure 7-6

Flashing for Masonry and Stone Veneer Locations and Installation

1. Install flashing for masonry and stone veneer at:
   a) the first course above finished ground level, and
   b) structural floors, and
   c) above and below window and door openings, and
   d) all veneer wall and roof intersections such as chimneys and where veneer is supported by steel angles.
2. Lap water-resistive paper over the top of flashing covered by veneer such as at the finished ground level flashing and at the flashing above openings.
3. Install base and counter flashing at veneer wall flashing such as at chimneys and steel angles.

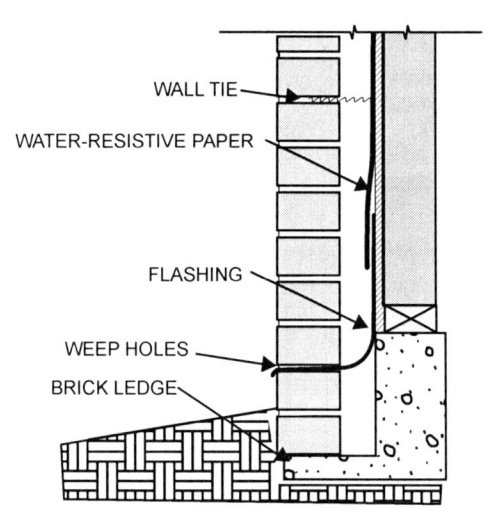

Brick Flashing at Foundation and Floors (R703.7-2)
Figure 7-7

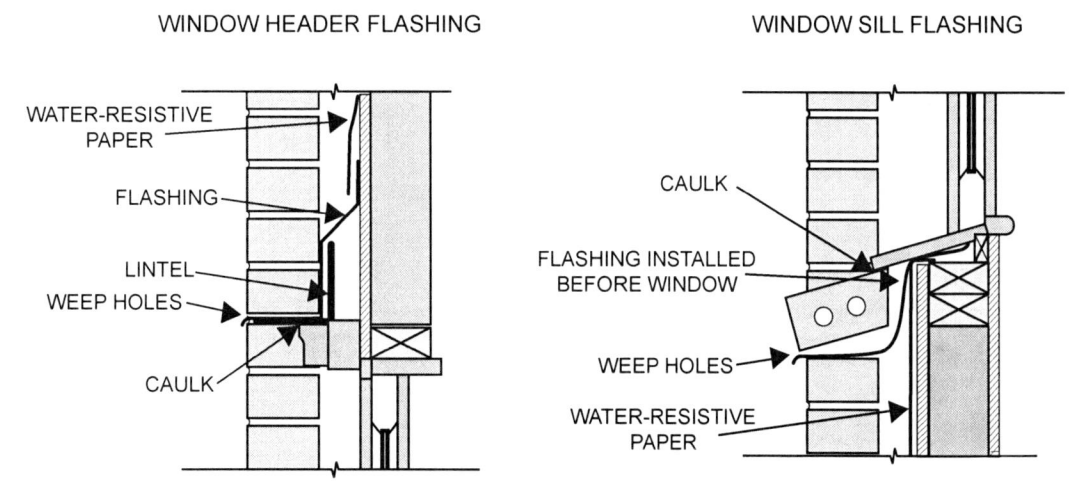

Brick Window Flashing (R703.7-3)
Figure 7-8

Weep Holes at Flashing

1. Install weep holes at all masonry and stone veneer flashing points so that allow water can escape.
2. Install the weep holes at the bottom part of the flashing.
3. Make weep holes at least (≥) 3/16 inch diameter and space them not more than (≤) 33 inches on center.

Air Space Between Masonry and Stone Veneer and Sheathing

1. Provide an air space between masonry and stone veneer and sheathing of between at least (≥) 1 inch and not more than (≤) 4 ½ inches. This is the most common method of applying masonry and stone veneer in residential construction.
2. You may fill the air space completely with mortar or grout as an alternative to providing the air space. Install water-resistive paper or liquid-water-resistive house wrap over studs and

sheathing when filling the airspace or you may attach approved wire mesh or paper-backed reinforcement directly to the studs.

Wall Anchors (Ties) for Masonry and Stone Veneer

1. Anchor masonry and stone veneer to the building wall using corrugated metal wall ties or other approved methods, to provide lateral support.
2. Extend metal wall ties at least (≥) 1 ½ inches into the mortar and leave at least (≥) 5/8 inch of mortar covering the outside edge of the wall tie.
3. Space wall ties not more than (≤) 24 inches on center horizontally and space wall ties vertically so that they support not more than (≤) 2.67 square feet of veneer.
4. Place additional wall ties around openings (greater than 16 inches in either direction) not more than (≤) 3 feet on center and not more than (≤) 12 inches from the opening.
5. Support not more than (≤) 2 square feet of veneer in seismic and high wind areas.
6. Do not exceed (≤) a 1 inch air space between wood framing and the veneer when using corrugated metal wall ties.
7. Do not exceed (≤) 4 ½ inches air space between wood framing and the veneer when using metal strand wire ties.

Masonry and Stone Veneer Height Limits

1. Build masonry and stone veneer walls not more than (≤) 30 feet above the non-combustible foundation plus 8 feet at wall ends such as gable ends. This height limit assumes that the veneer is applied over wood or steel framing. Other restrictions and requirements apply in the D and E seismic design areas.

Masonry and Stone Veneer Support by Framing General Requirements

1. You may use wood or steel framing to support masonry and stone veneer, except in seismic design areas. Example: a one-story roof (such as a garage roof) intersects with an adjacent second story sidewall (such as the second story of the home).
2. Do not exceed (≤) 40 pounds per square foot for the installed weight of the masonry or stone veneer over wood or steel framing. Most commercially available brick veneer satisfies this requirement.
3. Provide a movement joint between veneer supported by framing and veneer supported by the foundation.

Masonry and Stone Veneer Support by Steel Angle

1. You may use a steel angle attached to a framed sidewall to provide the structural support for masonry and stone veneer. The wall framing provides the support in this case.
2. Frame the wall to which the angle will be attached using at least (≥) 2x4 double studs spaced not more than (≤) 16 inches on center.
3. Use at least (≥) a 6 inches by 4 inches by 5/16 inch thick steel angle and place the long side vertically.

4. Attach the angle to each double stud using at least (≥) two lag screws that are at least (≥) 7/16 inch thick by 4 inches long.
5. Use washers or other spacers to leave at least (≥) 1/16 inch between the angle and the sheathing or other framing.
6. Weld stops to the angle that are at least (≥) 3 inches by 3 inches by ¼ inch thick and spaced not more than (≤) 24 inches on center, if the roof slope is at least (≥) 7/12 and not more than (≤) 12/12.
7. Do not exceed (≤) 12 feet 8 inches of masonry and stone veneer above the steel angle.

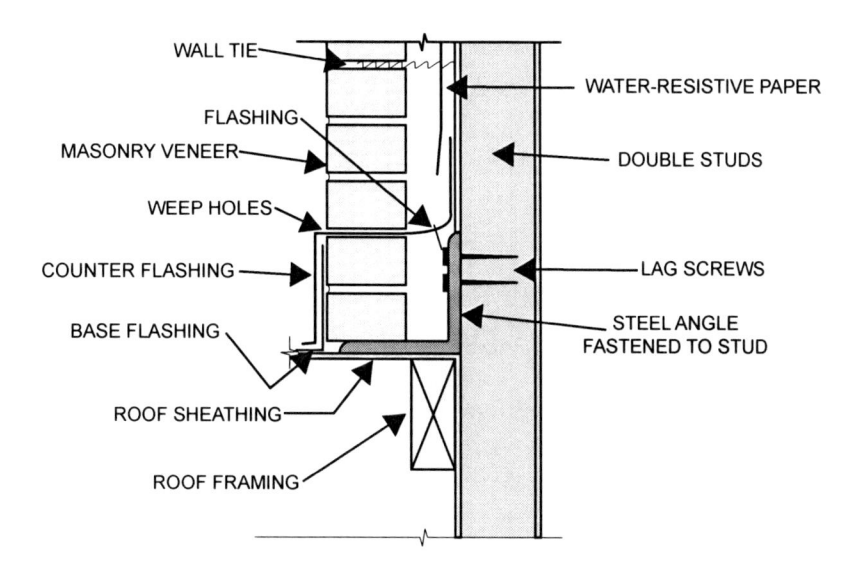

Brick Support Over Roof by Steel Angle (R703.7-4)
Figure 7-9

Masonry and Stone Veneer Support by Roof Framing

1. You may use a steel angle over framed rafters to provide structural support for masonry and stone veneer. The rafters provide structural support in this case.
2. Install at least (≥) three rafters under the veneer that are at least (≥) 2x6.
3. Attach the first rafter to each stud using at least (≥) three lag screws that are at least (≥) ⅝ inch thick by 5 inches long.
4. Attach each remaining rafter to the first rafter at each stud using at least (≥) two nails that are at least (≥) 10d.
5. Place a steel angle (no size specified) on the supporting rafters and do not attach the angle to the framing.
6. Place at least (≥) two-thirds of the veneer thickness on the angle.
7. Weld stops to the angle that are at least (≥) 3 inches by 3 inches by ¼ inch thick and spaced not more than (≤) 24 inches on center, if the roof slope is at least (≥) 7/12 and not more than (≤) 12/12.

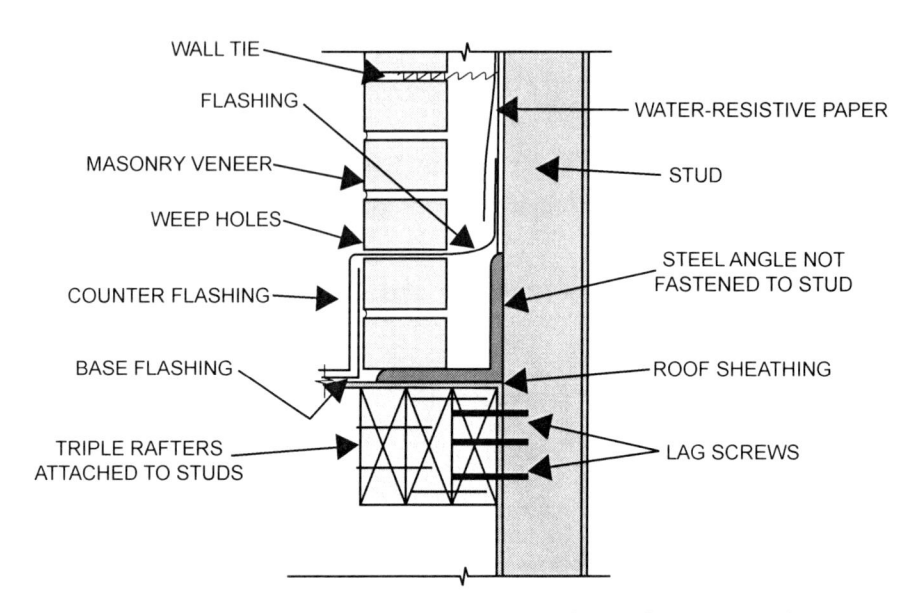

Brick Support Over Roof by Rafters (R703.7-5)
Figure 7-10

Masonry and Stone Veneer Support Over Openings (Lintels)

1. Support masonry and stone veneer over openings, such as windows and doors, by non-combustible material called a lintel. In wood-framed construction, lintels are usually "L" shaped steel and are often called angle iron. In masonry wall construction, lintels are often steel reinforced masonry.
2. Support lintels on structural supports (usually masonry on each side of the opening) bearing at least (≥) 4 inches on each side.
3. Place the lintel's long side vertically.
4. Use steel lintels that have a shop applied rust-resistant coating. You may use other approved rust-resistant lintel materials.
5. Some typical sizes and permitted clear spans for lintels are in Table R703.7. You may use other lintel sizes and spans with engineering approval.
6. You may use the following method to install a lintel with a clear opening span of not more than (≤) 18 feet – 3 inches.
    a) support the lintel on at least (≥) 18 inches of masonry on both sides, and
    b) use at least (≥) 5 inches by 3 ½ inches by 5/15 inch steel lintel, and
    c) support the lintel independently of the masonry for at least (≥) 7 days, and
    d) install double-wire joint reinforcement for at least (≥) 12 inches beyond both sides of the opening (lap any joints at least (12) inches, and use 3/16 diameter wire in the first 2 joints above the opening, or use 9 gage wire in the first 3 joints above the opening.

TABLE R703.7
Lintel Span Distances Over Openings Supporting Brick and Stone Veneer

size of angle (inches)	0 stories above feet - inches	1 story above feet - inches	2 stories above feet - inches
3 x 3 x 1/4	6 - 0	4 - 6	3 - 0
4 x 3 x 1/4	8 - 0	6 - 0	4 - 6
5 x 3.5 x 5/16	10 - 0	8 - 0	6 - 0
6 x 3.5 x 5/16	14 - 0	9 - 6	7 - 0
2-6 x 3.5 x 1/16	20 - 0	12 - 0	9 - 6

Brick and Stone Veneer Installation Discussion

Moisture will penetrate behind masonry and stone veneer at some point during the building's life. There is no practical way to avoid it. Proper installation of a water-resistive barrier combined with flashing and weep holes provides a means to drain the water harmlessly away from the vulnerable wood framing. Masonry and stone veneer provides no structural support to a building. In fact, it creates a structural load that must be carried by the foundation and by the structure's framing. It is important to support the veneer's vertical loads with proper framing and lateral loads with properly installed wall ties.

FLASHING (R703.8)

Flashing General Requirements

1. Use only corrosion-resistant flashing material. This includes fasteners or other materials used to secure the flashing.
2. Use flashing, fasteners and other materials that are compatible with each other and with surrounding materials. Incompatible materials will react with each other and degrade over time.
3. Flash and seal all openings and vulnerable areas so that moisture will not enter the structure. Flash and seal any point where moisture could enter the structure regardless of whether it is mentioned in the list of areas where flashing is specifically required.
4. Install flashing "shingle fashion" so that upper flashing laps over lower flashing resulting in a drainage plane that will drain water toward a designed discharge point.

THE WALL DRAINAGE PLANE

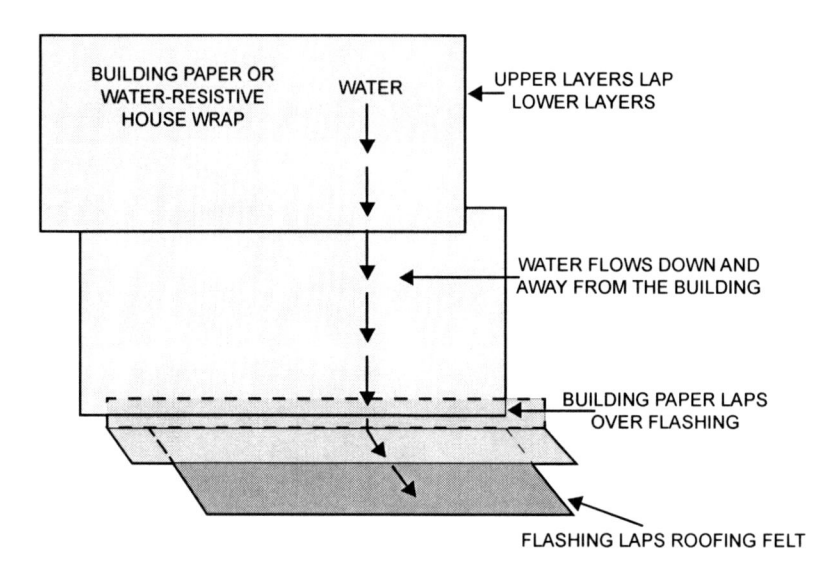

The Wall Drainage Plane (R703.8-1)
Figure 7-11

Flashing Required Locations

1. Install flashing at all window and door openings. Refer to the window manufacturer's installation instructions and to the instructions for any house wrap material.
2. Install sidewall flashing where chimneys or other masonry construction intersect with walls.
3. Install projecting lips (sometimes called kick-out flashing) at chimneys and other sidewalls where a roof and vertical sidewall intersect. Kick-out flashing helps divert water away from this vulnerable intersection.
4. Install header/sidewall flashing under and at the ends of all copings and sills including masonry, metal, and wood.
5. Install header/sidewall flashing above all wood trim that projects from the adjoining wall and forms a shelf where water can collect.
6. Install flashing at the attachment point of exterior porches, decks, balconies, stairs, or floor assemblies to wood-framed construction.
7. Install sidewall flashing at all roof and wall intersections.
8. Install flashing at all built-in gutters.

7 : Interior and Exterior Wall Covering 141

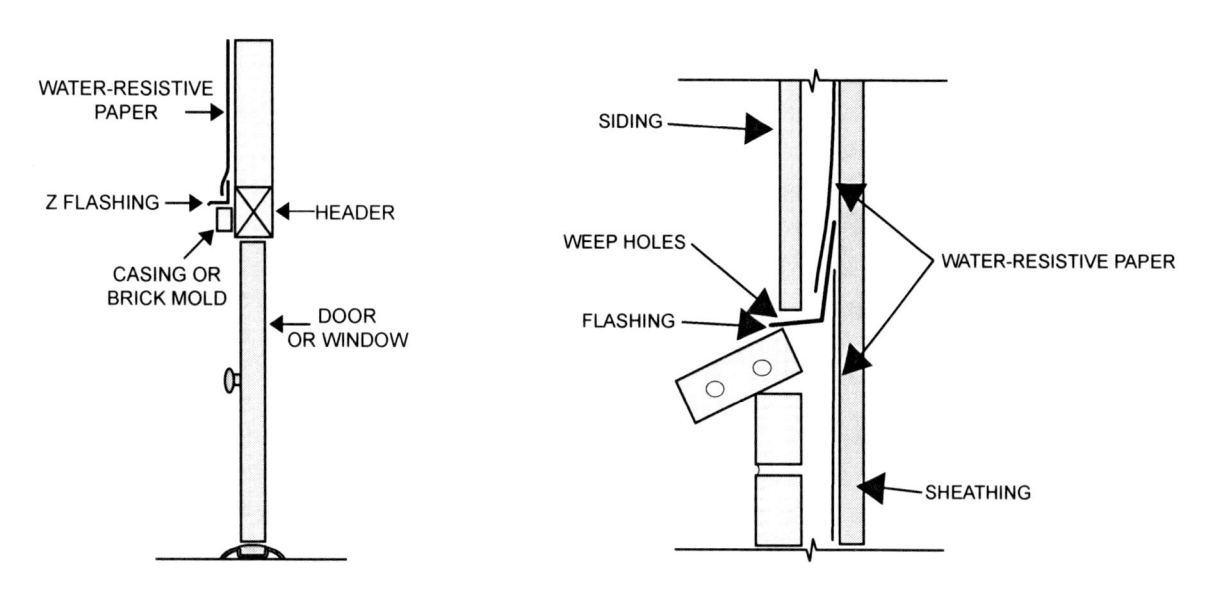

Flashing Above Doors and Windows (R703.8-2)
Figure 7-12

Flashing at Different Siding Materials (R703.8-3)
Figure 7-13

Kick-out Flashing (PR703.8-0)
Figure 7-14

Flashing Discussion

It is not possible to overstate the importance of flashing to the long-term integrity and health of the structure. Sealants such as caulk degrade over time and require maintenance. Exterior wall coverings move and crack creating gaps into which moisture can flow. Relying on building occupants to perform regular inspection and maintenance is not realistic. The best long term solution to avoiding moisture intrusion is a combination of a water-resistive building wrap and flashing integrated to form a drainage plane that prevents moisture from reaching vulnerable wood framing materials and drains the moisture away from the structure.

Flashing Best Practice

The IRC is mostly silent about how to install flashing. This leaves local building officials considerable latitude about what flashing techniques may be acceptable. The illustrations in this book present some recommended best practices. One of the best resources about flashing and water management in residential constructions is the Water Management Guide that should be available at www.eeba.org.

8

ROOF AND CEILING CONSTRUCTION

GUTTERS (R801.3)

When Gutters are Required

1. Provide gutters or other means to control roof runoff in areas with expansive or collapsible soil. Discharge the gutter water at least (≥) 5 feet away from the foundation or into an approve drainage system.

Gutters Best Practice

Install gutters on all homes at all horizontal rooflines regardless of whether they are required. Gutters help keep the foundation around the home dry. A dry foundation is less vulnerable to moisture problems such as water leaking into basements and crawl spaces or wicking up through the foundation. Dry soil is less attractive to most termites.

CEILING JOIST AND RAFTER FRAMING DETAILS (R802.3)

Ridge, Valley, and Hip Rafter Framing

1. Install at least (≥) a 1 inch (nominal thickness) ridge board at roof ridges. Install a ridge board that is at least (≥) as deep as the (plumb) cut end of the rafter. Install rafters directly across from each other at the ridge board. You may omit the ridge board if you secure the rafters to each other with a gusset plate.
2. Install at least a (≥) 2 inch (nominal thickness) hip rafter and valley rafter at all hips and valleys, including valleys formed when one roof is framed on top of another.
3. Support hip and valley rafters at the ridge with a brace to a load-bearing wall, or design the hip and valley rafters to bear the load at the ridge.
4. Toe nail rafters to the ridge and to valley and hip rafters using at least (≥) four 16d nails, or face nail rafters using at least (≥) three 16d nails. Toe nail rafters to the top plate using at least (≥) two 16d nails.
5. Design and support ridge, hip and valley rafters as beams, when the roof pitch is less than (<) 3/12.
6. Design and support the ridge as a beam and design the walls supporting the ridge board to bear the ridge board load, when framing cathedral and vaulted ceilings without ceiling joists and rafter ties.

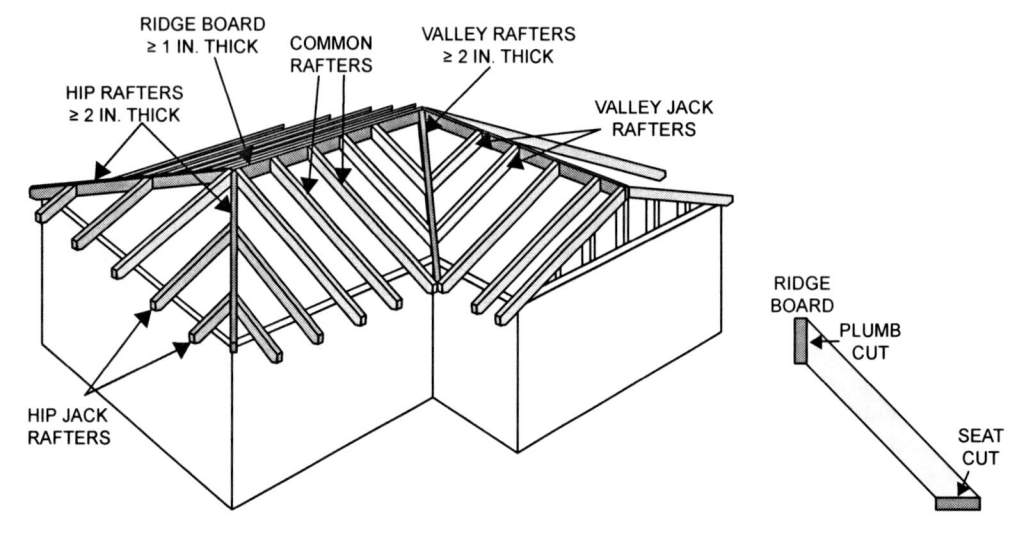

Rafter Type Names (R802.3-1)
Figure 8-1

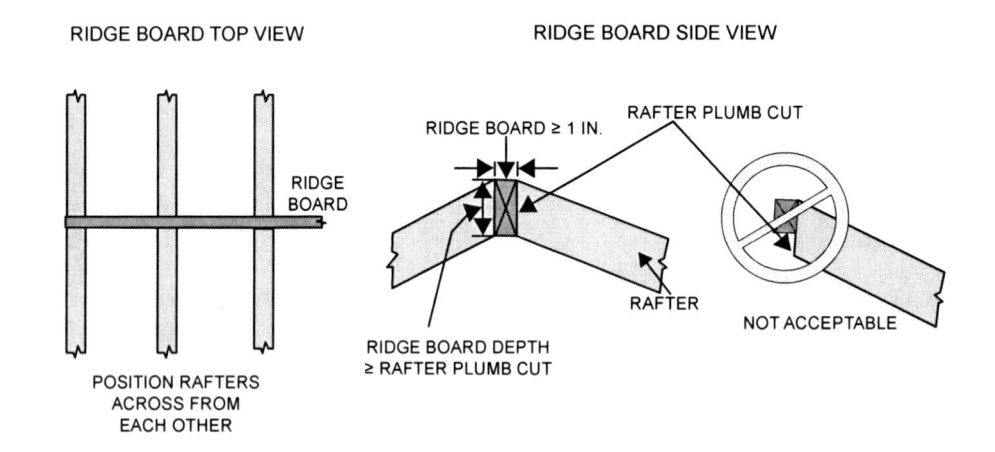

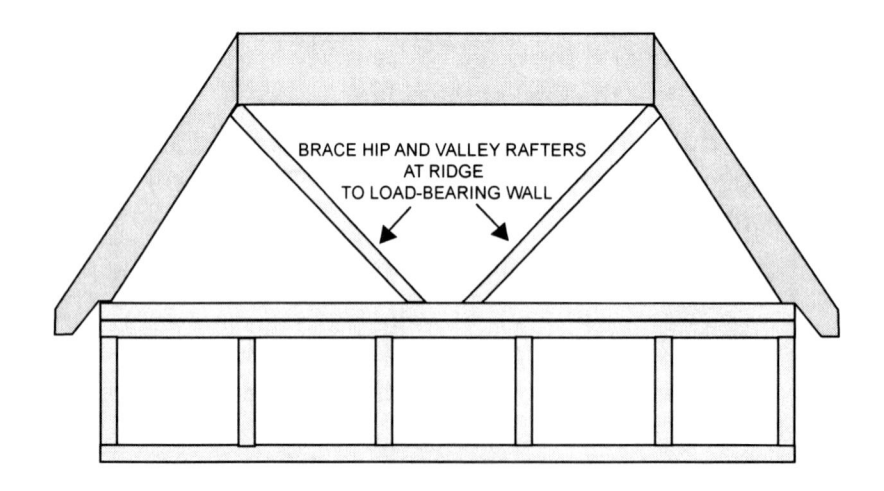

Rafter Attachment to Ridge (R802.3-2)
Figure 8-2

Purlins (802.5.1)

1. You may use purlins to support rafters that would otherwise span a greater distance than allowed by the IRC. Example: a properly installed purlin at the center of an 18 feet long rafter would allow you to use 9 feet as the rafter span distance.
2. Install purlins that are at least (≥) the same depth as the rafters they support. Example: use a 2x6 purlin to support a 2x6 rafter.
3. Use at least (≥) one 2x4 purlin brace to carry the purlin load to a load-bearing wall. The purlin brace length should not exceed (≤) 8 feet without additional bracing (usually an additional 2x4 nailed to the brace). Purlin braces should bear on a load-bearing wall and may not slope at less than (<) a 45-degree angle from horizontal. Space the purlin braces not more than (≤) 4 feet apart.

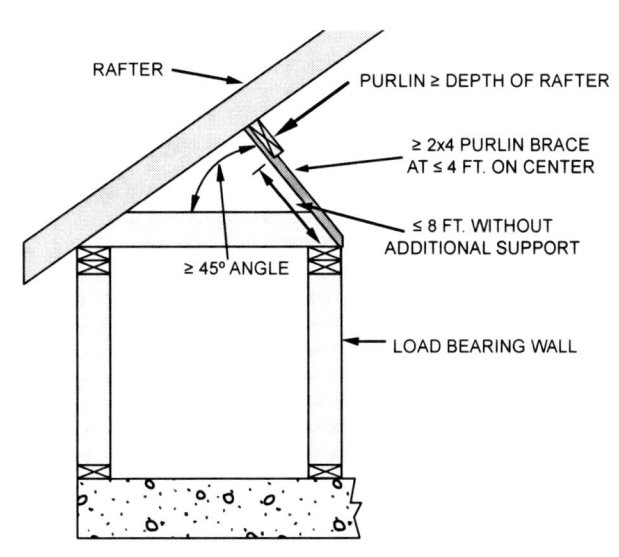

Purlins Supporting Rafters (R802.3-3)
Figure 8-3

Ceiling Joist Nailing to Rafter

1. Toe nail all rafters to the top plate using at least (≥) two 16d nails regardless of whether the rafter is or is not parallel to the ceiling joist.
2. Connect one rafter to one ceiling joist <u>when the ceiling joists are parallel to the rafters</u>. Face nail these ceiling joists to rafters using the quantity of 16d common nails or 40d box nails indicated in Table R802.3-1.
3. Connect one rafter to one rafter tie and connect the rafter tie to a ceiling joist <u>when the ceiling joists are not parallel to the rafters</u>. Face nail these rafters to rafter ties and the rafter ties to ceiling joists using the quantity of 16d common nails or 40d box nails indicated in Table R802.3-1. Use 2x4 or larger lumber for rafter ties. Connecting rafters to ceiling joists or to rafter ties helps the walls resist outward thrust pressure from the roof.
4. Lap ceiling joists that meet over interior walls or beams at least (≥) 3 inches and face nail using same quantity and type of nails indicated in Table R802.3-1. You may butt the ends of ceiling joists together over interior walls or beams and toe nail the ceiling joists to the supporting member using three 10d nails if the ceiling joists are not designed to resist rafter lateral thrust. Ceiling joists are often designed to resist rafter lateral thrust, so this butt end exception may not apply.

Ceiling Joist Nailing to Rafter Exceptions

1. Note the following exceptions to the quantity of nails required in Table R802.3-1:
   a) you may reduce the required quantity of nails by 25% if the nails are clinched (the pointed ends sticking out from the wood are bent over),
   b) you need not use Table R802.3-1 if you support the ridge board on load-bearing walls or if you design and support the ridge as a beam,
   c) you may use a smaller roof span column in Table R802.3-1 if you install purlins to support the rafters, Example: if you install purlins at the center of rafters with a roof span of 24 feet, you may reduce the roof span by 50% and use the 12 feet roof span column,
   d) you may reduce the actual rafter slope by one-third if you substitute rafter ties for ceiling joists, Example: if the actual rafter slope is 9/12, use 6/12 as the adjusted rafter slope, but because there is no 6/12 slope row, use the nearest more conservative 5/12 row,
   e) increase the quantity of nails in the table if the ceiling joists or rafter ties are not located at the bottom of the attic space, and use Table 802.3-2 to calculate the nail quantity increase. Refer to the Rafter Span Measurement and Span Adjustment for Ceiling Joist Location section for explanations and examples of how to calculate values for Table 802.3-2.

TABLE R802.3-1
Nail Quantities when Nailing Ceiling Joists and Rafter Ties to Rafters

rafter slope	rafter spacing (inches)	20 / 12	20 / 20	20 / 28	20 / 36	30 / 12	30 / 20	30 / 28	30 / 36	50 / 12	50 / 20	50 / 28	50 / 36	70 / 12	70 / 20	70 / 28	70 / 36
3/12	12	4	6	8	10	4	6	8	11	5	8	12	15	6	11	15	20
3/12	16	5	8	10	13	5	8	11	14	6	11	15	20	8	14	20	26
3/12	24	7	11	15	19	7	11	16	21	9	16	23	30	12	21	30	39
4/12	12	3	5	6	8	3	5	6	8	4	6	9	11	5	8	12	15
4/12	16	4	6	8	10	4	6	8	11	5	8	12	15	6	11	15	20
4/12	24	5	8	12	15	5	9	12	16	7	12	17	22	9	16	23	29
5/12	12	3	4	5	6	3	4	5	7	3	5	7	9	4	7	9	12
5/12	16	3	5	6	8	3	5	7	9	4	7	9	12	5	9	12	16
5/12	24	4	7	9	12	4	7	10	13	6	10	14	18	7	13	18	23
7/12	12	3	4	4	5	3	3	4	5	3	4	5	7	3	5	7	9
7/12	16	3	4	5	6	3	4	5	6	3	5	7	9	4	6	9	11
7/12	24	3	5	7	9	3	5	7	9	4	7	10	13	5	9	13	17
9/12	12	3	3	4	4	3	3	3	4	3	3	4	5	3	4	5	7
9/12	16	3	4	4	5	3	3	4	5	3	4	5	7	3	5	7	9
9/12	24	3	4	6	7	3	4	6	7	3	6	8	10	4	7	10	13
12/12	12	3	3	3	3	3	3	3	3	3	3	3	4	3	3	4	5
12/12	16	3	3	4	4	3	3	3	4	3	3	4	5	3	4	5	7
12/12	24	3	4	4	5	3	3	4	6	3	4	6	8	3	6	8	10

Column headers show ground snow load (psf) / roof span (feet): 20 psf {12, 20, 28, 36}, 30 psf {12, 20, 28, 36}, 50 psf {12, 20, 28, 36}, 70 psf {12, 20, 28, 36}.

TABLE 802.3-2
Nail Quantity Adjustment Factor when Ceiling Joists and Rafter Ties are not at the Bottom of the Attic

Hcj/Hrr	nail quantity increase factor
0.33	1.50
0.25	1.33
0.20	1.25
0.167	1.20
0.10 or less	1.11

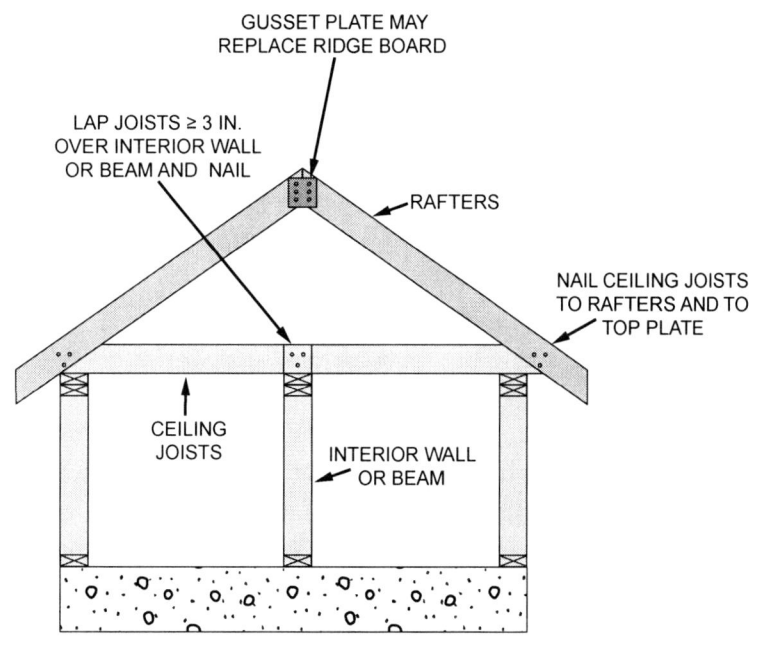

Ceiling Joists Parallel to Rafters (R802.3-4)
Figure 8-4

Collar Ties

1. Install 1x4 or larger collar ties or use a 1 ¼ inch x 20 gage ridge strap between rafters to resist ridge uplift by wind force. You may omit collar ties in vaulted and cathedral ceilings when you design and support the ridge as a beam.
2. Space collar ties not more than (≤) 4 feet on center.
3. Locate collar ties in the upper one-third of the attic space.
4. Connect collar ties and rafters using at least (≥) three 10d nails, face nailed.
5. Verify collar tie requirements with the local building official and with the Wood Frame Construction Manual in high wind design areas, and when the roof slope is less than (<) 3/12, and when the roof span is greater than (>) 36 feet.

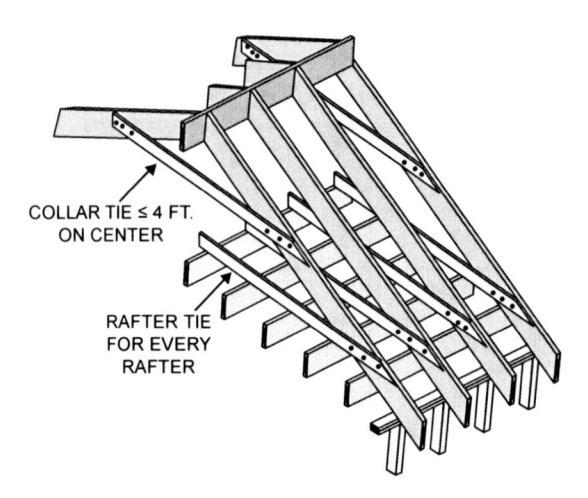

Rafter Ties and Collar Ties (R802.3-5)
Figure 8-5

Rafter and Ceiling Joist Bearing on Support

1. Install rafters and ceiling joists with at least (≥) 1 ½ inches of the rafter or joist bearing on supporting wood members(such as a top plate or a valley rafter) and at least (≥) 3 inches of the rafter or joist bearing on masonry or concrete.
2. Toe nail rafters to the top plate using at least (≥) two 16d nails.

Rafter and Ceiling Joist Bridging and Lateral Support

1. Install bridging on rafters and ceiling joists deeper than (>) 2x12 (6 to 1 depth to thickness ratio). Space bridging not more than (≤) every 8 feet. Bridging should consist of solid full depth blocking, wood or metal diagonal bridging, or by nailing at least (≥) a 1x3 wood strip to each rafter or ceiling joist. Bridging is required by some building officials on ceiling joists smaller than 2x12.
2. Install lateral support <u>at bearing points</u> (such as exterior walls and interior support walls) on rafters and ceiling joists deeper than (>) 2x10 (5 to 1 depth to thickness ratio).

CEILING JOIST AND RAFTER SPANS (R802.4 AND R802.5)

Ceiling Joist and Rafter Span Definitions

Attics without storage An attic without storage, <u>built with joists and rafters</u>, has less than (<) 42 inches between the top of the ceiling joists and the bottom of the rafters. An attic without storage, <u>built with trusses</u>, has not more than (≤) 2 adjacent trusses with the same web configuration that could contain a cube not more than (≤) 42 inches wide and 24 inches tall located in the same plane (area) of the truss.

Attic with limited storage An attic with limited storage, <u>built with joists and rafters</u>, has at least (≥) 42 inches between the top of the ceiling joists and the bottom of the rafters. An attic without storage, <u>built with trusses</u>, has at least (≥) 3 adjacent trusses with the same web configuration that could contain a cube more than (>) 42 inches wide and 24 inches tall located in the same plane (area) of the truss.

The definitions in this section determine which ceiling joist span table you should use. These definitions do not affect requirements for access to attics. Refer to Section R807 for attic access requirements. Access to attics with limited storage may be through a scuttle-hole or by pull-down stairs. If attic access is by permanent stairs, then you should consider the attic to be habitable space and you should size the joists using the bedroom floor joist span tables rather than the ceiling span joist tables.

An attic with limited storage is designed with an additional 10 pounds per square foot live load compared to an attic without storage. Verify the storage capacity of truss-built attics with the truss engineer before using the attic for storage.

Attic Storage Definition (R802.4-0)
Figure 8-6

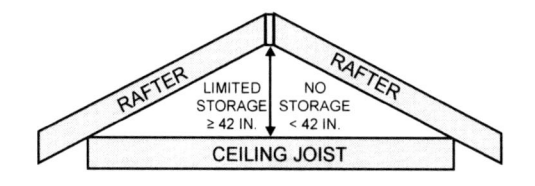

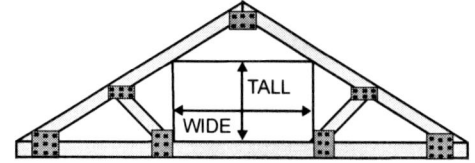

Roof live and snow load Use the roof live load 20 PSF tables in areas where the design ground snow load is less than (<) 30 PSF. Use the rafter snow load tables in areas of the country with ground snow loads of 30 PSF or more. Verify the design ground snow load with the local building official.

Rafter dead loads Use the 10 PSF rafter dead load columns when using one layer of roof coverings such as fiberglass shingles and wood. Use the 20 PSF rafter dead load columns when using roof coverings such as tile and slate.

Ceiling Joist and Rafter Deflection

1. All ceiling joist spans in the tables use L/240 deflection, where L is the length of the joist or rafter in inches divided by 240.
2. All rafter spans in the tables use L/180 deflection.

Ceiling Joist and Rafter Span Tables

1. Use the following tables to determine the maximum unsupported horizontal distance that ceiling joists and rafters can span.
2. Refer to the IRC or to the AF&PA Span Tables for Joists and Rafters to determine spans for lumber widths, species, grades, and snow load factors not in these tables.
3. These tables apply to roof systems framed using standard 2 inch (nominal thickness) dimension lumber. An engineer must design roof truss systems.

TABLE R802.4-1
Ceiling Joist Spans Sixteen Inches on Center
Uninhabitable Attics Without Storage

species	grade	2 x 6 feet-inches	2 x 8 feet-inches	2 x 10 feet-inches
douglas fir	2	17-8	23-0	>26-0
douglas fir	3	13-9	17-5	21-3
hem fir	2	16-6	21-9	>26-0
hem fir	3	13-9	17-5	21-3
southern pine	2	17-8	23-4	>26-0
southern pine	3	14-9	18-9	22-2
spruce pine fir	2	16-11	22-4	>26-0
spruce pine fir	3	13-9	17-5	21-3

TABLE R802.4-2
Ceiling Joist Spans Twenty-four Inches on Center
Uninhabitable Attics Without Storage

species	grade	2 x 6 feet-inches	2 x 8 feet-inches	2 x 10 feet-inches
douglas fir	2	14-10	18-9	22-11
douglas fir	3	11-2	14-2	17-4
hem fir	2	14-5	18-6	22-7
hem fir	3	11-2	14-2	17-4
southern pine	2	15-6	20-1	23-11
southern pine	3	12-0	15-4	18-1
spruce pine fir	2	14-9	18-9	22-11
spruce pine fir	3	11-2	14-2	17-4

TABLE R802.4-3
Ceiling Joist Spans Sixteen Inches on Center
Uninhabitable Attics With Limited Storage

species	grade	2 x 6 feet-inches	2 x 8 feet-inches	2 x 10 feet-inches
douglas fir	2	12-10	16-3	22-11
douglas fir	3	9-8	12-4	17-4
hem fir	2	12-8	16-0	22-7
hem fir	3	9-8	12-4	17-4
southern pine	2	13-6	17-5	23-11
southern pine	3	10-5	13-3	18-1
spruce pine fir	2	12-10	16-3	22-11
spruce pine fir	3	9-8	12-4	17-4

TABLE R802.4-4
Ceiling Joist Spans Twenty-four Inches on Center
Uninhabitable Attics With Limited Storage

species	grade	2 x 6 feet-inches	2 x 8 feet-inches	2 x 10 feet-inches
douglas fir	2	10-6	13-3	16-3
douglas fir	3	7-11	10-0	12-3
hem fir	2	10-4	13-1	16-0
hem fir	3	7-11	10-0	12-3
southern pine	2	11-0	14-2	16-11
southern pine	3	8-6	10-10	12-10
spruce pine fir	2	10-6	13-3	16-3
spruce pine fir	3	7-11	10-0	12-3

TABLE R802.4-5
Rafter Spans Sixteen Inches on Center
Roof Live Load 20 PSF, Ceiling not Attached to Rafters

dead load	10 psf	10 psf	10 psf	20 psf	20 psf	20 psf
species-grade	2 x 6 feet-inches	2 x 8 feet-inches	2 x 10 feet-inches	2 x 6 feet-inches	2 x 8 feet-inches	2 x 10 feet-inches
douglas fir - 2	14-4	18-2	22-3	12-5	15-9	19-3
douglas fir - 3	10-10	13-9	16-9	9-5	11-11	14-6
hem fir - 2	14-2	17-11	21-11	12-3	15-6	18-11
hem fir - 3	10-10	13-9	16-9	9-5	11-11	14-6
southern pine - 2	15-1	19-5	23-2	13-0	16-10	20-1
southern pine - 3	11-8	14-10	17-6	10-1	12-10	15-2
spruce pine fir - 2	14-4	18-2	22-3	12-5	15-9	19-3
spruce pine fir - 3	10-10	13-9	16-9	9-5	11-11	14-6

TABLE R802.4-6
Rafter Spans Twenty-four Inches on Center
Roof Live Load 20 PSF, Ceiling not Attached to Rafters

dead load	10 psf	10 psf	10 psf	20 psf	20 psf	20 psf
species-grade	2 x 6 feet-inches	2 x 8 feet-inches	2 x 10 feet-inches	2 x 6 feet-inches	2 x 8 feet-inches	2 x 10 feet-inches
douglas fir - 2	11-9	14-10	18-2	10-2	12-10	15-8
douglas fir - 3	8-10	11-3	13-8	7-8	9-9	11-10
hem fir - 2	11-7	14-8	17-10	10-0	12-8	15-6
hem fir - 3	8-10	11-3	13-8	7-8	9-9	11-10
southern pine - 2	12-3	15-10	18-11	10-8	13-9	16-5
southern pine - 3	9-6	12-1	14-4	8-3	10-6	12-5
spruce pine fir - 2	11-9	14-10	18-2	10-2	12-10	15-8
spruce pine fir - 3	8-10	11-3	13-8	7-8	9-9	11-10

TABLE R802.4-7
Rafter Spans Twenty-four Inches on Center
Roof Live Load 20 PSF, Ceiling Attached to Rafters

dead load	10 psf	10 psf	10 psf	20 psf	20 psf	20 psf
species-grade	2 x 6 feet-inches	2 x 8 feet-inches	2 x 10 feet-inches	2 x 6 feet-inches	2 x 8 feet-inches	2 x 10 feet-inches
douglas fir - 2	11-9	14-10	18-2	10-2	12-10	15-8
douglas fir - 3	8-10	11-3	13-8	7-8	9-9	11-10
hem fir - 2	11-5	14-8	17-10	10-0	12-8	15-6
hem fir - 3	8-10	11-3	13-8	7-8	9-9	11-10
southern pine - 2	12-3	15-10	18-11	10-8	13-9	16-5
southern pine - 3	9-6	12-1	14-4	8-3	10-6	12-5
spruce pine fir - 2	11-9	14-10	18-2	10-2	12-10	15-8
spruce pine fir - 3	8-10	11-3	13-8	7-8	9-9	11-10

TABLE R802.4-8
Rafter Spans Sixteen Inches on Center
Roof Live Load 20 PSF, Ceiling Attached to Rafters

dead load	10 psf	10 psf	10 psf	20 psf	20 psf	20 psf
species-grade	2 x 6 feet-inches	2 x 8 feet-inches	2 x 10 feet-inches	2 x 6 feet-inches	2 x 8 feet-inches	2 x 10 feet-inches
douglas fir - 2	14-1	18-2	22-3	12-5	15-9	19-3
douglas fir - 3	10-10	13-9	16-9	9-5	11-11	14-6
hem fir - 2	13-1	17-3	21-11	12-3	15-6	18-11
hem fir - 3	10-10	13-9	16-9	9-5	11-11	14-6
southern pine - 2	14-1	18-6	23-2	13-0	16-10	20-1
southern pine - 3	11-8	14-10	17-6	10-1	12-10	15-2
spruce pine fir - 2	13-5	17-9	22-3	12-5	15-9	19-3
spruce pine fir - 3	10-10	13-9	16-9	9-5	11-11	14-6

TABLE R802.4-9
Rafter Spans Sixteen Inches on Center
Ground Snow Load 30 PSF, Ceiling not Attached to Rafters

dead load	10 psf	10 psf	10 psf	20 psf	20 psf	20 psf
species-grade	2 x 6 feet-inches	2 x 8 feet-inches	2 x 10 feet-inches	2 x 6 feet-inches	2 x 8 feet-inches	2 x 10 feet-inches
douglas fir - 2	11-11	15-1	18-5	10-8	13-6	16-6
douglas fir - 3	9-0	11-5	13-11	8-1	10-3	12-6
hem fir - 2	11-9	14-11	18-2	10-6	13-4	16-3
hem fir - 3	9-0	11-5	13-11	8-1	10-3	12-6
southern pine - 2	12-6	16-2	19-3	11-2	14-5	17-3
southern pine - 3	9-8	12-4	14-7	8-8	11-0	13-0
spruce pine fir - 2	11-11	15-1	18-5	10-8	13-6	16-6
spruce pine fir - 3	9-0	11-5	13-11	8-1	10-3	12-6

TABLE R802.4-10
Rafter Spans Twenty-four Inches on Center
Ground Snow Load 30 PSF, Ceiling not Attached to Rafters

dead load	10 psf	10 psf	10 psf	20 psf	20 psf	20 psf
species-grade	2 x 6 feet-inches	2 x 8 feet-inches	2 x 10 feet-inches	2 x 6 feet-inches	2 x 8 feet-inches	2 x 10 feet-inches
douglas fir - 2	9-9	12-4	15-1	8-8	11-0	13-6
douglas fir - 3	7-4	9-4	11-5	6-7	8-4	10-2
hem fir - 2	9-7	12-2	14-10	8-7	10-10	13-3
hem fir - 3	7-4	9-4	11-5	6-7	8-4	10-2
southern pine - 2	10-2	13-2	15-9	9-2	11-9	14-1
southern pine - 3	7-11	10-1	11-1	7-1	9-0	10-8
spruce pine fir - 2	9-9	12-4	15-1	8-8	11-0	13-6
spruce pine fir - 3	7-4	9-4	11-5	6-7	8-4	10-2

TABLE R802.4-11
Rafter Spans Sixteen Inches on Center
Ground Snow Load 30 PSF, Ceiling Attached to Rafters

dead load	10 psf	10 psf	10 psf	20 psf	20 psf	20 psf
species-grade	2 x 6 feet-inches	2 x 8 feet-inches	2 x 10 feet-inches	2 x 6 feet-inches	2 x 8 feet-inches	2 x 10 feet-inches
douglas fir - 2	11-11	15-1	18-5	10-8	13-6	16-6
douglas fir - 3	9-0	11-5	13-11	8-1	10-3	12-6
hem fir - 2	11-5	14-11	18-2	10-6	13-4	16-3
hem fir - 3	9-0	11-5	13-11	8-1	10-3	12-6
southern pine - 2	12-3	16-2	19-3	11-2	14-5	17-3
southern pine - 3	9-8	12-4	14-7	8-8	11-10	13-0
spruce pine fir - 2	11-9	15-1	18-5	10-8	13-6	16-6
spruce pine fir - 3	9-0	11-5	13-11	8-1	10-3	12-6

TABLE R802.4-12
Rafter Spans Twenty-four Inches on Center
Ground Snow Load 30 PSF, Ceiling Attached to Rafters

dead load	10 psf	10 psf	10 psf	20 psf	20 psf	20 psf
species-grade	2 x 6 feet-inches	2 x 8 feet-inches	2 x 10 feet-inches	2 x 6 feet-inches	2 x 8 feet-inches	2 x 10 feet-inches
douglas fir - 2	9-9	12-4	15-1	8-8	11-0	13-6
douglas fir - 3	7-4	9-4	11-5	6-7	8-4	10-2
hem fir - 2	9-7	12-2	14-10	8-7	10-10	13-3
hem fir - 3	7-4	9-4	11-5	6-7	8-4	10-2
southern pine - 2	10-2	13-2	15-9	9-2	11-9	14-1
southern pine - 3	7-11	10-1	11-11	7-1	9-0	10-8
spruce pine fir - 2	9-9	12-4	15-1	8-8	11-0	13-6
spruce pine fir - 3	7-4	9-4	11-5	6-7	8-4	10-2

TABLE R802.4-13
Rafter Spans Sixteen Inches on Center
Ground Snow Load 50 PSF, Ceiling not Attached to Rafters

dead load	10 psf	10 psf	10 psf	20 psf	20 psf	20 psf
species-grade	2 x 6 feet-inches	2 x 8 feet-inches	2 x 10 feet-inches	2 x 6 feet-inches	2 x 8 feet-inches	2 x 10 feet-inches
douglas fir - 2	9-9	12-4	15-1	9-0	11-5	13-11
douglas fir - 3	7-4	9-4	11-5	6-10	8-8	10-6
hem fir - 2	9-7	12-2	14-10	8-11	11-3	13-9
hem fir - 3	7-4	9-4	11-5	6-10	8-8	10-6
southern pine - 2	12-2	13-2	15-9	9-5	12-2	14-7
southern pine - 3	7-11	10-1	11-11	7-4	9-4	11-0
spruce pine fir - 2	9-9	12-4	15-1	9-0	11-5	13-11
spruce pine fir - 3	9-9	12-4	15-1	6-10	8-8	10-6

TABLE R802.4-14
Rafter Spans Twenty-four Inches on Center
Ground Snow Load 50 PSF, Ceiling not Attached to Rafters

dead load	10 psf	10 psf	10 psf	20 psf	20 psf	20 psf
species-grade	2 x 6 feet-inches	2 x 8 feet-inches	2 x 10 feet-inches	2 x 6 feet-inches	2 x 8 feet-inches	2 x 10 feet-inches
douglas fir - 2	7-11	10-1	12-4	7-4	9-4	11-5
douglas fir - 3	6-0	7-7	9-4	5-7	7-1	8-7
hem fir - 2	7-10	9-11	12-1	7-3	9-2	11-3
hem fir - 3	6-0	7-7	9-4	5-7	7-1	8-7
southern pine - 2	8-4	10-9	12-10	7-9	10-0	11-11
southern pine - 3	6-5	8-3	9-9	6-0	7-7	9-0
spruce pine fir - 2	7-11	10-1	12-4	7-4	9-4	11-5
spruce pine fir - 3	6-0	7-7	9-4	5-7	7-1	8-7

TABLE R802.4-15
Rafter Spans Sixteen Inches on Center
Ground Snow Load 50 PSF, Ceiling Attached to Rafters

dead load	10 psf	10 psf	10 psf	20 psf	20 psf	20 psf
species-grade	2 x 6 feet-inches	2 x 8 feet-inches	2 x 10 feet-inches	2 x 6 feet-inches	2 x 8 feet-inches	2 x 10 feet-inches
douglas fir - 2	9-9	12-4	15-1	9-0	11-5	13-11
douglas fir - 3	7-4	9-4	11-5	6-10	8-8	10-6
hem fir - 2	9-7	12-2	14-10	8-11	13-3	13-9
hem fir - 3	7-4	9-4	11-5	6-10	8-8	10-6
southern pine - 2	10-2	13-2	15-9	9-5	12-2	14-7
southern pine - 3	7-11	10-1	11-11	7-4	9-4	11-0
spruce pine fir - 2	9-9	12-4	15-1	9-0	11-5	13-11
spruce pine fir - 3	7-4	9-4	11-5	6-10	8-8	10-6

TABLE R802.4-16
Rafter Spans Twenty-four Inches on Center
Ground Snow Load 50 PSF, Ceiling Attached to Rafters

dead load	10 psf	10 psf	10 psf	20 psf	20 psf	20 psf
species-grade	2 x 6 feet-inches	2 x 8 feet-inches	2 x 10 feet-inches	2 x 6 feet-inches	2 x 8 feet-inches	2 x 10 feet-inches
douglas fir - 2	7-11	10-1	12-4	7-4	9-4	11-5
douglas fir - 3	6-0	7-7	9-4	5-7	7-1	8-7
hem fir - 2	7-10	9-11	12-1	7-3	9-2	11-3
hem fir - 3	6-0	7-7	9-4	5-7	7-1	8-7
southern pine - 2	8-4	10-9	12-10	7-9	10-0	11-11
southern pine - 3	6-5	8-3	9-9	6-0	7-7	9-0
spruce pine fir - 2	7-11	10-1	12-4	7-4	9-4	11-5
spruce pine fir - 3	6-0	7-7	9-4	5-7	7-1	8-7

Rafter Span Measurement and Span Adjustment for Ceiling Joist Location

1. Measure common rafter spans horizontally beginning at the exterior wall and ending at the ridge board. Measure jack rafter spans horizontally beginning at the hip or valley rafter and ending at the ridge board. Do not measure rafter spans along the actual length of the rafter.

2. The rafter span tables assume that ceiling joists or rafter ties are located at or near the wall top plate. If the ceiling joists or rafter ties are located higher on the rafter, reduce the rafter spans in the tables using the following method. Measure the height of the ceiling joists or rafter ties above the top plate. This is the (H^{CJ}). Measure the height of the ridge board above the top plate. This is the (H^{RR}). Divide (H^{CJ}) by (H^{RR}) to calculate the ratio of the vertical height of the ceiling joists or rafter ties (H^{CJ}) to the vertical height of the roof ridge (H^{RR}). Reduce the rafter spans by the factor in the following table.

TABLE R802.4-17
Rafter Span Reduction for Ceiling Joist Location

H^{CJ} / H^{RR}	rafter span distance reduction factor
0.33	0.67
0.25	0.76
0.20	0.83
0.167	0.90
0.133 or less	1.00

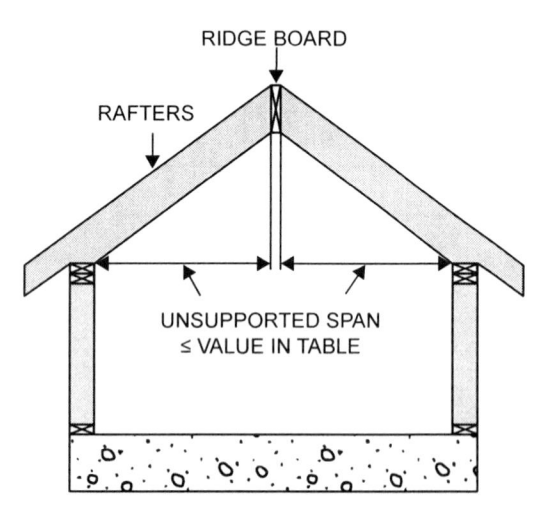

Rafter Span Distance Measurement (R802.5-1) Figure 8-7

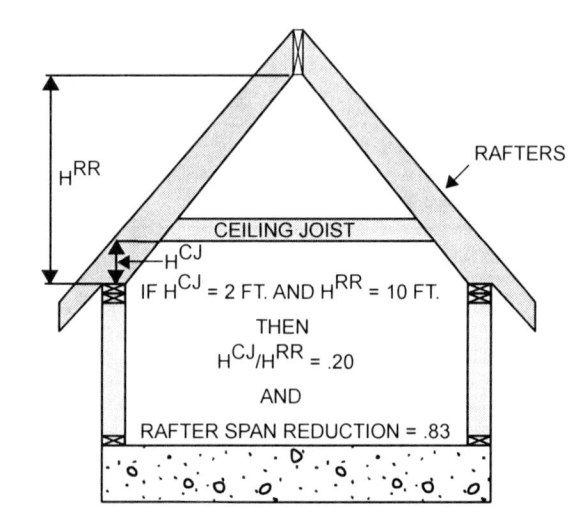

Rafter Span Distance Reduction for Ceiling Joist Location (R802.5-2) Figure 8-8

CEILING JOIST AND RAFTER BORING AND NOTCHING (R802.7)

Boring and Notching Definition

Bore A bore is a hole drilled in a stud or joist. Use the actual dimensions to determine the depth of framing lumber and when calculating the maximum hole diameter.

Notch A notch is a piece cut from the smaller dimension of framing lumber such as a stud or joist. Use the actual dimensions to determine the depth of framing lumber and when calculating the maximum notch depth. Actual dimensions are the dimensions of framing lumber after finishing at the mill. Example: the nominal dimensions of a 2x6 are 2 inches by 6 inches and the actual dimensions, after finishing, are about 1 ½ inches by 5 ½ inches.

Ceiling Joist and Rafter Notching

1. Notch dimension lumber ceiling joists, rafters, blocking, and beams not deeper than (≤) one-sixth of the depth of the member. You may notch the end of the member not deeper than (≤) one-quarter of the depth of the member. Notch the member not longer than (≤) one-third of the depth of the member. Do not place any notches in the middle one-third of the member. Example: notch a 2x8 ceiling joist not more than (≤) 1 ¼ inches deep and not more than (≤) 2 ½ inches long, except at the end where you may notch it not more than (≤) 1 7/8 inches deep.
2. Notch the tension side (bottom) of a ceiling joist, rafter, or beam that is more than (>) 4 inches thick only at the ends.
3. You may notch the cantilever portion of rafters (rafter tails) if the remaining rafter wood is at least (≥) 4 inches deep and the cantilever length is not more than (≤) 24 inches.

Ceiling Joist and Rafter Boring

1. Bore holes in dimension lumber ceiling joists, rafters, and beams not more than (≤) one-third of the depth of the member. Place holes at least (≥) 2 inches from the edge of the member and at least (≥) 2 inches from the edge of any other hole or notch. Example: bore a hole in a 2x6 rafter not more than (≤)1 7/8 inches in diameter.

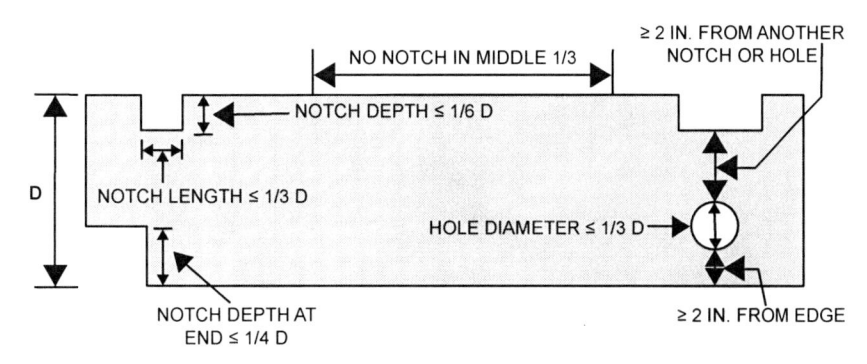

Ceiling Joist and Rafter Notching and Boring (R802.7-0)
Figure 8-9

I-Beam Ceiling Joist and Rafter Notching and Boring

1. Notch and bore wood I-Beam ceiling joists and rafters only according to manufacturer's instructions.
2. Do not notch the top and bottom flange unless allowed by the manufacturer.
3. Bore holes in the middle third of the span and not near the ends unless allowed by the manufacturer.

Roof Truss Notching and Boring

1. Do not notch or bore wood roof trusses unless specifically permitted in writing by the manufacturer or by an engineer.

Engineered Wood Notching and Boring

1. Do not notch or bore laminated veneer lumber and glue-laminated lumber unless specifically permitted in writing by the manufacturer or by an engineer.

CEILING JOIST AND RAFTER OPENINGS (R802.9)

Joist and Rafter Openings Description

Common reasons for openings in ceiling joists and rafters include openings for attic access (scuttle holes and pull-down stairs), openings for whole house fans and skylights, and framing for dormers or similar structures. The header joists distribute the load of the tail joists to the trimmer joists.

Openings Not More than (≤) Four Feet Wide

1. Install double trimmer joists on both sides of header joists. You may use a single trimmer joist on both sides of the header joists if the header is not more than (≤) 3 feet from the trimmer bearing point.
2. You may use a single header joist if the header joist span is not more than (≤) 4 feet wide.

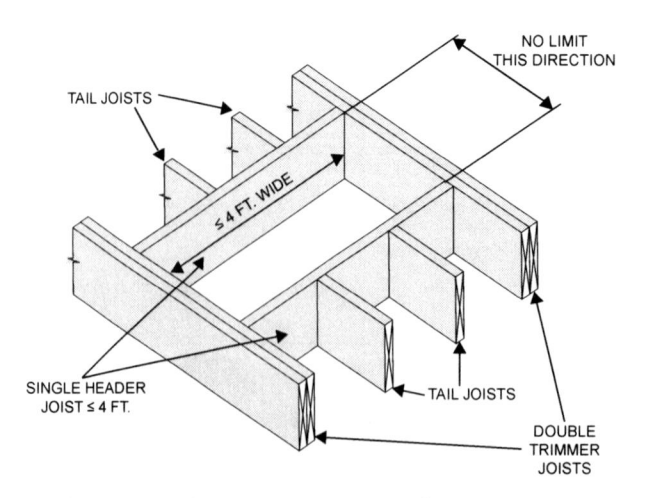

Rafter and Ceiling Joist Openings Not More than Four Feet Wide (R802.9-1)
Figure 8-10

Openings More than (>) Four Feet Wide

1. Install double trimmer joists and header joists if the header joist span is more than (>) 4 feet wide.
2. Install approved joist hangers to connect header joists to trimmer joists if the header joist span is more than (>) 6 feet wide.
3. Install approved joist hangers or a 2x2 ledger strip to connect tail joists to header joists if the tail joists are more than (>) 12 feet long.

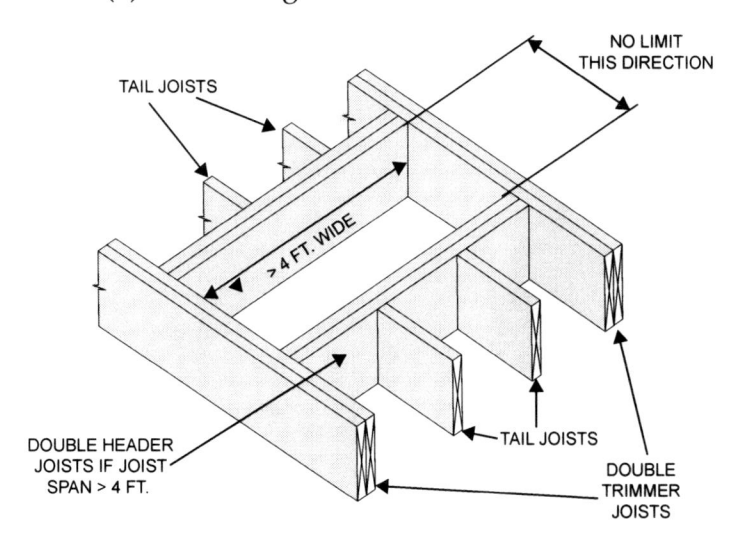

Rafter and Ceiling Joist Openings More than Four Feet Wide (R802.9-2)
Figure 8-11

WOOD TRUSS INSTALLATION AND BRACING (R802.10)

Truss Design and Bracing Written Specifications Requirements

1. Use a qualified engineer to design all wood trusses such as roof and floor trusses. The engineer and/or truss manufacturer should provide written truss design and installation specifications and deliver them to the job site with the trusses. These specifications should include engineering information, such as chord live and dead loads, and assembly information, such as the size, species, and grade of each truss member, and installation instructions, such as where each truss should be located on the structure and how the trusses should be permanently braced.

Truss Installation Tolerance Recommendations

1. Install trusses according to the installation tolerances contained in the written truss specifications. Use the following installation tolerances from the booklet Guide to Good Practice for Handling, Installation & Bracing of Metal Plate Connected Wood Trusses (BCSI-2008) only if the engineer and/or truss manufacturer does not provide installation instructions. The IRC does not specifically require installation to these tolerances; however, installation to these tolerances is implied by the general IRC requirement that components be installed according to manufacturer's installation instructions.

2. Install trusses so that a bow in either the top or bottom chord is not more than (≤) L/200 or 2 inches, whichever is less. L is the length of the truss chord in inches.
3. Install trusses that are out-of-plumb (vertical) by not more than (≤) D/50 or 2 inches, whichever is less. D is the depth of the truss in inches at the point of measurement.
4. Install trusses at load-bearing points not more than (≤) ¼ inch from the location on the plans.
5. Install trusses that use the top chord as the weight bearing point with a gap of not more than (≤) ½ inch between the inside of the load bearing support and the first diagonal or vertical truss web.

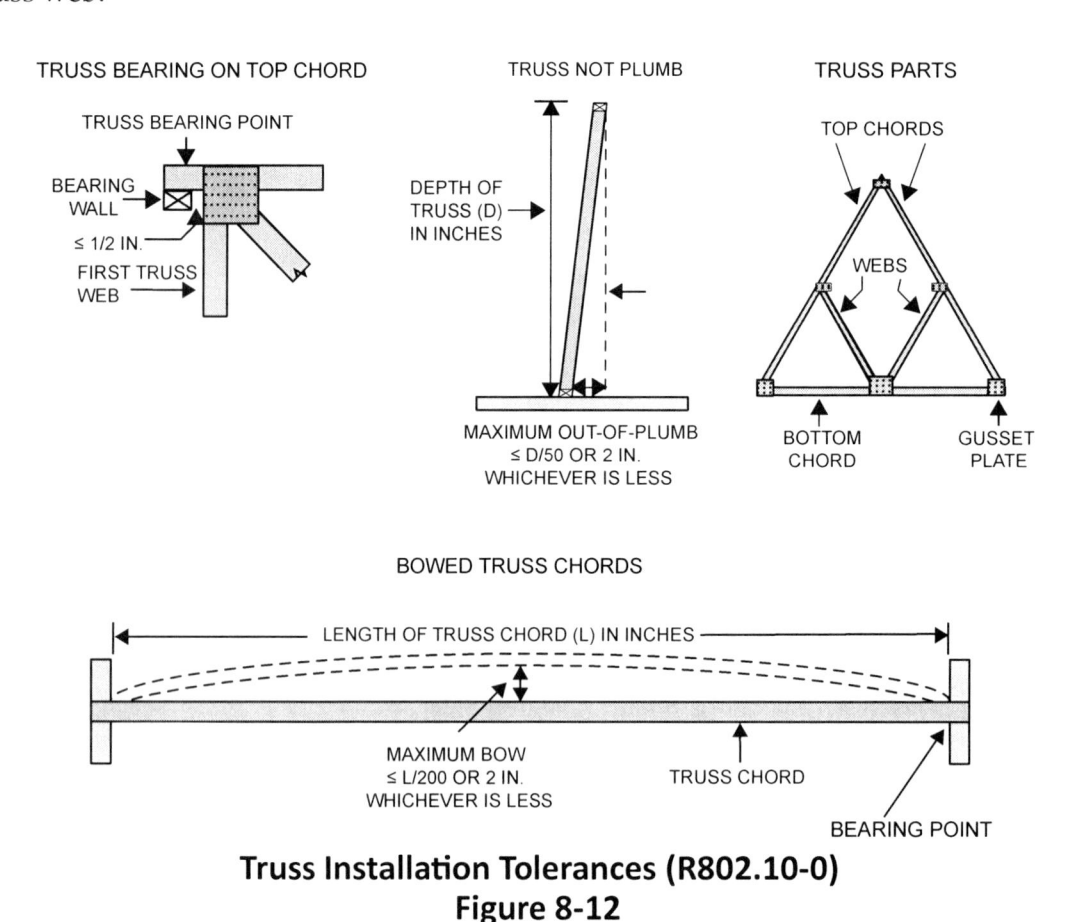

Truss Installation Tolerances (R802.10-0)
Figure 8-12

Truss Permanent Bracing Recommendations

1. Use the permanent bracing specifications in the written truss specifications. Use permanent truss bracing recommendations in BCSI-2008 only if the engineer and/or truss manufacturer does not provide permanent bracing instructions.
2. You may not need to install additional truss top chord bracing if the roof has properly installed structural sheathing. An example of properly installed structural sheathing is structural OSB installed with long dimension perpendicular to the trusses, and staggered sheathing joints, and proper type and spacing of fasteners.
3. You may need to install gable end bracing between the top chords and gable end walls to resist lateral movement of the entire gable roof structure.
4. You may not need to install permanent bottom chord bracing if drywall is attached to the

bottom chords such that the drywall provides necessary lateral bracing. Drywall that provides lateral bracing would be installed as previously described for structural OSB.

5. You may need to install permanent lateral bottom chord bracing across the chords to resist wind and snow load stresses. You may need to attach this permanent lateral bracing to a bearing or shear wall. You may also need to attach diagonal bracing between the lateral braces.
6. You may need to install lateral bracing, cross bracing, strongbacks, or diagonal cross bracing on truss webs (especially longer webs).
7. You may need to install permanent lateral bracing on parallel chord trusses (such as floor trusses) to resist truss movement. This bracing is usually attached either to webs or the bottom chords.

Gable End Truss Brace (PR802.10-1)
Figure 8-13

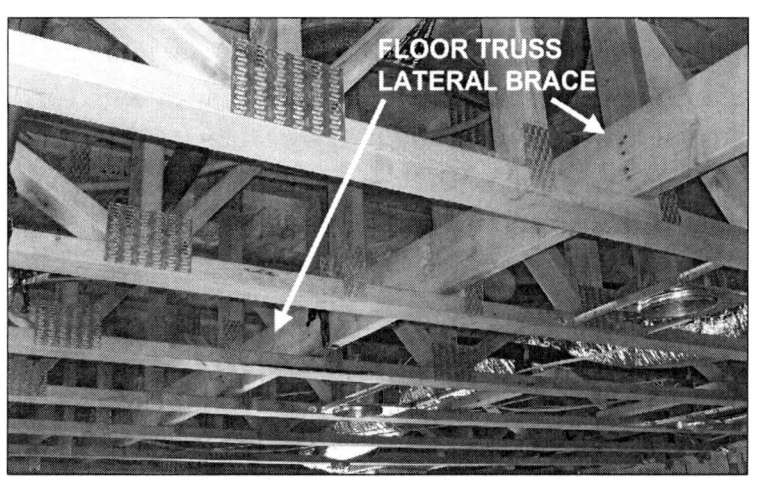

Floor Truss Lateral Brace (PR802.10-2)
Figure 8-14

Connection Between Roof Trusses and Walls

1. Install approved connectors capable of resisting an uplift force of at least (≥) 175 pounds between each roof truss and its supporting wall top plates. This requirement is for roof assemblies subject to wind uplift pressures of less than (<) 20 pounds per square foot.
2. Refer to the IRC for additional requirements for roof assemblies subject to roof uplift pressures of 20 pounds per square foot or more.

Alteration and Repair of Trusses

1. Do not alter trusses in any way, including cutting, notching, boring, and splicing, without written instructions from a qualified engineer.
2. Do not use trusses to carry the weight of equipment (such as furnaces or water heaters), or use the attic area for storage, or hang storage units from trusses unless the trusses have been designed to carry the additional weight.
3. Do not repair damaged trusses without written instructions from a qualified engineer.

Truss Discussion

Trusses are engineered systems designed to bear and distribute loads in a specific manner. If trusses are altered, damaged, or not installed according to the design assumptions, excess deflection (bouncing), sagging, and structural failure can occur. At this time, you may obtain BCSI-2008 at www.sbcindustry.com/bcsi.php.

ATTIC VENTILATION (R806)

Attic Ventilation Requirements

1. Provide ventilation to attic spaces, unless you design and build the attic as an unventilated, conditioned attic assembly. Provide ventilation when ceilings are applied directly to roof rafters, such as cathedral and vaulted ceilings, and in attics over unconditioned spaces, such as garage attics. Provide ventilation to each individual attic and ceiling space, unless there is effective means for air to move between spaces.
2. Protect ventilation openings from entry of rain or snow.
3. Make attic ventilation openings at least (≥) 1/16 inch and not more than (≤) ¼ inch.
4. Cover attic ventilation openings that are larger than ¼ inch with corrosion-resistant wire mesh with openings at least (≥) ⅛ inch and not more than (≤) ¼ inch.
5. Provide at least (≥) 1 inch clearance between insulation and roof sheathing. Do not cover ventilation openings with insulation.

Attic Ventilation Openings Area

1. Provide a net free ventilation opening area of at least (≥) 1 square foot for every 150 square feet of ventilated area, unless one of the reduction exceptions applies. The ventilated area is usually defined as the floor area under the attic. The net free ventilation opening area is the total opening area minus the area of any screens and/or louvers that protect the opening.
2. You may reduce the net free ventilation opening area to at least (≥) 1 square foot for every 300 square feet of ventilated area: (a) if at least (≥) 50 percent but not more than (≤) 80 per-

cent of the ventilation openings are located at least (≥) 3 feet above the eave vents and the balance of the ventilation openings are eave vents, or (b) by installing a Class I or Class II vapor retarder on the warm side of the ceiling.

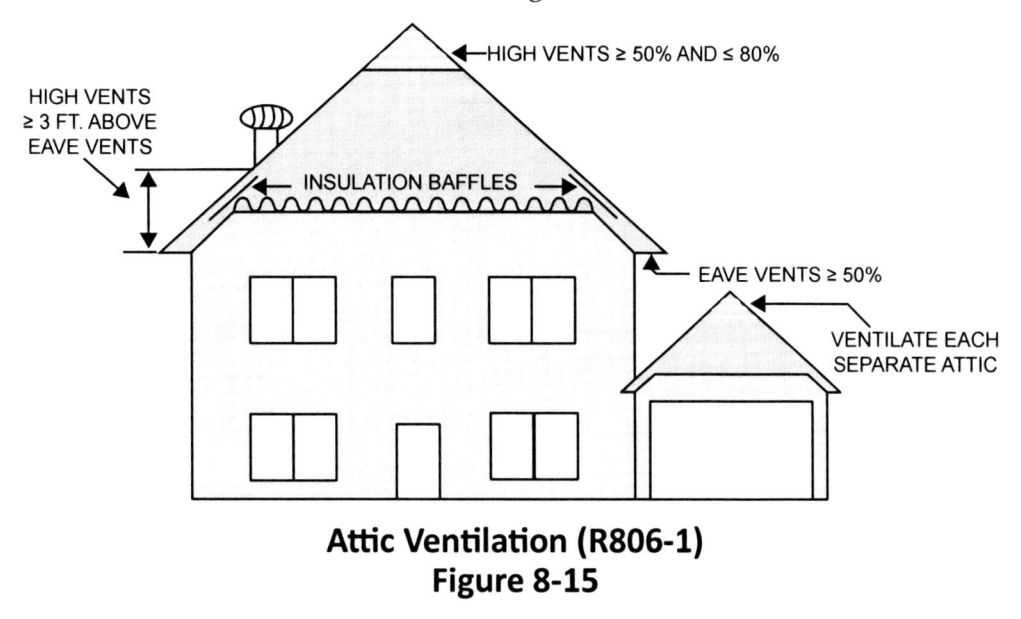

Attic Ventilation (R806-1)
Figure 8-15

Conditioned Attic Assemblies

1. Refer to the IRC and to your local building official to determine your climate zone before installing a conditioned attic assembly. You are not required to make attics conditioned.

2. Comply with all of the following when installing a conditioned attic assembly:

    A) Build and seal the entire attic area so it is completely within the building thermal envelope (see Chapter 11 for information about the building thermal envelope), and

    B) Do not install a vapor retarder on the attic floor, and

    C) Provide at least (≥) a ¼ inch a continuous ventilated air space between the exterior roof sheathing and the roofing underlayment and wood shingles and shakes roof covering materials, and

    D) Use insulation material that is a vapor retarder or install a vapor retarder in direct contact with the underside (conditioned side) of the insulation in climate zones 5, 6, 7, and 8, and

    E) Install insulation in the rafter and roof sheathing area by one of the following methods:

    a) Install air impermeable insulation directly in contact with the inside (unconditioned side) of the roof sheathing, or

    b) Install air permeable insulation directly in contact with the inside (attic side) of the roof sheathing and install rigid board or sheet insulation directly in contact with the outside (exterior side) of the roof sheathing according to Table R806, or

    c) Install rigid board or sheet insulation directly in contact with the inside (attic side) of the roof sheathing according to Table R806 and install air permeable insulation directly in contact with the rigid board or sheet insulation.

TABLE R806
Minimum Rigid Board or Sheet Insulation R-Value

climate zone	minimum R-value
2B and 3B tile roof only	none required
1, 2A, 2B, 3A, 3B, 3C	5
4C	10
4A, 4B	15
5	20
6	25
7	30
8	35

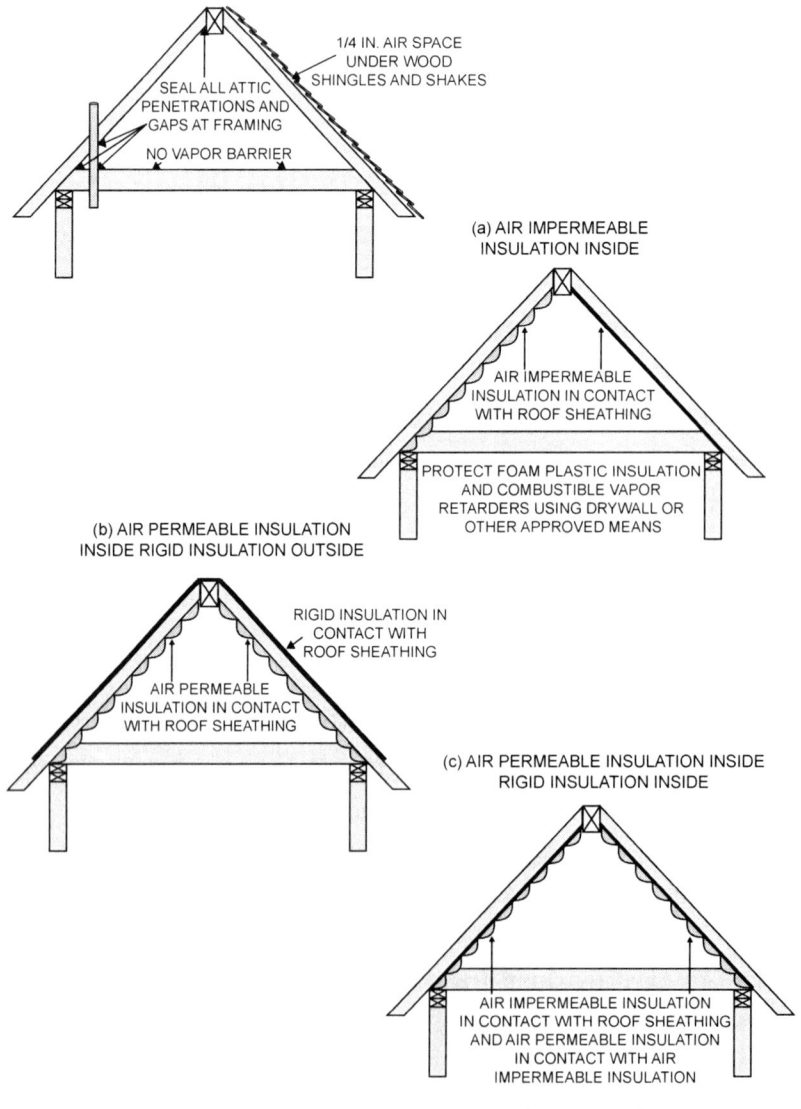

Conditioned Attic Assembly (R806-2)
Figure 8-16

Attic Ventilation Discussion

Screens and louvers will reduce the ventilation opening area. Use manufacturer's specifications to determine the net free ventilation opening area of commercially available ventilation opening covers. If manufacturer's specifications are not available, a safe assumption is that metal louvers provide a net free area of 75 percent of the gross louver area and that wood louvers provide a net free area of 25 percent of the gross louver area.

Attic Ventilation Best Practice

Use cardboard baffles or similar materials to keep insulation from blocking soffit vent openings, and to keep it from blocking the space between insulation and roof sheathing in cathedral and vaulted ceilings. Use baffles or other means to keep attic ventilation air currents from disturbing loose fill insulation. Air currents can blow loose fill insulation out of position, reducing or even eliminating insulation coverage over an area. Loose fill fiberglass insulation is particularly vulnerable to being disturbed by air currents.

Instruct painters to mask or otherwise protect soffit vent openings. It is common that, over time, these openings become restricted by paint buildup.

Consider making the attic a conditioned assembly. Conditioned attics help HVAC equipment and ducts located in the attic function more efficiently because energy is retained inside conditioned space instead of being lost to the outdoors. Recent building science research indicates that ventilated attics in warm humid climates may do more harm than good. This is because water may condense out of the humid air near where cool conditioned air leaks into the attic from openings such as recessed ceiling lights. In some cases, this water can damage the building and provide moisture for fungal growth.

Attic Ventilation Examples

Given a 2,100 square feet single story home with a 600 square feet attached garage, the required total net free ventilation area is at least (≥) 18 square feet at the 1/150 ventilation ratio or at least (≥) 9 square feet at the more commonly used 1/300 ventilation ratio. For best results, the ventilation openings should be evenly distributed between the home and garage attics. If the garage and home attics are separated so that air flow between the two is limited, the ventilation openings must be distributed between the two attics with at least (≥) 7 square feet in the main home attic and at least (≥) 2 square feet in the garage attic.

Given a 1,800 square feet two story home with a 300 square feet attached garage and given that the first and second floors each have an area of 900 square feet, the total net free ventilation area is at least 4 square feet at the 1/300 ventilation ratio. Because the home and garage attics are almost certainly separated so that no air flows between them, the ventilation openings must be distributed between the two attics with at least 3 square feet in the main home attic and at least 1 square foot in the garage attic.

ATTIC ACCESS (R807)

Attic Access Requirements

1. Provide an access opening to every attic with at least (≥) 30 square feet of attic area and

a vertical height of at least (≥) 30 inches at some point in the 30 square feet. Measure the vertical height from the top of the ceiling joists (or truss bottom chord) to the bottom of the rafters (or truss top chord).

2. Provide a rough opening (size before finishing) for a ceiling attic access of at least (≥) 22 inches by 30 inches. Locate the opening in a hallway or other readily accessible location. Locate the opening so that at least (≥) 30 inches of unobstructed head room exists at some point above the opening.
3. Provide a rough opening (size before finishing) for a wall attic access of at least (≥) 22 inches wide by 30 inches high.
4. You do not need to provide attic access if the ceiling and roof systems are built using non-combustible materials. This is rare in residential construction.
5. Refer to Chapter 13 for additional access requirements if appliances are located in the attic.

Attic Access Best Practice

Avoid locating attic access in places such as reach-in closets, along the edges of walk-in closets and in pantries where shelves will be located, and over spaces where appliances such as laundry appliances will be located. At some point during the home's existence, attic access will be required. A convenient and safe access opening is best for workers, inspectors, and homeowners alike.

9
ROOF COVERINGS AND FLASHING

ROOF FLASHING AND DRAINAGE (R903)

Roof Flashing Locations and Materials

1. Install flashing:
   a) at all intersections between roofs and sidewalls, and
   b) at all points where a roof changes direction or pitch, and
   c) at all intersections between parapet walls and roofs, and
   d) where roofs contact or drain water on moisture-permeable material such as masonry and concrete, and
   e) at all penetrations through a roof such as plumbing vents, gas and oil equipment vents, chimneys, exhaust ducts, dormers, and skylights.

2. Use corrosion-resistant metal flashing at least (≥) 26 gage galvanized sheet, if using metal as flashing material. You may use other approved flashing material that is compatible with the surrounding materials. Caulk and roofing mastic are sealants and are not flashing materials.

Parapet Wall Coping

1. Install noncombustible and weatherproof coping material on the top of all parapet walls. The coping should be at least as wide as the parapet wall and should be sloped to drain water.

Enclosed Roof Drainage Methods and Installation

1. Install a properly designed drainage system on any roof not designed to drain water off the roof edge. Such roofs are usually low slope roofs surrounded by parapet walls.
2. Install a primary drainage system to drain the water off the roof. You may use openings in the parapet walls (called scuppers) or you may use roof drains connected by pipes.
3. Place primary scuppers level with the surrounding roof and slope the roof surface toward the scuppers. Flash scuppers so they will not leak.
4. Provide a secondary drainage system when using piped roof drains (not scuppers) as the primary roof drainage system. You may use additional piped roof drains or you may use scuppers as the secondary drains. Make secondary piped roof drains the same size as the main roof drainage system. Locate secondary piped roof drains 2 inches above the low point of the roof. Make secondary scuppers at least (≥) three times the size of the main roof

drains, with at least (≥) a 4 inch opening height, and locate them 2 inches above the low point of the roof.
5. Design and install secondary piped drains and associated pipes to comply with the International Plumbing Code.
6. Discharge secondary overflow drains to an approved location, preferably one that will alert the occupants to a problem with the main roof drains. Do not connect the secondary overflow drains to the main roof drains.

Scupper (PR903-0)
Figure 9-1

Crickets at Chimneys

1. Install a cricket (saddle) at all chimneys where a roof drains against the chimney and the chimney is more than (>) 30 inches wide.
2. Use sheet metal or other approved materials to cover the cricket.

Roof Flashing and Drainage Discussion

Roofs that are not properly flashed or have poorly designed or installed drainage systems will eventually leak. Piped roof drains run the risk that the roof drains may become clogged. In the best case, the roof may simply leak. In the worst case, the water, which is very heavy, can cause structural failure.

ASPHALT (FIBERGLASS) SHINGLE ROOF COVERING MATERIALS AND INSTALLATION (R905.2)

Shingle Roof Covering Description

Shingle roof covering materials discussed in this section are the fiberglass strip shingles used in modern residential construction. Strip shingles are the most common roof covering material in modern residential construction.

Roof slopes are shown as x/y where x is the number of vertical units rise and y is the number of horizontal units run. A 4/12 roof has 4 vertical units rise for every 12 horizontal units run.

Roof Slope Restriction

1. Do not install shingles on roofs with a slope less than (<) 2/12.
2. Install a double underlayment layer under shingles on roofs with a slope between 2/12 and 4/12.
3. Verify manufacturer's instructions about minimum roof slope.

Roof Deck Type Restriction

1. Install shingle roof covering only on solid sheathed roofs.

Underlayment Specifications

1. Use at least (≥) 15 pound (per 100 square feet) roofing felt. This is the most common shingle underlayment. Other material, such as modified bitumen sheets, may be acceptable. Refer to the IRC for other acceptable underlayment materials.

Underlayment Application for Roof Slopes 4/12 and Greater

1. Begin at the eaves and apply at least (≥) a 36 inches wide strip of underlayment parallel to the eaves.
2. Lap horizontal joints at least (≥) 2 inches with the upper strip over the lower strip.
3. Lap end joints at least (≥) 6 inches.
4. Use sufficient fasteners to hold underlayment in place. The IRC does not specify fastener type and quantity.
5. Lap underlayment over drip edge at eaves, if using drip edge. Apply drip edge over underlayment at rakes, if using drip edge. The IRC does not require a drip edge, but shingle manufacturers often recommend it.

UNDERLAYMENT INSTALLATION FOR ROOF SLOPE ≥ 4/12 WITHOUT ICE DAM

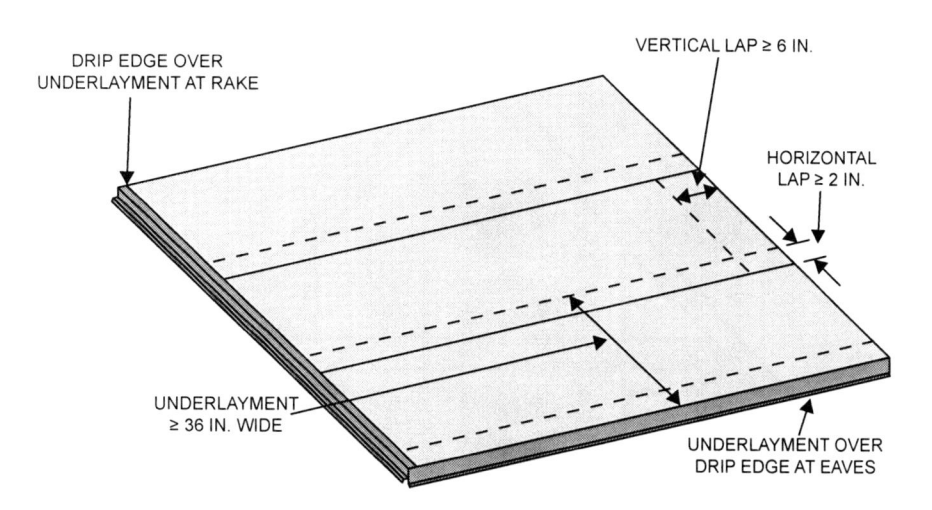

Underlayment Installation Roof Slope ≥ 4/12 (R905.2-1)
Figure 9-2

Underlayment Application for Roof Slopes Between 2/12 and 4/12

1. Begin at the eaves and apply at least (≥) a 19 inches wide strip of underlayment parallel to the eaves.
2. Begin again at the eaves and apply at least (≥) a 36 inches wide strip of underlayment.
3. Lap each successive layer at least (≥) 19 inches over the previous layer with the upper layer over the lower layer.
4. Lap end joints at least (≥) 6 inches.
5. Use sufficient fasteners to hold underlayment in place. The IRC does not specify fastener type and quantity.
6. Install drip edge as previously described, if using drip edge.

Underlayment Application in 110+ mph Wind Areas

1. Apply underlayment according to the roof slope.
2. Install corrosion-resistant fasteners according to manufacturer's instructions and space them along the overlaps at not more than (≤) 36 inches on center.

Underlayment Application in Ice Dam Areas

1. Install ice dam underlayment where there is a history of water backup at the eaves caused by ice. Verify ice dam requirements with the local building official. You need not install ice dam underlayment on unconditioned detached accessory structures.
2. Install either a sheet of self-adhering polymer modified bitumen roofing or at least (≥) two layers of roofing felt cemented together. Begin the ice dam underlayment at the lowest edge of all roof surfaces and extend it at least (≥) 24 inches beyond the exterior wall of the building.
3. Measure distances horizontally, not up the roof sheathing. Begin the 24 inches measurement from the interior side of the wall. Example: if the eaves extend 12 inches, horizontally, from the exterior wall of the building, extend the ice dam underlayment at least (≥) 39 ½ inches, horizontally, from the edge of the eaves (assuming a 2x4 wall).

EXTEND ICE DAM UNDERLAYMENT ≥ 2 FT. BEYOND EXTERIOR WALL

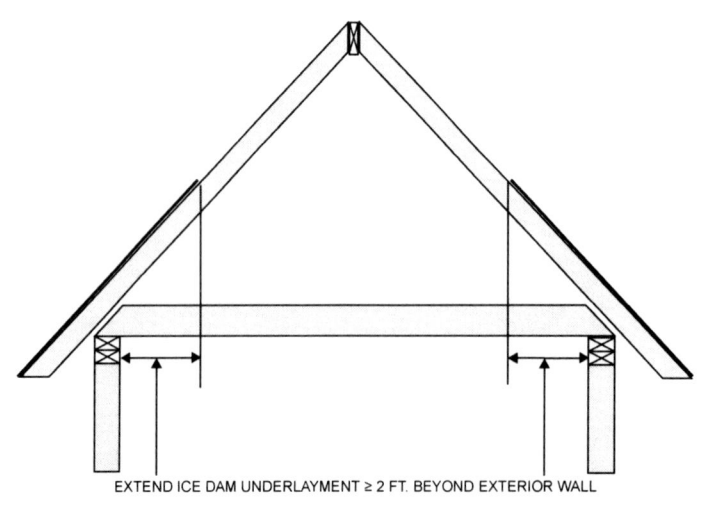

Ice Dam Underlayment Installation (R905.2-2)
Figure 9-3

Closed-Cut Valley Flashing

1. Install closed valley flashing material according to manufacturer's instructions before installing the shingles. You may use at least (≥) a 36 inches wide strip of smooth roll roofing material as closed valley flashing material with at least (≥) 18 inches on each side of the valley or you may use any open valley lining material.
2. Place nails at least (≥) 6 inches away from the valley centerline, unless other spacing is approved by the shingle manufacturer.
3. Apply the shingles across one side of the valley at least (≥) 12 inches or as recommended by the shingle manufacturer.
4. Apply shingles from the other direction to before the valley centerline and trim the edges as recommended by the shingle manufacturer. Seal the cut shingles in a closed-cut valley as recommend by the manufacturer. Sealing the cut shingles is frequently omitted.

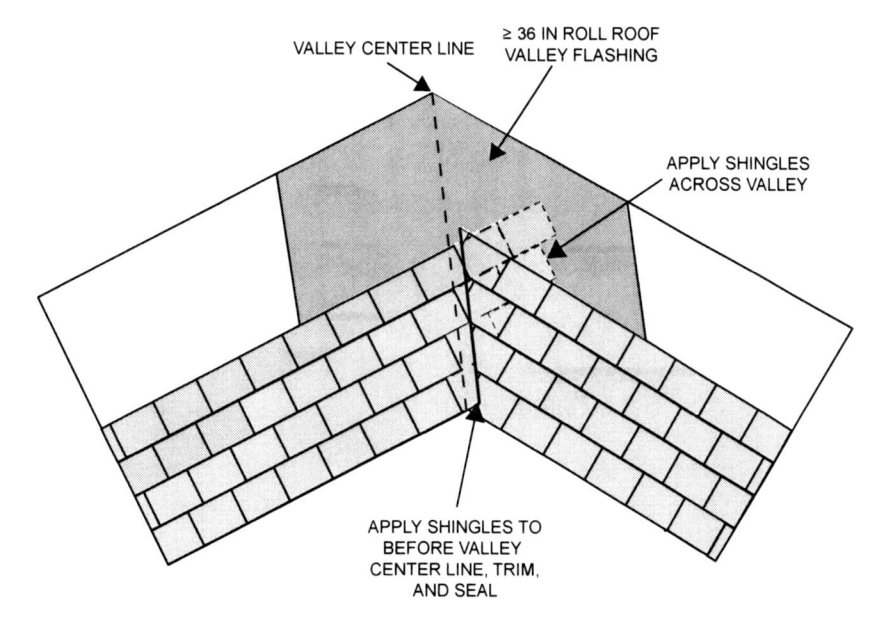

Closed-Cut Shingle Valley (R905.2-3)
Figure 9-4

Open Valley Flashing

1. Install at least (≥) a 24 inches wide strip of metal with 12 inches on each side of the valley. The metal will usually be 0.024 inch thick aluminum or 0.0179 inch thick galvanized steel. You may use other metals. Refer to the IRC.
2. You may install at least (≥) an 18 inches wide roll of mineral surfaced roll roofing under at least (≥) a 36 inches wide roll of the same material as an alternative to the metal valley material.
3. Place nails at least (≥) 6 inches away from the valley centerline, unless other spacing is approved by the shingle manufacturer.

Sidewall and Penetration Flashing

1. Install step flashing at the intersections of a sloped roof and a vertical sidewall. Use flashing

that is at least (≥) 4 inches wide by 4 inches high. Install kick out flashing at the end of the wall that directs water away from the sidewall.
2. Flash the intersection of a sloped roof and a chimney according to the shingle manufacturer's instructions. This typically includes step flashing covered with counter flashing.
3. Flash other roof penetrations, such as plumbing and gas vents, according to the shingle manufacturer's instructions.
4. Flash skylights according to the skylight manufacturer's instructions.

Fastener Type and Quantity in Standard Conditions

1. Use the type and quantity of fasteners recommended by the shingle manufacturer. Locate nails on the shingle strip precisely as recommended by the shingle manufacturer. Some manufacturers recommend installing nails below the black adhesive seal strip. Other manufacturers leave a gap in the seal strip for installing nails. Do not install nails above the seal strip unless allowed by the manufacturer. Failure to comply with manufacturer's installation instructions is a code violation and may void the manufacturer's warranty.
2. Use corrosion-resistant nails (usually galvanized steel) with at least (≥) a 12 gage shank and at least (≥) a ⅜ inch diameter head. Use nails long enough to penetrate into the roof sheathing at least (≥) ¾ inch and completely through any sheathing that is less than (<) ¾ inch thick.
3. Install at least (≥) 4 nails per shingle strip with a nail at 1 inch from each end and two nails equally spaced in the center of the strip, in wind speed areas less than (<) 110 mph.

Fastener Type and Quantity in Special Conditions

1. Install additional fasteners as recommended by the shingle manufacturer in wind speed areas greater than (>) 110 mph and for very steep roof slopes such as Mansard roofs. Install at least (≥) 6 nails per strip in these applications and verify fastening recommendations with the shingle manufacturer.
2. Use shingles labeled on the wrapper as complying with ASTM D3161 in wind speed areas greater than (>) 110 mph.

Staples as Shingle Fasteners

1. Staples are not mentioned in the IRC as a code approved shingle fastener. Some shingle manufacturers allow staples, but seldom recommend them. Avoid using staples as shingle fasteners in both new construction and when replacing an existing shingle roof.

CONCRETE AND CLAY TILE ROOF COVERING MATERIALS AND INSTALLATION (R905.3)

Tile Roof Covering Description

Roof tiles are made using concrete or clay and come in several shapes. The most common shapes are flat and an S shape. Clay tiles are very delicate and are easily broken. Concrete tiles are more durable. Avoid walking on tile roof unless you are trained how to do so. Concrete and clay tiles are among the most expensive roof covering materials and usually have a long useful life.

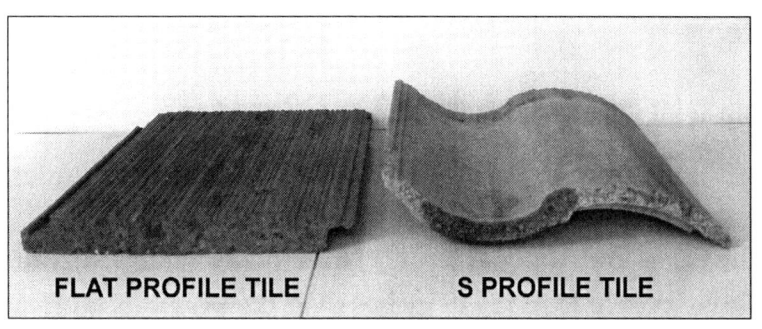

Flat and S Profile Concrete Tiles (PR905.3-1)
Figure 9-5

The underlayment material and the flashing are the waterproof membrane that seals the home from water penetration. The tile serves only to protect the underlayment from exposure to sunlight and excessive moisture and to look good.

The provisions for tile application in this section are general and primarily for moderate climates. Refer to tile manufacturer's installation instructions and local installation requirements for your area.

Roof slopes are shown as x/y where x is the number of vertical units rise and y is the number of horizontal units run. A 4/12 roof has 4 vertical units rise for every 12 horizontal units run.

Roof Slope Restriction

1. Do not install tiles on roofs with a slope less than (<) 2 ½ /12.
2. Install a double underlayment layer under tiles on roofs with a slope between 2 ½ /12 and 4/12.

Roof Deck Type Restriction

1. Install tile roof covering on solid sheathed roofs or on spaced structural sheathing.

Underlayment Specifications

1. Use at least (≥) 30 pound (per 100 square feet) roofing felt. This is the most common tile roof underlayment. Other materials, such as mineral surfaced roll roofing, are often superior to roofing felt. Refer to the IRC for other acceptable underlayment for tile roofs.

Underlayment Application for Roof Slopes 4/12 and Greater

1. Begin at the eaves and apply at least (≥) a 36 inches wide strip of underlayment parallel to the eaves.
2. Lap horizontal joints at least (≥) 2 inches with the upper strip over the lower strip.
3. Lap end joints at least (≥) 6 inches.
4. Lap underlayment at least (≥) 1 inch over rake edges. (industry recommendation).

5. Use sufficient fasteners to hold underlayment in place. The IRC does not specify fastener type and quantity.

Underlayment Application for Roof Slopes Between 2 ½ /12 and 4/12

1. Begin at the eaves and apply at least (≥) a 19 inches wide strip of underlayment parallel to the eaves.
2. Begin again at the eaves and apply at least (≥) a 36 inches wide strip of underlayment.
3. Lap each successive layer at least (≥) 19 inches over the previous layer with the upper layer over the lower layer.
4. Lap end joints at least (≥) 6 inches.
5. Lap underlayment at least (≥) 1 inch over rake edges. (industry recommendation).
6. Use sufficient fasteners to hold underlayment in place. The IRC does not specify fastener type and quantity.
7. Refer to the illustration in Section R905.2.

Underlayment Application in 110+ mph Wind Areas

1. Apply underlayment according to the roof slope.
2. Install corrosion-resistant fasteners according to manufacturer's instructions and space them along the overlaps at not more than (≤) 36 inches.

Batten Installation (Industry Recommendation)

1. You are not required to use battens when installing a tile roof, unless recommended by the manufacturer. If you use battens, follow these industry installation recommendations.
2. Install battens that are at least (≥) 1x2 utility grade wood, not longer than (≤) 4 feet, and installed with at least (≥) a ½ inch gap between each batten for drainage. Alternative installations that allow drainage under or between battens are acceptable.
3. Space battens based on the size and type of tile and on the tile manufacturer's recommendations.
4. Attach battens using at least (≥) 8d corrosion-resistant nails spaced not more than (≤) 24 inches on center and long enough to penetrate at least (≥) ¾ inch into or through the sheathing. Alternative fasteners are corrosion-resistant staples at least (≥) 16 gage, 7/16 inch crown, 1 ½ inches long, and long enough to penetrate at least (≥) ¾ inch into the sheathing, and spaced not more than (≤) 12 inches on center.

Valley Flashing

1. Install at least (≥) a 22 inches wide strip of metal with at least (≥) 11 inches on each side of the valley. Use metal valley flashing with at least (≥) a 1 inch high splash diverter rib running down the valley center. The metal should be at least (≥) 0.019 inch thick galvanized steel or equivalent corrosion-resistant metal. Metal flashing sections should end lap at least (≥) 4 inches with the upper section over the lower section.
2. Install at least (≥) a 36 inches wide roll of ASTM D 2626 Type I roll roofing under the metal valley material, if the roof slope is at least (≥) 3/12.

3. Apply adhesive between the Type I roll roofing and the underlayment or install a self-adhering polymer modified bitumen sheet instead of the Type I roll roofing where the average daily January temperature is 25º F or less.

Sidewall and Penetration Flashing

1. Install roof penetration flashing, such as plumbing vent flashing, according to the flashing manufacturer's instructions. Install roof and sidewall intersection flashing using base flashing and counter flashing installed according to manufacturer's instructions.

Fastener Type

1. Install corrosion-resistant nails with at least (≥) an 11 gage shank and a 5/16 inch diameter head. The nails should be long enough to penetrate into the roof sheathing at least (≥) ¾ inch and completely through any sheathing that is less than (<) ¾ inch thick.

Perimeter Tile Nailing

1. The roof perimeter includes both sides of hips and ridges, gable rake edges, and eave edges.
2. Install at least (≥) one nail per tile within at least (≥) 3 tile courses of the perimeter and at least (≥) 36 inches from the perimeter edge, whichever is greater.

Perimeter Nailing Locations (PR905.3-2)
Figure 9-6

Field Tile Nailing in Standard Conditions

1. Field tiles are all tiles other than perimeter tiles and cap tiles on ridges and hips. Standard conditions are design wind speed of not more than (≤) 100 mph, and buildings with a roof 40 feet or less above the ground, and areas not subject to snow.
2. Install at least (≥) one nail per field tile when tiles cover solid roof sheathing and no battens are installed.
3. You are not required to install nails in field tiles when battens are installed and the roof slope is less than (<) 5/12.
4. Install at least (≥) one nail per tile when tiles weigh less than 9 pounds per square foot.
5. Install two nails per tile in areas subject to snow.

Field Tile Nailing in Special Conditions

1. You may be required to install nails in most or all tiles if the roof slope exceeds (>) 5/12, or if the design wind speed exceeds (>) 100 mph, or if the roof is higher than (>) 40 feet above the ground, or if the roof is subject to snow. Verify fastening requirements with the tile manufacturer and the local building official if any of these special conditions exist.

Tile Roof Covering Best Practice

Tile is usually a very heavy roof covering material. Verify that the rafters or trusses are designed and braced to carry the load. Do not install tile on a roof that was previously covered by another roof covering material without evaluation of the roof framing and support by a qualified engineer or contractor.

A good quality concrete tile roof can have a useful life exceeding 80 years. Thirty pound felt underlayment can start to deteriorate in as few as 10 years and may need replacement before the end of the tile's useful life. Consider installing mineral-surfaced roll roofing as tile underlayment instead of thirty pound felt. Good quality underlayment and flashing materials should perform well for the entire life of the tile roof.

METAL SHINGLE ROOF COVERING MATERIALS AND INSTALLATION (R905.4)

Metal Shingle Roof Covering Description

Metal shingles have a weather exposure area of less than (<) 3 square feet per shingle. This distinguishes them from metal panel roof coverings that have a larger weather exposure area. Metal shingles must be made from naturally corrosion resistant metal or from metals treated with a corrosion resistant coating.

Roof slopes are shown as x/y where x is the number of vertical units rise and y is the number of horizontal units run. A 4/12 roof has 4 vertical units rise for every 12 horizontal units run.

Roof Slope Restriction

1. Do not install metal shingles on roofs with a slope less than (<) 3/12.

Roof Deck Type Restriction

1. Install metal shingles on solid sheathed roofs or on roof decks with close fitted sheathing, unless the manufacturer's installation instructions state otherwise.

Underlayment Specifications

1. Use at least (≥) 15 pound (per 100 square feet) roofing felt. Other materials are acceptable. Refer to the IRC for other acceptable underlayment materials.

Underlayment Application in Ice Dam Areas

1. Install ice dam underlayment where there is a history of water backup at the eaves caused

by ice. You need not install ice dam underlayment on unconditioned detached accessory structures.

2. Install either a sheet of self-adhering polymer modified bitumen roofing or at least (≥) two layers of roofing felt cemented together. Begin the ice dam underlayment at the lowest edge of all roof surfaces and extend it at least (≥) 24 inches beyond the exterior wall of the building.

3. Measure distances horizontally, not up the roof sheathing. Begin the 24 inches measurement from the interior side of the wall. Example: if the eaves extend 12 inches, horizontally, from the exterior wall of the building, extend the ice dam underlayment at least (≥) 39 ½ inches, horizontally, from the edge of the eaves (assuming a 2x4 wall).

4. Refer to the illustration in Section R905.2.

Metal Shingle Installation

1. Install and secure metal shingles according to manufacturer's installation instructions.

Valley Flashing

1. Use metal valley flashing made from the same material as the metal shingles.
2. Install metal valley flashing with at least (≥) 8 inches on each side of the valley, and at least (≥) a ¾ inch high splash diverter rib running down the valley center. Lap metal flashing sections at least (≥) 4 inches with the upper section over the lower section.
3. Install at least (≥) a 36 inches wide roll of underlayment under the metal valley material. Extend the underlayment over the full length of the valley. This underlayment is in addition to the underlayment for the shingles.
4. Apply adhesive between the metal flashing and the underlayment or install a self-adhering polymer modified bitumen sheet instead of the valley underlayment where the average daily January temperature is 25º F or less and where the roof slope is less than (<) 7/12.

MINERAL-SURFACED ROLL ROOF COVERING MATERIALS AND INSTALLATION (R905.5)

Mineral-Surfaced Roll Roof Covering Description

Mineral-surfaced roll roofing material usually comes in 36 inch wide rolls. It is usually a lower quality and less expensive roof covering material compared to other roof covering materials. It is commonly used on temporary buildings, accessory buildings, low slope porch roofs, and in other applications where long life is not critical.

Roof slopes are shown as x/y where x is the number of vertical units rise and y is the number of horizontal units run. A 4/12 roof has 4 vertical units rise for every 12 horizontal units run.

Roof Slope Restriction

1. Do not install roll roof covering on roofs with a slope less than (<) 1/12 or as recommended by the manufacturer.

Roof Deck Type Restriction

1. Install roll roof covering only on solid sheathed roofs.

Underlayment Application in Ice Dam Areas

1. Install ice dam underlayment where there is a history of water backup at the eaves caused by ice. You need not install ice dam underlayment on unconditioned detached accessory structures.
2. Install either a sheet of self-adhering polymer modified bitumen roofing or at least (≥) two layers of roofing felt cemented together. Begin the ice dam underlayment at the lowest edge of all roof surfaces and extend it at least (≥) 24 inches beyond the exterior wall of the building.
3. Measure distances horizontally, not up the roof sheathing. Begin the 24 inches measurement from the interior side of the wall. Example: if the eaves extend 12 inches, horizontally, from the exterior wall of the building, extend the ice dam underlayment at least (≥) 39 ½ inches, horizontally, from the edge of the eaves (assuming a 2x4 wall).
4. Refer to the illustration in Section R905.2.

Roll Roof Covering Installation

1. Install mineral-surfaced roll roof covering according to manufacturer's installation instructions. These instructions usually include covering nailed seams with the overlapping course of roll roof covering.

SLATE AND SLATE TYPE SHINGLE ROOF COVERING MATERIALS AND INSTALLATION (R905.6)

Slate and Slate Type Shingle Roof Covering Description

Slate is a natural stone material. Artificial slate is also available. Natural slate is very heavy and requires roof framing designed to carry the load. Natural slate has a very long useful life. When high quality natural slate is properly maintained, it can last as long as the home. Natural slate is not commonly used in modern residential construction.

Install slate shingles according to the shingle manufacturer's installation instructions. If the manufacturer does not publish installation instructions, the National Roofing Contractors Association publishes authoritative information about proper installation and flashing for most common roof covering materials.

Roof slopes are shown as x/y where x is the number of vertical units rise and y is the number of horizontal units run. A 4/12 roof has 4 vertical units rise for every 12 horizontal units run. Any reference to slate shingles includes artificial slate type shingles.

Roof Slope Restriction

1. Do not install slate shingles on roofs with a slope less than (<) 4/12.

9 : Roof Coverings and Flashing   181

Roof Deck Type Restriction

1. Install slate shingles on solid sheathed roofs.
2. Verify acceptable roof deck material (e.g., plywood) with the slate manufacturer.

Underlayment Application

1. You are not required to install underlayment under slate shingles, except in ice dam prone areas, unless the slate manufacturer requires it. Underlayment is often used under slate shingles and is recommended by some experts.
2. Install slate shingles and underlayment according to the slate manufacturer's recommendations. Verify underlayment requirements with the slate shingle manufacturer.

Underlayment Application in Ice Dam Areas

1. Install ice dam underlayment where there is a history of water backup at the eaves caused by ice. You need not install ice dam underlayment on unconditioned detached accessory structures.
2. Install either a sheet of self-adhering polymer modified bitumen roofing or at least (≥) two layers of roofing felt cemented together. Begin the ice dam underlayment at the lowest edge of all roof surfaces and extend it at least (≥) 24 inches beyond the exterior wall of the building.
3. Measure distances horizontally, not up the roof sheathing. Begin the 24 inches measurement from the interior side of the wall. Example: if the eaves extend 12 inches, horizontally, from the exterior wall of the building, extend the ice dam underlayment at least (≥) 39 ½ inches, horizontally, from the edge of the eaves (assuming a 2x4 wall).
4. Refer to the illustration in Section R905.2.

Slate Roof Covering Installation

1. Install slate shingles according to manufacturer's installation instructions.
2. Use two fasteners per slate shingle or as recommended by the slate shingle manufacturer.
3. Install slate shingles with at least (≥) a 4 inches head lap on roofs with a slope at least (≥) 4/12 and less than (<) 8/12. Use at least (≥) a 3 inches head lap on roofs with a slope at least (≥) 8/12 and less than (<) 20/12. Use at least (≥) a 2 inches head lap on roofs with a slope of (≥) 20/12 or more.

Valley Flashing Material

1. Install at least (≥) a 15 inches wide strip of at least (≥) 0.0179 inch thick galvanized steel. Verify valley flashing requirements with the slate shingle manufacturer.

Sidewall and Penetration Flashing

1. Flash roof penetrations and roof sidewall intersections using metal flashing and counter flashing installed according to the slate shingle manufacturer's instructions.

2. Install special flashing at chimneys and brick and stucco sidewalls according to the slate shingle manufacturer's instructions.

Slate Roof Covering Best Practice

Slate is a very heavy roof covering material. Verify that the rafters are designed and braced to carry the load. Do not install slate on a roof that was previously covered by another roof covering material without an evaluation of the roof framing and support by a qualified engineer or contractor.

WOOD SHINGLE ROOF COVERING MATERIALS AND INSTALLATION (R905.7)

Wood Shingle Roof Covering Description

Wood shingles are usually sawn on all sides and have a uniform width and butt thickness. They are usually tapered with a relatively smooth and uniform surface. The butt end of a shingle is the thicker end of the shingle. Wood shingles are laid with the butt end toward the eaves.

Roof slopes are shown as x/y where x is the number of vertical units rise and y is the number of horizontal units run. A 4/12 roof has 4 vertical units rise for every 12 horizontal units run.

Application of the Material in this Section

Apply this section to wood shingles. Do not apply to wood shakes. Refer to R905.8 for wood shakes.

Roof Slope Restriction

1. Do not install wood shingles on roofs with a slope less than (<) 3/12.

Roof Deck Type Restriction

1. Install wood shingles on solid sheathed roofs or on spaced sheathing.
2. Use at least (≥) 1x4 wood spaced as recommended by the shingle manufacturer, if using spaced sheathing. Install spaced sheathing using the same on center spacing as the shingle weather exposure.
3. Install solid sheathing under the ice dam protective underlayment.
4. Verify acceptable roof deck material with the wood shingle manufacturer. OSB may not be acceptable as roof sheathing under wood shingles.

Underlayment Application

1. You are not required to install underlayment with wood shingles, except in ice dam prone areas, unless recommended by the wood shingle manufacturer.
2. Install eave protection underlayment strips, "breather" type underlayment, or furring strips if installing wood shingles over solid sheathing and/or if recommended by the wood shingle manufacturer. Verify underlayment requirements with the wood shingle manufacturer and the local building official.

Underlayment Application in Ice Dam Areas

1. Install ice dam underlayment where there is a history of water backup at the eaves caused by ice. You need not install ice dam underlayment on unconditioned detached accessory structures.
2. Install either a sheet of self-adhering polymer modified bitumen roofing or at least (≥) two layers of roofing felt cemented together. Begin the ice dam underlayment at the lowest edge of all roof surfaces and extend it at least (≥) 24 inches beyond the exterior wall of the building.
3. Measure distances horizontally, not up the roof sheathing. Begin the 24 inches measurement from the interior side of the wall. Example: if the eaves extend 12 inches, horizontally, from the exterior wall of the building, extend the ice dam underlayment at least (≥) 39 ½ inches, horizontally, from the edge of the eaves (assuming a 2x4 wall).
4. Refer to the illustration in Section R905.2.

Wood Shingle Installation

1. Install wood shingles according to the manufacturer's installation instructions and local building official requirements.
2. Install at least (≥) a double starter course of wood shingles at the eaves. Extend the butt end of the shingles as a starter course about 1 ½ inches over the eaves and extend the shingles about 1 inch over rakes, or as recommended by the manufacturer.
3. Use only two fasteners per wood shingle long enough to penetrate at least (≥) ½ inch into the sheathing and through sheathing less than (<) ½ inch thick. Position fasteners not more than (≤) ¾ inch from each wood shingle edge and not more than (≤) 1 inch above the exposure line. Verify recommended fastener materials, size, and placement with the wood shingle manufacturer.
4. Space the side edge joints of wood shingles at least (≥) 1 ½ inches away from the side edge joints in the courses above and below. Do not allow any two joints in any three adjacent courses to be in direct alignment.
5. Leave a joint (slot) between the side edge of each shingle of at least (≥) ¼ inch and not more than (≤) ⅜ inch.
6. Drive nails flush with the wood shingle. Do not allow nails to protrude above the shingle or be driven into the shingle.

Wood Shingle Exposure

1. Install wood shingles with the exposure specified in the following table. Exposure is the amount of visible shingle in each shingle course.

TABLE R905.7
Wood Shingle Exposure

shingle length (inches)	shingle grade	exposure (inches) 3/12 to < 4/12	exposure (inches) 4/12 and steeper
16	1	3.75	5
16	2	3.5	4
16	3	3	3.5
18	1	4.25	5.5
18	2	4	4.5
18	3	3.5	4
24	1	5.75	7.5
24	2	5.5	6.5
24	3	5	5.5

Valley Flashing Material

1. Use at least (≥) a 0.019 inch, 26-gage, corrosion-resistant metal valley flashing.
2. Install valley flashing at least (≥) 10 inches on each side of the valley centerline for roof slopes less than (<) 12/12.
3. Install valley flashing at least (≥) 7 inches on each side of the valley centerline for roof slopes (≥) 12/12 or more.
4. Verify valley flashing requirements with the wood shingle manufacturer.

Sidewall and Penetration Flashing

1. Install flashing of roof penetrations and roof sidewall intersections according to the wood shingle manufacturer's instructions.

Wood Shingle Roof Covering Best Practice

Wood that is exposed to moisture on a continuous basis tends to deteriorate more rapidly. This is true even for naturally decay resistant wood. Wood shingles need to dry both from underneath and from the top for maximum useful life. Follow manufacturer's recommendations when installing wood shingles in high humidity and cold weather environments.

Wood shingles will dry and deteriorate over time. Comply with the shingle manufacturer's recommendations about periodic shingle cleaning and sealing.

For more information about installing wood shingles, see the following web site: www.cedar-bureau.org.

WOOD SHAKE ROOF COVERING MATERIALS AND INSTALLATION (R905.8)

Wood Shake Roof Covering Description

Wood shakes are usually sawn on one or two sides and do not have a uniform width and butt thickness. They may be tapered and may not have uniform surface.

Roof slopes are shown as x/y where x is the number of vertical units rise and y is the number of horizontal units run. A 4/12 roof has 4 vertical units rise for every 12 horizontal units run.

Application of the Material in this Section

1. Apply this section to wood shakes. Do not apply to wood shingles. Refer to R905.7 for wood shingles.

Roof Slope Restriction

1. Do not install wood shakes on roofs with a slope less than (<) 3/12.

Roof Deck Type Restriction

1. Install wood shakes on solid sheathed roofs or on spaced sheathing.
2. Use at least (≥) 1x4 wood spaced as recommended by the shake manufacturer, if using spaced sheathing. Install spaced sheathing using the same on center spacing as the shake weather exposure. Install an additional 1x4 between the spaced sheathing, if using the maximum 10 inches shake weather exposure.
3. Install solid sheathing under the ice dam protective underlayment.
4. Verify acceptable roof deck material with the wood shake manufacturer. OSB may not be acceptable as roof sheathing under wood shakes.

Underlayment Application

1. You are not required to install underlayment with wood shakes, except in ice dam prone areas, unless recommended by the wood shake manufacturer.
2. Install eave protection underlayment strips, "breather" type underlayment, or furring strips if installing wood shakes over solid sheathing and/or if recommended by the wood shake manufacturer. Verify underlayment requirements with the wood shake manufacturer and the local building official.

Underlayment Application in Ice Dam Areas

1. Install ice dam underlayment where there is a history of water backup at the eaves caused by ice. You need not install ice dam underlayment on unconditioned detached accessory structures.
2. Install either a sheet of self-adhering polymer modified bitumen roofing or at least (≥) two layers of roofing felt cemented together. Begin the ice dam underlayment at the lowest edge of all roof surfaces and extend it at least (≥) 24 inches beyond the exterior wall of the building.

3. Measure distances horizontally, not up the roof sheathing. Begin the 24 inches measurement from the interior side of the wall. Example: if the eaves extend 12 inches, horizontally, from the exterior wall of the building, extend the ice dam underlayment at least (≥) 39 ½ inches, horizontally, from the edge of the eaves (assuming a 2x4 wall).
4. Refer to the illustration in Section R905.2.

Interlayment Material and Installation

1. Use at least (≥) 30 pound felt that is 18 inches wide as wood shake interlayment.
2. Place the interlayment between each course of shakes so that no felt is exposed to the weather. Place the lower edge of the interlayment strip above the butt end of the shake it covers at a distance of twice the shake's exposure.

Wood Shake Installation

1. Install wood shakes according to the manufacturer's installation instructions and local building official requirements.
2. Install a double starter course at the eaves using 15, 18, or 24 inches wood shakes or wood shingles.
3. Use only two corrosion-resistant fasteners per wood shake long enough to penetrate at least (≥) ½ inch into the sheathing and through sheathing less than ½ inch thick. Position fasteners not more than (≤) 1 inch from each wood shake edge and not more than (≤) 2 inches above the exposure line. Verify recommended fastener materials, size, and placement with the wood shake manufacturer.
4. Space the side edge (slot) of wood shakes at least (≥) 1 ½ inches from slots in the courses above and below.
5. Leave a slot (gap) between shakes in the same course according to the following table.
6. Install shakes so they hang over the eaves between 1 ½ and 2 inches. You may leave a ¾ inch overhang at the eaves if a gutter is installed.
7. Install shakes so they hang over roof rakes between 1 and 2 inches.

Wood Shake Exposure

1. Install wood shakes with the exposure and slot size specified in the following table.

TABLE 905.8
Wood Shake Exposure and Slot Size

shake material	shake length	shake grade	exposure (inches) 4/12 and steeper	slot size (inches)
naturally durable wood	18 24	1 1	7.5 10	3/8 to 5/8
preservative-treated taper-sawn southern yellow pine	18 24 18 24	1 1 2 2	7.5 10 5.5 7.5	3/8 to 5/8
taper-sawn durable wood	18 24 18 24	1 1 2 2	7.5 10 5.5 7.5	3/8 to 5/8

Valley Flashing Material

1. Use at least (≥) 0.019-inch, 26 gage, corrosion-resistant metal valley flashing.
2. Install valley flashing at least (≥) 11 inches on each side of the valley centerline.
3. Lap ends of valley flashing at least (≥) 4 inches with the top section lapping over the bottom section.
4. Verify valley flashing requirements with the wood shake manufacturer.

Sidewall and Penetration Flashing

1. Install flashing of roof penetrations and roof sidewall intersections according to wood shake manufacturer's instructions.

Wood Shake Roof Covering Best Practice

Wood that is exposed to moisture on a continuous basis tends to deteriorate more rapidly. This is true even for naturally decay resistant wood. Wood shakes need to dry both from underneath and from the top for maximum useful life. Follow manufacturer's recommendations when installing wood shakes in high humidity and cold weather environments.

Wood shakes will dry and deteriorate over time. Comply with the shake manufacturer's recommendations about periodic shake cleaning and sealing.

For more information about installing wood shakes see the following web site: www.cedarbureau.org.

LOW SLOPE (FLAT) ROOF COVERING MATERIALS AND INSTALLATION (R905.9 AND 11-15)

Low Slope Roof Covering Description

Roofs that are often described as "flat" are not supposed to be flat. They must be sloped to drain water toward scuppers or roof drains.

Roof slopes are shown as x/y where x is the number of vertical units rise and y is the number of horizontal units run. A 4/12 roof has 4 vertical units rise for every 12 horizontal units run.

Low Slope Roof Types

1. The traditional low slope roof covering is the built-up roof covering consisting of multiple layers of roofing felt or other sheet material covered with asphalt or coal tar bitumen or other similar material. The last layer is usually covered with stone aggregate.
2. Other low slope roof coverings include: modified bitumen membrane, thermoset single-ply roofing, thermoplastic single-ply roofing, sprayed polyurethane foam roofing, foam plastics, and liquid-applied coatings.

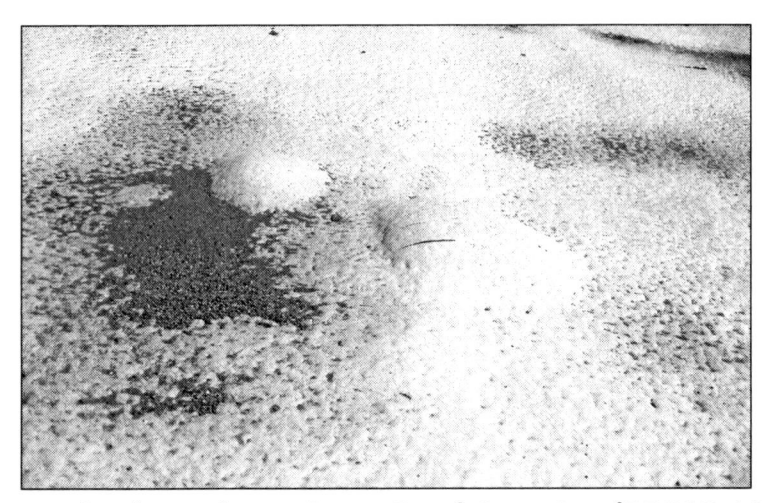

Sprayed Polyurethane Foam Roof Covering (PR905.14-0)
Figure 9-7

Minimum Roof Slope

1. Install most low slope roofs with at least (≥) a ¼ /12 (2 percent) slope toward scuppers or roof drains.

Low Slope Roof Covering Installation

1. Install all low slope roof coverings according to the manufacturer's instructions.

METAL PANEL ROOF COVERING MATERIALS AND INSTALLATION (R905.10)

Metal Panel Roof Covering Description

Metal panel roof coverings have an exposure of at least 3 square feet per panel. This distinguishes metal panels from metal shingles. Metal panels may be flat lapped panels that are either unsealed at the laps or are sealed or soldered at the laps. Metal panels may also be a standing seam type where the seams between panels are raised above the roof surface. Standing seam metal roof coverings are a good selection in high wind areas because they resist being blown off by high winds.

Roof slopes are shown as x/y where x is the number of vertical units rise and y is the number of horizontal units run. A 4/12 roof has 4 vertical units rise for every 12 horizontal units run.

Roof Slope Restriction

1. Do not install lapped, nonsoldered seam metal panel roof covering <u>without lap sealant</u> on a roof slope less than (<) 3/12.
2. Do not install lapped, nonsoldered seam metal panel roof covering <u>with lap sealant</u> on a roof slope less than (<) ½ /12.
3. Do not install a standing seam metal panel roof covering on a roof slope less than (<) ¼ /12

Roof Deck Type Restriction

1. Install metal panel roof coverings on solid-sheathed roofs or on spaced sheathing.
2. Install metal panel roof coverings on spaced sheathing only if the material is designed for such sheathing.
3. Verify roof deck recommendations with the metal panel roof manufacturer.

Underlayment Application

1. You are not required to install underlayment with metal roof covering unless recommended by the metal roof covering manufacturer.
2. Install any required underlayment according to manufacturer's instructions.

Fastener Types

1. Use the type and quantity of fasteners specified by the metal roof manufacturer's instructions. Locate the fasteners as specified by the metal roof manufacturer's instructions.

REPAIR AND REPLACEMENT OF ROOF COVERINGS (R907)

Definition of Repair versus Replacement of Roof Coverings

1. You may repair existing roof covering material using the same materials and methods used on the existing roof, <u>if you repair less than (<) 25 percent of the roof area in a 12 month period</u>.
2. Comply with IRC provisions for new roof covering material, if you repair more than (≥) 25 percent of the roof in a 12 month period.
3. Refer to the International Building Code for additional information.

Permit Requirements

1. Verify permit requirements with the local building official before major roof covering repair and before roof covering replacement. A permit may be required for major repairs and replacement of roof covering.

Structural Loads Imposed by New Roof Covering Material

1. Verify that the building is capable of supporting the loads imposed by the new roof covering. This is particularly important when adding new roof covering material over existing

material and when replacing lighter roof covering material, such as fiberglass shingles, with heavier roof covering material such as concrete tile or slate.

Installing Additional Layers Over Existing Roof Covering Material

1. Do not install new roof covering material directly over existing roof covering material that is water-soaked, or otherwise deteriorated, or if the existing material will not be a satisfactory base for the new material.
2. Do not install new roof covering material directly over wood shakes, slate, and tiles of clay and cement.
3. Do not install new roof covering material directly over any roof with two or more existing layers of roof covering material.
4. Do not install new asphalt shingles over existing roof covering material in areas subject to moderate or severe hail exposure. Refer to the IRC Chapter 9 for a map showing hail exposure areas.
5. You may be allowed to install metal roofing systems over existing roof coverings, under certain conditions.
6. You may be allowed to install metal roofing systems and concrete and clay tiles over wood shakes if the building can accommodate the additional structural load and if roof covering does not create a combustible concealed space.

Wood Roof Concealed Spaces

1. Do not allow uncovered spaces and gaps between existing wood shingles and shakes and new roof covering material. This condition could occur when installing some metal panel roofing systems and when installing various types of curved profile roofing materials such as clay and concrete tiles.
2. Cover the entire existing wood roof covering with gypsum board, mineral fiber, or other approved material securely fastened in place, if spaces or gaps create combustible sealed spaces.

Reuse of Materials and Flashing

1. Do not reuse materials and flashing that are damaged, deteriorated, or rusted.
2. Materials and flashing that are in good condition may be reused according to manufacturer's instructions.

Roof Covering Repair and Replacement Best Practice

Obtain a building permit for roof covering replacement work regardless of whether one is required, or at least have the work independently inspected by a qualified person. Do not install any new roof covering material over existing material regardless of whether such work is allowed. A tear-off will cost more, but you will get a better long-term result. Do not reuse any existing flashing or other materials regardless whether it is allowed. New materials will cost more, but you will get a better long-term result. Employ a qualified engineer or contractor to verify roof structural integrity when adding new roof covering material over existing material or when replacing a lighter roof covering material with a heavier material.

10

FIREPLACES AND CHIMNEYS

MASONRY FIREPLACES (R1001)

Components Governed by this Chapter

The material in this chapter applies to masonry chimneys and fireplaces unless otherwise indicated. For rules governing factory-built fireplaces and chimneys, refer to sections of this chapter that specifically address factory-built chimneys and fireplaces and to the manufacturer's instructions for those components. If there is a difference between manufacturer's instructions and code provisions, use the manufacturer's instructions unless the IRC specifically states that you should use code provisions.

Masonry Fireplace Parts Definitions

Firebox or combustion chamber The firebox is the area in the fireplace where the fuel is burned.

Firebox opening The firebox opening is at the widest and highest dimension at the front of the firebox. The firebox opening extends vertically from the top of the hearth to the bottom of the lintel and horizontally across the front of the firebox walls.

Hearth The hearth is the floor of the firebox.

Hearth extension The hearth extension is the area in front of the firebox, made of noncombustible material, upon which sparks and hot materials from the firebox may land without starting a fire.

Lintel A lintel is a piece of noncombustible material, usually a piece of steel, located above the firebox opening that supports the masonry above the firebox opening.

Throat The throat is the opening above the firebox through which combustion products leave the firebox.

Damper The damper is a piece of ferrous metal that seals the firebox or chimney from the outdoors. The damper is usually located in the fireplace throat, but it may be located anywhere between the throat and the top of the chimney.

Smoke chamber The smoke chamber is an area above the firebox between the throat and the chimney.

Smoke shelf The smoke shelf is an optional dip at the bottom of the smoke chamber.

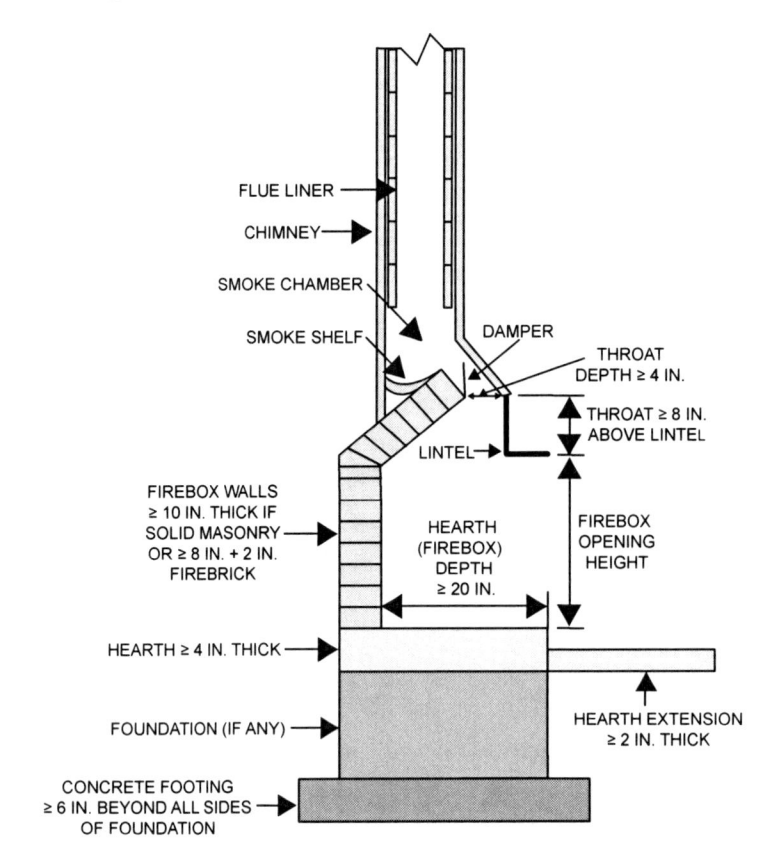

Fireplace Parts (R1001-1)
Figure 10-1

Masonry Firebox Construction

1. Build a masonry firebox (hearth) at least (≥) 20 inches deep. The IRC does not define a minimum width.
2. Build firebox walls using solid masonry, solid grouted hollow masonry, stone, or concrete.
3. Build firebox side and back walls at least (≥) 8 inches thick, including the lining, if using firebrick that is at least (≥) 2 inches thick or if using other approved lining material.
4. Build firebox side and back walls at least (≥) 10 inches thick, if not using firebrick or other approved lining material.
5. Lay firebrick using medium-duty refractory mortar with joints not more than (≤) ¼ inch.

Masonry Hearth Construction

1. Build a masonry firebox (hearth) at least (≥) 20 inches deep and at least (≥) 4 inches thick.
2. Build a masonry hearth and hearth extension using concrete or masonry. Reinforce both to carry their own weight and any imposed loads.
3. Do not leave any combustible material under the hearth and hearth extension when construction is complete.

Masonry Hearth Extension Construction

1. Build a hearth extension for a masonry fireplace at least (≥) 2 inches thick. You may use ap-

proved noncombustible material at least (≥) ⅜ inch thick, if the firebox bottom is at least (≥) 8 inches above the top of the hearth extension.

2. Build a hearth extension for a masonry fireplace at least (≥) 16 inches in front of the firebox opening and at least (≥) 8 inches to the sides of the firebox opening, if the firebox opening is less than (<) 6 square feet.
3. Build a hearth extension for a masonry fireplace at least (≥) 20 inches in front of the firebox opening and at least (≥) 12 inches to the side of the firebox opening, if the firebox opening is (≥) 6 square feet or more.
4. Build a hearth extension for a factory-built fireplace according to the fireplace manufacturer's instructions. The hearth extension size is often the same as for a masonry fireplace.

Lintels

1. Use noncombustible material for the lintel that is adequate to carry the load of the masonry above.
2. Place the lintel so that it bears at least (≥) 4 inches beyond each side of the fireplace opening.

Masonry Fireplace Throat Construction

1. Locate a masonry fireplace throat at least (≥) 8 inches above the lintel.
2. Make the masonry fireplace throat opening depth at least (≥) 4 inches.
3. Make the cross-sectional area of the masonry fireplace parts above the firebox, including the throat, damper, and smoke chamber, at least (≥) as large as the cross-sectional area of the flue. Example: a 7 inch round flue has an area of 38 square inches. The throat, damper, and smoke chamber must each have an area at least (≥) 38 square inches.

Masonry Fireplace Damper Location and Installation

1. You may locate the masonry fireplace damper anywhere between at least (≥) 8 inches above the lintel and the top of the chimney.
2. Use ferrous metal for the damper.
3. Locate the damper control in the room containing the fireplace.

Masonry Fireplace Smoke Chamber Construction

1. Build a masonry fireplace smoke chamber using solid masonry, solid grouted hollow masonry, stone, or concrete. Do not leave the cores of hollow masonry exposed in the smoke chamber.
2. Build the smoke chamber side and back walls at least (≥) 6 inches thick, including the lining, if using at least (≥) 2 inch thick firebrick or if using a lining of vitrified clay at least (≥) ⅝ inch thick.
3. Build smoke chamber side and back walls at least (≥) 8 inches thick, if not using firebrick or vitrified clay lining.
4. Lay firebrick using medium-duty refractory mortar.

5. Build the inside height of the smoke chamber (from the throat to the start of the flue) not higher than (≤) the inside width of the fireplace opening.
6. Incline the smoke chamber not more than (≤) 45 degrees from vertical, if using a prefabricated smoke chamber or when rolling or sloping the smoke chamber walls.
7. Corbel the smoke chamber not more than (≤) 30 degrees from vertical, if using corbelled masonry for the smoke chamber walls. Parge the inside of a corbelled smoke chamber so that the chamber has a smooth finish.

Masonry Fireplace Clearances to Combustible Materials

1. Leave at least (≥) 2 inches clearance between the front and sides of a masonry fireplace and combustible materials such as wood studs, joists, and beams. Leave at least (≥) 4 inches clearance between the back of the fireplace and combustible materials.
2. You are not required to leave space between combustible materials and:
   a) fireplaces listed and labeled for contact with combustible materials and installed according to manufacturer's instructions, and
   b) masonry fireplaces that are part of masonry wall or concrete walls if combustible materials are at least (≥) 12 inches from the inside surface of the firebox, and
   c) the edges of combustible materials, such as wood sheathing, wood siding, and wood flooring, if the materials abut the edges of a masonry fireplaces and if the edges are at least (≥) 12 inches from the inside surface of the firebox.

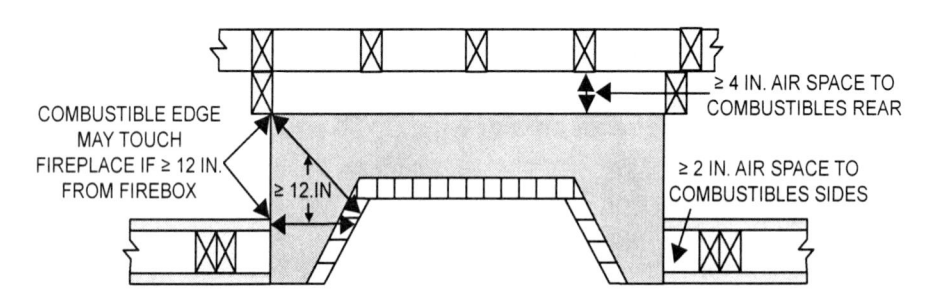

Fireplace Clearances to Combustible Materials (R1001-2)
Figure 10-2

Masonry Fireplace Mantels and Trim

1. Locate all combustible mantels and combustible trim at least (≥) 6 inches from a masonry fireplace opening.
2. Provide at least (≥) 1 inch clearance to the firebox opening for every ⅛ inch that combustible material projects from the fireplace surround. This applies to materials within (≤) 12 inches of the fireplace opening. Example: locate 1 inch thick fireplace mantel legs at least (≥) 8 inches from the fireplace opening. Example: locate greater than (>) 12 inches from the fireplace opening any part of a fireplace mantel or mantel leg that is more than (>) 1 ½ inches thick.

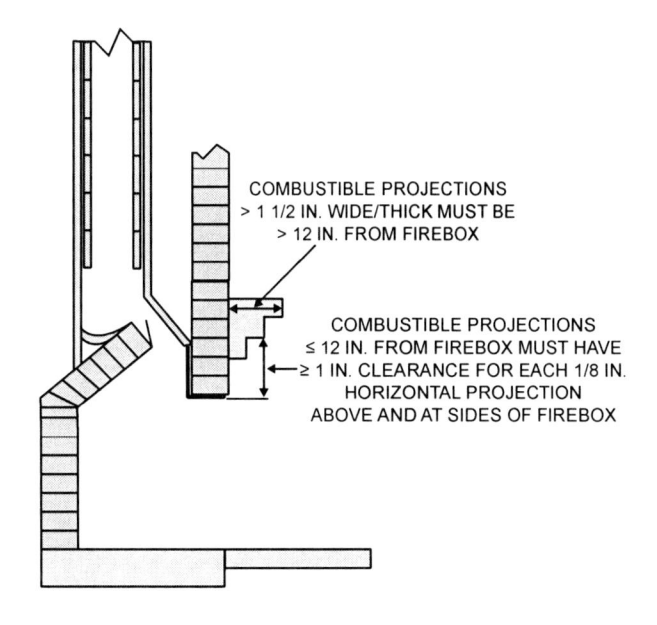

Fireplace Clearances to Projecting Combustible Trim (R1001-3)
Figure 10-3

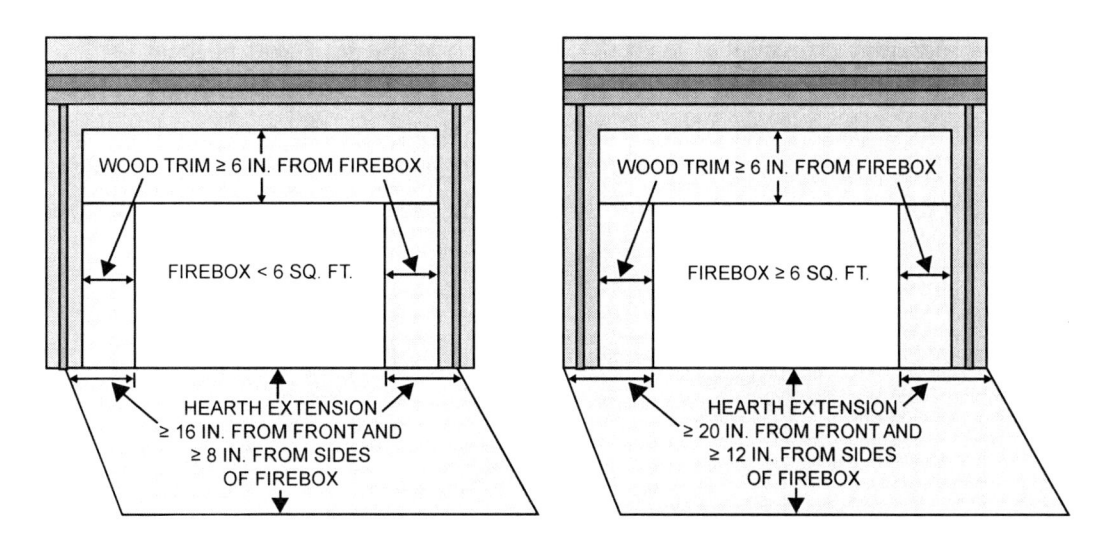

Fireplace Clearances to Combustible Trim (R1001-4)
Figure 10-4

Masonry Fireplace Fireblocking

1. Install noncombustible fireblocking material at all spaces where the fireplace passes through floors and ceilings.
2. Place the fireblocking material on metal strips or metal lath and provide at least (≥) 1 inch depth of fireblocking material and fasten the fireblocking material securely in place.
3. Do not fill the space around the fireplace other than to install required fireblocking.

Masonry Fireplace Foundation

1. Provide a masonry chimney and fireplace with a solid masonry or concrete foundation at

least (≥) 12 inches thick and at least (≥) 6 inches beyond every side of the chimney and fireplace wall. The usual frost line and undisturbed soil requirements apply to chimney and fireplace foundations.

MASONRY CHIMNEYS (R1003)

Chimney Definition

Chimney A chimney is a generally vertical, non-combustible structure that contains at least one flue and exhausts combustion products to the outdoors. A chimney may be constructed using masonry or it may be a factory-built system using a metal flue. Chimneys are usually built for use with solid-fuel-burning fireplaces, but may serve as vents for other fuel-burning devices such as gas and oil-burning equipment.

A properly sized chimney may serve as a vent for gas and oil-burning equipment, but chimneys and vents are constructed differently. The rules that apply to chimneys do not always apply to vents. Refer to Chapter 18 for oil-burning equipment vents and Chapter 24 for gas-burning equipment vents.

Chimney Termination Height

1. Terminate a masonry chimney at least (≥) 3 feet above the roof and at least (≥) 2 feet above any part of the building within 10 feet of the chimney. Measure termination height above the roof from the highest point where the chimney penetrates the roof to where the flue exits the chimney. This provision also applies to many factory-built chimneys. Confirm factory-built chimney termination height using the manufacturer's installation instructions.

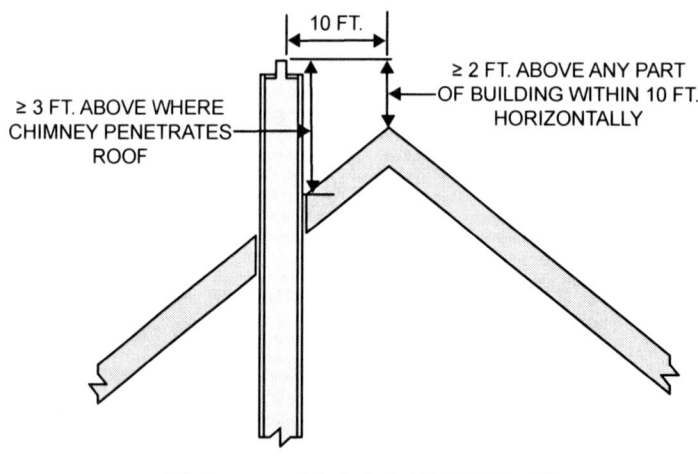

Chimney Height (R1003-1)
Figure 10-5

Chimney Crickets

1. Install a cricket (also called a saddle) on chimneys that are more than (>) 30 inches wide in the dimension parallel to the roof ridgeline. A cricket is not required if the chimney intersects the roof ridgeline. This also applies to factory-built chimneys that are installed inside a wood chimney chase.

2. Flash the cricket at the chimney wall using base and step counter flashing that is compatible with the roof covering material.
3. Install the cricket with a vertical height at the chimney based on the following table. W is the width of the chimney. Leave at least (≥) a 1 inch air space between a wood framed cricket and a masonry chimney wall.

TABLE R1003-1
Chimney Cricket Height

roof slope	cricket height
12/12	1/2 W
8/12	1/3 W
6/12	1/4 W
4/12	1/6 W
3/12	1/8 W

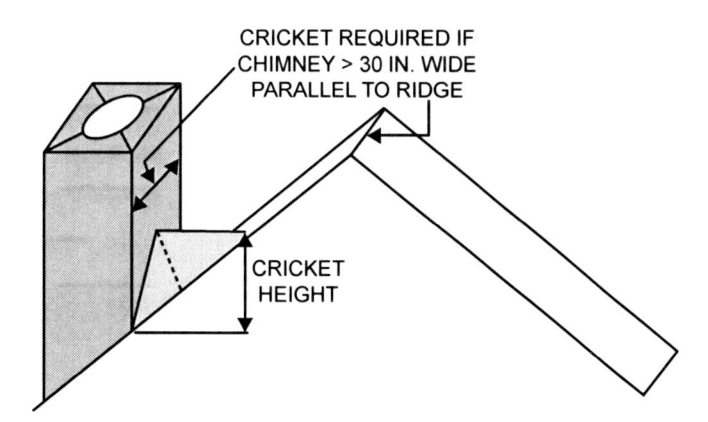

Chimney Cricket Height (R1003-2)
Figure 10-6

Spark Arrestors

1. You are not required to install a spark arrestor on a masonry chimney, unless the local building official requires one. They are, however, recommended to protect the home and surrounding area from fire and to protect the chimney from water damage.
2. Comply with all of the following requirements for installed spark arrestors:
   a) make the unobstructed arrestor area at least (≥) four times the area of the flue it serves;
   b) make the arrestor screen using heat and corrosion resistance equal to 19 gage galvanized steel or 24 gage stainless steel;
   c) build the arrestor screen so it does not pass ½ inch diameter spheres and does not obstruct ⅜ inch diameter spheres;
   d) make the arrestor accessible for cleaning and make the cap removable to allow flue cleaning.

Masonry Chimney Clearances to Combustible Materials

1. Leave at least (≥) 2 inches of clear air space between combustible materials and any part of a masonry chimney located within a building or within the exterior wall of a building. A chimney is within a building or within a building exterior wall if any side of the chimney abuts a building wall or if any side of the chimney is surrounded by the building walls. Example: a chimney built along the outside wall of a building is within the building exterior wall until the chimney penetrates the roof.
2. Leave a clear air space of at least (≥) 1 inch between combustible materials and masonry chimneys located entirely outside a building. A chimney is entirely outside a building if all chimney sides are open to the outdoors. Example: a chimney passing through a cornice or soffit is entirely outside the building.
3. Do not fill the clear air space, except to install required fireblocking.

Masonry Chimney Clearances to Combustible Materials Exceptions

1. You are not required to leave clear air space between combustible materials and:
    a) listed chimney lining systems labeled for contact with combustible materials and installed according to manufacturer's recommendations, and
    b) masonry chimneys that are part of masonry or concrete walls if the combustible materials are at least (≥) 12 inches away from the inside surface of the flue liner, and
    c) the edges of combustible materials, such as wood sheathing, wood siding, and wood flooring, if the combustible material edges abut the edges of a masonry chimney and if the combustible material edges are at least (≥) 12 inches away from the inside surface of the flue liner. The combustible material edges may project beyond the edge of the chimney not more than (≤) 1 inch.

Masonry Chimney Fireblocking

1. Install noncombustible fireblocking material at all spaces where the masonry chimney passes through floors and ceilings.
2. Place the fireblocking material on metal strips or metal lath and fasten the fireblocking material securely in place.
3. Install fireblocking material that is at least (≥) 1 inch thick.

10 : Fireplaces and Chimneys   199

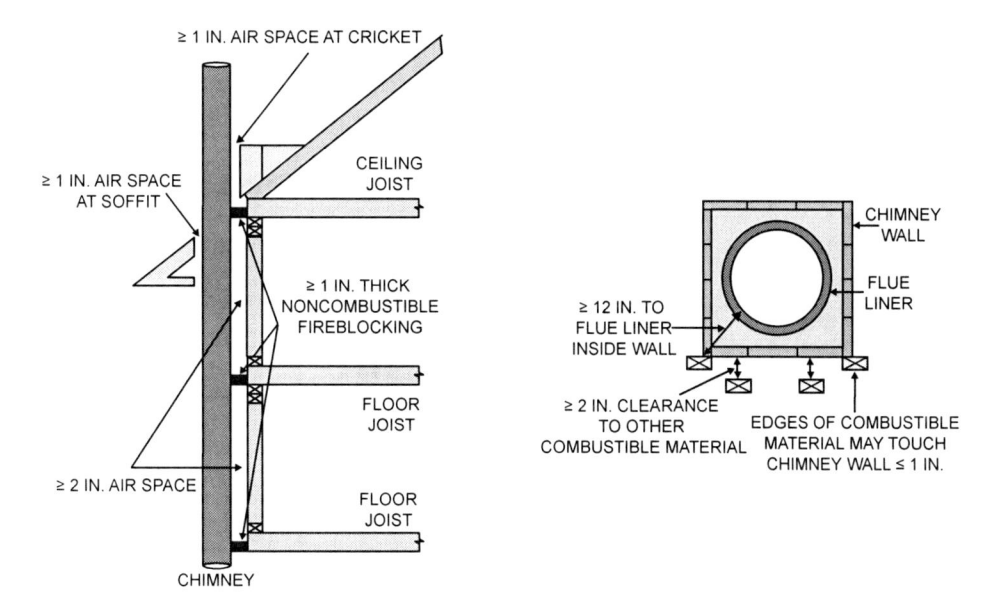

Chimney Clearance to Combustible Materials and Fireblocking (R1003-3)
Figure 10-7

Masonry Chimney Flue Liners

1. Line masonry chimneys with a fireclay liner, a listed chimney lining system, or other approved materials or systems if the chimney is built using 4 inch masonry (bricks).

Fireclay Flue Liner Installation

1. Install fireclay flue liners beginning at least (≥) 8 inches below the lowest appliance flue inlet or at the top of the fireplace smoke chamber and ending above the chimney walls.
2. Install fireclay flue liners with a slope from vertical of not more than (≤) 30 degrees.
3. Provide an air space between the fireclay flue liner and the masonry chimney walls that is not more than (≤) the thickness of the flue liner. Do not use the air space to vent or exhaust any other appliances.
4. Use medium-duty refractory mortar to seal joints between flue liner sections. Use only enough mortar to seal the joints and hold the liner in place. The liner should be smooth on the inside and the mortar should not restrict the air space between the liner and the chimney walls.

Masonry Chimney Flue Sizes

1. Measure masonry chimney flues using the net cross-sectional <u>area</u>. You may use the area in the following tables, or you may use the manufacturer provided area, or you may measure the area.
2. Determine a flue's aspect ratio by comparing the flue's length to its width.
3. Use a rectangular flue that has a net cross-sectional area of at least (≥) 1/10 of the fireplace opening when the flue's aspect ratio is less than (<) 2 to 1.
4. Use a rectangular flue that has a net cross-sectional area of at least (≥) 1/8 of the fireplace opening when the flue's aspect ratio at least (≥) 2 to 1.

5. Use a round flue that has a net cross-sectional area of at least (≥) 1/12 of the fireplace opening.
6. You may, as an alternative, use graphs in the IRC to determine masonry chimney flue sizes.

TABLE R1003-2
Fireplace Opening Sizes for Rectangular Flue Liners

flue size outside dimensions (inches)	net cross-sectional area (sq. in.)	aspect ratio	maximum fireplace opening size (sq. in.)
4 ½ x 13	34	2.9 to 1	272
8 x 8	42	1 to 1	420
8 ½ x 8 ½	49	1 to 1	490
8 x 12	67	1.5 to 1	670
8 ½ x 13	76	1.5 to 1	760
12 x 12	102	1 to 1	1020
8 ½ x 18	101	2.1 to 1	808
13 x 13	127	1 to 1	1,270
12 x 16	131	1.3 to 1	1,310
13 x 18	173	1.4 to 1	1,730
16 x 16	181	1 to 1	1,810
16 x 20	222	1.3 to 1	2,222
20 x 20	298	1 to 1	2,980

TABLE R1003-3
Fireplace Opening Sizes for Round Flue Liners

flue size inside diameter (inches)	net cross-sectional area (sq. in.)	maximum fireplace opening size (sq. in.)
6	28	336
7	38	456
8	50	600
10	78	936
10 ¾	90	1,080
12	113	1,356
15	176	2,112

Masonry Chimneys with Multiple Flues

1. Provide every fireplace and appliance with its own independent flue.
2. Separate chimney flues by at least (≥) one 4 inches masonry wythe bonded into the chimney walls.
3. You are not required to separate flues if the flues are used to vent only one appliance. The two flues may touch in the chimney with only the flue lining walls separating the flues. Stagger the adjacent flue joints at least (≥) 4 inches.

Masonry Chimney Changes in Size and Shape

1. Do not change the size or shape of a masonry chimney wall or masonry chimney flue lining within (≤) 6 inches above and below where the chimney passes through a floor, ceiling or roof.
2. Do not offset (slope from vertical) a fireclay flue liner so that the centerline of the flue liner above the offset extends beyond the centerline of the chimney wall below the offset. This restriction does not apply if the chimney wall is more than one wythe thick or if the offset is supported in an approved manner. The IRC does not define an approved support for chimney offsets.
3. Comply with the following restrictions when changing the shape or size (corbelling) of a masonry chimney:
    a) project (corbel) a single course of masonry not more than (≤) ½ of the masonry unit's height or more than (>) 1/3 of the masonry unit's bed depth, whichever is less, and
    b) project (corbel) a chimney not more than (≤) ½ of the chimney's wall thickness, and
    c) you may project (corbel) the chimney not more than (≤) the chimney wall thickness on the exterior of the enclosing walls on the second story of a two-story home, and
    d) extend or project (corbel) a chimney equally on both sides if the chimney has a wall thickness less than (<) 12 inches.

202 Everybody's Building Code

CENTERLINE OF FLUE ABOVE OFFSET

CENTERLINE OF WALL BELOW OFFSET

ONE WYTHE CHIMNEY WALLS

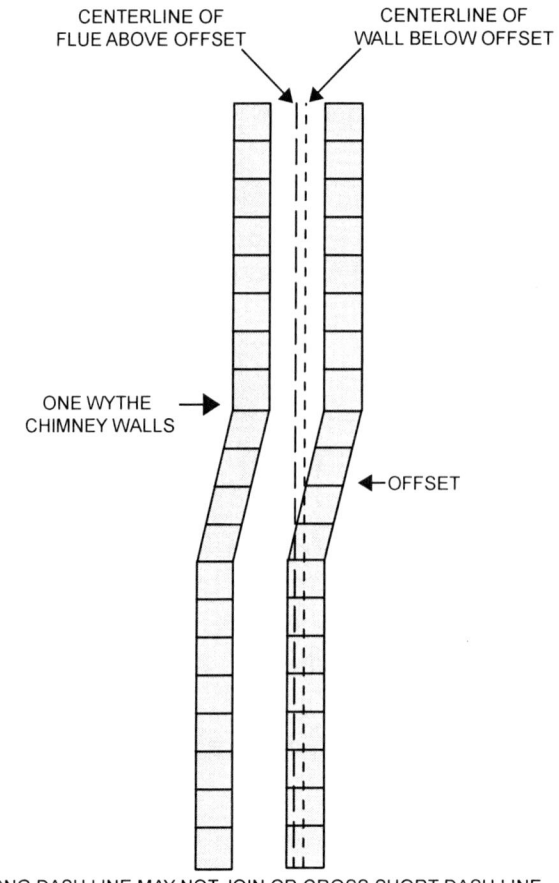

OFFSET

LONG DASH LINE MAY NOT JOIN OR CROSS SHORT DASH LINE

Maximum Chimney Offset (R1003-4)
Figure 10-8

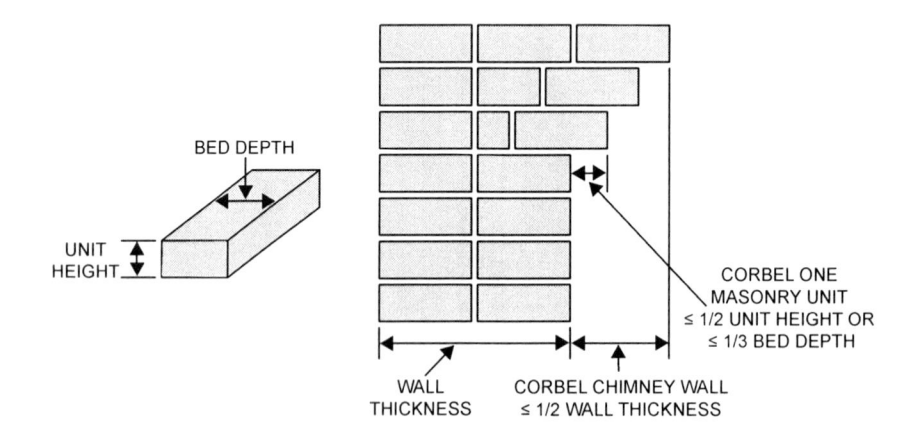

BED DEPTH

UNIT HEIGHT

CORBEL ONE MASONRY UNIT
≤ 1/2 UNIT HEIGHT OR
≤ 1/3 BED DEPTH

WALL THICKNESS

CORBEL CHIMNEY WALL
≤ 1/2 WALL THICKNESS

Brick Corbels (R1003-5)
Figure 10-9

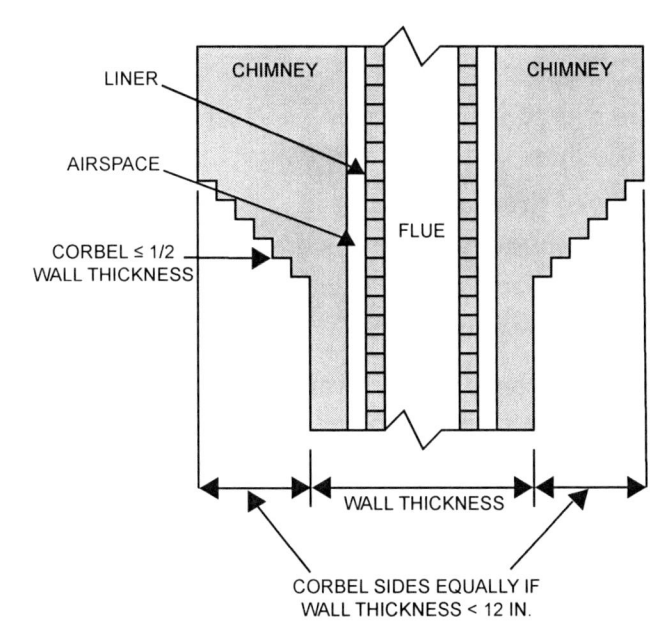

Brick Chimney Corbelling at Second Story (R1003-6)
Figure 10-10

Masonry Chimney Wall Thickness

1. Build masonry chimney walls using solid masonry, or hollow masonry with mortar in all holes, that is at least (≥) 4-inches nominal thickness.

Masonry Chimney Cleanout Openings

1. Install a cleanout opening with a noncombustible door and an opening height of at least (≥) 6 inches within not more than (≤) 6 inches from the base of each masonry chimney flue.
2. You are not required to install a cleanout opening if a masonry fireplace can be cleaned through the fireplace opening.

Masonry Chimney Foundation

1. Provide the masonry chimney and fireplace with a solid masonry or concrete foundation at least (≥) 12 inches thick and that extends at least (≥) 6 inches beyond every side of the chimney wall. The usual frost line and undisturbed soil requirements apply to masonry chimney foundations.

Masonry Chimney Additional Structural Loads

1. Do not use a masonry chimney to support loads other than that of the chimney itself unless the chimney is designed to support the additional loads. Structural loads include roof and floor framing and attachments such as antennas.

Fuel-Burning Appliance Connection to Masonry Chimneys

1. Do not connect an appliance vent to a masonry chimney flue if the area of the appliance connector is larger than (>) the area of the chimney flue.

2. Connect gas appliance vents to masonry chimney flues according to the provisions for gas appliance vents in IRC Chapter 24.
3. Connect appliances, such as pellet fuel-burning and oil fuel-burning appliances, to masonry chimney flues only if the flue:
   a) is built with an approved fire-clay liner, or if
   b) has been relined with a chimney lining system listed for use in a masonry chimney and listed for use with the appliance, or if
   c) is built using approved materials.
4. Install a permanent label in a conspicuous location warning occupants if a chimney has been relined and warning them what types of appliances may be connected to the chimney.

Masonry Chimney Seismic Reinforcing

1. Reinforce masonry chimneys and fireplaces in seismic activity areas with vertical and horizontal reinforcing. Vertical reinforcing usually consists of four number 4 reinforcing bars. Horizontal reinforcing usually consists of ¼ inch ties placed every 18 inches of vertical height to form a cage with the vertical reinforcing bars.
2. Anchor chimneys to the building if any part of the chimney is outside of building's exterior walls.
3. Refer to IRC 1003.3 for more about chimney seismic reinforcing.

FIREPLACE COMBUSTION AIR (R1006)

Combustion Air Required

1. Provide combustion air from outside the building for masonry and factory-built fireplaces.

Masonry Fireplace Combustion Air

1. Draw combustion air from outdoors, or from attics or crawl spaces that are not sealed or mechanically ventilated. Do not draw combustion air from a basement or garage.
2. Locate the combustion air intake source below the firebox.
3. Cover the exterior combustion air intake terminal with a corrosion-resistant ¼ inch mesh screen.
4. Provide the combustion air duct with an area at least (≥) 6 square inches and not more than (≤) 55 square inches. The combustion air duct must be large enough to provide all combustion air for the fireplace.
5. Provide unlisted ducts with at least (≥) 1 inch clearance between the duct and combustible materials within at least (≥) 5 feet of where the duct terminates in the home (the duct outlet).
6. Locate the duct outlet in the back or sides of the firebox or not more than (≤) 24 inches from the firebox opening, either on or near the floor.
7. Provide a means to close the duct outlet and design it to ensure that burning material cannot drop into concealed combustible spaces.

Factory-Built Fireplace Combustion Air

1. Provide combustion air for factory-built fireplaces according to the fireplace manufacturer's instructions. Manufacturer's instructions may differ from the IRC provisions for masonry fireplaces.

FACTORY- BUILT FIREPLACES AND CHIMNEYS (R1004, R1005, G2430, G2432, AND G2433)

Factory-Built Fireplace and Chimney Discussion

Factory-built fireplaces and chimneys include components tested, listed, and labeled to be installed together as a system. Such fireplaces are usually designed to burn solid fuels, such as wood, although they may be converted to use gas logs if approved by the fireplace manufacturer. Do not mix components from different manufacturers unless approved by the fireplace manufacturer.

Fireplaces designed to burn only gas are not really fireplaces. They are decorative gas appliances. Vented decorative gas appliances are more like a water heater than like a fireplace. Unvented decorative gas appliances are more like a gas range than like a fireplace. Install and use decorative gas appliances according to manufacturer's instructions and IRC Chapter 24. Note that some jurisdictions do not allow unvented decorative gas appliances. Also note that manufacturers of unvented decorative gas appliances recommend opening a window during use and recommend limits on the duration of use.

Factory-Built Fireplace and Chimney Installation

1. Install factory-built chimneys and fireplaces according to the manufacturer's instructions. These instructions include requirements for hearth extensions, clearances to combustible materials, and installation of combustion air ducts.

Decorative Chimney Covers

1. Do not install decorative chimney covers, shrouds, or similar components at the chimney termination unless the component is listed and labeled for use with the particular fireplace system.

Structural Support for Factory-Built Fireplaces

1. Provide adequate structural support for factory-built fireplaces and chimneys according to manufacturer's recommendations.

Gas Logs and Gas Log Lighters (G2432 and G2433)

1. Install and use gas log sets and gas log lighters in masonry and factory-built fireplaces according to the manufacturer's instructions for the fireplace and the manufacturer's instructions for the gas logs and/or gas log lighters.

11

ENERGY EFFICIENCY

LIMITATIONS OF THE MATERIAL IN THIS CHAPTER

IRC Chapter 11 offers a comparatively simple method to comply with the IRC energy efficiency requirements. This method is explained and clarified in subsequent parts of this book chapter. If each individual component complies with the value stated in the table, then the building complies with the energy efficiency requirements.

IRC Chapter 11 and the International Energy Conservation Code (IECC) also provide alternate methods of compliance. These alternate methods are complex and require documentation explaining how compliance is achieved. We will not cover the alternate methods in this book. Refer to IRC Commentary Chapter 11 or to the IECC, or to a qualified energy contractor for more information about alternate energy efficiency compliance methods.

BUILDINGS GOVERNED BY IRC ENERGY EFFICIENCY REQUIREMENTS

1. Apply IRC Chapter 11 or IECC requirements to all residential buildings governed by the IRC. This IRC Chapter does not apply to parts of the building that do not contain conditioned space, such as an attached, unconditioned garage.
2. Verify energy efficiency requirements with the local building official. Interpretation and enforcement of this IRC Chapter varies between jurisdictions.

INSULATION INSTALLATION GENERAL REQUIREMENTS

1. Install insulation according to manufacturer's installation instructions and applicable provisions of the IRC. Manufacturer's instructions are an enforceable extension of the code.
2. Install insulation so that the manufacturer's R-value identification mark is readily observable for inspection. The manufacturer is required to place an R-value mark on each piece of insulation more than 12 inches wide or the insulation contractor may provide written certification of the manufacturer and R-value of the insulation installed if there is no manufacturer's R-value mark.
3. Install insulation that has a rigid, opaque, and water-resistive covering that will protect it from the elements when installing insulation on the exterior of basement walls, on crawl space walls, and on the perimeter of slab-on-grade floors. Extend the protective coating at least (≥) 6 inches below grade.
4. Affix an energy certificate on or in the electrical panel. The builder or registered design professional should complete the certificate. Provide the following information on the certificate: (a) the predominant insulation R-values in the attic/ceiling, walls, foundation, and HVAC ducts not in conditioned areas, and (b) the U-value and SHGC of fenestration, and

(c) the type and efficiency of the HVAC and water heating equipment, and (d) notice if home contains a gas unvented room heater, an electric furnace, or baseboard electric heaters. If there is more than one value for a component, use the value covering the largest area. You may place additional information on the certificate.
5. Refer to IRC Table N1102.4.2 for specific requirements regarding air barrier and insulation installation requirements. These requirements differ significantly from current common installation practices and codify generally accepted best installation practices.

ENERGY EFFICIENCY DEFINITIONS

Basement wall A basement wall is a wall with at least (≥) 50 percent of its area below grade (covered by earth on the outside). A wall with less than (<) 50 percent of its area below grade is an exterior wall. Examine each individual below grade wall to determine if it is a basement or exterior wall. This definition is not the same as the definition for story above grade.

Building or thermal envelope The building or thermal envelope is the conditioned (heated and/or cooled) area of the dwelling. The envelope boundary between conditioned and unconditioned space includes walls, ceilings, floors, basement walls and slab-on-grade foundations. The thermal envelope may include the attic and the crawl space if these areas are designed and built as conditioned space.

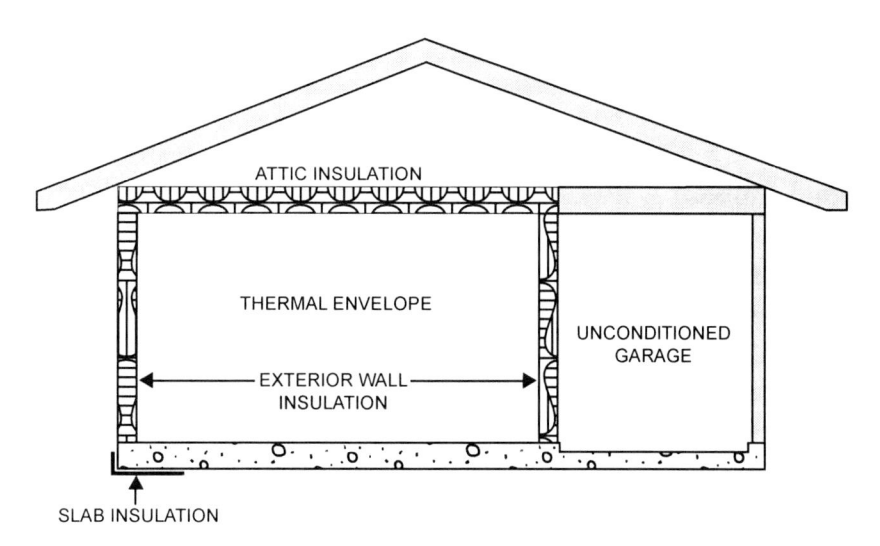

Thermal Envelope One Story Slab Foundation (N1102-1)
Figure 11-1

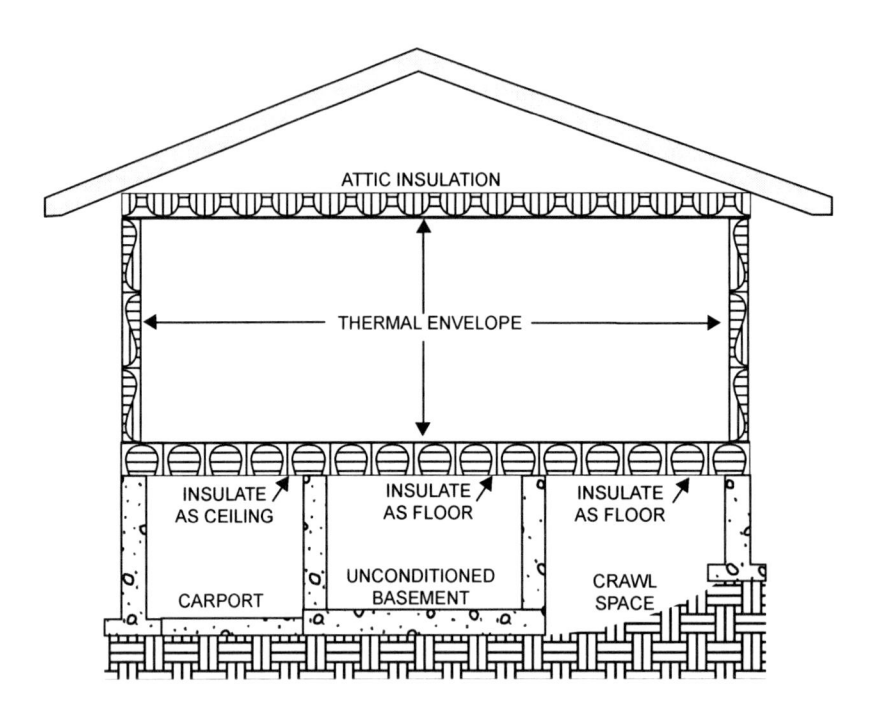

Thermal Envelope One Story Raised Foundation (N1102-2)
Figure 11-2

Ceilings Ceilings include all standard truss and rafter constructed flat, vaulted, and cathedral ceilings.

Exterior wall (wood framed) A wood framed exterior wall is a vertical wall (not a basement wall) that surrounds the building envelope. Exterior walls include: (a) walls between an unconditioned garage and conditioned space, and (b) below grade walls with less than (<) 50 percent of the area below grade, and (c) knee walls, dormer walls, skylight walls in attics, walls at ceiling height changes, and similar walls surrounding conditioned space, and (d) rim joists and similar structures between floors.

Fenestration Fenestration means any door, window, glass block, or skylight whether glazed or opaque.

Mass wall Mass walls, for Chapter 11 purposes, are vertical exterior walls (not basement walls) built with concrete blocks, concrete, insulated concrete forms, masonry cavity walls, brick (not brick veneer), adobe, compressed earth block, rammed earth, and solid timber/logs. Masonry and concrete mass walls should weigh at least (≥) 30 pounds per square foot. Solid timber and log walls should weigh at least (≥) 20 pounds per square foot.

R-value R-value is a measure of a material's resistance to conductive heat flow. R-value is the material's insulating value. A higher R-value indicates higher resistance to conductive heat flow. Only components designed to provide insulation, such as fiberglass batts and insulated sheathing, have an R-value for Chapter 11 purposes. Do not use any R-value for components such as drywall, structural sheathing, and siding when calculating the total R-value for an insulated assembly such as a wood-framed wall.

Solar heat gain coefficient (SHGC) SHGC is a measure of the amount of solar radiation that passes through a window. A lower SHGC means that less solar radiation passes through a window.

U-factor U-factor is a measure of a material's capacity to allow conductive heat flow. The U-factor is the reciprocal of the R-value. A lower U-factor indicates a higher resistance to conductive heat flow. The U-factor is most often used to describe the thermal efficiency of windows, glazed and opaque doors, and skylights. Chapter 11 contains an alternative compliance method based on the U-factor values of the building's components.

INSULATION AND FENESTRATION REQUIREMENTS (N1102)

Insulation and Fenestration Requirements Table

1. Use the following table to determine the insulation and fenestration requirements to comply with IRC energy efficiency provisions.
2. Refer to individual component sections when an option is indicated in the table. Example: refer to the mass wall section for an explanation of the options in the mass wall column.

TABLE N1102-1
Insulation and Fenestration Requirements

climate zone	fenestration U-factor max.	skylight U-factor max.	glazed fenestration and skylight SHGC max.	ceiling R-value min.	wood-framed wall R-value min.	mass wall R-value min.	floor R-value min.	basement wall R-value min.	slab R-value/ depth min.	crawl space walls R-value min.
1	1.2	0.75	0.40	30	13	3/4	13	0	0	0
2	0.75	0.75	0.40	30	13	4/6	13	0	0	0
3	0.65	0.65	0.40	30	13	5/8	19	0	0	5/13
4 except marine	0.40	0.60	none	38	13	5/10	19	10/13	10/ 2 ft.	10/13
5 and marine 4	0.35	0.60	none	38	19 or 13 + 5	13/13	30	10/13	10/ 2 ft.	10/13
6	0.35	0.60	none	49	19 or 13 + 5	15/19	30	10/13	10/ 4 ft.	10/13
7 and 8	0.35	0.60	none	49	21	19/21	30	10/13	10/ 4 ft.	10/13

Fenestration U-factor and SHGC Requirements

1. Obtain U-factor and SHGC ratings from the manufacturer's label on the fenestration. If the manufacturer does not provide the fenestration's ratings, use the default ratings from IRC Chapter 11.
2. You may calculate an area-weighted average U-factor for all fenestration when individual fenestration components do not comply with the U-factor requirements.
3. You may calculate an area-weighted average SHGC when individual fenestration components do not comply with the SHGC requirements. You need not include components that are less than (<) 50% glazed in the area-weighted average SHGC calculation. Example: you need not include doors with small windows in the area-weighted average SHGC calculation.
4. You may exclude not more than (≤) 15 square feet of glazed fenestration from both the U-factor and SHGC requirements. You may also exclude one opaque door from the fenestration U-factor requirement. This means that you do not have to include 15 square feet of glazed fenestration, such as cut glass or stained glass, and one opaque door when using Table N1102.1 and when performing an area-weighted average calculation. This allows some design flexibility when selecting windows and doors.
5. You need not comply with SHGC requirements in Marine climate zones.
6. Example (for both U-factor and SHGC area-weighted average): assume one window with a glazed area of 10 square feet and a SHGC of .35 and assume one window with a glazed area of 15 square feet and a SHGC of .45. The area-weighted average SHGC of the two windows is ((10 x .35) + (15 x .45)) / (10 + 15) = .41. If these were the only two windows in a home in climate zones one, two, or three, these windows would not comply with the Table N1102.1 requirement.

Window Energy Efficiency Rating Label (PN1102-0)
Figure 11-3

Replacement Window Efficiency Requirements

1. Comply with the U-factor and SHGC values in the Table N1102.1 when replacing windows in an existing building with new windows, including new frames, sash, and glazing. This requirement does not apply when replacing only glazing.

Ceiling Insulation Requirements

1. You may substitute R-30 insulation for R-38, and you may substitute R-38 insulation for R-49, near the top plate, if the distance between the ceiling and roof framing does not allow for full insulation thickness near the outer edge at the top plate. You may extend the reduced insulation only until the distance between the ceiling and the roof allows for the full thickness of the required insulation.

2. You may install at least (≥) R-30 insulation in some ceilings without attic spaces, such as vaulted and cathedral ceilings, even if Table N1102.1 requires more insulation. You may apply this exception to not more than (≤) 500 square feet of ceiling space in the entire home. The exception accounts for the fact that it is not possible to place more than R-30 insulation in many framed vaulted and cathedral ceilings.

Exterior (Wood-Framed) Walls Insulation Requirements

1. Insulate exterior walls that face or are open to unconditioned space. Example: walls surrounding a furnace closet are exterior walls when the closet has combustion air openings to the outside, or to an attic, or to a crawl space. Install an exterior door, including weather strip and threshold, at such furnace closets. Example: walls surrounding a skylight chase are exterior walls where they face the attic or other unconditioned area.

2. You may use R-13 wall cavity insulation plus R-5 insulated sheathing to satisfy the exterior wall insulation requirements in climate zones five and six. This is a common method for insulating 2x4 exterior walls. You may substitute structural sheathing for R-5 insulated sheathing if the structural sheathing covers not more than (≤) 25% of the exterior wall surface. Add at least (≥) R-2 insulated sheathing to the structural sheathing if the structural sheathing covers more than (>) 25% of the exterior wall surface.

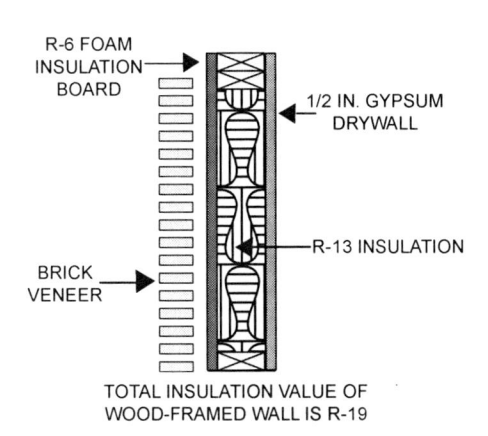

Wood-Framed Wall Insulation (N1102-3)
Figure 11-4

Steel-Framed Wall Insulation Requirements

1. Refer to the IRC for more information about insulating steel-framed walls.

Mass Wall Insulation Requirements

1. Use the first value in the mass wall column of Table N1102-1 to determine mass wall insulation requirements when at least (≥) 50% of the insulation R-value is on the wall's exterior or is integrated into the wall structure. Example: a concrete block wall with R-5 insulated sheathing applied to the exterior would satisfy Table N1102-1 requirements in climate zones four and below. Example: a concrete block wall with insulated cores would satisfy Table N1102-1 requirements for insulation integrated into the wall structure.
2. Use the second value in the mass wall column of Table N1102-1 to determine mass wall insulation requirements when more than (>) 50% of the insulation R-value is on the wall's interior. Building a stud wall on the inside of the mass wall and filling the wall cavity with insulation is a common method for satisfying the Table N1102-1 insulation requirement. You may install insulation on the interior of a mass wall according to the following table instead of using the Table N1102-1 exterior wall values.

Floor Insulation Requirements

1. Secure floor insulation so that it maintains permanent contact with the subfloor decking.
2. You may install less than R-30 floor insulation climate zones five through eight if it is not possible to properly install R-30 insulation in the floor cavity. Install at least (≥) R-19 insulation in such floor cavities.

Basement Wall Insulation Requirements

1. Insulate either the basement walls or the basement ceiling, as required by Table N1102.1, if the basement is unconditioned space.
2. Insulate the basement walls, if the basement is conditioned space. Insulate the band joists or rim boards at the first floor system when insulating basement walls.
3. Insulate the basement ceiling using the floor values in the table, if you elect to insulate the basement ceiling.
4. Insulate basement walls from the top of the wall to a depth of 10 feet below grade or to the basement floor, whichever is less.
5. You may use continuous insulation at R-10, such as insulated sheathing, or you may use framed-wall cavity insulation at R-13 to satisfy basement wall insulation requirements.

Slab-on-grade Floor Insulation Requirements

1. Insulate slab-on-grade floors under conditioned spaces unless the floor surface is at least (≥) 12 inches below grade. You may install the insulation either on the interior or exterior of the slab.
2. You need not insulate slab-on-grade floors in areas with very heavy termite infestation probability.
3. Install the insulation downward from the top of the slab to the bottom of the slab or until

reaching the depth in Table N1102.1. If necessary to reach the depth in the table, extend the insulation horizontally until reaching the required depth in the table.
4. Protect any horizontal insulation extending away from the building with pavement or at least 10 inches of soil.
5. Add R-5 to the table values if the slab contains heating elements.

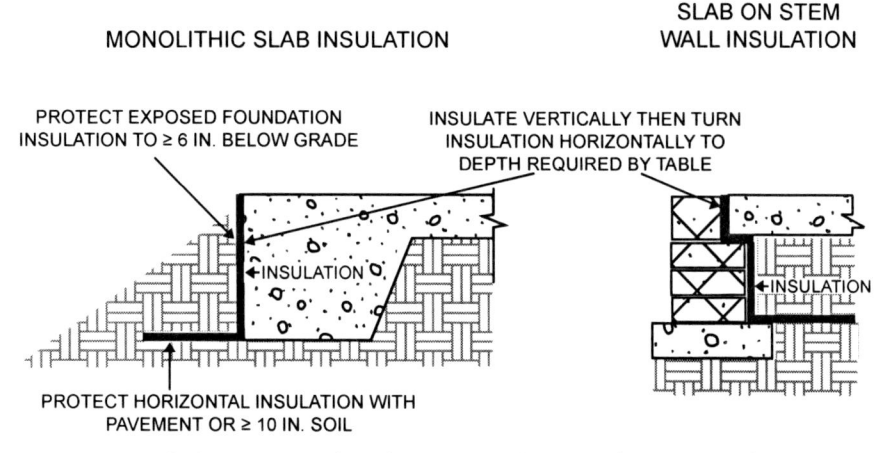

Slab-on-grade Floor Insulation (N1102-4)
Figure 11-5

Crawl Space Foundation Insulation Requirements

1. You may either insulate the floor above ventilated crawl space foundations or insulate crawl space foundation walls of unventilated crawl spaces.
2. Install crawl space wall insulation on the inside of the crawl space walls beginning at the sill plate and extending to <u>exterior finished grade</u>, then extending for an additional 24 inches either vertically along crawl space wall or horizontally along the ground.
3. Install a continuous vapor retarder over all exposed earth in unventilated crawl spaces as described in Section 408. The most common vapor retarder material is 6 mil polyethylene.

Blown and Sprayed Insulation Installation Requirements

1. Provide written certification of the insulation type, insulation manufacturer, installed density and R-value when insulation is blown or sprayed in walls.
2. Provide written certification of the insulation's settled R-value, installed density, installed and settled thickness, coverage area, and the number of bags used when insulation is blown or sprayed in an attic. Place the signed and dated certificate in a conspicuous place. The written certification is often placed in the attic at the attic access opening.
3. Provide written certification of the installed thickness and R-value of sprayed polyurethane foam insulation.
4. Place markers having 1 inch high numbers every 300 square feet to indicate the installed thickness of the insulation before installing attic insulation. Face the markers toward the attic access opening.
5. The insulation contractor is responsible for providing all certifications and markers.

Sealing Openings in the Thermal Envelope

1. Seal all openings in the thermal envelope using caulk, weather stripping, gaskets, or other approved materials. Use sealing materials that are flexible and will allow for different rates of expansion and contraction between different materials. Openings include: (a) joints and gaps between framing materials (such as tees and corners in exterior stud walls), (b) space between sill plates and the foundation, (c) spaces around doors, windows and skylights, (d) penetrations for utility cables and pipes, (e) openings in walls and ceilings for electrical boxes and recessed lights, (f) spaces behind tubs and showers on exterior walls, (g) dropped ceilings, soffits, and chases, (h) walls and ceilings that separate an attached garage from conditioned space, (i) attic access openings, and any other joints, seams, and penetrations. Lack of sealing allows air movement that can reduce insulation effectiveness and can allow moisture in the air to enter and condense in the wall cavity.
2. Verify air sealing and insulation installation by either a blower door test or by visual inspection by an approved person.

Access Doors and Openings

1. Install weather stripping and insulation on doors and access openings between conditioned and unconditioned spaces. Doors and openings include: attic access hatches covered with drywall, plywood, and similar materials, pull-down attic stairs, doors into furnace closets that have combustion air openings to the outside, and outside doors into conditioned crawl spaces. Use the same weather stripping and insulation as required for the surrounding area.
2. Install a wood-framed baffle or similar structure around attic access hatches to prevent loose-fill insulation from falling out when the hatch cover is removed.

Recessed Light Types and Installation

1. Install recessed lights that are Type IC rated and labeled as complying with ASTM E.
2. Seal recessed lights by caulking or installing a gasket between the light housing and the wall or ceiling covering.

Vapor Retarders

1. Design wall, ceiling, and floor systems so that water vapor will not enter into and condense in the systems. Water vapor will migrate from warm and moist areas into cool areas and it will condense when the temperature in the cool area drops below the dew point. Water vapor that condenses in wood-framed systems will damage the wood, reduce the R-value of any insulation in the system, and provide moisture for fungal growth.
2. Install vapor retarders on the warm-in-winter side of insulation in climate zones Marine 4, 5, 6, 7, and 8. You may eliminate vapor retarders in climate zones four and lower and you may install vapor retarders on the warm-in-summer side of insulation in these climate zones, based on local conditions.

Duct Insulation and Sealing

1. Insulate HVAC supply ducts to at least (≥) R-8. Insulate all other ducts to at least (≥) R-6
2. You are not required to insulate ducts that are completely within conditioned space.
3. Verify duct sealing with a duct pressure test. You may perform this test during rough-in or after final installation of the HVAC system. Refer to the IRC for test requirements.

Thermostats

1. Install at least (≥) 1 set back type thermostat in each home.
2. Install an adaptive recovery type thermostat on heat pumps that prevents operation of supplemental heat strips if the heat pump compressor can satisfy the heating load.

Pipe Insulation

1. Insulate to at least (≥) R-2 pipes in mechanical systems that can carry fluids above 105° F or below 55° F. Examples of such pipes include air conditioning refrigerant suction tubes (the larger tube) and pipes in hot water and steam heating systems.

Hot Water Circulating Systems

1. Provide hot water circulating systems with a timer or with a readily accessible switch that can turn of the pump.
2. Insulate pipes or tubes used in a hot water circulating system to at least (≥) R-2. One common interpretation of this provision requires insulation of all hot water pipes if the water distribution system is designed and plumbed for installation of a hot water recirculating pump. A less common, but reasonable, interpretation of this provision requires insulation of all hot water pipes because hot water circulating systems can be retrofitted on most hot water distribution systems.

Air Intake and Exhaust Systems

1. Provide an automatic or gravity operated damper for mechanical air intake and exhaust systems that will close the damper when the system is not operating.

Fireplaces

1. Install gasketed doors and outdoor combustion air on all new wood-burning fireplaces. This includes new masonry and factory-built fireplaces.

Swimming Pools

1. Install a readily accessible on/off switch on any swimming pool heater.
2. Install a timer switch on all pool heaters and pumps.
3. Install a vapor retardant cover on heated pools. Some exceptions exist to this requirement, but the exceptions are rare in residential pools. Refer to IRC Section N1103.8

Light Bulbs

1. Install compact fluorescent or similar approved light bulbs in at least (≥) 50% of all light fixtures in the home. Refer to IRC Chapter 2 for bulb specifications.

Energy Efficiency Best Practice

In very warm areas of the country where solar heat gain is significant, consider installing a radiant barrier in the attic. A properly installed radiant barrier can be far more effective than insulation in reducing heat transfer between conditioned space and attics.

Warning: installers have been known to blow insulation at the required thickness near the markers and blow less insulation in more inaccessible areas of an attic.

For more information about energy efficiency and green building, refer to sources such as the National Association of Home Builders Green Building Guidelines (www.nahbgreen.org) and similar guidelines from the U. S. Green Building Council (www.usgbc.org).

12

MECHANICAL SYSTEMS CHANGES AND MAINTENANCE

MECHANICAL SYSTEMS CHANGES AND MAINTENANCE (M1201 AND M1202)

Mechanical Systems Governed by the IRC

Mechanical systems governed by the IRC are permanently installed heating, ventilation, and air conditioning systems. The IRC does not govern temporary and portable equipment and it does not govern most plug-and-cord connected heating and cooling equipment. HVAC is a common acronym that refers to mechanical systems and stands for heating, ventilation, and air conditioning.

Updates and Changes to HVAC Systems

1. Comply with IRC provisions <u>in effect when the work is performed</u> when making additions, alterations, and major repairs to existing HVAC systems. Only the new system components must comply with current IRC provisions. You are not required to make existing HVAC system components comply with current IRC provisions.

2. You do not need to comply with current IRC provisions when making minor additions, adjustments, alterations, and repairs to existing HVAC systems, if the work is performed using methods and materials equivalent to existing methods and materials, and if the work does not cause the existing system to become unsafe, and if the work is approved by the local building official.

Grandfathering Existing HVAC Systems

1. You are not required to abandon, remove, or alter an HVAC system that is lawfully in existence and safely functioning. Lawfully in existence means the system was inspected and complied with the code when installed and/or modified.

Maintenance of Existing HVAC Systems Required

1. Maintain HVAC systems so that they remain safe and operate according to their original design. Maintenance is the responsibility of the building owner or owner's agent. The building official may require reinspection of HVAC systems to confirm safety and maintenance.

13

MECHANICAL SYSTEMS GENERAL REQUIREMENTS

ACCESS TO MECHANICAL APPLIANCES (M1305)

Access Requirements for Mechanical Appliances

1. Provide access to mechanical appliances that does not require removing or damaging permanent construction. Access means the ability to inspect, repair, remove, and replace the largest piece of the appliance without removing or damaging permanent construction. Permanent construction means structural materials such as studs and joists and means finish materials such as drywall and wood trim. Permanent construction includes other appliances and other piping and ducts not connected to the appliance being serviced. Example: two furnaces are located in an attic. A duct or pipe from furnace one may not block the access path or service platform for furnace two.
2. Provide a level work space or platform at least (≥) 30 inches deep and wide in front of the appliance control side, or more if recommended by the manufacturer.
3. Provide room heaters with at least (≥) 18 inches on the control side. No working platform is required in front of room heaters.

Access to Appliances Installed in Compartments, Closets, and Alcoves

1. Provide a total working space for furnaces and air handlers installed in compartments, closets, and alcoves at least (≥) 12 inches wider than the appliance and provide at least (≥) 3 inches working space on each side, back, and top of the appliance. Working space means the space required to maintain the appliance. Working space is different from clearance to combustible materials.
2. Provide at least (≥) 6 inches working space in front of the combustion chamber side of furnaces with a firebox open to the atmosphere. This includes most furnaces.
3. Apply these minimum working space requirements even if the manufacturer's instructions allow lesser clearances.
4. You are not required to apply these working space requirements to replacement appliances if they are installed according to manufacturer's instructions.

Access to Appliances in Rooms where the Appliance Is Not Accessible from the Service Opening

1. Provide the following access for appliances located in rooms or alcoves where the appliance is not directly accessible from the service opening: (a) a door or opening and an unobstructed passageway to the appliance that is at least (≥) 24 inches wide or large enough to remove the largest piece of appliance, whichever is greater, and (b) a level service platform at the

service side of the appliance that is at least (≥) 30 inches deep and as high as the appliance or 30 inches high, whichever is greater.

Access to Appliances in Attics.

1. Provide the following service access for appliances located in an attic:
   a) an unobstructed finished (clear) access opening at least (≥) 20 inches by 30 inches, and large enough to remove the largest piece of the appliance, whichever is larger, and
   b) a continuous and unobstructed path of solid flooring at least (≥) 24 inches wide, and at least (≥) 30 inches high, and not more than (≤) 20 feet long measured along the center line of the floor beginning at the opening of the appliance, and
   c) a level service platform at least (≥) 30 inches wide and 30 inches deep and 30 inches high on all sides of the appliance that require service access, and
   d) a light fixture controlled by a switch located at the access opening and a receptacle near the appliance.

2. You may provide an unobstructed service access path not more than (≤) 50 feet long if the entire pathway is at least (≥) 6 feet high and at least (≥) 22 inches wide over its entire length.

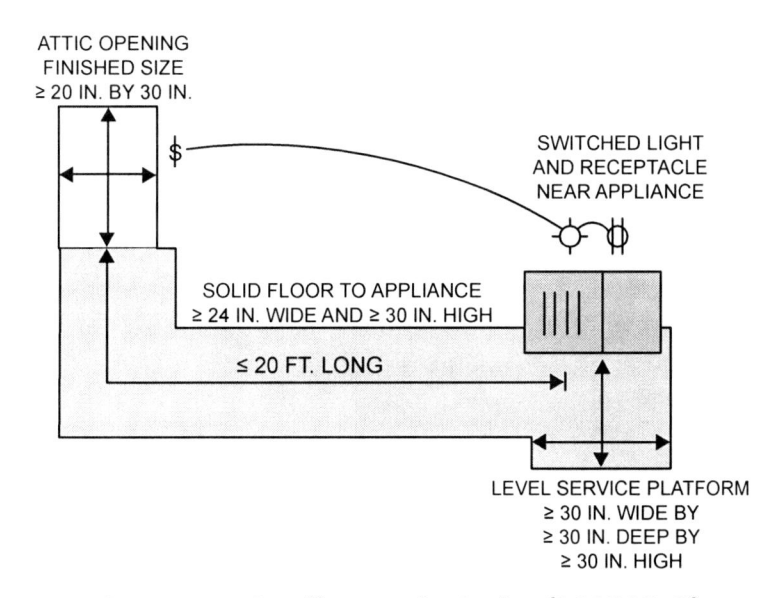

Access to Appliances in Attics (M1305-0)
Figure 13-1

Access to Appliances in Crawl Spaces

1. Provide the following service access for appliances located in a crawl space:
   a) an access rough opening at least (≥) 22 inches by 30 inches, and large enough to remove the largest piece of the appliance, whichever is larger, and
   b) a continuous and unobstructed path at least (≥) 22 inches wide and at least (≥) 30 inches high and not more than (≤) 20 feet long measured along the center line of the path beginning at the opening of the appliance, and
   c) a level service space at least (≥) 30 inches wide and 30 inches deep on the appliance's front or service side, and

d) a light fixture controlled by a switch located at the access opening and a receptacle near the appliance.

2. You may provide an unobstructed service access path of unlimited length if the entire pathway is at least (≥) 6 feet high and at least (≥) 22 inches wide over its entire length.
3. Line the sides of the access path with concrete or masonry to at least (≥) 4 inches above adjoining grade if the service access path is more than (>) 12 inches below adjoining grade.
4. Provide at least (≥) 6 inches clearance between appliances suspended from the floor and soil and extend the clearance at least (≥) 12 inches on all sides of the appliance.
5. Provide a firm and level concrete pad or other approved support pad that extends at least (≥) 3 inches above the surrounding soil for appliances mounted on the ground.

OIL AND SOLID-FUEL APPLIANCE CLEARANCE REDUCTION TO COMBUSTIBLE MATERIALS (M1306)

Appliances Governed by these Code Provisions

1. Apply these clearances to combustible reduction provisions to oil and solid fuel-burning appliances and apply these provisions to related equipment such as vents and chimneys.
2. Do not apply these provisions to gas-burning appliances. Refer to the IRC for clearance reductions that apply to gas-burning appliances.

Clearance to Combustible Materials Definition and Discussion

Heat-generating appliances, such as furnaces, boilers, water heaters, wood stoves, factory-built fireplaces, and their chimneys and vents, must be separated from combustible materials. Combustible materials include wood, drywall (the drywall paper is combustible), some roof covering materials, and insulation. Without separation, heat generated by the appliance or vent could ignite the combustible material causing a fire.

The ideal method of providing separation is physical distance. Most heat-generating appliances and vents have a recommended physical separation distance to combustible materials as part of their listing. If space limits do not allow the full physical separation distance, then the IRC allows various clearance reduction devices that protect the combustible material and reduce the physical separation distance recommended by the appliance or vent manufacturer.

Most clearance reduction devices rely on sheet metal, insulation, and an air circulation space in various combinations. We provide one example here. Refer to IRC Section M1306.2 for more clearance reduction devices.

Clearance Reduction Device Requirements

1. Measure clearance reductions from the nearest outer surface of the heat-generating appliance or vent to the nearest outer surface of the combustible material.
2. Install the clearance reduction device so that it covers all combustible material within the appliance manufacturer's recommended physical separation distance. Example: if the manufacturer's recommended physical separation distance is 12 inches, then the clearance reduction device should extend beyond the appliance or vent by at least (≥) 12 inches.

3. Provide an air circulation space of at least (≥) 1 inch when using clearance reduction devices that require an air circulation space. Provide at least (≥) 1 inch between the heat-generating appliance or vent and the clearance reduction device.
4. Do not use combustible spacers, ties or other combustible material when assembling the clearance reduction device. Do not place spacers or ties directly opposite the heat generating appliance or vent.
5. Leave at least (≥) 1 inch open at the top and bottom or the top and sides of the clearance reduction device if the clearance reduction device is installed along a straight wall and not in or near corners.
6. Leave at least (≥) 1 inch open at the top and bottom of the clearance reduction device if the clearance reduction device is installed in a corner.
7. Use mineral wool and fiberglass batts or boards with a minimum density of 8 pounds per cubic foot, and a minimum melting point of 1,500º F.
8. Do not allow the clearance reduction device to interfere with draft hood clearances, combustion air, safety devices, and service access.
9. Do not use clearance reduction devices if the appliance or equipment manufacturer's instructions prohibit them.

Clearance Reduction for Solid Fuel-Burning Appliances

1. Do not use clearance reduction devices if the solid fuel-burning appliance manufacturer's recommended physical separation distance is 12 inches or less.
2. Do not use clearance reduction devices to reduce the clearance for any solid fuel-burning appliance to less than 12 inches. Solid fuel-burning appliances, such as wood stoves, can generate too much heat to safely reduce the clearance to less than 12 inches.

Clearance Reduction Device Example

1. Use the following table to determine the clearance reductions allowed using a clearance reduction device constructed of 24 gage galvanized sheet steel with at least (≥) 1 inch air circulation space between the sheet steel and the combustible material. The first row in the table gives the manufacturer's recommended physical separation distance from combustible material for the heat-generating appliance or vent without using a protection device. The second row identifies whether the protection device separates the top or the sides and rear of the heat generating appliance from the combustible material. The third row gives the minimum allowed distance between the heat generating appliance or vent and combustible material using the protection device. Refer to the IRC for more clearance reduction devices.

TABLE M1306
Sheet Metal and Air Space Clearance Reduction Device Clearance to Combustible Materials Reduction

manufacturer's recommended clearance from combustible materials (inches)	36	36	18	18	12	12	9	9	6	6
clearance above or at sides or rear	above	sides & rear	above	sides & rear	above	sides & rear	above	sides & rear	above	sides & rear
clearance from combustible materials with reduction device (inches)	18	12	9	6	6	4	5	3	3	3

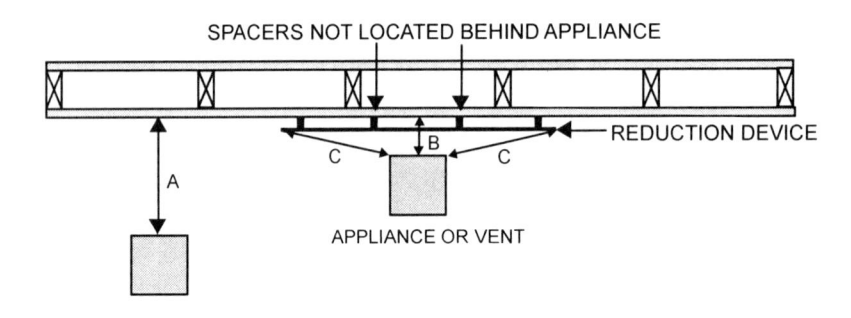

A = MANUFACTURER RECOMMENDED CLEARANCE TO COMBUSTIBLES
B = REDUCED CLEARANCE WITH REDUCTION DEVICE
C = LENGTH OF REDUCTION DEVICE SO C = A

Sheet Metal Clearance to Combustibles Reduction Device (M1306-0)
Figure 13-2

APPLIANCE INSTALLATION, ANCHORAGE, ELEVATION, AND PROTECTION

Appliances Governed by these Code Provisions

1. Apply these code provisions to all fuel-burning mechanical appliances including appliances using natural and propane gas, oil, and solid fuels.
2. Note that similar provisions for gas burning appliances exist in IRC Chapter 24.

Flood-Resistant Installation (M1301.1.1)

1. Install mechanical appliances above design flood elevation or install them to prevent entry of water into the system and to withstand the force of flood waters. Apply this rule to flood-prone areas defined by the local building official.

Appliance Installation by Manufacturer's Instructions (M1307.1)

1. Install mechanical appliances according to manufacturer's installation instructions.

2. Use the more restrictive provision if a difference exists between the manufacturer's instructions and the IRC.
3. Provide the manufacturer's operating and installation instructions on site during installation and inspection and leave them attached to the appliance after appliance startup.
4. Note that manufacturer's instructions are an important part of the listing requirements of the IRC. As such, they are an enforceable extension of the IRC.

Seismic Anchorage of Water Heaters (M1307.2)

1. Secure water heaters to walls at the upper one-third and the lower one-third of the water heater tank in Seismic Design Categories above D_1. Maintain at least (≥) 4 inches clearance between the strap and the controls. This requirement includes electric and fuel-burning water heaters.
2. Use at least (≥) 1 ½ inches wide by 16 gage metal, or similar material, for straps around the water heater tank. Use ½ inch EMT tubing with ends flattened, or similar material, for anchors from the straps to the wall. Use fasteners of adequate size to attach straps and anchors to the studs.
3. Verify other acceptable methods of seismic anchorage with the local building official.

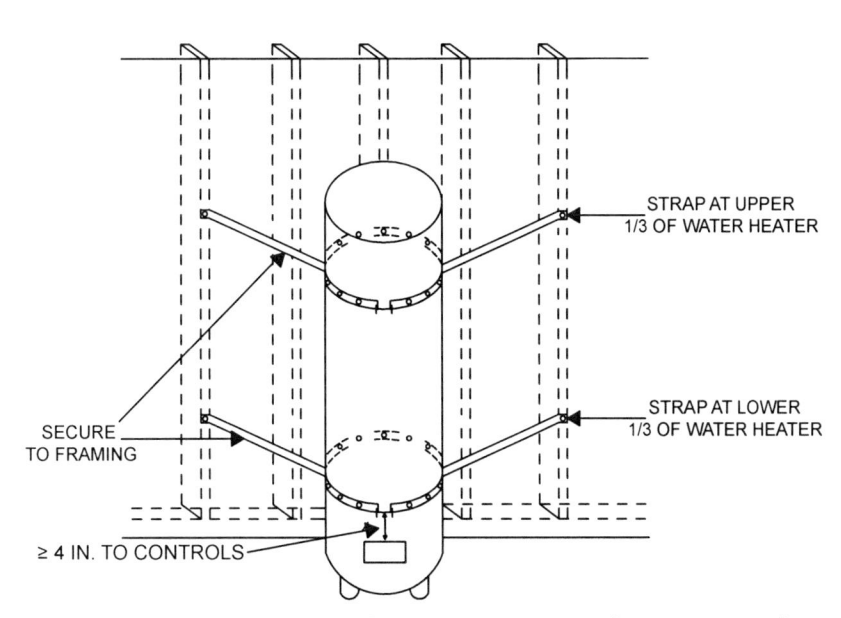

Seismic Anchorage of Water Heaters (M1307.2-0)
Figure 13-3

Elevation of Appliances in Garages (M1307.3 and G2408.2)

1. Elevate the appliance <u>ignition source</u> at least (≥) 18 inches above the floor when the appliance is located in a garage or is located in an unconditioned room that opens directly into the garage. Appliances with a potential ignition source include gas and electric water heaters, gas and electric clothes dryers, gas and electric furnaces, and heat pumps with auxiliary resistance heating elements. Rooms that open directly into the garage include storage and utility rooms that are not part of the conditioned living space. These rooms include rooms separated from the garage by a door opening into the garage.

2. Measure the elevation distance to the <u>ignition source</u> in the equipment, not to the bottom of the equipment (unless the ignition source is at the bottom of the equipment).
3. You may install appliances on the floor in rooms that are adjacent to a garage but do not have an opening into the garage.
4. Refer to Chapter 24 for similar provisions covering gas appliances.

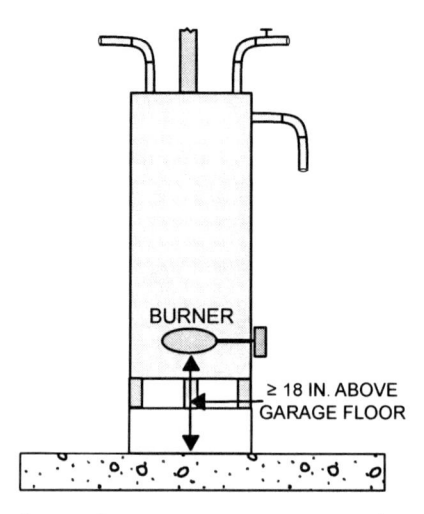

Elevation of Appliances in Garages (M1307.3-0)
Figure 13-4

Protection of Appliances from Vehicle Impact (M1307.3.1)

1. Protect HVAC appliances and water heaters from vehicle impact. The appliance or water heater does not need to be located in a garage or carport to qualify for protection from vehicle impact. The IRC does not specify how to provide this protection. Common protection methods include steel poles called bollards, vehicle tire stops, and encasing the equipment in substantial framing.
2. Refer to Chapter 24 for similar provisions covering gas appliances.

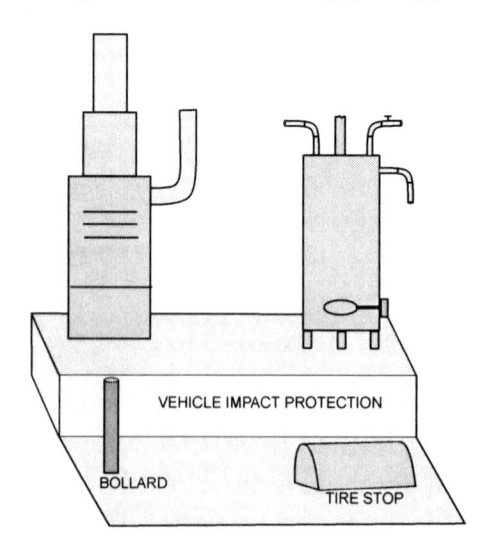

Protection of Appliances from Vehicle Impact (M1307.3.1-0)
Figure 13-5

Elevation of Outdoor HVAC Equipment Above Grade (M1308.3 and M1403.2)

1. Raise HVAC equipment, such as condensers, located outdoors at least (≥) 3 inches above grade or more if required by manufacturer's installation instructions. Measure from the highest point of the ground to the lowest part of the equipment's supports, such as attached feet.

Avoiding Fuel Pipe Strain (G2408.6)

1. Install and support appliance so that they do not place undue stress on fuel pipes and fittings.

14

HEATING AND COOLING EQUIPMENT

HVAC EQUIPMENT GENERAL INSTALLATION REQUIREMENTS (M1401)

Equipment Installation by Manufacturer's Instructions

1. Install heating and cooling equipment according to manufacturer's installation instructions and provisions of the IRC.
2. Apply the more restrictive provision, if a conflict occurs between the manufacturer's instructions and the IRC provisions.

Equipment Sizing

1. Size heating and cooling equipment according to The Air Conditioning Contractors of America (ACCA) Manual S or similar approved method. Manual S and Manual J account for conditions such as the direction the structure faces, the size and type of windows and doors, local temperature conditions, and insulation. Contractors should provide a copy of the sizing calculations for all new construction and when replacing existing appliances.

Duct Design (M1601.1)

1. Design duct systems according to ACCA Manual D or similar approved method. Contractors should provide a copy of the duct design calculations for all new construction.

ELECTRIC RADIANT HEATING SYSTEMS INSTALLATION REQUIREMENTS (M1406)

Electric Radiant Heating Description

Electric radiant heating systems provide heat to a single room. They usually have no fan and provide heat by natural movement of the heated air and by thermal radiation. They are common in small seasonally occupied buildings, some rural homes, and in buildings without ducts for forced-air heating and cooling. These elements become very hot and proper installation is important to prevent fires and electrical problems.

Installation Requirements

1. Install electric radiant heating panels according to manufacturer's installation instructions and provisions of the IRC.
2. Install radiant panels parallel to wood framing members and fasten the panels to the surface of the framing members or mount the panels between framing members.
3. Install fasteners in areas of the radiant panel designed for fasteners. Install fasteners at least ($\geq$) ¼ inch away from a heating element.

4. Install radiant panels as complete units, unless listed and labeled for field modifications.
5. Do not install radiant panels on drywall unless the panel's maximum operating temperature is not more than (≤) 125º F.

ELECTRIC HEATING ELEMENTS INSTALLED IN HVAC DUCTS, HEAT PUMPS, AND AIR CONDITIONERS (M1407)

Electric Heating Element Description

Electric resistance heating elements are often installed in heat pumps when they are used cold climates. These supplemental electric heating elements activate if the temperature becomes too cold for the heat pump to provide adequate heat. These elements become very hot and proper installation is important to prevent fires and electrical problems.

Installation Requirements

1. Install electric heating elements according to manufacturer's installation instructions and provisions of the IRC.
2. Provide access to all electric heating elements for service and replacement.
3. Provide a fan interlock to prevent heater operation without fan operation.

Clearance to Combustible Materials

1. Provide clearance, as recommended by the heating element manufacturer, between electric heating elements and Class I duct material such as flexible ducts and duct board. Clearance is not required if the heating elements are listed for zero clearance to combustible materials.
2. Install electric heating elements at least (≥) 4 feet away from heat pumps unless both the heating element manufacturer's instructions and the heat pump manufacturer's instructions list the equipment for use together.

VENTED FLOOR FURNACES (M1408 AND G2437)

Vented Floor Furnace Description

Vented floor furnaces provide heat to a single room or a small home with a few rooms. If they have no fan, they provide heat by natural movement of the heated air and by thermal radiation. They are most common in small seasonally occupied buildings and some rural homes. These furnaces become very hot and proper installation is important to prevent fires.

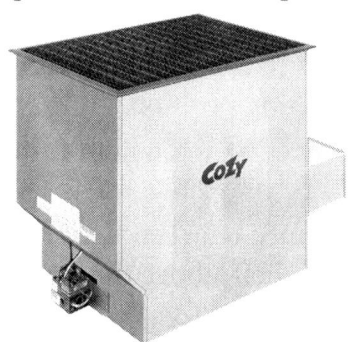

Vented Floor Furnace (MM1408-0]
Figure 14-1

Installation Requirements

1. Install floor furnaces according to manufacturer's installation instructions and provisions of the IRC.
2. Locate the thermostat for the floor furnace in the room where the floor furnace floor register is located.
3. Support the floor furnace independently of its floor register.
4. Do not locate a floor furnace in areas such as hallways, doorways, stair landings, or in an exit from any room or space.
5. Provide at least (≥) one walkway with at least (≥) 18 inches clearance between the floor furnace and a wall. This allows occupants to walk around the floor furnace, not over the hot furnace discharge cover.

Crawl Space Installations

1. Do not support floor furnaces on the ground.
2. Locate the floor furnace at least (≥) 6 inches above the ground. You may reduce the clearance to at least (≥) 2 inches if the lower 6 inches of the floor furnace is sealed to prevent water entry.
3. Extend any excavation that is necessary to obtain clearance to ground at least (≥) 30 inches beyond the control side of the floor furnace and at least (≥) 12 inches beyond all other sides. Slope the excavation outward from the furnace base at an angle not more than (≤) 45 degrees from horizontal.

Upper Floor Installations (G2437.6)

1. Do not install a floor furnace where it will project into habitable space. A floor furnace cabinet must project only into uninhabitable space.
2. Use noncombustible materials to separate the uninhabitable space from habitable space.
3. Provide access of at least (≥) 6-inches to all sides and the bottom of the floor furnace.

Clearance to Combustible Materials

1. Provide at least (≥) 6 inches clearance between floor furnace floor registers and any wall.
2. Provide at least (≥) 6 inches clearance between floor furnace wall registers and the inside corner of an adjoining wall.
3. Provide at least (≥) 12 inches clearance between floor furnace floor registers and a swinging door in any open, closed, and swinging position.
4. Provide at least (≥) 12 inches clearance between floor furnace registers and any combustible materials such as draperies.
5. Provide at least (≥) 60 inches clearance between floor furnace floor registers and any combustible projection, such as a wood shelf, above the floor register.
6. Do not install floor furnaces in concrete slab-on-grade foundations.

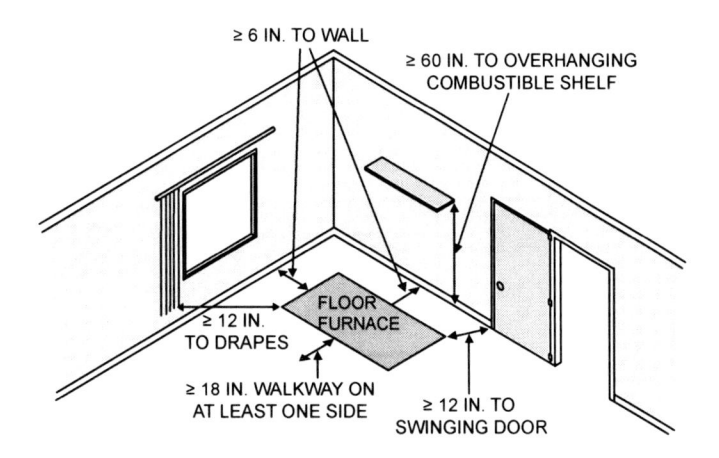

Vented Floor Furnace Clearance to Combustible Materials (M1408.3-0)
Figure 14-2

Service Access

1. Provide a service opening using either a foundation opening of at least (≥) 18 inches by 24 inches or a trap door floor of at least (≥) 22 inches by 30 inches opening for service. The opening must allow replacement of the floor furnace.

VENTED WALL FURNACES (M1409 AND G2436)

Vented Wall Furnace Description

Vented wall furnaces provide heat to a single room or adjacent rooms. If they have no fan, they provide heat by natural movement of the heated air and by thermal radiation. They are most common in small seasonally occupied buildings, room additions, and homes in warm climates where heating demand is minimal and occasional. These furnaces become very hot and proper installation is important to prevent fires.

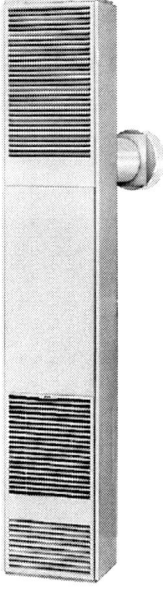

Vented Wall Furnace (MM1409-0)
Figure 14-3

Installation Requirements

1. Install vented wall furnaces according to manufacturer's installation instructions and provisions of the IRC.
2. Do not attach ducts to vented wall furnaces. Attach boots and other parts intended to distribute air into other rooms only if listed in the wall furnace manufacturer's installation instructions.
3. Do not install vented wall furnaces so that air can circulate from a bathroom into other rooms in the building.
4. Install a manual fuel shutoff valve ahead of all wall furnace controls.

Clearance to Combustible Materials

1. Provide at least (≥) 12 inches clearance between the wall furnace and a swinging door in any open, closed, and swinging position. Do not use doorstops or closers to obtain this clearance.
2. Provide clearance to all combustible walls, floors, and furnishings as recommended by the manufacturer.

Service Access

1. Provide access to the wall furnace as recommended by the manufacturer for cleaning, service, and parts replacement.
2. Do not attach the wall furnace to the framing parts that must be removed for normal service and maintenance.

VENTED ROOM HEATERS (M1410)

Vented Room Heater Description

Vented room heaters provide heat to a single room or adjacent rooms. If they have no fan, they provide heat by natural movement of the heated air and by thermal radiation. They are most common in small seasonally occupied buildings, room additions, and homes in warm climates where heating demand is minimal and occasional. These heaters become very hot and proper installation is important to prevent fires.

Vented Room Heater (MM1410-0)
Figure 14-4

Installation Requirements

1. Install vented room heaters according to manufacturer's installation instructions and provisions of the IRC.

Clearance to Combustible Materials

1. Install vented room heaters on non-combustible floors or on non-combustible assemblies approved for use with the room heater. This is not required if the room heater is listed in the manufacturer's instructions as being approved on for placement on combustible floors without protection.
2. Extend non-combustible assemblies at least (≥) 18 inches beyond all sides of the room heater.
3. Provide clearance to all combustible walls, floors, and furnishings as recommended by the manufacturer.

AIR CONDITIONING CONDENSATE DISPOSAL (M1411)

Condensate Description

The process of removing heat from the air is often called air conditioning. Water is a byproduct of air conditioning because water vapor condenses out from the air when the air temperature is reduced. In areas with high humidity, air conditioning can produce significant amounts of water. The water removed from the air during air conditioning is called condensate.

Condensate Disposal Location Requirements

1. Do not discharge condensate on to a street, alley, or any other place that would create a nuisance. Some jurisdictions, particularly in warm moist areas, require that you discharge condensate away from the foundation. Verify discharge location requirements with the local building official.

Condensate Discharge Pipe Requirements

1. Use at least (≥) ¾ inch internal diameter pipe for primary and auxiliary condensate discharge pipes. Do not decrease pipe size between the collection and discharge point.
2. Install horizontal pipe sections with a uniform slope in the direction of the discharge point of at least (≥) 1/8 inch in 12 inches.
3. Use fittings, primers, cements, hangers, and other components that are compatible with the pipe material. Install the pipe according to the provisions in Chapter 30.
4. Use pipe material and use a pipe size that will accommodate the condensate temperature, pressure, and flow rate produced by the air conditioning system.
5. You may use most water supply and drain pipes for condensate discharge pipes. The most common condensate discharge pipes are PVC, CPVC, and ABS.

Condensate Auxiliary (Backup) System Requirements

1. Install an auxiliary condensate system when the air conditioner evaporator coil is located

where building damage may occur if the primary condensate discharge system malfunctions. This usually applies to evaporator coils installed in or above finished space. Many jurisdictions require auxiliary condensate systems for all air conditioning systems, unless all of the equipment is located outside the building.

2. Install one of the following auxiliary condensate systems when an auxiliary condensate system is required.

Condensate Auxiliary Drain Pan with Discharge Pipe

1. Install an auxiliary drain pan under the evaporator coil. Use a pan that is at least (≥) 1 ½ inches deep and at least (≥) 3 inches larger than the evaporator coil in both length and width. Construct the pan using either at least (≥) 0.0276 inch galvanized sheet metal or at least a (≥) 0.0625 inch nonmetallic pan.
2. Slope the pan toward the discharge pipe connection.
3. Install the auxiliary discharge pipe using the same materials and methods as the primary discharge pipe.
4. Terminate the auxiliary discharge pipe at a conspicuous point so that the occupants can see that the primary condensate discharge system is not functioning properly. A conspicuous point often means above a window.

Condensate Auxiliary Drain Pan with Water Level Cutoff Switch

1. Install an auxiliary drain pan under the evaporator coil. Use a pan that is at least 1 ½ inches deep and at least 3 inches larger than the evaporator coil in both length and width. Construct the pan using either at least (≥) 0.0276-inch galvanized sheet metal or at least (≥) a 0.0625 inch nonmetallic pan.
2. Install a water level cutoff switch in the pan that will shut off the air conditioner before the pan overflows.

Condensate Auxiliary Discharge Pipe Attached to Evaporator Coil

1. Install an auxiliary condensate discharge pipe at the evaporator coil interior condensate pan. Connect the auxiliary condensate discharge pipe above the primary condensate discharge pipe.
2. Use the same type and size pipe for the auxiliary discharge pipe as required for the primary discharge pipe. Slope the auxiliary discharge pipe toward the discharge point with a slope of at least (≥) 1/8 inch in 12 inches.
3. Terminate the auxiliary pipe at a conspicuous point so that the occupants can see that the primary condensate discharge system is not functioning properly. A conspicuous point often means above a window.

Water Level Cutoff Switch

1. Install a water level cutoff switch above where the primary condensate discharge pipe connects to the evaporator coil and below the evaporator coil interior condensate pan overflow rim, or you may install the switch in the primary or secondary discharge pipes. The switch

location should allow the switch to shut off the air conditioner before water overflows into the building.

Water Level Cutoff Switch (PM1411-0)
Figure 14-5

Water Level Cutoff Switch for Downflow Air Conditioners

1. Install a water level cutoff switch on air conditioners where the supply air is directed downwards. This also applies to any air conditioner where it is not possible to install an auxiliary drain pan under the evaporator coil. Install the switch below the evaporator coil interior condensate pan overflow rim.
2. You may not substitute water level cutoff switches located on the exterior of the evaporator coil or located in the condensate drain lines for the interior cutoff switch.

Auxiliary Drain Pan Separation from Appliances

1. Install all parts of appliances and insulation that could be damaged by water in the auxiliary drain pan above the flood level of the pan.
2. Use supports located in the drain pan that are water resistant and approved for the intended use. Example: do not use wood blocks in the drain pan to support an appliance.

Condensate Auxiliary (Backup) System Requirements for Category IV Appliances

1. Install an auxiliary condensate drain pan under most Category IV condensing appliances. The pan is required when the appliance is located where building damage may occur if the primary condensate discharge system becomes blocked or does not function. This usually applies to appliances installed in or above finished space. A common example of a Category IV appliance is a high efficiency gas furnace.
2. Install the pan and the disposal pipe using one of the previously discussed methods.
3. You do not need to install a drain pan if the fuel-fired appliance automatically shuts down when the primary condensate discharge system malfunctions.

Condensate Disposal Best Practice

In areas with warm and humid summer conditions, the cold condensate can cause moisture to condense on the outside of the primary condensate disposal pipe. This condensation can, over time, damage wood and drywall and provide moisture for fungal growth. Insulate the primary condensate disposal pipes in areas with warm and humid summers.

COOLANT ACCESS CAPS (M1411.6)

1. Install locking-type, tamper-resistant caps on refrigerant line access ports located outdoors.

EVAPORATIVE COOLING EQUIPMENT INSTALLATION REQUIREMENTS (M1413)

Evaporative Cooling Equipment Description

Evaporative coolers (also called swamp coolers) are usually located on the roof or on the ground outside the home. They work by running a stream of water over one or more media that look similar to a sponge. A fan draws air through the media and the evaporation of the water lowers the air temperature. The fan blows this cooled air through ducts into the home. Evaporative coolers work only in dry areas of the country and are most effective when the dew point is less than about 55º F.

Evaporative (Swamp) Cooler (PM1413-0)
Figure 14-6

Installation Requirements

1. Install evaporative coolers according to manufacturer's installation instructions and relevant parts of the IRC.
2. Install evaporative coolers on the roof or on a level base or platform that is at least 3-inches above the ground. Secure the evaporative cooler to prevent movement.

Water Supply Protection

1. Install an approved backflow prevention device on the evaporative cooler water supply. Refer to IRC P2902.

15

KITCHEN AND CLOTHES DRYER EXHAUST SYSTEMS

VENTILATION FAN DISCHARGE LOCATION

1. Discharge ventilation fans, such as bathroom, toilet room, and laundry room fans, directly outdoors. Discharging a ventilation fan exhaust duct into or toward an attic, soffit, or crawl space vent does not comply with this provision. The duct must discharge directly outdoors.

CLOTHES DRYER EXHAUST SYSTEMS (M1502 AND G2439)

Installation Requirements

1. Construct, install, and terminate clothes dryer exhaust ducts according to the clothes dryer manufacturer's installation instructions. If the clothes dryer manufacturer is not known during construction, use the IRC requirements. The clothes dryer manufacturer is rarely known during construction, so the manufacturer's installation instruction exception rarely applies.
2. Do not connect clothes dryer exhaust ducts to any other system such as bathroom exhaust fan ducts, plumbing vents, and fuel-burning equipment vents and flues.
3. Do not install clothes dryer exhaust ducts in or through any fireblocking, draftstopping, or fire-resistance rated assembly unless the duct is constructed and installed to maintain the code required fireblocking or draftstopping.
4. Do not run clothes dryer exhaust ducts into or through other ducts or plenums. Example: do not run a clothes dryer exhaust duct into or through an HVAC supply or return duct or into or through a combustion air duct.
5. Install the clothes dryer exhaust duct during construction if space for clothes dryer is provided.

Duct Construction

1. Use a 4 inch diameter smooth wall metal clothes dryer exhaust duct, unless the clothes dryer manufacturer's instructions allow another size.
2. Install duct joints so that the inside part of the joint fits into the outside part of the joint in the direction of the air flow.
3. Do not use screws or other fasteners that penetrate the duct and could trap lint. Pop rivets (1/4 inch) are usually considered acceptable fasteners.
4. Support the duct at least (≥) every 4 feet. Joints and elbows are vulnerable areas for separation.
5. Protect the duct with at least (≥) 16 gage shield plates if the duct is within (≤) 1 ¼ inches from

the edge of a framing member. Extend the shield plate at least (≥) 2 inches above sole plates and below top plates. Protect the duct with shield plates at any other location where it is likely to be penetrated by fasteners.

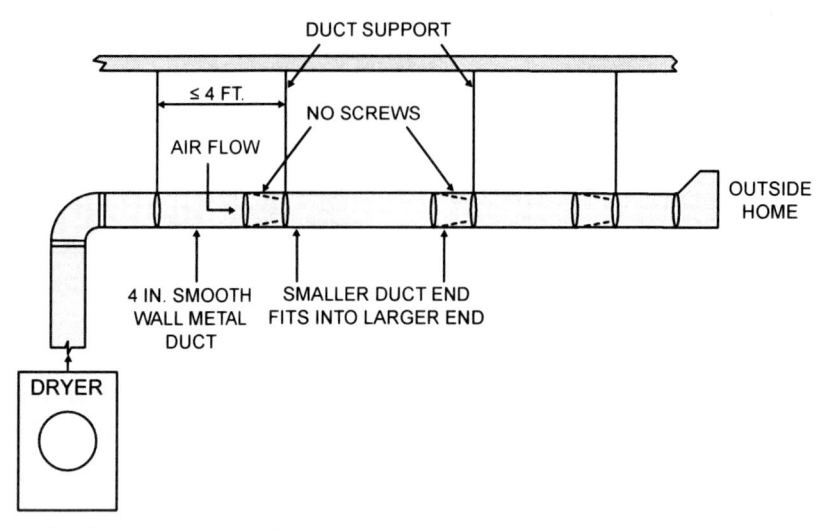

Clothes Dryer Exhaust Duct Construction (M1502-1)
Figure 15-1

Duct Length

1. Do not exceed (≤) 25 feet developed length between the beginning of the clothes dryer exhaust duct and the duct termination, unless the clothes dryer manufacturer's installation instructions allow a longer length. Developed length means the straight line length of the duct, reduced by bends in the duct.
2. Reduce developed duct length by 2 ½ feet for every 45 degree bend and by 5 feet for every 90 degree bend. You may use the manufacturer provided developed length for smooth radius bends. You may use the IRC table for smooth radius bend developed length if the manufacturer's instruction are not available.
3. Do not include the transition duct in the dryer duct developed length.
4. Locate a permanent label within 6 feet of the clothes dryer exhaust duct connection that shows the exhaust duct's developed length. This requirement applies only when the duct is concealed.
5. Note that IRC Section G2439.5.5.1 specifies a developed clothes dryer duct length of not more than (≤) 35 feet. Verify with the local building official which length applies in your area.

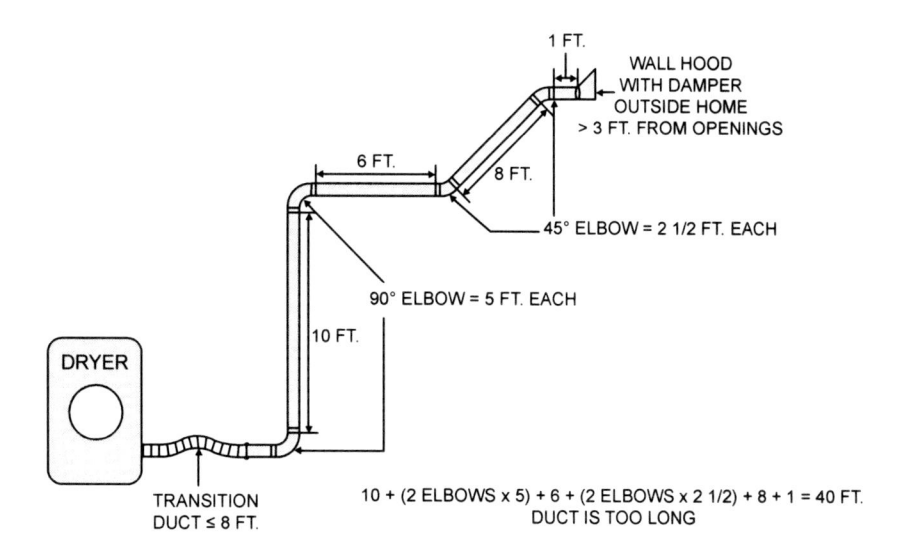

15 : Kitchen and Clothes Dryer Exhaust Systems 237

Clothes Dryer Exhaust Duct Length (M1502-2)
Figure 15-2

Duct Termination

1. Terminate clothes dryer exhaust ducts outside the building. Outside the building does not include attics and crawl spaces.
2. Locate the clothes dryer exhaust duct termination at least (≥) 3 feet from any opening to the building, unless the clothes dryer manufacturer's installation instructions specify another location. The clothes dryer manufacturer is rarely known during construction, so the manufacturer's installation instruction exception rarely applies.
3. Provide a backdraft damper at the duct termination or at another approved location.
4. Do not install a screen at the exhaust duct termination. A screen will trap lint.

Transition Duct

1. The transition duct is the duct (usually flexible duct) between the dryer and the start of the smooth wall dryer exhaust duct.
2. Limit the transition duct length to 8 feet.
3. Use only one piece of listed and labeled transition duct. Do not splice together two or more lengths of transition duct material.
4. Do not run the transition duct through walls or in concealed spaces.

Clothes Dryer Makeup Air (G2439.4)

1. Provide makeup air for clothes dryers that exhaust more than (>) 200 cubic feet per minute. The IRC does not specify how to provide makeup air and it does not specify that the makeup air come from outdoors.
2. Provide a net free opening of at least (≥) 100 square inches when clothes dryers are installed in closets or provide makeup air by other approved means.

Clothes Dryer Installation Discussion

Beware of locating clothes dryers in the same room with other devices that consume or exhaust large amounts of air. Examples of other devices include water heaters, furnaces and boilers, fireplaces, and other fuel-burning appliances. Devices that use large amounts of air could draw poisonous combustion gasses, such as carbon monoxide, from the fuel-burning appliance vent into the home. This could create a dangerous situation.

Proper installation of clothes dryer exhaust ducts improves clothes dryer energy efficiency and fire safety. If lint collects in the clothes dryer exhaust duct, it can decrease the airflow through the clothes dryer and through the exhaust duct. Decreased airflow through the clothes dryer can increase drying times and increase energy use. Decreased airflow through the exhaust duct can allow more lint to become trapped in the duct. Flammable lint and high temperatures create a fire hazard.

Some people use larger diameter dryer exhaust ducts to get around the 35 feet duct length limit. Larger diameter ducts can reduce the air speed in the duct and allow lint to collect in the duct. Do not use larger diameter clothes dryer exhaust ducts unless allowed by the clothes dryer manufacturer. If the clothes dryer manufacturer does not allow a larger diameter dryer exhaust duct, then the exhaust duct system should be replaced with one that complies with manufacturer's recommendations.

Many heat pump and air conditioner manufacturers do not recommend locating clothes dryer exhaust duct terminations near the outside condenser units. The hot moist air from the clothes dryer can reduce the efficiency and effectiveness of the condenser. Chemicals in the clothes dryer exhaust air can damage the condenser. Verify the condenser manufacturer's installation instructions when clothes dryer exhaust ducts are closer than 3 feet to a condenser.

Use only metal clothes dryer transition ducts. Do not use plastic covered transition ducts. Plastic covered transition ducts are a fire safety hazard.

Clothes dryers can exhaust 200 cubic feet per minute of air or more. Significant makeup air is required to replace this exhausted air. If the clothes dryer is in a closed laundry room, install an opening in the wall or door to provide makeup air for the dryer. If an opening is not possible or not desired, do not close the interior laundry room door when the clothes dryer is operating.

KITCHEN RANGE HOODS AND EXHAUST SYSTEMS (M1503)

Installation Requirements

1. Discharge kitchen exhaust ducts to the outdoors when natural or mechanical ventilation is not provided in the kitchen area. Natural ventilation usually means an operable window in the kitchen area. Mechanical ventilation usually means a central heating system. Most homes have either natural or mechanical ventilation in the kitchen area, so external discharge of range hoods is rarely required.
2. You may install a ductless, recirculating, kitchen hood if the kitchen is provided with natural or mechanical ventilation.
3. You need not install a recirculating or an externally ducted kitchen exhaust hood in most

homes; however, externally ducted kitchen exhaust hoods are recommended. Verify kitchen exhaust hood requirements with the local building official.

Above Ground Exhaust Duct Construction

1. Use smooth, single wall galvanized steel, stainless steel, or copper to construct kitchen exhaust ducts.
2. Seal the exhaust duct air tight to avoid leaking flammable grease into wall or floor cavities or between the kitchen exhaust hood and the kitchen cabinet.

Downdraft Exhaust Duct Construction in Concrete

1. You may use Schedule 40 PVC pipe to construct exhaust ducts for downdraft exhaust fans if all of the following conditions are met:
   a) install the PVC duct only in a concrete slab on grade foundation, and
   b) backfill and compact the duct's trench with sand or gravel, and
   c) extend the PVC duct not more than (≤) 1 inch above the indoor concrete floor, and
   d) extend the PVC duct not more than (≤) 1 inch above grade outside the building.
2. Use solvent cement for all PVC duct joints and fittings.
3. Provide a backdraft damper at the duct termination or at the downdraft exhaust fan.

Exhaust Duct Termination

1. Terminate kitchen exhaust hood ducts outside the building. Outside the building does not include attics and crawl spaces.
2. Provide a backdraft damper at the duct termination or other approved location. Many kitchen hoods and cabinet-mounted microwave ovens have backdraft dampers integrated into the equipment.

Exhaust Fan Rates

1. Provide an exhaust rate of at least (≥) 100 cubic feet per minute for intermittently operated exhaust hoods or at least (≥) 20 cubic feet per minute for continuously operating exhaust hoods.
2. Provide makeup air for exhaust fans with a capacity of more than (>) 400 cubic feet per minute. Install a damper or other means to close the makeup air duct that automatically opens and closes with the operation of the exhaust fan.

Domestic Open-top Broiler Hoods

1. Refer to the IRC Chapter 15 for provisions covering hoods for domestic open-top broilers.

Range Hood Best Practice

Install and use externally discharged range hoods in all homes, particularly when using a gas range. These hoods improve indoor air quality and reduce the amount of moisture that cooking can place in the air.

16

HVAC DUCT SYSTEMS

FLEXIBLE DUCT INSTALLATION (M1601.3)

General Installation Requirements

1. Install flexible ducts according to manufacturer's installation instructions. The installation instructions that follow are from the Air Diffusion Council and may be downloaded at www.flexibleduct.org.
2. Use flexible ducts that are labeled at least (≥) every 36 inches with information such as the manufacturer's name and the R-value of the duct insulation.
3. Do not expose flexible ducts to direct sunlight such as may occur under roof vents. Direct sunlight can damage the duct outer cover.
4. Extend flexible duct to its full length. Do not leave excess duct material in a duct run and do not compress the duct.
5. Seal flexible duct connections to flanges of plenums and fittings using mechanical fasteners such as straps and using pressure-sensitive tape or mastic marked as complying with UL 181B-FX for tape and UL 181B-M for mastic.

Duct Support

1. Support flexible ducts using material at least (≥) 1 ½ inches wide. You may support flexible ducts on 1 ½ inch wide framing.
2. Support flexible ducts at not more than (≤) 5 feet intervals. You may use a fitting or distribution plenum to provide initial flexible duct support.
3. Do not allow flexible duct to sag between supports more than (>) ½ inch per foot.
4. Support bends in long horizontal runs of flexible duct at not more than (≤) one duct diameter on both sides of the bend.
5. Support bends in flexible duct that occur near the plenum connection. Allow flexible ducts to run at least several inches beyond a plenum connection before making a bend.
6. Provide independent support for duct fittings and distribution plenums. Support duct fittings at not more than (≤) 1 foot from the fitting.
7. Support vertical runs of flexible duct at more than (≤) 6 feet intervals.

Duct Bends

1. Do not bend flexible ducts at sharp angles across obstructions such as framing lumber and pipes.

2. Do not bend flexible ducts so that the bend radius at the centerline is less than (<) one duct diameter.
3. Avoid changing the shape of the duct. The area of a round duct is greater than the area of the same duct compressed into an ellipse.

Duct Connections and Splices

1. Connect and splice ducts according to manufacturer's instructions.
2. Connect flexible ducts to a beaded metal collar that is at least ($\geq$) 2 inches long.
3. Splice two ducts together using a beaded metal sleeve that is at least ($\geq$) 4 inches long.
4. Use an approved clamp and at least ($\geq$) 2 wraps of tape to secure a nonmetallic flexible duct to a metal collar and sleeve. Use clamps and tape labeled as complying with UL181B.

Flexible Duct Installation Discussion

Improper flexible duct installation is a common problem. Improper installation can reduce the volume of air that moves through the duct and can increase the friction between the air and the duct walls. This can cause the HVAC system to work harder and longer than necessary, wasting energy and money.

UNACCEPTABLE SHARP DUCT BENDS

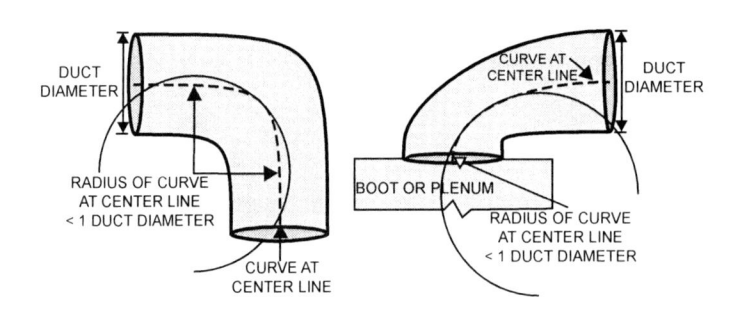

UNACCEPTABLE CHANGE IN DUCT SHAPE

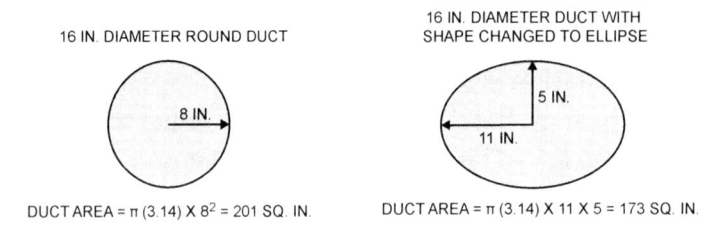

16 IN. DIAMETER ROUND DUCT

16 IN. DIAMETER DUCT WITH SHAPE CHANGED TO ELLIPSE

DUCT AREA = π (3.14) X 8² = 201 SQ. IN.

DUCT AREA = π (3.14) X 11 X 5 = 173 SQ. IN.

Unacceptable Flexible Duct Installation (R1601.3-1)
Figure 16-1

UNACCEPTABLE DUCT SPLICING WITHOUT METAL SLEEVE

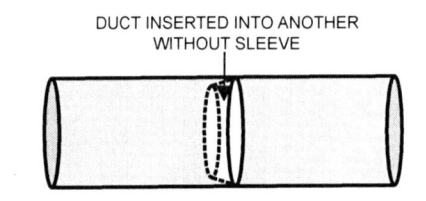

DUCT INSERTED INTO ANOTHER WITHOUT SLEEVE

UNACCEPTABLE DUCT SUPPORT SPACING AND DUCT SAG

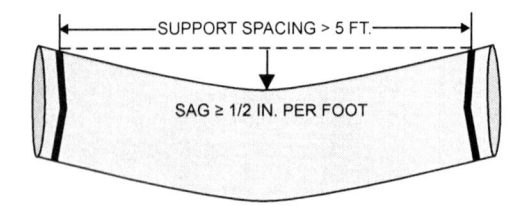

SUPPORT SPACING > 5 FT.

SAG ≥ 1/2 IN. PER FOOT

Unacceptable Flexible Duct Installation (R1601.3-2)
Figure 16-2

16 : Hvac Duct Systems   243

ACCEPTABLE DUCT BENDS

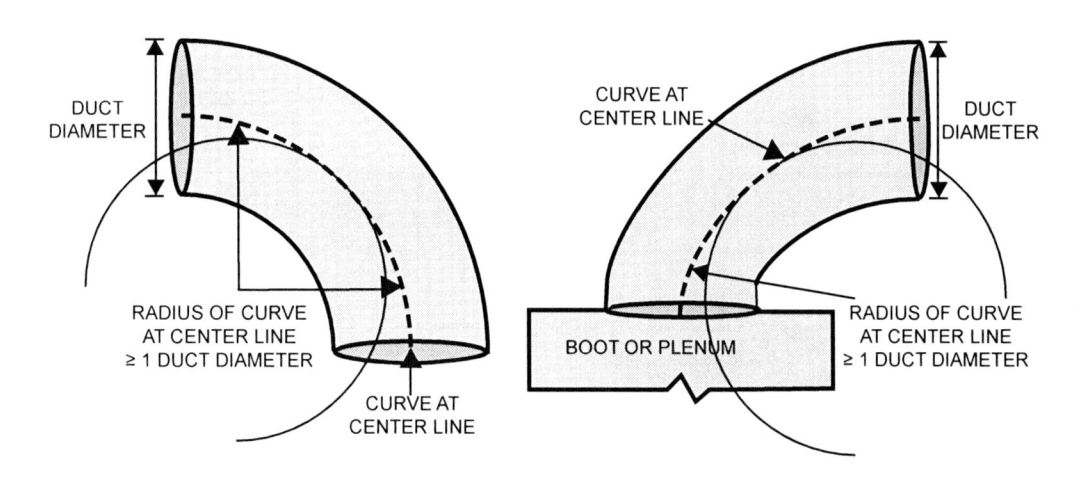

- DUCT DIAMETER
- RADIUS OF CURVE AT CENTER LINE ≥ 1 DUCT DIAMETER
- CURVE AT CENTER LINE

- CURVE AT CENTER LINE
- DUCT DIAMETER
- BOOT OR PLENUM
- RADIUS OF CURVE AT CENTER LINE ≥ 1 DUCT DIAMETER

ACCEPTABLE DUCT SPLICE USING METAL SLEEVE

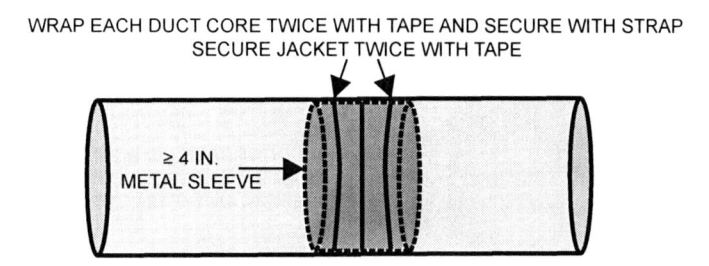

WRAP EACH DUCT CORE TWICE WITH TAPE AND SECURE WITH STRAP
SECURE JACKET TWICE WITH TAPE

≥ 4 IN. METAL SLEEVE

ACCEPTABLE DUCT SUPPORT AND SAG

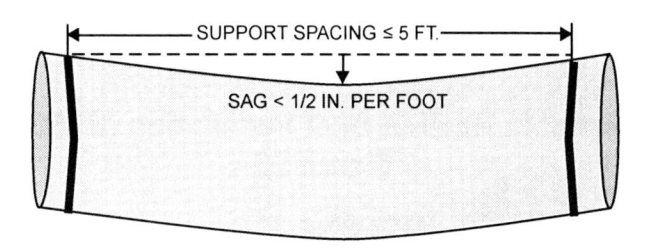

SUPPORT SPACING ≤ 5 FT.
SAG < 1/2 IN. PER FOOT

Acceptable Flexible Duct Installation (R1601.3-3)
Figure 16-3

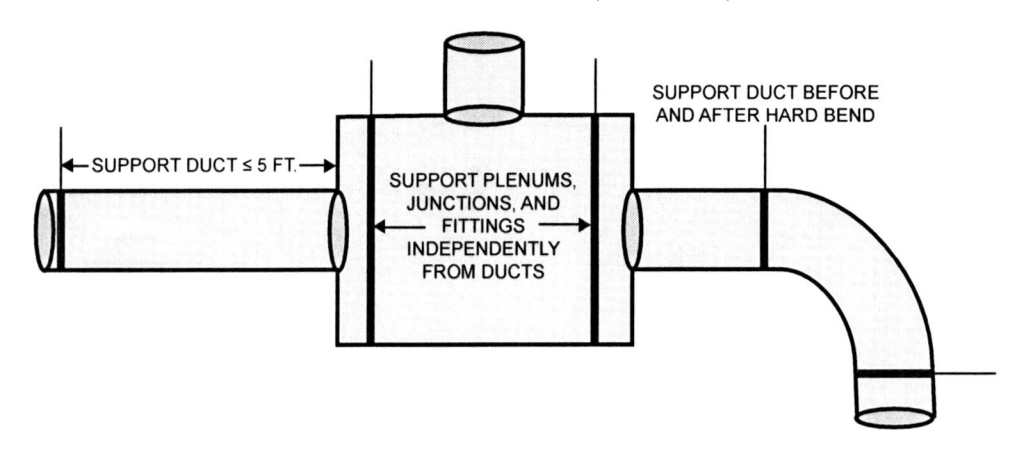

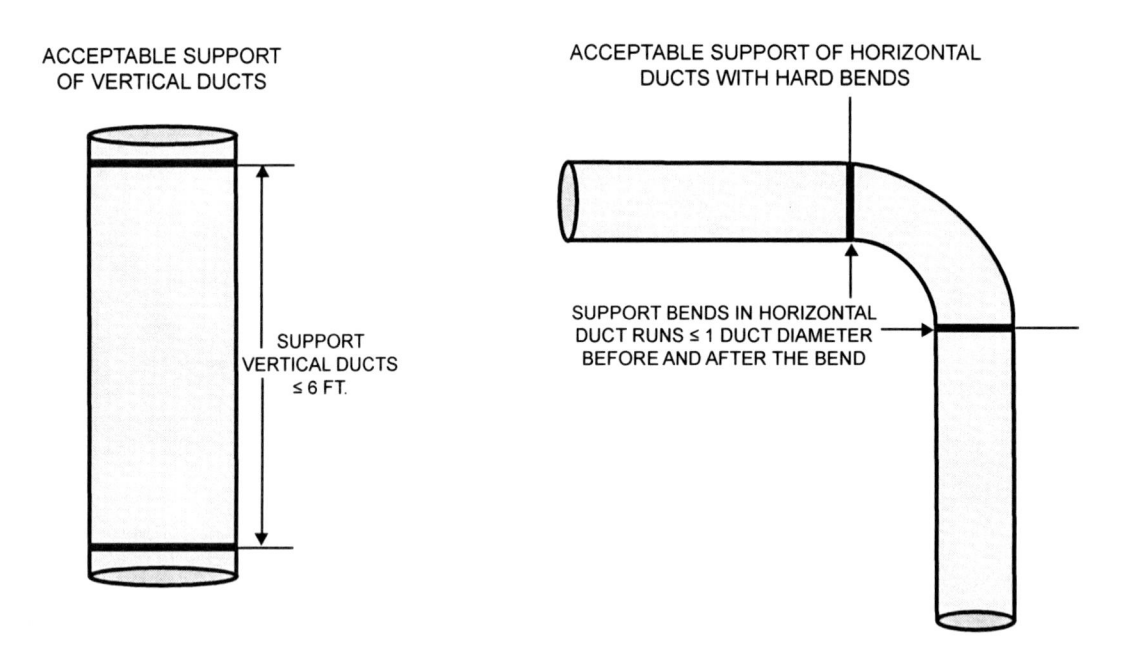

Acceptable Flexible Duct Installation (R1601.3-4)
Figure 16-4

FRAMING CAVITY RETURN DUCTS (M1601.1.1)

Return Ducts in Framing Cavities Installation Requirements

1. You may use framing cavities, such as cavities in stud wall and between solid floor joists, as return ducts or plenums. Do not use framing cavities for supply ducts or plenums.
2. Do not use framing cavities as ducts or plenums if the cavities are part of a required fire-resistance assembly.
3. Do not run wall cavity ducts or plenums through more than one floor level.
4. Install fireblocking in framing cavity plenums.
5. Use drywall (gypsum) in framing cavity ducts and plenums only when the air temperature will not exceed 125º F. and when the surfaces are not subject to condensation.
6. Seal framed return cavities airtight (M1602.2).

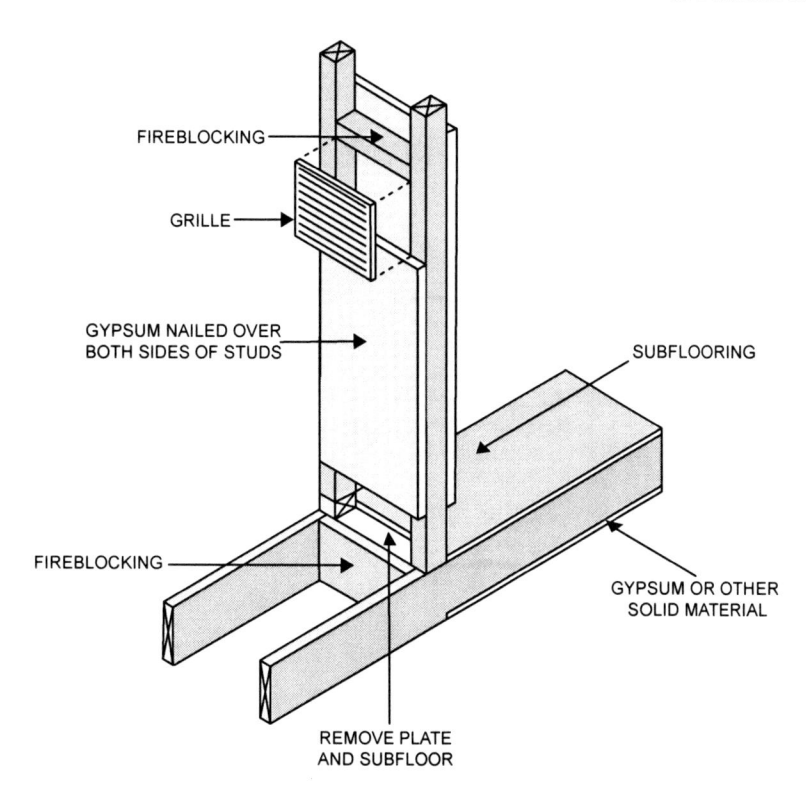

Framing Cavity Return Duct (M1601.1.1-0)
Figure 16-5

UNDERGROUND DUCTS (M1601.1.2)

Ducts Installed Underground or in Concrete

1. Use approved concrete, clay, metal, or plastic for HVAC ducts that are installed underground or in concrete.
2. Protect metal ducts from corrosion or completely surround them with concrete at least (≥) 2 inches thick.
3. Install nonmetallic ducts according to manufacturer's installation instructions.
4. Do not install flexible ducts underground or in concrete.
5. Seal and secure all ducts before pouring concrete.
6. Slope all ducts to an accessible point for drainage of any condensation or liquid that may enter the ducts.
7. Do not exceed 150º F. air temperature in plastic ducts.

Underground Duct Installation Best Practice

Avoid installing metal ducts underground or in concrete. Metal ducts will often deteriorate over time regardless of the protective coatings used.

CRAWL SPACE USED AS HVAC SUPPLY PLENUM (M1601.5)

Crawl Space Prohibited as HVAC Supply Plenum

1. Do not use crawl spaces and similar under-floor spaces as an HVAC supply plenum in new buildings.

2. You may continue to use and maintain existing under-floor plenums. Refer to the IRC for requirements regarding maintaining these existing under-floor plenums.

OUTDOOR AND RETURN AIR LOCATION AND INSTALLATION (M1403, M1602 AND G2442)

Appliances Governed by these Code Provisions

1. Apply these code provisions to forced-air furnaces, and to air conditioning systems, and to heat pumps.

Return Air General Installation Requirements (M1602.1)

1. Draw return air only from inside the home. You may dilute return air with air from outdoors.
2. Do not circulate air from one dwelling unit into another dwelling unit.

Prohibited Sources of Return Air (M1602.2)

1. Do not draw return air from a closet, bathroom, toilet room, kitchen, garage, mechanical room, furnace room, closet, unconditioned attic, or alcove.
2. Do not draw return air from a room or space if the volume of the room or space is less than (<) 25 percent of the total volume of all space served by the HVAC system. Include spaces connected by permanent openings to other rooms when calculating the volume of a space. You may ignore this minimum volume requirement if the supply air to the room is at least (≥) as much as the return air. Example: do not locate the only return air duct in a 240 square feet bedroom of a 1,000 square feet house.
3. Use airtight ducts to bring return air directly into the furnace blower housing from outside the furnace room, closet, or alcove.

Prohibited Sources of Outdoor Air (M1602.2)

1. Locate outdoor air intake openings <u>connected to forced-air heating and cooling systems</u> at least (≥) 10 feet horizontally from contaminant sources including gas equipment vents, chimneys, plumbing vents, or the discharge outlet of an exhaust fan.
2. You may locate outdoor air intake openings closer than 10 feet horizontally to a contaminant source if the outdoor air intake opening is at least (≥) 3 feet below the contaminant source. Note that this differs from the gravity air intake rules in Chapter 3.
3. Do not locate outdoor air intake openings where objectionable odors, fumes or flammable vapors may be present.
4. Locate outdoor air intake openings at least (≥) 10 feet above a public walkway or driveway.
5. Do not locate outdoor air intake openings at grade level next to a sidewalk, street, alley, or driveway.
6. Provide an automatic or gravity operated damper for air intake systems that will close the damper when the system is not operating (Chapter 11).
7. Note that similar provisions exist in Chapter 24.

See Table 303.4 for a summary of outdoor air intake opening location requirements.

Return Air Drawn from Rooms with Fuel-Burning Appliances (M1602.2 and G2442.8)

1. Do not draw return air from a room or space containing a fuel-burning appliance if the room or space is the sole source of return air for the system. Common fuel-burning appliances include furnaces, fireplaces, and water heaters This restriction does not apply if: (a) the appliance is a direct-vent appliance or does not require a vent, or if (b) the volume of the room exceeds 1 cubic foot for each 10 Btu/hour input rating for all fuel-burning appliances in the room, and the volume of supply air approximately equals the volume of return air, and return air inlets are located at least (≥) 10 feet from the appliance firebox or draft hood.
2. Draw return air for a gas furnace from rooms where the furnace is not located if the furnace supply air goes to other rooms.

Minimum Furnace Duct Size (G2442.2)

1. Install supply and return ducts for a forced-air furnace sized according to manufacturer's instructions. If the manufacturer does not provide duct size instructions, provide a total unobstructed area of at least (≥) 2 square inches 1,000 Btu/hour output rating of the furnace for the supply duct system and for the return duct system. Estimate the output rating by multiplying the furnace input rating by the furnace efficiency.

Minimum Heat Pump Return Duct Size (M1403)

1. Install outside air and return ducts for heat pumps according to manufacturer's instructions. If the manufacturer does not provide return duct size instructions, provide outside air and return ducts with a total unobstructed area of at least (≥) 6 square inches per 1,000 Btu/hour output rating of the heat pump. Estimate the output rating by multiplying the heat pump input rating by the heat pump average coefficient of performance. Note that a heat pump's coefficient of performance is difficult to find. Refer to the manufacturer's instructions if there is a question about return duct size.

TABLE M1602
Round Duct Areas

duct diameter (in.)	duct area (sq. in.)	maximum Btu/hr output for 80% efficient gas furnace served by indicated return duct (approximate)	maximum Btu/hr input for heat pump served by indicated return duct (approximate)
14	153.9	76,000 Btu/hr	24,000 Btu/hr (2 ton)
16	201.1	100,000 Btu/hr	36,000 Btu/hr (3 ton)
18	254.5	127,000 Btu/hr	48,000 Btu/hr (4 ton)
20	314.2	157,000 Btu/hr	60,000 Btu/hr (5 ton)

17
COMBUSTION AIR

This chapter is effectively deleted in IRC 2009

18

CHIMNEYS AND VENTS FOR LIQUID AND SOLID-FUEL APPLIANCES

APPLIANCES GOVERNED BY THIS CHAPTER

1. Apply the provisions in this chapter to chimneys and vents used by solid and liquid-fuel-burning mechanical appliances. The most common modern appliances governed by this chapter are oil-burning appliances such as boilers and furnaces. Do not apply these requirements to fireplaces. Refer to Chapter 10 for information about fireplace chimneys. Do not apply these requirements to gas-burning appliances. Note that similar provisions for gas appliances begin at IRC Chapter 24.

CHIMNEYS AND VENTS FOR LIQUID AND SOLID-FUEL APPLIANCES GENERAL REQUIREMENTS (M1801)

Use of Flue Space Around Flue Liner Systems (M1801.4)

1. Do not vent other appliances into the space surrounding a flue liner system inside a masonry chimney flue. You may install another flue liner system inside the same masonry chimney flue if both liners are installed according to manufacturer's instructions.

Connecting Negative and Positive Pressure Draft Systems (M1801.5)

1. Do not connect vents and flues designed for natural (negative pressure) draft appliances to appliances using positive pressure draft.
2. Provide a safety device that will stop the flow of fuel to positive pressure draft appliances if the positive pressure draft system is not operating.

Running Vents in HVAC Ducts (M1801.8)

1. Do not run vents, vent connectors, and chimneys into or through HVAC supply and return ducts and plenums.

Sealing Unused Openings (M1801.10)

1. Seal all unused openings in all vent and chimney systems using an approved method.

Common Vent Connected to Multiple Appliances (M1801.11)

1. Locate two or more appliances that are connected to the same common vent on the same floor of the home.
2. Offset vent inlets so they are not directly across from each other.
3. Do not connect natural (negative pressure) draft appliances and positive pressure draft appliances to the same vent.

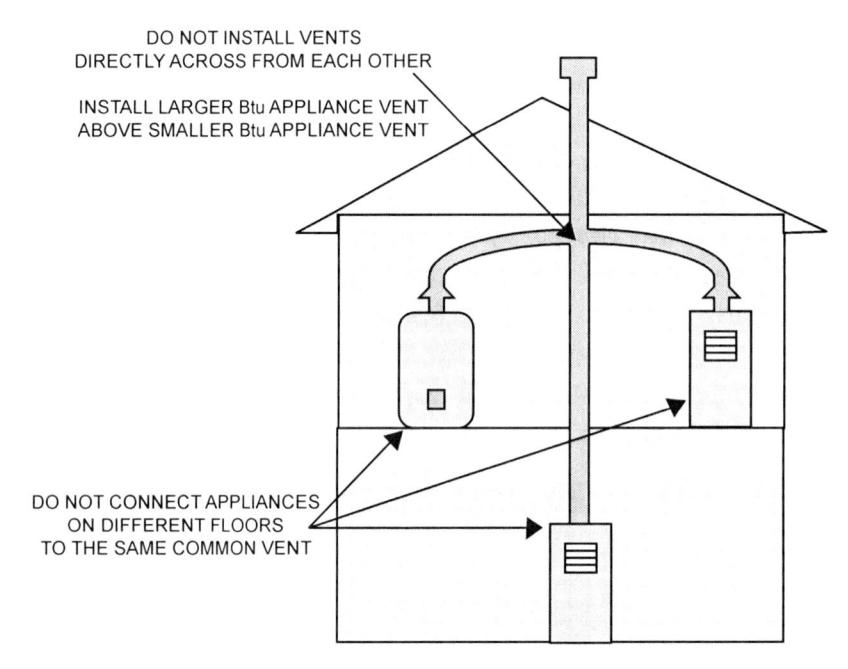

Vents Connected to Multiple Appliances (M1801-11-0)
Figure 18-1

Flues for Multiple Solid-Fuel Appliances (M1801.12)

1. Do not use the same common flue for multiple solid-fuel-burning appliances. Provide each solid-fuel-burning appliance with its own separate flue.

Vents for Appliances Using Different Fuels (M1801.12)

1. Do not use the same flue for solid-fuel-burning appliances and appliances using other fuels such as oil and gas.

ADDING OR REMOVING LIQUID AND SOLID-FUEL APPLIANCES FROM CHIMNEYS AND VENTS (M1801.3)

Description of Potential Problems when Adding or Removing Fuel-Burning Appliances

Every fuel-burning appliance has different characteristics that will affect the operation of a chimney or vent. Adding or removing appliances may cause a chimney or vent that once operated properly to operate improperly. Problems that may occur include backdrafting of exhaust gasses into the home and condensation of moisture that can quickly damage the chimney or vent. Backdrafting and damaged chimneys and vents are a significant safety hazard.

Recalculate Size of Chimneys and Vents when Adding or Removing Appliances

1. Recalculate the size of a chimney or vent when adding or removing a fuel-burning appliance. The new chimney or vent size could increase, decrease, or remain the same depending on the type and efficiency of the appliance added or removed. Account for the new size requirements based on all fuel-burning appliances attached to the chimney or vent. To calculate the required size of a masonry chimney used to vent an oil-burning appliance, use NFPA 31. To calculate the required size of a gas appliance vent, use IRC Chapter 24.

Cleaning and Inspection of Chimneys and Vents when Adding or Removing Appliances

1. Inspect chimneys and vents when adding or removing fuel-burning appliances. Ensure that the flue is continuous and free of cracks, damage, or deterioration that could allow escape of combustion products. Ensure required clearances to combustible materials and ensure that required firestops and fireblocks are installed.
2. Clean flues that have been used for solid or liquid-fueled appliances before inspecting the flue.

Chimney Cleanouts

1. Install a cleanout opening with a tight-fitting, noncombustible door and with an opening height of at least ($\geq$) 6 inches and located at least ($\geq$) 6 inches below the lowest chimney inlet opening.

DRAFT HOODS, DRAFT REGULATORS, AND DAMPERS FOR LIQUID AND SOLID-FUEL APPLIANCES (M1802)

Draft Hood Location

1. Locate an appliance's draft hood in the same room or space where the combustion air openings are located.

Dampers

1. Install manually operated dampers only with solid-fuel-burning appliances.
2. Install automatically operated dampers that contain a safety device that prevents operation of the fuel-burning appliance if the damper is not open to a safe position. Install automatically operated dampers according to manufacturer's instructions.

Draft Regulators

1. Install a draft regulator on all oil-burning appliances that use a chimney as a vent.
2. Locate the draft regulator in the same space as the appliance.
3. Install draft regulators according to manufacturer's instructions.

CONNECTION OF VENT CONNECTORS TO CHIMNEYS FOR LIQUID AND SOLID-FUEL APPLIANCES (M1803 AND 1805)

Vent Connector Definition

Vent connector A vent connector is a pipe that conducts the combustion products from a fuel-burning appliance to a vertical vent or flue. A vent connector is required when the appliance draft hood or vent connection does not line up with the vent or flue. Vent connectors may be single wall metal pipe, or a factory-built chimney material, or a listed Type L double-wall pipe.

Liquid and Solid-Fuel Vent Connector Material

1. Use at least (≥) 26 gage galvanized sheet metal for any single-wall connectors less than (<) 6 inches diameter.
2. Use at least (≥) 24 gage galvanized sheet metal for any single wall vent connectors at least (≥) 6 inches and not more than (≤) 10 inches diameter.
3. Use factory-built listed Type L vents or listed factory-built chimney material for double wall vent connectors.

Liquid and Solid-Fuel Vent Connector Installation

1. Locate a liquid or solid-fuel-burning appliance as close as possible to the vent or flue.
2. Install connectors in the same room or space where the appliance is located.
3. Install connectors across the shortest possible distance and using as few bends as possible.
4. Slope connectors up toward the vent at least (≥) ¼ inch per foot.
5. Support connectors securely over their run.
6. Fasten connector joints with sheet metal screws or rivets unless the connector material uses a manufacturer supplied locking system.
7. Do not install a connector that is smaller than the flue collar of the appliance.
8. Install factory-built connectors according to manufacturer's instructions.
9. Provide access to all connectors for inspection, cleaning, and replacement.
10. Do not connect an appliance to a factory-built chimney unless the appliance and the chimney are specifically listed for such connection. Make all connections to factory-built chimneys according to the chimney manufacturer's instructions.

Liquid and Solid-Fuel Vent Connector Through Walls and Ceilings

1. Do not run connectors through floors or ceilings.
2. Do not run connectors through walls unless the connector manufacturer lists the connector to run through walls or unless the connector is run through a listed wall pass-through device.
3. Comply with the following when running a single wall connector through a wall if the appliance is listed for use with a Type L vent: (a) protect the single wall connector with a ventilated metal thimble at least (≥) 4 inches larger than the connector, and (b) maintain at least (≥) 6 inches between the thimble and combustible material.

Liquid and Solid-Fuel Vent Connector Length

1. Comply with the following when running a connector to a natural draft chimney: (a) install a single wall connector with a horizontal length not more than (≤) 75 percent of the vertical height of the chimney above the connector, and (b) install a factory-built listed connector with a horizontal length not more than (≤) 100 percent of the vertical height of the chimney above the connector.

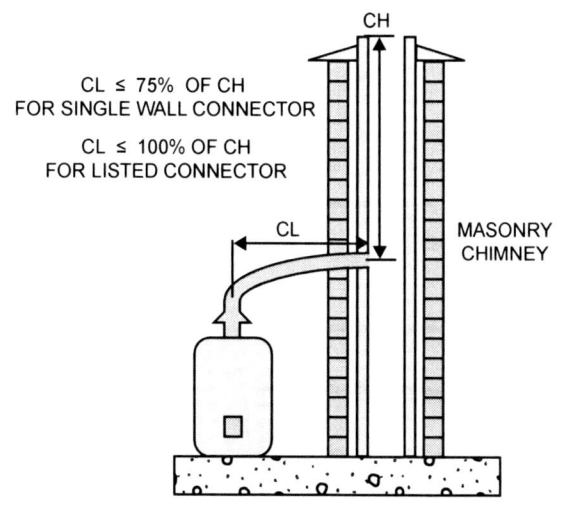

Vent Connector Length to Natural Draft Chimney (M1803-0)
Figure 18-2

Liquid and Solid-Fuel Vent Connector Clearance to Combustibles

1. Provide connectors with clearance to combustible materials in the following table. The clearances in the table assume unlisted connectors. Use manufacturer's instructions for clearances when using factory-built listed connectors.

TABLE M1803
Liquid and Solid-Fuel Vent Connector Minimum Clearance to Combustibles

connector type	minimum distance to combustibles (inches)
Single wall metal Oil and solid-fuel appliances Oil appliances listed for Type L vents	18 9
Type L Oil and solid-fuel appliances Oil appliances listed for Type L vents	9 3

Vent Connector Connection Through a Fireplace Firebox

1. Terminate a connector directly into a masonry fireplace flue. Do not terminate the connector in the damper or smoke chamber. Provide access the connector for inspection and cleaning.

2. Seal the flue below where the connector enters the flue so that air from the fireplace opening cannot enter the flue above the connector.
3. Provide access to the flue for inspection and cleaning. The IRC does not specify how to provide this access.
4. Do not attach any appliance to a factory-built fireplace chimney unless the fireplace manufacturer's instructions specifically permit attachment of the appliance.

Vent Connector Connection Directly to a Masonry Chimney (M1805.2)

1. Terminate a vent connector directly into a fireplace flue at least ($\geq$) 6 inches above the bottom of the flue. If connection less than (<) 6 inches above the bottom of the flue is the only way to install the connector, provide a capped tee in the connector next to the chimney as a cleanout.
2. Terminate vent connectors flush with the inner face of the flue liner. Do not extend the connector into the flue.
3. Cement connectors and thimbles firmly to the masonry.

Size of Chimney Flue Used as Appliance Vent (M1805.3)

1. Comply with the following when using a natural draft chimney to vent one or more appliances: (a) ensure that the effective area of the chimney flue is at least ($\geq$) as large as the area of one vent connector entering the flue, and (b) ensure that the effective area of the chimney flue is at least ($\geq$) as large as the area of the largest vent connector entering the flue plus 50 percent of the areas of any additional vent connectors entering the flue.

Example:

Question:
May you connect one 6 inches diameter round connector and two 4 inches diameter round connectors to one 8 inches round chimney flue?

Answer:
The area of the chimney flue is 4^2 (flue radius squared) x 3.14(π) = 50.3 sq. in. The area of the 6 inches round connector is 3^2 (connector radius squared) x 3.14(π) = 28.3 sq. in. The area of each 4 inches round connector is 2^2 (connector radius squared) x 3.14(π) = 12.6 sq. in. Add 28.3 sq. in. plus 12.6 sq. in. (two times 50 percent of 12.6 sq. in.) equals 40.9 sq. in. You may connect these connectors to the chimney.

Size of Chimney Flue for Solid-Fuel Appliance (M1805.3.1)

1. Ensure that the area (not the diameter) of a chimney flue connected to a solid-fuel-burning appliance is at least ($\geq$) as large as the appliance flue collar area or connector area and not more than ($\leq$) three times as large as the appliance flue collar area. Use manufacturer's installation instructions if the instructions conflict with this provision.

VENTS FOR LIQUID AND SOLID-FUEL APPLIANCES (M1804)

Appliances Governed by these Code Provisions

1. Apply these code provisions to vents (not chimneys) used by liquid and solid-fuel-burning appliances.
2. Do not apply these code provisions to direct vent appliances.
3. Note that similar venting provisions for gas appliances begin in Chapter 24.

Liquid and Solid-Fuel Vent Types

1. Use a listed Type L vent for oil-burning appliances.
2. Use a listed pellet vent for pellet fuel-burning appliances.

Liquid and Solid-Fuel Vent Flashing and Shrouds

1. Install flashing according to manufacturer's recommendations on all vents that pass through a roof. This usually includes a metal thimble sized to surround the vent with no significant gaps between the vent and thimble and usually includes a storm collar ring.
2. Do not install a shroud or similar decorative cover around a vent unless the shroud or cover is listed for use with the specific venting system and is installed according to manufacturer's instructions.

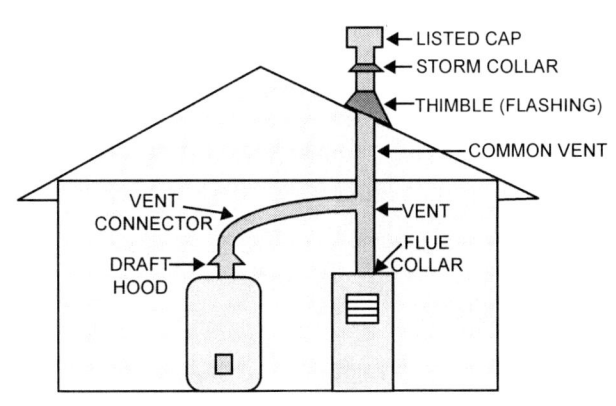

Vent System Parts (M1804-1)
Figure 18-3

Liquid and Solid-Fuel Natural Draft Vent Height

1. Terminate the vent for a natural draft hood equipped appliance at least 5 feet above the highest connected appliance outlet. Measure from the draft hood to the bottom of the vent cap.

Type L Vent Roof Termination Height

1. Terminate a Type L vent at least ($\geq$) 2 feet above the roof and at least ($\geq$) 2 feet above any part of the home within ($\leq$) 10 feet of the vent. Measure termination height above the roof from the highest point where the vent penetrates the roof to the bottom of the vent cap.
2. Install a listed vent cap on a Type L vent.

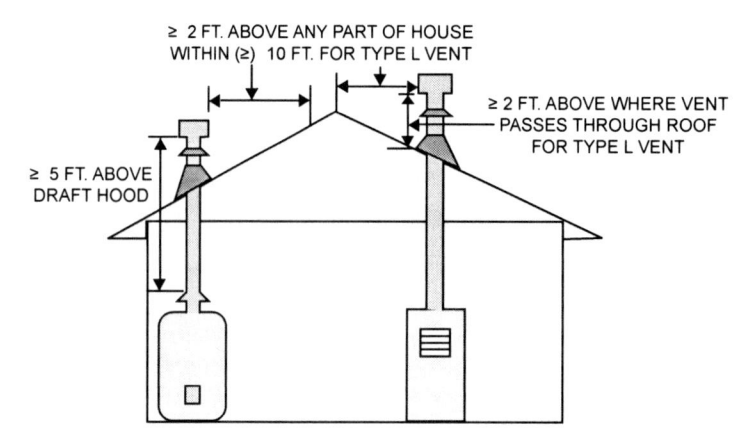

Vent Height and Termination – Natural Draft Appliances (M1804-2)
Figure 18-4

Liquid and Solid-Fuel Powered Vent System Termination

1. Comply with all of the following requirements when terminating a <u>vent</u> connected to an internal or external power exhauster and when terminating a <u>vent</u> equipped with a draft inducer:

   a) terminate the vent at least (≥) 3 feet above any forced-air inlet located within (≤) 10 feet, and

   b) terminate the vent at least (≥) 4 feet below, or at least (≥) 4 feet horizontally, or at least (≥) 1 foot above any window or gravity air inlet into the home, and

   c) terminate the vent at least (≥) 3 feet from any interior corner formed by the intersection of two exterior walls that are perpendicular to each other, and

   d) terminate the bottom of the vent at least (≥) 12 inches above finished ground level, and

   e) do not terminate the vent directly above or closer than (≤) 3 feet horizontally from an oil tank vent or gas meter, and

   f) direct the vent discharge away from the home.

2. Note that a <u>vent</u> equipped with a draft inducer is different from an <u>appliance</u> equipped with a draft inducer. A vent draft inducer pulls combustion products through a vent and an appliance draft inducer pulls combustion products through an appliance.

Liquid and Solid-Fuel Single Appliance Vent Size

1. Install a single appliance vent that has an area at least (≥) as large as the appliance's vent connector area and at least (≥) 7 square inches. This provision does not apply if the vent is an integral part of a listed and labeled appliance such as a swimming pool heater.

19

SPECIAL FUEL-BURNING EQUIPMENT

KITCHEN COOKING EQUIPMENT (M1901 AND G2447)

Range and Cooktop Clearance to Combustible Material

1. Provide at least (≥) 30 inches vertical clearance between built-in or freestanding ranges and cooktops and combustible materials, including kitchen cabinets made from wood or metal. This provision applies to gas and other fuel-fired ranges and cooktops. This provision also applies to electric ranges and cooktops when required by manufacturer's installation instructions.
2. You may reduce the clearance to at least (≥) 24 inches if:
   a) a cooking appliance or microwave oven is installed according to manufacturer's instructions above the range or cooktop, or
   b) a metal ventilating hood is installed above the range or cooktop with a clearance of at least (≥) ¼ inch between the hood and the cabinet, or
   c) the underside of the combustible material is covered with at least (≥) ¼ inch of sheet metal covered insulating millboard.
3. Do not use cooking appliances listed for commercial use in any home.

SAUNA HEATERS (M1902 AND G2440)

Sauna Heater Installation Requirements

1. Install sauna heaters according to manufacturer's instructions.
2. Protect sauna heaters and any hot parts, such as draft hood or combustion air inlet, from accidental contact. Use guards, such as wood, that do not easily transfer heat. Provide any required clearance between combustible guards and hot surfaces.
3. Provide combustion air to sauna heaters as required by the IRC and manufacturer's instructions.
4. Provide a thermostat that will limit sauna room temperature to not more than (≤) 194º F.
5. Use a timer, if provided, that has a one hour limit. Locate the timer, if provided, outside the sauna.
6. Install the heat sensor not more than (≤) 6 inches from the ceiling if the thermostat is not incorporated into the sauna heater.
7. Do not obtain combustion air from inside the sauna.
8. Do not locate a sauna draft hood inside the sauna.
9. Install a ventilation opening into the sauna at least (≥) 4 inches by 8 inches located near the top of the door into the sauna.

20

BOILERS AND WATER HEATERS

HOT WATER AND STEAM BOILERS (M2001 AND G2452)

Labeling and Instructions Requirements

1. Attach to the boiler a permanent and complete set of operating instructions, rating data, and the manufacturer's nameplate.
2. Provide a complete control diagram and complete operating instructions when the boiler is installed.
3. Install boilers according to manufacturer's instructions, including requirements for clearances to combustible materials and provisions for combustion air.

Shutoff Valves

1. Provide all boilers and modular boilers with a shutoff valve on both the supply and return piping. Each individual boiler in a multiple or modular boiler system must have these shutoff valves. Shutoff valves are not required for a single low pressure steam boiler.

Gauges

1. Provide hot water boilers with a pressure gauge and a temperature gauge or a combined pressure and temperature gauge. These gauges should show actual pressure and temperature and the normal operating range of pressure and temperature.
2. Provide steam boilers with a water gauge (sight glass) and a pressure gauge. The pressure gauge should show actual pressure and the normal operating range of pressure. Install the water gauge so that the gauge midpoint is at the normal water level.

Pressure Relief Valve

1. Provide all boilers with a pressure relief valve. Set the valve at the maximum rating of the boiler. Install the valve discharge pipe so that it slopes to the discharge point. The discharge point should be not more than ($\leq$) 18 inches from the floor or should drain into an open receptor.

Low Water Cutoff

1. Provide all boilers with a low water cutoff device. This device should automatically stop the boiler heating system if the water level drops below the manufacturer defined minimum safe level.

Hot Water Boiler Expansion Tanks (Non-pressurized)

1. Provide hot water boilers with either a non-pressurized or pressurized expansion tank. Calculate the tank size according to the following table.
2. Fasten non-pressurized securely to the building or boiler and support the tank so that it will support two times the weight of the water when the tank is full.
3. Provide a means to drain non-pressurized tanks without emptying the boiler system.

Hot Water Boiler Expansion Tanks (Pressurized)

1. Provide hot water boilers with either a non-pressurized or pressurized expansion tank. Calculate the tank size according to the following table.
2. Design pressurized tanks so that they can withstand a hydrostatic test pressure at least (≥) 2 ½ times the allowable working pressure of the system.

Hot Water Boiler Expansion Tank Capacity

1. Calculate system volume including water in the boiler, convectors, and piping. This does not include any water in the expansion tank.

TABLE M2001
Boiler Expansion Tank Size

system volume (gallons)	pressurized expansion tank (gallons)	non-pressurized expansion tank (gallons)
10	1	1.5
20	1.5	3
30	2.5	4.5
40	3	6
50	4	7.5
60	5	9
70	6	10.5
80	6.5	12
90	7.5	13.5
100	8	15

WATER HEATER INSTALLATION AND ACCESS (M2005)

Water Heater General Installation Requirements

1. Install water heaters according to the manufacturer's instructions and applicable IRC provisions. Refer to Chapter 13 for water heater service access requirements.

Water Heater Prohibited Locations

1. Do not install fuel-fired water heaters in rooms used as storage closets. You may install water heaters in closets used solely to store the water heater if you provide adequate combustion air in the closet. You may install electric water heaters in any closet when allowed by the manufacturer.
2. Do not install fuel-fired water heaters in bedrooms or bathrooms unless the water heater is installed in a sealed enclosure where combustion air does not come from the living space. This restriction does not apply to direct vent water heaters.
3. You may provide access to water heaters located in attics or crawl spaces through bedrooms, bathrooms, or their closets if ventilation of the bedroom, bathroom, or closet complies with the IRC.

POOL HEATER INSTALLATION (M2006)

Pool Heater General Installation Requirements

1. Install pool heaters according to the manufacturer's instructions and applicable IRC provisions. If a conflict exists between the manufacturer's instructions and the IRC, the more restrictive provision applies.

Pool Heater Relief Valves

1. Provide pool heaters with a temperature relief valve.

Pool Heater Bypass Valve

1. Provide either an integrated or a field installed water supply bypass valve on pool heaters between the inlet and outlet pipes.

21

HYDRONIC PIPING

HYDRONIC PIPING SYSTEMS (M2101)

Hyronic Piping System Discussion

A hydronic piping system consists of pipes or tubes, fittings, and valves used in a building heating and/or cooling system. Hydronic piping systems are used to distribute hot water or steam in boiler type heating systems. Hydronic piping systems are also used in space cooling systems such as chilled water systems, although hydronic cooling is rare in homes.

Limitations of the Material in this Section

Selection and installation of hydronic piping systems is complex. The risk of injury and property damage is significant if the system fails. Hydronic piping should be left to qualified and licensed contractors. We will present general information about hydronic piping in this section. Confirm specific hydronic piping requirements in IRC Chapter 21 and in the manufacturer's instructions.

Hydronic Piping System Materials

1. You may use most types of metal and plastic pipes and tubes that are suitable for potable water supply pipes in hydronic piping systems. Most metal pipes are restricted to above ground use, except for copper tubing and steel pipes. Most plastic pipes and tubes (such as CPVC and PEX) may be used either above ground or as embedded radiant systems.

Hydronic Piping System Installation

1. Use fittings and fitting attachment materials (e.g., solvent cement) for hydronic piping as though it were being used for potable water. Embedded (and inaccessible) fittings must be welded, soldered, heat-fused or cemented as appropriate for the type of pipe.
2. Support hydronic piping as though it were being used for potable water.
3. Protect hydronic piping that passes through concrete or masonry with a sleeve.
4. Protect hydronic piping from contact with other materials that are not compatible with the hydronic piping materials and could cause the hydronic piping to degrade.
5. Install hydronic piping so that it will not be subject to excess stress and so that expansion, contraction, and settlement of the structure will not affect the hydronic piping.

Protection of Potable Water

1. Install a backflow prevention device to protect the potable water supply system as specified in Section P2902.

22

OIL PIPING AND STORAGE SYSTEMS

OIL PIPING AND STORAGE SYSTEMS (M2201)

Oil Storage Tanks Above Ground

1. Use only oil storage tanks that are listed and labeled for above ground oil storage.
2. Limit the total amount of oil stored above ground, both inside and outside the home, to not more than (≤) 660 gallons, unless the storage system complies with NFPA 31.
3. Install indoor oil storage tanks so that the tanks can be removed from the home as whole units.
4. Locate oil storage tanks that have more than (>) a 10 gallon capacity at least (≥) 5 feet from any flame.
5. Support oil storage tanks using rigid and non-combustible supports that prevent shifting and settling.
6. Protect oil storage tanks from the weather and from physical damage.
7. Locate oil storage tanks at least (≥) 5 feet from an adjoining property line.

Oil Storage Tanks Below Ground

1. Use only oil storage tanks that are listed and labeled for below ground oil storage.
2. Do not undermine the building foundation when excavating for underground oil storage tanks. While not specifically required by the IRC, restrictions on excavations for pipes near foundations are a good guide for safe oil storage tank excavations.
3. Do not locate oil storage tanks closer than 1 foot to a basement wall, pit, or property line.
4. Place oil storage tanks on clean, well-tamped, non-corrosive materials such as clean soil, sand, or gravel.
5. Cover oil storage tanks with at least (≥) 1 foot of soil.
6. Protect oil storage tanks from corrosion using appropriate coatings or by using corrosion-resistant materials.

Oil Gauges

1. Provide indoor oil storage tanks with a device that indicates when the oil in the tank reaches a predetermined safe level.
2. Do not use sight glasses or similar devices that could break and cause a liquid oil or oil vapor leak.

Oil Pipes and Connector Materials

1. Use steel pipe or tubing, or copper tubing for oil supply piping. Use at least Type L copper tubing and fittings, if using copper tubing. Do not use aluminum tubing.
2. Use flexible metal hoses for oil piping only where rigid piping is impractical or when isolation from vibration is a concern. Use only flexible metal hoses that are listed and labeled for oil piping and install them according to manufacturer's instructions.
3. Install oil piping to avoid stressing the pipe and to allow for normal expansion and contraction of the piping materials.
4. Install oil supply piping that is at least ($\geq$) ⅜ inch diameter.

Oil Pipe Fittings

1. Use only fittings and materials compatible with the type pipe material being used.
2. Do not use cast iron fittings, unions that require packing or gaskets, left or right couplings, or soldered fittings using solder with a melting point less than (<) 1,000º F.
3. Use a compatible lubricant or pipe thread compound to ensure tight fitting oil pipe fitting joints.

Oil Fill Pipe

1. Locate oil fill pipes outside the building and at least ($\geq$) 2 feet from any building opening at the same or lower level.
2. Install a tight metal cover on an oil fill pipe.

Oil Tank Vent Pipe

1. Use at least ($\geq$) 1 ¼ inches diameter vent pipe.
2. Install the vent pipe so that it drains toward the oil storage tank without any sagging or traps that can collect liquid.
3. Do not connect a vent pipe with fill pipes, pipes from burners, or overflow pipes from auxiliary tanks.
4. Install the tank end of the vent pipe at the top of the tank.
5. Do not insert the tank end of the vent pipe more than 1 inch into the tank.
6. Locate the vent pipe termination at least ($\geq$) 2 feet, measured both vertically and horizontally, from any building opening.
7. Install on the vent pipe a weatherproof cap or fitting with an unobstructed area at least as large as the cross-sectional area of the vent pipe.

8. Locate the vent pipe vertically above ground so that snow and ice will not obstruct the vent.

Oil Tank Connection Between Two Tanks

1. Locate the tanks on the same horizontal level so that gravity causes the flow of oil from one tank to another.
2. Do not exceed (≤) 660 gallons total capacity between the two oil tanks.
3. Connect together not more than (≤) two tanks.

Oil Pumps and Valves

1. Use only listed and labeled oil pumps and install them according to the manufacturer's instructions.
2. Use oil pumps that automatically shut off when the oil flow stops.
3. Provide a readily accessible oil shutoff valve between the oil supply and the oil burner.
4. Install a pressure-relief valve on the discharge line of an oil pump if a shutoff valve is installed on the discharge line. The relief valve should discharge into a return line to relieve excess pressure.
5. Install a pressure-relief valve on oil lines using a heater in the fuel oil supply system. The relief valve should discharge into a return line to relieve excess pressure.

Oil Pressure

1. Do not exceed (≤) 3 pounds per square inch oil pressure at the inlet of the appliance.

23

SOLAR ENERGY SYSTEMS

SOLAR ENERGY SYSTEMS (M2301)

Solar Energy Systems Governed by this Chapter

Solar energy systems governed by this chapter capture solar radiation in a liquid thermal mass such as water or a solid thermal mass such as stone to provide space heating and water heating. This chapter does not address solar systems that use photoelectric cells to produce electric energy.

Solar Energy Systems Installation Requirements

1. Install only listed and labeled solar energy systems according to manufacturer's instruction.
2. Provide access to solar energy system collectors, controls, dampers, fans, blowers, and pumps for inspection, maintenance, and replacement.
3. Design or reinforce building structural components to support the additional weight of any solar energy system components. Thermal mass collectors can be extremely heavy and engineering assistance may be required to determine necessary reinforcement of roof and ceiling framing to support the additional weight.
4. Provide solar energy systems that use liquid as the thermal mass and/or circulation medium with temperature and pressure relief valves, vacuum relief valves, expansion tanks, and backflow protection as recommended by the manufacturer for the system being installed.
5. Protect solar energy system liquids from freezing unless the winter design temperature is greater than (>) 32° F.
6. Do not use flammable gasses and liquids as a circulation medium.

24

FUEL GAS

GAS APPLIANCES AND GAS PIPING SYSTEMS GENERAL REQUIREMENTS (G2401, G2403-G2405)

Gas Types Governed by the IRC

The IRC governs natural gas (methane) and liquified petroleum (LP) gas (propane and butane) in permanent systems beginning after the point of delivery by the gas supplier. The IRC does not govern liquified natural gas systems and temporary and portable LP gas systems.

Gas Appliance Listing and Labeling

1. Use gas appliances that are listed and labeled for the intended purpose. This means that an appliance listed and labeled for one purpose may not be used for another purpose. Example: a gas cooking appliance listed and labeled only for indoor use cannot be used outdoors.

Gas Appliance Replacement Parts

1. Repair or replace defective gas appliance parts with similar parts that do not change the terms of the appliance listing. This usually means using only parts supplied and/or approved by the appliance manufacturer.

Gas Appliance Seismic and Weather Protection

1. Support gas appliances to resist wind loads and exposure to weather when the appliance is located outdoors.
2. Support gas appliances to resist seismic forces when the appliance is located in a seismic design area.
3. Use only gas appliances designed and listed for exterior use when installing the gas appliances outdoors or protect the appliance from outdoor conditions that might affect its proper operation, safety, or useful life.

Gas Appliance and Piping Effects on Building Structural Members

1. Do not cut, notch, bore, or drill building structural members (such as studs and joists) except as allowed the IRC. Refer to Chapters 5 and 6.
2. Do not cut, notch, bore, drill or otherwise alter trusses in any way unless approved in writing by the truss manufacturer or by a qualified design professional.
3. Do not add gas appliances that increase the weight carried by structural members (joists and trusses) without determining if the structural members will safely carry the additional weight.

Condensate Auxiliary (Backup) System Requirements for Category IV Appliances

1. Install an auxiliary condensate drain pan under most Category IV condensing appliances. The pan is required when the appliance is located where building damage may occur if the primary condensate discharge system becomes blocked or does not function. This usually applies to appliances installed in or above finished space. A common example of a Category IV appliance is a high efficiency gas furnace.
2. Install the pan and the disposal pipe using one of the methods described in Chapter 14.
3. You do not need to install a drain pan if the fuel-fired appliance automatically shuts down when the primary condensate discharge system malfunctions.

GAS APPLIANCES PROHIBITED LOCATIONS AND PROHIBITED COMBUSTION AIR SOURCES (G2406)

Gas Appliance Prohibited Installation Locations

1. Do not locate gas or other fuel-burning appliances in: (a) bedrooms, (b) bathrooms, (c) toilet rooms, or (d) storage closets. Do not draw combustion air for any fuel-burning appliance from these rooms regardless of where the appliance is located.
2. Do not locate appliances anywhere that is not approved by the manufacturer's instructions.

Gas Appliance Prohibited Installation Locations Exceptions

1. You may install direct vent appliances in prohibited locations if the appliance draws all combustion air directly from the outdoors.
2. You may install vented room heaters, vented wall furnaces, vented decorative appliances, and decorative appliances listed for installation in vented solid fuel-burning fireplaces (such as gas logs) in prohibited locations if the room satisfies combustion air volume requirements.
3. You may install one listed wall-mounted unvented room heater in a bathroom if the appliance has an oxygen depletion safety shutoff system, and if the appliance input rating is not more than ($\leq$) 6,000 Btu/hour, and if the bathroom satisfies combustion air volume requirements.
4. You may install one listed wall-mounted unvented room heater in a bedroom if the appliance has an oxygen depletion safety shutoff system, and if the appliance input rating is not

more than (≤) 10,000 Btu/hour, and if the bedroom satisfies combustion air volume requirements.
5. You may install appliances in an enclosure accessible from the prohibited locations if all combustion air is drawn directly from the outdoors and if the enclosure is equipped with a self-closing door that is weather-stripped.
6. The standard combustion air volume requirement is at least (≥) 50 cubic feet per 1,000 Btu/hour appliance input rating. This standard volume requirement does not apply if the home is tightly sealed with a known air infiltration rate of less than 0.40 air changes per hour. Tightly sealed homes are rare.

COMBUSTION AIR FOR GAS APPLIANCES GENERAL REQUIREMENTS (G2407)

Combustion Air Description

Fuel-burning appliances, such as gas furnaces, boilers, and water heaters, need air to support the fuel burning (combustion) process. These appliances also need air for cooling and ventilation of the appliance, and for proper operation of the vent system that expels combustion byproducts outside. The air required to support operation of fuel-burning appliances is called combustion air.

Without adequate combustion air, incomplete fuel combustion may occur. Byproducts of incomplete fuel combustion can include carbon monoxide and soot that can damage the appliance and its vent. This is a health and safety hazard. Appliances operating without adequate combustion air can cost more to operate and maintain.

Do not confuse combustion air with the similar term makeup air. Makeup air replaces air that is exhausted by clothes dryers, exhaust fans, fireplaces, and similar devices.

Appliances Needing Combustion Air

1. Provide combustion air for Category I gas appliances according to the appliance manufacturer's recommendations and to the IRC Chapter 24 requirements. Category I gas appliances include the furnaces and water heaters found in most homes.
2. Provide combustion air for direct vent and for Category II, III, and IV appliances according to the appliance manufacturer's instructions. Do not apply IRC combustion air requirements to these appliances. Category II appliances do not currently exist. Category III and IV appliances include medium and high efficiency gas appliances that operate with positive vent pressure.
3. Do not apply IRC combustion air requirements to fireplaces and fireplace stoves. Refer to IRC Chapter 10 for fireplace combustion air requirements.

Combustion Air Depletion by Other Systems

1. Provide makeup air when air exhausted by appliances (such as clothes dryers, bathroom and kitchen exhaust fans, fireplaces) interferes with appliance operation. Account for combustion air used by other fuel-burning appliances when determining combustion air requirements. This is important when drawing all combustion air from inside the home.

Other appliances compete with gas and oil-burning appliances for combustion air. This can create negative pressure that can interfere with operation of the gas and oil-burning appliances and their vents. The IRC does not define how to account for air exhausted by other appliances. Gas and oil-burning appliances located in or near rooms containing clothes dryers, exhaust fans, and fireplaces require special attention to ensure that combustion air and venting needs are satisfied.

Combustion Air Opening Covers Area

1. Use the net free area of covers installed over combustion air openings when calculating the area of combustion air openings. The net free area is the area of the opening minus the area of screens, louvers, or grilles.
2. Use screens that have openings at least (≥) ¼ inch on combustion air opening covers.

Combustion Air Opening Louvers and Grilles

1. Use manufacturer's specifications, if available, to determine the net free area of louvers and grilles. If manufacturer's specifications are not available, assume that metal louvers provide a net free area of 75 percent of the gross louver area. Assume that wood louvers provide a net free area of 25 percent of the gross louver area.
2. Lock nonmotorized louvers and grilles in the full open position.
3. Provide a safety interlock system for motorized louvers that prevents appliance burner ignition until after the louvers are fully open and prevents burner operation if the louvers are closed.

Combustion Air Duct Materials and Construction

1. Use galvanized steel to construct combustion air ducts. Refer to IRC Chapter 16 for duct material specifications.
2. You may use unobstructed stud and joist spaces as combustion air ducts if only one required fireblock is removed.
3. Terminate combustion air ducts in unobstructed space that allows free air movement.
4. Do not open combustion air ducts into more than one room or enclosure.
5. Do not use the same combustion air duct for both the upper and lower duct openings.
6. Do not install a screen on any combustion air duct opening in the attic.
7. Do not slope horizontal combustion air ducts downward toward the source of combustion air. Make the duct level or slope it toward the appliance.
8. Do not use the space in a masonry, metal, or factory-built chimney that surrounds a chimney liner, gas vent, plastic piping or other devices as a combustion air duct.
9. Locate the lowest point of an exterior combustion air opening at least (≥) 12 inches above exterior grade.

Homes Built Using Air Tight Construction Techniques Description

Homes built using air tight construction techniques do not allow enough air infiltration into the home to safely support fuel combustion. Lack of adequate combustion air can cause many problems including production of carbon monoxide and soot that can be a health hazard and can damage appliances and vents. <u>Do not draw combustion air only from inside the home if it is built using air tight construction techniques</u>.

This fuel gas code section limits use of the standard method for obtaining all combustion air from inside the home to homes having a known air infiltration rate of at least (≥) 0.40 air changes per hour. Homes with fewer than (<) 0.40 air changes per hour may not allow enough air infiltration to safely support combustion.

It is very rare to know the actual air infiltration rate for a home. Homes that satisfy all of the following requirements probably have fewer than (<) 0.40 air changes per hour and if so cannot use the standard method: (1) home thermal envelope walls have a continuous water vapor retarder with a rating of 1 perm or less and any openings in the vapor barrier are sealed, and (2) doors and operable windows meet air leakage requirements of the International Energy Conservation Code, and (3) gaps and spaces are sealed including gaps and spaces between windows and doors and the surrounding framing, between sole plates and floors, between wall and ceiling joints, between wall panels, and at wall penetrations for utilities such as plumbing, electrical, and gas.

Older homes rarely satisfy these requirements. Newer homes may satisfy the first two requirements, but it is still rare for most builders to seal all framing and utility penetration gaps as intended by the third requirement. Most homes may use the standard method for obtaining all combustion air from inside the home, but you should verify with the builder if the home was built using air tight construction techniques.

COMBUSTION AIR FOR GAS APPLIANCES FROM INSIDE THE BUILDING (G2407.5)

Combustion Air from the Room where the Appliance is Located (Standard Method)

1. You may draw combustion air from the room where the appliance is located if the room's volume is at least (≥) 50 cubic feet per 1,000 Btu/hour input rating for all appliances in the room. You may add the volume of rooms directly adjacent to the room where the appliance is located if there are no doors or other closable obstructions between the rooms.
2. Do not draw combustion air only from inside the home if it is built using air tight construction techniques.

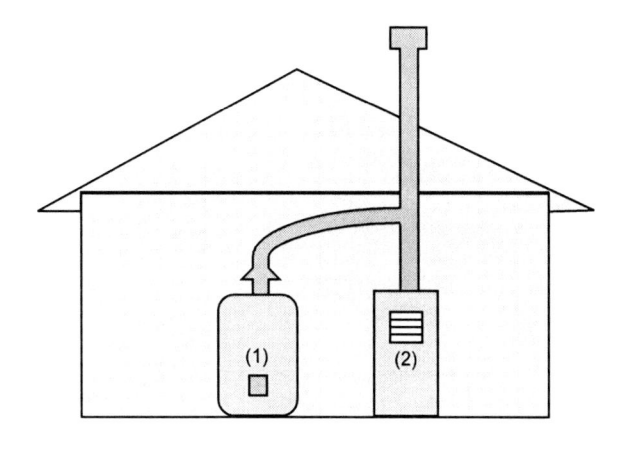

(1) 40,000 Btu WATER HEATER   (2) 110,000 Btu FURNACE

MINIMUM ROOM VOLUME IS ≥ 50 CU. FT. PER 1,000 Btu
TOTAL INPUT FOR ALL APPLIANCES

EXAMPLE:
40,000 Btu + 110,000 Btu = 150,000 Btu
150,000 Btu / 1,000 Btu = 150
150 X 50 CU. FT. = 7,500 CU. FT. MINIMUM ROOM VOLUME

Combustion Air from Room where Appliance is Located (G2407.5-1)
Figure 24-1

Combustion Air from the Room where the Appliance is Located (Calculated Method)

1. Use the following calculated volume equations to determine if the room where the appliance(s) are located has sufficient volume to provide all combustion air for the appliance(s) only if the number of air changes per hour is known.
2. Use the following equation for appliances without draft inducer fans:

$$\text{Room Volume Greater Than Or Equal To } (\geq)$$
$$(21 \text{ ft}^3/\text{ACH}) (I_o/1,000 \text{ Btu/hour})$$

3. Use the following equation for appliances with draft inducer fans:

$$\text{Room Volume Greater Than Or Equal To } (\geq)$$
$$(15 \text{ ft}^3/\text{ACH}) (I_f/1,000 \text{ Btu/hour})$$

ACH = Air Changes per Hour expressed as a decimal such as 0.40. Do not use an ACH greater than 0.60.
I_o = Btu input per hour of all appliances in the room without draft inducer fans.
I_f = Btu input per hour of all appliances in the room with draft inducer fans.

Combustion Air from Other Rooms on the Same Floor Level

1. You may draw combustion air from rooms that are on the same floor level by installing permanent openings between the rooms. Ensure that the total volume of the connected rooms complies with either the standard or calculated volume method.
2. Install two permanent openings between the room where the appliance(s) are located and each room from which you wish to draw combustion air. Start one opening not more than

(≤) 12 inches from the room ceiling and the other not more than (≤) 12 inches from the room floor.

3. Provide each opening with a net free area of at least (≥) 1 square inch per 1,000 Btu/hour input rating of all appliances in the room and at least (≥) 100 square inches per opening.

4. Provide each opening with a minimum dimension of at least (≥) 3 inches.

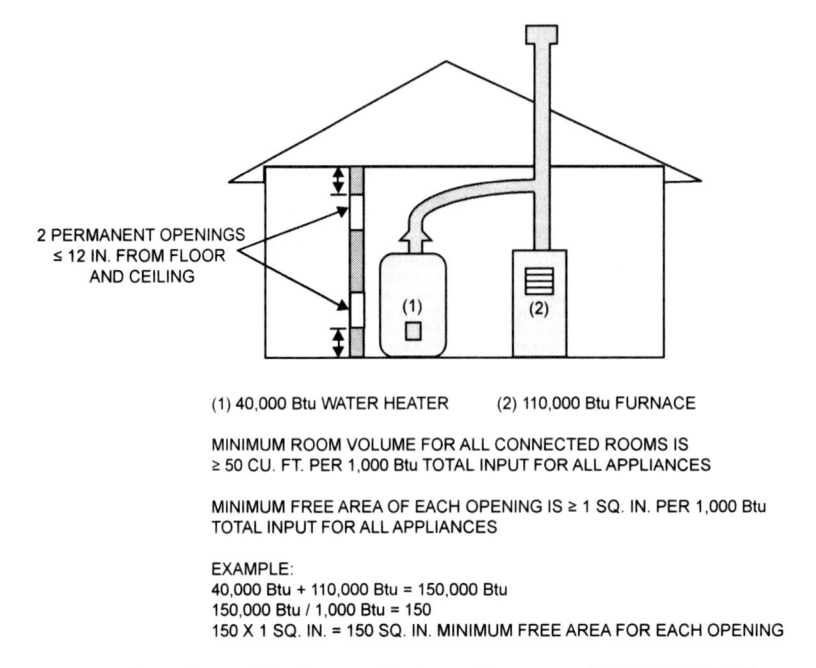

2 PERMANENT OPENINGS
≤ 12 IN. FROM FLOOR
AND CEILING

(1) 40,000 Btu WATER HEATER   (2) 110,000 Btu FURNACE

MINIMUM ROOM VOLUME FOR ALL CONNECTED ROOMS IS
≥ 50 CU. FT. PER 1,000 Btu TOTAL INPUT FOR ALL APPLIANCES

MINIMUM FREE AREA OF EACH OPENING IS ≥ 1 SQ. IN. PER 1,000 Btu
TOTAL INPUT FOR ALL APPLIANCES

EXAMPLE:
40,000 Btu + 110,000 Btu = 150,000 Btu
150,000 Btu / 1,000 Btu = 150
150 X 1 SQ. IN. = 150 SQ. IN. MINIMUM FREE AREA FOR EACH OPENING

Combustion Air from Other Rooms (G2407.5-2)
Figure 24-2

Combustion Air from Other Rooms on Different Floor Levels

1. You may draw combustion air from areas that are on different floor levels by installing at least (≥) one permanent opening between the levels. The opening can be in a floor/ceiling assembly or in a louvered door between the levels. Ensure that the total volume of the connected rooms complies with either the standard or calculated volume method.

2. Provide the opening with a total net free area of at least (≥) 2 square inches per 1,000 Btu/hour input rating of all appliances in the room.

(1) 40,000 Btu WATER HEATER   (2) 110,000 Btu FURNACE

MINIMUM ROOM VOLUME IS ≥ 50 CU. FT. PER 1,000 Btu TOTAL INPUT FOR ALL APPLIANCES

MINIMUM FREE AREA OF OPENING OR DOOR IS ≥ 2 SQ. IN. PER 1,000 Btu TOTAL INPUT FOR ALL APPLIANCES

EXAMPLE:
40,000 Btu + 110,000 Btu = 150,000 Btu
150,000 Btu / 2,000 Btu = 150
150 X 2 SQ. IN. = 300 SQ. IN. MINIMUM FREE OPENING AREA OF DOOR OR OPENING

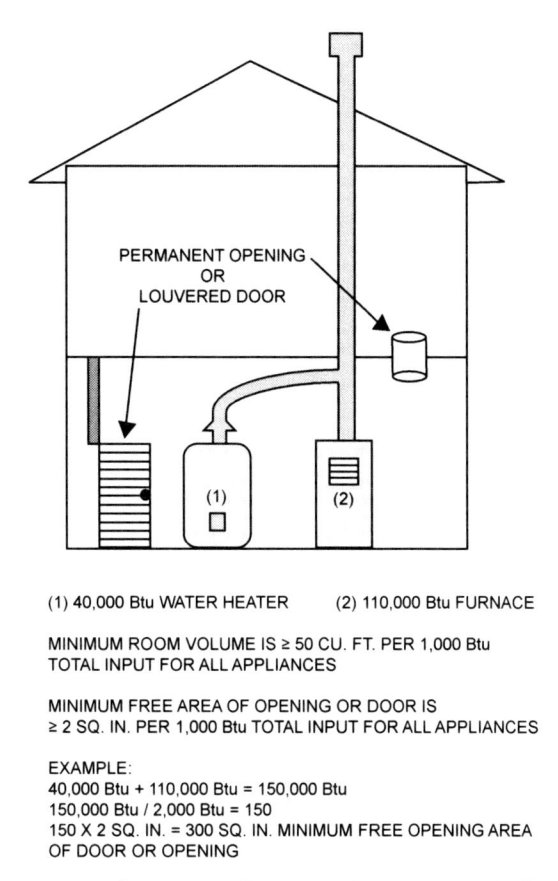

Combustion Air from Different Floor Levels (G2407.5-3)
Figure 24-3

COMBUSTION AIR FOR GAS APPLIANCES FROM OUTSIDE THE BUILDING (G2407.6)

Combustion Air Openings Directly Outside or Ducts Run Vertically

1. Install two permanent combustion air openings between the room where the appliance(s) are located and outside the building. The outside space may be an adequately ventilated attic or crawl space or it may be outside the home. The openings may open directly to the outside or may communicate with the outside using vertical ducts. Do not use one common vertical combustion air duct for both the upper and lower duct openings.
2. Provide openings with the smallest dimension of at least (≥) 3 inches.
3. Start one opening not more than (≤) 12 inches from the room ceiling and the other not more than (≤) 12 inches from the room floor.
4. Provide each opening with a net free area of at least (≥) 1 square inch per 4,000 Btu/hour input rating of all appliances in the room.
5. Ensure that the attic and/or crawl space ventilation openings have a net free area of at least 1 square inch per 4,000 Btu/hour input rating of all appliances that depend on the attic and/or crawl space for combustion air <u>and</u> ensure that the attic and/or crawl space ventilation openings also have enough additional net free area to provide required attic and/or crawl space ventilation.

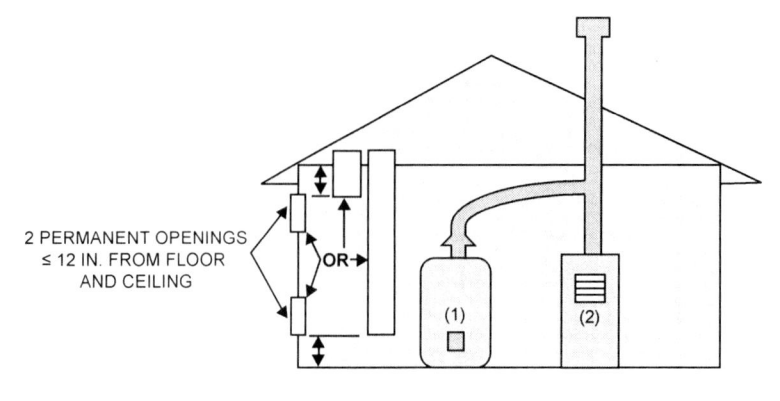

(1) 40,000 Btu WATER HEATER   (2) 110,000 Btu FURNACE

MINIMUM AREA OF EACH OPENING IS
≥ 1 SQ. IN. PER 4,000 Btu TOTAL INPUT FOR ALL APPLIANCES

EXAMPLE:
40,000 Btu + 110,000 Btu = 150,000 Btu
150,000 Btu / 4,000 Btu = 37 1/2
37 1/2 x 1 SQ. IN. = 37 1/2 SQ. IN. MINIMUM FREE AREA FOR EACH OPENING

Combustion Air from Outside (G2407.6-1)
Figure 24-4

Combustion Air Ducts Run Horizontally

1. Install two permanent horizontal combustion air ducts between the room where the appliance(s) are located and outside the building.
2. Use ducts with the smallest dimension of at least (≥) 3 inches.
3. Start one duct not more than (≤) 12 inches from the room ceiling and the other not more than (≤) 12 inches from the room floor.
4. Provide each duct with a net free area of at least (≥) 1 square inch per 2,000 Btu/hour input rating of all appliances in the room.

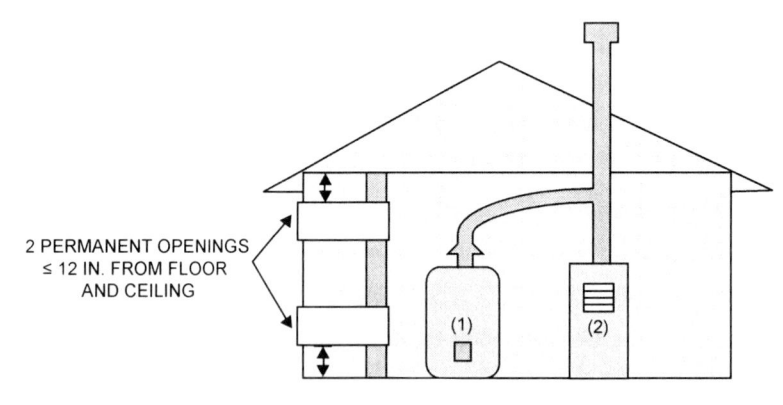

(1) 40,000 Btu WATER HEATER   (2) 110,000 Btu FURNACE

MINIMUM FREE AREA OF EACH OPENING IS ≥ 1 SQ. IN. PER 2,000 Btu
TOTAL INPUT FOR ALL APPLIANCES

EXAMPLE:
40,000 Btu + 110,000 Btu = 150,000 Btu
150,000 Btu / 2,000 Btu = 75
75 x 1 SQ. IN. = 75 SQ. IN. MINIMUM FREE AREA FOR EACH OPENING

Combustion Air from Outside – Horizontal Ducts (G2407.6-2)
Figure 24-5

Combustion Air One Permanent Opening

1. Install one permanent combustion air opening between the room where the appliance(s) are located and outside the building. You may use an adequately ventilated attic as the outside space. The opening may open directly to the outside or it may communicate with the outside using a duct.
2. Use an opening with the smallest dimension of at least (≥) 3 inches.
3. Start the opening not more than (≤) 12 inches from the room ceiling.
4. Provide at least (≥) 1 inch clearance from the opening to the sides of the appliance and at least (≥) 6 inches clearance to the front of the appliance.
5. Provide the opening with a net free area of at least (≥) 1 square inch per 3,000 Btu/hour input rating of all appliances in the room and a net free area that is at least as large as the sum of the areas of all vent connectors in the space. Example: if the vent connector diameters are 3 inches and 4 inches, then the net free opening area must be at least (≥) 78.6 square inches, or at least (≥) 1 square inch per 3,000 Btu/hour input rating, whichever is larger.
6. Ensure that attic ventilation openings have a net free area of at least (≥) 1 square inch per 3,000 Btu/hour input rating of all appliances that depend on the attic space for combustion air and ensure that attic ventilation openings also have enough additional net free area to provide required attic ventilation.

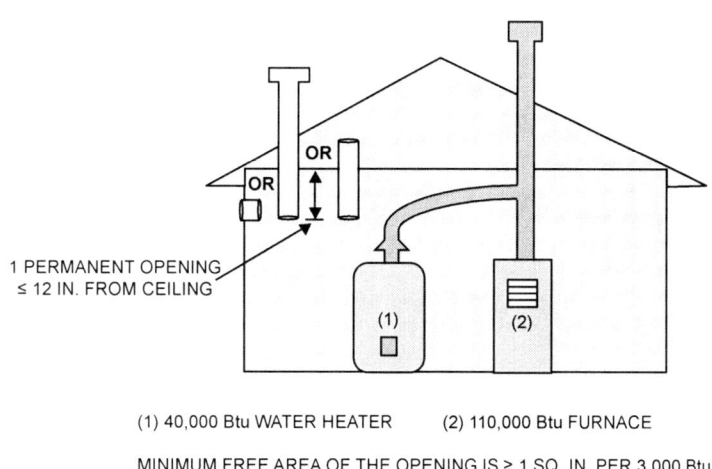

(1) 40,000 Btu WATER HEATER   (2) 110,000 Btu FURNACE

MINIMUM FREE AREA OF THE OPENING IS ≥ 1 SQ. IN. PER 3,000 Btu TOTAL INPUT FOR ALL APPLIANCES

EXAMPLE:
40,000 Btu + 110,000 Btu = 150,000 Btu
150,000 Btu / 3,000 Btu = 50
50 X 1 SQ. IN. = 50 SQ. IN. MINIMUM FREE AREA FOR THE OPENING

Combustion Air – One Permanent Opening (G2407.6-3)
Figure G24-6

COMBUSTION AIR FOR GAS APPLIANCES FROM INSIDE AND OUTSIDE THE BUILDING (G2407.7)

Combustion Air Combining Inside and Outside Sources

1. You may combine the available volume of inside space where the appliance(s) are located with outside combustion air openings or ducts. This combination allows you to reduce the size of the outside combustion air openings and/or ducts.

2. Calculate the reduced size of the outside combustion air openings and/or ducts by calculating the ratio of the actual available indoor air volume to the actual volume required by all gas appliances in the room or space.

Combustion Air Indoor Volumes

1. Calculate the total required indoor air volume (TRV) required by all gas appliances in the room or space. Use the standard or calculated method.
2. Measure the actual available indoor air volume (AIV) in the room or space where the appliance(s) are located. You may include spaces that communicate to the room or space through openings or ducts as described in the IRC.

Combustion Air Outside Opening Size

1. Calculate the full outside air opening or duct size (FSO) for the type of opening or duct you intend to use. Use the horizontal, vertical, or single opening method from the IRC.

Combustion Air Outside Opening Size Reduction Equation

1. Use the following equation to calculate the reduced size combustion air openings or ducts:

$$(1 - (AIV / TRV)) \times FSO = \text{reduced outdoor air opening size}$$

AIV = Actual Available Indoor Air Volume
TRV = Total Required Indoor Air Volume
FSO = Full Outside Air Openings Size

2. Use a duct or opening dimension of at least (≥) 3 inches regardless of the calculated reduced air opening size.

Example:

Question:

Given two 100,000 Btu/hour furnaces and one 40,000 Btu/hour water heater located in a garage measuring 25 feet wide by 20 feet deep by 10 feet high, what size combustion air openings are required using two openings open directly to outdoors.

Answer:
AIV = 25 x 20 x 10 = 5,000 cubic feet
TRV = ((100,000 + 100,000 + 40,000)/1,000) x 50 = 12,000 cubic feet
FSO = (100,000 + 100,000 + 40,000)/4000 = 60 sq. in.

$$(1 - (5,000/12,000)) = .583 \times 60 \text{ sq. in.} = 35 \text{ sq. in.}$$

Each opening should be at least (≥) 35 sq. in. net free area

GAS APPLIANCE INSTALLATION (G2408)

1. Provide a firm and level concrete pad or other approved support pad that extends at least (≥) 3 inches above the surrounding soil for appliances mounted on the ground.

GAS APPLIANCE CLEARANCE REDUCTION TO COMBUSTIBLE MATERIALS (G2409)

Appliances and Equipment Governed by these Code Provisions

1. Apply these clearance to combustible reduction provisions to gas-burning appliances and apply these provisions to related equipment such as vents and chimneys.
2. Note that similar provisions for other fuel-burning appliances exist in IRC Chapter 13.

Clearance to Combustible Materials Definition and Discussion

Heat generating appliances, such as furnaces, boilers, water heaters, and the vents for gas burning appliances, must be separated from combustible materials. Combustible materials include wood framing and drywall (the drywall paper is combustible). Without separation, heat generated by the appliance or vent could ignite the combustible material causing a fire.

The ideal method of providing separation is physical distance. Most heat generating appliances and vents have a recommended physical separation distance as part of their listing. If space limits do not allow the full physical separation distance, then the IRC allows various clearance reduction devices that protect the combustible material and reduce the physical separation distance recommended by the appliance or vent manufacturer.

Most clearance reduction devices rely on sheet metal, insulation, and an air circulation space in various combinations. We provide an example here.

Clearance Reduction Device Requirements

1. Measure clearance reductions from the nearest outer surface of the heat generating appliance or vent to the nearest outer surface of the combustible material.
2. Install the clearance reduction device so that it covers all combustible material within the clearance reduction area. Example: if the manufacturer's recommended clearance distance is 12 inches, then the clearance reduction device should extend beyond the appliance or vent by at least (≥) 12 inches.
3. Provide an air circulation space of at least (≥) 1 inch when using clearance reduction devices that require an air circulation space. Provide at least (≥) 1 inch between the heat generating appliance or vent and the clearance reduction device.
4. Do not use combustible spacers, ties or other combustible material when assembling the clearance reduction device. Do not place spacers or ties directly opposite the heat generating appliance or vent.
5. Leave at least (≥) 1 inch open at the top and bottom or the top and sides of the clearance reduction device to provide air circulation behind the protection device. This applies to devices installed along a straight wall and not in or near corners.
6. Leave at least (≥) 1 inch open at the top and bottom of the clearance reduction device to pro-

vide air circulation behind the clearance reduction device. This applies to devices installed in a corner.
7. Use mineral wool and fiberglass batts or boards with a density of at least (≥) 8 pounds per cubic foot, and a melting point of at least (≥) 1,500º F.
8. Do not allow the clearance reduction device to interfere with draft hood clearances, combustion air, safety devices, and service access.
9. Do not use clearance reduction devices if the appliance or equipment manufacturer's instructions prohibit them.

Clearance Reduction for Appliances in Small Rooms

1. Do not use clearance reduction devices if the gas appliance is installed in a small room such as a closet or alcove. Provide full the full distance clearances required by manufacturer's installation instructions for appliances installed in small rooms.

Clearance to Gas Appliance Supply Plenums and Supply Ducts

1. Provide clearance to a supply plenum and supply ducts within (≤) 3 feet of a supply plenum as required by the appliance manufacturer's installations instructions.

Clearance to Doors, Drawers, and Projections

1. Provide clearance to combustible doors, drawers, windows, and other projections that could swing or otherwise intrude into the required clearance space. This means that if the projection can swing into the required clearance area, then you must provide clearance to the projection assuming that it will be left open in the clearance area.
2. Do not use closers, door stops, or similar devices to provide clearance to the appliance.

Clearance Reduction Device Example

1. The following table presents the clearance reductions allowed using a clearance reduction device constructed of 24 gage sheet metal with at least (≥) a 1 inch air circulation space between the sheet metal and the combustible material. The first row in the table gives the manufacturer's recommended physical separation distance from combustible material for the heat generating appliance or vent without using a protection device. The second row identifies whether the protection device separates the top or the sides and rear of the heat generating appliance from the combustible material. The third row gives the minimum allowed distance between the heat generating appliance or vent from combustible material using the protection device.

TABLE G2409
Sheet Metal and Air Space Clearance Reduction Device Clearance to Combustible Materials Reduction

manufacturer's recommended clearance from combustible materials (inches)	36	36	18	18	12	12	9	9	6	6
clearance above or at sides or rear	above	sides & rear	above	sides & rear	above	sides & rear	above	sides & rear	above	sides & rear
clearance from combustible materials with reduction device (inches)	18	12	9	6	6	4	5	3	3	3

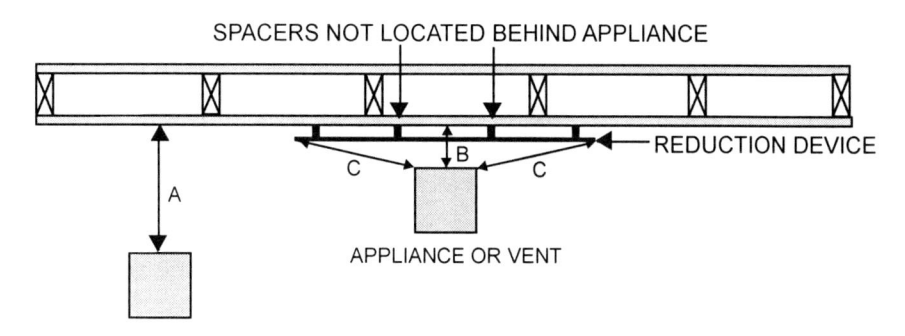

A = MANUFACTURER RECOMMENDED CLEARANCE TO COMBUSTIBLES
B = REDUCED CLEARANCE WITH REDUCTION DEVICE
C = LENGTH OF REDUCTION DEVICE SO C = A

Sheet Metal Clearance to Combustibles Reduction Device (G2409-0)
Figure 24-7

GAS PIPING SYSTEM GROUNDING AND BONDING (G2410 AND G2411)

Gas Piping System Use as a Grounding Electrode

1. Do not use gas pipes as a grounding electrode and do not use gas pipes as part of the grounding electrode system.

Gas Piping System Bonding

1. Connect all above ground parts of the gas piping system together as an electrically continuous path and bond it to an effective ground fault path. This means that you must bond (connect) metal gas pipe to the building's grounding electrode system. Refer to Chapter 36 for more information about bonding.
2. You may consider gas pipe (other than CSST tubing) bonded where the gas pipe is connected to the appliance's equipment grounding wire.
3. Bond CSST tubing to the electrical service grounding electrode where the gas service pipe enters the building.

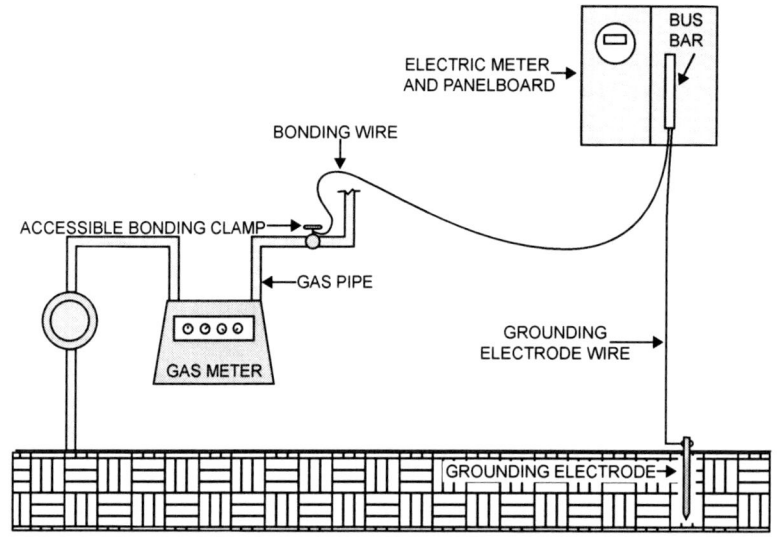

Gas Pipe Bonding (G2410-0)
Figure 24-8

GAS PIPING GENERAL INSTALLATION, MODIFICATION, AND IDENTIFICATION (G2412)

Gas Piping Governed by the IRC

1. Apply IRC gas piping provisions beginning at the outlet connection of the gas provider's gas meter and apply the provisions beginning at the second stage regulator of a liquefied petroleum (LP) gas system.

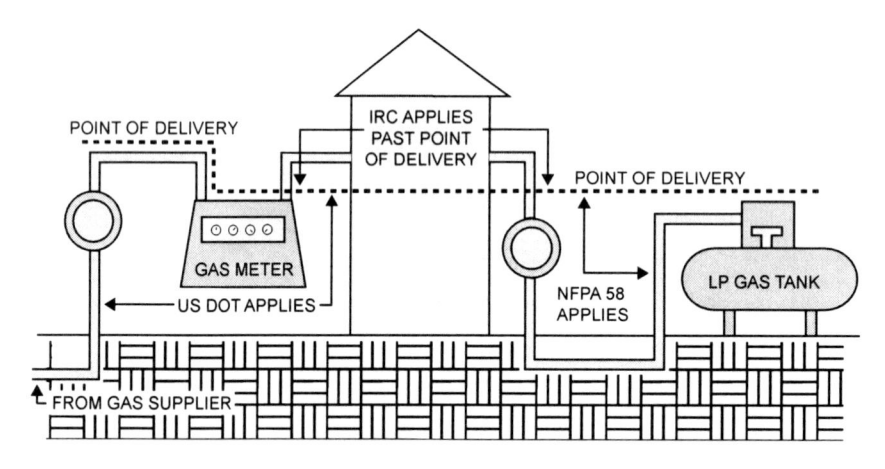

Gas Piping Governed by the IRC (G2412-0)
Figure 24-9

Gas Provider Piping Located Inside the Home

1. Apply IRC provisions to gas provider piping, if any, located inside the home. This includes provisions governing gas pipe support, gas pipe penetration of fire resistive walls, and gas pipes run through structural components (studs, joists).

Recalculation of Gas Pipe Size when Modifying Piping or Adding Gas Appliances

1. Do not modify or add to existing gas piping or add new gas appliances to existing gas piping without determining if the existing gas piping and any new gas piping can satisfy the gas volume demand requirements. Recalculate gas pipe sizing according to IRC gas pipe sizing requirements when modifying or adding gas piping and when adding a new gas appliance. Adding new gas appliances or new gas piping can cause new and existing gas appliances to perform improperly and create dangerous conditions. Most readers should let a qualified contractor calculate gas pipe size.

Gas Pipe Labeling

1. Label all exposed gas piping, other than black steel pipe, using a yellow label with "GAS" printed in black letters. Locate the labels not more than (≤) every 5 feet. The label is not required on gas piping in the same room as the gas appliance served. Exposed gas piping is any gas piping not concealed in walls or underground. Gas piping in attics, basements, and crawl spaces is exposed. This labeling provision will apply, in most common situations, to copper pipe and tubing used as gas piping.

Multiple Gas Meters for One Building

1. Do not connect gas pipes from one user's gas meter another user's gas pipes at any point after the outlet side of the meter. This prevents one user from paying for another user's gas and prevents gas shut off at one meter from feeding into pipes that are thought to be shut off.
2. Label piping from multiple meters, using an approved permanent labeling system, so that the piping from each meter can be readily identified.

GAS PIPE SIZING (G2413)

Limitations of the Material in this Section

Determining the correct size of gas pipes requires knowledge of the type(s) of gas pipes to be installed, the length of each part of the gas pipe system (trunks and branches), the Btu/hour input ratings of all gas appliances to be installed and the appliance location in the home, the type of gas (natural or LP), the gas supply inlet pressure, and the number of bends and fittings in the piping system. This knowledge is beyond most readers of this book; therefore, we will not discuss how to determine gas pipe sizes. Leave calculation of correct gas pipe size calculations to qualified contractors. Refer to the IRC Commentary for gas pipe size tables and examples of how to determine gas pipe size.

We will present two examples of gas pipe sizes for average homes. Do not assume that your gas pipe sizes are wrong if your home has different size pipes from the following examples. Your pipes may have been sized using different assumptions or sizing methods. In practice, gas pipe installers often use "rules of thumb" to install gas pipes using a limited number of pipe sizes that are larger than the minimum required size. This makes gas pipe installation easier and relieves the installer from performing detailed gas pipe size calculations.

Input Rating for Typical Gas Appliances

1. Use the actual Btu/hour input rating for the installed appliance to determine if the gas pipe size is correct. The actual Btu/hour input rating should be on the appliance label.
2. Use the assumed values in the following table if the actual Btu/hour input rating is not known.

TABLE G2413-1
Assumed Btu/hour Ratings for Common Gas Appliances

gas appliance	input Btu/hour
boiler-space heating	100,000
forced-air furnace	100,000
30-40 gallon storage water heater	35,000
50 gallon storage water heater	50,000
cooktop	40,000
range	65,000
barbecue	40,000
clothes dryer	35,000
gas fireplace-direct vent	40,000
gas log lighter	2,500
fireplace gas logs	80,000

Gas Pipe Size Example 1

1. The following table shows approximate gas pipe size for the main gas pipe entering from the gas meter and for the branches to the individual appliances. This example assumes Schedule 40 black steel pipe (a common type of gas pipe) and natural gas at 0.5 psi inlet pressure.

TABLE EX2413-1
Gas Pipe Size Example 1

gas appliance (pipe length – feet)	input Btu/hour	minimum gas pipe size (inch)
A – B (30)	315,000 add demands at C+D+F+G+I+J	1
B – C (20) furnace	100,000	1/2
B – D (20) water heater	35,000	3/8
B – E (20)	180,000 add demands at F+G+I+J	3/4
E – F (25) range	65,000	1/2
E – G (20) clothes dryer	40,000	3/8
E – H (20)	75,000 add demands at I+J	1/2
H – I (30) barbecue	35,000	3/8
H – J (20) fireplace	40,000	3/8

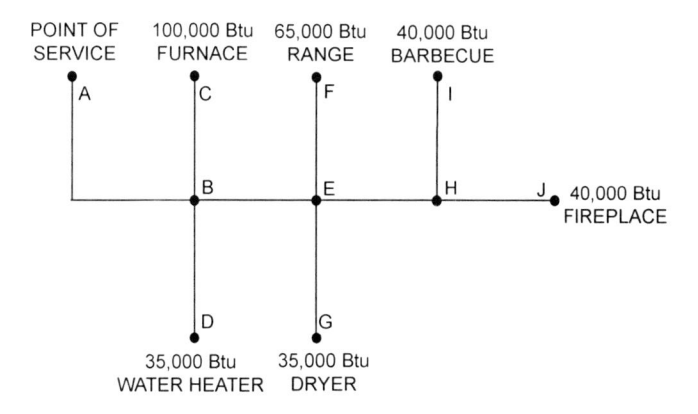

Gas Pipe Size Example – All Gas House (G2413-1)
Figure 24-10

Gas Pipe Size Example 2

1. The following table shows approximate gas pipe size for the main gas pipe entering from the gas meter and for the branches to the individual appliances. This example assumes Schedule 40 black steel pipe (a common type of gas pipe) and natural gas at 0.5 psi inlet pressure.

TABLE EX2413-2
Gas Pipe Size Example 2

gas appliance (pipe length – feet)	input Btu/hour	minimum gas pipe size (inch)
A – B (30)	170,000 Add demands at C+D+E	¾
B – C (20) furnace	100,000	1/2
B – D (20) water heater	35,000	3/8
B – E (20) clothes dryer	35,000	3/8

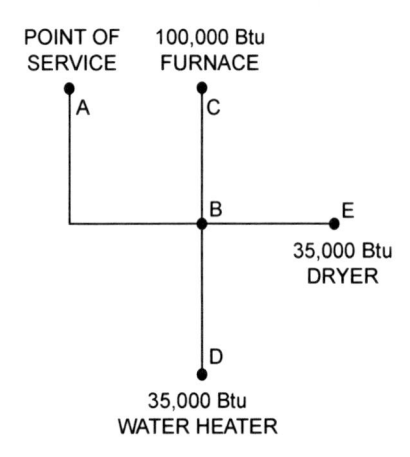

Gas Pipe Size Example – Gas Heat and Water Heating (G2413-2)
Figure 24-11

GAS PIPE MATERIALS (G2414)

Materials Permitted for Use as Gas Pipes in Buildings

1. You may use Schedule 40 or thicker steel or wrought iron pipe for gas pipes. Black steel is one of the most common types of gas pipe.
2. You may use seamless copper tubing, aluminum alloy tubing, or steel tubing for gas pipes. Do not use these materials if the gas contains materials that would corrode the tubing. Do not use copper tubing if the gas contains more than 0.3 grains of hydrogen sulfide per 100 standard cubic feet of gas. Verify with the local gas supplier and with the local building official if copper gas pipe is approved in your area.
3. You may use corrugated stainless steel tubing (CSST) for gas pipe. CSST is a recent alternative to other types of gas pipe. It is a semi-rigid tube with some flexibility. It is covered in a yellow plastic jacket.

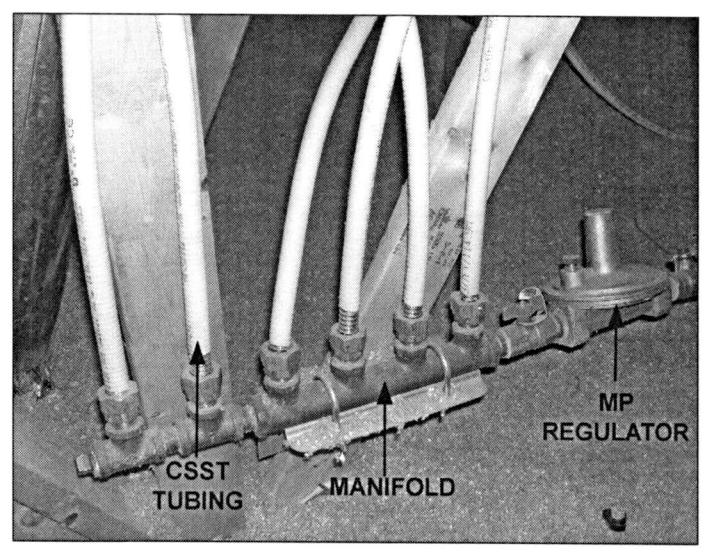

Corrugated Stainless Steel Tubing (PG2414-0)
Figure 24-12

Plastic Gas Pipe (G2415.14)

1. Do not use plastic pipe and tubing as gas pipe in or under buildings or within slabs. Use plastic pipe, tubing, and fittings only underground.

Used Gas Pipe and Materials

1. Reuse gas pipe, fittings, and valves only if they are free of foreign materials and in satisfactory condition for their intended use.

Defective Pipe and Materials

1. Do not repair defects in gas pipe, fittings, and valves. Replace defective materials.

Corrosion Protection of Gas Pipe and Materials

1. Use metallic gas pipe and fittings protected with an approved corrosion-resistant material if the pipe or fittings may be subject to corrosion Corrosion-resistant materials include wraps, tapes, enamels, sleeves, and factory-applied coatings. Corrosion may be caused by contact with corrosive materials such as concrete or masonry, by exposure to soil, or by exposure to the weather. Gas pipe located outdoors may be subject to corrosion even if protected by a roof or by an equipment enclosure such as a barbecue island.

Metallic Gas Pipe Threads

1. Use tapered pipe threads for metallic gas pipes and fittings.
2. Do not use metallic gas pipe threads that are stripped, chipped, corroded, or otherwise damaged. Replace pipe with defective threads.
3. Use metallic pipe with the proper number of threads given the size of the pipe as described in the following table.

TABLE 2414
Minimum Metallic Gas Pipe Threads

steel pipe size (inches)	length of threads (inches)	number of threads
½	¾	10
¾	¾	10
1	⅞	10
1 ¼	1	11
1 ½	1	11

GAS PIPE INSTALLATION AND PROTECTION (G2415)

Gas Pipe Prohibited Installation Locations

1. Do not install gas pipes in or through an HVAC supply or return air duct, exhaust duct, clothes (laundry) chute, chimney, gas vent, dumbwaiter, or elevator shaft.
2. Install gas pipe from a gas meter only in the townhouse served by the gas meter. Do not install gas pipe from a gas meter in or through another townhouse.

Gas Pipe in Masonry and Concrete Walls

1. Do not install gas pipes in solid walls, such as concrete and masonry, unless the pipe is in an open chase or in a casing (sleeve). This protects the pipe from settlement stress and corrosion.

Gas Pipe in Solid Floors

1. You may install gas pipes in a channel in a solid floor (such as a groove in concrete slab) and cover the pipe so that access is possible with minimum damage to the building.
2. Protect the gas pipe and any conduit from corrosion. Install conduit that is designed to withstand any imposed loads.
3. You may install gas pipes in a conduit (sleeve) of Schedule 40 steel, wrought iron, PVC, or ABS pipe with one end terminating indoors and one end terminating outdoors. Seal the indoor end of the conduit to prevent gas leakage. Extend the indoor end of the conduit into an accessible space and at least (≥) 2 inches above where the conduit emerges from the floor. Extend the outdoor end of the conduit at least (≥) 4 inches outdoors, vent the conduit to outdoors above final grade, and protect the vent opening from entry of water and insects.
4. You may install gas pipe in a conduit (sleeve) using the same materials as in #2 and with both ends terminating indoors. Extend both ends of the conduit into an accessible space and at least (≥) 2 inches above where the conduit emerges from the floor. Do not seal the conduit ends.

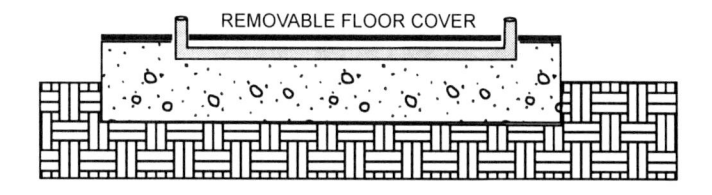

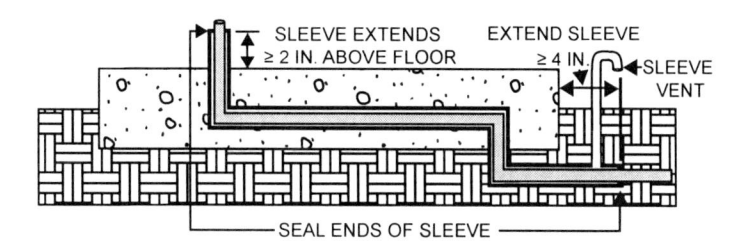

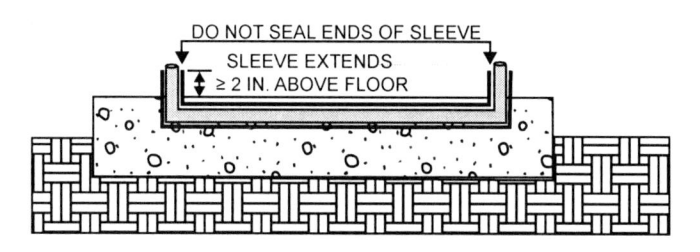

Gas Pipe Installation in Solid Floors (G2415-1)
Figure 24-13

Gas Pipe Fittings in Concealed Locations

1. Do not use unions, tubing fittings, left and right couplings, bushings, compression couplings, and swing joints made by combinations of fittings in concealed locations. You may use fittings listed for use in concealed locations and you may join tubes by brazing.

Gas Pipe Run Underground Through Foundations

1. Do not run gas pipe <u>that is not encased in conduit</u> through underground foundation walls. Gas pipe must enter and leave buildings through above ground walls and the space between the gas pipe and the wall must be sealed.
2. Enclose gas pipes that run through underground foundations or through foundation walls in approved conduit. Install the conduit and gas pipe as described in the Gas Pipe in Solid Floors section.

Gas Pipe Shield Plates in Wood Framing

1. Protect gas pipe (other than black or galvanized steel) with shield plates if the pipe is closer than (<) 1 ½ inches from the edge of wood studs, joists, rafters, or similar framing members.

Extend the shield plate at least (≥) 4 inches below top plates, at least (≥) 4 inches above bottom plates, and at least (≥) 4 inches beyond both sides of a stud, joist, or rafter.

2. Use manufacturer recommended shield plates for CSST gas tubing.

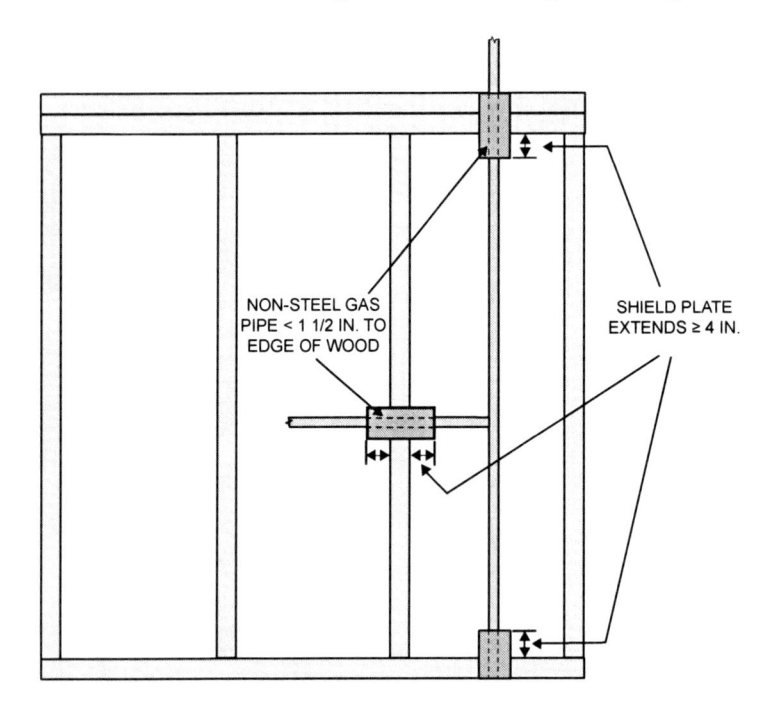

Gas Pipe Protection in Wood Framing (G2415-2)
Figure 24-14

Gas Pipe Installed Above Ground Outdoors

1. Elevate gas pipes at least 3 ½ inches above ground and above a roof surface.
2. Protect gas pipes installed outdoors against physical damage.
3. Support gas pipes in a secure manner and at required intervals.
4. Protect gas pipes that penetrate an exterior wall with an approved coating or wrapping.
5. Fill the space between a gas pipe and any protective sleeve that penetrates an exterior wall. Use caulk or other appropriate material to fill the space.

Gas Pipe Protection from Corrosion

1. Protect metallic gas pipe in an approved manner if exposed to corrosion. See also a similar requirement in G2414.
2. Use factory-applied protective coatings on metallic gas piping and fittings. You may use field-applied coatings and wrappings on nipples, fittings, and places where the factory-applied coating has been damaged. Apply these coatings and wrappings according to manufacturer's instructions.
3. Use insulating couplings or fittings when joining dissimilar metals underground.
4. Do not place metallic gas pipe in contact with cinders (including concrete blocks that contain cinders).

Gas Pipe Burial Depth

1. Bury most underground pipes at least (≥) 12 inches below finished grade.
2. Bury individual gas pipes to exterior gas lights, grills, and similar appliances at least (≥) 8 inches below finished grade if the installation is approved and is located where the gas pipe is not subject to physical damage.
3. Apply these provisions to gas pipe governed by the IRC, not to gas pipes controlled by gas suppliers. See Figure G2412-0.

Gas Pipe Burial in Trenches

1. Grade trenches for gas pipes so that the pipe has firm and continuous support on the trench bottom.

Closure of Gas Outlets

1. Seal gas-tight most gas outlets that do not connect to appliances. Listed and labeled flush-mounted quick disconnect devices and listed and labeled gas convenience outlets do not need gas-tight caps if the outlets are installed according to manufacturer's instructions.

Extension of Gas Pipes Beyond Walls, Ceilings, and Floors

1. Extend the unthreaded portion of gas pipes at least (≥) 1 inch beyond finished walls and ceilings.
2. Extend the unthreaded portion of gas pipes at least (≥) 2 inches above floors, outdoor patios, and slabs.
3. Support the outlet fitting or pipe in a secure manner. Listed and labeled flush mounted quick disconnect devices and listed and labeled gas convenience outlets do not require the pipe extension lengths if the outlets are installed according to manufacturer's instructions.

Gas Outlet Location

1. Do not place gas outlets behind doors.
2. Locate gas outlets in the same room or space where the appliance is installed.

GAS PIPE INSPECTION, PRESSURE TESTING, AND PURGING (G2417)

Limitations of the Material in this Section

Most readers of this book should not inspect, pressure test, leak test, or purge gas piping. Allow qualified contractors to perform these important tasks. We will discuss only some basic testing requirements in this section to give the reader a basic understanding of inspecting, testing, and purging gas piping systems. Refer to the IRC for more information.

When to Inspect and Test Gas Pipe

1. Inspect and pressure test all new gas piping, new additions to existing gas pipes, and major repairs of existing gas pipes. Pressure testing of minor additions and repairs is not required if the work is inspected and tested with non-corrosive leak detection fluid.

Gas Pressure Test Gases

1. Use air, nitrogen, carbon dioxide, or an inert gas to test gas piping. Do not use oxygen.

Appliance Isolation from Gas Pipe Testing

1. Isolate or disconnect appliances that could be damaged by the test pressure. The high pressures often used to test gas piping can damage gas appliances.

Gas Test Gauges

1. Use a gas pressure gauge that is calibrated in units small enough to detect and indicate a pressure decrease in the gas piping being tested. If using a mechanical gauge, do not use a gauge that has a highest end scale of greater than five times the test pressure.

Gas Test Pressure

1. Apply test pressure at least (≥) 1 ½ times the gas system design working pressure and at least (≥) 3 psig.

Gas Test Duration

1. Test the gas piping for at least (≥) 10 minutes.

Gas Leak Testing

1. Inspect gas piping to ensure that all fittings and valves at unused outlets are closed prior to turning on gas to the gas piping.
2. Test new gas pipes and gas pipes that have been out of service for leaks when the gas is first introduced into the pipes. This leak testing can be done by observing the gas meter for evidence of gas flow when all gas appliances are off (and pilot lights are not lit).

Purging of Air from Gas Pipes

1. Purge air from gas piping before operating gas appliances.

GAS PIPE SUPPORT (G2418 AND G2424)

Gas Pipe Support Materials and Installation (G2418)

1. Support gas pipes with pipe hooks, metal straps, metal bands, metal brackets, or other suitable hangers. Use gas pipe supports made of material that is compatible with the gas piping material and will not cause corrosion by galvanic action. Example: do not use copper pipe supports with steel gas pipe. Use gas pipe supports that are strong enough to support the gas piping without allowing excessive gas pipe sagging and without straining fittings, joints, and valves. Use gas pipe supports that allow for natural expansion and contraction of gas piping material.
2. Attach gas pipe supports securely so they do not fail due to the weight or movement of the supported piping.

3. Do not use combustible pipe hangers.
4. Do not support gas piping by using other piping.
5. Do not use gas appliances to support gas piping and do not use gas piping to support gas appliances.

Gas Pipe Support Intervals (G2424)

1. Support gas pipes at intervals in the following table. Support for CSST piping is based on Gastite brand CSST installation instructions. Refer to manufacturer's instructions for CSST support spacing requirements.

TABLE G2424
Gas Pipe Support Intervals

black steel pipe size (inches)	steel pipe support spacing (feet)	copper, steel, aluminum tubing size (inches)	tubing support spacing (feet)	CSST size (inches/EHD)	CSST support spacing (feet)
½ horizontal and vertical support	6	½ horizontal and vertical support	4	⅜ / 13 horizontal and vertical support	4
¾ or 1 horizontal and vertical support	8	⅝ or ¾ horizontal and vertical support	6	½ / 18 horizontal and vertical support	8
1 ¼ and larger horizontal and vertical support	10	7/8 or 1 horizontal and vertical support	8	¾ / 23 or larger horizontal support	10
1 ¼ and larger vertical support	every floor level	1 or larger vertical support	every floor level	concealed vertical runs all sizes	10

DRIPS AND SEDIMENT TRAPS (G2419)

Drips (Drip Tees)

1. Install a drip (also known as a drip leg or drip tee) when the gas utility provides gas containing moisture. Wet gas is very rare in modern gas utility systems. Drips are rarely necessary.
2. Install any required drip at every point in the piping system where moisture could accumulate.
3. Locate a drip so it is readily accessible for cleaning.
4. Do not install a drip where it is subject to freezing.

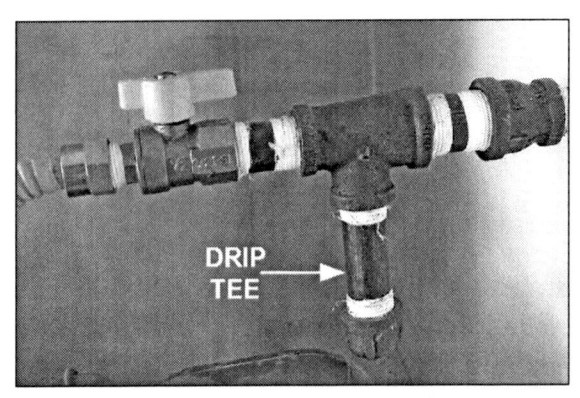

Drip Tee (PG2419-1)
Figure 24-15

Sediment Traps

1. Install a sediment trap in the gas piping to gas appliances such as furnaces, boilers, and water heaters. Gas lights, ranges, clothes dryers, outdoor grills, and appliances with an integrated sediment trap do not require sediment traps.
2. Install the sediment trap after the appliance gas shut off valve and as close as possible to the gas appliance inlet.
3. Refer to gas appliance manufacturer's installation instructions about sediment trap installation. The appliance manufacturer may require sediment traps and if so, a sediment trap should be provided to comply with manufacturer's instructions.

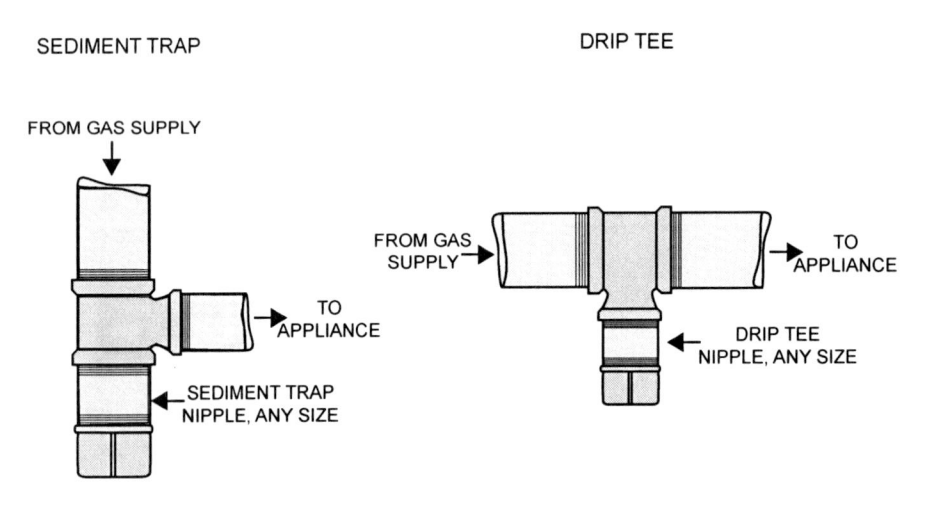

Sediment Trap and Drip Tee (G2419-0)
Figure 24-16

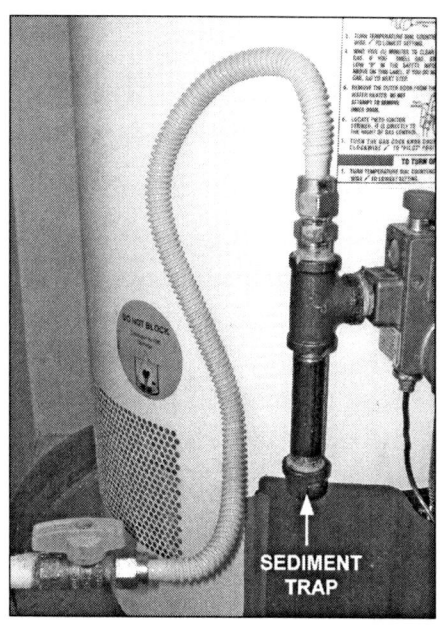

Sediment Trap (PG2419-2)
Figure 24-17

GAS SHUTOFF VALVES (G2420)

Gas Shutoff Valve Access for Appliances

1. Install accessible gas shutoff valves for appliances. Ready access to gas shutoff valves is not required. Removing access panels or moving the appliance to access the valve is acceptable.
2. Do not locate gas shutoff valves in concealed locations. A concealed location requires damaging a building component (such as drywall) to gain access.
3. Protect gas shutoff valves from damage.

Gas Shutoff Valves Location for Appliances

1. Install a gas shutoff valve in the same room as the appliance it serves and not less than 6 feet from the appliance. Install this shutoff valve in addition to any valve inside the appliance. Install this shutoff valve before any union, connector, or quick disconnect device served by the valve.
2. You may install a gas shutoff valve more than six feet from the appliance if the valve serves a vented decorative gas appliance (such as a vented gas fireplace), a vented room heater, or a decorative gas appliance (such as gas logs) installed in a vented fireplace. Permanently label the valve as the appliance's shutoff valve and make the valve readily accessible.
3. You may install a gas appliance shutoff valve at a gas distribution manifold. Locate the manifold not more than ($\leq$) 50 feet from the appliance. Permanently label valve as the appliance's shutoff valve and make the valve readily accessible. Gas distribution manifolds are commonly installed in CSST gas distribution systems.

Gas Shutoff Valves for Buildings

1. Install at least (≥) one gas shutoff valve outside each building served by a gas piping system. This valve is usually at the gas meter or at the gas supply tank.

Gas Shutoff Valves for MP Regulators

1. Install a gas shutoff valve immediately before every MP (medium pressure) regulator. These regulators are often placed before manifold gas distribution systems using CSST or copper tubing and may be placed before some gas appliances to reduce the gas pressure to the appliance. These regulators must be installed in the correct direction for gas to flow. Install these regulators according to manufacturer's instructions.

Gas Shutoff Valves in Fireplaces

1. Install gas shutoff valves in fireplaces according to the valve manufacturer's instructions. These valves are often used for gas logs installed in solid-fuel-burning fireplaces.

GAS PRESSURE REGULATORS (G2421)

Gas Pressure Regulators General Requirements

1. Install a gas pressure regulator before a gas appliance when the appliance operates at a lower gas pressure than the supply pressure.
2. Install gas pressure regulators where they are accessible. Ready access to gas pressure regulators is not required. Removing access panels or moving the appliance to access the valve is acceptable.
3. Do not locate gas pressure regulators in concealed locations. A concealed location requires damaging a building component (such as drywall) to gain access.
4. Protect gas pressure regulators from damage.
5. Vent gas regulators located indoors to the outdoors or use a gas regulator with a leak limiting device.

Service Gas Pressure Regulator (PG2421-1)
Figure 24-18

Gas Pressure Regulators (MP Regulators)

1. 1. Use only MP (medium pressure) gas regulators that are listed and approved for both the inlet and outlet gas pressure.
2. Use the manufacturer's instructions to determine if the MP gas regulator will supply gas at the proper pressure to the appliance served.
3. Vent MP gas regulators located indoors to the outdoors or use an MP gas regulator with a leak-limiting device.
4. Install a tee fitting between the MP gas regulator and its upstream shutoff valve. Position the tee fitting to allow connection of a pressure measuring device and to allow the fitting to act as a sediment trap.
5. Install a tee fitting not more than (≤) 10 pipe diameters downstream of the of the MP gas regulator outlet. Position the tee fitting to allow connection of a pressure measuring device.

MP Gas Pressure Regulator (PG2421-2)
Figure 24-19

GAS CONNECTIONS TO APPLIANCES (G2422)

Gas Connection to Appliances General Requirements

1. Use any of the following to connect gas piping to gas appliances: (a) rigid metal pipes and fittings, or (b) field fabricated copper or aluminum tubing approved for use with gas, or (c) listed and labeled manufactured gas connectors, including their associated quick-disconnect devices and convenience outlets, or (d) CSST tubing.
2. Install manufactured gas connectors according to manufacturer's instructions.
3. Protect manufactured gas connectors against physical damage.
4. Limit the length of manufactured gas connectors to not more than (≤) 3 feet, except not more than (≤) 6 feet for ranges and clothes dryers.
5. Do not run manufactured gas connectors into an appliance case, or through walls, ceilings, floors, or into concealed locations. Manufactured gas connectors may run into some fireplace inserts if the opening is factory-equipped with a protective device and the fireplace is listed for entry of a manufactured gas connector.
6. Install a shutoff valve, with an opening at least (≥) as large as the manufactured gas connector fitting, upstream of the manufactured gas connector.
7. Size the manufactured gas connector to supply the total gas demand of the appliance.

8. Use special manufactured gas connectors listed for periodic movement on appliances equipped with casters or otherwise intended for movement. Movement may be required for periodic cleaning and maintenance.
9. Install an accessible union not more than (≤) 6 feet from a gas appliance that is served by a rigid steel gas pipe connector.
10. Install appliances and gas connections so that undue strain is not placed on the gas connections (G2408.6).

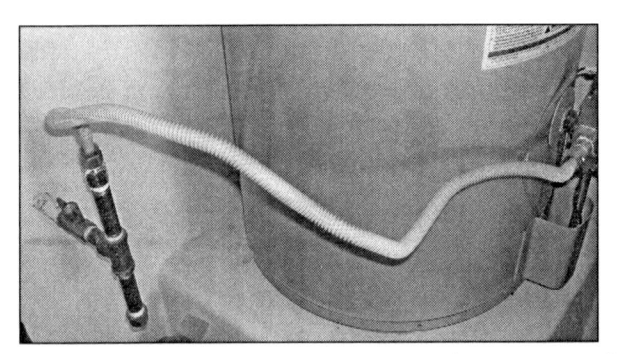

Manufactured Gas Connector (PG2422-0)
Figure 24-20

Manufactured Gas Connectors Best Practice

Most manufactured gas connectors are not designed for repeated movement. Movement can weaken the connector and cause a gas leak. Locate gas connectors where they will not be subjected to repeated movement or physical damage. Do not reuse most gas connectors. Install a new gas connector when installing a new gas appliance.

Manufactured gas connector manufacturers often recommend that any bends in the connector not exceed 1 ½ inches radius and recommend leaving about 2 inches of slack in the connector to allow for movement and to reduce strain on the connections.

VENTS FOR GAS APPLIANCES GENERAL REQUIREMENTS (G2425, G2426, G2427)

Appliances and Equipment Governed by these Code Provisions

1. Apply these code provisions to chimneys and vents used by gas-burning appliances.
2. Note that similar provisions for solid and liquid-fuel appliances begin in IRC Chapter 18.

Manufacturer's Installation Instructions (G2426.5, G2426.6, and Other Sections)

1. Size, install, terminate, and support all vents according to the vent manufacturer's and the gas appliance manufacturer's installation instructions. This includes direct vented appliances and appliances with an integral vent such as roof mounted gas furnaces and swimming pool heaters.

Unused Vent and Chimney Openings (G2425.5)

1. Seal all unused openings in all vent and chimney systems using an approved method. Vinyl concrete patch is a common approved method.

Positive Pressure Gas Vent Systems Use Restrictions (G2425.6)

1. Do not use vents and flues designed for natural draft (negative pressure) appliances with appliances and equipment using positive pressure draft. This means do not use single wall vents, Type B vents, and most chimneys to vent gas appliances that place their vents under positive pressure. An example of a positive vent pressure gas appliance is a Category IV condensing furnace. A Category I medium efficiency furnace with an induced draft does not operate under positive vent pressure.
2. Provide a safety device that will stop the flow of fuel to positive pressure draft appliances if the positive pressure draft system is not operating.

Gas Vent Entry into Fireplace Flue (G2425.7)

1. Install an air tight, noncombustible seal below the point where the gas vent or connector enters the fireplace flue. This reduces unintended dilution air that could adversely affect the flue's draft.
2. Provide access to the fireplace flue for inspection and cleaning.
3. Do not connect a gas vent to a factory-built fireplace flue unless the fireplace is specifically listed for such installation. Connect the gas vent according to the fireplace or flue manufacturer's instructions.
4. Extend the gas appliance vent or connector into a masonry fireplace flue so that the vent gasses are vented directly into the flue. Do not simply insert the vent into the fireplace throat. Provide access to the vent or connector for inspection and cleaning of both the vent and connector and of the flue.

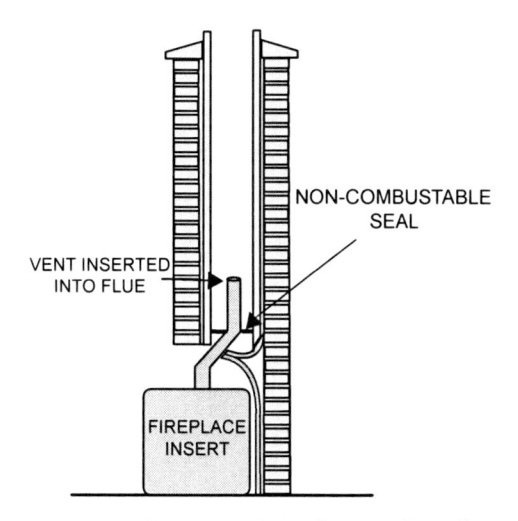

Gas Vent Connection to Fireplace Flue (G2425.7-0)
Figure 24-21

Gas Appliances for which Vents are Not Required (G2425.8)

1. You are not required to vent the following gas appliances:
    a) ranges and other domestic cooking appliances listed and labeled for optional venting,
    b) domestic (Type 1) clothes dryers,
    c) portable, countertop, and similar small kitchen and laundry appliances,

d) gas-fueled refrigerators,
e) listed unvented room heaters, and
f) listed unvented decorative gas appliances (unvented gas fireplaces).

2. Provide a venting system or other approved means of removing combustion gasses outdoors if the sum of the input ratings for appliances (c), (d), and (e) located in the same room exceeds (≥) 20 Btu/hour per cubic foot of room volume. You may add the volume of rooms adjacent to the room where the appliances are located if there is a door or other similar opening that cannot be closed between the rooms.
3. Verify venting requirements using manufacturer's instructions.

Vents and Chimneys with Power Exhausters (G2425.10)

1. Connect vents and connectors to vents and chimneys equipped with power exhausters on the inlet (negative pressure) side of the power exhauster.
2. Seal joints on the positive pressure side of the exhauster to prevent flue gas leaks according to the exhauster manufacturer's instructions.

Flue Lining Systems (G2425.12, 13, 14)

1. Use systems for relining masonry chimney flues that are listed and approved for the appliances to be vented. Example: use relining systems approved for solid fuels in a wood-burning fireplace. Do not use relining systems approved for use only with Category I gas appliances in a wood-burning fireplace. Install the relining systems and connect the appliances according to manufacturer's instructions.

Gas Vent Insulation Shields (G2426.4)

1. Install an insulation shield around any vent that passes through an attic or other insulated area (such as a floor/ceiling assembly).
2. Use at least (≥) 26 gage sheet metal for the insulation shield.
3. Extend the shield at least (≥) 2 inches above attic insulation material.
4. Secure the insulation shield to prevent movement of the shield.

Gas Vent Protection Against Damage (G2426.7)

1. Protect gas vents with shield plates when the vent is closer than (<) 1 ½ inches from the edge of concealed studs, joists, rafters, or similar framing members. Extend the shield plate at least (≥) 4 inches below top plates, and at least (≥) 4 inches above bottom plates, and at least (≥) 4 inches beyond both sides of a stud, joist, or rafter. This applies to all gas vents including plastic vents used with some high efficiency gas appliances. This requirement is similar to the requirement for protecting gas pipes. See Illustration G2415-2.

Gas Vent Labeling in Cold Climates (G2427.6.10)

1. Label gas vents that are intended for use only with gas appliances in areas that have both cold climates and extensively use liquid and solid fuels. The local building official deter-

mines where labeling is required. The label should read: "This gas vent is for appliances that burn gas. Do not connect to solid or liquid fuel-burning appliances or incinerators."

Gas Vents Run Along Exterior Walls (G2427.6.7)

1. Do not run Type B vents, and most other gas vents, along an outside wall. Do not terminate them adjacent to a wall or below eaves or below parapet walls unless the venting system is designed by a qualified engineer or the venting system is installed according to manufacturer's instructions. This restriction does not apply to direct vent appliances or to mechanical vent exhaust systems installed according to manufacturer's instructions.

ADDING OR REMOVING GAS APPLIANCES FROM CHIMNEYS AND VENTS (G2425.15)

Appliances and Equipment Governed by these Code Provisions

Apply these code provisions to chimneys and vents used by gas-burning appliances. Note that similar provisions for solid and liquid fuel-burning appliances exist in IRC Chapter 18.

Description of Potential Problems when Adding or Removing Fuel-Burning Appliances

Every fuel-burning appliance has different characteristics that will affect the operation of a chimney or vent. These characteristics include the quantity of flue gasses from the appliance, the temperature of the flue gasses, and the amount of water vapor in the flue gasses. Adding or removing appliances may cause a chimney or vent that once operated satisfactorily to operate improperly. Problems that may occur include backdrafting of exhaust gasses into the home and condensation of moisture that can quickly damage the chimney or vent. Backdrafting and damaged chimneys and vents are a significant safety hazard.

Recalculate Chimney or Vent Size when Adding Gas Appliances

1. Recalculate the size of a chimney or a vent when adding or removing a gas appliance. The new chimney or vent size could increase, decrease, or remain the same depending on the type and efficiency of the appliance added or removed. Account for the new size requirements based on all gas appliances connected to the chimney or vent. To calculate the size of a gas appliance vent, use Section G2428.
2. Do not vent solid-fuel-burning appliances (such as a wood-burning fireplace) and appliances using other fuels (such as a gas furnace) into the same flue. Provide each solid-fuel-burning appliance with its own separate flue.

Cleaning and Inspection of Chimneys and Vents

1. Inspect chimney flues and vents when adding or removing gas appliances. Ensure that the flue is continuous and free of cracks, damage, or deterioration that could allow escape of combustion products. Ensure required clearances to combustible materials and ensure that required firestops are installed.
2. Clean flues that have been used for solid or liquid-fueled appliances before inspecting the flue.

Chimney Cleanout Openings

1. Install in chimneys a cleanout opening that has a tight-fitting, noncombustible door with an opening height of at least (≥) 6 inches. Locate the upper edge of the door at least (≥) 6 inches below the lowest chimney inlet opening.

VENTING GAS APPLIANCES USING A MASONRY CHIMNEY (G2427.5)

Masonry Chimney Used for Gas Appliance Venting General Requirements

1. Construct the chimney according to IRC Chapter 10.
2. Use approved clay flue liners, listed chimney lining systems, or other approved materials that will resist deterioration by vent gasses at temperatures of at least (≥) 1,800º F.
3. You may use a chimney liner that is approved only as a gas appliance vent in masonry chimney if the liner is approved for: (a) Category I gas appliances, or (b) listed gas appliances with draft hoods, or (c) gas appliances listed for use with Type B vents. Install the liner according to manufacturer's instructions. Attach a permanent label where the appliance vent connects to the chimney liner. The label should read: "Do not connect to solid or liquid fuel-burning appliances or incinerators."

Masonry Chimney Termination Height

1. Extend masonry chimneys at least (≥) 3 feet above highest point where the chimney passes through the roof and extend the chimney at least (≥) 2 feet above any part of the roof or building within (≤) 10 feet horizontally. This helps reduce the chance that wind currents may interfere with the chimney's drafting.
2. Extend masonry chimneys at least (≥) 5 feet above the highest connected appliance draft hood or flue collar. This helps ensure that the chimney has enough height to develop the necessary draft to expel the flue gasses.

Masonry Chimney Flue Size for Gas Appliance Venting

1. Use one of the following methods to determine the proper size of a chimney flue used to vent a Category I gas appliance, or to vent a listed vent hood-equipped gas appliance, or to vent a gas appliance listed for use with a Type B vent. The methods are:
   a) use the provisions of Section G2428, or
   b) for a single draft hood appliance vented into a masonry chimney flue, make the chimney flue area and the appliance vent connector area at least (≥) as large as the appliance draft hood outlet area but not more than (≤) seven times the appliance draft hood outlet area, or
   c) for two draft hood appliances vented into a masonry chimney flue, make the chimney flue area at least (≥) as large as the larger appliance draft hood outlet area plus 50 percent of the smaller draft hood outlet area but are not more than (≤) seven times the smaller appliance draft hood outlet area.
2. You may use other approved engineering methods to determine the proper size of a chimney flue for gas appliances.

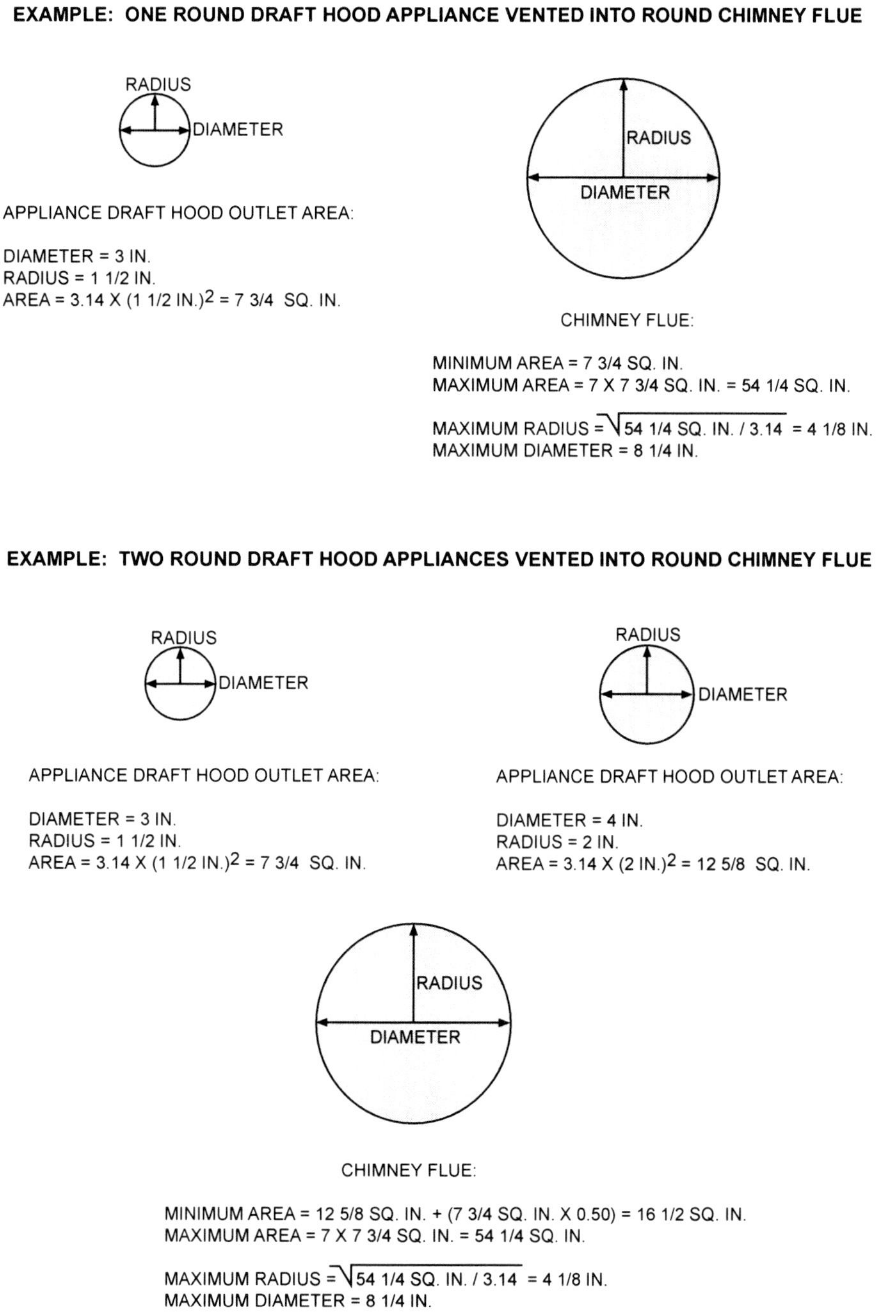

EXAMPLE: ONE ROUND DRAFT HOOD APPLIANCE VENTED INTO ROUND CHIMNEY FLUE

APPLIANCE DRAFT HOOD OUTLET AREA:

DIAMETER = 3 IN.
RADIUS = 1 1/2 IN.
AREA = 3.14 X (1 1/2 IN.)^2 = 7 3/4 SQ. IN.

CHIMNEY FLUE:

MINIMUM AREA = 7 3/4 SQ. IN.
MAXIMUM AREA = 7 X 7 3/4 SQ. IN. = 54 1/4 SQ. IN.

MAXIMUM RADIUS = $\sqrt{54\ 1/4\ \text{SQ. IN.} / 3.14}$ = 4 1/8 IN.
MAXIMUM DIAMETER = 8 1/4 IN.

EXAMPLE: TWO ROUND DRAFT HOOD APPLIANCES VENTED INTO ROUND CHIMNEY FLUE

APPLIANCE DRAFT HOOD OUTLET AREA:

DIAMETER = 3 IN.
RADIUS = 1 1/2 IN.
AREA = 3.14 X (1 1/2 IN.)^2 = 7 3/4 SQ. IN.

APPLIANCE DRAFT HOOD OUTLET AREA:

DIAMETER = 4 IN.
RADIUS = 2 IN.
AREA = 3.14 X (2 IN.)^2 = 12 5/8 SQ. IN.

CHIMNEY FLUE:

MINIMUM AREA = 12 5/8 SQ. IN. + (7 3/4 SQ. IN. X 0.50) = 16 1/2 SQ. IN.
MAXIMUM AREA = 7 X 7 3/4 SQ. IN. = 54 1/4 SQ. IN.

MAXIMUM RADIUS = $\sqrt{54\ 1/4\ \text{SQ. IN.} / 3.14}$ = 4 1/8 IN.
MAXIMUM DIAMETER = 8 1/4 IN.

Calculating Flue Areas (G2427.5-0)
Figure 24-22

Gas Venting with Solid-Fuel Appliances

1. Do not use the same flue to vent both solid-fuel-burning appliances and gas appliances. Provide each solid-fuel-burning appliance with its own separate flue.

Common Venting of Gas and Oil Appliances

1. You may use the same common flue to vent separate gas and liquid-fuel (oil) appliances.

Connect the appliances to the common flue by openings at different levels or by one suitable fitting located as close as possible to the common flue.

2. Determine the proper size of a common flue serving both gas and liquid fuel (oil) appliances using approved engineering methods.

Venting Dual Fuel Appliances

1. You may vent an appliance designed to burn both gas and solid-fuel into one masonry flue if the appliance is equipped with a manual reset device to shut off gas flow if there is a sustained backdraft of vent gasses.
2. You may vent an appliance designed to burn both gas and oil into one masonry flue if the flue is appropriately sized.

Use of Flue Space Around Flue Liner Systems

1. Do not vent any appliance in the space surrounding a flue liner system or in the space surrounding other gas vents inside a masonry chimney flue. You may install another flue liner system inside the same masonry chimney flue if both liners are installed according to manufacturer's instructions.
2. Do not use the space surrounding a flue liner system inside a masonry chimney flue to provide combustion air to any appliance. You may use the space to provide combustion air to a direct vent appliance if installed according to manufacturer's instructions.

GAS VENT ROOF TERMINATION (G2427.6)

Gas Vent Roof Flashing and Cap

1. Use manufacturer recommend components when extending a gas vent through a roof. These usually include flashing, a roof jack or thimble, a storm collar, and a listed cap.

Gas Vent Height Above the Roof

1. Use the following table to determine the minimum height above the roof of a Type B gas vent not more than (≤) 12 inches diameter. Measure termination height above the roof from the highest point where the vent penetrates the roof to the bottom of the listed cap. For thick roof covering materials such as tile, measure from the tile to the bottom of the listed cap.
2. Do not use the following table if a Type B vent is closer than (≤) 8 feet to a vertical sidewall, gable end, or similar vertical obstruction. Terminate these vents at least (≥) 2 feet higher than the highest point where the vent penetrates the roof and at least (≥) 2 feet higher than any part of the roof or building within (≤) 10 feet horizontally.
3. Do not use the following table for other venting systems including single wall vents, vents for direct vent appliances, appliances with integral vents such as roof mounted furnaces, vents for Category II, III, and IV gas appliances, and vents using mechanical draft equipment.
4. Terminate Type B gas vents larger than (>) 12 inches diameter at least (≥) 2 feet higher than the highest point where the vent penetrates the roof and at least (≥) 2 feet higher than any part of the roof or building within (≤) 10 feet horizontally.

TABLE G2427.6
Type B Gas Vent Height Above Roof

roof pitch	minimum vent height (inches)
flat to 6/12	12
over 6/12 to 7/12	15
over 7/12 to 8/12	18
over 8/12 to 9/12	24
over 9/12 to 10/12	30
over 10/12 to 11/12	39
over 11/12 to 12/12	48
over 12/12 to 14/12	60
over 14/12 to 16/12	72
over 16/12 to 18/12	84
over 18/12 to 20/12	90

Type B Gas Vent Roof Termination (PG2427.6-0)
Figure 24-23

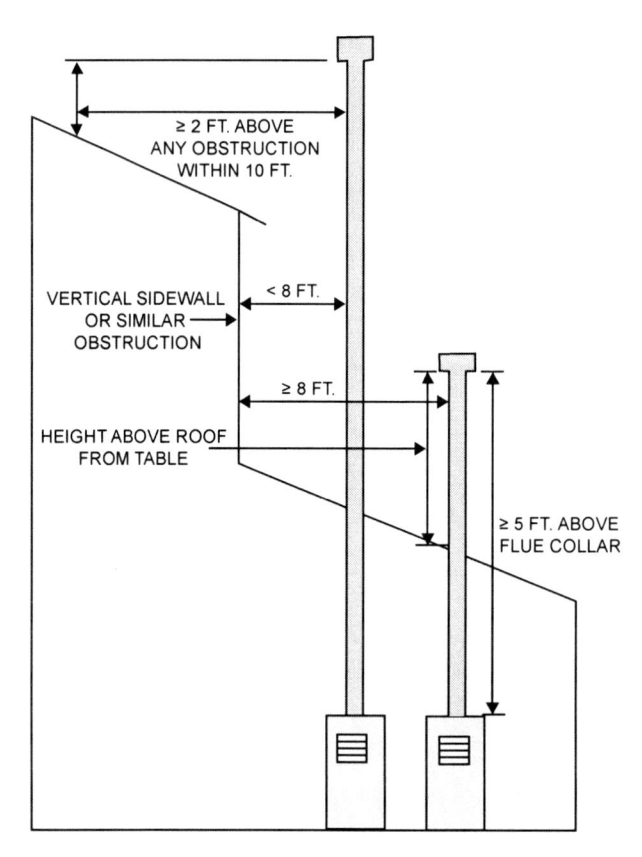

Gas Vent Roof Termination (G2427.6-0)
Figure 24-24

Gas Vent Height Above Appliance

1. Install a Type B or a Type L gas vent at least (≥) 5 feet above the highest connected appliance draft hood or flue collar.
2. Install a Type BW gas vent at least (≥) 12 feet above the bottom of the wall furnace.
3. Note that the vent sizing tables in IRC G2728 require a vent height of at least (≥) 6 feet above the draft hood or flue collar. This means that most Type B gas vents should terminate at least (≥) 6 feet above the draft hood or flue collar unless an engineer approves a lower height.

Decorative Shrouds for Gas Vents

1. Do not install a decorative shroud or surround at a gas vent termination unless the shroud or surround is listed for use with the specific gas venting system and unless the shroud or surround is installed according to manufacturer's instructions. This prevents an unlisted shroud from interfering with the drafting characteristics of the vent system.

SINGLE WALL VENTS FOR GAS APPLIANCES (G2427.7)

Single Wall Gas Vent Description

A single wall gas vent is constructed of at least (≥) 22 gage galvanized steel or similar material and serves as the vent for a gas appliance. Do not apply these provisions to single wall vent connectors used to connect a gas appliance to a listed venting system such as a Type B vent.

Single Wall Gas Vent Use Restrictions

1. Do not use a single wall gas vent unless permitted by the gas appliance manufacturer's instructions. Many modern gas appliance manufacturers do not permit use of single wall vents.
2. Do not install a single wall gas vent outdoors in cold climates. This effectively limits these vents to southern states. Ask the local building official if this restriction applies.
3. Do not originate or run a single wall gas vent in or through attics, floors, interior walls, or other concealed spaces. Run them only directly through a roof or directly through an exterior wall to the outdoors.

Single Wall Gas Vent Roof Flashing and Termination

1. Install a single wall gas vent at least (≥) 5 feet above the highest connected appliance draft hood or flue collar.
2. Extend single wall gas vent at least (≥) 2 feet higher than the highest point where the vent penetrates the roof and at least (≥) 2 feet higher than any part of the roof or building within (≤) 10 feet horizontally.
3. Install an approved cap or roof assembly at the top end of the single wall gas vent.
4. Install a noncombustible, non-ventilating thimble around the single wall gas vent where it penetrates a combustible roof assembly. Use a thimble that extends at least (≥) 18 inches above the roof and at least (≥) 6 inches below the roof. Leave the thimble open at the bottom and close the space between the vent and the thimble only at the top. Size the thimble according to Section G2427.10.15.

Single Wall Gas Vent Clearance to Combustible Material

1. Use the following table to determine the required clearance between single wall gas vent and combustible material.

TABLE G2427.7
Single Wall Gas Vent Clearance to Combustible Material

appliance	minimum clearance to combustibles (inches)
listed draft hood appliances and appliances listed for Type B vents	6
residential boilers and furnaces with listed gas conversion burner and a draft hood	9
residential appliances listed for Type L vents	9
unlisted residential draft hood appliances	9
residential and low heat appliances not listed above	18

Single Wall Gas Vent Size and Shape

1. Use the appliance manufacturer's venting installation instructions to determine the size and shape of a single wall gas vent. You may use one of the following IRC sizing methods if it does not conflict with manufacturer's instructions:

   a) you may use the single wall metal connector table for draft hood appliances in G2428, or

   b) you may install a single wall vent on a draft hood appliance if the single wall vent area is at least as large as the draft hood outlet area and not more than (≤) seven times the draft hood outlet area. Refer to illustration G2427.5-0 for an example.

2. You may use any shape single wall gas vent if the effective area of the vent is at least as large as the vent for which it is substituted and the minimum dimension of the vent is at least (≥) 2 inches.

Single Wall Gas Vent Support

1. Provide adequate support for single wall gas vent according to the weight of the material and the length and number of fittings in the vent run. The IRC does not specify what adequate support means.

VENT TERMINATION FOR MECHANICAL DRAFT AND DIRECT VENT APPLIANCES (G2427.8)

Direct Vent and Mechanical Draft Appliance Definitions

Direct vent appliance A direct vent appliance obtains all combustion air directly from the outside and vents all combustion gasses directly outside. Combustion air intake and venting usually occurs through a short length of concentric pipes run through a rear or side wall near the appliance.

Mechanical draft appliance A mechanical draft appliance creates positive pressure in the vent system that forces combustion gasses through the vent system. Contrast with natural draft appliances that rely on the negative pressure caused by the natural tendency of hot gas to rise. Category I fan-assisted appliances, including most medium efficiency furnaces, are not mechanical draft appliances. They are natural draft appliances.

Appliances and Equipment Governed by these Code Provisions

1. Apply these code provisions to gas vent systems using mechanical draft (positive pressure) venting equipment such as internal and external power exhausters and draft inducers.

2. Apply these code provisions to direct vent gas appliances.

3. <u>Do not apply these code provisions to Category I gas appliances including those with internal fan-assisted draft such as most medium efficiency gas furnaces.</u>

Mechanical Draft Vent Termination Locations

1. Locate the vent terminal of a mechanical draft vent at least (≥) 3 feet above any <u>forced-air inlet</u> within (≤) 10 feet. A forced-air inlet is an opening where air is drawn into the home by mechanical means, such as a furnace fan or a fan-powered outside air circulation system.

Do not apply this provision to separate the combustion air intake and vent terminal of direct vent appliances. Do not apply this provision to separate the combustion air intake and vent terminal of appliances with integral air inlet and flue discharge that are listed for outdoor use (such as a roof-mounted furnace).

2. Locate the vent terminal of a mechanical draft vent at least (≥) 4 feet below, or at least (≥) 4 feet horizontally, or at least (≥) 1 foot above any gravity-air inlet and at least (≥) 1 foot above finished grade. A gravity-air inlet is an operable window, door, or similar opening such as combustion air openings. Do not apply this provision to direct vent appliances.
3. Locate the terminal of a mechanical draft vent at least (≥) 12 inches above finished grade and at least (≥) 12 inches above, below, or to the side of any porch, deck, balcony or similar structure.

Mechanical Draft Water Heater (PG2427.8-0)
Figure 24-25

Direct Vent Appliance Vent Termination Locations

1. Locate the terminal of a direct vent appliance with an input rating not more than (≤) 10,000 Btu/hour at least (≥) 6 inches from any air inlet into the home. An air inlet is any forced-air or gravity-air inlet as described in the Mechanical Draft Vent Termination section.
2. Locate the terminal of a direct vent appliance with an input rating more than (>) 10,000 Btu/hour and not more than (≤) 50,000 Btu/hour at least (≥) 9 inches from any air inlet into the home.
3. Locate the terminal of a direct vent appliance with an input rating more than (>) 50,000 Btu/hour at least (≥) 12 inches from any air inlet into the home.
4. Locate the terminal of a direct vent appliance at least (≥) 12 inches above finished grade and at least (≥) 12 inches above, below, or to the side of any porch, deck, balcony or similar structure.

Condensate Disposal from Through-the-wall Vent Terminations

1. Do not locate through-the-wall vents (such as direct vents) over public walkways, or where condensate or vapor might create a nuisance or hazard, or where condensate could interfere with or damage other equipment. Apply this provision to all Category II and IV appliances

and to any gas appliance where local experience indicates that vent condensate is a problem. This provision will apply more often in cold climates. Verify with the local building official if this provision applies in your area.

VENT CONNECTORS FOR CATEGORY I GAS APPLIANCES (G2427.10)

Vent Connector Definition

Vent connector A vent connector is a pipe that connects a gas appliance to its vent or flue. A vent connector is required if the gas appliance is not located directly under its vent. A vent connector for a Category I gas appliance may be a listed vent material, such as a Type B vent, or a listed flexible vent connector, or a field constructed single wall metal pipe made of at least 26 gage galvanized steel. While a vent connector is part of the venting system, it is not the vent itself. This IRC section contains provisions applicable to vent connectors for Category I gas appliances. Section G2428 contains provisions applicable to the vent itself.

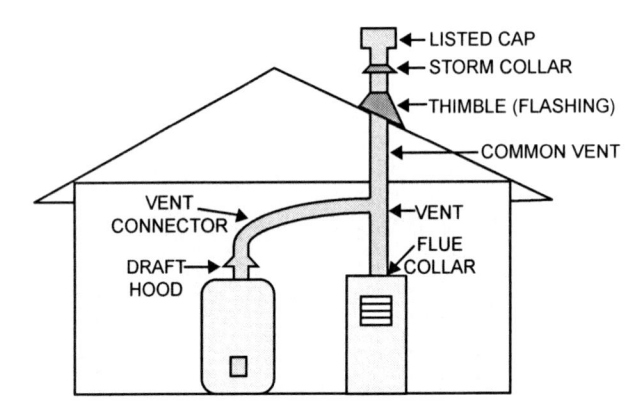

Vent System Components (G2427.10-1)
Figure 24-26

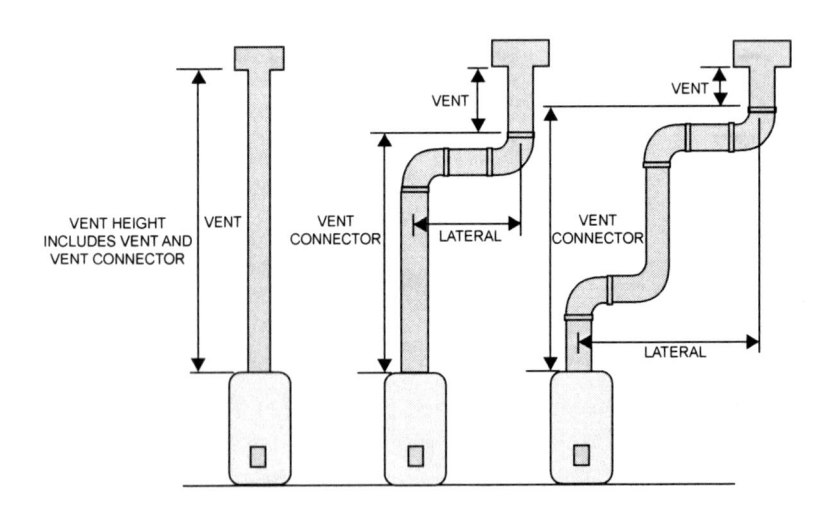

Vents and Vent Connectors (G2427.10-2)
Figure 24-27

Flexible Vent Connector (PG2427.10-0)
Figure 24-28

Vent Connectors in Unconditioned Space

1. Use Type B or Type L vent connectors with Category I gas appliances when the vent connectors are located in unconditioned areas, such as attics, crawl spaces, garages, and basements. You may use single wall pipe for a vent connector in an unconditioned garage or basement if the local 99 percent winter design temperature is at least (≥) 5º F. You may not use single wall pipe as a vent connector in any attic or crawl space.

Vent Connector Joints.

1. Secure joints between the vent connector and the flue collar or draft hood, and between vent connector sections, and between the vent connector and the vent using: (a) sheet metal screws (usually 3), or (b) listed interlocking vent material (such as Type B vent) connected according to the vent manufacturer's instructions, or (c) other approved means.

Vent Connector Slope

1. Slope vent connectors up toward the chimney or vent at least (≥) ¼ inch per foot. Do not allow any dips or sags in the vent connector.

Vent Connector Length

1. Locate gas appliances and their vents as close as possible to each other so that the vent connector length is as short as possible.
2. Do not install a horizontal single wall vent connector longer than (>) 75 percent of the chimney or vent height.
3. Do not install a horizontal Type B vent connector longer than (>) 100 percent of the chimney or vent height.
4. Do not install a horizontal vent connector that connects to a common vent longer than (>) 100 percent of the chimney or vent height.

5. Consider any angle greater than (>) 45º from vertical as horizontal.
6. <u>Do not use this vent connector length restriction section when using the vent sizing tables in Section G2428. The Section G2428 tables will apply in almost all cases; therefore, this section rarely applies.</u>

Vent Connector Support and Inspection

1. Provide adequate support for vent connectors according to the weight of the material and the length and number of fittings in the pipe run.
2. Provide ready access to the entire length of vent connectors for inspection, cleaning, and replacement. Do not conceal vent connectors. This includes concealment behind operable or removable panels.

Vent Connector Size for Single Gas Appliance

1. Use Section G2428 tables to determine the size of the vent connector for a single Category I or a single draft hood gas appliance.

Vent Connector Size for Single Gas Appliances with Multiple Draft Hoods

1. Use the appliance manufacturer's instructions or approved engineering methods to determine the size of the vent connector for a single gas appliance that has multiple draft hoods.

Vent Connector Size for Multiple Appliances with a Common Vent

1. Use Section G2428 tables to determine the size of each vent connector when two or more Category I gas appliances connect to a single, common vent.
2. You may use a vent connector that has an effective area at least as large as the gas appliance draft hood outlet to connect each draft hood gas appliance to the common vent. You may use this exception only if all the gas appliances are draft hood equipped and if each vent connector connects separately to the common vent.

Vent Connector Size for Multiple Appliances with a Common Connector

1. Use the appliance manufacturer's instructions or approved engineering methods to determine the size of the vent connector when two or more gas appliances use a common vent connector (also called a manifold).
2. Locate the common vent connector as high as possible in the space given available headroom and required clearances to combustible materials.
3. You may size a common vent connector, that serves only two draft hood appliances, by using a pipe and junction fittings for the common vent connector that are at least (≥) as large as the area of the larger draft hood outlet plus 50 percent of the area of the smaller draft hood outlet.

Vent Connector Size Increase

1. Use an appropriate increaser fitting at the appliance flue outlet to attach a vent connector

that is larger than the appliance flue outlet. This occurs when the Section G2428 tables or other vent connector sizing methods require a vent connector that is larger than the appliance flue outlet.
2. Do not increase the vent connector size more than two sizes greater than the diameter of the appliance flue collar or draft hood. Refer to Section G2428.2.11.

Different Size Vent Connectors Connecting to a Common Vent

1. Install the smaller vent connector above the larger vent connector and install the smaller vent connector as high as possible in the space given available headroom and required clearances to combustible materials.

Vent Connector Connection to a Chimney

1. Install a vent connector at least (≥) 12 inches above the bottom of a chimney flue.
2. You may use a thimble or slip joint to firmly attach the vent connector to the chimney flue.
3. Do not leave the vent connector loose so that flue gasses can escape or so that the vent connector could become disconnected from the chimney flue.
4. Attach the vent connector so that it will not enter the flue far enough to allow its end to be near the opposite wall of the chimney flue.
5. Do not attach a vent connector to a chimney serving a fireplace unless the fireplace flue opening is permanently sealed. Failure to seal the flue near where it connects to the fireplace can allow air to enter the chimney and reduce the draft created by the appliance vent gasses.

Vent Connector Passage Through Floors, Ceilings, or Walls

1. Do not pass single wall vent connectors through any floor or ceiling.
2. You may use a Type B vent as a vent connector through a floor or ceiling. Maintain required clearance between the Type B vent and combustible materials.

Single Wall Vent Connector Passage Through Combustible Exterior Wall

1. Use a ventilated metal thimble to guard a single wall vent connector passing through a combustible exterior wall.
2. Use a thimble at least (≥) 4 inches larger than the vent connector for a listed draft hood appliance and for an appliance listed for use with a Type B vent if the connector is less than (<) 6 feet long. You may use a thimble at least (≥) 2 inches larger than the vent connector if the connector is at least (≥) 6 feet long.
3. Use a thimble at least (≥) 6 inches larger than the vent connector for an unlisted draft hood appliance.
4. Use a thimble at least (≥) 12 inches larger than the vent connector for other residential and low heat appliances.
5. You may eliminate the thimble if you remove all combustible material for the required distance around the single wall vent connector and fill the opening with noncombustible material.

GAS VENT DRAFT HOODS AND DAMPERS (G2427.12, G2427.13, G2427.14)

Draft Hoods (G2427.12)

1. Install draft hoods according to manufacturer's instructions. Do not alter a manufacturer supplied draft hood except as specified by the manufacturer.
2. Install draft hoods and draft control devices in the same room as the appliance and so that there will be no difference in pressure between the hood or control device and the combustion air supply.
3. Install draft hoods with its opening at least (≥) 6 inches from any surface or with the clearance required by manufacturer's instructions, whichever is greater. Surfaces do not include the appliance itself and the vent attached to the draft hood.

Draft Hood (PG2427.12-0)
Figure 24-29

Draft Control Devices (G2427.12)

1. Install only listed draft control devices, such as barometric dampers, according to manufacturer's instructions.
2. Install draft control devices either horizontally or vertically as intended by the manufacturer.
3. Install draft control devices so that the relief opening is accessible to verify proper vent operation.

Manual Vent Dampers (G2427.13)

1. Do not install any manually operated damper on any gas appliance vent. Fixed baffles are not considered manually operated dampers.

GAS VENT SIZE TABLES DEFINITIONS (G2428.1)

Definitions of Terms Used to Calculate Gas Vent Size

Category I gas appliance A Category I gas appliance expels combustion products into a vent under negative static pressure and with a (higher) vent gas temperature that does not produce excessive moisture condensation in the vent. Most residential water heaters and furnaces are Category I appliances. Category I appliances can be either draft hood equipped (most water heaters) or fan-assisted appliances (most newer furnaces). The fan in a fan-assisted Category I appliance assists movement the combustion products within the heat exchanger of the furnace. The fan does not place the vent under positive static pressure.

Category II gas appliance A Category II gas appliance expels combustion products into a vent under negative static pressure and with a (lower) vent gas temperature that can produce excessive moisture condensation in the vent. At this time, the author knows of no available Category II appliances.

Category III gas appliance A Category III gas appliance expels combustion products into a vent under positive static pressure and with a (higher) vent gas temperature that does not produce excessive moisture condensation in the vent. Some mid-efficiency, sidewall vented residential furnaces and water heaters fall into this category.

Category IV gas appliance A Category IV gas appliance expels combustion products into a vent under positive static pressure and with a (lower) vent gas temperature that can produce excessive moisture condensation in the vent. This category includes high efficiency, condensing residential furnaces and boilers.

Common vent A common vent is a vent connected to two or more gas appliances located on the same level or floor. A common vent begins at the bottom of the fitting where the highest connecting gas appliance connects to the common vent. You may connect multiple Category I (negative vent pressure) fan-assisted and/or draft hood appliances to a common vent. You may not connect Category I gas appliances and Category III and IV (positive vent pressure) gas appliances to the same common vent.

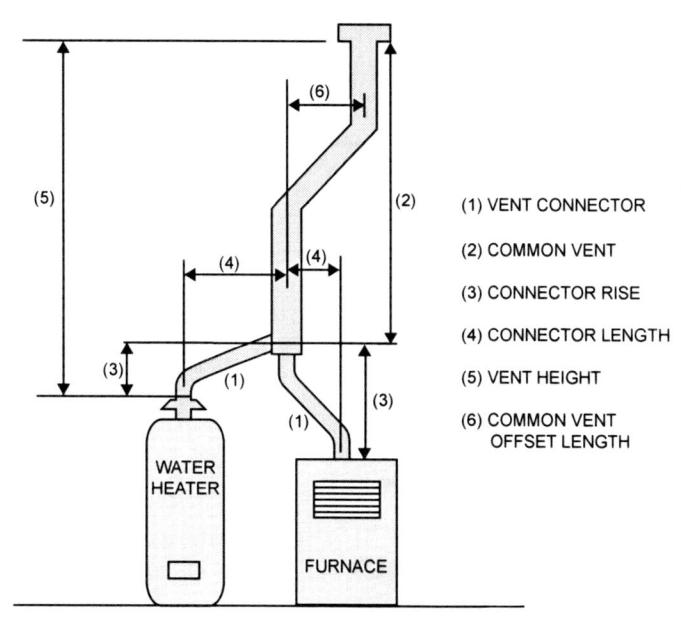

Common Vent Components (G2428.1-0)
Figure 24-30

Common vent offset A common vent offset is any part of a common vent that runs in a direction other than vertical.

Connector length Connector length is the total horizontal length of a vent connector in a common vent system measured from the center of the vent connector at the draft hood or flue collar to the center of the vent where the connector connects with the vent.

Connector rise Connector rise is the total vertical height of a vent connector in a common vent system measured from the appliance flue collar or draft hood outlet to the center of the fitting where the vent gas streams join.

Lateral A lateral is a vent connector direction other than vertical <u>in a single appliance vent system</u>.

Lateral length Lateral length is the total horizontal length of the vent connector in a single appliance vent system measured from the center of the vent connector at the draft hood or flue collar to the center of the vent where the connector connects with the vent.

Vent A vent is a generally vertical component, such as a metal pipe, that conducts combustion products from a gas appliance to the outdoors. A vent for a single gas appliance begins at the fitting where the vent connector, if any, connects to the vent. A common vent for multiple gas appliances begins at the highest connector fitting. If a vent is located directly over the appliance draft hood or flue collar, or if the vent connects directly to the gas appliance (as in Category III and IV gas appliances), then the vent begins at the gas appliance and there is no vent connector.

Vent diameter (D) The vent diameter is the length in inches of the vent opening.

Vent height Vent height is the total height of the vent and any vent connector measured from the draft hood or flue collar of the highest connected appliance on one building level or floor to the bottom of the listed vent cap or the end of the chimney flue.

Fan Min The Fan Min column in the tables lists the minimum input capacity, in Btu/hour, of one fan-assisted Category I gas appliance connected directly a vent or to a vent connector. Example: the minimum Btu/hour input capacity of a Category I fan-assisted furnace connected to a 4 inches diameter Type B vent connector with a vent height of 10 feet and a lateral length of 5 feet is 32,000 Btu/hour. See Table G2428.2-1.

Fan Max The Fan Max column in the tables lists the maximum input capacity, in Btu/hour, of one fan-assisted gas appliance connected directly a vent or to a vent connector. Example: the maximum Btu/hour input capacity of a Category I fan-assisted furnace connected to a 4 inches diameter single wall vent connector with a vent height of 10 feet and a lateral length of 5 feet is 111,000 Btu/hour. See Table G2428.2-2.

Fan + Fan The Fan + Fan column in the tables lists the maximum combined input capacity, in Btu/hour, of two or more Category I fan-assisted gas appliances connected to a common vent.

Fan + Nat The Fan + Nat column in the tables lists the maximum combined input capacity, in

Btu/hour, of one or more Category I fan-assisted gas appliances and one or more draft hood appliances connected to a common vent.

Nat + Nat The Nat + Nat column in the tables lists maximum combined input capacity, in Btu/hour, of two or more draft hood gas appliances connected to a common vent.

Nat Max The Nat Max column in the tables lists the maximum input capacity, in Btu/hour, of one draft hood gas appliance connected directly a vent or to a vent connector. Example: the maximum Btu/hour input capacity of a draft hood water heater connected to a 3 inches diameter Type B vent connector with a vent height of 10 feet and a lateral length of 5 feet is 40,000 Btu/hour. See Table G2428.2-1.

TYPE B GAS VENT SIZE FOR ONE APPLIANCE GENERAL INSTALLATION REQUIREMENTS AND EXAMPLES (G2428.2)

Application of these Tables

Use these tables to determine the size of Type B gas vents that serve only one Category I draft hood or fan-assisted gas appliance. Do not use these tables for: (a) Type BW vents, and (b) vents for decorative gas fireplaces, and (c) vents for gas appliances not listed for use with Type B vents, and (d) vents for appliances listed only for connection to chimneys, and (e) for factory-built chimneys, and (f) Category II, III, and IV gas appliances. Do not use these tables when connecting a single Category I appliance to a chimney. Use the tables in Section G2428.3 for this purpose.

Vent Obstructions

1. Do not use these tables if obstructions are installed in the vent or vent connector. Obstructions include vent dampers, draft regulators, and heat reclaimers.
2. Use equipment manufacturer's instructions to determine proper vent and connector size if vent obstructions are installed.

Vent Size from Tables Smaller than Draft Hood Size

1. You may use the vent size from these tables when the vent size from the tables is smaller than the size of the appliance draft hood or flue collar. Comply with all of the following requirements if you use a vent size from the tables that is smaller than the appliance draft hood or flue collar:
    a) use a vent height of at least (≥) 10 feet, and
    b) reduce the vent size not more than (≤) one table size for draft hoods and flue collars not more than (≤) 12 inches diameter, and
    c) reduce the vent size not more than (≤) two table sizes for draft hoods and flue collars larger than (>) 12 inches diameter, and
    d) reduce the values in the fan max column by 10 percent, and
    e) do not connect a 3 inch diameter vent to a 4 inch draft hood. Requirement (e) does not apply to fan-assisted appliances.

Vent Connector Laterals (Elbows)

1. Do not install any elbows in a vent system sized when using the zero lateral length table rows. The vent must attach directly to the appliance with no vent connector.
2. You may install not more than (≤) two 90 degree elbows in a vent system using the positive lateral length table rows without reducing the values in the tables. This includes any combination of fittings that total not more than (≤) 180 degrees.
3. Reduce the maximum capacity in the tables by 5 percent for each additional elbow not more than (≤) 45 degrees.
4. Reduce the maximum capacity in the tables by 10 percent for each additional elbow more than (>) 45 degrees and not more than (≤) 90 degrees.
5. Add the length of all offsets to determine the total lateral length when a vent connector system has multiple offsets.

Example:

Question:
What is the maximum Btu/hour input allowed for a 3 inches diameter vent with Type B vent connectors serving a natural draft water heater in the following illustration?

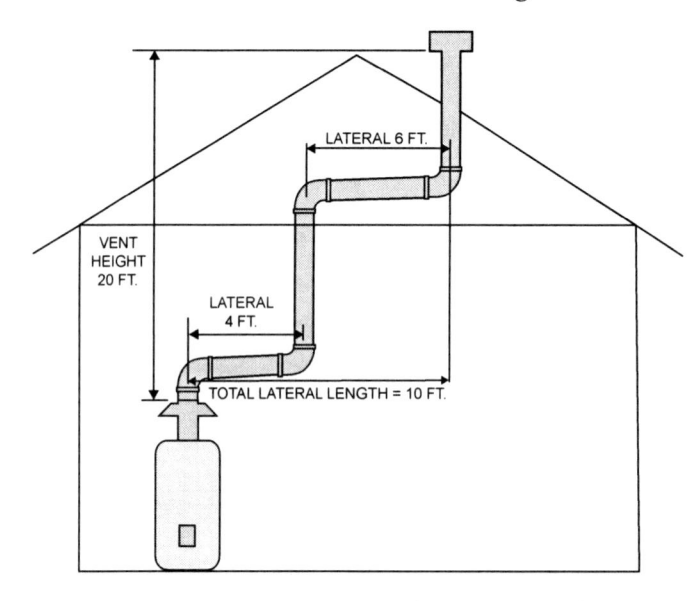

Vent Connector Laterals (G2428.2-0)
Figure 24-31

Answer:
Find the Btu/hour value in Table G2428.2(1) in the vent height 20 feet and connector lateral 10 feet row and the 3 inches nat max column. The value is 44,000 Btu/hour. Reduce the value by 20 percent to account for the two additional 90 degree elbows.

44,000 − (44,000 × .2) = 35,200

Appliance Btu/hour Input Reduction for High Altitude Installation

1. Use the appliance input rating, reduced (derated) for altitude, when using the fan min col-

umn in the tables. Refer to appliance manufacturer's instructions for altitude derating adjustments.

Appliance with Multiple Input Rates

1. Obtain the lowest and highest Btu/hour input rates for the appliance from the appliance label.
2. Select the input capacity from the fan min column that is less than the lowest Btu/hour appliance input rating.
3. Select the input capacity from the fan max or nat max column that is more than the highest Btu/hour appliance input rating.

Corrugated Chimney Liner System Sizing

1. Reduce the maximum input ratings from the tables by 20 percent to determine the input ratings for a corrugated metallic chimney liner system. The 20 percent reduction includes one long radius 90 degree bend. Reduce the maximum input ratings from the tables as described in Vent Connector Laterals (Elbows) if the vent system contains any additional bends.
2. You do not need to adjust the minimum input ratings.
3. Do not use a corrugated vent connector that is smaller in diameter than the appliance flue collar or draft hood diameter.

Vent Connector Size Smaller than Vent

1. Use the diameter of the vent connector to determine the vent system maximum capacity and use the diameter of the vent to determine the vent system minimum capacity when the diameter of the vent connector is smaller than the diameter of the vent. Note that vent system minimum capacity applies only to fan-assisted gas appliances. Example: In a vent system serving a Category I fan-assisted furnace, if the vent connector diameter is 3 inches and the vent diameter is 4 inches, use the fan max column in the 3 inches columns to determine the maximum vent Btu/hour capacity and use the fan min column in the 4 inches columns to determine the minimum vent Btu/hour capacity.
2. Do not install a vent with an area (not diameter) more than (>) seven times the area of the appliance flue collar or draft hood outlet unless the vent is sized using approved engineering methods.

Chimneys and Vents Exposed to Outdoors

1. Do not use the gas vent size tables for vents and chimneys exposed to the outdoors more than the minimum required to obtain the code required clearances to the roof and any sidewall. In cold climates, outdoors could include chimneys and vents in the attic. Verify with the local code official if chimneys and vents in attics are considered outdoors in your area.
2. Do not consider Type B vents and chimney liners installed in a masonry chimney flue as being exposed to the outdoors.
3. You may disregard this provision if the vent is sized according to the appliance manufacturer's instructions.

Vent Connector Size Larger than Flue Collar

1. Do not increase the vent connector size more than (>) two sizes greater than the diameter of the appliance flue collar or draft hood. Example: if the flue collar or draft hood diameter is 4 inches, do not use a vent connector with a diameter larger than 6 inches.

Use of Different Vent and Connector Materials

1. You may use different types and sizes of vent and connector materials in a vent system if all materials used are permitted by the gas vent size tables.

Table Interpolation and Extrapolation

1. You may interpolate to obtain values for vent input capacities that fall within the table values.
2. You may not extrapolate vent input capacities beyond the lower and upper ranges of the tables. This means you may not use the table values for vent heights less than 6 feet and more than 50 feet.
3. Use approved engineering methods to calculate vent capacities beyond the table ranges.

Table Interpolation Formulae

1. Use these formulae to determine vent capacities when the tables do not contain values for the actual vent system. If you do not wish to interpolate, you may use the closest (more conservative) value in the table.

Interpolated Maximum Vent Capacity = (A/B x C) + D
Interpolated Minimum Vent Capacity = E – (A/B x F)

A = The actual (or design) vent height minus the next lower height entry in the applicable table.

B = The difference between adjacent vent heights in the applicable table above and below the actual (or design) vent height.

C = The difference between maximum vent capacity entries in the column for the actual vent diameter. Use the vent height rows from B.

D = The smaller maximum vent capacity used to determine C.

E = The larger minimum vent capacity used to determine C.

F = The difference between minimum vent capacity entries in the column for the actual vent diameter. Use the vent height rows from B.

Example 1:

Question:
What are the minimum and maximum vent capacities for a single fan-assisted appliance given the following:

    Actual vent height 22 feet

    Vent diameter 4 inches

Lateral length 10 feet

Vent connector B vent

Answer:

Use Table G2428.2(1)

Interpolated Maximum Vent Capacity

A = 22-20 = 2 using the vent height feet column

B = 30-20 = 10 using the vent height feet column

C = 150,000-133,000 = 17,000 using the 4 inches fan max column

D = 133,000 using the 4 inches fan max column

(2/10 x 17,000) + 133,000 = 136,400

Interpolated Minimum Vent Capacity

A = 22-20 = 2 using the vent height feet column

B = 30-20 = 10 using the vent height feet column

E = 38,000 using the 4 inches fan min column

F = 38,000-37,000 = 1,000 using the 4 inches fan min column

38,000 – (2/10 x 1,000) = 37,800

Example 2:

Question:
May you vent a 45,000 Btu natural draft water heater into this vent system?

Actual vent height 14 feet

Vent diameter 3 inches

Lateral length 2 feet

Vent connector single wall

Answer:
Use Table G2428.2(2)

Interpolated Maximum Vent Capacity

A = 14-10 = 4 using the vent height feet column

B = 15-10 = 5 using the vent height feet column

C = 47,000-41,000 = 6,000 using the 3 inches nat max column

D = 41,000 using the 3 inches nat max column

(4/5 x 6,000) + 41,000 = 45,800

45,800 is more than 45,000 so you may use this vent system.

TYPE B GAS VENT SIZE TABLE FOR ONE APPLIANCE USING TYPE B VENT CONNECTOR (G2428.2-1)

Appliances and Equipment Covered by this Table

1. Apply this table to Category I gas appliances and natural draft appliances that would be classified as Category I appliances if they were classified. These appliances include most draft hood water heaters and most fan-assisted gas furnaces. Do not apply this table to Category II, III, and IV gas appliances, wall furnaces that use Type BW vents, decorative gas appliances, and other appliances not listed for use with a Type B vent.

2. Use this table for installations involving one gas appliance directly connected to one vent or using a Type B vent connector. The values in the table are appliance input ratings in thousands of Btu/hour.

TABLE G2428.2-1
Type B Gas Vent Size for One Appliance Using Type B Vent Connector

vent height feet	connector lateral length feet	vent D inches 3 fan min	vent D inches 3 fan max	vent D inches 3 nat max	vent D inches 4 fan min	vent D inches 4 fan max	vent D inches 4 nat max	vent D inches 5 fan min	vent D inches 5 fan max	vent D inches 5 nat max	vent D inches 6 fan min
6	0	0	78	46	0	152	86	0	251	141	0
6	2	13	51	36	18	97	67	27	157	105	32
6	4	21	49	34	30	94	64	39	153	103	50
6	6	25	46	32	36	91	61	47	149	100	59
8	0	0	84	50	0	165	94	0	276	155	0
8	2	12	57	40	16	109	75	25	178	120	28
8	5	23	53	38	32	103	71	42	171	115	53
8	8	28	49	35	39	98	66	51	164	109	64
10	0	0	88	53	0	175	100	0	295	166	0
10	2	12	61	42	17	118	81	23	194	129	26
10	5	23	57	40	32	113	77	41	187	124	52
10	10	30	51	36	41	104	70	54	176	115	67
15	0	0	94	58	0	191	112	0	327	187	0
15	2	11	69	48	15	136	93	20	226	150	22
15	5	22	65	45	30	130	87	39	219	142	49
15	10	29	59	41	40	121	82	51	206	135	64
15	15	35	53	37	48	112	76	61	195	128	76
20	0	0	97	61	0	202	119	0	349	202	0
20	2	10	75	51	14	149	100	18	250	166	20
20	5	21	71	48	29	143	96	38	242	160	47
20	10	28	64	44	38	133	89	50	229	150	62
20	15	34	58	40	46	124	84	59	217	142	73
20	20	48	52	35	55	116	78	69	206	134	84
30	0	0	100	64	0	213	128	0	374	220	0
30	2	9	81	56	13	166	112	14	283	185	18
30	5	21	77	54	28	160	108	36	275	176	45
30	10	27	70	50	37	150	102	48	262	171	59
30	15	33	64	NA	44	141	96	57	249	163	70
30	20	56	58	NA	53	132	90	66	237	154	80
30	30	NA	NA	NA	73	113	NA	88	214	104	346
50	0	0	101	67	0	216	134	0	397	232	0
50	2	8	86	61	11	183	122	14	320	206	15
50	5	20	82	NA	27	177	119	35	312	200	43
50	10	26	76	NA	35	168	114	45	299	190	56
50	15	59	70	NA	42	158	NA	54	287	180	66
50	20	NA	NA	NA	50	149	NA	63	275	169	76
50	30	NA	NA	NA	69	131	NA	84	250	NA	99

TABLE G2428.2-1
Type B Gas Vent Size for One Appliance Using Type B Vent Connector

vent height feet	connector lateral length feet	vent D inches 6 fan max	vent D inches 6 nat max	vent D inches 7 fan min	vent D inches 7 fan max	vent D inches 7 nat max	vent D inches 8 fan min	vent D inches 8 fan max	vent D inches 8 nat max	vent D inches 9 fan min	vent D inches 9 fan max	vent D inches 9 nat max
6	0	375	205	0	524	285	0	698	370	0	897	470
6	2	232	157	44	321	217	53	425	285	63	543	370
6	4	227	153	66	316	211	79	419	279	93	536	362
6	6	223	149	78	310	205	93	413	273	110	530	354
8	0	415	235	0	583	320	0	780	415	0	1006	537
8	2	263	180	42	365	247	50	483	322	60	619	418
8	5	255	173	70	356	237	83	473	313	99	607	407
8	8	247	165	84	347	227	99	463	303	117	596	396
10	0	447	255	0	631	345	0	847	450	0	1096	585
10	2	289	195	40	402	273	48	533	355	57	684	457
10	5	280	188	68	392	263	81	522	346	95	671	446
10	10	267	175	88	376	245	104	504	330	122	651	427
15	0	502	285	0	716	390	0	970	525	0	1263	682
15	2	339	225	38	475	316	45	633	414	53	815	544
15	5	330	217	64	463	300	76	620	403	90	800	529
15	10	315	208	84	445	288	99	600	386	116	777	507
15	15	301	198	98	429	275	115	580	373	134	755	491
20	0	540	307	0	776	430	0	1057	575	0	1384	752
20	2	377	249	33	531	346	41	711	470	50	917	612
20	5	367	241	62	519	337	73	697	460	86	902	599
20	10	351	228	81	499	321	95	675	443	112	877	576
20	15	337	217	94	481	308	111	654	427	129	853	557
20	20	322	206	107	464	295	125	634	410	145	830	537
30	0	587	336	0	853	475	0	1173	650	0	1548	855
30	2	432	280	27	613	394	33	826	535	42	1072	700
30	5	421	273	58	600	385	69	811	524	82	1055	688
30	10	405	261	77	580	371	91	788	507	107	1028	668
30	15	389	249	90	560	357	105	765	490	124	1002	648
30	20	374	237	102	542	343	119	743	473	139	977	628
30	30	219	131	131	507	321	149	702	444	171	929	594
50	0	663	363	0	932	518	0	1297	708	0	1730	952
50	2	497	314	22	715	445	26	975	615	33	1276	813
50	5	487	308	55	702	438	65	960	605	77	1259	798
50	10	471	298	73	681	426	86	935	589	101	1230	773
50	15	455	288	85	662	413	100	911	572	117	1203	747
50	20	440	278	97	642	401	113	888	556	131	1176	722
50	30	410	259	123	605	376	141	844	522	161	1125	670

TYPE B GAS VENT SIZE TABLE FOR ONE APPLIANCE USING SINGLE WALL VENT CONNECTOR (G2428.2-2)

Appliances and Equipment Covered by this Table

1. Apply this table to Category I gas appliances and natural draft appliances that would be classified as Category I appliances if they were classified. These appliances include most draft hood water heaters and most fan-assisted gas furnaces. Do not apply this table to Category II, III, and IV gas appliances, wall furnaces that use Type BW vents, decorative gas appliances, and other appliances not listed for use with a Type B vent.

2. Use this table for installations involving one gas appliance connected to one vent using a single wall connector. The values in the table are appliance input ratings in thousands of Btu/hour.

TABLE G2428.2-2
Type B Gas Vent Size for One Appliance Using Single Wall Vent Connector

vent height feet	connector lateral length feet	vent D inches 3	vent D inches 3	vent D inches 3	vent D inches 4	vent D inches 4	vent D inches 4	vent D inches 5	vent D inches 5	vent D inches 5	vent D inches 6
		fan min	fan max	nat max	fan min	fan max	nat max	fan min	fan max	nat max	fan min
6	0	38	77	45	59	151	85	85	249	140	126
6	2	39	51	36	60	96	66	85	156	104	123
6	4	NA	NA	33	74	92	63	102	152	102	146
6	6	NA	NA	31	83	89	60	114	147	99	163
8	0	37	83	50	58	164	93	83	273	154	123
8	2	39	56	39	59	108	75	83	176	119	121
8	5	NA	NA	37	77	102	69	107	168	114	151
8	8	NA	NA	33	90	95	64	122	161	107	175
10	0	37	87	53	57	174	99	82	293	165	120
10	2	39	61	41	59	117	80	82	193	128	119
10	5	52	56	39	76	111	76	105	185	122	148
10	10	NA	NA	34	97	100	68	132	171	112	188
15	0	36	93	57	56	190	111	80	325	186	116
15	2	38	69	47	57	136	93	80	225	149	115
15	5	51	63	44	75	128	86	102	216	140	144
15	10	NA	NA	39	95	116	79	128	201	131	182
15	15	NA	NA	NA	NA	NA	72	158	186	124	220
20	0	35	96	60	54	200	118	78	346	201	114
20	2	37	74	50	56	148	99	78	248	165	113
20	5	50	68	47	73	140	94	100	239	158	141
20	10	NA	NA	41	93	129	86	125	223	146	177
20	15	NA	NA	NA	NA	NA	80	155	208	136	216
20	20	NA	NA	NA	NA	NA	NA	186	192	126	254
30	0	34	99	63	53	211	127	76	372	219	110
30	2	37	80	56	55	164	111	76	281	183	109
30	5	49	74	52	72	157	106	98	271	173	136
30	10	NA	NA	NA	91	144	98	122	255	168	171
30	15	NA	NA	NA	115	131	NA	151	239	157	208
30	20	NA	NA	NA	NA	NA	NA	181	223	NA	246
30	30	NA	NA	NA	NA	NA	NA	NA	NA	NA	NA
50	0	33	99	66	51	213	133	73	394	230	105
50	2	36	84	61	53	181	121	73	318	205	104
50	5	48	80	NA	70	174	117	94	308	198	131
50	10	NA	NA	NA	89	160	NA	118	292	186	162
50	15	NA	NA	NA	112	148	NA	145	275	174	199
50	20	NA	NA	NA	NA	NA	NA	176	257	NA	236
50	30	NA	NA	NA	NA	NA	NA	NA	NA	NA	315

24 : Fuel Gas   323

TABLE G2428.2-2
Type B Gas Vent Size for One Appliance Using Single Wall Vent Connector

vent height feet	connector lateral length feet	vent D inches 6 fan max	vent D inches 6 nat max	vent D inches 7 fan min	vent D inches 7 fan max	vent D inches 7 nat max	vent D inches 8 fan min	vent D inches 8 fan max	vent D inches 8 nat max	vent D inches 9 fan min	vent D inches 9 fan max	vent D inches 9 nat max
6	0	373	204	165	522	284	211	695	369	267	894	469
6	2	231	156	159	320	213	201	423	284	251	541	368
6	4	225	152	187	313	208	237	416	277	295	533	360
6	6	220	148	207	307	203	263	409	271	327	526	352
8	0	412	234	161	580	319	206	777	414	258	1002	536
8	2	261	179	155	363	246	197	482	321	246	617	417
8	5	252	171	193	352	235	245	470	311	305	604	404
8	8	243	163	223	342	225	280	458	300	344	591	392
10	0	444	254	158	628	344	202	844	449	253	1093	584
10	2	287	194	153	400	272	193	531	354	242	681	456
10	5	277	186	190	388	261	241	518	344	299	667	443
10	10	261	171	237	369	241	296	497	325	363	643	423
15	0	499	283	153	713	388	195	966	523	244	1259	681
15	2	337	224	148	473	314	187	631	413	232	812	543
15	5	326	217	182	459	298	231	646	400	287	795	526
15	10	308	203	228	438	284	284	592	381	349	768	501
15	15	290	192	272	418	269	334	568	367	404	742	484
20	0	537	306	149	772	428	190	1053	573	238	1379	750
20	2	375	248	144	528	344	182	708	468	227	914	611
20	5	363	239	178	514	334	224	692	457	279	896	596
20	10	344	224	222	491	316	277	666	437	339	866	570
20	15	325	210	264	469	301	325	640	419	393	838	549
20	20	306	196	309	448	285	374	616	400	448	810	526
30	0	584	334	144	849	472	184	1168	647	229	1542	852
30	2	429	279	139	610	392	175	823	533	219	1069	698
30	5	417	271	171	595	382	215	806	521	269	1049	684
30	10	397	257	213	570	367	265	777	501	327	1017	662
30	15	377	242	255	547	349	312	750	481	379	985	638
30	20	357	228	298	524	333	360	723	461	433	955	615
30	30	NA	NA	389	477	305	461	670	426	541	895	574
50	0	629	361	138	928	515	176	1292	704	220	1724	948
50	2	495	312	133	712	443	168	971	613	209	1273	811
50	5	482	305	164	696	435	204	953	602	257	1252	795
50	10	461	292	203	671	420	253	923	583	313	1217	765
50	15	441	280	244	646	405	299	894	562	363	1183	736
50	20	420	267	285	622	389	345	866	543	415	1150	70
50	30	376	NA	373	573	NA	442	809	502	512	1086	649

TYPE B GAS VENT SIZE FOR MULTIPLE APPLIANCES GENERAL INSTALLATION REQUIREMENTS AND EXAMPLES (G2428.3)

Application of these Tables

1. Use these tables to determine the size of:
   a) Type B common vents for gas appliances,
   b) masonry chimney flues when used as common vents for gas appliances, and
   c) vent connectors, when more than one Category I draft hood or fan-assisted gas appliance is connected to a common vent.

2. Do not use this section for:
   a) Type BW vents, and
   b) vents for decorative gas fireplaces, and
   c) vents for gas appliances not listed for use with Type B vents, and

d) vents for appliances listed only for connection to chimneys, and
e) for factory-built chimneys.

3. Use this section to determine the size of gas vent connectors and masonry chimney flues that serve one Category I draft hood or fan-assisted gas appliance when the appliance is vented using a masonry chimney flue.

Vent Obstructions

1. Do not use the gas vent size tables if obstructions are installed in the vent or vent connector. Obstructions include vent dampers, draft regulators, and heat reclaimers.
2. Use equipment manufacturer's instructions to determine proper vent and connector size if vent obstructions are installed.

Vent Connector Length Limit

1. Install vent connectors between the appliances and the common vent by the most direct possible route from the appliance to the common vent.
2. Limit the vent connector length to not more than (≤) 1.5 feet times the vent connector diameter in inches unless you reduce the Btu/hour values in the tables. Example: a 4 inches diameter vent connector should have a maximum length of 6 feet.

Long Length Vent Connectors

1. You may use vent connectors that are longer than 1.5 times the vent connector diameter if you account for the additional vent connector length as follows: (a) reduce the values in the maximum columns (fan max and nat max) by 10 percent for each multiple of the maximum connector length, (b) use the single appliance tables G2428.2-1 or G2428.2-2 to determine the fan min column values for a fan-assisted appliance. Determine the vent height and connector lateral length as required for single appliances.

Example: A 4 inches diameter vent connector has a maximum length of 6 feet (1.5 x 4). Reduce the fan max and nat max capacity of the vent connector by 10 percent for connector lengths greater than (>) 6 feet but not more than (≤) 12 feet (2.0 times the maximum connector diameter). Reduce the capacity by 20 percent for lengths greater than (>) 12 feet (2.0 times the maximum connector diameter) but not more than (≤) 18 feet (3.0 times the maximum connector diameter).

Example 1:

Question:
What are the Btu/hour input capacity limits for a 4 inches diameter Type B vent connector 10 feet long with a rise of 2 feet and a common vent height of 20 feet?

Answer:
Find the fan max and nat max Btu/hour input capacities in Table G2428.3-1 in the 20 feet vent height and 2 feet connector rise row and the 4 inches connector diameter column. The Btu/hour input capacities are fan max 105,000 Btu/hour and nat max 66,000. Reduce these capacities by

10 percent to account for the vent connector length more than (>) 1.5 the connector diameter but not more than (≤) 2.0 times the connector diameter.

Fan max = 105,000 − (105,000 x .10) = 94,500 Btu/hour
Nat max = 66,000 − (66,000 x .10) = 59,400 Btu/hour

Find the fan min capacity in Table G2428.2-1 in the 20 feet vent height and 10 feet lateral length row and the 4 inches fan min column.

Fan min = 38,000 Btu/hour.

Example 2:

Question:
May you vent a 75,000 Btu/hour fan-assisted medium efficiency furnace and a 35,000 Btu/hour natural draft water heater into the following vent system?

> Common vent 5 inches diameter Type B vent with no offsets and 20 feet vent height
>
> Furnace connector 4 inches diameter Type B connector with 10 feet lateral length and 3 feet rise
>
> Water heater connector 3 inches diameter single wall connector with 5 feet lateral length and 3 feet rise

Answer:
Find the furnace vent connector fan max capacity in Table G2428.3-1. The fan max capacity in the 20 feet vent height and 3 feet connector rise row and 4 inches connector diameter column is 110,000 Btu/hour. Find the water heater vent connector nat max capacity in Table G2428.3-2. The nat max capacity in the 20 feet vent height and 3 feet connector rise row and 3 inches connector diameter column is 40,000 Btu/hour.

Reduce the furnace vent connector fan max capacity by 10 percent to account for the connector length more than (>) 1.5 times the connector diameter but not more than (≤) 2.0 times the maximum connector diameter.

Fan max. = 110,000 − (110,000 x .1) = 99,000 Btu/hour

Reduce the water heater vent connector nat max capacity by by 10 percent to account for the connector length more than (>) 1.5 times the connector diameter but not more than (≤) 2.0 times the maximum connector diameter.

Nat max. = 40,000 − (40,000 x .1) = 36,000 Btu/hour

Find the furnace vent connector fan min capacity in Table G2428.2-1 in the 20 feet vent height and 10 feet lateral length row and 4 inches vent diameter column.

Fan min. = 38,000 Btu/hour

The furnace input capacity of 75,000 Btu/hour is more than the fan min capacity and less than

326   Everybody's Building Code

the fan max capacity of the vent connector. You may use this vent connector in this application.

The water heater input capacity of 35,000 Btu/hour is less than the nat max capacity of the vent connector. You may use this vent connector in this application.

Add the furnace and water heater input ratings.

75,000 + 35,000 = 110,000 Btu/hour

Use the 20 feet vent height and fan+nat column in the common vent capacity table in Table G2428.3-2 to determine the common vent capacity. Use Table G2428.3-2 because single wall and Type B vent connectors are both used in the vent system. The common vent maximum capacity is 177,000 Btu/hour, which is more than the combined input ratings of the furnace and water heater. You may use this vent system in this application.

Common Vent Offset Length

1. Limit the use of common vent offsets.
2. Install a common vent offset that is not more than (≤) 1.5 feet per inch of common vent diameter. Example: a 6 inches diameter common vent may have an offset that is not more than (≤) 9 feet.
3. Add the length of all offsets to determine the total lateral length when a vent connector system has multiple offsets.

Common Vent Offsets (Elbows)

1. Reduce the maximum capacity in the common vent tables by 5 percent for each common vent elbow not more than (≤) 45 degrees.
2. Reduce the maximum capacity in the tables by 10 percent for each common vent elbow more than (>) 45 degrees and not more than (≤) 90 degrees.

Example:

Question:
What is the common vent Btu/hour capacity in the following vent system serving a fan-assisted medium efficiency furnace and a natural draft water heater?

Common vent	5 inches diameter Type B vent 20 feet high with an offset that is 7 feet long with two 60 degree elbows
Furnace connector	4 inches diameter Type B connector with 10 feet lateral length and 3 feet rise
Water heater connector	3 inches diameter single wall connector with 5 feet lateral length and 3 feet rise

Answer:
Use the 20 feet vent height and fan+nat column in the common vent capacity table in Table

G2428.3-2 to determine the common vent capacity. Use Table G2428.3-2 because single wall and Type B vent connectors are both used in the vent system. The common vent maximum capacity is 177,000 Btu/hour. Reduce the common vent capacity by 20 percent to account for two 60 degree elbows.

Maximum common vent Btu/hour capacity =

177,000 – (177,000 x .20) = 141,600

Vent Connector Laterals (Elbows)

1. You may install up to two 90 degree elbows in a vent connector system. This includes any combination of fittings that total less than (<) 180 degrees.
2. Reduce the maximum capacity in the vent connector tables by 5 percent for each additional elbow not more than (≤) 45 degrees.
3. Reduce the maximum capacity in the tables by 10 percent for each additional elbow more than (>) 45 degrees and not more than (≤) 90 degrees.

Example:

Question:
What are the Btu/hour capacities of a 4 inches diameter single wall vent connector with connector rise of 3 feet, a connector lateral length of 10 feet, four elbows consisting of two 45 degree elbows and two 90 degree elbows in the vent connector, and a common vent system 20 feet high?

Answer:
Find the connector fan max and nat max capacities in Table G2428.3-2 in the 20 feet vent height and 3 feet connector rise row and 4 inches connector diameter column. The fan max capacity is 100,000 Btu/hour and the nat max capacity is 70,000 Btu/hour. Reduce these capacities by 10 percent to account for the vent connector length more than (>) 1.5 the connector diameter but not more than (≤) 2.0 times the connector diameter and an additional 10 percent to account for the two extra 45 degree elbows.

Fan max = 107,000 – (107,000 x .20) = 85,600 Btu/hour
Nat max = 72,000 – (72,000 x .20) = 57,600 Btu/hour

Find the fan min capacity in Table G2428.2-2 in the 20 feet vent height and 10 feet lateral length row and the 4 inches fan min column.

Fan min = 93,000 Btu/hour

Reduce this capacity by 10 percent to account for the two extra 45 degree elbows.

Fan min = 93,000 – (93,000 x .10) = 83,700 Btu/hour

Common (Vertical) Vent Maximum Size

1. Do not use a vent or chimney with an area (not diameter) more than (>) seven times the area of the smallest appliance flue collar or draft hood outlet unless the vent or chimney is sized using approved engineering methods.

Example:

Question:
What is the maximum common vent or chimney area that may be used in a vent system serving a 3 inches diameter vent hood water heater and a 4 inches diameter fan-assisted furnace?

Answer:
Calculate the vent area of the smallest connected appliance. In this example, the 3 inches diameter vent hood is the smallest connected appliance.

Maximum vent area =

(3.1416($\prod$) x (1.5 inches)²) x 7 = 49.48 square inches

Common (Vertical) Vent Minimum Size

1. Use a common vent that has an area (not diameter) at least as large as the area of the largest vent connector.
2. Use a tee or wye fitting that has an opening size, where it connects to the common vent, that is at least as large as the common vent. The fitting may have smaller openings for the vent connectors.

Vent Connector Size Larger than Flue Collar

1. Do not increase the vent connector size more than two sizes greater than the diameter of the appliance flue collar or draft hood.

Vent Size from Tables Smaller than Appliance Outlet Size

1. Do not use a vent connector for a draft hood appliance that is smaller than the draft hood outlet diameter.
2. You may use the vent size from the tables for a fan-assisted appliance if the vent size from the tables is smaller than the size of the appliance flue collar if you comply with all of the following requirements:
   a) do not reduce the vent size more than one table size for flue collars 12 inches diameter or smaller, and
   b) do not reduce the vent size more than two table sizes for flue collars larger than (>) 12 inches diameter, and
   c) use a common vent to vent the fan-assisted appliance(s) with draft hood appliance(s), and

d) use vent connectors with a smooth interior wall. Do not use corrugated metal vent connectors.

Appliance Btu/h Input Reduction for High Altitude Installation

1. Use the appliance input, reduced (derated) for altitude, when using the fan min column in the tables. Refer to appliance manufacturer's instructions for altitude derating adjustments.

Appliance with Multiple Input Rates

1. Obtain the lowest and highest Btu/hour input rates for the appliance from the appliance label.
2. Select the input capacity from the fan min column that is less than the lowest Btu/hour appliance input rating.
3. Select the input capacity from the fan max or nat max column that is more than the highest Btu/hour appliance input rating.

Corrugated Chimney Liner System Sizing

1. Reduce the maximum input capacity from the tables by 20 percent to determine the size for a corrugated metallic chimney liner system. The 20 percent reduction includes one long radius 90 degree bend. Reduce the maximum input capacity from the tables as described in Common Vent Offsets (Elbows) if the vent system contains any additional bends.
2. You do not need to adjust the minimum input capacity.
3. Do not use a corrugated vent connector that is smaller in diameter than the appliance flue collar or draft hood diameter.

Chimneys and Vents Exposed to Outdoors

1. Do not use the gas vent size tables for vents and chimneys exposed to the outdoors more than the minimum required to obtain the code required clearances to the roof and any sidewall. In cold climates, outdoors could include chimneys and vents in the attic. Verify with the local code official if chimneys and vents in attics are considered outdoors in your area.
2. Do not consider Type B vents and chimney liners installed in a masonry chimney flue as being exposed to the outdoors.
3. You may disregard this provision if the vent is sized according to the appliance manufacturer's instructions.

Vent Connector Manifold

1. Reduce the common vent capacity in the tables by 10 percent if vent connectors are connected together to form a manifold prior to entering the common vent.
2. Use a vent connector manifold not longer than (≤) 1.5 feet times the manifold diameter in inches. Measure the manifold length from the common vent to most distant manifold vent connector fitting.

Use of Different Vent and Connector Materials

1. You may use different types and sizes of vent and connector materials in a vent system if all materials used are permitted by the gas vent size tables.

Table Interpolation and Extrapolation

1. You may interpolate to obtain values for vent input capacities that fall within the table values.
2. You may not extrapolate vent input capacities beyond the lower and upper ranges of the tables. This means you may not use the table values for vent heights less than 6 feet and more than 50 feet.
3. Use approved engineering methods to calculate vent capacities beyond the table ranges.
4. Refer to interpolation examples in 2428.2.

TYPE B GAS VENT SIZE TABLE FOR MULTIPLE APPLIANCES USING TYPE B VENT CONNECTOR (G2428.3-1)

Appliances and Equipment Covered by this Table

1. Apply this table to Category I gas appliances and natural draft appliances that would be classified as Category I appliances if they were classified. These appliances include most draft hood water heaters and most fan-assisted gas furnaces. Do not apply this table to Category II, III, & IV gas appliances, wall furnaces that use Type BW vents, decorative gas appliances, and other appliances not listed for use with a Type B vent.
2. Use this table for installations involving multiple gas appliances connected to one common vent using Type B vent connectors. The values in the table are appliance input ratings in thousands of Btu/hour.

TABLE G2428.3-1
Type B Gas Vent Size for Multiple Appliances Using Type B Vent Connector
Type B Vent Connector Capacity

vent height feet	connect rise feet	connect D inches 3	connect D inches 3	connect D inches 3	connect D inches 4	connect D inches 4	connect D inches 4	connect D inches 5	connect D inches 5	connect D inches 5	connect D inches 6	connect D inches 6
		fan min	fan max	nat max	fan min	fan max	nat max	fan min	fan max	nat max	fan min	fan max
6	1	22	37	26	35	66	46	46	106	72	58	164
6	2	23	41	31	37	75	55	48	121	86	60	183
6	3	24	44	35	38	81	62	49	132	96	62	199
8	1	22	40	27	35	72	48	49	114	76	64	176
8	2	23	44	32	36	80	57	51	128	90	66	195
8	3	24	47	36	37	87	64	53	139	101	67	210
10	1	22	43	28	34	78	50	49	123	78	65	189
10	2	23	47	33	36	86	59	51	136	93	67	206
10	3	24	50	37	37	92	67	52	146	104	69	220
15	1	21	50	30	33	89	53	47	142	83	64	220
15	2	22	53	35	35	96	63	49	153	99	66	235
15	3	24	55	40	36	102	71	51	163	111	68	248
20	1	21	54	31	33	99	56	46	157	87	62	246
20	2	22	57	37	34	105	66	48	167	104	64	259
20	3	23	60	42	35	110	74	50	176	116	66	271
30	1	20	62	33	31	113	59	45	181	93	60	288
30	2	21	64	39	33	118	70	47	190	110	62	299
30	3	22	66	44	34	123	79	48	198	124	64	309
50	1	19	71	36	30	133	64	43	216	101	57	349
50	2	21	73	43	32	137	76	45	223	119	59	358
50	3	22	75	48	33	141	86	46	229	134	61	366

TABLE G2428.3-1
Type B Gas Vent Size for Multiple Appliances Using Type B Vent Connector
Type B Vent Connector Capacity

vent height feet	connect rise feet	connect D inches 6	connect D inches 7	connect D inches 7	connect D inches 7	connect D inches 8	connect D inches 8	connect D inches 8	connect D inches 9	connect D inches 9	connect D inches 9
		nat max	fan min	fan max	nat max	fan min	fan max	nat max	fan min	fan max	nat max
6	1	104	77	225	142	92	296	185	109	376	237
6	2	124	79	253	168	95	333	220	112	424	282
6	3	139	82	275	189	97	363	248	114	463	317
8	1	109	84	243	148	100	320	194	118	408	248
8	2	129	86	269	175	103	356	230	121	454	294
8	3	145	88	290	198	105	384	258	123	492	330
10	1	113	89	257	154	106	341	200	125	436	257
10	2	134	91	282	182	109	374	238	128	479	305
10	3	150	94	303	205	111	402	268	131	515	342
15	1	120	88	298	163	110	389	214	134	493	273
15	2	142	91	320	193	112	419	253	137	532	323
15	3	160	93	339	218	115	445	286	140	565	365
20	1	125	86	334	171	107	436	224	131	552	285
20	2	149	89	354	202	110	463	265	134	587	339
20	3	168	91	371	228	113	486	300	137	618	383
30	1	134	83	391	182	103	512	238	125	649	305
30	2	158	85	408	215	105	535	282	129	679	360
30	3	178	88	423	242	108	555	317	132	706	405
50	1	145	78	477	197	97	627	257	120	797	330
50	2	172	81	490	234	100	645	306	123	820	392
50	3	194	83	502	263	103	661	343	126	842	441

TABLE G2428.3-1
Type B Gas Vent Size for Multiple Appliances Using Type B Vent Connector
Common Vent Capacity

vent height feet	vent D inches 4	vent D inches 4	vent D inches 4	vent D inches 5	vent D inches 5	vent D inches 5	vent D inches 6	vent D inches 6	vent D inches 6	vent D inches 7	vent D inches 7	vent D inches 7
	fan +fan	fan +nat	nat +nat	fan +fan	fan +nat	nat +nat	fan +fan	fan +nat	nat +nat	fan +fan	fan +nat	nat +nat
6	92	81	65	140	116	103	204	161	147	309	248	200
8	101	90	73	155	129	114	224	178	163	339	275	223
10	110	97	79	169	141	124	243	194	178	367	299	242
15	125	112	91	195	164	144	283	228	206	427	352	280
20	136	123	102	215	183	160	314	255	229	475	394	310
30	152	138	118	244	210	185	361	297	266	547	459	360
50	167	153	134	279	244	214	421	353	310	641	547	423

TABLE G2428.3-1
Type B Gas Vent Size for Multiple Appliances Using Type B Vent Connector Common Vent Capacity

vent height feet	vent D inches 8 fan +fan	vent D inches 8 fan +nat	vent D inches 8 nat +nat	vent D inches 9 fan +fan	vent D inches 9 fan +nat	vent D inches 9 nat +nat	vent D inches 10 fan +fan	vent D inches 10 fan +nat	vent D inches 10 nat +nat
6	404	314	260	547	434	335	672	520	410
8	444	348	290	602	480	378	740	577	465
10	477	377	315	649	522	405	800	627	495
15	556	444	365	753	612	465	924	733	565
20	621	499	405	842	688	523	1035	826	640
30	720	585	470	979	808	605	1209	975	740
50	854	706	550	1164	977	705	1451	1188	860

TYPE B GAS VENT SIZE TABLE FOR MULTIPLE APPLIANCES USING SINGLE WALL VENT CONNECTOR (G2428.3-2)

Appliances and Equipment Covered by this Table

1. Apply this table to Category I gas appliances and natural draft appliances that would be classified as Category I appliances if they were classified. These appliances include most draft hood water heaters and most fan-assisted gas furnaces. Do not apply this table to Category II, III, & IV gas appliances, wall furnaces that use Type BW vents, decorative gas appliances, and other appliances not listed for use with a Type B vent.

2. Use this table for installations involving multiple gas appliances connected to one common vent using single wall metal vent connectors. The values in the table are appliance input ratings in thousands of Btu/hour.

TABLE G2428.3-2
Type B Gas Vent Size for Multiple Appliances Using Single Wall Vent Connector
Single Wall Vent Connector Capacity

vent height feet	connect rise feet	connect D inches 3	connect D inches 3	connect D inches 3	connect D inches 4	connect D inches 4	connect D inches 4	connect D inches 5	connect D inches 5	connect D inches 5	connect D inches 6	connect D inches 6
		fan min	fan max	nat max	fan min	fan max	nat max	fan min	fan max	nat max	fan min	fan max
6	1	NA	NA	26	NA	NA	46	NA	NA	71	NA	NA
6	2	NA	NA	31	NA	NA	55	NA	NA	85	168	182
6	3	NA	NA	34	NA	NA	62	121	131	95	175	198
8	1	NA	NA	27	NA	NA	48	NA	NA	75	NA	NA
8	2	NA	NA	32	NA	NA	57	125	126	89	184	193
8	3	NA	NA	35	NA	NA	64	130	138	100	191	208
10	1	NA	NA	28	NA	NA	50	119	121	77	182	186
10	2	NA	NA	33	84	85	59	124	134	91	189	203
10	3	NA	NA	36	89	91	67	129	144	102	197	217
15	1	NA	NA	29	79	87	52	116	138	81	177	214
15	2	NA	NA	34	83	94	62	121	150	97	185	230
15	3	NA	NA	39	87	100	70	127	160	109	193	243
20	1	49	56	30	78	97	54	115	152	84	175	238
20	2	52	59	36	82	103	64	120	163	101	182	252
20	3	55	62	40	87	107	72	125	172	113	190	264
30	1	47	60	31	77	110	57	112	175	89	169	278
30	2	51	62	37	81	115	67	117	185	106	177	290
30	3	54	64	42	85	119	76	122	193	120	185	300
50	1	46	69	34	75	128	60	109	207	96	162	336
50	2	49	71	40	79	132	72	114	215	113	170	345
50	3	52	72	45	83	136	82	119	221	123	178	.353

TABLE G2428.3-2
Type B Gas Vent Size for Multiple Appliances Using Single Wall Vent Connector
Single Wall Vent Connector Capacity

vent height feet	connect rise feet	connect D inches 6	connect D inches 7	connect D inches 7	connect D inches 7	connect D inches 8	connect D inches 8	connect D inches 8	connect D inches 9	connect D inches 9	connect D inches 9
		nat max	fan min	fan max	nat max	fan min	fan max	nat max	fan min	fan max	nat max
6	1	102	207	223	140	262	293	183	325	373	234
6	2	123	215	251	167	271	331	219	334	422	281
6	3	138	222	273	188	279	361	247	344	462	316
8	1	106	226	240	145	285	316	191	352	403	244
8	2	127	234	266	173	293	353	228	360	450	292
8	3	144	241	287	197	302	381	256	370	489	328
10	1	110	240	253	150	302	335	196	372	429	252
10	2	132	248	278	183	311	369	235	381	473	302
10	3	148	257	299	203	320	398	265	391	511	339
15	1	116	238	291	158	312	380	208	397	482	266
15	2	138	246	314	189	321	411	248	407	522	317
15	3	157	255	333	215	331	438	281	418	557	360
20	1	120	233	325	165	306	425	217	390	538	276
20	2	144	243	346	197	317	453	259	400	574	331
20	3	164	252	363	223	326	476	294	412	607	375
30	1	129	226	380	175	296	497	230	378	630	294
30	2	152	236	397	208	307	521	274	389	662	349
30	3	172	244	412	235	316	542	309	400	690	394
50	1	137	217	460	188	284	604	245	364	768	314
50	2	164	226	473	223	294	623	293	376	793	375
50	3	186	235	486	252	304	640	331	387	816	423

TABLE G2428.3-2
Type B Gas Vent Size for Multiple Appliances Using Single Wall Vent Connector
Common Vent Capacity

vent height feet	vent D inches 4	vent D inches 4	vent D inches 4	vent D inches 5	vent D inches 5	vent D inches 5	vent D inches 6	vent D inches 6	vent D inches 6	vent D inches 7	vent D inches 7	vent D inches 7
	fan +fan	fan +nat	nat +nat	fan +fan	fan +nat	nat +nat	fan +fan	fan +nat	nat +nat	fan +fan	fan +nat	nat +nat
6	NA	78	64	NA	113	99	200	158	144	304	244	196
8	NA	87	71	NA	126	111	218	173	159	331	269	218
10	NA	94	76	163	137	120	237	189	174	357	292	236
15	121	108	88	189	159	140	275	221	200	416	343	274
20	131	118	98	208	177	156	305	247	223	463	383	302
30	145	132	113	236	202	180	350	286	257	533	446	349
50	159	145	128	268	233	208	406	337	296	622	529	410

TABLE G2428.3-2
Type B Gas Vent Size for Multiple Appliances Using Single Wall Vent Connector
Common Vent Capacity

vent height feet	vent D inches 8	vent D inches 8	vent D inches 8	vent D inches 9	vent D inches 9	vent D inches 9	vent D inches 10	vent D inches 10	vent D inches 10
	fan +fan	fan +nat	nat +nat	fan +fan	fan +nat	nat +nat	fan +fan	fan +nat	nat +nat
6	398	310	257	541	429	332	665	515	407
8	436	342	285	592	473	373	730	569	460
10	467	369	309	638	512	398	787	617	487
15	544	434	357	738	599	456	905	718	553
20	606	487	395	824	673	512	1013	808	626
30	703	570	459	958	790	593	1183	952	723
50	833	686	535	1139	954	689	1418	1157	838

MASONRY CHIMNEY SIZE TABLE WHEN CHIMNEY USED AS VENT FOR GAS APPLIANCES USING TYPE B VENT CONNECTOR (G2428.3-3)

Appliances and Equipment Covered by this Table

1. Apply this table to Category I gas appliances and natural draft appliances that would be classified as Category I appliances if they were classified. These appliances include most draft hood water heaters and most fan-assisted gas furnaces. Do not apply this table to Category II, III, & IV gas appliances, wall furnaces that use Type BW vents, decorative gas appliances, and other appliances not listed for use with a Type B vent.
2. Use this table for installations involving gas appliances connected to one masonry chimney

flue using Type B vent connectors. The values in the table are appliance input ratings in thousands of Btu/hour.

TABLE G2428.3-3
Masonry Chimney Size for Gas Appliances Using Type B Vent Connector
Type B Vent Connector Capacity

vent height feet	connect rise feet	connect D inches 3 fan min	connect D inches 3 fan max	connect D inches 3 nat max	connect D inches 4 fan min	connect D inches 4 fan max	connect D inches 4 nat max	connect D inches 5 fan min	connect D inches 5 fan max	connect D inches 5 nat max	connect D inches 6 fan min	connect D inches 6 fan max
6	1	24	33	21	39	62	40	52	106	67	65	194
6	2	26	43	28	41	79	52	53	133	85	67	230
6	3	27	49	34	42	92	61	55	155	97	69	262
8	1	24	39	22	39	72	41	55	117	69	71	213
8	2	26	47	29	40	87	53	57	140	86	73	246
8	3	27	52	34	42	97	62	59	159	98	75	269
10	1	24	42	22	38	80	42	55	130	71	74	232
10	2	26	50	29	40	93	54	57	153	87	76	261
10	3	27	55	35	41	105	63	58	170	100	78	284
15	1	24	48	23	38	93	44	54	154	74	72	277
15	2	25	55	31	39	105	55	56	174	89	74	299
15	3	26	59	35	41	115	64	57	189	102	76	319
20	1	24	52	24	37	102	46	53	172	77	71	313
20	2	25	58	31	39	114	56	55	190	91	73	335
20	3	26	63	35	40	123	65	57	204	104	75	353
30	1	24	54	25	37	111	48	52	192	82	69	357
30	2	25	60	32	38	122	58	54	208	95	72	376
30	3	26	64	36	40	131	66	56	221	107	74	392
50	1	23	51	25	36	116	51	51	209	89	67	405
50	2	24	59	32	37	127	61	53	225	102	70	421
50	3	26	64	36	39	135	69	55	237	115	72	435

TABLE G2428.3-3
Masonry Chimney Vent Size for Gas Appliances Using Type B Vent Connector
Type B Vent Connector Capacity

vent height feet	connect rise feet	connect D inches 6 nat max	connect D inches 7 fan min	connect D inches 7 fan max	connect D inches 7 nat max	connect D inches 8 fan min	connect D inches 8 fan max	connect D inches 8 nat max	connect D inches 9 fan min	connect D inches 9 fan max	connect D inches 9 nat max
6	1	101	87	274	141	104	370	201	124	479	253
6	2	124	89	324	173	107	436	232	127	562	300
6	3	143	91	369	203	109	491	270	129	633	349
8	1	105	94	304	148	113	414	210	134	539	267
8	2	127	97	350	179	116	473	240	137	615	311
8	3	145	99	383	206	119	517	276	139	672	358
10	1	108	101	324	153	120	444	216	142	582	277
10	2	129	103	366	184	123	498	247	145	652	321
10	3	148	106	397	209	126	540	281	147	705	366
15	1	114	100	384	164	125	511	229	153	658	297
15	2	134	103	419	192	128	558	260	156	718	339
15	3	153	105	448	215	131	597	292	159	760	382
20	1	119	98	437	173	123	584	239	150	752	312
20	2	138	101	467	199	126	625	270	153	805	354
20	3	157	104	493	222	129	661	301	156	851	396
30	1	127	96	504	187	119	680	255	145	883	337
30	2	145	99	531	209	122	715	287	149	928	378
30	3	163	101	554	233	125	746	317	152	968	418
50	1	143	92	582	213	115	798	294	140	1049	392
50	2	161	95	604	235	118	827	326	143	1085	433
50	3	180	98	624	260	121	854	357	147	1118	474

TABLE G2428.3-3
Masonry Chimney Vent Size for Gas Appliances
Using Type B Vent Connector
Chimney Flue Capacity

vent height feet	chim area inches 12	chim area inches 12	chim area inches 12	chim area inches 19	chim area inches 19	chim area inches 19	chim area inches 28	chim area inches 28	chim area inches 28	chim area inches 38	chim area inches 38	chim area inches 38
	fan +fan	fan +nat	nat +nat	fan +fan	fan +nat	nat +nat	fan +fan	fan +nat	nat +nat	fan +fan	fan +nat	nat +nat
6	NA	74	25	NA	119	46	NA	178	71	NA	257	103
8	NA	80	28	NA	130	53	NA	193	82	NA	279	119
10	NA	84	31	NA	138	56	NA	207	90	NA	299	131
15	NA	NA	36	NA	152	67	NA	233	106	NA	334	152
20	NA	NA	41	NA	NA	75	NA	250	122	NA	368	172
30	NA	NA	NA	NA	NA	NA	NA	270	137	NA	404	198
50	NA	NA	NA	NA	NA	NA	NA	NA	NA	NA	NA	NA

TABLE G2428.3-3
Masonry Chimney Vent Size for Gas Appliances
Using Type B Vent Connector
Chimney Flue Capacity

vent height feet	chim area inches 50	chim area inches 50	chim area inches 50	chim area inches 63	chim area inches 63	chim area inches 63	chim area inches 78	chim area inches 78	chim area inches 78	chim area inches 113	chim area inches 113	chim area inches 113
	fan +fan	fan +nat	nat +nat	fan +fan	fan +nat	nat +nat	fan +fan	fan +nat	nat +nat	fan +fan	fan +nat	nat +nat
6	NA	351	143	NA	458	188	NA	582	246	1041	853	NA
8	NA	384	163	NA	501	218	724	636	278	1144	937	408
10	NA	409	177	606	538	236	776	686	302	1226	1010	454
15	523	467	212	682	611	283	874	781	365	1374	1156	546
20	565	508	243	742	668	325	955	858	419	1513	1286	648
30	615	564	278	816	747	381	1062	969	496	1702	1473	749
50	NA	620	328	879	831	461	1165	1089	606	1905	1692	922

MASONRY CHIMNEY SIZE TABLE WHEN CHIMNEY USED AS VENT FOR GAS APPLIANCES USING SINGLE WALL VENT CONNECTOR (G2428.3-4)

Appliances and Equipment Covered by this Table

1. Apply this table to Category I gas appliances and natural draft appliances that would be classified as Category I appliances if they were classified. These appliances include most draft hood water heaters and most fan-assisted gas furnaces. Do not apply this table to

Category II, III, & IV gas appliances, wall furnaces that use Type BW vents, decorative gas appliances, and other appliances not listed for use with a Type B vent.

2. Use this table for installations involving gas appliances connected to one masonry chimney flue using single wall metal vent connectors. The values in the table are appliance input ratings in thousands of Btu/hour.

TABLE G2428.3-4
Masonry Chimney Vent Size for Gas Appliances Using Single Wall Vent Connector
Single Wall Vent Connector Capacity

vent height feet	connect rise feet	connect D inches 3 fan min	connect D inches 3 fan max	connect D inches 3 nat max	connect D inches 4 fan min	connect D inches 4 fan max	connect D inches 4 nat max	connect D inches 5 fan min	connect D inches 5 fan max	connect D inches 5 nat max	connect D inches 6 fan min	connect D inches 6 fan max
6	1	NA	NA	21	NA	NA	39	NA	NA	66	179	191
6	2	NA	NA	28	NA	NA	52	NA	NA	84	189	227
6	3	NA	NA	34	NA	NA	61	134	153	97	193	258
8	1	NA	NA	21	NA	NA	40	NA	NA	68	195	208
8	2	NA	NA	28	NA	NA	52	137	139	85	202	240
8	3	NA	NA	34	NA	NA	62	143	156	98	210	264
10	1	NA	NA	22	NA	NA	41	130	151	70	202	225
10	2	NA	NA	29	NA	NA	53	136	150	86	210	255
10	3	NA	NA	34	97	102	62	143	166	99	217	277
15	1	NA	NA	23	NA	NA	43	129	151	73	199	271
15	2	NA	NA	30	92	103	54	135	170	88	207	295
15	3	NA	NA	34	96	112	63	141	185	101	215	315
20	1	NA	NA	23	87	99	45	128	167	76	197	303
20	2	NA	NA	30	91	111	55	134	185	90	205	325
20	3	NA	NA	35	96	119	64	140	199	103	213	343
30	1	NA	NA	24	86	108	47	126	187	80	193	347
30	2	NA	NA	31	91	119	57	132	203	93	201	366
30	3	NA	NA	35	95	127	65	138	216	105	209	381
50	1	NA	NA	24	85	113	50	124	204	87	188	392
50	2	NA	NA	31	89	123	60	130	218	100	196	408
50	3	NA	NA	35	94	131	68	136	231	112	205	422

TABLE G2428.3-4
Masonry Chimney Vent Size for Gas Appliances Using Single Wall Vent Connector
Single Wall Vent Connector Capacity

vent height feet	connect rise feet	connect D inches 6	connect D inches 7	connect D inches 7	connect D inches 7	connect D inches 8	connect D inches 8	connect D inches 8	connect D inches 9	connect D inches 9	connect D inches 9
		nat max	fan min	fan max	nat max	fan min	fan max	nat max	fan min	fan max	nat max
6	1	100	231	271	140	292	366	200	362	474	252
6	2	123	239	321	172	301	432	231	373	557	299
6	3	142	247	365	202	309	491	269	381	634	348
8	1	103	250	298	146	313	407	207	387	530	263
8	2	125	258	343	177	323	465	238	397	607	309
8	3	145	266	376	205	332	509	274	407	663	356
10	1	106	267	316	151	333	434	213	410	571	273
10	2	128	276	358	181	343	489	244	420	640	317
10	3	147	284	389	207	352	530	279	430	694	363
15	1	112	268	376	161	349	502	225	445	646	291
15	2	132	277	411	189	359	548	256	456	706	334
15	3	151	286	439	213	368	586	289	466	755	378
20	1	117	265	425	169	345	569	235	439	734	306
20	2	136	274	455	195	355	610	266	450	787	348
20	3	154	282	481	219	365	644	298	461	831	391
30	1	124	259	492	183	338	665	250	430	864	330
30	2	142	269	518	205	348	699	282	442	908	372
30	3	160	277	540	229	358	729	312	452	946	412
50	1	139	252	567	208	328	778	287	417	1022	383
50	2	158	262	588	230	339	806	320	429	1058	425
50	3	176	271	607	255	349	831	351	440	1090	466

TABLE G2428.3-4
Masonry Chimney Vent Size for Gas Appliances
Using Single Wall Vent Connector
Chimney Flue Capacity

vent height feet	chim area inches 12	chim area inches 12	chim area inches 12	chim area inches 19	chim area inches 19	chim area inches 19	chim area inches 28	chim area inches 28	chim area inches 28	chim area inches 38	chim area inches 38	chim area inches 38
	fan +fan	fan +nat	nat +nat	fan +fan	fan +nat	nat +nat	fan +fan	fan +nat	nat +nat	fan +fan	fan +nat	nat +nat
6	NA	NA	25	NA	118	45	NA	176	71	NA	255	102
8	NA	NA	28	NA	128	52	NA	190	81	NA	276	118
10	NA	NA	31	NA	136	56	NA	205	89	NA	295	129
15	NA	NA	36	NA	NA	66	NA	230	105	NA	335	150
20	NA	NA	NA	NA	NA	74	NA	247	120	NA	362	170
30	NA	NA	NA	NA	NA	NA	NA	NA	135	NA	398	195
50	NA	NA	NA	NA	NA	NA	NA	NA	NA	NA	NA	NA

TABLE G2428.3-4
Masonry Chimney Vent Size for Gas Appliances
Using Single Wall Vent Connector
Chimney Flue Capacity

vent height feet	chim area inches 50	chim area inches 50	chim area inches 50	chim area inches 63	chim area inches 63	chim area inches 63	chim area inches 78	chim area inches 78	chim area inches 78	chim area inches 113	chim area inches 113	chim area inches 113
	fan +fan	fan +nat	nat +nat	fan +fan	fan +nat	nat +nat	fan +fan	fan +nat	nat +nat	fan +fan	fan +nat	nat +nat
6	NA	348	142	NA	455	187	NA	579	245	NA	846	NA
8	NA	380	162	NA	497	217	NA	633	277	1136	928	405
10	NA	405	175	NA	532	234	771	680	300	1216	1000	450
15	NA	400	210	677	602	280	866	772	360	1359	1139	540
20	NA	503	240	765	661	321	947	849	415	1495	1264	640
30	NA	558	275	808	739	377	1052	957	490	1682	1447	740
50	NA	612	325	NA	821	456	1152	1076	600	1879	1672	910

UNVENTED GAS ROOM HEATERS (G2445)

Unvented Room Heater Description

Unvented room heaters provide supplemental heat to a single room or adjacent rooms. If they have no fan, they provide heat by natural movement of the heated air and by thermal radiation. Because these heaters become very hot, proper installation is important to prevent fires. Because they are unvented, proper installation is important to prevent carbon monoxide poisoning.

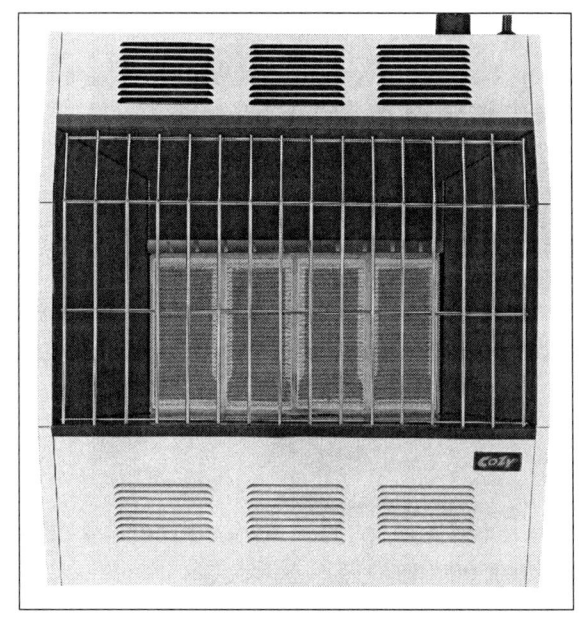

Unvented Room Heater (MG2445-0]
Figure 24-32

General Installation Requirements

1. Install unvented room heaters according to manufacturer's installation instructions and relevant provisions of the IRC.
2. Do not use unvented room heaters as the sole heat source for a home.
3. Use unvented room heaters that have in input rating not more than (≤) 40,000 Btu/hour.
4. Equip unvented room heaters with an oxygen depletion safety shutoff system that shuts off gas supply to the main and pilot burners when the surrounding oxygen levels are less than the manufacturer's setting. Do not allow field adjustment of the oxygen-depletion set point.
5. Do not install unvented room heaters in a space where the total Btu input rating of all unvented appliances exceeds (>) 20 Btu per cubic foot of space volume. You may add the volume of other spaces that are open to the space where the room heater is located if the space(s) are permanently open with no door between them.

Unvented Gas Room Heater Prohibited Locations

1. Do not locate or use an unvented gas room heater in: (a) bedrooms, (b) bathrooms, (c) toilet rooms, and (d) storage closets unless an exception applies.
2. You may install one listed wall-mounted unvented room heater in a bathroom if the appliance has an oxygen depletion safety shutoff system, and if the appliance Btu/hour input rating is not more than (≤) 6,000, and if the bathroom satisfies the volume requirements of Chapter 24.
3. You may install one listed wall-mounted unvented room heater in a bedroom if the appliance has an oxygen depletion safety shutoff system, and if the appliance Btu/hour input rating is not more than (≤) 10,000, and if the bedroom satisfies the volume requirements of Chapter 24.

Unvented Log Heaters

1. Do not install unvented log heaters in a factory-built fireplace unless the fireplace system is listed and labeled for installation of these log heaters.

GAS COOKING APPLIANCES (G2447)

Appliances and Equipment Governed by these Code Provisions

1. Apply these code provisions to gas cooking appliances intended for permanent installation. This does not include portable appliances with portable gas supplies such as outdoor grills.

Commercial Cooking Appliances

1. Do not use gas appliances listed and labeled for commercial use in a dwelling unit or in an area where domestic cooking occurs.
2. Use only gas appliances listed and labeled for domestic use in a dwelling unit or in an area where domestic cooking occurs.

Gas Ranges on Combustible Floors

1. Install gas ranges that rest on a combustible floor on manufacturer supplied legs or base.
2. Provide clearances to combustible materials on all sides, top, and bottom of the range according to manufacturer's instructions.

Gas Cooking Appliance Clearance Above Cooktop

1. Provide at least (≥) 30 inches above a gas range or cooktop and any combustible material and metal cabinets.
2. You may reduce the clearance to at least (≥) 24 inches if you install a microwave oven or other cooking appliance according to manufacturer's instruction or if you install a metal kitchen exhaust hood with at least (≥) ¼ inch between the hood and any combustible material and metal cabinets.

GAS LIGHTING (G2450)

Gas Lighting General Installation Requirements

1. Install gaslights according to manufacturer's instructions.
2. Attach gaslights to substantial supports, such as framing members, when installing gaslights on walls or ceilings. Do not rely on the gas pipe for support of gaslights.
3. Use a 2 ½ inch diameter, 0.064 inch steel post, or a 1 inch, Schedule 40 steel pipe, or materials of equal strength to mount gaslights on posts more than (>) 3 feet high.
4. Use at least (≥) ¾ inch, Schedule 40 steel pipe to mount gaslights on posts not more than (≤) 3 feet high.
5. Provide drain holes at the post base if water may collect inside the post.

Gaslight Pressure Regulator

1. Provide a gas pressure regulator of appropriate capacity and gas outlet pressure for gas pipes serving gas lights if the gas light does not come with a manufacturer supplied gas pressure regulator and if an appropriate gas pressure regulator does not already exist on the gas line serving the light. You may use one gas pressure regulator of sufficient capacity for multiple gaslights.

25

PLUMBING ADMINISTRATION

PLUMBING SYSTEMS CHANGES, INSPECTION, TESTING, AND MAINTENANCE (P2502 AND P2503)

Updates and Changes to Plumbing Systems

1. Comply with IRC provisions <u>in effect when the work is performed</u> when making additions, adjustments, alterations, and major repairs to existing plumbing systems. Only the new system components must comply with current IRC provisions. You are not required to make existing plumbing system components comply with current IRC standards, unless the new work causes the existing plumbing system to become unsafe, unsanitary, or overloaded.
2. You do not need to comply with current IRC provisions when making minor additions, adjustments, alterations, and repairs to existing plumbing systems, if the work is performed using methods and materials equivalent to existing methods and materials, and if the work does not cause the existing system to become unsafe, and if the work is approved.

Using Existing Building Sewers

1. You may use the existing building sewer and building drain when making changes to an existing plumbing system if the existing building sewer and drain is examined or tested and conforms to current IRC provisions.

Plumbing System Inspection Notice to Inspector

1. Notify the building official when the plumbing system is ready for inspection and do not cover or conceal work requiring inspection until approved by the building official.
2. Provide all test equipment, materials, and labor required by the building official for testing the plumbing system. Test materials and equipment include water and/or air for testing pipes and any required test gauges.

Plumbing System Inspection Materials and Procedures

1. Test the building sewer by inserting a test plug at the connection point with the public sewer and then filling the building sewer with water to a point at least (≥) 10 feet above the highest point of the building sewer pipe. Maintain the test without visible leaks for at least (≥) 15 minutes.
2. Test the rough plumbing drain system pipes by inserting a test plug at the connection point with the building sewer (or the end of a section of pipes to be tested) and filling the pipes with water to a point at least (≥) 10 feet above the highest point of the drain system pipes

being tested. You may, as an alternative, fill the pipes with at least (≥) 5 psi of air. Maintain the test without visible leaks for at least (≥) 15 minutes.
3. Test the rough plumbing water supply system with water under at least (≥) the working pressure of the water supply system. You may, as an alternative for pipes other than plastic, fill the pipes with at least (≥) 50 psi of air.
4. Test the finished plumbing traps and fixture connections by filling and draining the fixtures and visually determining that they are water-tight. You may, as an alternative, use a smoke test or a peppermint test. These tests are not commonly used.
5. Test site-built shower receptors according to the procedures in IRC Section P2503.6.

Backflow Prevention Devices Inspection and Testing

1. Inspect and test backflow prevention devices when installed.
2. Test the following devices after repairs or relocation and not less than annually: (a) reduced pressure backflow preventers, (b) double check valve assemblies, (c) double-detector check valve assemblies, (d) pressure vacuum breaker assemblies.

Test Gauges

1. Use test gauges that register in increments small enough to accurately display the required test pressures. Example: use a gauge that registers in 1 psi or fewer increments when the test pressure is between 10 and 100 psi.

26

GENERAL PLUMBING INSTALLATION REQUIREMENTS

PLUMBING PIPE GENERAL INSTALLATION REQUIREMENTS

Connection of Drainage Pipes and Fixtures to Sewer Systems (P2602.1)

1. Connect all plumbing drainage pipes, fixtures, and appliances to the building's sanitary sewer system (sewer or septic system). No part of the plumbing system should receive water from the system without providing a means to dispose of the water into the building's sanitary sewer system.
2. You may connect bathtubs, showers, sinks, and clothes washers to an approved gray water recycling system. Refer to IRC Appendix O for gray water recycling system requirements.

Flood-Resistant Installation (P2602.2)

1. Install water supply and drainage systems (pipes) so that they will not admit or discharge contents during flooding. Apply this rule to flood prone areas defined by the local building official.

Plumbing Pipe Protection Against Punctures (P2603.2.1)

1. Protect plumbing pipes (other than cast-iron or galvanized steel) with at least (≥) 16 gage thick shield plates if the pipe is closer than (<) 1 ½ inch from the edge of studs, joists, rafters, or similar framing members. Extend the shield plate at least (≥) 2 inches below top plates and at least (≥) 2 inches above bottom plates.
2. Apply these rules to pipes running through holes and notches in framing materials. While not required by the IRC, it is a best practice to protect pipes (other than cast-iron or galvanized steel) that are closer than (<) 1 ½ inch from the edge of framing materials. The most common example of such pipes is a pipe installed parallel to the edge of a stud or joist.

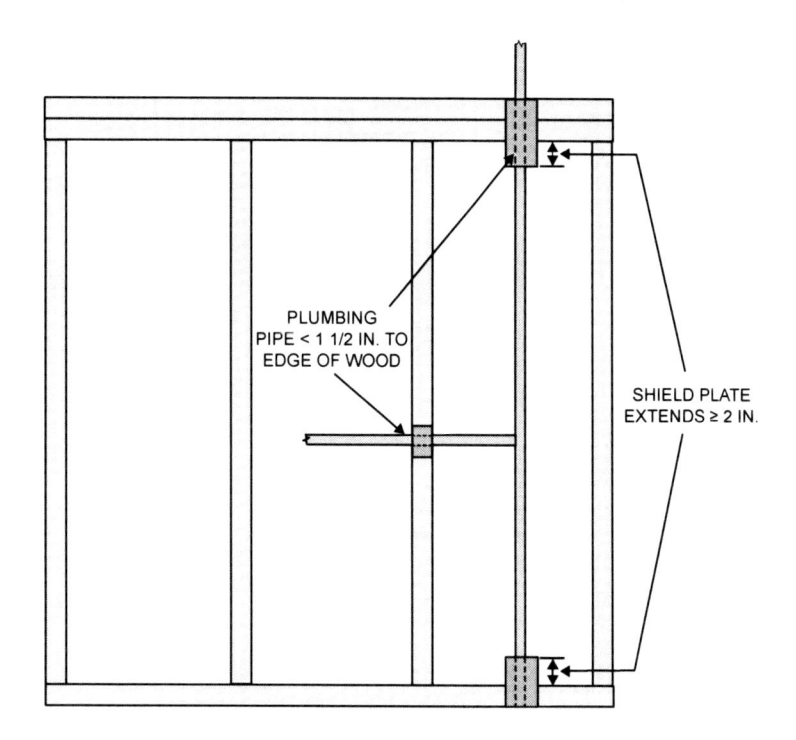

Water Pipe Protection Against Punctures (P2603.2.1-0)
Figure 26-1

Plumbing Pipe Protection Against Corrosion (P2603.3)

1. Protect metal plumbing pipes against external corrosion if they are contained in or pass through or under concrete or masonry walls and floors, steel framing, or other corrosive materials. Use sheathing or wrapping material that is at least (≥) 0.025 inch thick. Install the protective material so that any expansion or contraction of the pipe will not cause rubbing.

Plumbing Pipe Protection Against Breaking (P2603.4 and P2603.5)

1. Install a pipe sleeve or an arch that relieves pressure from the pipe if the pipe passes under a footing or through a foundation wall. Use a pipe sleeve that is two pipe sizes larger than the pipe passing through the footing or wall.
2. Fill the space between the pipe and pipe sleeve with caulk or other material approved by the building official. Use fire-resistant material if the pipe sleeve is in a fire-resistive assembly.
3. Protect all plumbing pipes from breakage if the pipe passes through or under any walls. The IRC does not specify the type of protection required for above grade walls.

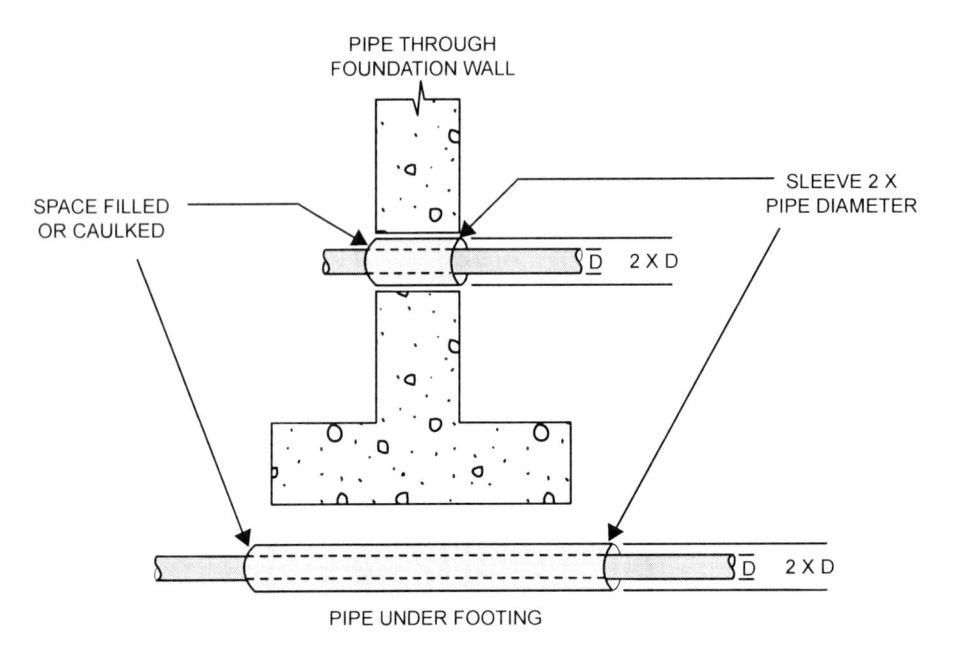

Water Pipe Protection Against Breaking (P2603.4-0)
Figure 26-2

Plumbing Pipe Protection Against Freezing (P2603.6)

1. Do not install water supply and waste pipes outside of a building, or in exterior building walls, or in attics and crawl spaces, or in any other place subject to freezing temperatures unless the pipes are protected by insulation or heat or both.
2. Install water service pipe at least (≥) 12 inches deep or at least (≥) 6 inches below the frost line.
3. Verify minimum building sewer depth with the local building official.
4. Apply these requirements only to areas with a winter design temperature of (≤) 32° F. or less.

Plumbing Pipe Trenching and Backfilling (P2604)

1. Install plumbing pipes in trenches so that the pipe rests on continuous support consisting of either undisturbed soil or stable and compacted fill. Use compacted fine soil, sand, fine gravel, or similar material when filling the bottom of trenches before placing plumbing pipes. Do not place pipes on unstable soils or soils containing large rocks, construction debris, or plant limbs, roots, or stumps. Do not use these types of materials to backfill a trench until the trench is filled to at least (≥) 12 inches above the pipe.
2. Excavate trenches in rocky or unstable soil at least (≥) two pipe diameters larger than the pipe and backfill the trench with compacted fine soil, sand, fine gravel, or similar material.
3. Backfill trenches with material not more than (≤) 6 inches thick before tamping the material in place. Continue backfilling the trench in tamped layers not more than (≤) 6 inches thick until the trench is filled. This helps avoid trench sagging after construction is complete and helps reduce stress on the pipe.

Trenches Parallel to Footings (P2604.4)

1. Do not dig trenches or install plumbing pipes that run parallel to a footing or wall if the trench or pipe is more than (>) 45 degrees below the bearing plane of the wall or footing.

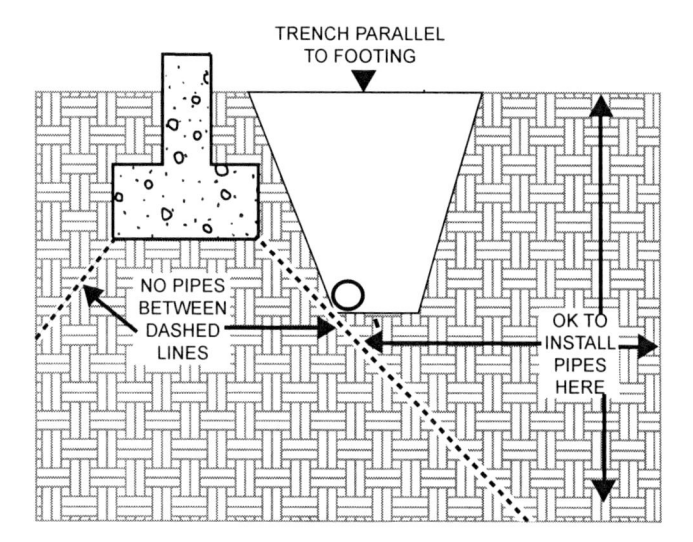

Trenches Parallel to Footings (P2604.4-0)
Figure 26-3

Plumbing Pipe Support (P2605)

1. Support pipes so they will maintain alignment and will not sag.
2. Support and install pipes so they can move with the normal expansion and contraction of the piping system without scraping or rubbing against supports or framing materials.
3. Use pipe supports that will carry the weight of the pipe and that are sufficiently wide to prevent crimping and distortion of the pipe.
4. Use pipe supports that will not cause corrosion or galvanic reaction between the pipe and the support. Example: do not use steel supports with copper pipe or copper supports with cast-iron pipe.
5. Provide rigid sway bracing at changes in pipe direction more than (>) 45 degrees for pipe sizes at least (≥) 4 inches diameter.
6. Provide horizontal and vertical support for pipes according to the following table.

TABLE P2605
Plumbing Pipe Support

pipe material	maximum horizontal spacing (inches)	maximum vertical spacing (inches)	mid story guide required for pipe diameters ≤ 2 inches
ABS pipe	48	120	yes
Cast-iron pipe	60 (a)	180	no
Copper pipe	144	120	no
Copper tubing (≤ 1 ¼ inches diameter)	72	120	no
Copper tubing (≥ 1 ½ inches diameter)	120	120	no
CPVC pipe or tubing (≤ 1 inch diameter)	36	120	yes
CPVC pipe or tubing (≥ 1 ¼ inch diameter)	48	120	yes
Polybutylene (PB) pipe or tubing	32	48	no
PEX	32	120	yes
PEX-AL-PEX and PE-AL-PE	32	48	yes
PVC pipe	48	120	yes
Steel pipe	144	180	no

a) You may increase cast-iron pipe horizontal spacing to 120 inches when using 10 feet pipe lengths.

Plumbing Pipe Roof and Wall Penetrations (P2606)

1. Make all exterior penetrations of roofs and walls by plumbing pipes water-tight. You may use any approved material such as lead, copper, galvanized steel, or approved elastomeric material.
2. Do not decrease the internal pipe diameter when installing flashing inside the pipe.

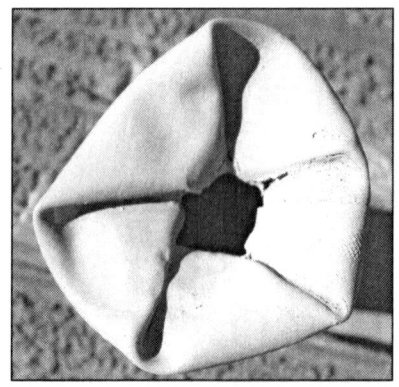

Plumbing Vent Size Restricted by Flashing (PP2606-0)
Figure 26-4

27

PLUMBING FIXTURES

DEFINITIONS OF TERMS USED IN PLUMBING SYSTEMS

Air admittance valve An air admittance valve is a one-way valve attached to a plumbing vent pipe. It is used when extending a vent to the roof or to another vent is impractical or not desirable. The valve allows air into the vent system when there is negative pressure in the vent pipe and closes to limit the flow of sewer gas into the home.

Branch drain A branch drain is a drainage pipe that takes soil and/or waste from fixture drains to a stack or to the building drain.

Branch vent A branch vent connects individual vents to a vent stack or stack vent.

Braze (Brazing) Brazing is a method of joining metal pipe (such as copper and brass) at temperatures exceeding 1,000° F. Brazing is sometimes called silver soldering because it uses a silver alloy as the brazing material. Brazed joints are stronger than soldered joints.

Building drain (sub-drain) The building drain is usually the lowest horizontal drain pipe in the building and collects material from branches and stacks. It extends to 30 inches beyond the foundation where it connects with the building sewer. A building with fixtures below the building drain (such as in a basement) has a building sub-drain. Material in a sub-drain must be pumped up to the building drain.

Building sewer Building sewer usually refers to the pipes beginning at the building drain and ending at the public sewer or septic tank.

Drain pipe Drain pipe usually refers to the pipes inside the building that take soil and waste to the building sewer pipe.

Fittings A fitting is a device that connects parts of the plumbing system together and allows pipes to change direction. Drainage fittings include wyes, sweeps, bends, tees, and couplings. Water supply fittings include elbows, tees, couplings, and valves.

Fixture A fixture is a device that connects to water supply pipes and connects to plumbing waste pipes. Fixtures include toilets (water closets), bathroom sinks (lavatories), kitchen and laundry sinks, bathtubs, and showers.

Fixture drain A fixture drain is the horizontal pipe between a trap outlet and the fitting connecting it to another drain pipe. A fixture drain is sometimes called a trap arm. Any pipe after the fitting is not part of the fixture drain.

Hub (hubless) A hub is an enlarged opening molded on the end of a pipe or a fitting into which a section of pipe (the spigot) is inserted. In older plumbing, cast iron hubs and spigots were sealed with oakum or hemp and lead. In modern plumbing, you may seal cast iron hubs and spigots with an elastomeric O-ring gasket or you may remove the hub and convert the pipe into a hubless pipe. A hubless pipe is one without a hub. Hubless pipe joints are often sealed by an elastomeric sleeve held in place by stainless steel rings.

Laundry tray A laundry tray is a sink, usually located in a laundry area, used for various laundry related and other purposes. It is also known as a laundry sink or a deep sink. You may discharge a clothes washing machine into a laundry tray instead of into a standpipe.

Offset An offset in a vertical drain pipe (stack) is a change in direction in the pipe from vertical to an angle other than vertical then back to vertical. Offsets are most often used to run a stack around an obstruction (such as a wall or beam) that cannot be drilled or notched. An offset that is not more than (≤) 45 degrees from vertical is defined to be vertical.

Receptor (indirect waste) The term receptor refers to a device such as a floor sink or a floor drain. Indirect waste receptors have a source of water that is not directly and permanently connected to the receptor. Example: a floor drain could receive condensate water from an air conditioning system. The condensate drain is not directly and permanently connected to the floor drain. Shower pans are referred to in the IRC as shower receptors.

Saddle fitting A saddle fitting is a connection between pipes where a new pipe is attached to an existing pipe by puncturing the existing pipe and clamping the new pipe to the existing pipe. Saddle fittings are sometimes used to tap existing water supply pipes for low volume applications such as refrigerator ice-makers and reverse osmosis water treatment systems. Saddle fittings are prohibited in drainage pipes, but are often found in low volume applications such as reverse osmosis water treatment system waste tubing connection to trap arms.

Slip joint A slip joint is a hand-tightened fitting at the inlet and outlet side of traps. Slip joints allow easy removal of the trap for cleaning. Slip joints must be accessible.

Soil Soil is material in the plumbing drainage system that contains urine or fecal material.

Solder (Soldering) Soldering is a method of joining metal pipe (such as copper and brass) at temperatures that do not exceed 800° F. Soldering usually uses a tin alloy as the joining material. Soldered joints are weaker than brazed joints.

Stack A stack is a vertical plumbing drain or waste pipe that extends one or more stories. A stack collects waste material from horizontal drainage pipes and conducts it to the building drain or other horizontal drain.

Stack vent A stack vent is a dry vent that connects to a soil or waste stack above the highest horizontal drainage connection and may extend through the roof to the outdoors or may terminate with a stack-type air admittance valve.

Standpipe A standpipe is a vertical pipe used as an indirect waste receptor. Standpipes are most often used as the receptor for a clothes washing machine.

Washing Machine Standpipe Rough-in (PP2700-1)
Figure 27-1

Stop-and-Waste Valve A stop-and-waste valve is a water supply valve with an opening that allows draining of the non-pressure side. These valves are most common in cold climates and are used to protect exterior water fixtures from freeze damage.

Tail piece A tail piece is a short piece of vertical pipe that runs from the plumbing fixture waste outlet (drain) to the inlet side of the fixture's trap.

Trap (P trap) A trap is a fitting, usually located either inside or under fixtures, that prevents sewer gasses from escaping from the plumbing waste pipes. Traps maintain a water seal (trap seal) extending from the trap's crown weir to its dip. Vents help protect the water seal from siphoning.

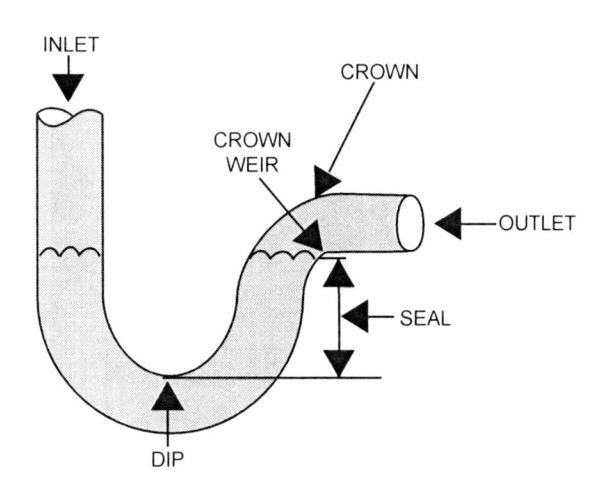

Trap Parts (P2700-0)
Figure 27-2

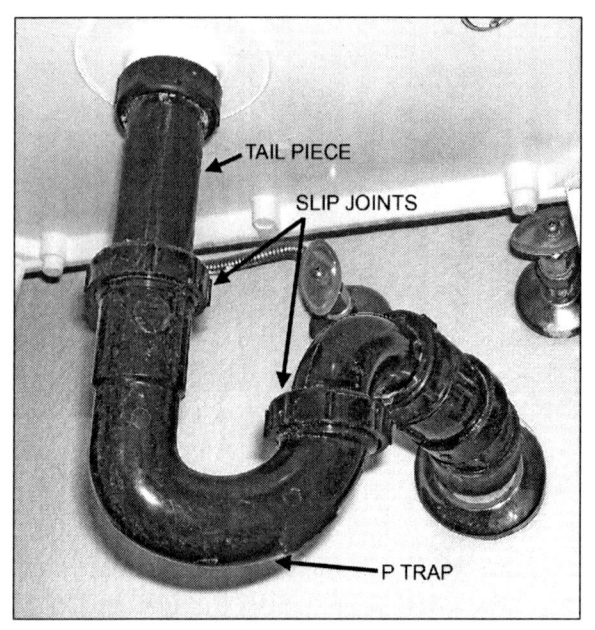

P Trap with Slip Joints (PP2700-2)
Figure 27-3

Vent A vent is pipe or mechanical device that allows air into the plumbing drain pipes to equalize air pressure in the pipes. Plumbing vents help avoid draining (siphoning) traps and help waste water flow freely through the system. Plumbing vents usually terminate on the roof, although mechanical vents (called air admittance valves) are allowed in some circumstances.

Individual Vent Rough-in (PP2700-3)
Figure 27-4

Vent stack A vent stack is a dry vent that connects at or near the connection of a soil or waste stack and a horizontal drain. A vent stack runs vertically and often runs parallel to the soil or waste stack that it vents.

27 : Plumbing Fixtures   357

Yard Hydrant (freeze proof) A freeze proof yard hydrant is an outdoor water supply outlet that has a valve and outlet above ground and a drain opening below the frost level. When the valve is opened, water flows. When the valve is closed, the water supply to the hydrant is shut off below the frost level and a drain hole is opened that allows the water in the yard hydrant pipe to drain into a gravel bed. This drains the yard hydrant and its riser so that the hydrant will not freeze.

Waste Liquid material in the plumbing drainage system that does not contain urine or fecal material. Waste is sometimes referred to as gray water. Waste comes from all plumbing fixtures except toilets and urinals.

PLUMBING FIXTURES GENERAL INSTALLATION REQUIREMENTS

Plumbing Fixtures Specifications (P2701.1)

1. Use approved plumbing fixtures and fittings made of approved materials that have been tested to comply with code approved standards. Most fixtures and fittings have the label of a testing company or some other seal that indicates code acceptance on the item or in its packaging.
2. Use fixtures and fittings that have smooth surfaces that are impervious to water flow. You may not use the ribbed, flexible traps and tail pieces sold in some home improvement stores.
3. Provide fixtures with a water supply that will keep them flushed and clean.
4. Do not allow water that has flowed into a plumbing fixture to connect to the potable water supply or to flow back from the fixture into the potable water supply.

Strainers for Plumbing Fixtures (P2702.1)

1. Provide each plumbing fixture, other than indirect receptors and toilets, with an approved strainer or similar device. Approved devices include pop-up stoppers and crossbars.

Tail Pieces (P2703)

1. Provide sinks, dishwashers, laundry tubs, and similar fixtures with tail pieces and traps at least (≥) 1 ½ inches diameter.
2. Provide vanity sinks, bidets, and similar fixtures with tail pieces and traps at least (≥) 1 ¼ inches.

Slip Joints (P2704)

1. Use slip joints only on a trap inlet, outlet, and within the trap seal.
2. Provide access to slip joints with access of at least (≥) 12 inches by 12 inches.

Fixture Installation (P2705)

1. Use corrosion-resistant screws, nuts, bolts, and washers to secure floor-outlet and floor-mounted fixtures such as toilets and bidets.

2. Support wall-mounted fixtures securely to the wall so that plumbing pipes do not carry the fixture's weight.
3. Make all contact points between fixtures and walls and floors water-tight. Contact points include between toilet bases and floors and between sinks and walls.
4. Do not install plumbing fixtures, pipes, or equipment so that they interfere with the operation of doors and windows.

Waste Receptor General Requirements (P2706.1 and 2706.3)

1. Use only approved waste receptors.
2. Install a removable strainer at the waste outlet of most waste receptors. The exception is an open hub or pipe extending at least (≥) 1 inch above a water-impervious floor.
3. Use waste receptors receiving indirect waste that are shaped and have the capacity to handle the waste flow without splashing or flooding. Provide ready access to these waste receptors for inspection and cleaning. Consider the rate of waste water flow and the height of the waste water source when determining the size and shape of an indirect waste receptor.
4. Install waste receptors in ventilated and accessible places. Do not install indirect waste receptors in bathrooms.
5. Do not discharge indirect waste into a plumbing fixture used for domestic or food preparation purposes. Such fixtures include kitchen and bathroom sinks, bathtubs, and showers. You may connect a dishwashing machine to a kitchen sink trap and you may discharge a clothes washing machine into a laundry tray.

Standpipes (P2706.2)

1. Extend a standpipe at least (≥) 18 inches and not more than (≤) 42 inches above the crown weir of the trap.
2. Provide access to standpipes for rodding.

Laundry Tray Connection to Standpipe (P2706.2.1)

1. You may connect a laundry tray waste pipe to a clothes washing machine standpipe if: (a) the standpipe is at least (≥) 30 inches tall measured from the standpipe trap weir, and if (b) the standpipe extends above the top rim of the laundry tray, and if (c) the laundry tray waste outlet is not more than (≤) 30 inches horizontally from the standpipe trap.

Disposal and Dishwasher Directional Fittings (P2707.1)

1. Use an approved directional fitting on the tail piece when connecting a disposal or dishwashing machine. This helps direct the waste down into the plumbing drain system and avoids blockage and blow back up the tail piece when these appliances discharge under pressure.

Toilets (Water Closets) (P2712)

1. Install toilets with an approved flushing mechanism that provides enough water to clear and refill the toilet bowl and refill the toilet's internal trap. Approved flushing mechanisms

are the common gravity feed flush tanks (one and two piece tanks) and power-assisted flushometer tanks or valves.

2. Install toilets that use an average of not more than (≤) 1.6 gallons per flush.
3. Provide the toilet with an adequate supply of water. Control the water supply with an automatic device (such as a float valve) that will refill the toilet tank after each flush and completely stop the flow of water to the tank when the tank is full. The device should also supply enough water to refill the toilet's internal trap.
4. Install toilets with a flush valve seat in the toilet tank that is at least (≥) 1 inch above the flood level of the toilet bowl. An alternate design (used by low-profile one piece toilets) is acceptable. This design closes the flush valve when the toilet is clogged and prevents water from flowing back into the tank.
5. Provide toilet tanks with an overflow pipe or mechanism that is sufficient to prevent the tank from flooding if the fill valve malfunctions.
6. Provide access to all parts in the toilet tank for repair and replacement.
7. Use toilet seats made of smooth, nonabsorbent material and are properly sized for the toilet bowl.
8. Use corrosion-resistant screws, nuts, bolts, and washers to secure toilets to the closet flange.

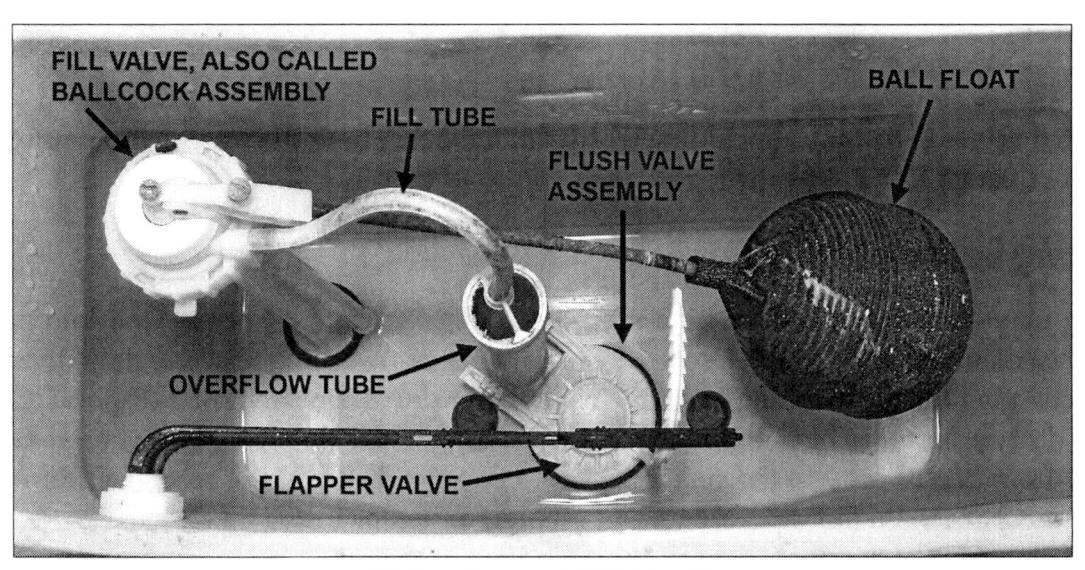

Toilet Parts (PP2712-0)
Figure 27-5

Plumbing Fixture Outlet Size

1. Use only fixtures with at least (≥) the outlet size the in the following table.

TABLE P2700
Plumbing Fixture Outlet Size

fixture	outlet size (inches)
shower	see Table 3201
bathtub	1 ½
bathroom sink (lavatory)	1 ¼
bidet	1 ¼
sinks & laundry tubs	1 ½
clothes washing machine standpipe	2
floor drain	2

Bathtub Temperature Control Valve (P2713.3)

1. Install valves in bathtubs (including whirlpool tubs) that limit the water temperature to not more than (≤) 120° F.

Dishwashing Machine Installation (P2717)

1. You may discharge a dishwashing machine, a disposal, and a kitchen sink into one 1 ½ inches diameter drain (trap). Use a ¾ inch diameter dishwashing machine drain tube when discharging the dishwashing machine into either a sink drain (trap) or a disposal. Connect the dishwashing machine drain tube to a wye fitting in the sink tail piece when connecting the drain line directly to the sink tail piece. Loop the dishwashing machine drain line as high as possible in the sink cabinet and securely fasten or install an air gap device. An air gap device is not required in the dishwashing machine drain tube.

Dishwashing Machine Air Gap Device (PP2717-1)
Figure 27-6

Clothes Washing Machine Installation (P2718)

1. Discharge the waste water from a clothes washing machine through an air gap. Do not connect the clothes washing machine drain line directly to the plumbing waste pipes. Inserting the clothes washing machine drain hose into the standpipe is the most common acceptable method of providing the required air gap.

Floor Drain Installation (P2719)

1. Install a removable strainer in floor drain.
2. Provide access to the floor drain so it can be cleaned. Do not restrict access to the floor drain with permanently installed appliances.
3. Install a floor drain with an outlet size of at least (≥) 2 inches.

Whirlpool Tub Installation (P2720)

1. Install whirlpool tubs according to manufacturer's instructions. This includes testing the tub for leaks and pump operation, usually prior to installation. This also includes providing adequate support for the tub, water, and occupants. Some whirlpool tub manufacturers allow plaster as a tub support method. Plaster is not the same as drywall joint compound. Do not use drywall joint compound to support bathtubs unless it is specifically approved by the tub manufacturer.
2. Provide a door or access panel large enough to allow service personnel to repair and replace the pump. The door size will depend on where the pump is located relative to the door. The door may have to be larger than the specified minimum size if the pump is located far away from the door.
3. Make the access opening at least (≥) 12 inches by 12 inches, if the manufacturer does not specify an opening size. Make the access opening at least (≥) 18 inches by 18 inches if the pump is more than (>) 2 feet from the opening. Do not place obstructions, such as tub support framing and pipes, between the access opening and the pump.
4. Locate the circulation pump above the crown weir of the trap.
5. Install circulation pipes and pump drain line so that they are self-draining and retain minimum possible water after using the tub.

Whirlpool Tub Motor Access Opening (PP2720-0)
Figure 27-7

Bidet Installation (P2721)

1. Install bidets with either an air gap between the water supply and the drain or a vacuum-breaker-type fixture supply fitting.
2. Install a device that limits the bidet water temperature to not more than (≤) 110° F.

Water Faucet and Valve Installation (P2722)

1. Install water faucet and valves so that hot water flows when the left side of the faucet or valve is active. You may use approved tub/shower valves that do not correspond to the hot on the left convention if the hot water flow corresponds to the markings on the valve.

SHOWERS (P2708 AND P2709)

Shower Size (P2708.1)

1. Provide showers with a finished area of at least (≥) 900 square inches and a finished minimum dimension at least (≥) 30 inches. Maintain the minimum dimensions from the top of the threshold to at least (≥) 70 inches above the shower drain outlet. Measure the shower from the center line of the threshold (curb). You may install valves, shower heads, soap dishes, and grab bars that encroach into the minimum dimensions. You may install a fold-down seat in the shower if the minimum dimensions are maintained when the seat is up.
2. You may provide a shower with a finished minimum dimension of at least (≥) 25 inches if the finished area is at least (≥) 1,300 square inches.
3. Provide shower compartment entry opening of at least (≥) 22 inch finished width.

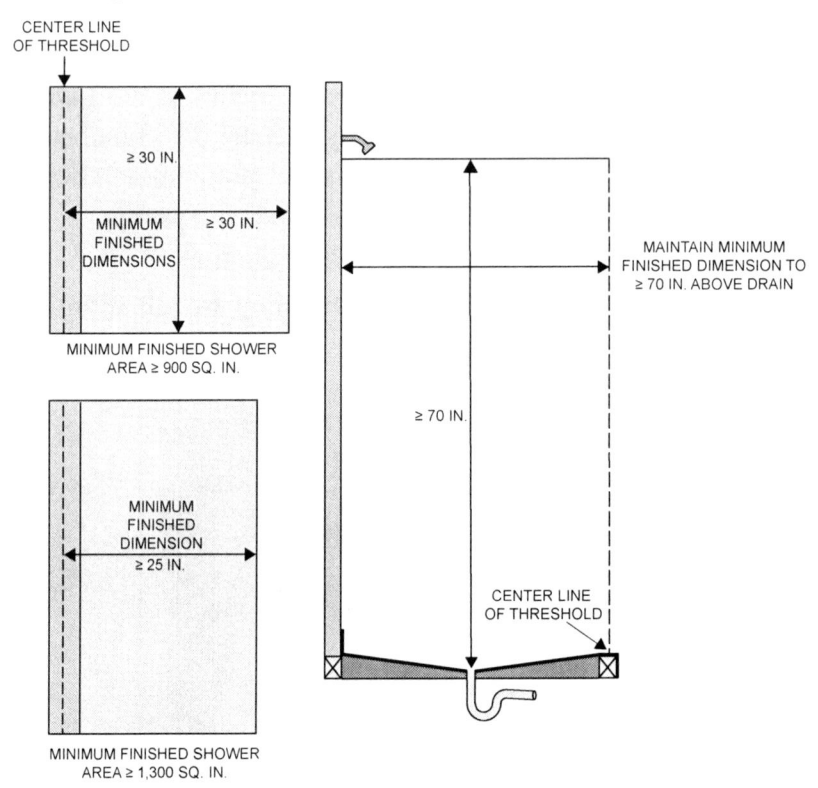

Shower Size (P2708-0)
Figure 27-8

Water Supply Riser (P2708.2)

1. Secure the pipe between the shower valve and the shower head to the permanent structure. This provision applies whether the riser is visible or concealed. Securing the riser helps avoid leaks if the riser twists and becomes loose at joints.

Shower Riser Rough-in (PP2708.2-1)
Figure 27-9

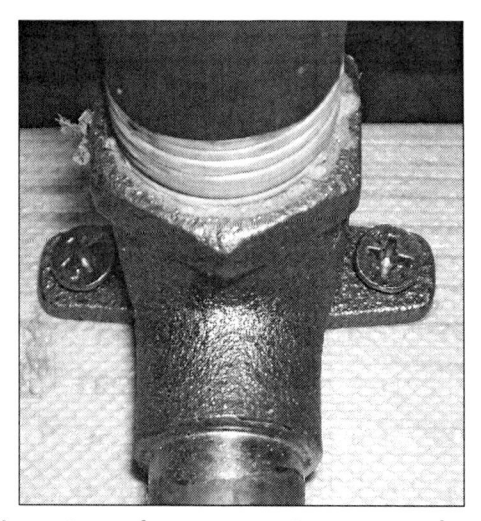

Shower Riser Attachment to Structure (PP2708.2-2)
Figure 27-10

Shower Temperature Control Valve (P2708.3)

1. Install shower valves and tub/shower valves that limit the water temperature to not more than (≤) 120° F. Use a pressure balance valve, a thermostatic mixing valve, or a valve that combines the two types. Do not use in-line thermostatic valves to comply with this section.

Shower Receptor Construction (P2709.1)

1. Install shower thresholds (curbs) at least (≥) 1 inch below the sides and back of the receptor.
2. Install shower thresholds (curbs) at least (≥) 2 inches and not more than (≤) 9 inches above the top of the drain.
3. Slope the shower floor at least (≥) ¼ unit in 12 units (2 percent slope) and not more than (≤) ½ unit in 12 units.
4. Use a flanged shower floor drain that provides a water-tight seal at the floor.

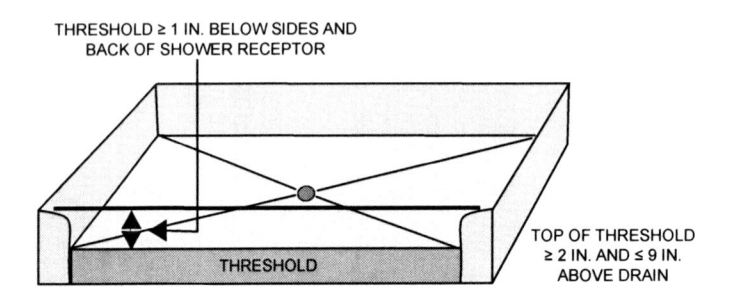

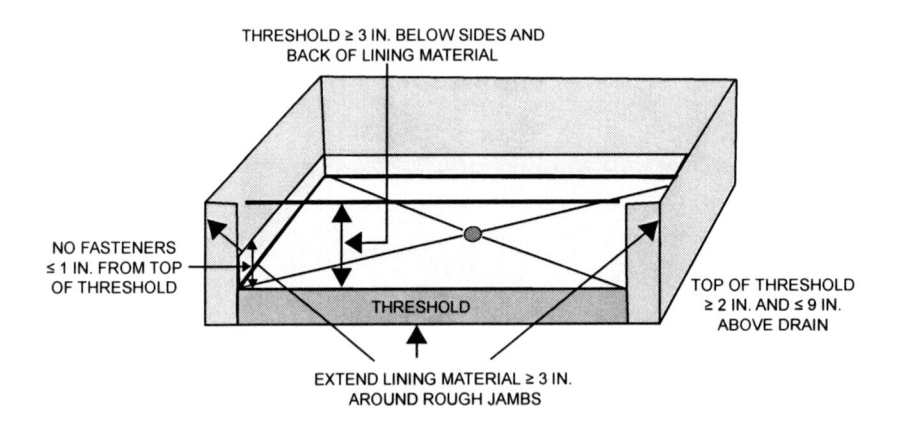

Shower Receptor Construction (P2709-0)
Figure 27-11

Site-Built Shower Receptor Linings (P2709.3)

1. Use hot-mopped felt, or approved sheet lead, or copper, or approved plastic lining material when installing a site-built shower receptor. Plastic liners (such as chlorinated polyethylene) are the most common modern site-built liner material.
2. Extend the lining material at least (≥) 3 inches beyond and around the rough jambs of the shower receptor. Extend the lining material at least (≥) 3 inches above the finished thresholds (curbs).
3. Slope the lining material at least ¼ unit in 12 units (2 percent slope) on a smooth and solid sub-base. Attach the lining material to an approved backing. Nail or perforate the lining at least (≥) 1 inch above the finished threshold. Seal joints in plastic lining material according to manufacturer's instructions.
4. Install an approved flanged shower drain that is equipped with weep holes into the drain and is equipped with a flange that makes a water-tight seal between the lining material and the drain.

28

WATER HEATERS

WATER HEATER DRIP PANS AND RELIEF VALVES

Water Heater Drip Pan Requirements (P2801.5)

1. Install a drip pan under water heaters located where leakage could cause damage. The IRC does not specify these locations. They often include attics and all areas within the conditioned area of the home, including finished basements.
2. Use a drip pan at least (≥) 1 ½ inches deep and made with at least (≥) 24 gage galvanized steel or other approved materials. Use a pan with a size and shape to catch all leaks and condensation from the water heater.

Water Heater Drip Pan Discharge Pipe (P2801.5)

1. Use at least (≥) a ¾ inch diameter discharge pipe to drain the drip pan. Use a larger discharge pipe if the connection to the drip pan is more than (>) ¾ inch diameter.
2. Run the discharge pipe to an indirect waste receptor (such as a floor drain) or to outside the building. If the discharge pipe terminates outside the building, locate the outlet at least (≥) 6 inches and not more than (≤) 24 inches above the adjacent ground surface.

Water Heater Relief Valves (P2803)

1. Install either a separate temperature relief valve and a separate pressure relief valve or a combination temperature and pressure relief valve on all appliances used to heat or store hot water. Combination temperature and pressure relief valves (T & P valves) are used almost exclusively in modern water heaters. This provision applies to tank-type, tankless, and swimming pool water heaters.
2. Install the temperature relief or T & P valve on the top of the water heater or on the side of the water heater within 6 inches of the top. Do not install an extension pipe between the water heater and the T & P valve.
3. Do not install a check valve or shutoff valve anywhere that might interfere with the operation of the relief valve or the flow of water or steam from the discharge pipe.

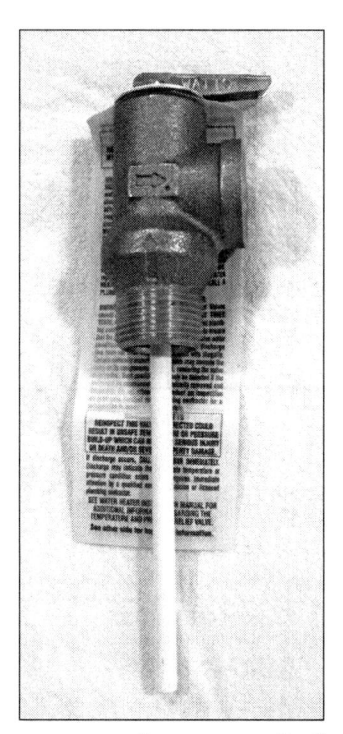

Water Heater Temperature Pressure Relief Valve (PP2803-0)
Figure 28-1

Water Heater Relief Valve Discharge Pipe (P2803.6.1)

1. Use water distribution pipe listed in Table P2905-2 as the relief valve discharge pipe. Copper and CPVC are the most commonly used discharge pipes. It is difficult to maintain uniform slope and fall on flexible pipes such as PEX.
2. Install the discharge pipe so hot water and steam will not cause personal injury or property damage if the relief valve discharges.
3. Install the discharge pipe so that any leaking from the pipe outlet is readily observable by the building occupants.
4. Use a discharge pipe that is at least (≥) as large as the relief valve opening. This size is usually ¾ inches diameter.
5. Run the discharge pipe full size to the floor, to an indirect waste receptor (such as a floor drain) inside the building, to the water heater drip pan or outside the building. If the area is subject to freezing, terminate the discharge pipe through an air gap into an indirect waste receptor located inside the building. You may use other discharge points in areas subject to freezing, if approved by the local building official.
6. Slope the discharge pipe so that it drains by gravity from the relief valve to the discharge point.
7. Do not connect the discharge pipe directly to the building's drain, waste, and vent system. Leave an air gap between the discharge pipe and the floor, ground, or other termination point.
8. Do not install a trap or a valve or a threaded outlet in the discharge pipe.
9. Terminate the discharge pipe through an air gap not more than (≤) 6 inches above the floor.

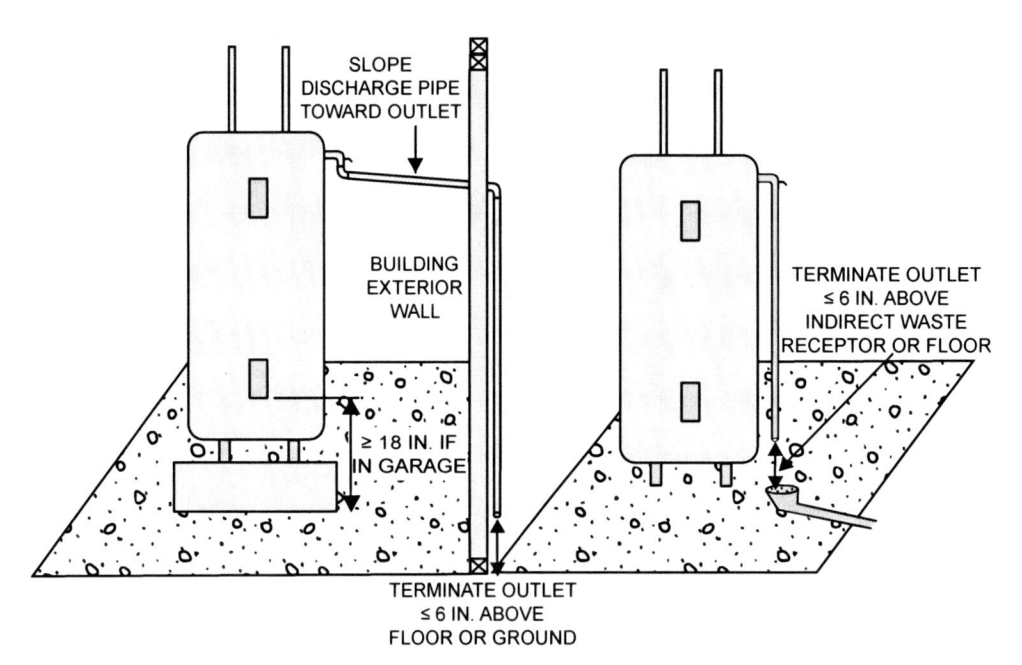

Water Heater Relief Valve Discharge Pipe Outside Termination (P2803.6.1-0)
Figure 28-2

Water Heater Relief Valve Discussion

Improper installation of the T & P valve and discharge pipe is a common problem, particularly when water heaters are replaced. Try to select a water heater that is similar in size and shape to the one being replaced. This will make it easier to install a discharge pipe that slopes toward the outlet point.

PVC pipe is commonly used for discharge pipes in manufactured homes and is acceptable in these homes. Refer to Appendix E for information about IRC application to manufactured homes.

29

WATER SUPPLY SYSTEM INSTALLATION REQUIREMENTS

BACKFLOW PROTECTION OF WATER SUPPLY (P2902)

Backflow and Cross-Connections Discussion

An important part of the design and use of the drinking (potable) water supply system is preventing contamination of the potable water. Contamination can occur when the potable water supply is intentionally or unintentionally connected to a contaminate source. Connection between the potable water supply and a contaminate source is called a cross-connection. Contamination occurs when contaminated material backflows into the potable water system through a cross-connection. A backflow is when material (usually liquid) travels in the reverse of the intended direction.

Some cross-connections are intended. Examples of intended cross-connections include toilet tank fill valves, automatic fill systems for swimming pools, and lawn irrigation systems. In all of these examples, the potable water supply is directly connected to a source of contaminated material that could backflow into the system under certain conditions. Some cross-connections are unintended. Examples of unintended cross-connections include spray hoses connected to a laundry tub faucet, hand-held shower heads with a hose long enough for the head to hang inside a tub or shower pan, and garden hoses. In all of these examples, a sudden loss of water pressure in the potable water supply system could allow any liquid at the end of these hoses to be drawn back into the potable water system. If the liquid were, such as weed killer in a spray bottle at the end of a garden hose, the weed killer could be drawn into the potable water system.

Backflow into the potable water system can occur by backpressure or by backsiphonage. Backpressure occurs when the pressure in the cross-connection source exceeds the pressure in the potable water supply system. Contaminated material is forced under pressure into the potable water system. Sources of backpressure include pumps, liquid storage tanks at a higher elevation than the cross-connection point, and thermal expansion from a heat source such as a water heater. Backsiphonage occurs when the pressure in the potable water supply system falls below atmospheric pressure. Air pressure can force contaminated material into the potable water supply system or negative pressure in the potable water supply system can draw contaminated material into the potable water supply system.

The IRC requires protections of all potable water supply outlets and all intentional cross-connections by an air gap or by an approved backflow prevention device.

BACKFLOW PROTECTION BY AIR GAPS (P2902.3.1)

Air Gap Definition

Air Gap An air gap is the unobstructed distance between a water supply fixture outlet opening and the flood rim level of a receptor. Example: the vertical distance between a bathtub spout and the highest level that the water in the bathtub could reach without overflowing is the air gap.

Air Gap Required Locations

1. Use clothes washing and dishwashing machines that contain an air gap device in the machine.
2. Provide an air gap at the discharge point of any relief valve and any relief valve piping (such as a water heater temperature and pressure relief valve discharge pipe).

Air Gap Distance Measurement

1. Measure the air gap distance between the plumbing fixture outlet opening and the flood rim of the fixture or receptor. Measure the fixture outlet opening diameter without the aerator attached. Measure the vertical air gap distance with the aerator attached.

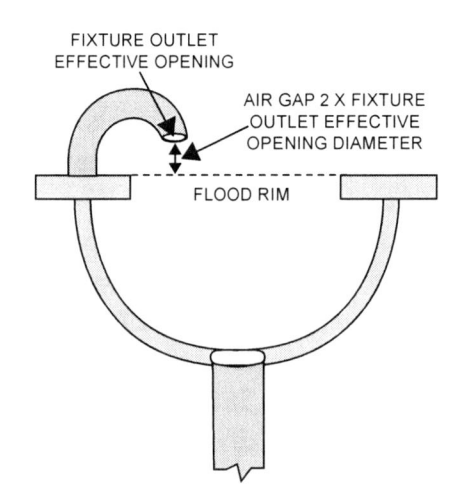

Air Gap Measurement (P2902.3.1-1)
Figure 29-1

Air Gap Minimum Distances

1. 1. Provide an air gap according to the following table when using an air gap as backflow prevention. Use the away from wall column when the closest edge of the fixture opening is more than (>) three times the effective opening diameter from a single wall and is more than (>) four times the effective opening diameter from two intersecting walls. Use the close to wall column when the closest edge of the fixture outlet effective opening is not more than (≤) three times the effective opening diameter from a single wall and is not more than (≤) four times the effective opening diameter from two intersecting walls.

TABLE P2902.3.1
Air Gap Minimum Distances

fixture effective opening size (inches)	minimum air gap when fixture effective opening is away from wall(s) (inches)	minimum air gap when fixture effective opening is close to wall(s) (inches)
≤ ½	1	1½
≤ ¾	1½	2½
≤ 1	2	3
> 1	two times the fixture effective opening diameter	three times the fixture effective opening diameter

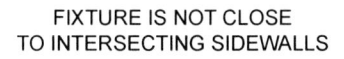

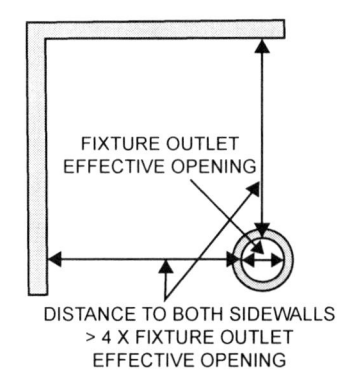

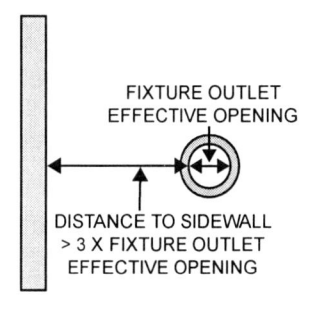

Air Gap Distance to Side Walls (P2902.3.1-2)
Figure 29-2

Example: If the fixture effective opening is ½ inch and the distance to a single sidewall is 1⅝ inches, then the minimum air gap is 1 inch because the distance is more than 3 times the opening size.

Example: If the fixture effective opening is 1 inch and the distance to a single sidewall is 3 inches, then the minimum air gap is 3 inches because the distance is not more than 3 times opening size.

Example: If the fixture effective opening is ½ inch and the distance to either intersecting sidewall is 1⅝ inches, then the minimum air gap is 1½ inches because the distance is not more than 4 times the opening size.

Example: if the fixture effective opening is 1½ inches and the distance to both intersecting sidewalls is 6 inches, then the minimum air gap is 4 ½ inches because the distance is not more than 4 times the opening size.

BACKFLOW PROTECTION USING BACKFLOW PREVENTION DEVICES (P2902.3 - P2902.6)

Backflow Protection Device General Installation Requirements

1. Protect all drinking (potable) water supply openings, outlets, and connections by an air gap or by an approved backflow preventer. This means that any place from which water flows must have either an air gap or have a backflow preventer installed. Examples of openings, outlets and connections include sinks, bathtubs, showers, hose bibbs, and water supply connections to water and steam heating systems, irrigation systems, swimming pools, fountains, ponds, and similar water features.
2. Install, inspect, and maintain backflow preventers according to manufacturer's instructions and the terms of the backflow preventer's listing.
3. Provide access to all backflow preventers for inspection and maintenance.
4. Protect backflow preventers from freezing by heat, insulation, or by making them removable.
5. Discharge backflow preventer relief port to an indirect waste receptor or to the outdoors.

Backflow Protection of Toilet Fill Valves

1. Protect toilets with an approved antisiphon fill valve.
2. Locate the backflow preventer at least (≥) 1 inch above the opening of the overflow pipe. Fill valves with all parts below the tank water line usually violate this provision.

Backflow Protection of Hose Bibbs

1. Protect water supply openings equipped with a hose connection with an approved atmospheric or pressure vacuum breaker or with a permanently attached hose connection vacuum breaker. Some jurisdictions require a backflow preventer on laundry sink and similar faucets with hose thread connections.
2. You are not required to install a backflow preventer on water heater and boiler hose connections if the connection is intended for tank draining. You are not required to install a backflow preventer on clothes washing machine hose connections if a backflow preventer is installed inside the machine.

Hose Connection Vacuum Breaker (PP2902.4.3-0)
Figure 29-3

Backflow Protection of Boilers

1. Protect boiler fill connections by installing an approved atmospheric backflow preventer when the boiler is filled only with water.
2. Protect boiler fill connections with an air gap or an approved reduced pressure backflow preventer when the boiler water contains chemicals.

Backflow Protection of Irrigation Systems

1. Protect lawn irrigation system water connections by installing an atmospheric vacuum breaker, a pressure vacuum breaker, or a reduced pressure backflow preventer.
2. Do not install a valve downstream from an atmospheric vacuum breaker.
3. Install a reduced pressure backflow preventer if chemicals are introduced into the irrigation system.

Pressure Vacuum Breaker (PP2902.5.3-0)
Figure 29-4

Backflow Protection of Automatic Fire Sprinkler Systems

1. Protect automatic fire sprinkler system water connections by installing a double check-valve assembly or a reduced pressure backflow preventer.
2. You are not required to protect the fire sprinkler water connection if the fire sprinkler pipes are installed as part of the building's potable water supply system according to IRC provisions and the sprinkler system does not have a fire department connection. This exception applies only when the fire sprinkler system and potable water supply system share some or all pipes and no fire department connection point is provided. If the fire sprinkler system and potable water supply system share only a connection to the main water service, then backflow protection is required.
3. Protect sections of the fire sprinkler system that contain chemicals or antifreeze or are connected to a non-potable water source by installing a reduced pressure backflow preventer. Protect the entire fire sprinkler system if the entire system contains chemicals, antifreeze, or non-potable water.

WATER SUPPLY GENERAL REQUIREMENTS (P2903)

Drinking Water Required (P2901)

1. Provide each dwelling with a supply of drinking (potable) water.
2. Identify any sources of non-potable water that may be supplied in a building. Use color, metal tags, or other approved means to identify both the potable and non-potable supply pipes and fixtures.

Minimum Water Pressure (P2903.3)

1. Provide each dwelling with at least ($\geq$) 40 psi of static water pressure. The local water utility determines the actual pressure at a dwelling. The minimum pressure applies to both public and private (well supplied) water supplies. Measure the water pressure as close as possible to where the water supply enters the building.

Maximum Water Pressure (P2903.3.1)

1. Do not exceed ($\leq$) 80 psi static water pressure.
2. Install an approved pressure-reducing valve at the main water supply connection to the dwelling if the static pressure exceeds the maximum. Measure the water pressure as close as possible to where the water supply enters the building.

Pressure-Reducing Valve (PP2903.3.1-0)
Figure 29-5

Thermal Expansion Devices (P2903.4)

1. Install a thermal expansion device on the cold water supply pipe when a:
   a) storage tank type water heater is installed, and
   b) check valve, backflow preventer, or other similar device is installed on the main water supply pipe.
2. Install the thermal expansion device between the water heater and the valve or backflow preventer. Some water meters contain a check valve. Many water heater manufacturers recommend installing thermal expansion devices on water systems closed by pressure-reduc-

ing valves and check valves and some manufacturers void the warranty if the a thermal expansion device is not installed when recommended.

Thermal expansion devices help reduce damage that can occur when heated water expands and increases pressure in the water supply pipes. This increased pressure can damage the water heater and can damage water supply pipes and hoses, such as washing machine hoses.

Thermal Expansion Tank
(PP2903.4-1)
Figure 29-6

Thermal Expansion Valve
(PP2903.4-2)
Figure 29-7

Water-Hammer Arrestors (P2903.5)

1. Install a water-hammer arrestor where required to control water flow and reduce the possibility of water hammer. A water hammer arrestor may be used near a quick-closing valve such as in a clothes washing machine.

Water-Hammer Arrestor (PP2903.5-0)
Figure : 29-8

Minimum Flow Rate at Fixtures (P2903.1)

1. Provide at least (≥) the water flow rate in the following table for the indicated fixtures. Water flow rate is measured in gallons per minute. Water flow rate means the water flow from the pipe <u>without the fixture attached</u>. The water flow rate in the table does not mean that the water flow from the fixture must be at least the amount in the table. Some fixtures contain required flow restrictors that will limit the actual water flow from the fixture to less than the water flow rate in the table. Example: the minimum water flow rate for a shower is 3 gallons per minute but the maximum flow-restricted rate from the shower head is 2.5 gallons per minute.

TABLE P2903.1 1
Minimum Water Flow Rate at Fixture Supply Pipe

fixture	minimum flow rate (gpm)
bathtub	4
bidet	2
dishwasher	2.75
laundry tub	4
lavatory	2
shower	3
hose bibb	5
sink	2.5

Maximum Flow Rate at Fixtures (P2903.2)

1. Use fixtures that allow a water flow rate that is not more than (≤) the flow rate in the following table. Water flow rate is measured in gallons per minute. If either the water supply pressure to the building or the water pressure loss in the pipes reduces the water pressure at the fixture to less than the design pressure, the flow rate at a flow-restricted fixture may be less than the maximum.

TABLE P2903.2 1
Maximum Water Flow Rate at Fixture

fixture	maximum water flow rate at design pressure
lavatory	2.2 gpm at 60 psi
shower head	2.5 gpm at 80 psi
sink	2.2 gpm at 60 psi

WATER SUPPLY PIPE SIZE (P2903.7)

Limitations of the Material in this Section

Determining the correct size of water pipes requires knowledge of the water pipe material(s) to be installed (e.g., copper or CPVC pipe), the length of each part of the water pipe system, the height of each fixture above the water source (e.g., water meter or well head), the water demand requirements of each fixture and fixture group, the water supply pressure, and the pressure loss induced by equipment such as water meters, backflow preventers, water softeners, and water filters. This knowledge is beyond most readers of this book; therefore, we will not discuss in detail how to determine water pipe sizes. Leave calculation of correct water pipe size calculations to qualified contractors.

We will present some basic information about how to calculate water pipe sizes and present an example of calculating water pipe sizes for an average home. Do not assume that your water pipe sizes are wrong if your home has different size pipes from the following example. Your pipes may have been sized using different assumptions or sizing methods. In practice, plumbers often use "rules of thumb" to install water pipes using a limited number of pipe sizes that may be larger than the minimum required size. This makes water pipe installation easier and relieves the plumber from performing detailed water pipe size calculations.

The material in this section applies to traditional plumbing piping using materials such as copper and CPVC pipe in a branch main and riser system. We do not address parallel water distribution systems using manifolds and individual distribution lines to each fixture.

Water Supply Fixture Units Description

1. Each water-using fixture and group of related fixtures has been assigned a water supply fixture unit (wsfu) value. This value is based on the typical water flow demand of the fixture or fixture group and the probability that the fixtures will be used simultaneously. Each fixture that uses both hot and cold water has a separate hot and cold wsfu value and a combined wsfu value. Use the combined wsfu value to calculate the building water service pipe size. Use the hot and cold wsfu values to calculate the hot and cold distribution pipe sizes. Fixtures that use only hot or cold water have a hot or cold wsfu value that is the same as the wsfu combined value.

TABLE P2903.7-1
Water Supply Fixture Units for Plumbing Fixtures

plumbing fixture	hot wsfu	cold wsfu	combined wsfu
bathtub with or without shower	1.0	1.0	1.4
clothes washing machine	1.0	1.0	1.4
dishwasher	1.4	-	1.4
full bath group with 1 lavatory, 1 bathtub or shower, 1 toilet	1.5	2.7	3.6
hose bibb (estimated value)	-	2.5	2.5
kitchen sink faucet	1.0	1.0	1.4
laundry tub	1.0	1.0	1.4
lavatory (bathroom sink)	0.5	0.5	0.7
shower	1.0	1.0	1.4
toilet (tank type)	-	2.2	2.2

Water Supply Pipe Size Table

1. The following table contains the water meter, water service pipe, and distribution pipe sizes for water pressures between 40 and 49 psi. Enter the table through the column listing the maximum developed length of the service and supply pipes between the source of water supply (the water meter or well head) and the most remote plumbing fixture in the home. Developed pipe length is the actual pipe length multiplied by 1.2 to account for pressure losses by fittings and valves. Find the row containing the number of wsfu at least (≥) the number of wsfu served by the distribution pipe run. Use the hot and cold wsfu values in the table to determine the size of hot and cold distribution pipes. Use the combined wsfu values in the table to determine the size of the water meter, service pipe and the main building distribution pipe. Read the water meter, service pipe, and main building distribution pipe size in the far left column and the distribution pipe size in the next column.

Because this is a summary discussion of water pipe sizing, we have not included all of the table values in the IRC. WSFU values for water pressures more and less than 40 to 49 psi are similar for developed lengths of 80 feet and fewer. Refer to IRC Appendix R for more detailed information about sizing water pipes.

29 : Water Supply System Installation Requirements

TABLE P2907.3-2
Water Service and Distribution Pipe Size at Water Pressures From 40 to 49 PSI

meter & service pipe size (inches)	distribution pipe size (inches)	40 feet	60 feet	80 feet	100 feet	150 feet	200 feet	250 feet	300 feet	400 feet	500 feet
¾	½	3	2.5	2	1.5	1.5	1	1	.5	.5	.5
¾	¾	9.5	9.5	8.5	7	5.5	4.5	3.5	3	2.5	2
¾	1	32	32	32	26	18	13.5	10.5	9	7.5	6
1	1	32	32	32	32	21	15	11.5	9.5	7.5	6.5
¾	1¼	32	32	32	32	32	32	32	27	21	16.5
1	1¼	80	80	80	80	65	52	42	35	26	20
1½	1¼	80	80	80	80	75	59	48	39	28	21
1	1½	87	87	87	87	87	87	87	78	65	55
1½	1½	151	151	151	151	151	130	109	93	75	63

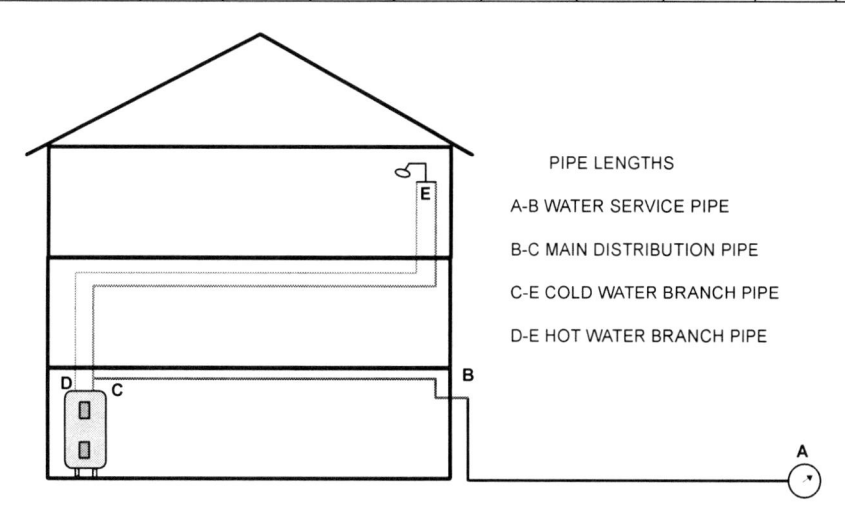

PIPE LENGTHS
A-B WATER SERVICE PIPE
B-C MAIN DISTRIBUTION PIPE
C-E COLD WATER BRANCH PIPE
D-E HOT WATER BRANCH PIPE

Water Supply Pipe Sizes (P2903.7-0)
Figure 29-9

Water Supply Pipe Size Example

1. Assume a new, four bedroom, 2 ½ bathrooms, home with the plumbing fixtures described in the following table.
2. Assume that the developed length of the water pipe from the water meter to the furthest plumbing fixture is 150 feet. Remember that developed length of water pipe is calculated by multiplying the actual pipe length by 1.2 to account for losses caused by fittings and valves.
3. Assume that the design water supply pressure is between 40 and 49 psi. Design water supply pressure is the actual water supply pressure leaving the water supply source reduced

by: (a) the height difference between the water supply source and the highest water fixture outlet; and (b) losses caused by equipment such as a water-pressure reducing valve, a backflow preventer, a water softener or whole house water filter, or any other equipment that reduces water pressure. Consult the equipment manufacturer's instructions to determine the water pressure reduction caused by equipment.

TABLE EX2903.7
Water Supply Pipe Size Example

plumbing fixtures
owner bathroom containing 1 bathtub, 1 shower, 2 lavatories, and 1 toilet
hall bathroom containing 1 bathtub with showerhead, 2 lavatories, and 1 toilet
half bathroom with 1 lavatory and 1 toilet
kitchen with 1 sink and disposal and 1 dishwasher
laundry with 1 clothes washing machine
2 hose bibbs

Example:

Question:
What is the minimum size water meter and service pipe that will serve this house?

Answer:
The minimum size water meter and service pipe is ¾ inch.

Refer to Table P2903.7-1. Add the combined wsfu for all fixtures in the house. Remember to use the fixture group values for the full bathroom groups and add the values for any extra individual fixtures. The combined wsfu total is 22.1. Enter the water supply pipe size Table P2903.7-2 in the 150 feet developed length column. The closest wsfu total that is at least (≥) 22.1 is 32 wsfu in the ¾ inch meter and 1¼ inches distribution pipe size row.

Example:

Question:
Assume that hot and cold water distribution pipes begin at the water heater to serve the owner bathroom, the hall bathroom, and one of the hose bibbs. Assume that the developed length of the hot and cold pipes is 60 feet to the furthest fixture. What are the minimum size distribution pipes that begin at the water heater and run to the first branch to serve the fixtures?

Answer:
The minimum hot water distribution pipe size is ¾ inch and the minimum cold water distribution pipe size is 1 inch.

Refer to Table P2903.7-1. Add the hot wsfu values and the cold wsfu values for the owner bathroom, the hall bathroom, and one hose bibb. Remember to use the fixture group values for the full bathroom groups and add the values for any extra individual fixtures. The hot wsfu value total is 5. The cold wsfu value total is 12.4. Enter the water supply pipe size Table P2903.7-2 in the 60 feet developed length column. The closest wsfu total that is at least (≥) 5 is 9.5 wsfu in the ¾ inch in the distribution pipe size row. The closest wsfu total that is at least (≥) 12.4 is 32 wsfu in the 1 inch in the distribution pipe size row.

WATER SUPPLY VALVES (P2903.9)

Water Supply Service Cutoff Valve

1. Provide each dwelling (including each unit of a two-family and townhouse building) with a water supply cutoff valve near where the water supply pipe enters the dwelling. Use a full-open type valve such as a gate or ball valve. Make this valve accessible.
2. Provide a means to drain the water supply pipes at the water supply cutoff valve. This means may be a bleed valve on the cutoff valve or it may be a hose bibb.
3. Provide each dwelling with a water supply cutoff valve at the curb or property line, if required by local authorities. This valve is usually installed at the water meter.

Water Heater Cutoff Valve

1. Provide each water heater with a cutoff valve on the cold water pipe near the water heater. Use a full-open type valve such as a gate or ball valve. Make this valve accessible.

Fixture Cutoff Valve (Angle Stop)

1. Provide each plumbing fixture, except for bathtubs and showers, with an accessible cutoff valve on the hot and cold water supply pipes. These valves are sometimes called angle stop valves. You may install cutoff valves at bathtubs and shower, but these valves are not required.

Valves and Outlets Installed Below Ground

1. Do not install water supply outlets and stop-and-waste valves below ground. Example: do not install a hose bibb below ground.
2. You may install a freeze-proof yard hydrant below ground if the water supply to the hydrant is protected with a backflow preventer and the yard hydrant is permanently labeled as a non-potable water source.

Hose Bibb Cutoff Valve (P2903.10)

1. Provide hose bibbs that are subject to freezing with a stop-and-waste valve inside the building. This includes frost-proof hose bibbs.
2. You need not install a stop-and-waste valve on a frost-proof hose bibb if the stem extends into an open heated or semi-conditioned area of the building.

FIRE SPRINKLER SYSTEM GENERAL REQUIREMENTS (P2904)

Limitations of the Material in this Section

The IRC provides detailed requirements for designing and installing residential fire sprinkler systems. Readers of this book should not attempt to design or install these systems. Consult qualified sprinkler system contractors when dealing with these systems. In this book section we present some general installation requirements to help readers better understand the nature and scope of residential fire sprinkler systems.

Note that this requirement is very controversial and may not be required in all jurisdictions. Verify with the local building official if this requirement applies in your area.

Sprinkler System General Installation Requirements

1. Install sprinkler system equipment that is listed for residential use and install the equipment according to manufacturer's instructions.
2. Protect sprinkler system pipes from freezing. Use dry heads when heads are required in areas subject to freezing.
3. Replace sprinkler system heads that have been painted, caulked, or damaged in any way.
4. Separate non-metallic sprinkler system pipes from interior space using material (such as 3/8 inch drywall) that has at least (≥) a 15 minute fire rating.
5. Do not install a shut off valve in the sprinkler system piping. This does not include the required main water shut off valve for the entire building.
6. Have a qualified contractor review the sprinkler system before installing devices that could reduce sprinkler system water pressure. This applies only if the device is installed in the piping system before the water connection to the sprinkler system. Such devices include pressure reducing valves, whole house water filters, and water softeners. Place a warning sign about such devices at the main water shut off valve.

Sprinkler System Heads Required Locations

1. Install sprinkler system heads in all areas of the building, except you are not required to install sprinkler system heads in these areas:
   a) attics, crawl spaces, and similar areas that are not normally occupied, and
   b) clothes closets, linen closets, and pantries with a floor area not more than (≤) 24 square feet, and with no dimension more than (>) 3 feet, and with a drywall ceiling, and
   c) bathrooms with a floor area not more than (≤) 55 square feet, and
   d) garages, carports, covered unheated areas (such as mud rooms), and similar areas.
2. Install a sprinkler system head above fuel-fired equipment located in attics, crawl spaces, and similar areas that are normally unoccupied. You are not required to install sprinkler system heads in the rest of the area.

Sprinkler System Head Type Required Locations

1. Install standard sprinkler heads in required locations, except for locations where intermedi-

ate sprinkler heads are required. Standard sprinkler heads have an activation temperature of between 135° F and 170° F.

2. Install intermediate sprinkler heads in and near heat sources such as attics, directly under skylights, concealed spaces directly under a roof, fuel-burning equipment and their vents and vent connectors, fireplaces and stoves, electric and gas cooking appliances, warm air HVAC registers, hot water pipes and lights. Refer to the IRC for required separation distances. Intermediate sprinkler heads have an activation temperature of between 175° F and 225° F.

Sprinkler Head Coverage Area and Obstructions

1. Install a sprinkler head so that it covers not more than (≤) 400 square feet and install the sprinkler head as specified by the manufacture's instructions.
2. Install ceiling-mounted (pendent) sprinkler heads at least (≥) 3 feet from the center of a ceiling fan, surface-mounted light fixture, or similar obstruction. You may install additional sprinkler heads around the obstruction to compensate for the obstruction.
3. Install wall-mounted sprinkler heads at least (≥) 5 feet from the center of a ceiling fan, surface-mounted light fixture, or similar obstruction. You may install additional sprinkler heads around the obstruction to compensate for the obstruction.

WATER SERVICE AND DISTRIBUTION PIPE GENERAL INSTALLATION REQUIREMENTS (P2905)

Water Pipe Installed in Contaminated or Corrosive Ground

1. Do not install water service or distribution pipe, fittings, valves, or other parts in soil or water that is contaminated with materials that may corrode or degrade the pipe or materials. The building official may require a soil analysis or may require alternate pipe routes or pipe materials if contaminated or corrosive soils are found or suspected.

Water Service Pipe Materials

1. Install water service pipe that has a working pressure rating of at least (≥) 160 psi at 73° F, or the highest available pressure, whichever is greater.
2. Common water service pipe materials used in modern residential construction include those in the following table. You may use other approved materials listed in the IRC.

TABLE P2905-1
Common Water Service Pipe Materials

CPVC plastic pipe
Copper & copper alloy pipe and tubing
Cross-linked polyethylene (PEX) tubing
PEX-AL-PEX pipe
PE-AL-PE pipe
Polyethylene (PE) pipe and tubing
Polypropylene (PP) pipe and tubing
PVC plastic pipe

Water Service Pipe Installation

1. You may install water service pipe in the same trench as the building sewer pipe if the building sewer pipe is listed in Chapter 30 for underground use within a building. Most modern building sewer pipes satisfy this requirement.

2. Separate the building sewer and water service pipes, if required: (a) in different trenches with the pipes separated by at least (≥) 5 feet measured horizontally or, (b) in the same trench with the pipes separated by a ledge of undisturbed or compacted soil that is at least (≥) 12 inches above and to the side of the building sewer pipe.

3. You do not need to separate the building sewer and water service pipes if the water service pipe crosses the building sewer pipe at an angle and the water service pipe is encased in a sleeve for at least (≥) 5 feet on either side of the building sewer pipe.

Physical separation of water service and building sewer pipe is rarely required in modern construction because the building sewer pipe is usually listed for underground use within a building. Physical separation of water service and building sewer pipe would be required when installing new water service pipe near an older existing building sewer pipe that is not listed for underground use within a building.

Water Distribution Pipe Materials

1. Install water distribution pipe that has a working pressure rating of at least (≥) 100 psi at 180° F.

2. Common water distribution pipe materials used in modern residential construction include those in the following table. You may use other approved materials listed in the IRC.

TABLE P2905-2
Common Water Distribution Pipe Materials

common water distribution pipe materials	approved for use under concrete slabs
CPVC plastic pipe	yes
copper and copper alloy pipe and tubing	copper tubing, minimum Type M
PEX-AL-PEX pipe	yes
PEX tubing	yes
PE-AL-PE pipe	yes

Plastic Pipe Joints

1. Use only tools, materials, and fittings recommended by the pipe manufacturer for use with the pipe material when joining fittings and valves to plastic pipe. Prepare pipes and fittings, apply primers and cement, and handle the joined pipes according to manufacturer's instructions. Do not use primers and cements designed for one type of plastic pipe on a different type of plastic pipe. Look for the correct ASTM standard on the primer and cement product label.

TABLE P2905-3
Plastic Pipe Approved Joining Methods

pipe type	approved joining method
ABS	solvent cement ASTM D 2235
CPVC	primer required solvent cement ASTM F 493
PVC	primer required ASTM F 656-96a solvent cement ASTM D2564
PEX	flared joints use only tool recommended by the pipe manufacturer mechanical joints use only fittings recommended by the pipe manufacturer
PP	heat-fusion and mechanical joints use only fittings recommended by the pipe manufacturer

Soldered Pipe Joints

1. Cut pipe edges square. Chamfer (bevel) the outside of the pipe and ream the inside of the cut pipe. Clean bright all surfaces to be soldered. Apply flux to all surfaces to be soldered. Apply heat to both the fitting and to the pipe to be soldered. Apply solder when both the fitting and the pipe are near the same temperature and at or above the solder's melting point. Use solder with not more than ($\leq$) 0.2 percent lead on potable water system pipes.

Joints in and Under Concrete

1. Install only wrought-copper fittings and brazed (silver soldered) joints in copper tubing installed in and/or under a concrete floor.

Joints Between Different Pipe Materials Within Buildings

1. You may use approved push-in mechanical fittings with a pressure-lock design to join copper pipe or CPVC tubing that have compatible outside diameters.
2. Use only brass fittings or dielectric fittings to join copper pipe or tubing to galvanized steel pipe. Join the fitting to the copper and then screw the fitting to the threaded galvanized steel pipe. Failure to comply with this requirement will cause corrosion at the fitting and possible failure and leaking of the fitting.
3. Use approved adapter fittings to join different types of plastic pipe and to join plastic pipe to other piping materials.

Bending Copper Tubing (P2906.1)

1. You may bend annealed and tempered drawn copper tubing by using forming equipment.
2. Do not deform or reduce the cross-sectional area of the tube when bending.
3. Make bends in copper tubing with a bend radius of not less than four tube diameters.

REVERSE OSMOSIS WATER TREATMENT UNITS (P2908.2)

Air Gap for Waste Discharge

1. Install an air gap or a backflow prevention device between the reverse osmosis waste or discharge line and the connection to the plumbing waste pipe. The reverse osmosis unit manufacturer should provide an air gap faucet or a backflow prevention device to comply with this provision. The faucet or device should be labeled as meeting the requirements of NSF 58.

30

SANITARY DRAINAGE SYSTEM INSTALLATION REQUIREMENTS

DRAINAGE AND SEWER PIPE MATERIALS, FITTINGS, AND JOINTS

Drainage and Sewer Pipe Materials (P3002.1 and P3002.2)

1. You may use any of the common drainage and sewer pipe materials listed in the following table. You may use other approved materials listed in the IRC.
2. Install galvanized steel drainage pipe at least (≥) 6 inches above the ground.
3. Use ABS, PVC, cast-iron, or any other pressure-rated pipe from Table P3002.2 in forced main sewers. Forced main sewers are rare in residential construction.

TABLE P3002.1
Common Drainage and Sewer Pipe Materials

common drainage & sewer pipe materials	used for drainage	used for sewer
cast-iron soil pipe	yes	yes
ABS-DWV pipe	yes	yes
PVC plastic pipe	yes	yes
Steel pipe (black or galvanized)	yes	no

Drainage and Sewer Pipe Fittings General Requirements (P3002.3)

1. Install fittings that have a smooth interior surface and are compatible with the pipe to which they are attached. Example: do not use ABS fittings with PVC pipe.
2. Do not use fittings that contain ledges, shoulders, or reductions that may retard or obstruct drainage flow.
3. Install fittings that maintain a 2 percent slope and are approved for use where installed. Example: do not use a vent tee in a drainage pipe where water flows.

Drainage and Sewer Pipe Prohibited Joints and Connections (P3003.2)

1. Do not use threaded connections in pipes where the threads run on the inside of the pipe and could retard or obstruct drainage flow.
2. Do not drill, tap, burn, or weld drainage, sewer, and vent pipes. Example: do not drill into a vent pipe to insert the discharge hose from a water softener.

3. Do not use the following types of joints and connections: (a) cement or concrete, (b) mastic or hot-pour bituminous, (c) fittings not approved for the specific type of pipe or installation, (d) joints between different pipe diameters made with elastomeric rolling O-rings, (e) solvent-cement joints between different types of plastic pipe, and (f) saddle fittings.

ABS Plastic Pipe Joints (P3003.3)

1. You may use approved elastomeric gaskets to join buried ABS pipes. You may use elastomeric gaskets above ground when other joints are not practical and when approved by the building official.
2. You may use solvent cement to join ABS pipes above and below ground. Clean and dry pipes and fittings before applying solvent cement to all joint surfaces. Make the joint while the solvent cement is wet. Use solvent cement that complies with ASTM D 2235. Do not use PVC cement with ABS pipe.
3. You may use threaded joints for Schedule 80 and heavier ABS pipe. The threads should be NPT type.

Cast-Iron Hub and Spigot Joints (P3003.6)

1. You may use lead-caulked joints to join cast-iron hub and spigot pipes. Pack the joint firmly with oakum (hemp) and fill with molten lead at least (≥) 1 inch deep and not more than (≤) ⅛ inch below the rim of the hub. Pour the lead in one continuous operation. This method is rare in modern residential plumbing.
2. You may use an approved positive-seal one piece elastomeric compression gasket to join cast-iron hub and spigot pipes. Place the gasket in the hub before the spigot is inserted.

Cast-Iron Hubless Pipe Joints (P3003.6)

1. Use an approved elastomeric sealing sleeve and stainless steel retaining rings to join cast-iron hubless pipes.

Elastomeric Sealing Sleeve (PP3003.6-0)
Figure 30-1

Copper and Brass Pipe and Copper Tubing Joints (P3003.5, P3003.10, and P3003.11)

1. You may braze joints in copper pipe and tubing and joints in brass pipe. Clean all pipes and fittings and use an approved flux where required. Copper and brass are rarely used as drainage pipes in modern residential construction.
2. You may use approved mechanical joints to join copper pipe and tubing and to join brass pipes. Install the mechanical joints according to manufacturer's instructions.
3. You may solder joints in copper pipe and tubing and joints in brass pipe. Soldering is the most common method of joining copper pipe and tubing and joining brass pipes. Soldering is sometimes called sweating. Cut pipe edges square. Chamfer (bevel) the outside of the pipe and ream the inside of the cut pipe. Clean all surfaces to be soldered to a bright finish. Apply flux to all surfaces to be soldered. Apply heat to both the fitting and to the pipe to be soldered. Apply solder when both the fitting and the pipe are near the same temperature and at or above the solder's melting point. Use solder with not more than ($\leq$) 0.2 percent lead on potable water system pipes.

Steel Pipe Joints (P3003.12)

1. You may use threaded joints for galvanized steel pipes. The threads should be NPT type.
2. You may use approved mechanical joints to join galvanized steel pipes. Install the mechanical joints according to manufacturer's instructions.

PVC Plastic Pipe Joints (P3003.14)

1. You may use approved elastomeric gaskets to join buried PVC pipes. You may use elastomeric gaskets above ground and when approved by the building official.
2. You may use solvent cement to join PVC pipes above and below ground. Clean and dry pipes and fittings before applying primer to all joint surfaces. Apply purple colored primer that complies with ASTM F 656. Apply solvent cement that complies with ASTM D 2564. Make the joint while the solvent cement is wet. Do not use ABS cement with PVC pipe.
3. You may use threaded joints for Schedule 80 and heavier PVC pipe. The threads should be NPT type.

Joints Between Different Types of Pipe (P3003.18)

1. Use compression or mechanical-sealing elastomeric fittings approved for joining the different types of pipe. Install all fittings according to manufacturer's instructions.
2. Use an approved brass ferrule with a caulked joint or a mechanical compression joint when joining copper tubing to cast-iron pipe.
3. Use a brass converter fitting or a dielectric fitting when joining copper tubing to galvanized steel pipe.

Toilet (Closet) Flange Joints (P3003.19)

1. Install a closet flange that is firmly attached to a structural support (floor) to connect a toilet to drainage piping. Use a closet flange that is compatible with the connected drainage pipe.

Example: do not use a PVC closet flange with ABS pipe. Do not use the closet flange to provide structural support to the toilet.

2. Use non-corrosive bolts and an approved gasket (O ring) or other approved setting compound to secure the toilet and closet flange and to make the seal water tight.

Drainage and Sewer Pipe Slope (P3005.3)

1. Install horizontal drainage and sewer pipe with a uniform slope and alignment.
2. Install pipe not more than (≤) 2 ½ inches diameter with at least (≥) a ¼ unit in 12 units (2 percent) slope.
3. Install pipe at least (≥) 3 inches diameter with at least (≥) a ⅛ unit in 12 units (1 percent) slope.

Drainage and Sewer Pipe Offset Size (P3006)

1. Use the vertical stack column in the <u>drainage pipe size</u> Table P3005.4-1 to determine the size of any offset pipe in a vertical drain pipe that is not more than (≤) 45 degrees from vertical.
2. Use the <u>sewer pipe size</u> Table P3005.4-2 to determine the size of any offset pipe below the lowest horizontal branch that is more than (>) 45 degrees from vertical.
3. Size an offset pipe above the lowest horizontal branch that is more than (>) 45 degrees from vertical as follows:
    a) use the vertical stack column in the drainage pipe size Table P3005.4-1 to determine the size of the stack pipe above the offset, and
    b) use the sewer pipe size Table P3005.4-2 to determine the size of the offset, and
    c) use the pipe size from the previous step (b) or the total number of dfu draining into the entire stack, whichever is larger, to determine the size of the stack below the offset.

DRAINAGE AND SEWER PIPE SIZE (P3005.4)

Limitations of the Material in this Section

Determining the correct size of drainage and sewer pipes requires knowledge that is beyond most readers of this book; therefore, we will not discuss in detail how to determine drainage and sewer pipe sizes. Leave calculation of correct drainage and sewer pipe size calculations to qualified contractors.

We will present some basic information about how to calculate drainage and sewer pipe sizes and present an example of calculating drainage and sewer pipe sizes for an average home. Do not assume that your drainage and sewer pipe sizes are wrong if your home has different size pipes from the following example. Your pipes may have been sized using different assumptions or sizing methods. In practice, plumbers often use "rules of thumb" to install drainage and sewer pipes using a limited number of pipe sizes that may be larger than the minimum required size. This makes drainage and sewer installation easier and relieves the plumber from performing detailed pipe size calculations.

Drainage Fixture Units Description (P3004.1)

1. Each plumbing fixture and group of related fixtures has been assigned a drainage fixture

unit (dfu) value. This value is based on the typical water flow demand of the fixture or fixture group and the probability that the fixtures will be used simultaneously.

2. Use the highest dfu value for a similar fixture if a fixture is not listed in the following table.

3. Use a dfu value of 1.5 dfu for every 1 gallon per minute flow of water into a drainage system from a continuous or semi-continuous source such as a sump pump.

4. Note that the actual pipe size required for a shower or a fixture group that includes a shower may be different from the pipe size calculated based on drainage fixture units. This is because the shower trap size may be larger when numerous shower heads and body sprays are installed. Refer to Table P3201 for shower trap size requirements and base the shower drainage pipe size on the required trap size, not on the dfu value.

TABLE P3004.1
Drainage Fixture Unit Values

plumbing fixture or fixture group	drainage fixture unit (dfu) value
bar sink	1
bathtub with or without shower	2
bidet	1
clothes washing machine standpipe	2
dishwasher	2
floor drain (not used as a receptor)	0
kitchen sink	2
kitchen group (dishwasher and sink)	2
laundry tub	2
laundry group (clothes washing machine and laundry tub)	3
lavatory	1
shower	2
toilet (1.6 gallons per flush)	3
toilet (more than 1.6 gallons per flush)	4
full-bath group (1.6 gallons per flush toilet and lavatory and bath tub or shower) (add 1 dfu for toilet > 1.6 gallons per flush)	5
half-bath group (1.6 gallons per flush toilet and lavatory) (add 1 dfu for toilet > 1.6 gallons per flush)	4
multiple-bath groups 1.5 baths 2 baths 2.5 baths 3 baths 3.5 baths add 2 dfu for each additional full bath	7 8 9 10 11

Drainage Pipe Size Table

1. Use the following table to determine how many dfu may flow through horizontal branch drainage pipes or through vertical stack drainage pipes. Use at least (≥) a 3 inch diameter pipe for toilets regardless of the values in the table.
2. Base the actual pipe size on the trap size required from Table P3201 when there is a difference between Table P3201 and Table P3005.4-1.

TABLE P3005.4-1
Drainage Pipe Maximum DFU Capacity Table

pipe diameter (inches)	max. dfu horizontal branch	max. dfu vertical stack
1 ¼	1 bidet or lavatory only	1 bidet or lavatory only
1 ½	3	4
2	6	10
2 ½	12	20
3	20	48
4	160	240

Sewer Pipe Size Table

1. Use the following table to determine how many dfu may flow through building drain or building sewer pipes. Use at least (≥) a 3 inch diameter pipe for building and sewer drain pipes that serve toilets regardless of the values in the table.

TABLE P3005.4-2
Sewer Pipe Maximum DFU Capacity Table

pipe diameter (inches)	1/8 inch slope per foot	1/4 inch slope per foot	1/2 inch slope per foot
1 ½	not allowed	limited, see IRC P3005.4.2	limited, see IRC P3005.4.2
2	not allowed	21	27
2 ½	not allowed	24	31
3	36	42	50
4	180	216	250

Drainage and Sewer Pipe Size Calculation Method

1. Use the following steps to determine the size of drainage and sewer pipes.
    a) Draw a line diagram of the plumbing system showing the relative location of each fixture.
    b) Assign the dfu value from Table P3004.1 to each fixture and fixture group.
    c) Begin at the top floor or most remote fixture. Work downstream adding the dfu values for each fixture or fixture group. Remember to use the reduced multiple-bath fixture group dfu values beginning where the pipes from the bathrooms connect. Remember to check Table P3201 for shower trap size.
    d) Assign sizes to the pipes using Tables P3005.4-1 and P3005.4-2. You may use larger pipes

than those in the table. You may not use smaller pipes and you may not reduce the pipe size in the direction of flow even if the diagram appears to allow it.

Drainage and Sewer Pipe Size Calculation Example

1. Assume a new, four bedrooms, 2 ½ bathrooms, home with the plumbing fixtures described in the following table. The full bathrooms are on the second floor. The remaining fixtures are on the first floor.

TABLE EX3005.4
Drainage and Sewer Pipe Size Calculation Example

plumbing fixture or fixture group
bathroom containing 1 bathtub, 1 shower with 1 showerhead, 2 lavatories, and 1 toilet
bathroom containing 1 bathtub with 1 showerhead, 2 lavatories, and 1 toilet
bathroom with 1 lavatory and 1 toilet
kitchen with 1 sink and disposal and 1 dishwasher
laundry with 1 clothes washing machine
2 hose bibbs

Example 1:

Question:
Assuming that both second floor bathrooms drain to one stack, what is the dfu load on the stack and what size pipe should be installed for that stack?

Answer:
The dfu load is 12 and the pipe size is at least (≥) 3 inches.

Refer to table P3004.1. Remember to use the bathroom group values and add for any extra fixtures. The dfu load for a two full bathroom group (containing 2 bathtubs or showers, 2 lavatory sinks, and 2 toilets) from the dfu table is 8. Add 2 dfu for the extra shower and 2 dfu for the two extra lavatory sinks. Refer to Table 3004.5-1. A 2 ½ inches diameter pipe can serve up to 20 dfu as shown in the vertical stack column,; however, the minimum pipe size serving a toilet is 3 inches.

Example 2:

Question:
What is the total dfu load for this home and what size building and sewer drain pipes should be installed?

Answer:
The total dfu load for this home is 17 and both the building drain and building sewer pipe sizes are at least (≥) 3 inches.

Refer to table P3004.1. Remember to use the bathroom and kitchen group values and add for any extra fixtures. The dfu load for two and one half bathroom groups (containing 2 bathtubs or showers, 3 lavatory sinks, and 3 toilets) from the dfu table is 9. Add 2 dfu for the extra shower and 2 dfu for the two extra lavatory sinks. Add 2 dfu for the kitchen group and 2 dfu for the laundry. The hose bibbs add no drainage load. A 3 inches diameter pipe is the minimum size for any building drain or building sewer pipe that connects to a toilet.

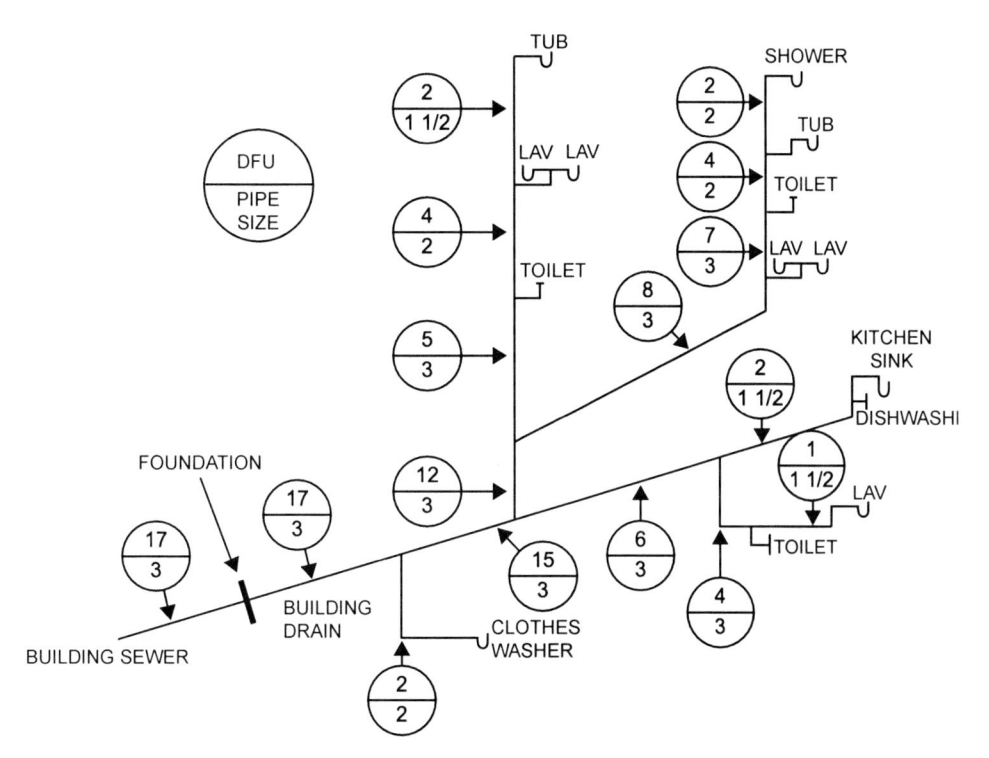

Drainage and Sewer Pipe Size Example (P3005.4-0)
Figure 30-2

DRAINAGE AND SEWER PIPE FITTINGS DEFINITIONS (P3005.1)

Drainage and Sewer Pipe Fittings Discussion

Drainage and sewer pipe fittings are used for changing the direction of drainage flow and are different from fittings used in water service and distribution pipes. Drainage and sewer pipe fittings must provide a gentle change in direction because drainage water flows by gravity and may contain solids. You cannot use elbows and other fittings intended for water under pressure with drainage and sewer pipes. You cannot use fittings intended only for vent pipes with pipes that carry liquids.

Drainage and sewer pipe fittings come in many different types and configurations. Some fittings have openings that are all the same size and some have reduced sizes for some openings. Some fittings are double fittings with openings on both sides of the fitting. Some fittings combine different types of fittings into one fitting, such as the combination wye and 1/8 bend.

Some fittings have all female openings (called hubs) and some fittings have a male and a female opening (called a street fitting). Fittings produced for some types of drainage and sewer pipe are not produced for others.

It is beyond the scope of this book to discuss all the possible types of drainage and sewer pipe fittings. We will discuss some of the more common ones used in modern residential plumbing.

Drainage and Sewer Pipe Fittings Definitions

Bend A bend is a fitting used to change the direction of waste flow. It is similar to an elbow used in water pressure pipes. Some people refer to a DWV bend as an elbow. A single bend has two openings. A double bend has three openings, two of which are directly across from each other. Some bends have side inlets. Use vent bends only in the dry vent sections of vent pipes. Bends are made with the following angles.

TABLE P3005.1-1
Bend Direction Change Table

bend name	direction change (degrees)
1/4 bend	90
1/6 bend	60
1/8 bend	45
1/16 bend	22 ½

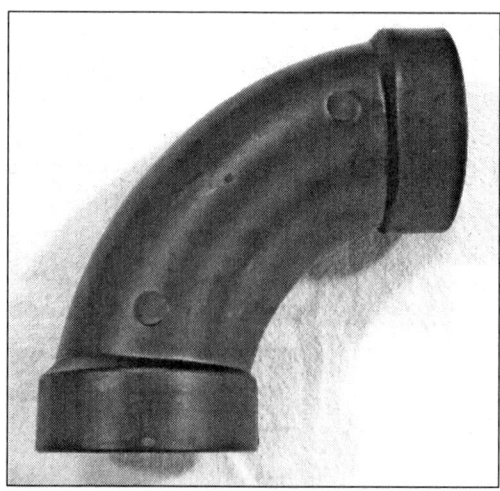

Long Turn ¼ Bend (PP3005.1-1)
Figure 30-3

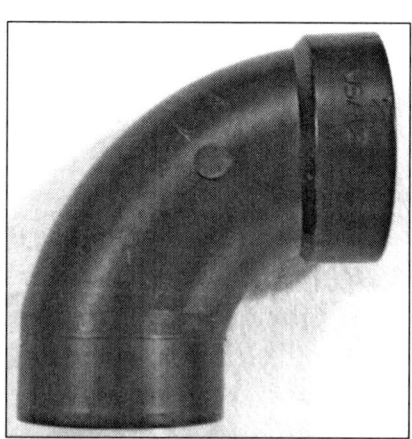

¼ Street Bend (PP3005.1-2)
Figure 30-4

1/8 Bend (PP3005.1-3)
Figure 30-5

¼ Bend Vent Elbow (PP3005.1-4) Figure 30-6

Closet bend A closet bend is a fitting used to connect a closet flange to other plumbing pipes. Closet bends often reduce the pipe size from the 4 inches of the closet flange to 3 inches.

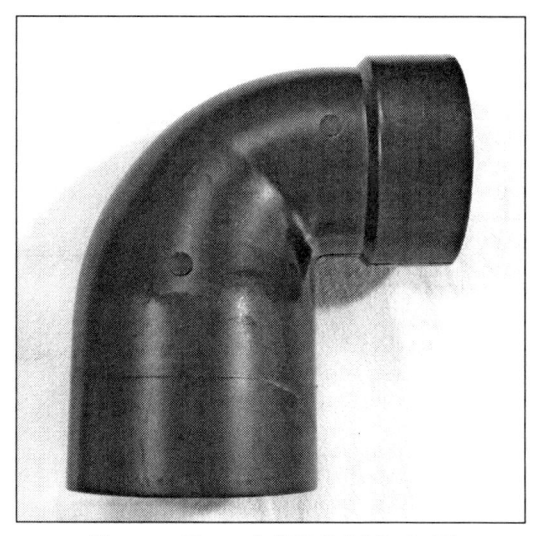

Closet Bend (PP3005.1-5)
Figure 30-7

Closet flange A closet flange is the fitting upon which a toilet (water closet) sits. Many different closet flanges are available to accommodate different fitting and pipe configurations. One type of closet flange allows you to offset the closet flange around a floor joist.

Closet Flange (PP3005.1-6)
Figure 30-8

Coupling A coupling is a fitting used to join two lengths of pipe in a straight line. It has two female openings, one on each end.

Inlet An inlet is an additional opening in a fitting. A low-heel-inlet is located in a straight line with one opening of the fitting. A high-heel-inlet is located above the curved portion of the fitting. A side-inlet occurs on one side of the fitting.

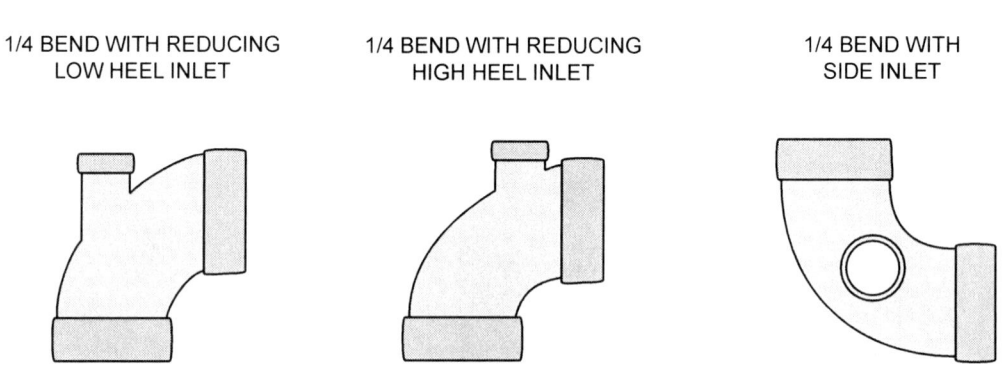

1/4 Bends with Inlets (P3005.1-1)
Figure 30-9

1/4 Bend with Reducing Low-Heel Inlet (PP3005.1-7)
Figure 30-10

Sanitary tee A sanitary tee is a tee fitting combined with a ¼ bend fitting.

Sanitary Tee
(PP3005.1-8)
Figure 30-11

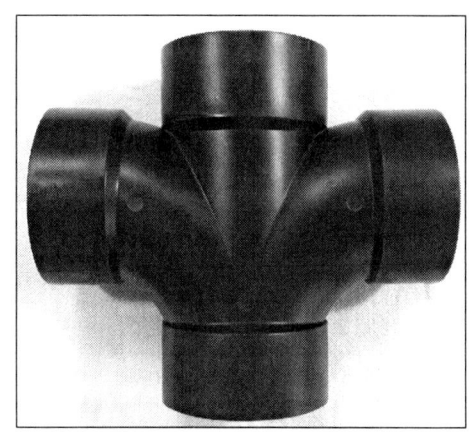

Double Sanitary Tee
(PP3005.1-9)
Figure 30-12

Street fitting A street fitting has a female opening (hub) on one end and a male opening (spigot) on the other end. Most drainage fittings have female openings on both ends.

Sweep A sweep is a fitting used to change the direction of waste flow. Sweeps have a large curvature radius. Short sweeps have a smaller radius than large sweeps.

Tee A tee is a fitting with 3 openings. Two openings are in a straight line and one opening is at an approximate 90° angle to the others. Double tees, with 4 openings, are also available. Use vent tees only in the dry vent sections of vent pipes.

Wye A wye is a fitting with 3 openings. Two openings are in a straight line and one opening is at an approximate 45° angle to the others. Wye fittings can be made with other fittings to make combination fittings such as a tee-wye and a combination wye and 1/8 bend. Double wye and double tee-wye fittings are also available.

Wye (PP3005.1-10)
Figure 30-13

Long Radius Reducing
Tee-Wye
(PP3005.1-11)
Figure 30-14

DRAINAGE AND SEWER PIPE FITTINGS INSTALLATION (P3005.1)

Drainage and Sewer Pipe Fittings for Changing Direction of Flow

1. Use the fittings in the following table to change the direction of flow in drainage and sewer pipes.

TABLE P3005.1-2
Approved Drainage Fittings for Changing Direction of Flow

type of fitting	horizontal to vertical	vertical to horizontal	horizontal to horizontal
1/16 bend	YES	YES	YES
1/8 bend	YES	YES	YES
1/6 bend	YES	YES	YES
1/4 bend	YES	YES for fixture drains ≤ 2 inches	YES for fixture drains ≤ 2 inches
short sweep	YES	YES for fixture drains ≤ 2 inches and for drains ≥ 3 inches	YES for fixture drains ≤ 2 inches
long sweep	YES	YES	YES
sanitary tee	YES with limits	NO	NO
wye	YES	YES	YES
long radius tee-wye	YES	YES	YES

Drainage and Sewer Pipe Fittings Changing from Horizontal to Vertical Using Multiple Fittings

1. You may use multiple fittings and double fittings (such as double sanitary tees) to connect back-to-back fixtures and two or more branch drains on the same level if: (a) directly opposite fitting connections are from the same size pipe, and if (b) directly opposite fitting connections are from similar fixture types or fixture groups.

2. Do not use a double sanitary tee to receive discharge from back-to-back toilets and from fixtures or appliances with pumping action (such as washing machines and dishwashers). You may use a double sanitary tee if the distance between the center of the closet flange and the inlet of the sanitary tee is at least (≥) 18 inches.

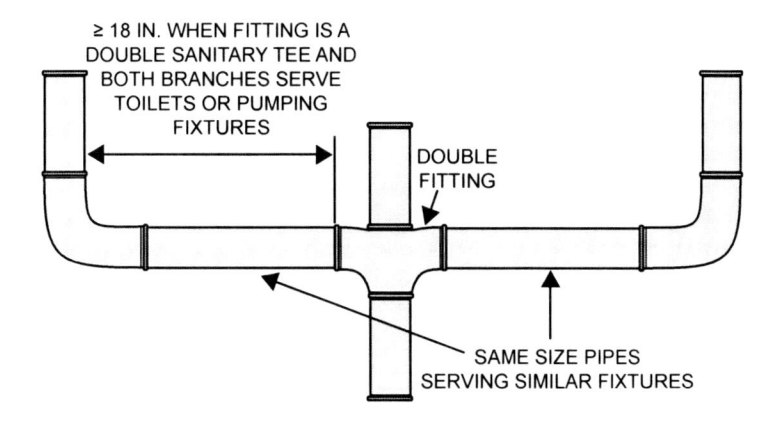

Approved Use of Double Fittings (3005.1-2)
Figure 30-15

Quarter Bends with Heel or Side-Inlet

1. You may use a heel-inlet quarter bend to change drainage flow direction, except:
   a) you may not discharge a toilet into any opening of a heel-inlet quarter bend unless the heel-inlet is used as a dry vent and the heel-inlet is installed vertically (facing up), and
   b) you may not discharge flow from a wet-vented fixture into the low-heel inlet of a quarter bend.

2. You may use a side-inlet quarter bend to change the flow direction in any drainage configuration. The side-inlet may accept drainage flow from any fixture.

3. You may connect a dry vent to a heel or side-inlet quarter bend only when the inlet is vertical (facing up). You may connect a dry vent to a quarter bend with a horizontal (side facing) inlet only if the entire quarter bend fitting is used as part of a dry vent.

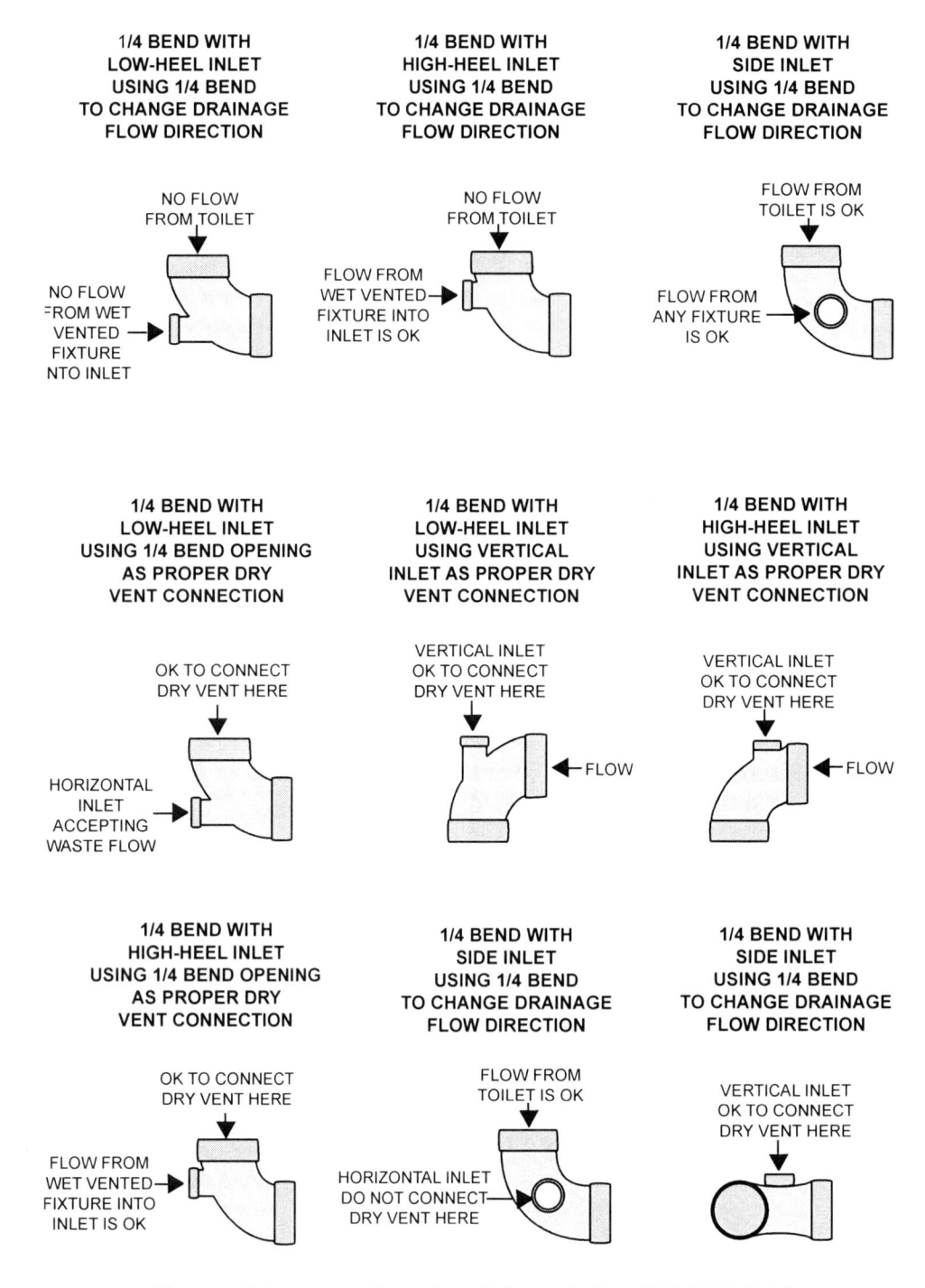

Uses of Quarter Bends with an Inlet (P3005.1-3)
Figure 30-16

Water Closet Connection Between Closet Flange and Pipe

1. You may use a 3 inch quarter bend to connect to a closet flange if you install a 4-inch-by-3-inch flange to receive the closet fixture horn.
2. You may use 4-inch-by-3-inch reducing closet bend to connect to the closet flange.

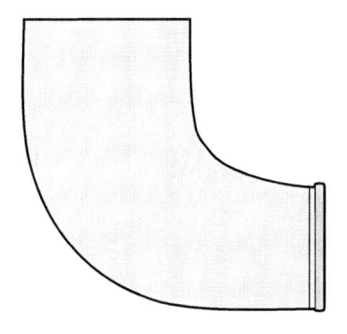

Reducing Closet Bend (P3005.1-4)
Figure 30-17

Drainage and Sewer Pipe Dead Ends

1. You may not extend a drainage or sewer pipe more than (>) 2 feet beyond the waste flow unless the extension is necessary to install a required cleanout or unless the extension is part of an approved rough-in for future fixtures.

Drainage and Sewer Pipe Sizing for Future Fixtures

1. Use pipe sizes that account for the drainage load imposed by all future fixtures that have been roughed-in and will connect to installed pipes.
2. Terminate rough-in pipes with an accessible permanent plug or cap fitting.

Drainage and Sewer Pipe Reduction in Size

1. Do not reduce drainage and sewer pipe size in the direction of the waste flow. A 4-inch-by-3-inch closet bend fitting is not a reduction in size. Example: do not drain a 2 inches trap into a 1 ½ inches drain pipe.

DRAINAGE AND SEWER PIPE CLEANOUTS (P3005.2)

Cleanout Locations and Spacing

1. Install a cleanout in every horizontal drain pipe so that the distance between cleanouts is not more than (≤) 100 feet, measured along the length of the pipe. Install at least (≥) one cleanout for every horizontal drain pipe regardless of length of the drain pipe. This provision applies to the building drain, building sewer, and horizontal branch drains.
2. Install a cleanout near the junction of the building drain and the building sewer. You may install this cleanout inside or outside the building. Make this cleanout accessible at the lowest floor level inside or at grade level outside. You may install this cleanout in at least (≥) a 3 inch diameter soil stack if the cleanout fitting is not more than (≤) 10 feet from the building drain connection to the building sewer. Measure the 10 feet along the developed length of the pipe from the cleanout fitting to the building drain and sewer junction.
3. Install a cleanout near the base of every vertical waste or soil stack. You may install this cleanout in the vertical stack or in the horizontal drain pipe.
4. Install a cleanout at every change of pipe direction of more than (>) 45 degrees when the direction change uses one fitting. You do not need to install a cleanout if the change in pipe

direction uses two or more fittings. When multiple direction changes occur in one pipe run, only one cleanout is required spaced not more than (≤) 40 feet apart. This provision applies to the building drain, building sewer, and horizontal branch drains. Example: A direction change using one 1/4 bend fitting requires a cleanout, but a change in direction using two 1/8 bend fittings does not require a cleanout.

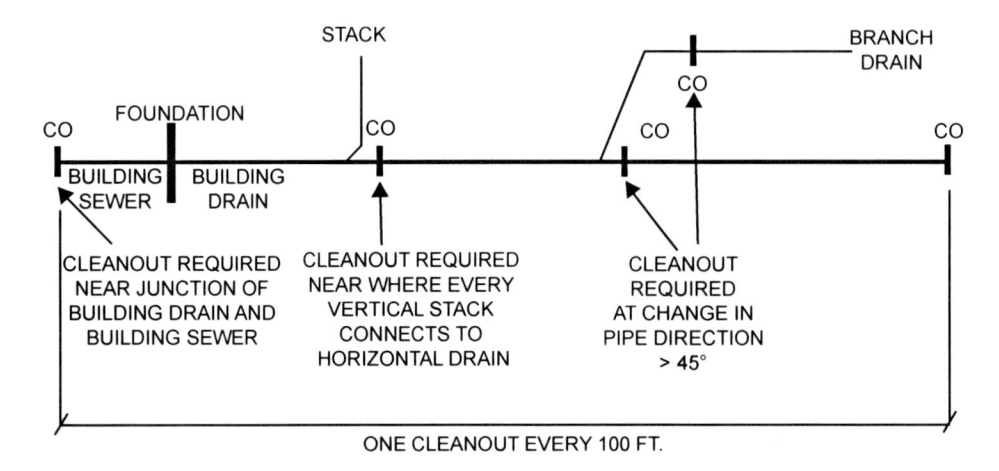

Cleanout Locations (P3005.2-1)
Figure 30-18

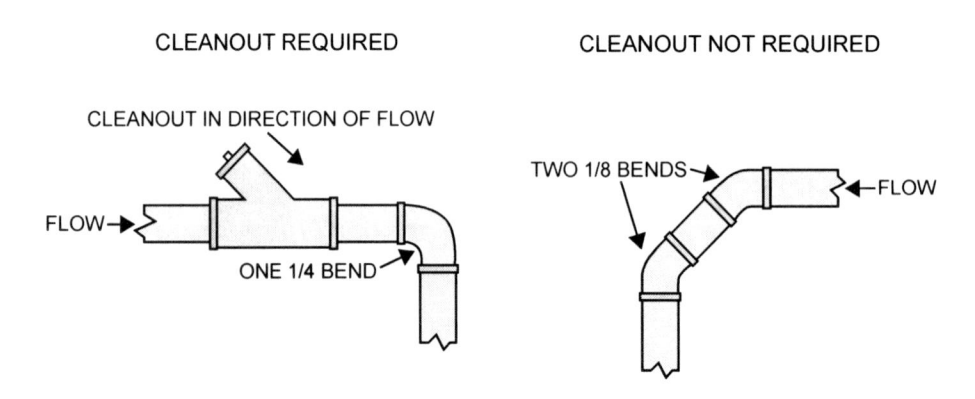

Cleanout at Direction Change (P3005.2-3)
Figure 30-19

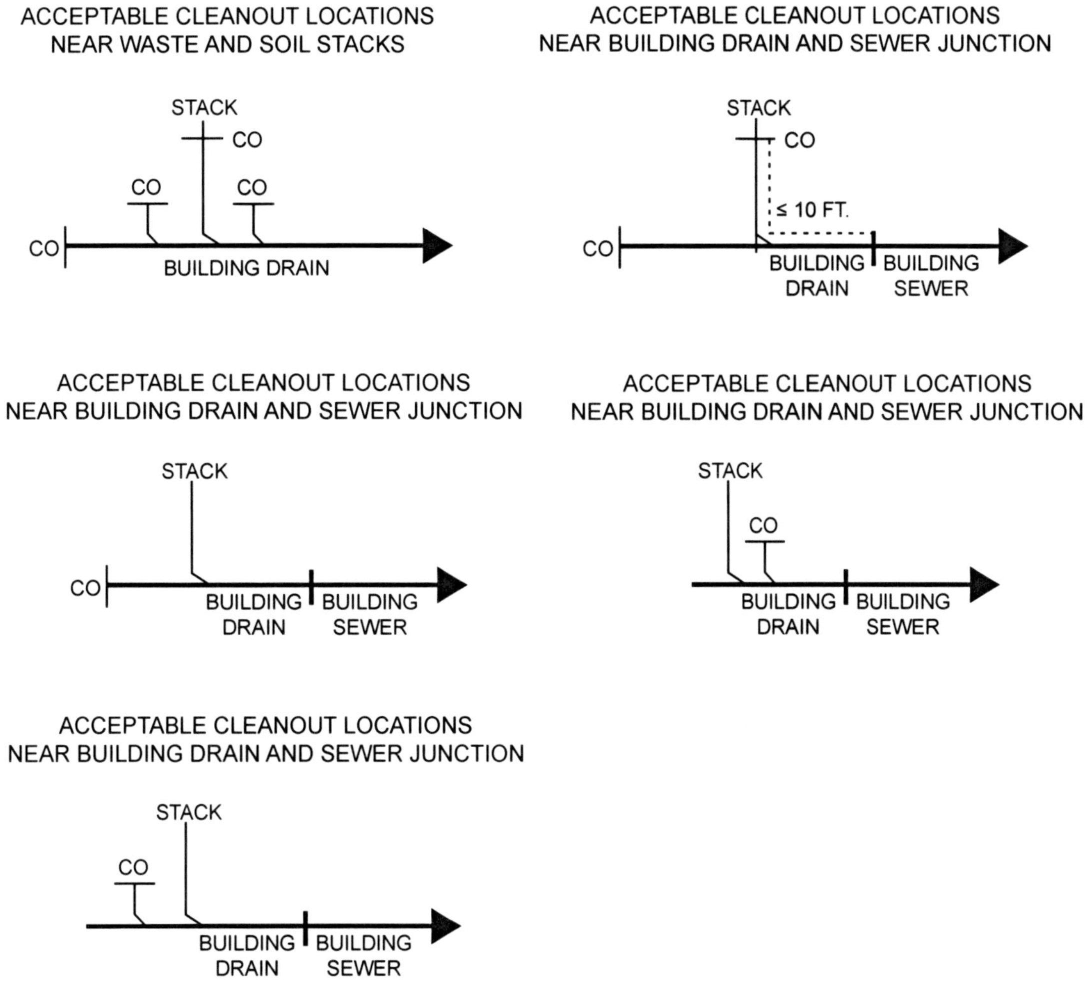

30 : Sanitary Drainage System Installation Requirements

ACCEPTABLE CLEANOUT LOCATIONS
NEAR WASTE AND SOIL STACKS

ACCEPTABLE CLEANOUT LOCATIONS
NEAR BUILDING DRAIN AND SEWER JUNCTION

ACCEPTABLE CLEANOUT LOCATIONS
NEAR BUILDING DRAIN AND SEWER JUNCTION

ACCEPTABLE CLEANOUT LOCATIONS
NEAR BUILDING DRAIN AND SEWER JUNCTION

ACCEPTABLE CLEANOUT LOCATIONS
NEAR BUILDING DRAIN AND SEWER JUNCTION

Acceptable Locations for Cleanout near Stack Base (P3005.2-2)
Figure 30-20

Cleanout Substitutes

1. You may use a fixture trap (such as a sink) or a fixture with an integral trap (such as a toilet) as a cleanout if the:
   a) trap or fixture is readily removable without disturbing concealed piping; and
   b) cleanout is accessible as defined in the IRC; and
   c) fixture trap or fixture provides the required cleanout size for all pipes that will be cleaned from the cleanout substitute.

2. Note that drainage pipes 3 inches and larger require a cleanout size that is larger than most fixture drains. You cannot use a 1 ½ or 2 inches fixture drain as a cleanout for pipes 3 inches and larger.

Cleanout Size

1. Install cleanouts at least as large as in the following table. You may install different size cleanouts in cast-iron drainage pipes because these pipes have different cap sizes.

TABLE 3005.2
Cleanout Size Table

pipe size (inches)	minimum cleanout size (inches)
1 ½	1 ½
2	1 ½
3	2 ½
≥ 4	3 ½

Cleanout Accessibility

1. Provide at least (≥) 18 inches in front of cleanouts (≥) 3 inches and larger and at least (≥) 12 inches in front of cleanout smaller than (<) 3 inches.
2. Provide enough access around concealed cleanouts to remove the cleanout plug and use the drain cleaning equipment.
3. Do not conceal cleanouts with permanent finishing materials.
4. Extend underground cleanouts to or above finished grade. Do not extend cleanouts above surfaces where they may become trip hazards or where they may be damaged by traffic.

Cleanout Plugs

1. Install brass or plastic plugs in cleanout fittings.
2. Make cleanouts gas and liquid tight.

Cleanout Direction

1. Install cleanouts so that they open toward the direction of the waste flow.

Cleanout Fixture Connections

1. Do not connect other pipes or fixtures to an existing cleanout unless the connection is approved by the local building official and you install an alternate cleanout. Example: do not remove a cleanout plug and use the cleanout opening as the drain for a laundry sink.

SEWAGE PUMPS AND EJECTORS (P3007)

Sewage Pump and Ejector Installation

1. Drain only plumbing fixtures located below the building sewer into a sewage pump or ejector. Drain all other plumbing fixtures into the building sewer. You may drain plumbing fixtures located above the building sewer into a sewage pump or ejector when you install a sewage pump or ejector in an existing plumbing system.
2. Install at least (≥) a 2 inches diameter discharge pipe on a nongrinding sewage pump or ejector.

3. Install at least (≥) a 1 ¼ inches diameter discharge pipe on a grinding sewage pump or ejector.
4. Install an accessible check valve and a full open valve on the discharge pipe between the sewage pump or ejector and the connection point to the building sewer or drain. Locate the full open valve on the discharge side of the check valve. Locate both valves above the sump pit cover. If the discharge pipe is below ground, locate the valves in an accessible pit with a removable cover.
5. Make the sump pit and cover accessible.
6. Connect the sump pit discharge pipe to the building sewer or use a wye fitting to connect the discharge pipe to a building drain. Make the building drain connection at least (≥) 10 feet from the where a soil stack, waste stack, or fixture drain connects with the building drain. Locate the wye opening at the top of the building drain pipe.
7. Locate the sump pit so that all materials flow into the pit by gravity.
8. Install and vent sewage pump and ejectors according to manufacturer's installation instructions.

Sewage Pump and Ejector Specifications

1. Install only automatic sewage pumps or ejectors. Do not rely on occupants to manually activate the sewage pump or ejector.
2. Install a sump pit that is at least (≥) 18 inches wide and 24 inches tall.
3. Construct the sump pit using concrete, steel, or plastic with a solid bottom capable of supporting the pump.
4. Install a gas and liquid tight cover for all sump pits.
5. Control the liquid level in the sump pit so that it does not rise to within (≤) 2 inches of the inlet pipe.
6. Install a sewage pump or ejector capable of handling 2 inches diameter solids if it serves a toilet. Install a sewage pump or ejector capable of handling 1 inch diameter solids if it does not serve a toilet.
7. Install a sewage pump or ejector according to Table P3007.

TABLE P3007
Sewage Pump or Ejector Capacity

discharge pipe diameter (inches)	minimum pump or ejector capacity (gallons per minute)
2	21
2 1/2	30
3	46

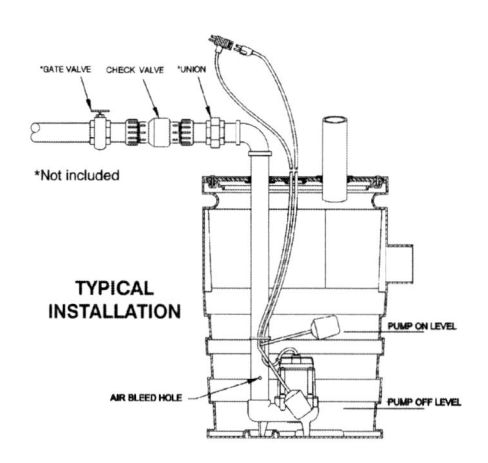

Sewage Ejector Pump (MP3007-1)
Figure 30-21

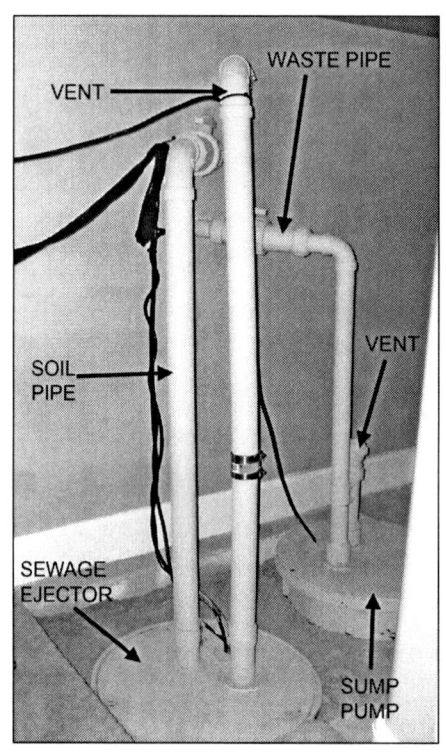

Sewage Ejector and Sump Pumps (PP3007-2)
Figure 30-22

Macerating Toilets Installation

1. A macerating toilet is a toilet with an internal mechanism that grinds and ejects soil materials under pressure to a soil pipe above the toilet. They are used when a toilet is located at a level below the building drain.
2. Install macerating toilets according to manufacturer's installation instructions.

BACKWATER VALVES (P3008)

Backwater Valves

1. Install a backwater valve to protect fixtures whose flood rim level is below the closest upstream public sewer manhole cover.
2. Install the backwater valve in the building drain or in any branch drain that serves the fixtures requiring protection.
3. Do not discharge fixtures that have flood rim levels above the closest upstream manhole cover through the backwater valve.
4. Provide access to the backwater valve through a water tight cover.
5. Use only approved backwater valves constructed with parts that will not corrode and will provide a positive mechanical seal.
6. Install a backwater valve that has at least (≥) the same capacity as the pipes served.

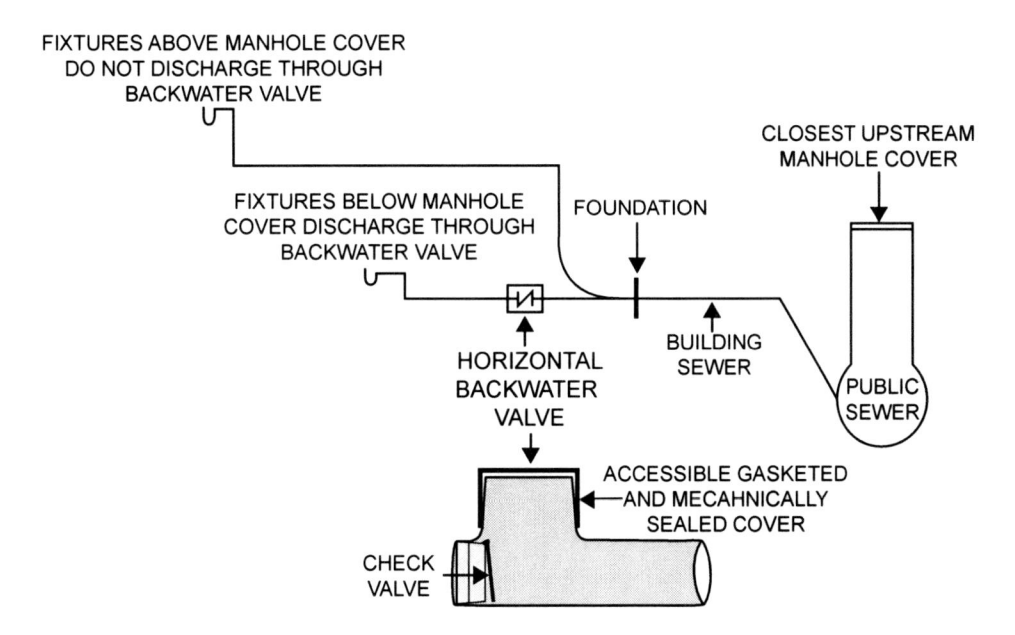

Backwater Valve Installation (P3008-0)
Figure 30-23

31

PLUMBING VENTS

PLUMBING VENTS GENERAL INSTALLATION

Plumbing Vents Required (P3101 and P3102)

1. Install an approved vent for every trap and trapped fixture. This means that every plumbing fixture (such as a sink or a shower) and every plumbing fixture with an integrated trap (such as a toilet) must be protected by an individual vent or an approved system where one vent protects multiple fixtures.
2. Terminate at least (≥) one vent outdoors. Connect the outdoor vent to the building drain or to a branch or extension of the building drain. The branch or extension cannot be an island fixture vent.

Flood Resistance (P3101)

1. Install vent pipes above the design flood elevation established by local regulations. Obtain this elevation from Section R323.1 or from the local building official.

Vent Slope and Support (P3104)

1. Install all vent pipes using adequate supports so that the vent pipes slope toward the soil or waste pipe. Moisture in any form should flow toward the soil or waste pipe by gravity. The IRC does not specify support intervals for vent pipes. Supporting vent pipes at the same interval required for drain pipes is recommended, but not required.

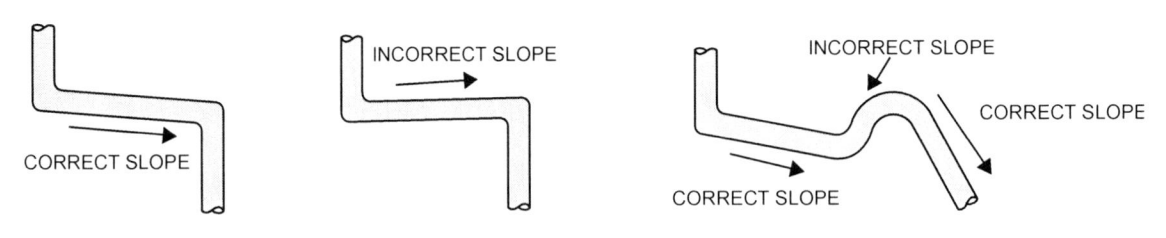

Vent Slope (P3104-1)
Figure 31-1

Vent Connection to Horizontal Drainage Pipes (P3104)

1. Connect vent pipes to horizontal drainage pipes above the center-line of the horizontal drainage pipe. This protects the vent pipe from filling with solid material.

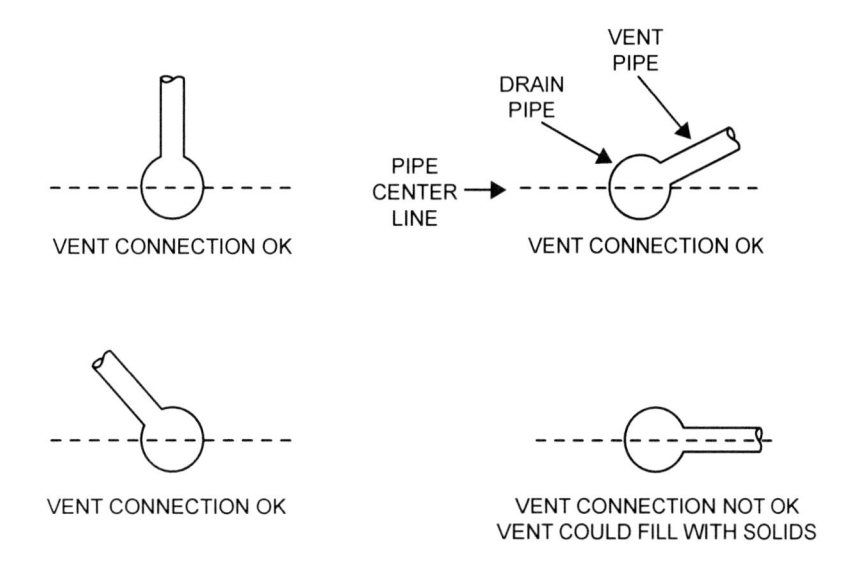

Vent Connection to Horizontal Drainage Pipe (P3104-2)
Figure 31-2

Vent Connection Height Minimums (P3104)

1. Connect dry vent pipes to vent stacks, stack vents, and to stack-type air admittance valves so that the connection point is at least (≥) 6 inches above the flood rim level of the highest fixture served by the vent. A common violation of this provision is when a dry vent runs parallel to the drainage pipes under the fixture. This provision helps protect the vent pipe from filling with solid material.
2. Install horizontal branch vent pipes at least (≥) 6 inches above the flood rim level of the highest fixture served by the vent.

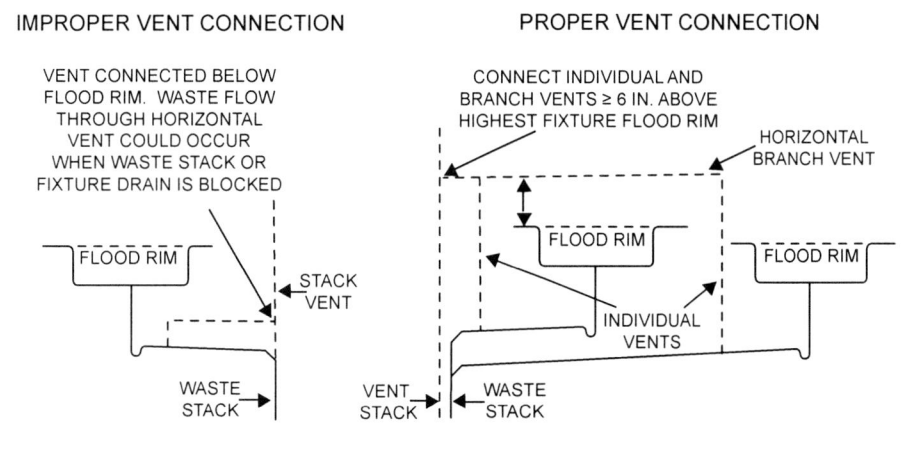

Minimum Height for Vent Connections (P3104-3)
Figure 31-3

Vent Rough-in for Future Fixtures (P3104)

1. Install a vent for roughed-in (future) fixtures that is at least (≥) one-half the diameter of the drain pipe rough-in.

2. Connect the roughed-in vent to the vent system or provide another approved means to terminate the roughed-in vent.
3. Label the roughed-in vent pipe to indicated that it is a vent.

VENT EXTERIOR TERMINATIONS (P3103)

Vent Height Above Roof

1. Extend vent pipes above the roof at least (≥) 6 inches, or the number of inches required by local snow accumulation and temperature conditions, whichever is higher. Measure height on the high side where the vent exits the roof. Obtain the snow accumulation height from the local building official.
2. Extend vent pipes at least (≥) 7 feet above any roof used as a balcony, observation deck, or similar accessible walking surface.

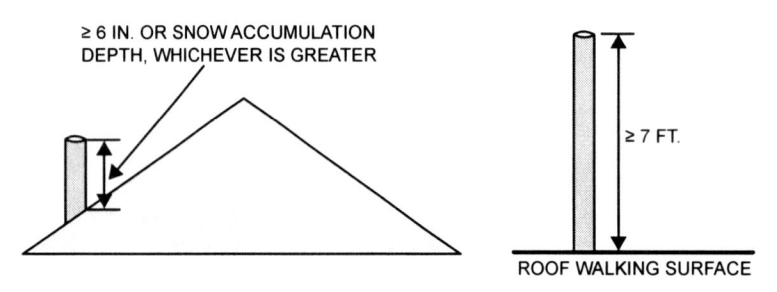

Vent Height Above Roof (P3103-1)
Figure 31-4

Vent Freezing and Frost Closure Protection

1. Protect exterior vent terminals from freezing by using heat, insulation or both.
2. Increase the diameter of exterior vent terminal pipes to at least (≥) 3 inches, beginning at least (≥) 1 foot below the roof or inside the wall.
3. These provisions apply only where the 97.5 percent winter design temperature is less than (<) 0° F. Obtain this information from IRC Chapter 3 and from the local building official.

Vent Flashing

1. Use approved flashing to make vent pipes extending through a roof water tight.
2. Use caulk to make vent pipes extending through a wall water tight.

Lead Plumbing Vent Flashing (PP3103-1)
Figure 31-5

Vent Prohibited Uses

1. Do not use a vent pipe to support flag poles, antennae, or similar items unless the vent pipe is structurally reinforced in an approved manner. Approved vent pipe structural reinforcement is very rare. It is best not to use vent pipes to support other components.
2. Do not use plumbing vents other than for venting the plumbing system (P3101.3). Example: do not discharge HVAC system condensate or waste water from a water softener or water filtration system into a vent pipe. You may be able to use vent pipes to receive discharge from these devices if the vent and connecting pipes have been designed and installed as waste pipes. Such design and installation is very rare. It is best not to discharge waste water into vent pipes.

Improper Connection of Water Softener to Vent (PP3103-2)
Figure 31-6

Vent Exterior Termination Locations

1. Locate plumbing vent terminations at least (≥) 4 feet below, or at least (≥) 2 feet above, or at least (≥) 10 feet horizontally from any:
   a) door or operable window, and
   b) other air intake opening of the building, and
   c) air intake opening of any adjacent building.
2. Locate plumbing vent terminations running through a sidewall at least (≥) 10 feet from the lot line and at least (≥) 10 feet above the highest grade within 10 feet horizontally from the vent termination.
3. Protect side wall vent terminations from entry by birds or rodents.
4. Do not locate vent terminations directly under the building's overhang if the overhang contains eave vents.

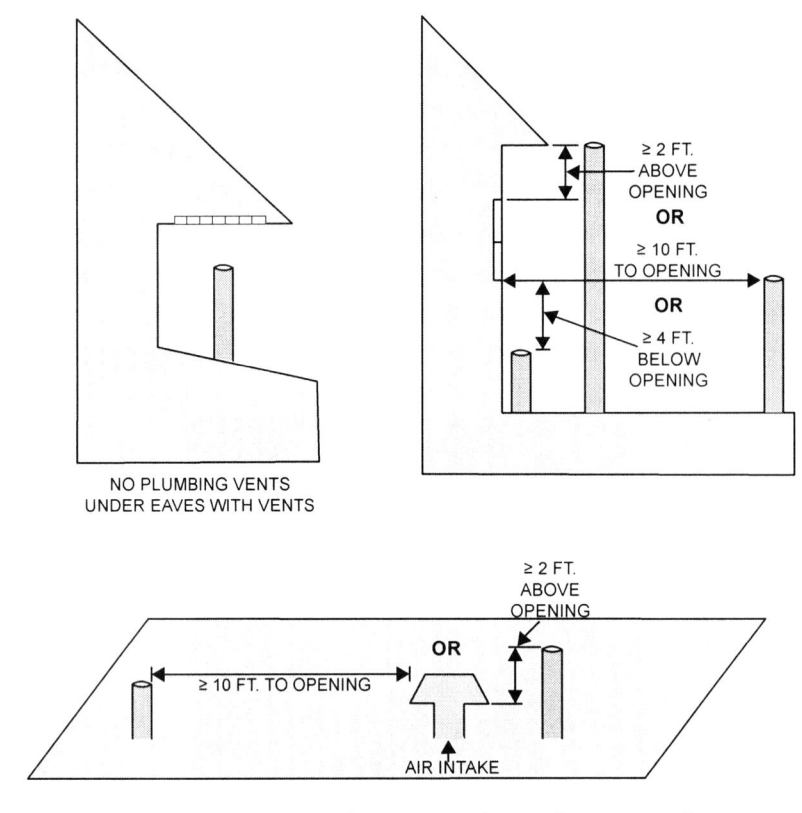

Vent Termination Locations (P3103-2)
Figure 31-7

FIXTURE DRAINS (P3105)

Vent Distance from Trap

1. Use the following table to determine the maximum length of a fixture drain between a trap weir and a vent fitting. The vent fitting may be at a vent pipe, such as an individual vent, or at a vented pipe, such as a wet vent.
2. The table does not apply to self-siphoning fixtures, such as toilets. No fixture drain length limitations apply to these fixtures.

TABLE P3105
Vent Distance from Trap Table

trap size	slope (inch per foot)	distance from trap to vent fitting (feet)
1 ¼	¼	5
1 ½	¼	6
2	¼	8
3	⅛	12
4	⅛	16

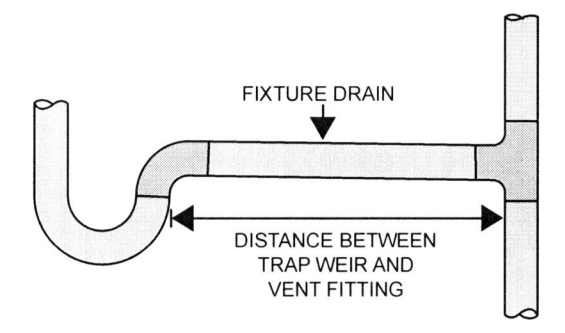

Vent Distance from Trap (P3105-1)
Figure 31-8

Fixture Drain Slope

1. Connect the fixture drain pipe with not more than (≤) one pipe diameter of fall between the bottom of the trap outlet and the bottom of the vent fitting inlet. This parallels the distance requirements in Table P3105 and reduces the chance that the trap will drain because the fitting is below the trap. Example: 5 feet x ¼ inch/foot = 1 ¼ inches. See the first row of Table P3105.
2. Connect the top of the fixture drain pipe to the vent fitting above the trap weir. This provision does not apply to toilet fixture drains.

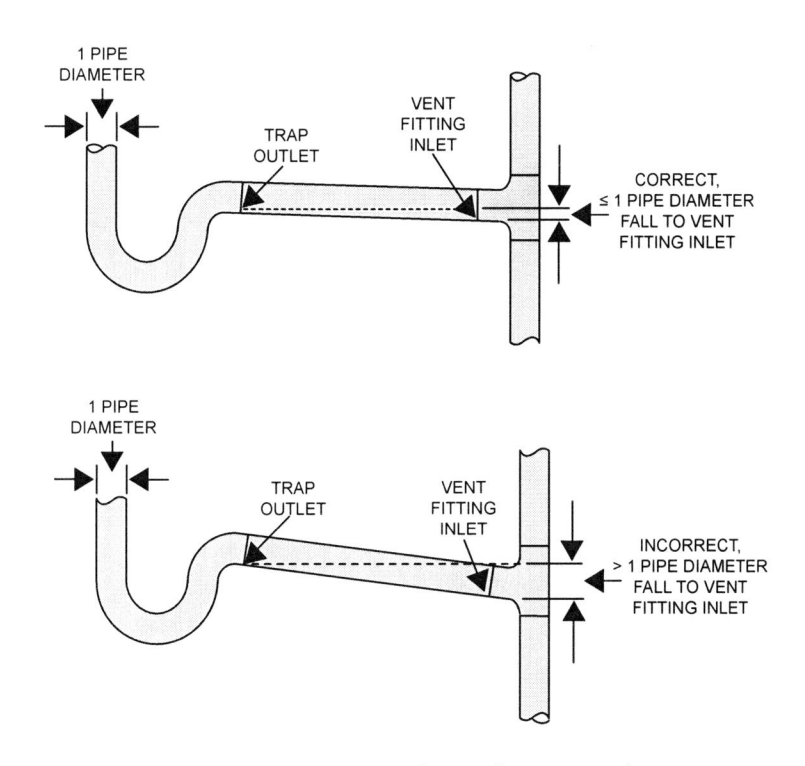

Fixture Drain Slope (P3105-2)
Figure 31-9

Crown Venting

1. Connect the vent fitting at least (≥) two pipe diameters from the trap weir.

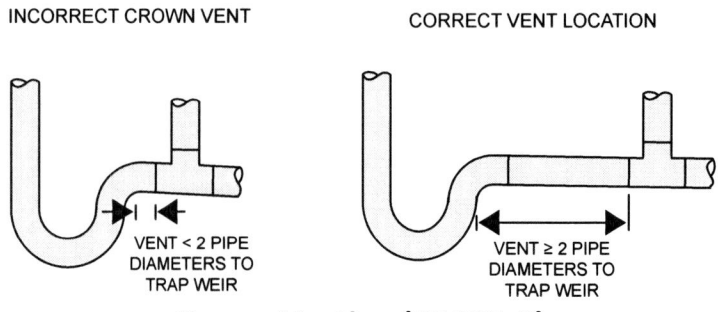

Crown Venting (P3105-3)
Figure 31-10

INDIVIDUAL VENTS (P3106)

1. Fixture Types: Use an individual vent to protect any fixture.
2. Number of Fixtures: Use an individual vent to protect only one fixture.
3. Fixture Location: Use an individual vent to protect one fixture located anywhere in the structure.
4. Individual Vent Connection Location: Connect the individual vent on the fixture drain of the fixture being vented or at the fixture drain connection to the drainage system.
5. Fixture Drain Length to Vent Connection: Use Table P3105 to determine the maximum distance between the fixture trap weir and the individual vent fitting.
6. Individual Vent Pipe Size: Use at least a (≥) 1 ¼ inches pipe or a pipe at least (≥) one-half the size of the drain pipe being vented, whichever is larger.

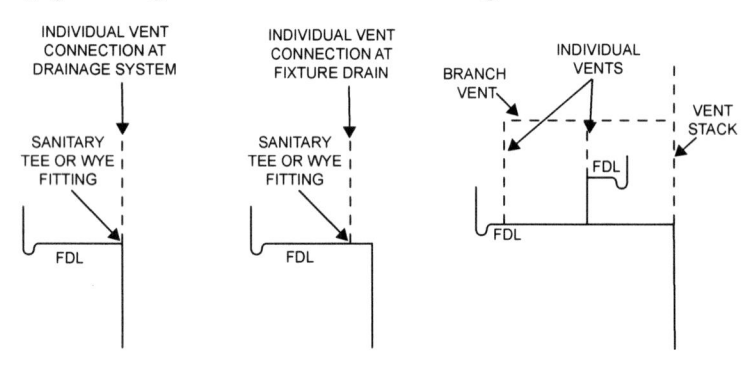

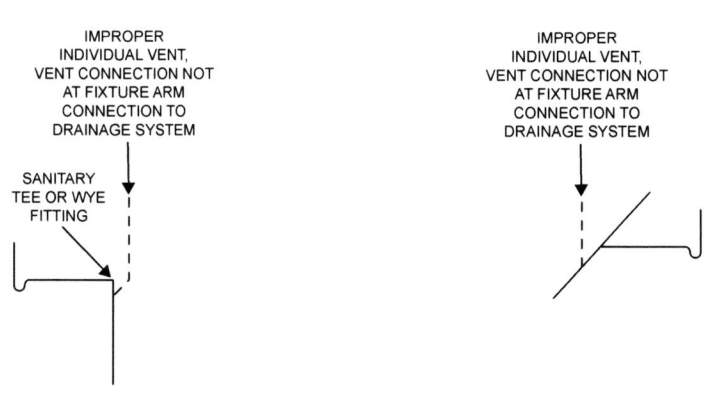

Individual Vent (P3106-0)
Figure 31-11

Individual Vent Rough-in (PP3106-0)
Figure 31-12

COMMON VENTS (P3107)

1. Fixture Types: Use a common vent to protect any two fixtures. You may common vent different types of fixtures, such as a sink and a shower or a shower and a toilet.

2. Number of Fixtures: Use a common vent to protect only two fixtures.

3. Fixture Location: Use a common vent only for fixtures located on the same floor level. You may connect the fixture drains at different vertical levels if the fixtures are on the same floor level.

4. Horizontal Common Vent Connection Location: You may connect the common vent where the fixture drains intersect. You may connect the common vent downstream from where the fixture drains intersect <u>only when the fixture drains connect to the branch drain pipe at the same horizontal level</u>.

5. Vertical Common Vent Connection Location: Connect the common vent as a vertical extension of the branch drain pipe when the fixture drains connect to the branch drain pipe at different vertical levels. Do not connect a toilet above another type of fixture when connecting two fixtures to a vertical common vent.

6. Fixture Drain Length to Vent Connection: Use Table P3105 to determine the maximum distance between each fixture trap weir and the common vent fitting.

7. Common Vent Pipe Size: (a) Use at least a (≥) 1 ¼ inches pipe or a pipe at least (≥) one-half the size of the drain pipe being vented, whichever is larger, for the common vent. (b) Use the following table to size the vertical pipe between the upper and lower fixture drain connections of a vertical common vent. Use the total dfu discharged by both fixtures and Table P3005.4-1 to size the vertical pipe below the lower fixture drain connection of a common vertical vent. You may not connect a toilet to a drainage pipe smaller than 3 inches regardless of what is allowed in the table.

TABLE P3107
Common Vent Vertical Pipe Size

pipe size (inches)	max. discharge from upper fixture drain (dfu)
1 ½	1
2	4
2 ½ to 3	6

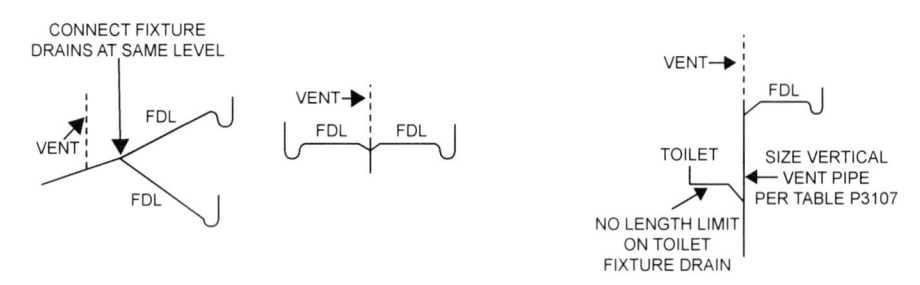

Common Vent (P3107-0)
Figure 31-13

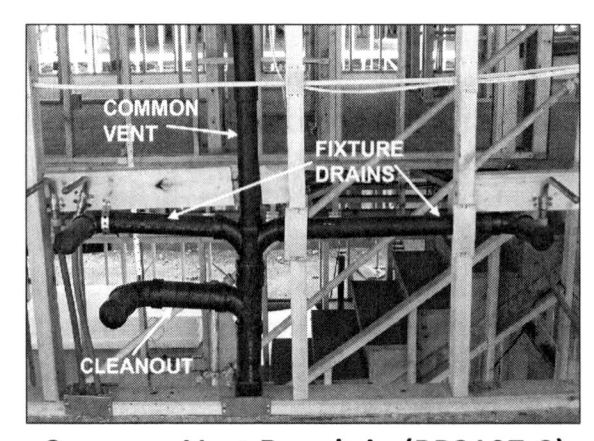

Common Vent Rough-in (PP3107-0)
Figure 31-14

WET VENTS (P3108)

1. Fixture Types: Use a wet vent to protect any combination of fixtures from not more than (≤) two bathroom groups.
2. Number of Fixtures: Use a wet vent to protect not more than (≤) two toilets, and two bathtubs or showers, and two lavatory sinks, and two bidets.
3. Fixture Location: Use a wet vent only for approved bathroom fixtures located on the same floor level.
4. Wet Vent Connection Location:
   a) Begin the wet vent with an individual or common vent for a lavatory, bidet, shower, or

bathtub. This vent does not need to be at the first wet vented fixture in a <u>horizontal</u> wet vent. This vent must be at the first wet vented fixture in a <u>vertical</u> wet vent. End the wet vent at the last wet vented fixture connection to the wet vented pipe.

    b) Do not connect more than one fixture upstream from the beginning individual or common vent in a horizontal wet vent.

    c) Connect each fixture individually to the wet vented pipe. Do not connect two or more fixtures together and connect that branch drain to the wet vented pipe.

5. Horizontal Wet Vent Fixture Drain Connection Location:

    a) Connect each individual fixture drain horizontally to the horizontal wet vented pipe. Example: you may not install a sanitary tee fitting vertically and connect a fixture drain to the vertical opening of the sanitary tee in a horizontal wet vent. You may install the sanitary tee horizontally and connect the horizontal fixture drain to the horizontal opening of the sanitary tee.

    b) You may connect a fixture drain vertically to a horizontal wet vented pipe if you install a dry vent on the vertically connected fixture. Example: you may install a sanitary tee fitting vertically if you connect an individual vent to the fixture.

    c) Do not connect any fixtures to the horizontal wet vented pipe other than those fixtures being wet vented. You may connect other fixtures to the horizontal pipe downstream after the wet vent ends. Example: do not connect a bedroom bar sink to a wet vented pipe.

6. Vertical Wet Vent Fixture Drain Connection Location:

    a) Connect all <u>toilet</u> fixture drains at the same vertical level.

    b) Connect fixture drains from bathtubs, showers, lavatory sinks, and bidets at or above where the toilet fixture drains connect to the vertical wet vent.

7. Fixture Drain Length to Wet Vented Pipe: Use Table P3105 to determine the maximum distance between each fixture trap weir and the fixture drain fitting at the wet vented drain pipe. You may use individual and common vents to protect any fixture where the fixture drain length limit is a problem.

8. Wet Vent Pipe Size: (a) Use a dry vent that is at least a (≥) 1 ¼ inches pipe or a pipe at least (≥) one-half the size of the wet vented pipe, whichever is larger, for the individual or common vent that begins the wet vent. (b) Use the following table to size the horizontal and vertical wet vented drainage pipe. You may not connect a toilet to a drainage pipe smaller than 3 inches regardless of what is allowed in the table.

TABLE P3108
Horizontal and Vertical Wet Vented Drainage Pipe Size

wet vented pipe size (inches)	max. dfu load
1 ½	1
2	4
2 ½	6
3	12
4	32

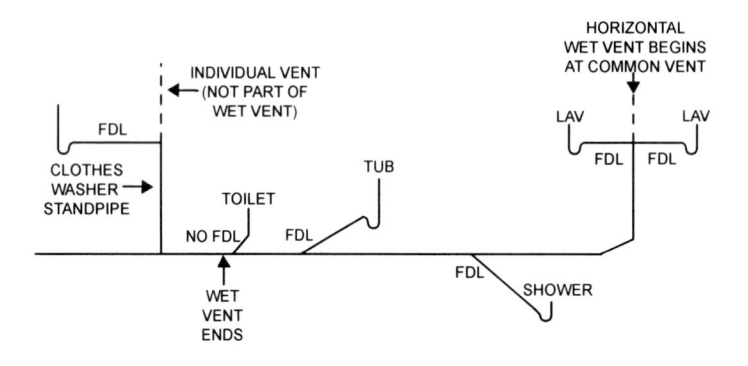

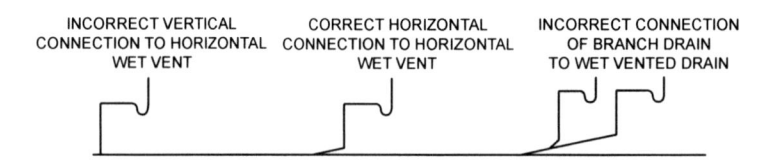

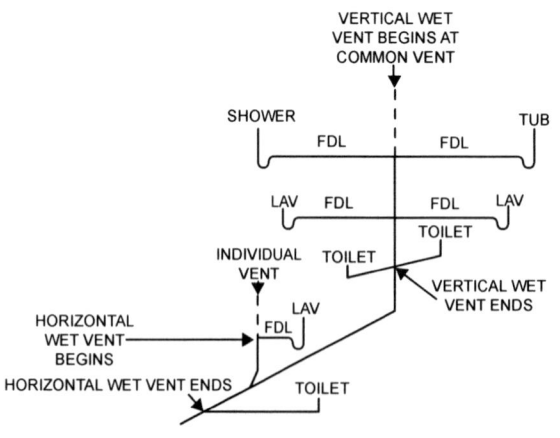

FDL = FIXTURE DRAIN LENGTH IS LIMITED PER TABLE P3105

Wet Vent (P3108-0)
Figure 31-15

WASTE STACK VENTS (P3109)

1. Fixture Types: Use a waste stack vent to protect any combination of fixtures, except toilets and urinals.
2. Number of Fixtures: Use a waste stack vent to protect any number of approved fixture types.
3. Fixture Location: Use a waste stack vent for fixtures located on the same or different floor levels.
4. Pipe Configuration:
    a) Use only a vertical pipe for a waste stack. Do not install vertical or horizontal offsets in the waste stack pipe between the highest and lowest vented fixtures. You may install offsets in the vertical pipe below the lowest fixture vented by the waste stack vent.
    b) Maintain at least (≥) the same pipe size for the entire length of the waste stack.
    c) Connect each fixture separately to the waste stack.
5. Waste Stack Dry Vent Connection Location: Connect the waste stack vent as a dry vertical extension of the waste stack. You may install offsets in the dry vent above the waste stack. Connect any offsets at least (≥) 6 inches above the highest fixture flood rim. See Section 3104.
6. Fixture Drain Length to Vent Connection: Use Table P3105 to determine the maximum distance between each fixture trap weir and the fixture drain fitting at the waste stack pipe. You may use individual and common vents to protect any fixture where the fixture drain length limit is a problem.
7. Waste Stack Vent Pipe Size:
    a) Use a dry stack vent pipe at least (≥) as large as waste stack being vented. Example: if the waste stack pipe is 3 inches, then the waste stack vent must be at least (≥) 3 inches.
    b) Use the following table to size the wet vertical waste stack pipe. Use the one branch interval column to determine the maximum dfu load in any single horizontal fixture drain connecting to the waste stack. Use the stack column to determine the maximum dfu load in the waste stack.

TABLE P3109
Vertical Waste Stack Drainage Pipe Size

stack pipe size (inches)	max. dfu load one fixture drain	max. dfu load for stack
1 ½	1	2
2	2	4
2 ½	no limit	8
3	no limit	24
4	no limit	50

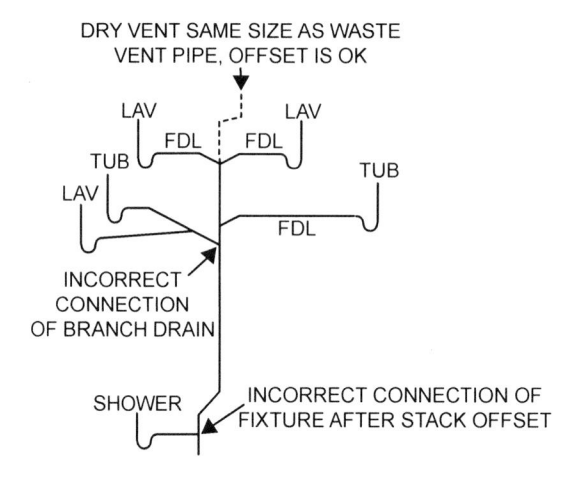

Waste Stack Vent (P3109-0)
Figure 31-16

CIRCUIT VENTS (P3110)

1. Fixture Types: Use a circuit vent to protect a combination of any fixture types.
2. Number of Fixtures: Use a circuit vent to protect not more than (≤) 8 fixtures.
3. Fixture Location: Use a circuit vent only for fixtures located on the same floor level and connecting to the same horizontal circuit vented pipe. You may connect other fixtures to the horizontal circuit vented pipe if: (a) the other fixtures are on the same floor level, and if (b) the other fixtures have their own individual or common vents. Do not include these fixtures in the eight fixtures limitation.
4. Pipe Configuration:
   a) Connect each individual fixture drain horizontally to the horizontal circuit vented pipe.
   b) Slope the horizontal circuit vented pipe not more than (≤) one unit in twelve units (8 percent slope).
   c) Use the total number of dfu discharged into the entire horizontal circuit vented pipe and use Table P3005.4-1 to determine the size of the horizontal circuit vented pipe at each point over its length.

5. Circuit Vent Connection Location: Connect the vent for the horizontal circuit vented pipe between the two most upstream fixtures.
6. Fixture Drain Length to Vent Connection: Use Table P3105 to determine the maximum distance between each fixture trap weir and the fixture drain fitting at the horizontal circuit vented pipe. You may use individual and common vents to protect any fixture where the fixture drain length limit is a problem.
7. Circuit Vent Pipe Size: Use at least a (≥) 1 ¼ inches pipe or a pipe at least (≥) one-half the size of the horizontal circuit vented pipe, whichever is larger.

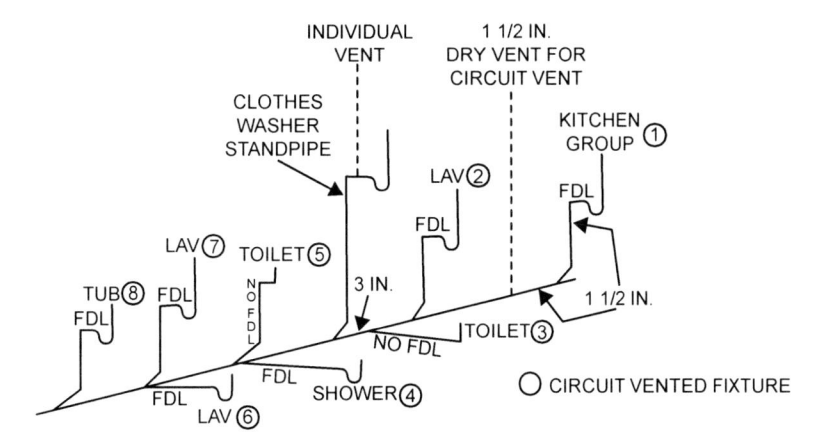

Circuit Vent (P3110-0)
Figure 31-17

COMBINATION WASTE AND VENT (P3111)

1. Fixture Types: Use a combination waste and vent to protect floor drains, sinks, and lavatories. Do not connect standpipes, toilets, urinals, or sinks with disposals to a combination waste and vent.
2. Number of Fixtures: Use a combination waste and vent to protect any number of approved fixture types.
3. Fixture Location: You may use a vertical pipe not more than (≤) 8 feet high between the fixture drain and the horizontal combination waste and vent pipe.
4. Pipe Configuration:
   a) Slope the horizontal combination waste and vent pipe not more than (≤) one-half unit in twelve units (4 percent slope).
   b) Use the following table to determine the size of the combination waste and vent pipe. Use the branch or stack column if the combination waste and vent pipe discharges into a horizontal branch or stack pipe. Use the building drain or subdrain column if the combination waste and vent pipe discharges into the building drain or a subdrain.

TABLE P3111
Combination Waste and Vent Pipe Size

combination waste and vent pipe size (inches)	max. dfu load discharge to branch or stack	max. dfu load discharge to building drain or subdrain
2	3	4
2 ½	6	26
3	12	31
4	20	50

5. Vent Connection Location: Connect an individual vent to the combination waste and vent pipe if the pipe does not discharge into the building drain or into another independently vented horizontal branch drain. Extend any individual vent at least (≥) 6 inches above the flood rim level of the highest fixture being vented before any horizontal offsets.

6. Fixture Drain Length to Vent Connection: (a) You may use Table P3105 to determine the maximum fixture drain length for the size of trap if you size the fixture drain as a fixture drain, or (b) You may use Table P3111 if you size the fixture drain as a combination waste and vent. When using Table P3111, the combination waste and vent pipe is oversized and allows enough air movement to avoid siphoning the trap, thus, there is no need for a fixture drain length limit.

7. Vent Pipe Size: Use at least a (≥) 1 ¼ inches pipe or a pipe at least (≥) one-half the size of the drain pipe being vented the dry vent, whichever is larger.

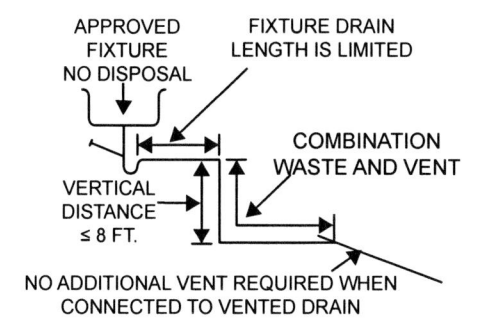

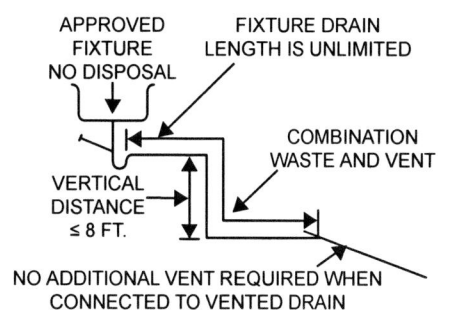

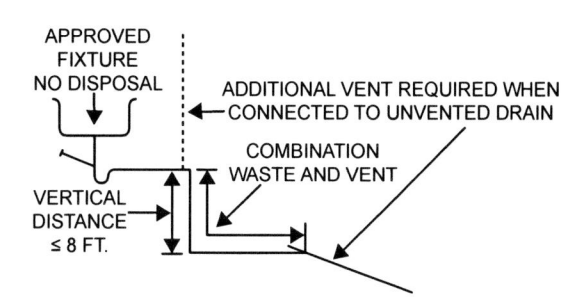

Combination Waste and Vent (P3111-0)
Figure 31-18

ISLAND FIXTURE VENTS (P3112)

1. Fixture Types: Use an island fixture vent to protect only sinks and lavatories. You may connect a dishwasher and disposal to a kitchen sink as a kitchen group.
2. Number of Fixtures: Use an island fixture vent to protect any number of approved fixtures types.
3. Fixture Location: Use an island fixture vent only for fixtures located in the same island and on the same floor level.
4. Pipe Configuration:
   a) Extend the loop portion of the island fixture vent vertically to above the drain outlet of the fixture being vented before extending the horizontal and/or vertical downward portion.
   b) Use drainage fittings and pipe slopes for any portion of the vent below the fixture flood rim level. Do not use vent fittings or slope the vent pipe as a vent below the fixture flood rim level.
   c) Connect the downward portion of the vent loop downstream from where the fixture drain connects with the horizontal drainage pipe. Make the connection using a full size fitting.

d) Provide cleanouts at the downward portion of the loop vent and in the vertical portion of the vent pipe before it connects to the exterior vent pipe.

5. Dry Vent Connection Location:
   a) Connect the dry vent to the drainage system using a full size fitting. Connect the dry vent to a vertical drain pipe or the top half of a horizontal drain pipe.
   b) Extend any dry vent at least (≥) 6 inches above the flood rim level of the highest fixture being vented before any connection to the outside vent.

6. Fixture Drain Length to Vent Connection: Use Table P3105 to determine the maximum distance between the fixture trap weir and the fixture drain connection to the island vent.

7. Vent Pipe Size: Use at least a (≥) 1 ¼ inches pipe or a pipe at least (≥) one-half the size of the drain pipe size being vented as the dry portion of the vent, whichever is larger.

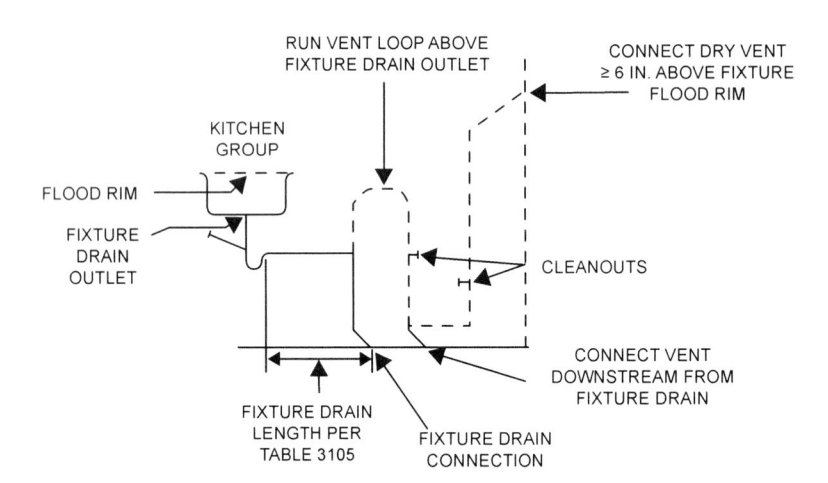

Island Fixture Vent (P3112-0)
Figure 31-19

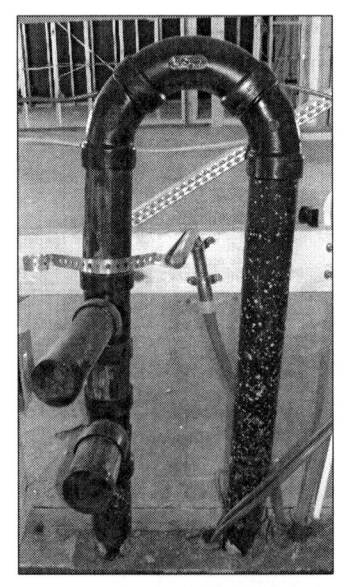

Island Fixture Vent Rough-in
Figure 31-20

VENT PIPE SIZE (P3113)

Vent Pipe Size

1. Use at least a (≥) 1 ¼ inches diameter vent pipe or a vent pipe at least (≥) one-half the diameter of the drain pipe being vented, whichever is larger, as the dry vent.
2. Increase the vent pipe diameter by at least (≥) one pipe size over the entire length of the vent pipe when the vent developed length is greater than (>) 40 feet.

Vent Pipe Developed Length

1. Measure the developed length of individual, branch, and circuit vents beginning where the vent connects to the drainage system and ending where the vent connects to a vent stack, stack vent, air admittance valve, or the vent's termination point outside the building.

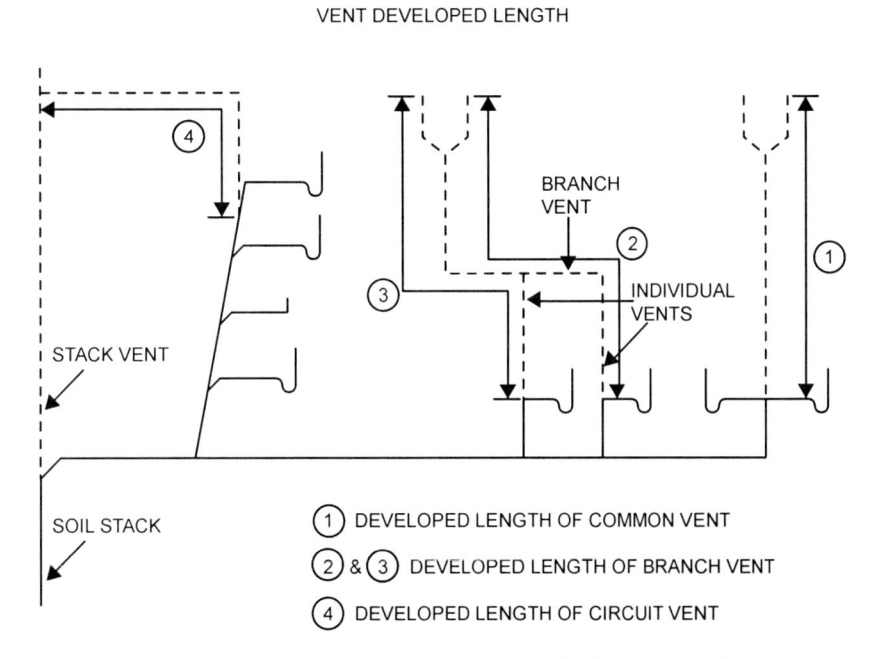

Vent Pipe Developed Length (P3113-0)
Figure 31-21

Branch Vent Size with Multiple Connected Vents

1. Determine the branch vent size by adding the total dfu load for all fixtures connected to the branch vent and sizing the branch vent using the horizontal branch drain column of Table P3005.4-1. Example: three vents with dfu loads of 5, 4, and 5 are connected to one branch vent. The size of the branch vent is 3 inches because the total dfu load of 14 is more than the maximum of 12 allowed for a 2 ½ inches pipe and less than the maximum of 20 allowed for a 3 inches pipe.

Sewage Pump and Ejector Vents

1. Install a 1 ½ inches diameter vent for sewage pumps and ejectors with not more than (≤) 20 gallons per minute discharge capacity.

2. Install a 2 inches diameter vent for sewage pumps and ejectors with not more than (≤) 40 gallons per minute discharge capacity.
3. Refer to the IRC for other pipe sizes and pump discharge capacities.
4. Apply the previous vent sizes for sewage pumps and ejectors that are not pneumatic. Use at least (≥) a 1 ¼ inches diameter vent for pneumatic pumps and ejectors.
5. Do not use an air admittance valve as a vent for a sump or any tank unless the valve is designed for use with sumps and tanks.

AIR ADMITTANCE VALVES (P3114)

General Installation Requirements and Approved Uses

1. Install air admittance valves according to manufacturer's installation instructions and provisions of the IRC.
2. You may use air admittance valves to vent individual vents, branch vents, circuit vents, and stack vents. Use individual and branch type air admittance valves to vent fixtures that are on the same floor level and that are connected to a horizontal branch drain.
3. Use air admittance valves that are rated for the vent size to which the valve is connected.

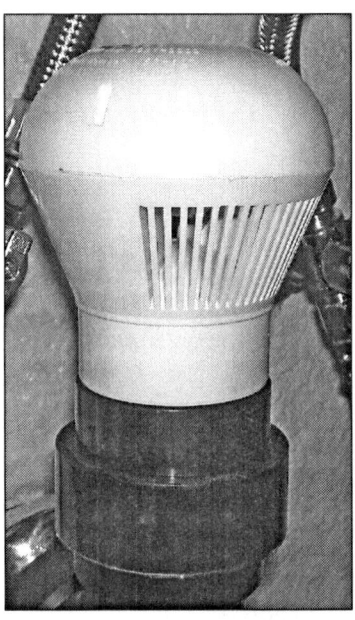

Air Admittance Valve (PP3114-0)
Figure 31-22

Installation Location Requirements

1. Locate individual and branch type air admittance valves at least (≥) 4 inches above the horizontal branch drain or fixture drain being vented.
2. Locate stack type air admittance valves at least (≥) 6 inches above the flood rim level of the highest fixture being vented.
3. Locate the air admittance valve within the vent's developed length limits.
4. Locate air admittance valves in attics at least (≥) 6 inches above insulation.
5. Provide air admittance valves with access and adequate ventilation.

6. Do not use an air admittance valve as a vent for a sump or any tank unless the valve is designed for use with sumps and tanks.

Outside Vent Required

1. Provide at least ($\geq$) one vent stack or stack vent that terminates outdoors for every plumbing system.

32

TRAPS

FIXTURE TRAPS (P3201)

Trap Size

1. Use the following table to determine the minimum trap size for most plumbing fixtures.
2. Do not install separate traps on toilets, urinals, and other fixtures that have traps in the fixture itself.
3. Do not install a trap that is larger than the drainage pipe into which the trap discharges. Example: do not connect a 2 inch trap to a 1 ½ inch pipe on the discharge side of the trap.

TABLE P3201
Minimum Trap Size for Plumbing Fixtures

plumbing fixture	minimum trap size (inches)
bath tub (equipped or not equipped with shower head or whirlpool)	1 ½
bidet	1 ¼
clothes washing machine standpipe	2
dishwasher (separately trapped)	1 ½
floor drain	2
kitchen sink (equipped or not equipped with dishwasher or disposal and trapped using one or two traps)	1 ½
laundry tubs (≥ 1 compartments)	1 ½
lavatory	1 ¼
shower (total flow rate of all showerheads and body sprays ≤ 5.7 gallons per minute (gpm) >5.7 gpm and ≤12.3 gpm >12.3 gpm and ≤25.8 gpm >25.8 gpm and ≤ 55.6 gpm	1 ½ 2 3 4

Trap Design

1. Install traps of standard design that: (a) have a smooth internal surface for water flow, and (b) are self-cleaning, and (c) do not have interior partitions or moving parts, and (d) are

constructed using cast iron, cast or drawn brass, or approved plastic. Standard design for modern fixture traps is the P trap.

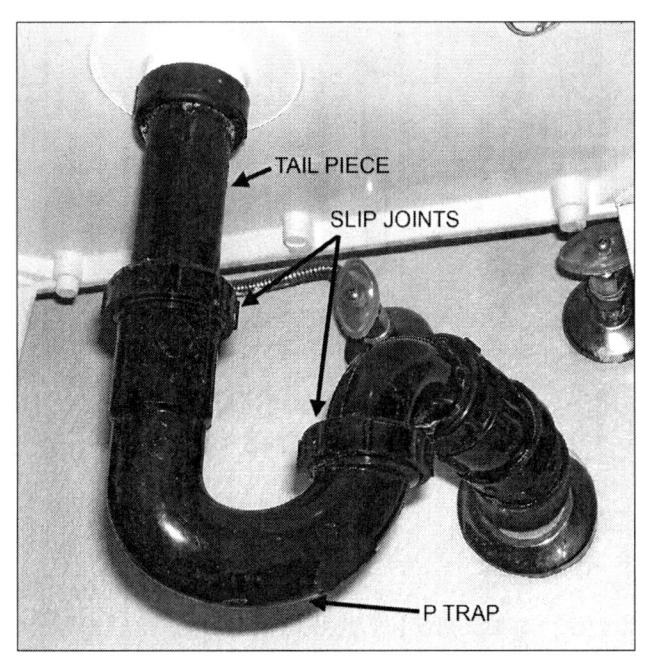

P Trap with Slip Joints (PP3201-0)
Figure 32-1

Trap Seal

1. Install traps with water seal of at least (≥) 2 inches and not more than (≤) 4 inches.
2. Install floor drain traps that have a deep seal (near 4 inches) design or a trap primer. Connect trap primer valves above the trap seal level.

Trap Installation

1. Set traps level with respect to their water seal.
2. Protect traps from freezing.
3. Provide access to traps with slip joints at the trap inlet or outlet.
4. Do not install more than one trap per fixture.
5. Limit the vertical distance between the fixture drain outlet and the trap weir to not more than (≤) 24 inches. Limit the vertical distance between the top of a washing machine standpipe and the trap weir to at least (≥) 18 inches and not more than (≤) 42 inches.
6. Limit the horizontal distance between the fixture drain outlet and the center of the trap inlet to not more than (≤) 30 inches. Note that this 30 inches horizontal distance may be eliminated or not enforced in some jurisdictions. Verify if this provision applies in your jurisdiction.

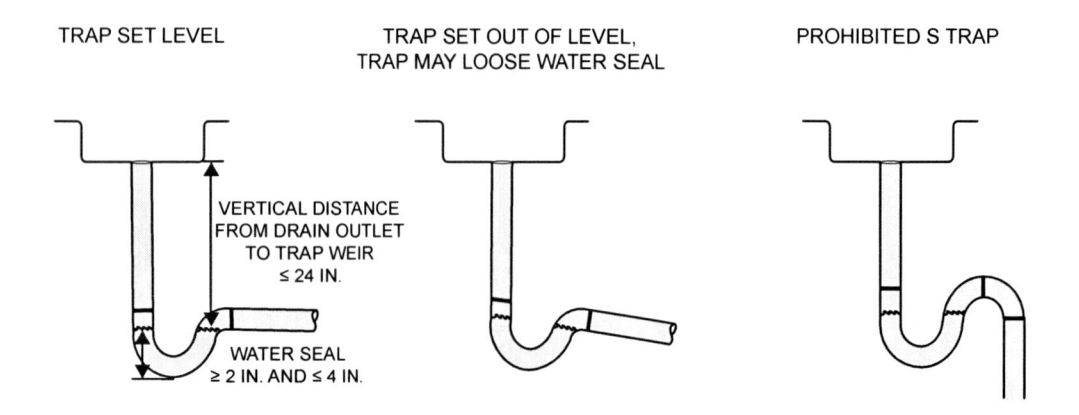

Trap Installation (P3201-1)
Figure 32-2

Prohibited Traps

1. Do not install the following types of traps: (a) bell traps, and (b) drum traps, and (c) S traps, and (d) traps with moving parts, and (e) building traps.

Traps Serving Multiple Fixture Drain Outlets

1. You may install one trap to serve not more than (≤) 3 kitchen sinks, or 3 lavatories, or 3 laundry tubs if the fixtures:
   a) are adjacent to each other and in the same room, and
   b) have drainage outlets not more than (≤) 30 inches apart, and
   c) have the trap installed at the center drainage outlet of three fixtures.

2. You may connect a laundry tray waste line to a clothes washing machine standpipe as described in Chapter 27.

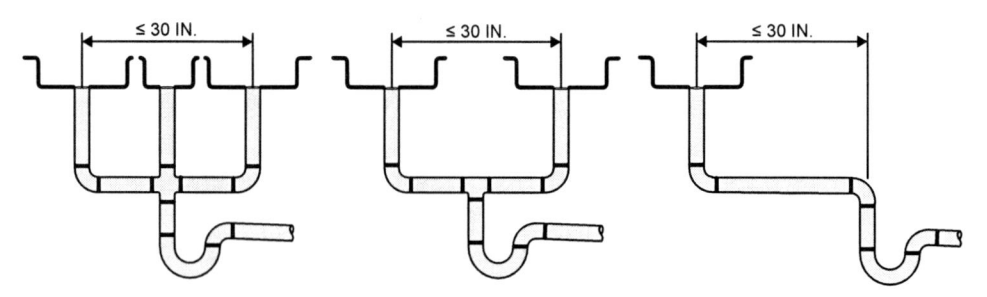

One Trap Serving Multiple Drain Fixture Outlets (P3201-2)
Figure 32-3

33

STORM WATER DRAINAGE

UNDERGROUND STORM WATER DRAINS

Underground Drain Materials and Installation Requirements

1. Use at least a (≥) 4 inches diameter pipe of an approved type. The most common pipe materials for underground storm water drains are solid and perforated corrugated polyethylene and PVC drain pipe.
2. Install an accessible backwater valve if the storm water drainage system could allow water to flow into the building.
3. Discharge the water to an approved location above ground or into a sump pit, dry well, or a trapped area drain.

SUMP PITS AND PUMPS

Sump Pit and Sump Pump Requirements

1. Install a sump pump that has the capacity to discharge storm water at the anticipated flow rate and to move water up any required vertical distance.
2. Install a sump pit that is at least (≥) 18 inches wide and 24 inches tall, unless the building official approves a different size.
3. Construct the sump pit using concrete, steel, or plastic with a solid bottom capable of supporting the pump.
4. Install an accessible full-flow check valve on the pump discharge pipe.
5. Install electrical circuits for the sump pump according to IRC requirements and the pump manufacturer's instructions.
6. Install discharge pipes, including the underground drain pipes, that are at least (≥) as large as the pump discharge outlet.

34

ELECTRICAL SYSTEM GENERAL REQUIREMENTS

ELECTRICAL SYSTEM GENERAL INSTALLATION REQUIREMENTS (E3401-E3104)

Electrical Systems Governed by the IRC

1. The IRC governs 120/240 volt, 0 to 400 ampere, single-phase residential electrical systems including wiring, equipment, light fixtures, appliances, and other devices involved in supplying, distributing, and using electricity in a home.
2. Electrical chapters of the IRC are a modified version of parts of the National Electrical Code ® (NEC ®) published and copyrighted by the National Fire Protection Association.
3. Electrical systems and components not governed by the IRC are usually addressed by the version of the NEC adopted by the local jurisdiction.
4. The IRC does not govern the electrical transmission and communication systems controlled by utilities. This often includes electrical service wires and equipment up to and including the electric meter and often includes cable TV and telephone wires up and including the utility interface boxes.
5. The IRC does not govern internal wiring of electrical equipment such as motors; however, it usually requires that electrical equipment be listed.

Updates and Changes to Electrical Systems

1. Comply with IRC provisions <u>in effect when the work is performed</u> when making additions, adjustments, and alterations to existing electrical systems. Only the new components must comply with current IRC provisions, unless new loads placed on existing components exceed loads allowed by current IRC provisions. Example: Existing kitchen receptacles, including the receptacle for a range hood, are supplied by two 20 amp circuits. You wish to replace the range hood with a microwave oven. You should add a new, dedicated 20 amp circuit to serve the microwave oven to comply with current IRC provisions and microwave manufacturer's installation instructions.
2. Comply with local permitting and inspection requirements when making minor repairs to existing electrical components. Refer to Chapter 1 and verify permitting and inspection requirements with the local building official.
3. Comply with the Smoke Alarm provisions in Chapter 3 when required by the local building official.

Changes to Building Structural Members

1. Do not cut, notch, bore, or drill building structural members (such as studs and joists) except as allowed the IRC.

2. Do not cut, notch, bore, drill or otherwise alter trusses in any way unless approved in writing by an approved design professional.

Penetrations of Firestops and Draftstops

1. Maintain the integrity of firestops, draftstops, and fire-resistance rated walls required by the IRC. Use approved materials and methods to seal any penetrations of firestops, draftstops, and fire-resistance rated walls.

Electrical Component Listing, Labeling, and Installation

1. Use only listed and labeled electrical components.
2. Install electrical materials and equipment according to the terms of their listing including manufacturer's installation instructions.

Panelboard Cabinet Selection

1. Install the type of electrical panel cabinet based on the environment where the cabinet is located.
2. Use the enclosure selection table in the IRC to determine the proper type of cabinet for the environment. Cabinets for interior use will usually have an enclosure-type number of 1 or 2. Cabinets for exterior use will usually have an enclosure-type number of 3, 3R, 3S, 3X, 3RX, or 3SX.

Electrical Component Protection During Construction

1. Protect electrical components intended for indoor use from water damage during construction. These components may be labeled as "Type I", or as "dry locations", or as "indoor use only".
2. Protect internal parts of electrical components and enclosures from damage or contamination by materials such as paints and sealants, drywall joint compound, cleaning supplies, and corrosive agents.
3. Remove foreign debris from electrical components.

Damaged Electrical Components

1. Replace electrical components that have been broken, cut, bent, deteriorated by corrosion or overheating, or otherwise damaged if the damage may prevent safe operation or mechanical strength of the component. This applies to all electrical components including insulation, bus bars, and terminals.

Openings in Boxes and Enclosures

1. Close unused openings in junction boxes, panel cabinets, and similar enclosures. Examples include knockouts in boxes and cabinets and circuit breaker tabs in panelboard cabinets. Use closure materials that provide protection similar to the original enclosure walls. This does not include tape, cardboard, and similar materials.

2. Recess plugs at least (≥) ¼ inch from the enclosure's outer surface when using metallic plugs in nonmetallic enclosures.

Identification of Circuit Breakers and Fuses

1. Provide a legible and permanent marking or label that identifies the purpose of circuit breakers, fuses, and other equipment used to disconnect power from a circuit. Identify the circuit in enough detail so that it can be distinguished from all other circuits. Example: Do not identify a circuit as general lighting. Identify the specific rooms or outlets served by the circuit. A marking or label is not required if the purpose of the disconnecting equipment is self-evident. Use marking or labeling materials that will withstand the environment where the disconnecting equipment is located.
2. Locate the circuit identification on the face of the panelboard enclosure or on the inside panelboard door.

Electrical Component Attachment

1. Attach electrical equipment securely to the surface to which it is mounted.
2. Do not use wooden plugs or similar materials to mount electrical equipment on masonry, concrete, plaster, or similar materials.

Electrical Component Protection Against Damage and Accidental Contact

1. Use approved enclosures to protect energized parts operating with at least (≥) 50 volts.
2. Use approved guards or other approved methods to protect electrical components against physical damage.

ELECTRICAL EQUIPMENT ACCESS AND CLEARANCES (E3405)

Clearances Around Electrical Panel Enclosures and Energized Equipment

1. Provide a clear working space in front of electrical panel cabinets and other equipment and enclosures that require access while interior parts are energized. Examples of other enclosures include air conditioner and furnace service disconnect boxes.
2. Make the clear working space at least (≥) 36 inches deep, and at least (≥) 30 inches wide (or as wide as the enclosure, if it is wider than 30 inches), and at least (≥) 78 inches high. Measure the clear working space in front of the enclosure beginning at the front of the enclosure. Measure the clear working space from the energized parts, if the parts requiring access are not in an enclosure.
3. Provide enough clearance so that the enclosure door can be opened at least (≥) 90 degrees.
4. Do not allow any objects located above or below the electrical enclosures to extend into the clear working space more than (>) 6 inches beyond the front of the electrical enclosure.
5. Provide access to the clear working space. Do not block access with shelves, workbenches, or other difficult to move objects.

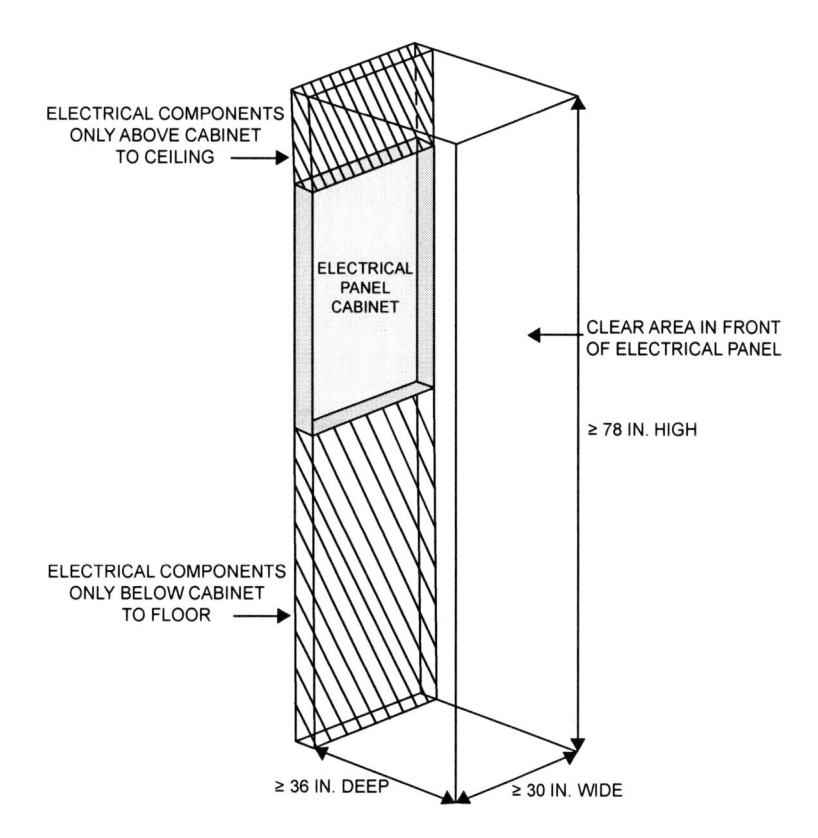

Clearances Around Electrical Panels (E3405-0)
Figure 34-1

Clear Space Above and Below Electrical Panel Enclosures

1. Provide a clear space directly above and below electrical panel enclosures that is free from any components not associated with the electrical system. This space is intended for wires entering and leaving the electrical panel. Do not install plumbing pipes, HVAC ducts, and similar components in this space.
2. Provide a clear space that is at least (≥) the width and depth of the electrical panel enclosure and extend the clear space from the floor to the structural ceiling or at least (≥) 6 feet above the enclosure, whichever is lower.

Electrical Panel Prohibited Locations and Access

1. Do not locate electrical panels and circuit breakers and fuses in clothes closets, bathrooms, over stairways, or in spaces designated for storage.
2. Install electrical panels circuit breakers and fuses where they are readily accessible. Readily accessible means not opening locks, moving objects, and using ladders.
3. Install electrical panels and circuit breakers and fuses so that the circuit breaker and fuse handle is not more than (≤) 78 inches above the floor or ground when the center of the handle is in its highest position

Electrical Panel Lighting

1. Provide an artificial light for service equipment and electrical panels installed indoors. The IRC does not specify how close the light should be to the equipment.

WIRE SPLICES AND GENERAL WIRE INSTALLATION REQUIREMENTS (E3406 AND E3407)

Wire Splices

1. Splice (join) wires using only listed devices such as appropriate size wire nuts. Use wire nuts according to manufacturer's recommendations about the number and size of wires that the wire nut can accommodate.
2. Cover spliced wires with material equal to the original insulation. This does not include electrical tape or similar materials.
3. Splice wires that will be buried in the ground using only devices listed for direct burial and install them according to manufacturer's instructions.
4. Provide access to spliced wires, unless the splice and splicing device are specifically allowed to be concealed. Access is usually provided by an accessible, covered junction box.
5. Do not place wire splices in a raceway unless the raceway has a removable cover.

Splicing Aluminum and Copper Wires

1. Splice (join) aluminum and copper wires together using devices listed for splicing aluminum and copper wires. Look for a mark or label such as AL/CU on the device or on the package for assurance that the device is listed for splicing aluminum and copper wires. Some wire nuts sold for residential use are not listed for splicing aluminum and copper wires.
2. Use only inhibitors and anti-oxidant compounds that are approved for splicing aluminum and copper wires. These materials should not degrade or damage the wires, wire insulation, or equipment. Read and follow manufacturer's instructions.

Length of Wires in Boxes

1. Extend wires at least (≥) 3 inches beyond the opening of any electrical box, junction, or switch point, if the opening is less than (<) 8 inches in any direction. This applies to most switch, receptacle, and light fixture mounting boxes used in residential electrical systems.
2. Extend wires at least (≥) 6 inches beyond where the wires emerge from the raceway or cable sheath. Example: NM cable enters a single residential switch box with 1 inch of intact sheathing (outer cover). Begin the 6 inches measurement where the sheathing ends. The cable should extend at least 7 inches from the rear of the box. The NM cable should also extend at least 3 inches beyond the outside edge of the box.

Connecting Wires to Terminals

1. Remove insulation from wires and connect wires to terminals without damaging the wire. Do not connect damaged wires to terminals. Example: if you nick, damage, or cut strands from a stranded wire, cut the wire back to where it is full size and use the full undamaged wire.

2. Connect more than (>) one wire to a terminal only if the terminal is identified to accept multiple wires. Example: many panelboards require one wire per terminal for the grounded (neutral) wires and allow two or more same gage wires per terminal for the equipment grounding wires. Example: many circuit breakers allow only one hot (ungrounded) wire per circuit breaker terminal.
3. Connect aluminum wires to terminals only if the terminal is identified to accept aluminum wires.

Wire Color Codes

1. Use wires with white or gray colored insulation or wires with three white stripes on other than green insulation as neutral (grounded) wires. You may use wires with other than white or gray colored insulation as neutral (grounded) wires if they are larger than (>) #6 AWG and if you mark them with a permanent white marking at all wire terminations.
2. Use wires with green colored insulation or wires with green colored insulation and at least (≥) 1 yellow stripe as equipment grounding wires. You may use uninsulated (bare) wires as equipment grounding wires in most circuits.
3. You may use any color other than white, gray, or green as hot (ungrounded) wires. The common colors are red and black. You may use a wire with white or gray insulation as a hot (ungrounded) wire if the wire is part of a cable (such as NM) and if you permanently mark it as a hot (ungrounded) conductor at all places where the wire is visible and accessible. This marking is usually done by wrapping the end of the wire with black or red electrical tape.

Wires Installed in Conduit

1. Install only stranded wire in raceways (such as conduit) if the wire is size #8 AWG or larger. You may install solid #8 AWG wire as a bonding wire and as a service grounding wire (the grounding electrode conductor).

Wires Run in Parallel

1. Limit running wires in parallel (two wires joined at each end to make one wire) to wire size #1/0 AWG and larger.
2. Use wires with the same characteristics including size of wire, type of insulation, type of wire conductor, length of wire, and termination method. Consult an experienced electrician before running wires in parallel.

Neutral and Equipment Grounding Wire Continuity

1. Connect neutral (grounded) wires together in device boxes if the neutral (grounded) wire is part of a multiwire branch circuit. Do not rely on any device, such as a receptacle or light fixture, to provide the connection for the neutral (grounded) wire in a multiwire branch circuit.
2. Connect equipment grounding wires together in all device boxes. Do not rely on any device, such as a receptacle or light fixture, to provide the connection for the equipment grounding wire in any circuit.
3. Install a wire (called a pigtail) between the connected wires and any device in the box.

Connection of Grounded and Grounding Wires in a Box (PE3406-0)
Figure 34-2

Wires Serving the Same Circuit

1. Run all wires that serve the same circuit in the same cable or raceway. This includes the neutral (grounded) and the equipment grounding wires. Example: do not serve a circuit using hot (ungrounded) and equipment grounding wires from one piece of NM cable and the neutral (grounded) wire from a piece of NM cable from a different circuit breaker or fuse. This is rarely an issue in residential construction.

Terminal Identification Markings

1. Use devices that have the neutral (grounded) terminal colored white, or labeled with the word "white", or labeled with the letter "W" if the device connects to both the hot (ungrounded) and neutral (grounded) wires. Common devices include receptacles, polarized plugs, polarized plug-and-cord assemblies, and other polarized devices. Most receptacles use a silver color for the neutral (grounded) terminal and a brass color for the hot (ungrounded) terminal. Some may also use a word or letter label. Terminal identification is not required if the device has a normal current rating more than (>) 30 amperes and if the device is not a polarized plug or receptacle device. Terminal identification by color or label is not required if the neutral (grounded) terminal is clearly evident.

35

DEFINITIONS OF TERMS USED IN ELECTRICAL SYSTEMS

Accessible (Wires) Wires are accessible if they can be exposed without removing or damaging permanent parts of the building and if a person can reach them for inspection, repair, or maintenance. Examples: wires are accessible if they are behind suspended ceiling panels, or if access requires opening a door, removing an access panel, or climbing a ladder. Wires are not accessible if you must cut drywall to expose the wires or if they are located in an area that cannot be reached for repair, inspection, or maintenance.

Accessible (Readily) Electrical components are readily accessible if they can be reached quickly without using keys, lock combinations, ladders, tools, or devices. Panelboards and service disconnect equipment must be readily accessible in case circuits need to be shut off during an emergency.

Ampacity Ampacity describes the current-carrying capacity of a wire, measured in amperes. The ampacity of a wire depends on how it is used. A wire's ampacity is higher when used as a service or feeder wire than when used as a branch circuit wire. Refer to Chapter 36 for wire service and feeder ampacities and to Chapter 37 for wire branch circuit ampacities.

Ampere An ampere is a measure of the rate of flow of electricity. One volt acting on one ohm of resistance equals one ampere of current flow. An ampere is similar to the gallon per minute rate of flow in a water pipe. Ampere is abbreviated amp and is expressed in Ohm's Law as the letter I.

Bonding Metallic components are bonded if they are physically and electrically connected together. Components are bonded when a bonding wire connects them together. Example: a bonding wire should connect a swimming pool motor and nearby metal parts of the electrical supply system. Components are bonded when there is an electrically conducting connection between metal parts. Example: metal conduit should be electrically and mechanically connected where it enters a panelboard cabinet.

Bonded metallic components are part of an electrically conductive path that will safely conduct current imposed by a ground fault. Example: when metal conduit containing a damage wire becomes energized, this is a ground fault. A proper bonding connection will conduct the fault current on the conduit safely to ground and allow proper operation of the circuit breaker or fuse. Otherwise, a person touching the energized conduit could become the current's path to ground and that person could receive a dangerous shock or the current flow could generate enough heat to start a fire.

Branch circuit A branch circuit begins at a circuit breaker or fuse in a panelboard and conducts electricity to where it is used. A branch circuit can serve one device, such as an oven, or it can serve multiple devices such as receptacles and light fixtures.

Branch circuit (general lighting) A general lighting branch circuit is one that serves multiple light fixtures and receptacles. This includes lights and receptacles in places such as bedrooms, living areas, hallways, garage and the home's exterior.

Cable A cable is two or more wires contained in an insulating sheath or jacket. Most "wire" used in residential construction is actually a cable called non-metallic cable and abbreviated NM. Romex® is brand name belonging to one manufacturer of NM cable.

Conductor A conductor, broadly defined, is any material that provides low resistance to the flow of electricity. Conductor is the preferred technical term for electrical wire. Conductors in a residential electrical system include: ungrounded (hot), grounded (neutral), grounding (equipment grounding), grounding electrode, service entrance, and feeders.

Dead front (dead front cover) A dead front means that a person cannot come in contact with energized components protected by a dead front cover. The term dead front cover usually describes part of an electrical cabinet that when removed allows access to energized parts.

Energized An electrical component is energized if it is connected to a voltage source. A common term for energized is that the component is "hot."

Equipment (fixed) Electrical equipment that is fixed in place is permanently connected to the building's electrical system. Light fixtures, while permanently connected, are not considered fixed equipment. Examples of fixed equipment include ranges, ovens, furnaces, air handlers, air conditioner condensers, water heaters, and permanently connected through-the-wall air conditioners. Examples of equipment that is similar to fixed equipment include clothes dryers and plug-and-cord connected window and through-the-wall air conditioners.

Feeder A feeder circuit consists of all wires that run between a voltage source and the final circuit breakers or fuses protecting branch circuits. In residential electrical systems, feeders may run between the service equipment and the main panelboard and between the main panelboard and any subpanels.

Ground (grounded) A ground (grounded) connection is the return path through which alternating current electricity flows to complete a circuit. A grounded conductor is connected to the earth or to some body that serves as the earth. A grounded connection may be intentional (as in a circuit's grounded conductor) or it may be unintentional (as in a ground fault).

Grounded wire A grounded conductor, broadly defined, is any conductor that is intentionally grounded. The common term for the grounded conductor in residential electrical systems is the "neutral" wire or conductor. The grounded conductor is a current-carrying conductor. You should treat it as such when working with electrical circuits. Grounded conductors are usually insulated with white or light gray colored insulation.

Grounding wire A grounding conductor, also called an equipment grounding conductor, connects electrical equipment directly to a grounding electrode. This connection usually occurs at a grounding bus or terminal bar at the service equipment that is in turn connected to a grounding electrode. Grounding conductors are bare wires or may be insulated with green colored insulation.

Grounding electrode A grounding electrode is a component in contact with the earth that provides the grounding connection for the electrical system. Common residential grounding electrodes include a copper rod driven at least (≥) 8 feet into the ground, or a copper water service pipe, or a piece of reinforcing steel embedded in the footing.

Grounding electrode wire The grounding electrode conductor is a wire that connects the grounding electrode to the grounded conductors. In most residential electrical systems, the only connection between the grounding electrode conductor and the grounded conductors should occur at the service equipment.

Ground fault A ground fault occurs when metal that is not normally energized becomes energized. Examples of a ground fault: (a) the hot (ungrounded) wire in a motor is damaged or disconnected and touches the motor's case energizing the case; (b) a screw penetrates the insulation of a hot (ungrounded) wire in an electrical panelboard and energizes the cabinet; (c) damaged insulation on a hot (ungrounded) wire allows the conductor to touch copper water pipe energizing the pipe.

Location (damp) Damp locations are subject to moderate levels of moisture but are not subject to direct saturation by liquids. Examples of damp locations include covered porches and some basements. Many inspectors consider ceilings over showers and bathtubs as damp locations but the IRC does not specifically cite these as damp locations.

Location (wet) Wet locations are subject to direct contact with liquids or the elements. Examples of wet locations include exterior house walls not protected by a roof, concrete and masonry in contact with the earth, and any components buried or in contact with the earth.

Ohm's law Ohm's law expresses the relationship between characteristics of an electric circuit. Power (watts) equals Voltage (volts) times Current (amps) and Voltage (volts) equals Current (amps) times Resistance (ohms). The common expressions of Ohm's law are $P = I \times E$ and $E = I \times R$.

Outlet An outlet is a connection point where electricity is taken for use. An outlet could be a receptacle, or a light fixture box, or junction box connected to an oven, or an air conditioning condenser disconnect box. Switch boxes, junction boxes, and panelboards are not outlets.

Overcurrent protection device An overcurrent protection device is a device that automatically interrupts the flow of electricity if the current flowing through the device exceeds a design maximum amount. Common examples in residential electrical systems are fuses and circuit breakers.

Panelboard (load center) A panelboard (also called a load center) is the equipment that distributes electricity to branch circuits. Fuses or circuit breakers are mounted on a panelboard and wires are connected to the fuses or circuit breakers and to busses (also called terminal bars). These connections distribute electricity to the branch circuits. A panelboard is the equipment inside a cabinet or enclosure to which the fuses or circuit breakers and wires are attached. It is not the cabinet or enclosure itself. Panelboards and cabinets are two separate components, although in residential electrical systems they are usually factory assembled and installed as one unit. Common terms used in residential electrical systems include main electrical panel and subpanel(s).

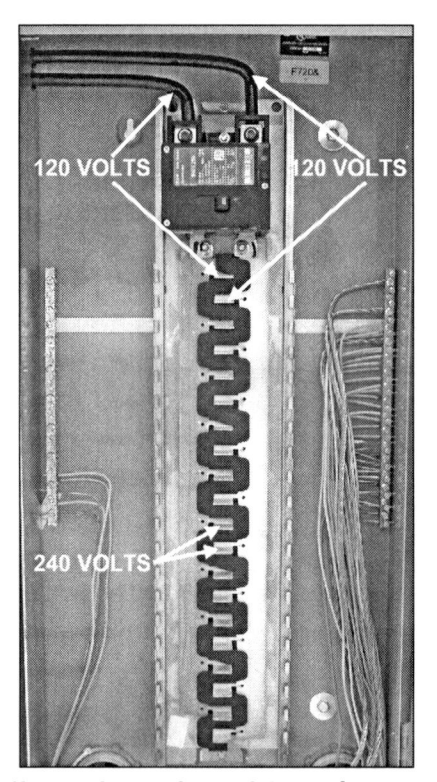

Panelboard Inside Cabinet (PE3500-0)
Figure 35-1

Power Power is a measure of the work performed by electricity. Power is measured in watts and is expressed on Ohm's Law as the letter P.

Raceway A raceway is a channel designed to enclose and protect electrical wires. Raceway is a generic term that describes conduit, tubing, surface raceways and other approved components through which electrical wires are run.

Receptacle A receptacle is a device into which a plug is inserted and through which electricity flows to equipment that uses electricity. Receptacles include the familiar single (one plug) and duplex (two plug) 120 volt devices and the 240 volt devices most often seen in laundry rooms to serve electric clothes dryers. All receptacles are outlets but not all outlets contain receptacles. See the definition of outlet.

Resistance Resistance is a measure of how difficult it is for electricity to flow through a material. Electricity flows more easily (lower resistance) through a conductor and does not flow easily (higher resistance) through an insulator. Resistance is measured in ohms and is expressed in Ohm's Law as the letter R.

Service Service is a generic term describing conductors and equipment that deliver electricity to a building. Service drop and service lateral conductors and equipment (such as meters) are usually installed and maintained by the electric utility.

Service drop The service drop describes overhead electrical wires beginning at the power pole and ending where the service drop wires connect to the service entrance wires. This is usually at the service point near the mast on the roof.

Service entrance wires Service entrance wires run from the service point to the service equipment. In an overhead service system (service drop), the service entrance conductors are often defined at those between the connection point at the utility's overhead wires and the service equipment. In an underground system (service lateral), the service entrance conductors are more difficult to define. If the utility's meter and the service equipment are mounted in the same cabinet, then there are no service entrance conductors because the service point is at the service equipment. If the utility's meter and the service equipment are mounted in different cabinets, then the service entrance conductors may be defined as running between the meter and the service equipment.

Service equipment The service equipment includes the circuit breakers, fuses, or switches that control and cut off power to the building's entire electric system. Other terms for service equipment include main service cut off and service disconnecting means. The service equipment may be located in the same cabinet as the main distribution panelboard or it may be located in a different cabinet.

Service lateral The service lateral describes the utility's underground electrical wires, often beginning at the utility's transformer cabinet near the street and often ending at a meter cabinet.

Service point The service point is where the utility's service wires connect to the home's service entrance wires. The service point in an overhead service drop is often where the utility's wires connect to the service entrance wires near the mast on the roof. The service point in an underground service lateral is often at a meter cabinet. The service point is defined by the local electric utility and determines where the utility's service and maintenance responsibilities end and where the homeowner's service and maintenance responsibilities begin. The service point varies depending on the utility and on how electric service is supplied to the home.

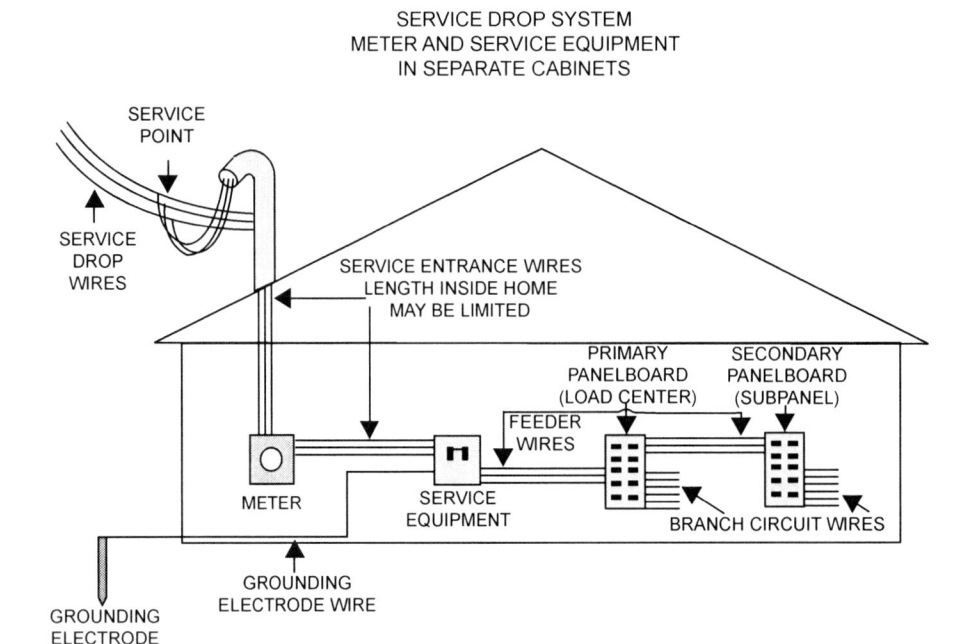

SERVICE DROP SYSTEM
METER AND SERVICE EQUIPMENT IN SEPARATE CABINETS

SERVICE LATERAL SYSTEM
METER AND SERVICE EQUIPMENT IN ADJACENT CABINETS

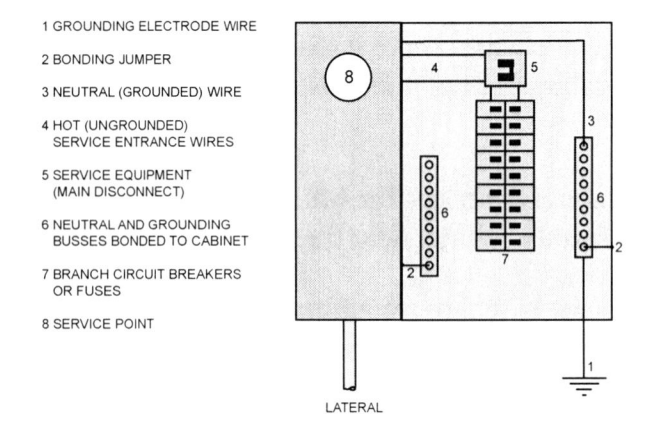

1 GROUNDING ELECTRODE WIRE
2 BONDING JUMPER
3 NEUTRAL (GROUNDED) WIRE
4 HOT (UNGROUNDED) SERVICE ENTRANCE WIRES
5 SERVICE EQUIPMENT (MAIN DISCONNECT)
6 NEUTRAL AND GROUNDING BUSSES BONDED TO CABINET
7 BRANCH CIRCUIT BREAKERS OR FUSES
8 SERVICE POINT

Electrical Component Definitions (P3501-0)
Figure 35-2

Ungrounded conductor An ungrounded conductor is one that intentionally carries electricity. The common term for an ungrounded conductor in residential electrical systems is the "hot" or "live" wire or conductor. Ungrounded conductors are usually insulated with red or black colored insulation.

Voltage Voltage is a measure of the potential difference between two conductors in a circuit. Voltage is similar to the water pressure in a pipe. In most residential electric systems, the nominal voltage potential between the two ungrounded (hot) wires is approximately 240 volts and the nominal voltage potential between an ungrounded (hot) wire and the grounded (neutral) wire is approximately 120 volts. The actual voltage in a circuit is usually different from the nominal voltage. Voltage is measured in volts and is expressed in Ohm's Law as the letter E.

Wire The term wire, defined as a conductor of electricity, is not formally used in the IRC. The preferred term is conductor. See the definition of conductor.

36

ELECTRICAL SERVICES

ELECTRICAL SERVICES GENERAL REQUIREMENTS (E3601)

One Electrical Service Per Dwelling Unit

1. Provide only one electrical service per dwelling unit. This usually means one electric meter and one main service disconnect per building. Attached townhouses are considered separate buildings and usually have one electrical service per townhouse unit. Duplex and other two-family buildings are not considered separate buildings, although they are separate dwelling units. Check with the local building official before any project that contemplates providing an additional electrical service to a building.

Electrical Service Run Through Building Interiors

1. Do not run service wires that serve one building through the interior of another building. A building's interior includes the attic, basement, and crawl space. Service wires are considered inside the building even if they are run in conduit. Service wires that are encased in concrete or buried underground are not considered inside a building's interior.

Electrical Service Entrance Wires Commingled with Other Wires

1. Do not run service entrance wires in the same raceway or cable with other wires. Other wires include 120/240 volt branch circuit wires, coaxial cable for cable and satellite television, and wire for telephone and alarm systems. You may run grounding wires, bonding wires, and load management controllers with overcurrent protection in service entrance raceways and cables.

Electrical Main Disconnecting (Service) Equipment

1. Provide equipment to disconnect all electrical service to a building using not more than (≤) six switches or circuit breakers located in the same area. This means that a person must be able to turn off all electrical power to a building in not more than (≤) six hand motions without moving from one position.
2. Label the service disconnecting equipment as such. The label must be permanent and clearly marked.
3. Use only service disconnecting equipment listed and labeled for that purpose. The electric meter and meter enclosure are not service equipment. Do not rely on removing the electric meter to disconnect electrical service.
4. Install the service disconnecting equipment in a readily accessible place where every building occupant has access. Refer to the definition of readily accessible.

5. Install the service disconnecting equipment outside the building or inside the building as close as possible to where the service entrance conductors enter the building. Check with the local building official about where interior service disconnecting equipment may be installed and about the maximum distance between where service entrance conductors enter the home and where they connect to the service disconnecting equipment. Fifteen feet is one typical maximum, but the distance may be less is some jurisdictions.
6. Do not install service disconnecting equipment in bathrooms.
7. Install the service disconnecting switches or circuit breakers not more than ($\leq$) 79 inches above the floor or ground.

ELECTRICAL SERVICE LOAD CALCULATION (E3602)

Limitations of the Material in this Section

We do not recommend that most readers of this book determine electrical service load. Leave this to experienced electrical contractors. For readers who are interested in how to calculate service loads, we provide the following explanation.

Electrical Service Minimum Size

1. Provide at least ($\geq$) 100 amp service to a single family dwelling unit.
2. Provide at least ($\geq$) 60 amp service to an accessory structure. Exceptions to the 60 amp minimum service exist for one and two circuit service to some accessory structures.

Service Load Formula

1. Use the following formula to determine the load and the minimum size for the hot (ungrounded) service conductors and service disconnect equipment.

$$((GL + SA + FE) - 10,000) \times .40 + 10,000 + HE$$

GL GL represents the load for 120 volt lighting and receptacle circuits. Calculate this load by multiplying 3 watts times the conditioned square footage of the home. Measure conditioned square footage based on the outside framed dimensions of the home. Do not include open porches, garages, and areas that cannot be converted into conditioned living space such as most attics and crawl spaces. Include unfinished basements if they can be converted into conditioned living space. Do not add any additional load for the 20 amp bathroom receptacle circuit. It is already included in the GL load.

SA SA represents the load for 20 amp, 120 volt kitchen appliance and laundry receptacle circuits. Calculate this load by multiplying 1,500 watts times the total number of 20 amp, 120 volt appliance kitchen appliance and laundry receptacle circuits. The IRC requires at least ($\geq$) 2 kitchen appliance circuits and 1 laundry circuit, so the minimum number of circuits in any home is three. Increase the number of circuits in the SA load if you run additional 120 volt receptacle circuits to the kitchen or laundry. If you run a separate dedicated circuit for a refrigerator, do not add this circuit to the SA load. The IRC allows a refrigerator to run off of one of the required kitchen receptacle circuits.

FE FE represents the load for 120 and 240 volt circuits serving a dedicated load or serving permanently wired (fixed) electrical equipment. Calculate this load by adding the nameplate wattage rating of all such equipment. Examples of dedicated loads and fixed equipment include ranges, wall ovens, microwave ovens, broilers and other permanent cooking appliances, disposals, dishwashers, electric (not gas) clothes dryers, water heaters, and heat pump and gas furnace blower motors. Do not include heat pump and air conditioning condensers and do not include heat pump heating strips in the FE load.

HE HE represents the load for heating or air conditioning equipment. Calculate this load by using the largest nameplate wattage rating for only one of the following:
   a) 100 percent of all air conditioning and heat pump condensers; or
   b) 100 percent of all electric heating systems (such as electric boilers and central electric resistance heating systems) where the usual load is likely to be continuous at the full nameplate wattage rating; or
   c) 100 percent of all heat pump condensers plus 65 percent of the heat pump supplemental (auxiliary/emergency) heat strips (do not include the heat pump condensers if the heat strips and the condensers cannot operate simultaneously); or
   d) 65 percent of electric radiant heating units if there are less than (<) four separately controlled units; or
   e) 40 percent of electric radiant heating units if there are at least (≥) four separately controlled units.

Adjusted Load Adjust the general lighting (GL), small appliance (SA), and dedicated equipment (FE) loads because all circuits will not be active at the same time. Calculate this adjustment by adding the total wattage for GL + SA + FE, subtracting 10,000 watts, multiplying the remainder by .40, and adding 10,000 watts to the result.

Example: assume GL + SA + FE equals 21,000 watts,

   1) subtract 10,000 watts from 21,000 watts equals 11,000 watts (21,000-10,000 = 11,000),
   2) multiply 11,000 watts by .40 equals 4,400 watts (11,000 x .40 = 4,400),
   3) add 10,000 watts to 4,400 watts equals 14,400 watts (10,000 + 4,400 = 14,400).

Service Load Calculation Example

1. Assume an all electric (no gas) home described in the following table.

TABLE EX3602-1
Service Load Calculation Example
Sample Home Electrical Equipment

home size and electrical equipment	name plate wattage rating
2,300 conditioned square feet	
3 – 20 amp, 120 volt kitchen small appliance circuits	
1 – 20 amp, 120 volt laundry circuit	
1 – 20 amp, 120 volt refrigerator circuit	
1 microwave oven	1,600
1 wall oven	6,600
1 surface cooking unit	8,100
1 dishwasher	1,200
1 disposal	800
1 clothes dryer	5,600
1 water heater	4,500
1 heat pump condenser	7,200
1 heat pump air handler	1,000
heat pump auxiliary heat strips (the heat strips do not operate when the condenser operates)	10,000

Step 1 Calculate GL Load

2,300 conditioned square feet x 3 watts/square foot =   6,900 watts
Total GL load   **6,900 watts**

Step 2 Calculate SA Load

Three kitchen circuits x 1,500 watts/circuit =   4,500 watts +
One laundry circuit x 1,500 watts/circuit =   1,500 watts +
Total SA load =   **6,000 watts**

Note that the 20 amp refrigerator circuit is not included in the SA load.

Step 3 Calculate FE Load

Microwave oven   1,600 watts +
Wall oven   6,600 watts +
Surface cooking unit   8,100 watts +
Dishwasher   1,200 watts +

Disposal	800 watts +
Clothes dryer	5,600 watts +
Heat pump air handler	1,000 watts +
Water heater	4,500 watts +
Total FE load =	**29,400 watts**

Step 4 Calculate HE Load

100% of heat pump condenser =	7,200 watts
Total HE load =	**7,200 watts**

Step 5 Calculate Adjusted Load

Total GL load	6,900 watts +
Total SA load	6,000 watts +
Total FE load	29,400 watts +
Total unadjusted load =	42,300 watts
Subtract first 10,000 watts	(10,000) watts -
Excess over first 10,000 watts =	32,300 watts
Multiply excess by .40	12,920 watts
Add first 10,000 watts	10,000 watts +
Total adjusted load =	**22,920 watts**

Step 6 Calculate Service Load in Watts

Adjusted load	22,920 watts +
Add HE load	7,200 watts +
Total service load =	**30,120 watts**

Step 7 Calculate Service Load in Amps

30,120 watts/240 volts = 125.5 amps

The next standard service size greater than 125.5 amps is a 150 amp service. The minimum hot (ungrounded) service wires for a 150 amp service are #1 AWG copper or 2/0 AWG aluminum.

The neutral (grounded) wire is often two sizes smaller than the hot (ungrounded) wires. This is because the 240 volt loads are either not included or are only partially included when calculating the potential unbalanced load on the neutral (grounded) wire. The two sizes smaller neutral (grounded) wire is a "rule-of-thumb" convention, and is not sanctioned by the IRC. The electrical contractor should calculate the neutral (grounded) wire size. Refer to Feeder Wire Sizing for a brief discussion of calculations for sizing a neutral (grounded) service wire.

Note that we use watts to represent equipment power ratings instead of volt-amps as used in the IRC. Volt-amps and watts are not always the same; however, watts is a more commonly used term for power and it is close enough for calculating service loads.

Some equipment name plates may not provide a wattage rating. The rating may consist of an amp draw rating at a nominal 120 or 240 volts or may consist of amp draw ratings at voltages other than 120 and 240. Use the 120 or 240 volt amp draw rating and multiply amps times volts to yield power in watts.

ELECTRICAL SERVICE, FEEDER, AND GROUNDING ELECTRODE WIRE SIZE (E3603)

Service, Feeder, and Grounding Electrode Wire Size

1. Use the following table to determine the minimum wire size for service entrance, feeder, and grounding electrode wires. This table applies to service entrance wires, and to feeder wires serving the entire dwelling, and to feeder wires serving accessory structures that require at least (≥) one 240 volt circuit or more than (>) two 120 volt circuits. This table applies only to wire with insulation types THHW, THW, THWN, USE, and XHHW.

2. Refer to Sections 3607 and 3608 for information about grounding electrode wires and grounding electrodes. Rod in this table means that the grounding electrode is a driven rod or a pipe installed according to Section 3608. Ufer in this table means that the grounding electrode is encased in concrete and installed according to Section 3608. Other in this table means that the grounding electrode is one of the other grounding electrodes allowed by Section 3608. Driven rods, water service pipes, and concrete encased electrodes are used as grounding electrodes in most homes.

TABLE E3603
Service Entrance and Feeder Wire Minimum Size

wire size copper (AWG)	wire size aluminum (AWG)	max. ampacity	min. grounding electrode wire size copper (AWG)	min. grounding electrode wire size aluminum (AWG)
4	2	100	8	6
3	1	110	8	6
2	1/0	125	8	6
1	2/0	150	6	4
1/0	3/0	175	6	4
2/0	4/0	200	6 rod or 4 ufer	4 rod or 2 other
3/0	250 kcmil	225	6 rod or 4 ufer	4 rod or 2 other
4/0	300 kcmil	250	6 rod or 4 ufer	4 rod or 1/0 other
250 kcmil	350 kcmil	300	6 rod or 4 ufer	4 rod or 1/0 other
350 kcmil	500 kcmil	350	6 rod or 4 ufer	4 rod or 1/0 other
400 kcmil	600 kcmil	400	6 rod or 4 ufer	4 rod or 3/0 other

Feeder Wire Size for Accessory Structures

1. Provide at least (≥) 60 amp service to accessory structures, unless the exception in #3 below applies.

2. Determine the load for an accessory structure using the feeder load calculations in Section 3704.
3. You may use the following wire sizes as a feeder when the load is limited to one or two 15 or 20 amp, 120 volt, branch circuits:
    a) use at least (≥) #10 AWG copper or #8 AWG aluminum wire if the accessory structure has not more than (≤) two 15 or 20 amp, 120 volt branch circuits,
    b) use at least (≥) #14 AWG copper or #12 AWG aluminum if the accessory structure has only one 15 amp, 120 volt branch circuit and use at least (≥) the same size feeder wire as used for the branch circuit.
4. Provide an equipment grounding wire with the feeder wires and refer to the grounding requirements in Section E3607 if there are at least (≥) 2 branch circuits in the accessory structure.

Grounding Electrode Wire Protection

1. Protect #8 AWG grounding electrode wires in metallic or non-metallic conduit. Bond grounding electrode wires that are in metallic conduit at both ends of the conduit and at any intermediate junction boxes or enclosures.
2. Run #6 AWG grounding electrode wires as close as possible to the structure for physical protection. Place wire supports not more than (≤) 24 inches apart and not more than (≤) 12 inches from any enclosure or termination.

Service Entrance Wire Overcurrent Protection

1. Install fuse(s) or circuit breaker (s) in series with each hot (ungrounded) service entrance wire. Use fuse(s) or circuit breaker(s) that have a rated ampacity not more than (≤) the connected wires. Example: use not more than (≤) a 200 amp circuit breaker with 2/0 AWG copper or 4/0 AWG aluminum service entrance wires. You may use a lower ampacity circuit breaker (such as a 150 amp circuit breaker), but not a higher one (such as a 225 amp circuit breaker).
2. Install the fuse(s) or circuit breaker(s) in or as close as possible to the service disconnecting equipment. In almost all cases, these fuse(s) or circuit breaker(s) also serve as the service equipment. Install these fuse(s) or circuit breaker(s) as close as possible to where the service entrance wires enter the home.
3. Do not install a fuse, circuit breaker, or switch on the neutral (grounded) wire.

Service Wire Entrance Overcurrent Protection - Multiple Fuses or Circuit Breakers

1. Install not more than (≤) six sets of fuses or circuit breakers in series with the hot (ungrounded) service entrance wires. Two pole circuit breakers with a tie handle and a fuse set of two or more fuses mounted so that the fuse set can be removed by pulling one handle count as one fuse or circuit breaker.
2. You may install between two and six sets of fuses or circuit breakers where the sum of the ampacity ratings of all devices exceeds the rated ampacity of the hot (ungrounded) service entrance wires. You may do this only when the calculated service load ampacity is not more than (≤) the hot (ungrounded) service entrance wire rated ampacity.

Wire and Circuit Ampacity Discussion

Don't be confused by the differences between the maximum wire ampacities listed in the Table 3603 and those listed in the branch circuit Table 3705-2. Example: #4 AWG copper wire has a maximum rated ampacity of 100 amps when used as a service wire but only 85 amps when used as a branch circuit wire. The difference is because it is more likely that the load on one individual branch circuit will be at a higher percentage of its maximum capacity for a longer period of time compared to all circuits in a home being active at the same time for a long period of time. Example: #4 AWG copper wire might serve an electric resistance forced air heating system. When the heating system is on, the load on the wire could be near the maximum allowed capacity for a long period of time. It is less likely that all circuits in a home would be on at the same time for the same duration.

Don't be confused by the service wire maximum number of service disconnecting means (6) and the maximum number of panelboard protection devices (2) in Section 3606. These are two different requirements serving two different purposes. The service disconnecting means requirement is intended to protect the structure and personnel by allowing rapid disconnection of electric service during an emergency. The panelboard protection requirement is intended to protect the panelboard from damage by excess electric current.

SERVICE DROP CLEARANCES AND INSTALLATION (E3604)

Service Drop Clearances to Decks and Openings

1. Provide at least (≥) 3 feet clearance between service drop and service entrance wires and porches, decks, stairs, ladders, fire escapes, balconies, sides of doors, and <u>sides and bottoms of operable windows</u> (not the tops of windows). Provide clearance only to service drops and service entrance wires that consist of individual wires and wires that are not protected by a raceway or outer jacket. This means that clearances are usually required for utility service drop wires and are not required for SE type service entrance cable and for wires or cables installed in conduit or tubing.

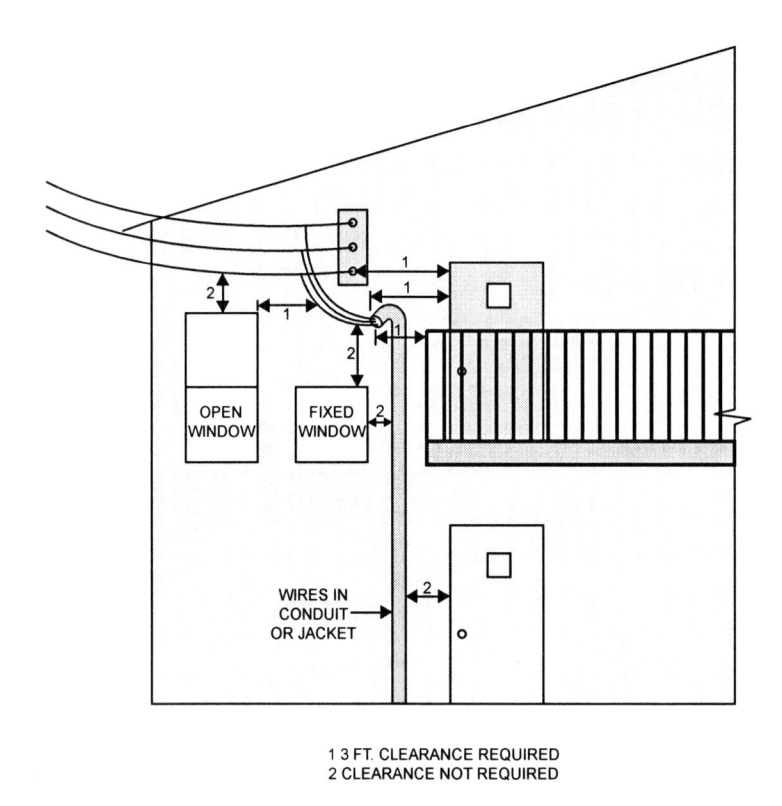

1 3 FT. CLEARANCE REQUIRED
2 CLEARANCE NOT REQUIRED

Service Drop Clearances to Openings (E3604-1)
Figure 36-1

Service Drop Clearance Above Roofs

1. Provide at least (≥) 8 feet vertical clearance between service drop wires and a roof not designed for regular pedestrian traffic with a slope less than (<) 4 inches in 12 inches. Access to such a roof would usually be by a ladder, through a window, or through a maintenance hatch.
2. Provide at least (≥) 10 feet vertical clearance between service drop wires and a roof designed for regular pedestrian traffic. Access to such a roof would usually be by stairs or by a door and the roof edges would be protected by a guard.
3. Provide at least (≥) 3 feet vertical clearance between service drop wires and roof with a slope at least (≥) 4 inches in 12 inches.
4. Provide at least (≥) 18 inches vertical clearance between service drop wires and a roof if:
   a) the wires pass only over the overhang portion of the roof, and if
   b) not more than (≤) 6 feet of wire pass over not more than (≤) 4 lineal feet of roof surface measured horizontally, and if
   c) the wires enter a through-the-roof mast or terminate at an approved support.

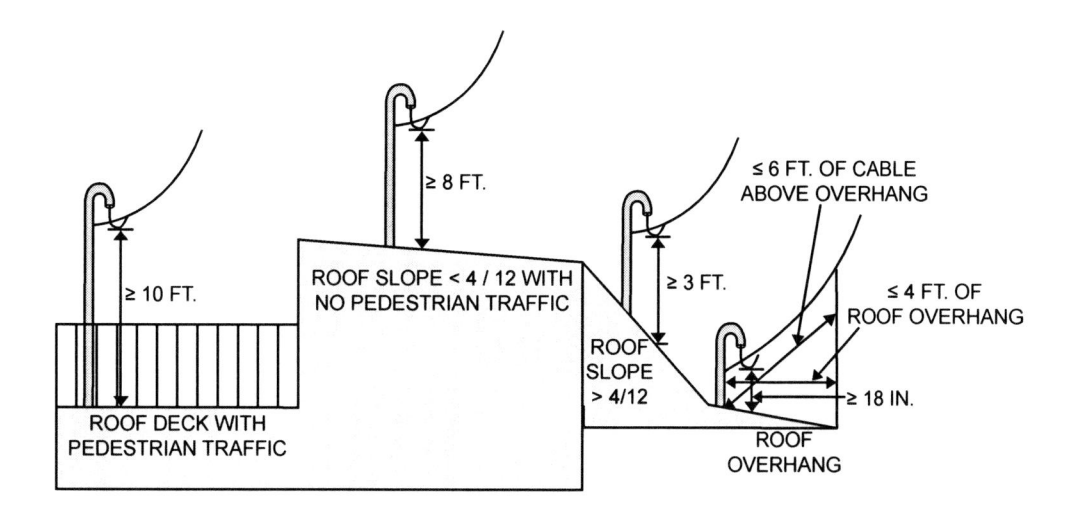

Service Drop Clearances Above Roofs (E3604-2)
Figure 36-2

Service Drop Clearance Above Ground

1. Measure the vertical clearance between service drop wires and the ground, walkway, driveway, or street beginning at the lowest point of the service drop wires and ending at the surface under the wire's lowest point. The lowest point of the service drop wires is often at the drip loop, but it could be at the point of attachment to the house or it could be where the wires enter the house.
2. Provide at least (≥) 10 feet vertical clearance between service drop wires and areas or sidewalks accessed by pedestrians only.
3. Provide at least (≥) 12 feet vertical clearance between service drop wires and residential property and driveways.
4. Provide at least (≥) 18 feet vertical clearance between service drop wires and public streets, alleys, roads, or parking areas subject to truck traffic.

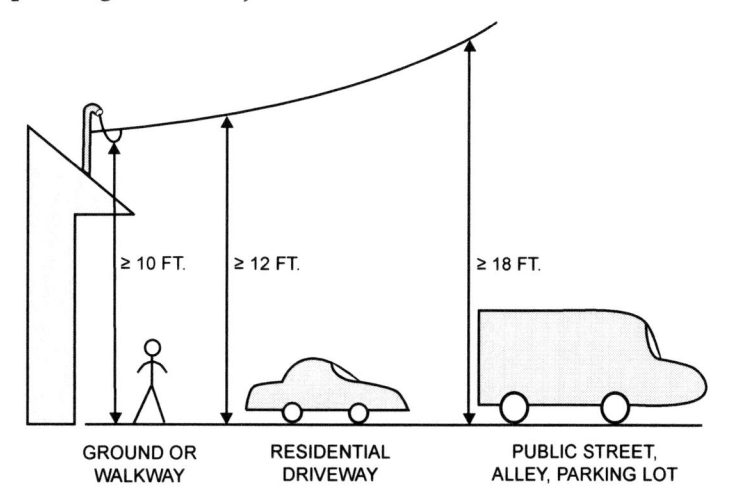

Service Drop Clearances Above Ground (E3604-3)
Figure 36-3

Service Drop Attachment and Support

1. Attach service drop wires to the building at least (≥) 10 feet above finished grade and at a point high enough to provide the required ground clearances over the entire length of the service drop.
2. Use only approved parts and fittings to attach service drop wires to buildings and use only parts and fittings that are strong enough to bear the loads imposed by the service drop wires.
3. Do not attach anything other than service drop wires and service mast guy wires to a service mast. This means do not attach antennas, satellite dishes, flags, or guy wires that are not part of the service mast supports.

SERVICE ENTRANCE WIRE AND MAST INSTALLATION (E3605)

Service Entrance Wire Insulation

1. Insulate hot (ungrounded) service entrance wires with approved insulation.
2. You may use uninsulated copper wire as the neutral (grounded) wire if it is inside a raceway or if it is part of a service entrance cable or if it is buried in an approved manner.
3. You may use uninsulated aluminum wire as the neutral (grounded) wire if it is part of a service entrance cable or if it buried in an approved manner.

Service Entrance Cable Protection Against Damage

1. Run above ground service entrance cable inside approved conduit or tubing (such as RMC, IMC, EMT, Schedule 80 PVC) if the wire is subject to physical damage and if required by the local building official. Places where service entrance cable might be subject to physical damage include near driveways and walkways and where doors, shutters, or awnings might impact the cable.
2. Use service entrance cable labeled as sunlight resistant if the cable is exposed to any direct sunlight.

Service Entrance Wire Splices

1. You may splice service entrance wires using approved clamps or bolts.
2. Use splicing materials listed for burial when splicing buried wires.

Service Mast Installation.

1. Install a rain-tight service head or goose neck on top of the service mast.
2. Install the service mast so that any condensation or water that enters can drain out before it gets to the service equipment or panelboard.
3. Form drip loops on each service wire.
4. Locate the service head or goose neck above the service wire attachment point. You may locate the service wire attachment point above the service head or goose neck if it is not more than (≤) 24 inches from the service head or goose neck and if it is not possible to locate the attachment point below the goose neck or service head.

5. Run each service entrance wire through a separate bushed opening in the service head or goose neck.

Service Mast with Goose Neck (PE3605-0)
Figure 36-4

SERVICE GROUNDING GENERAL REQUIREMENTS (E3607)

Service Grounding

1. Connect the neutral (grounded) wire to the grounding electrode wire at the nearest accessible point at or before the service equipment (main disconnect). The service equipment is usually the most convenient accessible grounding point because the meter enclosure and points before it are usually locked or secured and not accessible. The grounding electrode wire connects the neutral (grounded) wire to a grounding electrode.
2. Do not connect the neutral (grounded) wire to ground at any other place downstream from the service equipment grounding point. An exception to this rule exists when two buildings are supplied by one electric service.
3. Connect (bond) all metal parts of the electrical system to the neutral (grounded) wire. This includes service equipment and panelboard cases, any metal electrical conduit or tubing, all metal pipes in the building (such as metal water and gas pipe).

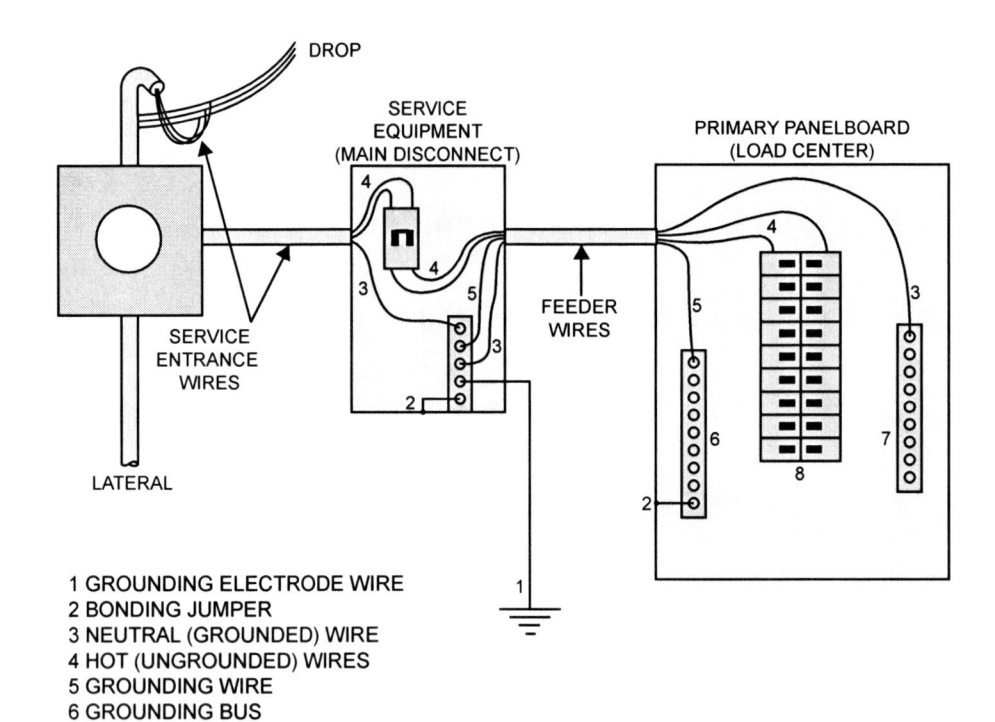

1 GROUNDING ELECTRODE WIRE
2 BONDING JUMPER
3 NEUTRAL (GROUNDED) WIRE
4 HOT (UNGROUNDED) WIRES
5 GROUNDING WIRE
6 GROUNDING BUS
7 NEUTRAL (GROUNDED) BUS ISOLATED FROM CABINET
8 BRANCH CIRCUIT BREAKERS OR FUSES

Service Grounding with Separate Service Equipment (E3607-1)
Figure 36-5

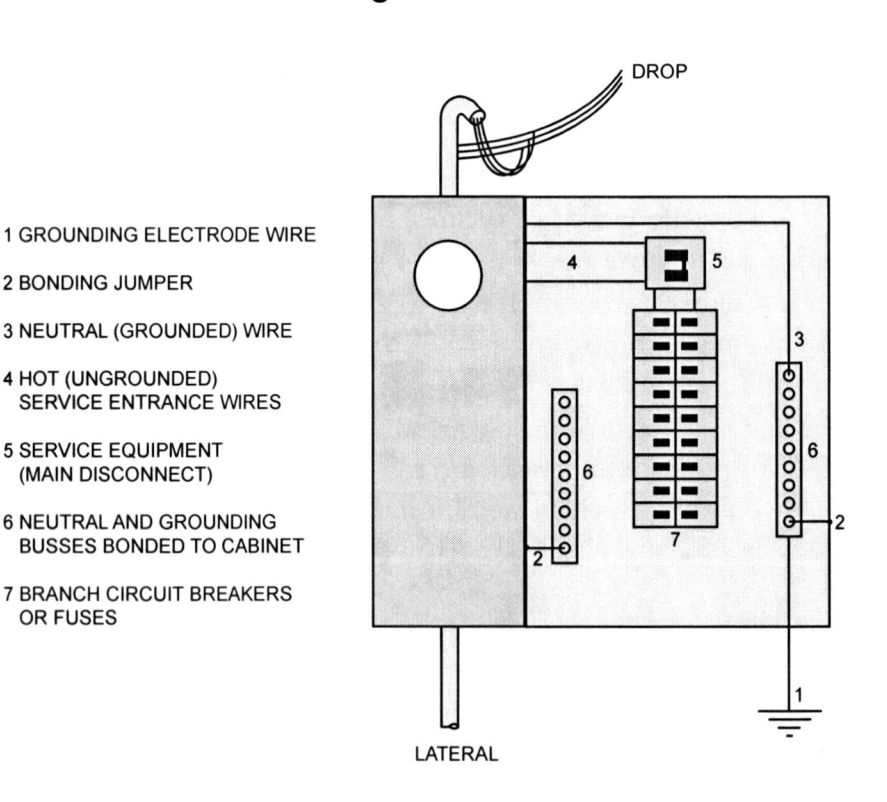

1 GROUNDING ELECTRODE WIRE

2 BONDING JUMPER

3 NEUTRAL (GROUNDED) WIRE

4 HOT (UNGROUNDED) SERVICE ENTRANCE WIRES

5 SERVICE EQUIPMENT (MAIN DISCONNECT)

6 NEUTRAL AND GROUNDING BUSSES BONDED TO CABINET

7 BRANCH CIRCUIT BREAKERS OR FUSES

Service Grounding with Panel and Service Equipment in One Cabinet (E3607-2)
Figure 36-6

Service Grounding at Two Buildings Using Four Wire Feeder

1. Use this procedure when installing a new feeder cable to a second building from the building with the primary electric service. You are not required to use this procedure if there is only one branch circuit in the second building and if the new feeder cable contains an equipment grounding wire.
    a) Install a feeder cable to the second building that contains an equipment grounding wire. Size the equipment grounding wire as required by Section E3908.
    b) Install a grounding electrode at both buildings.
    c) Connect the feeder cable equipment grounding wire to the grounding electrode wire at the second building subpanel grounding bus. Connect all second building branch circuit equipment grounding wires to the grounding bus.
    d) Bond the subpanel case to the grounding bus.
    e) Connect the feeder cable neutral (grounded) wire to an isolated grounded bus at the second building subpanel. Do not connect the grounded bus to the subpanel case or to the grounding bus.

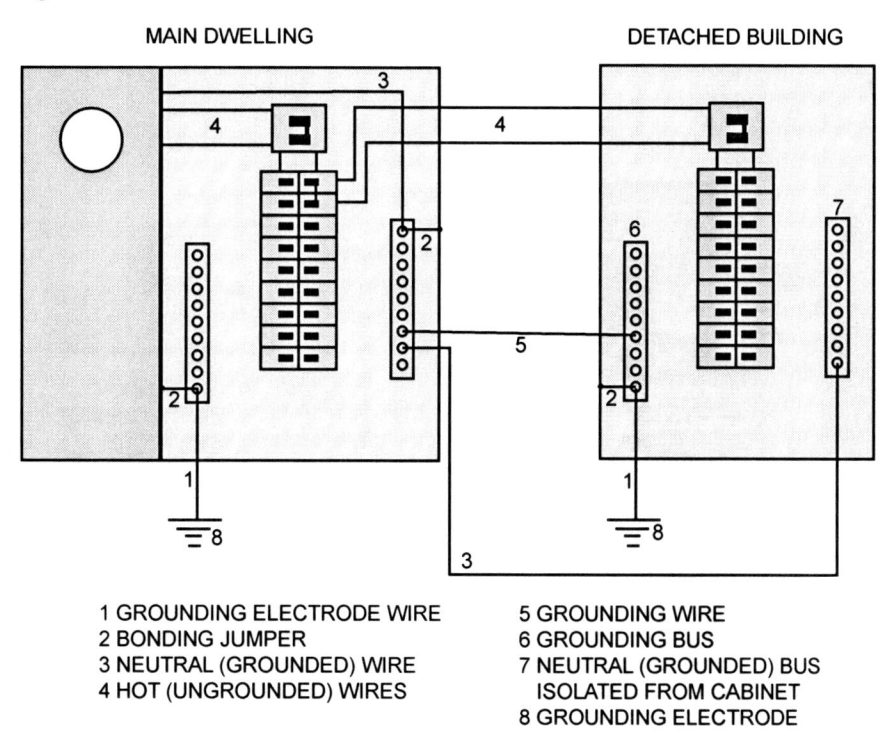

1 GROUNDING ELECTRODE WIRE
2 BONDING JUMPER
3 NEUTRAL (GROUNDED) WIRE
4 HOT (UNGROUNDED) WIRES
5 GROUNDING WIRE
6 GROUNDING BUS
7 NEUTRAL (GROUNDED) BUS
 ISOLATED FROM CABINET
8 GROUNDING ELECTRODE

Service Grounding at Two Buildings Using Four Wire Feeder (E3607-3)
Figure 36-7

Service Grounding at Two Buildings Using Three Wire Feeder

1. Use this procedure when two existing buildings are supplied by one electric service and when the existing feeder cable to the second building does not contain an equipment grounding wire.
    a) Install a grounding electrode at both buildings.

b) Connect the feeder cable neutral (grounded) wire to grounded bus at the second building subpanel.
c) Connect all second building branch circuit equipment grounding and neutral (grounded) wires to the grounded bus.
d) Bond the subpanel case to the grounded bus.
e) Do not connect any continuous metal path between the two buildings if the path is bonded to the electrical system in both buildings. Example: do not run metal water or gas pipe between the two buildings because such pipes are required to be bonded to the electrical system and because these pipes would provide an alternate path for the electricity.
f) Do not install ground fault protection on the feeder wires to the second building.

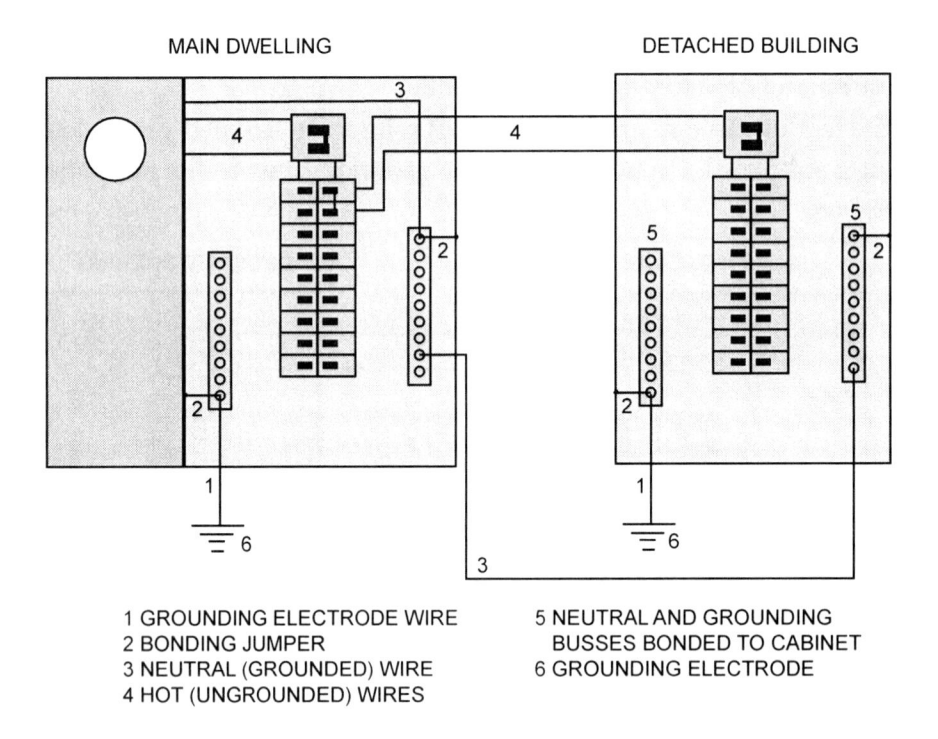

1 GROUNDING ELECTRODE WIRE
2 BONDING JUMPER
3 NEUTRAL (GROUNDED) WIRE
4 HOT (UNGROUNDED) WIRES
5 NEUTRAL AND GROUNDING BUSSES BONDED TO CABINET
6 GROUNDING ELECTRODE

Service Grounding at Two Buildings Using Three Wire Feeder (E3607-4)
Figure 36-8

Grounding Discussion

One of the important purposes of grounding and bonding can be summarized in this simple rule: Electricity wants to return to ground and will find the path of least resistance to get there. When the electrical system is working as intended, electricity enters through the hot (ungrounded) wire, does its work, and returns to ground through the neutral (ungrounded) wire. This is the path of least resistance.

When electricity finds its way out of the intended path, things get dangerous. Example: a rat sits on copper water pipe and chews through the insulation on electrical cable exposing the hot (ungrounded) wire. After electrocuting the unfortunate rat, the exposed wire lands on the water pipe. If the water pipe is connected without electrical interruption to ground (through bonding or because the water pipe is a grounding electrode), the electricity thinks that the water pipe is the neutral (grounded) wire and happily starts flowing through the water pipe. This is a ground fault. The electric current should quickly rise to the point where it trips a circuit breaker or blows a fuse, clearing the fault.

But what if the water pipe is not grounded or bonded to ground? Perhaps a water softener has been added to the system interrupting the electrical continuity of some or all of the water pipe. In our example, the water pipe is still energized but there is no way for the electricity to return to ground; that is, until someone grabs a metal water faucet handle and is standing on the ground or on some conducting surface. At that time, the electricity finds its path of least resistance to ground through the person. The person is injured or killed.

When trying to understand grounding and bonding, think like electricity. If metal can become energized, however unlikely that is, you must assume that it will become energized. Bonding metal together and connecting the metal to ground in an approved manner lets you, not the electricity, decide how electricity will flow in a fault condition.

GROUNDING ELECTRODES (E3608)

Connect (Bond) All Grounding Electrodes

1. Connect (bond) together all grounding electrodes that may be available at a building. This includes underground metal water pipe, reinforcing bars or wire in concrete, ground rings, and ground rods. The IRC does not require that all possible types of grounding electrodes be installed. It requires that if a grounding electrode is installed, it must be connected (bonded) to all other grounding electrodes and to the neutral (grounded) wire.
2. Use a bonding jumper at least (≥) as large as the grounding electrode wire to connect (bond) the grounding electrodes. You may connect bonding jumpers between grounding electrodes at any convenient point.
3. Connect the grounding electrode wire at any convenient grounding electrode.

Metal Underground Water Pipe Electrodes

1. Use metal underground water pipe that is in contact with the ground for at least (≥) 10 feet as a grounding electrode. This includes all metal water pipe materials such as copper and steel. Underground water pipe includes metal well casing pipe that is electrically connected (bonded) to the electrical system. It also includes water pipes other than water service pipes such as metal irrigation system pipes.
2. You must consider all underground water pipe that satisfies the previous conditions as a grounding electrode and connect (bond) underground water pipe to all other grounding electrodes.
3. Do not connect a grounding electrode wire to any interior metal water pipe at a point that is more than (>) 5 feet from where the underground water pipe enters the building. Do not use any interior metal water pipe that is more than (>) 5 feet from where the water pipe enters the building as a conductor for a grounding electrode. Example: do not connect the grounding electrode wire at a water heater cold water pipe if the pipe is more than (>) 5 feet from where the water pipe enters the building.
4. Do not use underground metal water pipe as the only grounding electrode. Install at least

one other type of grounding electrode and connect (bond) it to the underground metal water pipe.
5. Install bonding jumper wires around devices that might interrupt electrical continuity. Such devices include water meters, water pressure reducers, water softeners, and water filtration systems.

Concrete Encased Electrodes

1. You may use at least (≥) ½ inch diameter reinforcing bar or at least (≥) #4 AWG bare copper wire as a concrete encased grounding electrode. The electrode material must be at least (≥) 20 feet long.
2. Encase the reinforcing bar or wire in at least (≥) 2 inches of concrete. Place the bar or wire near the bottom of the concrete and place the concrete in direct contact with the ground. Do not place a moisture barrier between the concrete and the ground.
3. You may use wire ties or similar means to connect (bond) reinforcing bars together to achieve the 20 feet minimum length.
4. Concrete encased electrodes are also called ufer grounding electrodes after the man who designed this grounding electrode system.

Bare Copper Wire as Ufer Grounding Electrode (PE3608-0)
Figure 36-9

Ground Ring Electrodes

1. You may use at least (≥) #2 bare copper wire that is at least (≥) 20 feet long and is buried at least (≥) 30 inches below ground as a grounding electrode.

Rod and Pipe Electrode Materials

1. You may use metal pipe or conduit that is at least (≥) ¾ inch diameter and is at least (≥) 8 feet

long as a grounding electrode. Use galvanized materials or other corrosion-resistant coating on iron and steel pipes.
2. You may use a stainless steel, zinc-coated steel, or copper rod that is at least (≥) ⅝ inch diameter and is at least (≥) 8 feet long as a grounding electrode.
3. You may use a <u>listed</u> stainless steel or non-ferrous (such as copper) rod that is at least (≥) ½ inch diameter and is at least (≥) 8 feet long as a grounding electrode.
4. Do not use aluminum as rod and pipe electrodes.

Grounding Electrode Installation

1. Clean grounding electrodes of all non-conductive materials such as paint.
2. Place rod and pipe electrodes at least (≥) 6 feet away from any other type of grounding electrode. Example: place a grounding rod at least (≥) 6 feet from an underground metal water pipe.
3. Drive rod and pipe electrodes at least (≥) 8 feet into the ground. You may drive rod and pipe electrodes into the ground at not more (≤) than a 45 degree angle or bury them at least 30 inches deep in the ground if rock is encountered above the minimum 8 feet depth.
4. Leave the upper end of the electrode at or below ground level or protect the above ground electrode end and the attachment point of the grounding electrode conductor from physical damage.

Metal Underground Gas Pipe Electrode

1. Do not use metal underground gas pipe as a grounding electrode.

BONDING (E3609)

Bonding Metal Service Components

1. Connect (bond) together any non-current carrying components in an electrical system so that any current imposed on the components will be safely carried to ground. Such components include metallic conduit and tubing, cabinets, and junction boxes.
2. Connect (bond) together the following metallic, non-current carrying components <u>associated with the electric service wires and enclosures</u>:
   a) service raceways (such as service drop masts and service lateral risers) and armored cable surrounding service wires, and
   b) service enclosures (such as meter boxes, service equipment boxes, and panelboard enclosures), and
   c) raceways and armor surrounding a grounding electrode conductor, including all junction boxes and enclosures between the service equipment and the grounding electrode conductor.
3. Do not use standard locknuts or bushings as the only bonding connection device at enclosure knockouts <u>if any part of the knockout remains</u>. Use approved bonding connectors or bonding jumpers <u>unless the entire knockout is removed and only the enclosure body remains.</u> This provision applies only to components associated with the electric service wires and enclosures.

4. Make threaded couplings or threaded bosses wrench-tight at enclosures.
5. Make threadless couplings and connectors wrench-tight at enclosures.
6. You may use other approved devices for bonding such as bonding locknuts and bonding bushings.

Bonding Connections for Cable TV and Other Systems

1. Provide an accessible bonding terminal or bonding bar that is not inside the service equipment cabinet and not inside the subpanel cabinet at any accessory building. Provide capacity for at least (≥) 3 bonding wires. Do not install this terminal or bar so that it interferes with opening of any service or meter cabinet. Use this terminal or bar for bonding cable TV wires, satellite dishes and other antennae, and telephone wires to the electrical system.
2. You may install one of the following as the bonding terminal or bar:
   a) listed grounding and bonding terminals mounted to and electrically connected to the meter cabinet; or
   b) a bonding bar near the service equipment cabinet, meter cabinet, or a non-flexible metallic service wire raceway; connect the bonding bar to one of the cabinets or to the raceway using at least (≥) #6 AWG copper wire; or
   c) a bonding bar near the grounding electrode wire; connect the bonding bar to the grounding electrode wire using at least (≥) #6 AWG copper wire.

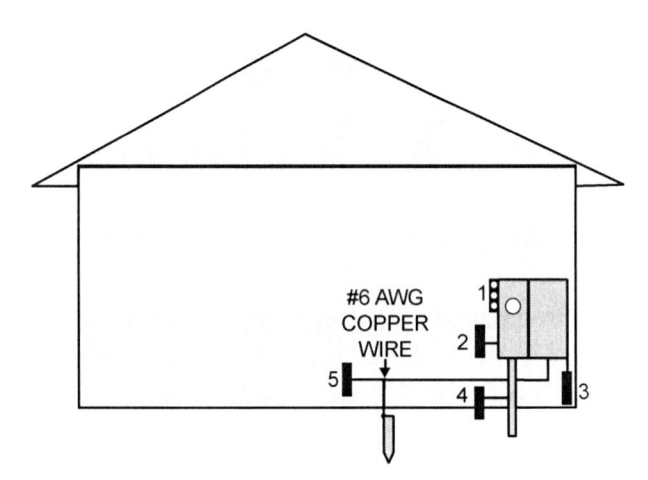

1 BONDING TERMINALS AT METER CABINET
2 BONDING BAR NEAR METER CABINET
3 BONDING BAR NEAR SERVICE EQUIPMENT CABINET
4 BONDING BAR NEAR NONFLEXIBLE METAL SERVICE WIRE RACEWAY
5 BONDING BAR NEAR GROUNDING ELECTRODE WIRE

Accessible Bonding Points for Cable TV and Other Systems (E3609-0)
Figure 36-10

Improper Bonding Strap Connection on Painted Service Raceway (PE3609-0)
Figure 36-11

Bonding Jumper Size

1. Use a bonding jumper at the service equipment that is at least (≥) as large as the grounding electrode wire. This applies to bonding jumpers and bonding wires, including the main bonding jumper at the service equipment, that occur downstream from the service equipment.

Metal Water Pipe Bonding

1. Connect (bond) interior metal water pipes to the service equipment enclosure, or to the neutral (grounded) wire at the service equipment, or to the grounding electrode conductor, or to any grounding electrode.
2. Use a bonding jumper or wire that is at least (≥) as large as the grounding electrode wire.
3. Make the bonding connection point accessible.

Metal Gas and Other Pipe Bonding

1. Connect (bond) interior metal gas pipes and other metal pipes to the service equipment enclosure, or to the neutral (grounded) wire at the service equipment, or to the grounding electrode conductor, or to any grounding electrode.
2. Use a bonding jumper or wire that is at least (≥) as large as the equipment grounding wire used on the circuit that might energize the pipe. You may use the equipment grounding wire that serves the equipment as the bonding wire. Example: you may use the equipment grounding wire that serves a furnace as the bonding wire for the gas pipe connected to the furnace.
3. Make the bonding connection point accessible.

GROUNDING ELECTRODE WIRES (E3610 AND E3611)

Aluminum Grounding Electrode Wires

1. Do not use aluminum or copper-clad aluminum grounding electrode wires if the wire is in direct contact with masonry or with the ground or if the wire is in a corrosive environment.

2. Do not install aluminum or copper-clad aluminum grounding electrode wires within 18 inches of the ground when the wire is installed outside.

Connecting Grounding Electrode Wires to the Electrode

1. Use one of the following methods to connect grounding electrode wires to grounding electrodes: (a) a pipe fitting, pipe plug or other approved device screwed into a pipe or pipe fitting, or (b) a listed bolted clamp made of cast bronze or brass, or plain or malleable iron.
2. You may use a listed metal strap ground clamp to connect indoor communications equipment grounding electrode wires to a grounding electrode.
3. Make accessible the connection point of grounding electrode wires and bonding jumpers to grounding electrodes. The connection point need not be accessible for buried or concrete encased grounding electrodes.
4. Clean grounding electrode wire connection points and all clamps and fittings of non-conductive materials such as paint.
5. Use ground clamps or fittings that are either approved for installation without physical protection or that are protected by enclosing them in metal, wood or an equivalent protective cover.

Connections Around Equipment and Insulated Fittings

1. Install bonding jumpers around equipment such as water meters, pressure reducing valves, water softeners, water filtration equipment, dielectric fittings and other equipment and fittings that interrupt the electrical continuity of metal piping used as a grounding electrode.
2. Make bonding jumpers long enough to permit removal of the equipment and maintain electrical continuity.

37

BRANCH CIRCUIT AND FEEDER REQUIREMENTS

MULTIWIRE BRANCH CIRCUITS (E3701.5)

Multiwire Branch Circuit Definition

Multiwire branch circuit A multiwire branch circuit is a three wire branch circuit with two hot (ungrounded) wires and one neutral (grounded) wire. In residential electrical systems, the voltage between the two hot (ungrounded) wires is 240 volts and the voltage between the hot (ungrounded) wires and the neutral (grounded) wire is 120 volts. When a multiwire branch circuit is operating as intended, the voltage on the shared neutral (grounded) wire is zero. Split-wired receptacles that provide the required two 20 amp kitchen countertop receptacle circuits are one example of a multiwire branch circuit. Clothes dryer and range circuits are another example. Water heater and air conditioning condenser circuits are usually not multiwire branch circuits because there is no neutral (ungrounded) wire in the circuit.

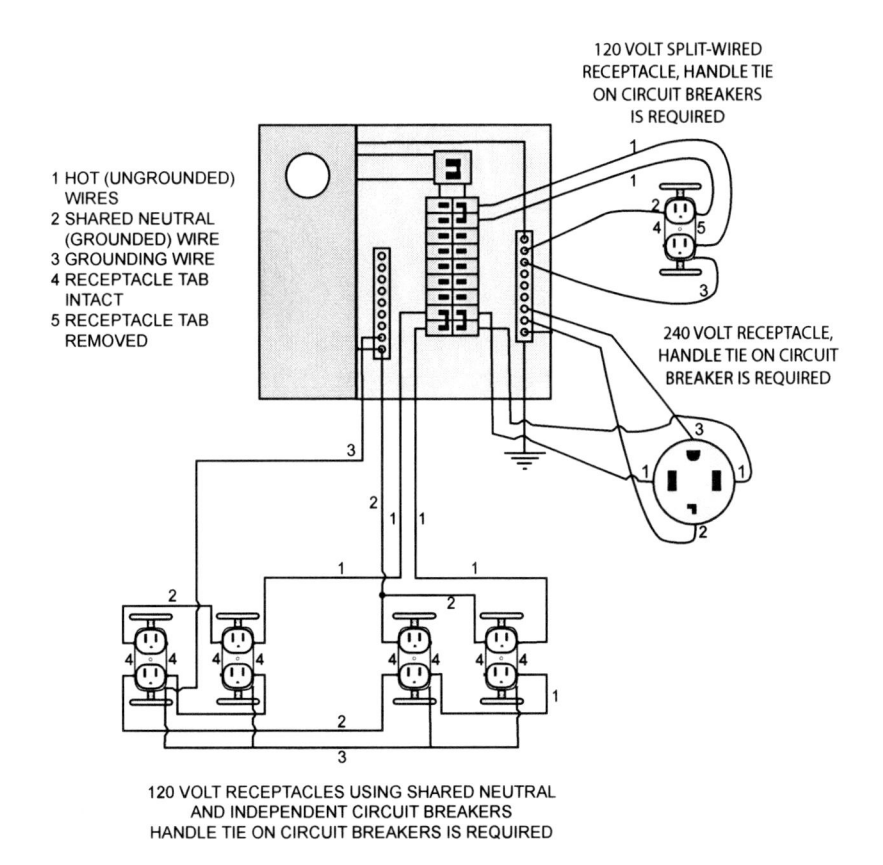

Multiwire Branch Circuits (E3701.5-0)
Figure 37-1

Multiwire Branch Circuit Requirements

1. Originate multiwire branch circuit wires from adjacent slots on the same panelboard.
2. Use a two-pole overcurrent device or two single pole devices that are connected by an approved handle tie to simultaneously disconnect power to all ungrounded (hot) a multiwire branch circuit wires. Do not connect circuit breaker handles with nails, wires, or other unapproved handle tie substitutes.
3. Use wire ties or similar devices to group all ungrounded (hot) and grounded (neutral) wires of each multi-wire branch circuit in the cabinet where the circuit originates.

BRANCH CIRCUIT VOLTAGE AND AMPERAGE RATINGS (E3702)

Multiple Outlet Branch Circuit Amperage and Voltage Rating Limits

1. Use only 15 amp and 20 amp, 120 volt, circuits for multiple outlet branch circuits. A multiple outlet branch circuit has more than one light fixture and/or receptacle on the same circuit. One duplex receptacle (the common receptacle with two openings for plugs) counts as two receptacles. A circuit that serves one duplex receptacle is a multiple outlet branch circuit. This provision does not apply to a circuit that serves one single receptacle or one single light fixture.
2. Use only 120 volt branch circuits to supply residential light fixtures, and to supply receptacles for plug-and-cord connected loads not more than ($\leq$) 1,440 watts, and to supply motor loads less than (<) .25 horsepower.
3. You may use either 120 or 240 volt branch circuits to supply one plug-and-cord connected or one permanently wired appliance rated more than (>) 1,440 watts. This means that branch circuits rated more than (>) 120 volts are effectively limited to serving a single receptacle or permanently wired fixed equipment.

Multiple Outlet Branch Circuit Load Limits

1. Do not connect one plug-and-cord device that exceeds 80 percent of a <u>multiple outlet branch circuit's</u> amperage rating. This means that that one device (such as a vacuum cleaner or a toaster oven) may not exceed 12 amps (about 1,440 watts) on a 15 amp multiple outlet branch circuit and may not exceed 16 amps (about 1,920 watts) on a 20 amp multiple outlet branch circuit.
2. Do not connect one or more fixed devices that in total exceed 50 percent of a <u>multiple outlet branch circuit's</u> amperage rating. Fixed devices do not include light fixtures. This means that that all fixed devices (such as a permanently wired disposal or hot water circulating pump) on a multiple outlet branch circuit may not exceed 7.5 amps (about 900 watts) on a 15 amp multiple outlet branch circuit and may not exceed 10 amps (about 1,200 watts) on a 20 amp multiple outlet branch circuit.

Thirty Amp Branch Circuit Load Limits

1. Do not connect one plug-and-cord device that exceeds 80 percent of a 30 amp branch circuit's amperage rating. This means that that one device (such as a clothes dryer) may not exceed 24 amps (about 5,760 watts) on a 30 amp, 240 volt branch circuit.

2. Do not use a 30 amp branch circuit to serve loads other than a fixed device such as a water heater or a single plug-and-cord connected device such as a welder.

Single-Motor Branch Circuit Wire Size

1. Use wires for a branch circuit that are rated at least (≥) 125 percent of one motor's full-load current rating when the motor is the only equipment on the circuit. This means that the wires serving one motor, such as a swimming pool pump with a full-load current rating of 15 amps, must be rated to carry at least (≥) 18.75 amps. Number 12 AWG copper wire would be the minimum size for this application. Note that equipment such as dishwashers and room air conditioners may appear to be single-motor devices, but are actually treated as combination motor and other loads because they contain equipment in addition to a single compressor or pump motor.

Combination Motor and Other Load / Branch Circuit Wire Size

1. Determine the wire size for a branch circuit serving one or more fixed motors that are at least (≥) .125 horsepower and serving other loads by:
   a) multiply the largest fixed motor's full-load current rating by 1.25, and
   b) add the result in (a) to the sum of the other loads.

   Example: determine if a ½ horsepower disposal rated at 6.9 amps and a dishwasher rated at 12 amps, including a 6.8 amp motor, should be on one 20 amp circuit. Multiply 1.25 times 6.9 amps (the largest motor's load). This equals 8.625 amps. Add 8.625 amps to 12 amps. This equals 20.625 amps. You need to place the disposal and the dishwasher on separate circuits.

   Example: determine the wire size for the dishwasher in the previous example. Multiply 1.25 times 6.8 amps. This equals 8.5 amps. Subtract 6.8 amps from 12 amps to determine the other loads for the dishwasher. This equals 5.2 amps. Add 5.2 amps to 8.5 amps. This equals 13.7 amps. You may place the dishwasher on a 15 amp circuit if it is the only device on the circuit and if allowed by the manufacturer's installation instructions.

2. Compute the wire size for a branch circuit serving one or more fixed motors that are less than (<) .125 horsepower and serving other loads by adding the full-load current ratings of all loads on the circuit. This means that for small motors, it is not necessary to use the 125 percent safety margin.

Fluorescent Light Circuit Loads

1. Compute the load of light fixtures that use ballasts (such as fluorescent lights) based on the fixture's total load including the ballast and the lamps. The current load rating is usually marked on the light fixture.

Cooking Appliance Circuit Loads

1. Use the appliance's nameplate rating to determine the load on one branch circuit serving one <u>wall oven</u> or one <u>counter-mounted cooktop</u>. Example: one wall oven has a nameplate

rating of 7,200 watts. The load on a 240 volt dedicated branch circuit serving this wall oven is 30 amps (7,200 watts divided by 240 volts).

2. You may use 8,000 watts as the load for one branch circuit serving one <u>range</u> or 11,000 watts as the load for one branch circuit serving two <u>ranges</u>. A range is a cooking appliance with a cooktop and oven in one cabinet. Each range must have a nameplate rating of not more than (≤) 12,000 watts. You must use at least (≥) a 40 amp branch circuit if the range's nameplate rating exceeds 8,750 watts. Example: one dedicated 240 volt branch circuit serves two ranges each with a nameplate rating of 8,000 watts. The calculated load on this circuit is 45.8 amps (11,000 watts divided by 240 volts). The minimum dedicated 240 volt branch circuit serving the two ranges is 50 amps.

3. You may calculate an adjusted load for one <u>counter-mounted cooktop</u> and not more than (≤) 2 <u>wall-mounted ovens</u> if:
   a) all appliances are in the same room and if,
   b) all appliances are supplied by one branch circuit, and if
   c) each appliance nameplate rating is at least (≥) 1,750 watts and not more than (≤) 8,750 watts, and if
   d) the sum of the nameplate ratings of all appliances is not more than (≤) 27,000 watts.

4. Use the following steps to calculate the adjusted load:
   1. Add the nameplate ratings of all appliances.
   2. Subtract 12,000 watts from the sum of the appliance nameplate ratings.
   3. If the result in step 2 is not an even multiple of 1,000 watts, round up if more than (>) 500 watts or round down if not more than (≤) 500 watts.
   4. Divide the result in step 3 by 1,000 watts.
   5. Multiply the result in step 4 by 0.05.
   6. Multiply the result in step 5 by 8,000 watts.
   7. Add the result in step 6 to 8,000 watts.
   8. Divide the result in step 7 by 240 volts. This is the adjusted load in amps.

Example:

Question:

Given a cooktop with a nameplate rating of 8,100 watts and 2 wall ovens with nameplate ratings of 7,600 watts and 6,600 watts, what is the adjusted branch circuit load in amps if all appliances are in the same room and all are supplied by one branch circuit?

Answer:
   1. Add 8,100 watts + 7,600 watts + 6,600 watts = 22,300 watts.
   2. 22,300 watts – 12,000 watts = 10,300 watts.
   3. Round the result in step 2 down to 10,000 watts.
   4. 10,000 watts / 1,000 watts = 10
   5. 10 x 0.05 = 0.5
   6. 0.5 x 8,000 watts = 4,000 watts
   7. 4,000 watts + 8,000 watts = 12,000 watts

8. 12,000 watts / 240 volts = 50 amps

Water Heating and Space Heating Branch Circuit Loads

1. Use a branch circuit that is at least (≥) 125 percent of the nameplate rating for electric water heaters and electric space heaters such as baseboard heaters. The load on these devices is considered continuous and an extra margin of safety is required. Example: an electric water heater with a nameplate rating of 4,500 watts at 240 volts should be served by a circuit rated at least (≥) 23.4 amps.

2. Use not more than (≤) a 30 amp branch circuit to supply electric space heaters.

Air Conditioning and Heat Pump Condenser Branch Circuit Size

1. Use the minimum circuit ampacity rating on a condenser nameplate to determine the minimum wire size and minimum fuse or circuit breaker for the branch circuit.

2. Use the maximum fuse or circuit breaker rating on the condenser nameplate to determine the maximum fuse or circuit breaker rating. The fuse or circuit breaker rating is often larger than the rating for the wire. This is because the fuse or circuit breaker rating is based on the surge needed to start the condenser and the wire size is based on the load needed to run the condenser.

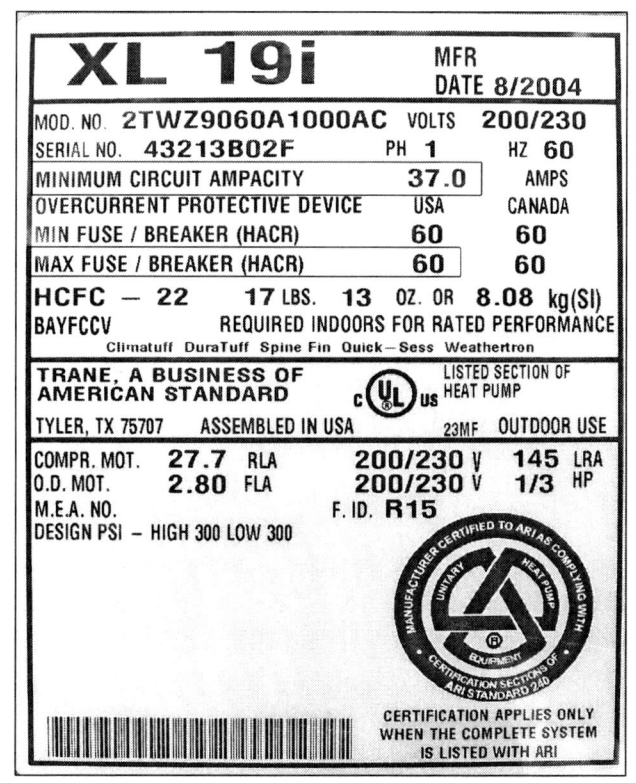

Condenser Nameplate (PE3702-0)
Figure 37-2

Room Air Conditioner Branch Circuits

1. Use wires that are rated at least (≥) 125 percent of a window or through-wall air conditioner's total rated current load if:

a) the air conditioner is connected to a receptacle by a plug-and-cord, and if
b) the air conditioner's total rated current load is shown on its nameplate (not just the individual motor load), and if
c) the air conditioner's total rated current load on the nameplate is not more than (≤) 40 amps and 250 volts, and if
d) the branch circuit overcurrent protection device does not exceed the branch circuit wire ampacity rating and the ampacity rating of the receptacle. Example: a plug-and-cord connected room air conditioner's total rated current load is 17 amps. Use wires rated for 1.25 times 17 amps equals 21.25 amps (#10 copper wire).

2. Do not install a window or through-wall air conditioner on a 15 or a 20 amp multiple outlet branch circuit if the air conditioner's total rated current load is more than (>) 50 percent of the branch circuit's rating.
3. Do not install a window or through-wall air conditioner on a 15 or a 20 amp branch circuit without other outlets if the air conditioner's total rated current load is more than (>) 80 percent of the branch circuit's rating. Example: a plug-and-cord connected window air conditioner's total rated current load is 11 amps. You may not install this air conditioner on either a 15 amp or 20 amp branch circuit with other outlets because the 11 amp total rated current load exceeds 50 percent of the branch circuit's rating. You may install this air conditioner on either a 15 amp or 20 amp branch circuit if the air conditioner outlet is the only outlet on the branch circuit. Any light or receptacle (including the second half of a duplex receptacle) on the same circuit is another outlet.

BRANCH CIRCUITS REQUIRED (E3703)

Central Heating Branch Circuit

1. Provide a dedicated branch circuit to serve central heating equipment such as gas furnaces and heat pump air handlers. You may use this circuit to serve directly related equipment such as pumps, motorized valves and dampers, humidifiers, and air filters.
2. Do not apply this rule to fixed space heating equipment such as electric baseboard heaters. You may supply more than one space heating unit on a branch circuit.

Kitchen Receptacle Branch Circuit

1. Provide at least (≥) two 20 amp, 120 volt branch circuits to serve only countertop, wall, and floor receptacles in the kitchen, pantry, breakfast and dining areas, and similar rooms. You may not use these branch circuits to supply light fixtures or other outlets in the listed rooms and you may not use these branch circuits to supply outlets in rooms other than those listed.
2. You may use a dedicated 15 amp branch circuit to provide power for a refrigerator.

Laundry Receptacle Branch Circuit

1. Provide at least (≥) one 20 amp, 120 volt branch circuit to serve only receptacles located in the laundry area. You may not use the laundry branch circuit to supply light fixtures or other outlets in the laundry and you may not use the laundry branch circuit to supply outlets in other rooms.

Bathroom Receptacle Branch Circuit

1. Provide at least (≥) one 20 amp, 120 volt branch circuit to <u>serve only receptacles</u> located in the bathroom(s). You may not use the bathroom branch circuit to supply light fixtures or other outlets in the bathroom and you may not use the bathroom branch circuit to supply outlets in other rooms.
2. You may provide each bathroom with its own dedicated 20 amp, 120 volt branch circuit. In this case, you may use the branch circuit to supply other bathroom outlets, such as light fixtures and exhaust fans.

General Lighting Branch Circuits

1. Provide at least (≥) the number of general lighting branch circuits determined when calculating the electrical service load size. This applies even if the known actual load is less than the calculated load.
2. Distribute the general lighting branch circuit load as evenly as possible among the general lighting branch circuits. Example: a 2,300 conditioned square feet house has a calculated general lighting load of 3 watts per square foot or 6,900 watts. To obtain the current load in amps, divide 6,900 watts by 120 volts and get 57.5 amps. Divide 57.5 amps by 15 amps to obtain 3.83 fifteen amp circuits. You may also divide 57.5 amps by 20 amps to obtain 2.875 twenty amp circuits. Round up to four 15 amp or three 20 amp general lighting circuits. Four is the minimum number of 15 amp general lighting circuits and three is the 20 amp general lighting circuits for this house.

Receptacle Quantity Limitation on Branch Circuit Discussion

A widely held belief exists that the IRC limits the number of receptacles on a residential branch circuit. This belief is incorrect. The IRC only requires that the number of branch circuits is sufficient to supply the connected load and that the load on any branch circuit does not exceed the IRC limits. This belief may come from restrictions on the number of outlets (both lights and receptacles) allowed for commercial electrical circuits. Commercial applications allow about 13 outlets on a 20 amp circuit and about 10 outlets on a 15 amp circuit. Wiring residential general lighting branch circuits based on these commercial outlet limits is often a good idea, but is not required by the IRC.

FEEDER LOAD CALCULATION (E3704)

Limitations of the Material in this Section

We do not recommend that most readers of this book determine feeder load. Leave this to experienced electrical contractors. For readers who are interested in how to calculate feeder loads, we provide the following explanation.

Feeder wire sizes based on the formula in this section are for wires run to subpanels that do not serve all (100 percent) of the home's electrical load. Use the electrical service formula to determine the feeder wire size for a feeder that serves the home's entire electrical load.

Feeder Load Formula

1. Use the following table to determine the minimum size for the hot (ungrounded) feeder wires.
2. You are not required to make the hot (ungrounded) feeder wires larger than the service entrance wires.
3. Provide an equipment grounding wire in a feeder cable if the circuits served by the feeder require equipment grounding wires. This will apply in most cases. See also Section 3607.

TABLE E3704-1
Ungrounded Feeder Load Formula

load type	demand factor
general lighting circuits + kitchen appliance circuits + laundry circuits	100 % of the first 3,000 watts plus 35 % of any excess over 3,000 watts
permanently wired appliances and motors	100 % of the load for ≤ 3 appliances/motors or 75 % of the load for ≥ 4 appliances/motors
motor surge load	25 % of the largest fixed motor load
clothes dryer	100 % of the clothes dryer actual load or 5,000 watts per clothes dryer, whichever is more
cooking appliances	refer to text for demand factor adjustment
largest of air conditioning or heat pump condenser load or fixed electric space heating load	100 % of the largest load

General lighting circuits Calculate the load for general lighting circuits served by the feeder branch circuits, if any. Multiply 3 watts times the conditioned square footage of the area served by the feeder branch circuits. Measure conditioned square footage based on the outside framed dimensions of the area served by the feeder branch circuits. Do not include open porches, garages, and areas that cannot be converted into conditioned living space such as most attics and crawl spaces. Include unfinished basements if they can be converted into conditioned living space. Do not include the 20 amp bathroom receptacle circuit. It is already included in this load.

Kitchen appliance and laundry Calculate the load for 20 amp, 120 volt kitchen appliance and laundry receptacle circuits served by the feeder branch circuits, if any. Multiply 1,500 watts times the total number of 20 amp, 120 volt appliance kitchen appliance and laundry receptacle circuits served by the feeder branch circuits. Do not add a separate dedicated circuit for a refrigerator to this load because the IRC allows a refrigerator to run off of the required kitchen receptacle circuit.

Permanently wired appliances and motors Calculate the load for 120 and 240 volt circuits serving dedicated or fastened-in-place electrical appliances and motors served by the feeder branch circuits, if any. Add the nameplate rating of all appliances and motors served by the feeder branch circuits. Examples of such appliances and motors include microwave ovens, dishwashers, water heaters, room air conditioners, disposals, spa, whirlpool tub, and swimming pool pump motors, garage door openers, and blowers for gas furnaces heat pump air handlers. Do not include clothes dryers, ranges, ovens, and similar cooking equipment, and condensers for heat pumps and air conditioning equipment.

Motor surge load Calculate the surge load for the single largest fixed motor served by the feeder branch circuits, if any. Multiply 0.25 times the largest motor nameplate rating. Examples of motors include spa, whirlpool tub, and swimming pool pump motors, garage door openers, and blowers for gas furnaces heat pump air handlers. Do not include auxiliary heat strips for heat pumps.

Electric clothes dryers Calculate the load for electric clothes dryers served by the feeder branch circuits, if any. Add the full nameplate wattage rating of all clothes dryers or add 5,000 watts per clothes dryer, whichever is larger.

Cooking appliances

1. You may add the full nameplate rating of all cooking equipment served by the feeder branch circuits, if any, to determine the cooking equipment load.
2. You may, as an alternative, use Table E3704-2 to calculate an adjusted cooking equipment feeder load. Note that the values in Table E3704-2 are from IRC Chapter 37 and from NEC 2005 Table 220.55. Examples of cooking equipment include ranges, surface-mounted cooktops, wall ovens, and boilers.
3. Refer to IRC Chapter 37 for information about adjustments for appliances with nameplate ratings more than 12,000 watts.

TABLE E3704-2
Cooking Appliance Demand Load Adjustment Table

number of appliances rated at least (≥) 1,750 watts and not more than (≤) 12,000 watts	adjusted demand for all appliances
1 appliance	8,000 watts
2 appliances	11,000 watts
3 appliances	14,000 watts
4 appliances	17,000 watts
5 appliances	20,000 watts

Heating and air conditioning load Calculate the load for electric heating or air conditioning equipment served by the feeder branch circuits, if any. Use the largest nameplate rating of:
   a) air conditioning or heat pump condensers; or
   b) central electric forced air heating equipment, including supplemental (auxiliary/ emergency) heat strips in heat pump air handlers; or
   c) electric radiant heating units.

Feeder Load Calculation Example

1. Assume that a feeder serves part of the home described in the following table.

TABLE EX3704-1
Feeder Load Calculation Example
Sample Home Electrical Equipment Served by a Feeder

home size and electrical equipment	nameplate rating
1,300 conditioned square feet	
2 – 20 amp, 120 volt kitchen small appliance circuits	
1 – 20 amp, 120 volt laundry circuit	
1 refrigerator	1,400
1 microwave oven	1,600
1 wall oven	6,600
1 surface cooking unit	8,100
1 dishwasher	1,200
1 disposal	800
1 clothes dryer	5,600
1 water heater	4,500
1 whirlpool tub motor (120 volt)	1,200
2 garage door openers (each)	900
1 heat pump condenser	7,200
1 heat pump air handler motor	1,000
heat pump auxiliary heat strips	10,000

Step 1 Calculate General Lighting and Kitchen/Laundry Load

Total lighting load = 1,300 conditioned square feet x 3 watts/square foot =	3,900 watts +
Two kitchen circuits x 1,500 watts/circuit =	3,000 watts +
One laundry circuit x 1,500 watts/circuit =	1,500 watts +
Total unadjusted load =	8,400 watts
Subtract first 3,000 watts	(3,000 watts) -
Excess over first 3,000 watts =	5,400 watts
Multiply excess by 0.35 =	1,890 watts
Add first 3,000 watts	3,000 watts +
Total adjusted general lighting and kitchen/laundry load =	**4,890 watts**

Note that the 20 amp refrigerator circuit is not included in the kitchen and laundry load.

Step 2 Calculate Permanently Wired Appliance and Motor Load

Microwave oven	1,600 watts +
Dishwasher	1,200 watts +
Disposal	800 watts +
Whirlpool tub motor	1,200 watts +
Two garage door openers (900 watts each)	1,800 watts +
Heat pump air handler	1,000 watts +
Water heater	4,500 watts +
Total unadjusted load =	12,100 watts
Multiply unadjusted load by 0.75 for ≥ 4 appliances =	9,075 watts
Total adjusted appliance load =	**9,075 watts**

Step 3 Calculate Motor Surge Load

Largest fixed motor load is whirlpool tub motor	1,200 watts
Multiply 1,200 watts x 0.25 =	300 watts
Total motor surge load =	**300 watts**

Step 4 Calculate Clothes Dryer Load

100% of actual clothes dryer load =	**5,600 watts**

Step 5 Calculate Cooking Appliance Load

Total adjusted cooking appliance load for two appliances each rated less than 12,000 per table E3604-2 =	**11,000 watts**

Step 6 Calculate Heating and Air conditioning Load

100% of heat pump auxiliary heat strips =	**10,000 watts**

Step 7 Calculate Adjusted Feeder Load

Total adjusted general lighting and kitchen/laundry load	4,890 watts +
Total adjusted appliance load	9,075 watts +
Total motor surge load	300 watts +
100% of actual clothes dryer load =	5,600 watts +
Total adjusted cooking appliance load	11,000 watts +
100% of heat pump auxiliary heat strips =	10,000 watts +
Total adjusted feeder load =	**40,865 watts**

Step 8 Calculate Service Load in Amps

40,865 watts/240 volts = 170.3 amps

The minimum hot (ungrounded) feeder wires for a 170.3 amp feeder are #1/0 AWG copper or 3/0 AWG aluminum, assuming wire with 90°C insulation is used. Note that these wire sizes come from the Table E3705-2 in this section, not from the service wire size Table E3603. The wire sizes in this section are used because this feeder does not supply the entire building electrical service.

Note that we use watts to represent equipment power ratings instead of volt-amps as used in the IRC. Volt-amps and watts are not always the same; however, watts is a more commonly used term for power and it is close enough for calculating feeder loads.

Some equipment name plates may not provide a wattage rating. The rating may consist of an amp draw rating at a nominal 120 or 240 volts or may consist of amp draw ratings at voltages other than 120 and 240. Use the 120 or 240 volt amp draw rating and multiply amps times volts to yield power in watts.

Feeder and Service Neutral (Grounded) Wire Load Calculation

1. Use the following steps to calculate the neutral (grounded) load and wire size for both feeder and service neutral (grounded) wires. The following steps are simplified and may not provide accurate results in all cases. Refer to the IRC Commentary or a residential electrical book for more information.
    a) Begin by using the Feeder Load Formula Table E3704-1 to calculate the load on the service or feeder hot (ungrounded) wire. The Feeder Load Formula will give a different result compared to the Service Load Formula.
    b) Subtract the nameplate rating of all two-wire, 240 volt circuits. These circuits do not place a load on the neutral (grounded) wire. Examples of such circuits include electric water heaters, heat pump and air conditioning condensers, 240 volt motors, and most electric resistance heating units.
    c) Subtract 30 percent of the nameplate rating of all three-wire, 240 volt circuits. Examples of such circuits include clothes dryers, ovens, ranges, and similar cooking equipment.

Feeder and Service Neutral Load Calculation Example

Begin with the previous Feeder Load Calculation Example and apply the adjustment steps.

Feeder load from previous example	40,865 watts
Subtract heat pump air handler motor if 240 volt motor	
do not subtract if 120 volt motor	(1,000) watts
Subtract heat pump heat strips	(10,000) watts
Subtract water heater	(4,500) watts
Subtract 30% of cooking equipment (11,000 watts x 0.30)	(3,300) watts
Subtract 30% of clothes dryer (5,600 watts x 0.30)	(1,680) watts
Total neutral load =	20,385 watts
Total neutral load in amps (20,385 watts/240 volts)	84.9 amps

The minimum neutral (grounded) feeder wire for a 84.9 amps is #4 AWG copper or #3 AWG aluminum, assuming wire with 90°C insulation is used.

WIRE SIZING AND OVERCURRENT PROTECTION (E3705)

NM Cable (Romex®) Ampacity and Overcurrent Protection

1. Use the following table to determine the maximum ampacity and overcurrent protection of NM cable. NM cable is often referred to by the trade name Romex®. This table will apply to almost all branch circuit and feeder wiring in modern residential electrical systems. Example: the maximum rating for a circuit breaker protecting Number 12 copper wire is 20 amps.

TABLE E3705-1
NM Cable Maximum Ampacity Table

wire size (AWG)	copper wire (amps)	aluminum wire (amps)
14	15	-
12	20	15
10	30	25
8	40	30
6	55	40
4	70	55
3	85	65
2	95	75
1	110	85

Wire Ampacity and Overcurrent Protection

1. Use the following tables to determine the maximum ampacity and overcurrent protection of electrical wires <u>other than NM cable</u>. Use these tables for branch circuit wires and feeder wires that serve less than 100 percent of the home's electrical service. Use the Table E3603 for service wires and feeder wires that serve 100 percent of the home's electrical service.

2. You may need to reduce the maximum ampacities in the following table to account for high air temperatures and multiple wires that run close together in cables, in raceways, and in bundles of wires installed close together. These calculated ampacity reductions are described in subsequent sections. These calculated ampacity reductions are seldom necessary in residential electrical systems because the defined ampacity of NM cable (in Table E3705-1) is below where the calculated ampacity reductions would have any effect.

TABLE E3705-2
Copper Wire Maximum Ampacity Table

wire size (AWG)	wire insulation temperature 60°C (140°F)	wire insulation temperature 75°C (167°F)	wire insulation temperature 90°C (194°F)
	insulation type TW, UF	insulation type RHW, THHW, THW, THWN, USE, XHHW	insulation type RHW-2, THHN, THHW, THHW-2, XHHW, XHHW-2
	maximum wire ampacity	maximum wire ampacity	maximum wire ampacity
14	20	20	25
12	25	25	30
10	30	35	40
8	40	50	55
6	55	65	75
4	70	85	95
3	85	100	110
2	95	115	130
1	110	130	150
1/0	125	150	170
2/0	145	175	195
3/0	165	200	225
4/0	195	230	260

TABLE E3705-3
Aluminum Wire Maximum Ampacity Table

wire size (AWG)	wire insulation temperature 60°C (140°F)	wire insulation temperature 75°C (167°F)	wire insulation temperature 90°C (194°F)
	insulation type TW, UF	insulation type RHW, THHW, THW, THWN, USE, XHHW	insulation type RHW-2, THHN, THHW, THHW-2, XHHW, XHHW-2
	maximum wire ampacity	maximum wire ampacity	maximum wire ampacity
14	-	-	-
12	20	20	25
10	25	30	35
8	30	40	45
6	40	50	60
4	55	65	75
3	65	75	85
2	75	90	100
1	85	100	115
1/0	100	120	135
2/0	115	135	150
3/0	130	155	175
4/0	150	180	205

Wire and Circuit Ampacity Discussion

The maximum ampacities in the previous tables are based on the type of insulation surrounding the individual wires, <u>not on the wiring method or type of cable in which the wires are run.</u> Example: most NM type cable used in residential construction has THHN insulation on each individual wire. THHN insulation is rated at 90°C; however, when used in an NM type cable assembly, the maximum ampacity of the NM cable assembly itself is defined by Table E3705-1.

Ampacity Reduction for High Temperature

1. Reduce the maximum wire ampacity in Tables E3705-2 and E3705-3 if the ambient air temperature where the wires are installed is more than 86°F (30°C). Calculate the wire's reduced ampacity rating by: (a) determining the wire size and type (copper or aluminum), and (b) determining the type of insulation covering the wire, and (c) multiplying the ampacity in Tables E3705-2 or E3705-3 by the reduction factor in Table E3705-4.

Example:

Question:
What is the maximum ampacity of #6 AWG copper NM cable with THHN insulation installed in an attic where the air temperature reaches 125°F.

Answer:
Find the maximum ampacity of #6 AWG copper wire with THHN insulation in the 90°C column in Table E3705-2. Number 6 AWG copper wire ampacity is 75 amps. Find the reduction factor for 90°C wire insulation in the right column of Table E3705-4 and in the 125°F row. The reduction factor is 0.76. Multiply 75 amps times 0.76 equals 57 amps. The maximum ampacity of this wire at this temperature is 57 amps. Note that the defined maximum ampacity of #6 copper NM cable in Table E3705-1 is 55 amps. Use the lesser defined maximum capacity instead of the temperature adjusted capacity.

TABLE E3705-4
Wire Ampacity Adjustment for Temperature Table

air temperature	wire insulation temperature 60°C (140°F) ampacity adjustment percentage	wire insulation temperature 75°C (167°F) ampacity adjustment percentage	wire insulation temperature 90°C (194°F) ampacity adjustment percentage
31°- 35°C 87°- 95°F	0.91	0.94	0.96
36°- 40°C 96°- 104°F	0.82	0.88	0.91
41°- 45°C 105°- 113°F	0.71	0.82	0.87
46°- 50°C 114°- 122°F	0.58	0.75	0.82
51°- 55°C 123°- 131°F	0.41	0.67	0.76
56°- 60°C 132°- 140°F	wire insulation temperature exceeded	0.58	0.71
61°- 65°C 141°- 158°F	wire insulation temperature exceeded	0.33	0.58

Ampacity Reduction for Proximity

1. Reduce the maximum wire ampacity in Tables E3705-2 and E3705-3 if:
   a) the number of current-carrying wires in a cable or raceway is at least (≥) 4, or if
   b) single wires or multiple wire cables (such as NM) are stacked or bundled for more than (>) 24 inches. Remember that neutral (grounded) wires are current-carrying wires. Calcu-

late the wire's reduced ampacity rating by: (1) determining the wire size and type (copper or aluminum), and (2) determining the type of insulation covering the wire, and (3) determining the number of current carrying wires in the cable, raceway, or bundle, and (4) multiplying the ampacity in Tables E3705-2 or E3705-3 by the reduction factor in Table E3705-5.

2. Reduce the maximum wire ampacity in Tables E3705-2 and E3705-3 if more than (>) 2 NM cables each containing at least (≥) 2 current-carrying wires pass through wood framing that will be fire or draftstopped using thermal insulation or sealing foam. Calculate the wire's reduced ampacity using the steps described in the previous item 1. This will apply to NM installations where cables run through top and bottom plates; however, as seen in the example, this provision may have little practical effect except where several NM cables are run through holes above or below an electrical panel.

Example:

Question:
Assume five copper 12/3 NM cables with THHN insulation are run from a panelboard inside a wall for a distance of more than 24 inches. Assume that the temperature inside the wall is less than 30°C. Calculate the reduced ampacity of the wires because of wire proximity.

Answer:
Find the maximum ampacity of #12 AWG copper wire with THHN insulation in the 90°C column of the Table E3705-2. The wire ampacity is 30 amps.

Determine the number of current carrying wires in five 12/3 NM cables. NM cable 12/3 has 4 wires: 2 hot (ungrounded), 1 neutral (grounded) wire, and 1 grounding wire. Count only the current carrying wires when reducing ampacity for wire proximity. Remember that both the hot (ungrounded) and neutral (grounded) wires carry current in 120 volt residential circuits. Five NM 12/3 cables contain 15 current carrying wires.

Find the reduction factor for 15 current carrying wires in Table E3705-5. The reduction factor is 0.50. Multiply 30 amps times 0.50 equals 15 amps. The maximum ampacity of these wires due to wire proximity is 15 amps.

Example:

Question:
Assume two copper 12/2 NM cables and one copper 14/2 NM cable are run through a hole in a top plate that has been firestopped with spray foam sealant. Assume that the temperature inside the wall is less than 30° C. Calculate the reduce ampacity of the wires because of wire proximity in a firestopped assembly.

Answer:
Find the maximum ampacity of #12 AWG and #14 AWG copper wire with THHN insulation in the 90°C column of the Table E3705-2. Number 12 AWG copper wire ampacity is 30 amps and #14 copper wire ampacity is 25 amps.

Determine the number of current carrying wires in two 12/2 NM cables and one 14/2 NM cable. Each 12/2 and 14/2 NM cable has 3 wires: 1 hot (ungrounded), 1 neutral (grounded) wire, and 1 grounding wire. Count only the current carrying wires when reducing ampacity for wire proximity. Remember that both the hot (ungrounded) and neutral (grounded) wires carry current in 120 volt residential circuits. Each 12/2 and 14/2 NM cable has two current carrying wires for a total of six current carrying wires.

Find the reduction factor for 6 current carrying wires in Table E3705-5. The reduction factor is 0.80. Multiply 30 amps by 0.80 equals 27 amps and multiply 25 amps by 0.80 equals 20 amps. The maximum ampacity of these wires due to wire proximity in a firestopped assembly is greater than that allowed by Table E3705-1, so use the ampacity values in that table. In this case, the ampacity reduction has no practical effect.

TABLE E3705-5
Wire Ampacity Adjustment for Proximity Table

number of current-carrying wires	ampacity reduction percentage
4-6	80
7-9	70
10-20	50
21-30	45
31-40	40
≥ 41	35

Ampacity Reduction Discussion

Hot (ungrounded) and neutral (grounded) wires are surrounded by insulation that is designed to remain intact up to a certain temperature. At temperatures above the design temperature, the insulation can break down and create an electrical shock and a fire hazard. The ampacity reduction because of high ambient air temperatures and wire proximity reduces the chance that the heat generated by electricity when it travels through wires plus the heat of the surrounding air will exceed the temperature rating of the wire's insulation.

Note that the ampacity reductions because of high temperature and wire proximity are cumulative. This means that if wires are subject both to high temperatures and wire proximity, then the reduced ampacity from one would be further reduced by the other. Example: if the #6 AWG copper wire with a high temperature reduced ampacity of 57 amps were in a bundle of cables containing 6 current carrying wires, then the 57 amps would be further reduced by multiplying 57 amps times 0.80 equals 45.6 amps.

Electrical Device Limit on Circuit Ampacity

1. Use the lowest rated temperature of any wire or device in the circuit to determine the circuit's maximum ampacity. Example: if a receptacle is rated at 60°C, then the maximum ampacity

of the entire circuit, including the wires and overcurrent device, is determined using 60°C values in the tables. This applies regardless of whether wires or other devices in the circuit are rated to operate at higher temperatures.

Overcurrent Protection

1. Protect all branch circuits and feeders with a fuse or circuit breaker installed where the circuit receives its electrical supply. This will usually be at the main panelboard or at a subpanel.
2. You may use the next largest fuse or circuit breaker if the ampacity of the circuit does not match a standard size fuse or circuit breaker and if the circuit does not supply multiple receptacles. This applies to branch circuits serving known loads from fixed equipment, not to general lighting branch circuits.
3. Standard amp ratings for fuses and circuit breakers are: 15, 20, 25, 30, 35, 40, 45, 50, 60, 70, 80, 90, 100, 110, 125, 150, 175, 200, 225, 250, 300, 350, 400.

PANELBOARD PROTECTION AND RATING (E3706)

1. Use a panelboard with an ampacity rating at least (≥) as large as the rating of the wires that supply the panelboard. You may use a panelboard with a higher ampacity rating, but not one with a lower rating than the service entrance or feeder wires that supply the panelboard.
2. Protect panelboards using not more than (≤) 2 main circuit breakers or 2 sets of fuses with a combined rating not more than (≤) the panelboard's maximum current rating. These circuit breakers or fuses will often be the service equipment in main panelboards. For subpanels, these circuit breakers or fuses may be at the main panelboard or in the subpanel.
3. Identify the purpose or function of all branch circuits in the panelboard. This identification should be permanent and legible and should be able to withstand the conditions at the panelboard. Locate this identification on the dead front cover or on the cabinet door.

38

WIRING METHODS

WIRING METHODS DEFINITION

Wiring methods Wiring methods describes wires, cables, conduit, and tubing that one may use as service entrance wires, feeder wires, and branch circuit wires. The most common wiring method in modern residential construction is nonmetallic sheathed cable, abbreviated NM, and often referred to by the trade name Romex®. Other common residential wiring methods include service entrance cable (SE), and various types of electrical conduit and tubing.

KNOB-AND-TUBE WIRING

Knob-and-tube wiring is found in some older homes built before about 1940. It consists of two separate wires supported on insulators (knobs) and running through insulating cylinders (tubes) when the wires pass through framing. You may tap into and extend existing knob-and-tube wiring if you use a currently approved wiring method (such as NM cable) for the extension and if you enclose the tap in an approved junction box.

Knob-and-tube wiring is often part of an obsolete and undersized electrical system that is easy to overload. Carefully calculate the existing and new load on the existing knob-and-tube circuit and do not overload the existing circuit. Do not use existing knob-and-tube wiring if the insulation is deteriorated. Do not place insulation around or over knob-and-tube wires. Insulation can allow the wires to overheat and cause a fire.

While extending existing knob-and-tube wiring is not prohibited, it is not recommended. It is usually wise to upgrade to a modern electrical system rather than extend an obsolete and potentially dangerous existing knob-and-tube system.

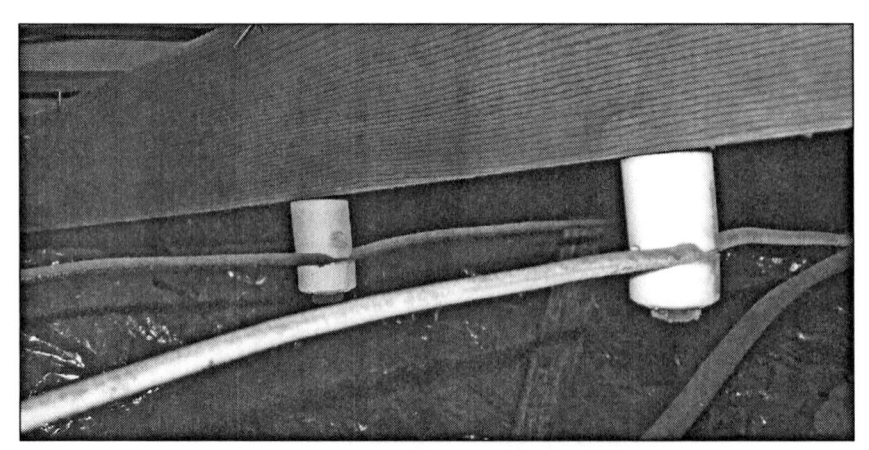

Knob-and-Tube Wiring (PE3800-0)
Figure 38-1

38 : Wiring Methods

WIRING METHODS AND ALLOWED USES (E3701)

Wiring Methods Currently Allowed

1. The following table lists the wiring methods currently allowed in residential construction. Note that certain wiring methods may not be used in certain applications.

TABLE E3801-1
Current Wiring Methods Table

wiring method	abbreviation
armored cable	AC
electrical metallic tubing	EMT
electrical nonmetallic tubing	ENT
flexible metal conduit	FMC
intermediate metal conduit	IMC
liquidtight flexible conduit	LFC
metal-clad cable	MC
nonmetallic sheathed cable	NM
rigid nonmetallic conduit	RNC
rigid metallic conduit	RMC
service entrance cable	SE
surface raceways	SR
underground feeder cable	UF
underground service cable	USE

Circuit Wires in Same Raceway

1. Run all wires for the same circuit, including grounding wires, in the same cable, raceway, or trench. This includes service, feeder, and branch circuit wires.
2. You may not run equipment grounding wires (e. g., for a receptacle or switch) to a water pipe, as is done in some older homes. This attempt at grounding violates this provision and grounding electrode provisions.

Wiring Method Allowed Uses

1. The following table lists when a wiring method may be used in a specific application. Note that some wiring methods have restrictions or limitations shown by the following superscripts: (1) use less than (<) 6 feet of LFC if the conduit walls are not reinforced, (2) insulate the neutral (grounded) wire unless the cable is used to supply other buildings on the same property, (3) insulate the neutral (grounded) wire, (4) use wires approved for wet locations and seal raceways to prevent water entry, (5) use materials listed as sunlight resistant, (6) protect metal raceways from corrosion, (7) use Schedule 80 RNC, (8) use materials listed as sunlight resistant if exposed to direct sunlight, (9) use less than (<) 6 feet of conduit.

TABLE E3801-2
Current Wiring Methods Allowed Uses Table

allowed application	AC	EMT	ENT	FMC	IMC RMC RNC	LFC1	MC	NM	SR	SE	UF	USE
service entrance	NO	OK	OK[8]	OK[9]	OK	OK[9]	OK	NO	NO	OK	NO	OK
feeder	OK	OK	OK	OK	OK	OK	OK	OK	NO	OK[2]	OK	OK[2]
branch circuits	OK	OK	OK	OK	OK	OK	OK	OK	OK	OK[3]	OK	NO
indoors (e.g., in stud walls)	OK	OK	OK	OK	OK	OK	OK	OK	OK	OK	OK	NO
wet locations and exposed to sunlight	NO	OK	OK[8]	OK[4]	OK	OK	OK	NO	NO	OK	OK[5]	OK[5]
damp locations	NO	OK	OK	OK[4]	OK	OK	OK	NO	NO	OK	OK	OK
embedded in concrete in dry location	NO	OK	OK	NO	OK	NO	NO	NO	NO	NO	NO	NO
embedded in concrete below grade	NO	OK[6]	OK	NO	OK[6]	NO	NO	NO	NO	NO	NO	NO
embedded in plaster in dry location	OK	OK	OK	OK	OK	OK	OK	NO	NO	OK	OK	NO
embedded in masonry	NO	OK	OK	NO	OK[6]	OK	OK	NO	NO	NO	NO	NO
in masonry voids & cells in damp location or below grade	NO	OK[6]	OK	OK[4]	OK[6]	OK	OK	NO	NO	OK	OK	NO
fished in masonry voids	OK	NO	NO	OK	NO	OK	OK	OK	NO	OK	OK	NO
in masonry voids & cells in dry location	OK	OK	OK	OK	OK	OK	OK	OK	NO	OK	OK	NO
exposed not subject to damage	OK	OK	OK	OK	OK	OK	OK	OK	OK	OK	OK	OK
exposed subject to damage	NO	NO	NO	NO	OK[7]	NO	NO	NO	NO	NO	NO	NO
direct burial	NO	OK[6]	NO	NO	OK[6]	OK	OK[6]	NO	NO	NO	OK	OK

ABOVE GROUND WIRING INSTALLATION (E3802)

NM and UF Cable Installation

1. Use NM and UF cable where the cable is not subject to physical damage. Physical damage can occur unless the cable is covered by drywall or other material or unless the cable is run in conduit or tubing. Physical damage includes damage by sunlight.

2. Protect NM and UF cable using RMC, IMC, EMT, or Schedule 80 RNC when the cable is subject to physical damage. Extend the protection at least (≥) 6 inches above the floor when the cable runs through the floor. This provision applies to exposed wall framing, such as

unfinished basements and garages, and to cable that runs through framed and concrete slab floors. This provision does not apply to cable run in attics and in basement ceiling joists.

3. Protect NM and UF cable using nail guards or other approved physical protection when the cable is installed:
   a) through holes, notches, or grooves that are closer than (<) 1 ¼ inches to the edge of a stud or joist, and
   b) in notches and grooves in places such as drywall, plaster and under carpet, unless the groove or notch is deeper than (≥) 1 ¼ inches, and
   c) through holes in metal framing (use grommets or bushings), and
   d) parallel to the edge of a stud, joist, or furring strip when the cable is closer than (<) 1 ¼ inches to the edge of the framing member.

4. Support NM and UF cable every 4 ½ feet. Use wire staples or other approved fasteners to secure vertical runs of NM and UF cable. Staple the cable only on the flat edge. NM and UF cable run across the tops of joists is usually considered supported.

5. Secure NM and UF cable not more than (≤) 8 inches from boxes and terminations that do not have cable clamps. This includes most plastic boxes. Secure NM and UF cable not more than (≤) 12 inches from boxes and terminations that have cable clamps. This includes most metal boxes. Measure the support distance from where the cable sheathing ends in the box, not from the box itself.

6. Use NM cable only in dry locations that are indoors and not within concrete or masonry that is exposed to the ground. Do not use NM cable in conduit that is buried in the ground. Buried conduit is considered a wet location. You may use UF cable in wet locations including outdoors and underground if it is not subject to damage.

Wires Protected by Nail Guards (PE3802-2)
Figure 38-2

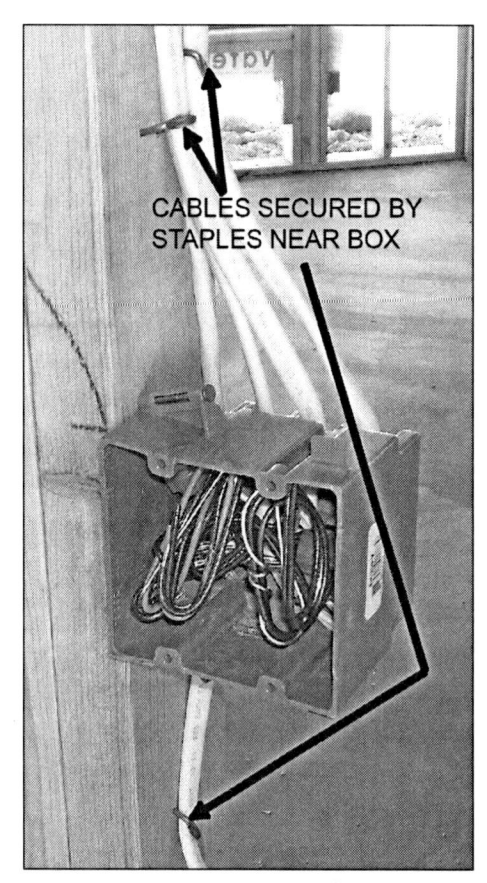

Wires Secured at Box (PE3802-1)
Figure 38-3

Conduit and Tubing Installation

1. Apply the following installation requirements to EMT, IMC, RMC, ENT, FMC, LFC, and RNC:

   a) limit the number of 90 degree bends between junction boxes to not more than (≤) four, and

   b) install bushings where conduit or tubing enters a box, fitting, or enclosure, unless the device provides equivalent protection against damage to any wires that may be pulled into the device, and

   c) remove rough edges from the ends of all conduit and tubing that may damage wires, and

   d) support EMT, IMC, and RMC not more than (≤) every 10 feet and within (≤) 3 feet of junction boxes or terminations, and

   e) support ENT not more than (≤) every 3 feet, unless the ENT is in an accessible ceiling, such as a drop ceiling, and if the distance between light fixtures is not more than (≤) 6 feet, and

   f) support FMC and LFC not more than (≤) every 4 ½ feet and within 12 inches of junction boxes and terminations, unless the FMC and LFC is in an accessible ceiling, such as a drop ceiling, and if the distance between light fixtures is not more than (≤) 6 feet.

2. You may allow not more than (≤) 36 inches between the last support and a light fixture or other equipment that may need to be moved for service or replacement.

Wiring Support Requirements

1. The following table lists the on center support requirements for wiring methods. Note that some wiring methods have special requirements shown by the following superscripts: (1) support is not required in accessible ceilings, such as drop ceilings, if the distance between light fixtures is not more than (≤) 6 feet, (2) you may allow not more than (≤) 24 inches between the last support and a light fixture or other equipment that may need to be moved for service or replacement, (3) you may allow not more than (≤) 36 inches between the last support and a light fixture or other equipment that may need to be moved for service or replacement, (4) support NM and UF cable not more than (≤) 8 inches from boxes and terminations that do not have cable clamps. This includes most plastic boxes. Measure the support distance from where the cable sheathing ends in the box, not from the box itself, (5) support NM and UF cable not more than (≤) 12 inches from boxes and terminations that have cable clamps. This includes most metal boxes. (6) support RNC not more than (≤) 5 feet for conduit sizes more than (>) one inch.

TABLE E3802
Wiring Method Support Table

	AC	MC	EMT IMC RMC	ENT	FMC LFC	NM UF	RNC	SE USE (service)	SE USE (branch circuit or indoor feeder)
maximum support spacing (feet)	4.5[1]	6[1]	10	3[1]	4.5[1]	4.5	3[6]	2.5	4.5
maximum support distance to box or termination (inches)	12[1,2]	12[1,2]	36	36	12[1,3]	8[4] 12[5]	36	12	12

Wiring Protection in Attics

1. Protect electrical cables in accessible attics by using substantial guard strips that are at least as tall as the cables electrical cables when:

   a) access to the attic is by permanent stairs or ladders (such as a pull-down attic ladder) and the cables are within (≤) 7 feet vertically from the top of attic floor joists or truss bottom chords or the cables run across the face (shortest dimension) of rafters, studs, or truss webs or chords, or

   b) access to the attic is by scuttle hole or similar opening and the cables described in (a) are within (≤) 6 feet horizontally from the nearest point of the attic access opening.

2. You need not protect electrical cables in accessible attics when the cables are installed:

a) running parallel to the edge of the framing and at least (≥) 1 ¼ inches from the edge of the framing, or
b) in holes that are at least (≥) 1 ¼ inches from the edge of the framing.

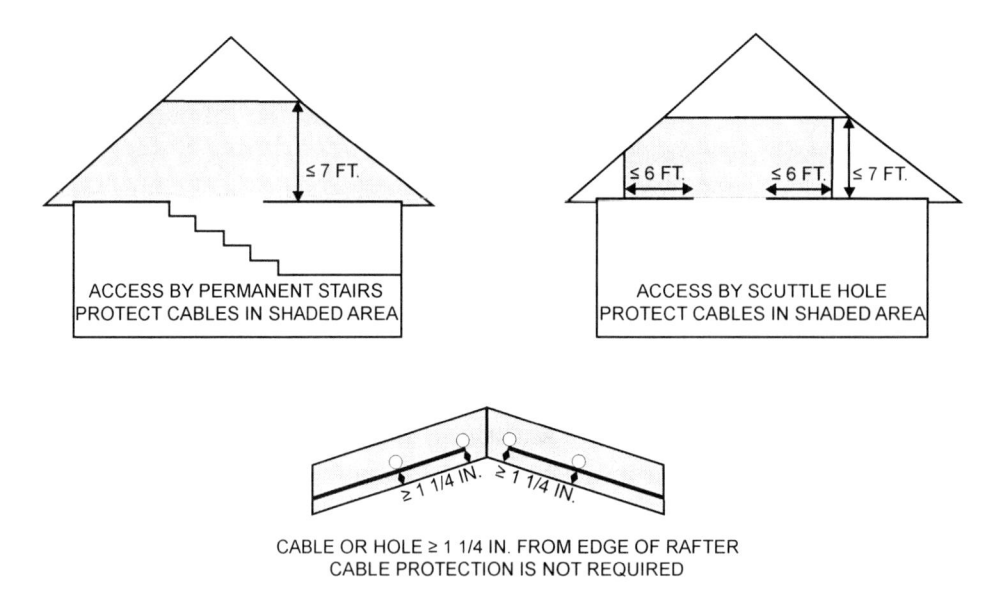

Wiring Protection in Attics (E3802-1)
Figure 38-4

Wiring in Unfinished Basement Ceiling Joists

1. Install small gage cables: (a) parallel with basement ceiling joists and at least (≥) 1 ¼ inches from the bottom of basement ceiling joists, or (b) through holes drilled through the ceiling joists. Do not install these cables directly along the bottom of basement ceiling joists, unless you install the cables on running boards. A running board is wood, such as a 1x6, attached to the bottom of the basement ceiling joists. This applies to cables containing wires #10 AWG and smaller.
2. You may install cables containing at least (≥) two #6 AWG or larger wires or at least three #8 AWG or larger wires directly along the bottom of basement ceiling joists without additional protection.

Bends in Cables and Conduit

1. Do not bend cables, conduit, tubing, or other raceways if the bend damages the wiring method or if the bend reduces the diameter of the conduit, tubing, or other raceway.
2. Bend NM, UF, and SE cable so that the radius of the curve on the inner edge of the cable is not smaller than (<) 5 times the diameter of the cable. Example: if the cable is ½ inch wide, any bend in the cable should have a radius of not smaller than (<) 2 ½ inches.

```
                    ↕ NM CABLE
                      1/2 IN. WIDE
```

BEND RADIUS ≥ 2 1/2 IN.

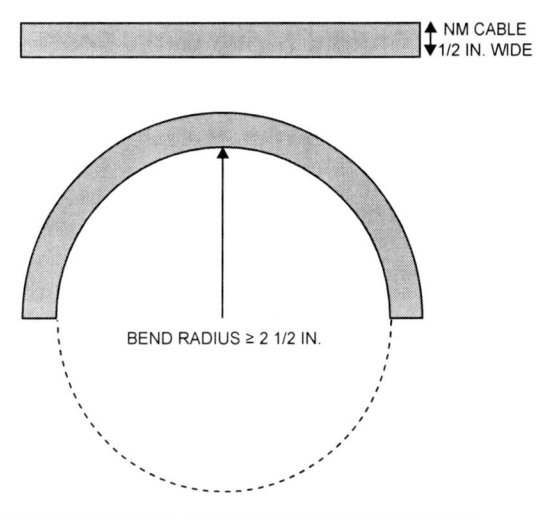

BEND RADIUS NOT SMALLER THAN 5 TIMES CABLE WIDTH

Bends in Electrical Cable (E3802-2)
Figure 38-5

Wiring Exposed to Direct Sunlight

1. Use cables and wires that are listed as sunlight resistant when they may be exposed to direct sunlight. You may cover wires and cables not listed as sunlight resistant with insulating tape or a sleeve that is listed as sunlight resistant.

Raceways and Cables Exposed to Different Temperatures

1. Seal conduit, tubing, cables, and sleeves against air movement if: (a) the assembly runs between a warm and moist area and a cool area, and if (b) condensation is known to be a problem. Use an approved material, such as electrical putty, to seal the assembly against air movement. Examples of when this situation can occur include: (a) during the winter in cold climates when an assembly runs between warm conditioned space and cold unconditioned space such as an attic or crawl space, and (b) during the summer in warm climates when an assembly runs between warm unconditioned space and cool conditioned space. This situation is more likely to occur in metallic conduit and tubing.

BELOW GROUND WIRING INSTALLATION (E3803)

Below Ground Wiring Burial Depth

1. The following table lists how much cover is required for wiring and conduit buried underground. Depths are in inches.

TABLE E3803
Below Ground Wiring Burial Depth

wiring method or circuit location	120 volt, 15 or 20 amp residential branch circuits with GFCI (inches)	30 volt or less irrigation or landscape lighting circuits (inches)	buried cables or individual wires (inches)	RMC or IMC (inches)	nonmetallic raceways listed for burial (inches)
all locations not specified below	12	6	24	6	18
covered by ≥ 2 inches of concrete or equivalent	6	6	18	6	12
covered by ≥ 4 inches of concrete, no vehicle traffic, slab extends ≥ 6 inches beyond wiring method	6 (buried) 4 (in raceway)	6 (buried) 4 (in raceway)	18	4	4
under building	0 (in raceway only)	0 (in raceway only)	0 (in raceway only)	0	0
under public & commercial streets, alleys, driveways, parking lots	24	24	24	24	24
under residential driveways and parking areas	12	18	18	18	18
in solid rock & covered by ≥ 2 inches of concrete extending to rock	2 (in raceway only)	2 (in raceway only)	2 (in raceway only)	2	2

Protection where Wires Emerge from Ground

1. Protect wires where they emerge from the ground using enclosures or raceways beginning at the wire's minimum burial depth or at least (≥) 18 inches below where the wires emerge from the ground, whichever is less. Extend the protection to at least (≥) 8 feet above finished grade.
2. Protect wires at the point where they enter the building.

Below Ground Splices and Taps

1. You may splice or tap below ground wires using approved methods and materials. Boxes are not required when using methods and materials approved for splicing and tapping buried wires.

Raceway Seals

1. Seal conduit and tubing at both ends where moisture could enter and damage wires.

39

RECEPTACLE, LIGHT, AND WIRING INSTALLATION

RECEPTACLE INSTALLATION (E3901)

Interior Receptacle General Installation Requirements

1. Install receptacles in living rooms, family rooms, bedrooms, dens, sunrooms, recreation rooms, dining rooms, breakfast rooms, libraries, and similar living areas. Kitchens, bathrooms, hallways, garages, laundry rooms, and exterior receptacles have their own installation requirements.

Interior Receptacle Height

1. Install receptacles not more than (≤) 66 inches above the finished floor. You may install receptacles at any height, but you may count only receptacles not more than (≤) 66 inches above the finished floor among the required receptacles.

Interior Receptacle Spacing

1. Install the required interior receptacles so that any point along a wall is not more than (≤) 6 feet from a receptacle. Do not include operable doors, fireplaces, closet interiors, and similar openings when measuring a wall. A wall begins at the edge of an opening and continues around any corners to the next opening. Walls include fixed (not sliding) panels in doors that are at least (≥) 2 feet wide. Walls include partial height walls that serve functions such as room dividers and walls that form breakfast bars and similar bar-type counters. Walls include guards and railings at balconies, raised floors, and other areas where furniture could be placed.

2. Locate floor receptacles intended to serve as required interior receptacles not more than (≤) 18 inches from the wall. You may install interior floor receptacles at any safe place, but you may count only receptacles not more than (≤) 18 inches from the wall among the required receptacles.

Interior Receptacle Spacing Discussion

Receptacle spacing is prescriptive, that is, spacing is based on a formula that requires receptacles in places where they may never be used. A receptacle could end up behind a door or along a wall in a room where furniture could not be placed. If the wall space fits the required receptacle spacing formula, place one there regardless of whether or not "common sense" says one is needed.

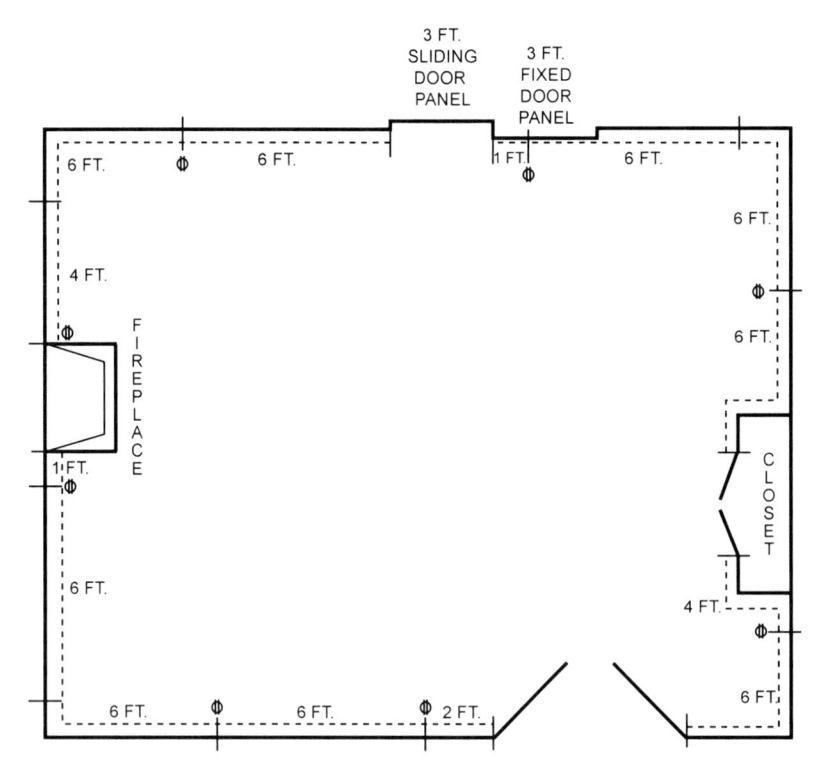

Interior Receptacle Spacing (E3901-1)
Figure 39-1

Kitchen Receptacles General Installation Requirements

1. Use the required two 20 amp small appliance receptacle circuits <u>only</u> for wall, countertop, and floor <u>receptacles</u> in the kitchen, dining room, and breakfast room. You may supply a refrigerator from one of the two small appliance receptacle circuits. You may install additional 20 amp receptacle circuits, including a dedicated 15 amp or 20 amp circuit for the refrigerator.
2. Do not use the required small appliance receptacle circuits to serve other outlets, such as lighting outlets.
3. Serve only one kitchen with the two 20 amp small appliance receptacle circuits.

Kitchen Countertop Receptacle Spacing

1. Install a GFCI protected receptacle at every kitchen countertop that is at least (≥) 12 inches wide.
2. Install kitchen countertop receptacles so that all points along the countertop wall are not more than (≤) 2 feet from a receptacle. A wall begins at the edge of an opening or appliance and continues around any corners and ends at the next opening or appliance. Include windows when measuring the wall unless the window is above a sink or cooking appliance.
3. Install receptacles behind a sink or cooking appliance located along a straight wall if the countertop behind the sink or cooking appliance is at least (≥) 12 inches wide. Install receptacles behind a sink or cooking appliance located along a wall corner if the countertop behind the sink or cooking appliance is at least (≥) 18 inches wide.

4. Install receptacles not more than (≤) 20 inches above the countertop. You may install receptacles at any height, but you may include only receptacles not more than (≤) 20 inches above the countertop among the required kitchen countertop receptacles.

5. Do not include among the required kitchen countertop receptacles:
   a) receptacles located in appliance garages, and
   b) receptacles dedicated for a fixed-in-place appliance, and
   c) receptacles not readily accessible for use by small appliances.

6. Do not install receptacles face up on work surfaces.

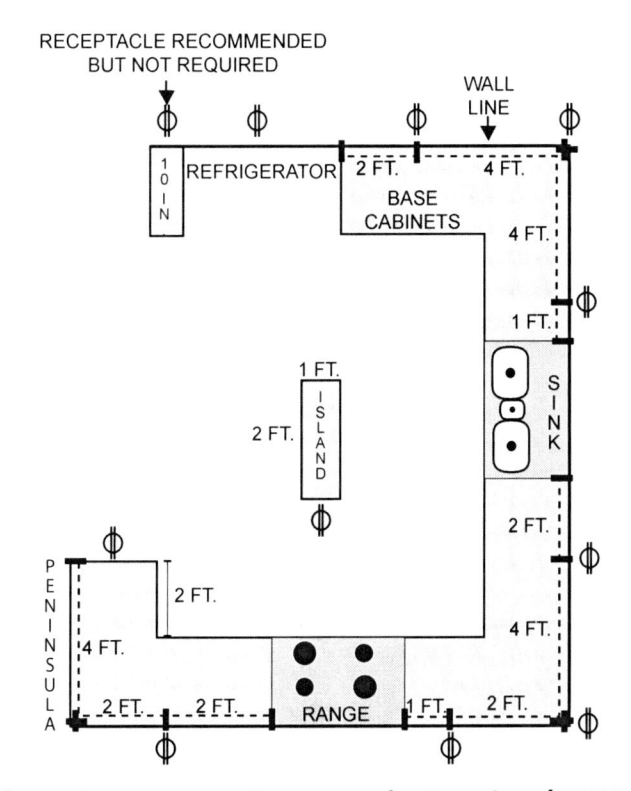

Kitchen Countertop Receptacle Spacing (E3901-2)
Figure 39-2

Kitchen Island and Peninsula Receptacles Without a Sink or Cooking Appliance

1. Install at least (≥) one GFCI protected receptacle at every kitchen island and peninsula that measures at least (≥) 24 inches by at least (≥) 12 inches. Measure a peninsula from the interior connecting edge of the countertop.

2. Install kitchen countertop receptacles along any wall space above an island or peninsula countertop. Such wall space occurs when an island or peninsula is installed at a partial height wall.

3. You may install receptacles not more than (≤) 12 inches below an island or peninsula countertop if the countertop is flat and there is no wall space above the countertop. Do not install the required kitchen island or peninsula receptacle below a breakfast bar or other countertop that extends more than (>) 6 inches beyond the supporting base.

4. Do not install receptacles face up on work surfaces.

Kitchen Island Receptacles with a Sink or Cooking Appliance

1. Install at least (≥) one GFCI protected receptacle not more than (≤) 24 inches from each side of a sink or cooking appliance installed in a kitchen island.
2. Install receptacles behind a sink or cooking appliance if the countertop behind the sink or cooking appliance is at least (≥) 12 inches wide or at least (≥) 18 inches wide if the sink or cooking appliance is installed in a corner.
3. Install kitchen countertop receptacles along any wall space above an island countertop. Such wall space occurs when an island is installed at a partial height wall.
4. You many install receptacles not more than (≤) 12 inches below an island countertop if the countertop is flat and there is no wall space above the countertop. Do not install the required kitchen island receptacles below a breakfast bar or other countertop that extends more than (>) 6 inches beyond the supporting base.
5. Do not install receptacles face up on work surfaces.

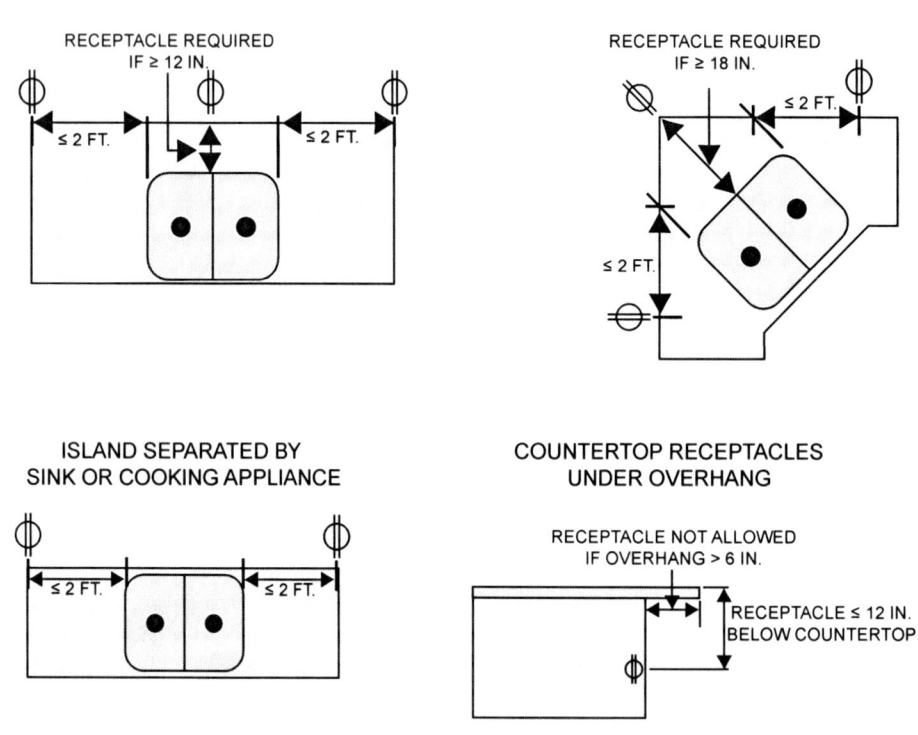

Island and Peninsula Receptacles (E3901-3)
Figure 39-3

Appliance Receptacles

1. Install receptacles for appliances (such as a refrigerator, a clothes washer, or clothes dryer) not more than (≤) 6 feet from the intended appliance location.

Bathroom Sink Receptacles

1. Install at least (≥) one GFCI protected receptacle not more than (≤) 36 inches from the outside edge of each sink basin in a bathroom. You may install the receptacle(s):
   a) between 2 sink basins if the receptacle is not more than (≤) 36 inches from each sink basin; or
   b) along a wall adjacent to the sink. An adjacent wall usually means the wall on which the mirror is usually placed or on the wall perpendicular to the "mirror wall"; or
   c) on the side or face of the basin cabinet if the receptacle is not more than (≤) 12 inches below the countertop.

   Receptacles in light fixtures do not count as the required sink receptacle.

2. Do not install receptacles face up on work surfaces.

Exterior Receptacles

1. Install at least (≥) one GFCI protected, 15 or 20 amp, 120 volt, receptacle on the front and back exterior wall of every home. Locate the receptacle so that it is accessible from grade level and is not more than (≤) 78 inches above finished grade level.
2. Install at least (≥) one GFCI protected, 15 or 20 amp, 120 volt, receptacle within the perimeter of any balcony, deck, or porch that: (a) is accessible from inside the home, and (b) a useable area of at least (≥) 20 square feet.

Laundry Receptacles

1. Install at least (≥) one 20 amp, 120 volt, receptacle in the laundry area. This required receptacle usually serves the clothes washing machine. The required laundry receptacle is in addition to any required garage or basement receptacle if the laundry is in the garage or basement.
2. Provide GFCI protection for the laundry receptacle in a garage or basement. You need not provide GFCI protection for this receptacle if you install a dedicated single receptacle serving one appliance or a dedicated duplex receptacle serving two appliances.
3. Provide GFCI protection for laundry receptacles within (≤) 6 feet of a sink. This includes the washing machine receptacle. There is no dedicated receptacle exception in this case.

Basement Receptacles

1. Install at least (≥) one GFCI protected, 15 or 20 amp, 120 volt, receptacle in an unfinished basement.
2. Install at least (≥) 1 GFCI protected receptacle in the unfinished part of a basement that is partially finished. If unfinished parts of a basement are separated by finished parts, install at least (≥) 1 receptacle in each unfinished part.

Garage Receptacles

1. Install at least (≥) one GFCI protected, 15 or 20 amp, 120 volt, receptacle in an attached garage. Install at least (≥) 1 GFCI protected receptacle in a detached garage if the garage is

supplied with electricity. You are not required to supply electricity to detached garages, but if you do you must install a receptacle.

Hallway Receptacles

1. Install at least (≥) one 15 or 20 amp, 120 volt, receptacle in any hallway that is at least (≥) 10 feet long. A hallway begins at an opening or wall and continues around any corners without passing through a doorway. Measure a hallway along the center line and around any corners.

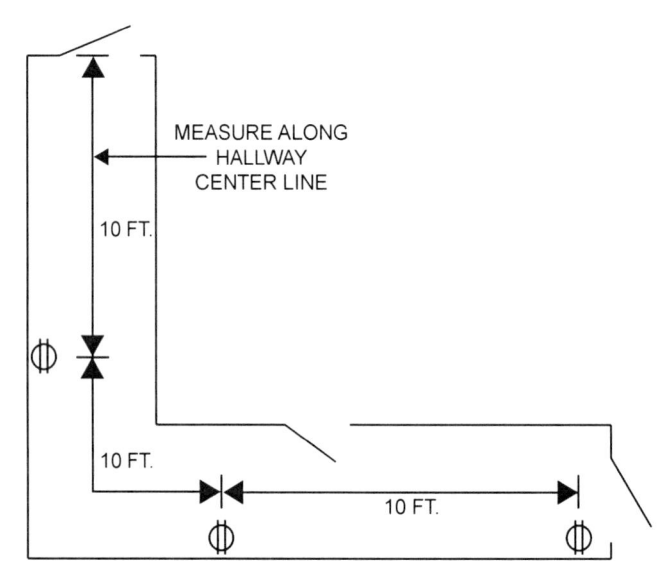

Hallway Receptacle Spacing (E3901-4)
Figure 39-4

HVAC Service Receptacles

1. Install at least (≥) one accessible 15 or 20 amp, 120 volt, service receptacle located not more than (≤) 25 feet from heating and air conditioning equipment. This includes interior and exterior equipment. Locate the receptacle on the same level as the equipment. Example: the service receptacle for attic equipment must be in the attic, not on the story under the attic.
2. Do not supply the receptacle from the load side of the equipment service disconnect. This means that if using the equipment service disconnect shuts off power to receptacle, the receptacle does not count as the service receptacle.
3. You need not install a service receptacle for evaporative coolers.

GROUND-FAULT AND ARC-FAULT PROTECTION REQUIRED LOCATIONS (E3902)

Bathroom Receptacles

1. Install ground-fault circuit interrupt (GFCI) protection on all 120 volt receptacles located in bathrooms. This applies to all receptacles regardless of where they are located in the bathroom and includes receptacles located at countertops, inside cabinets, and along bathroom walls.

Garage and Accessory Building Receptacles

1. Install ground-fault circuit interrupt (GFCI) protection on all 120 volt receptacles located in garages and grade-level areas of unfinished accessory buildings. You do not need to provide GFCI protection for receptacles that are not readily accessible such as receptacles in the garage ceiling. You do not need to provide GFCI protection for dedicated receptacles that serve an appliance that is not easily moved. Examples of dedicated receptacles include receptacles for water softeners, refrigerators, alarm systems, and central vacuums. The receptacle must be a single receptacle when serving a single appliance or a duplex receptacle if serving two appliances. A duplex receptacle serving one appliance is a violation.

Exterior Receptacles

1. Install ground-fault circuit interrupt (GFCI) protection on all 120 volt receptacles located outdoors. This does not apply to receptacles that are dedicated for deicing equipment and are located under the eaves. This applies to Christmas lighting receptacles located under the eaves.

Crawl Space Receptacles

1. Install ground-fault circuit interrupt (GFCI) protection on all 120 volt receptacles located in crawl spaces. Receptacles in crawl spaces are not required unless equipment requiring service is located there.

Basement Receptacles

1. Install ground-fault circuit interrupt (GFCI) protection on all 120 volt receptacles located in unfinished basements. An unfinished basement is not intended as habitable space and is limited to storage and work space. The exceptions for garage receptacles apply to unfinished basement receptacles.

Kitchen Countertop Receptacles

1. Install ground-fault circuit interrupt (GFCI) protection on all 120 volt receptacles that serve kitchen countertops. This does not include receptacles under the kitchen sink and receptacles located on kitchen walls that do not serve the countertop.

Laundry, Utility, and Bar Sink Receptacles

1. Install ground-fault circuit interrupt (GFCI) protection on all 120 volt receptacles that are located within ($\leq$) 6 feet of the outside edge of a laundry, utility, or bar sink. This includes wall, floor, and countertop receptacles. This includes any appliance receptacles within the 6 feet distance, such as the washing machine receptacle.

Boathouse Receptacles

1. Install ground-fault circuit interrupt (GFCI) protection on all 120 volt receptacles located in boathouses.

2. Install ground-fault circuit interrupt (GFCI) protection on all 120 volt and 240 volt receptacles that serve boat hoists.

Spas, Tubs, and Other Circuits Requiring Ground-Fault Protection

1. Install ground-fault circuit interrupt (GFCI) protection on all circuits serving spa tubs, whirlpool tubs, hot tubs, and similar equipment. Refer to Chapter 42 for more information about receptacles serving these components.
2. Install ground-fault circuit interrupt (GFCI) protection on all circuits serving electrically heated floors in bathrooms.

Arc-Fault Circuit Interrupters

1. Install a combination type arc-fault circuit interrupter (AFCI) on each 120 volt branch circuit serving sleeping, family, dining, living, sun, and recreation rooms, and parlors, libraries, dens, hallways, closets, and similar rooms and areas. This means that virtually all 120 volt branch circuits in a home are required to have AFCI protection.
2. Note that this requirement is controversial and may not be adopted in all areas. Verify adoption of this requirement with the local building official.
3. You may install the AFCI not more than (≤) 6 feet from the origination of the branch circuit if you run the wires in metal conduit or a metallic sheath. Measure the 6 feet along the branch circuit wires.

Arc-Fault Circuit Interrupters Discussion

An AFCI protects against fires caused by electrical arcing between different wires (parallel faults) and electrical arcing along one wire (series faults). Parallel faults are often caused by damaged wire insulation. Series faults are often caused by a break in the wire itself. Older branch/feeder AFCI are effective in detecting parallel faults, but less effective in detecting series faults. Newer combination AFCI are effective in detecting both types of faults not only in the branch circuit wires, but also in wires plugged into the receptacles.

LIGHT FIXTURE REQUIRED LOCATIONS (E3803)

Lights Required in Habitable Rooms

1. Install at least (≥) 1 switch-controlled light outlet in every habitable room and bathroom. This outlet may be a switched (half-hot) receptacle in habitable rooms other than kitchens and bathrooms. In kitchens and bathrooms, the outlet must be a switched wall or ceiling lighting outlet. You may use lights controlled by occupancy sensors if the sensors have a manual override that allows switch control of the light.

Lights Required in Other Interior Spaces

1. Install at least (≥) 1 switch-controlled light outlet in every hallway, stairway, attached garage, and detached garage if the detached garage is provided with electricity. Note that a light outlet may be a switched receptacle instead of a light fixture. A light fixture is usually a better, but not required, choice.

2. Install at least (≥) 1 switch at each floor to control stairway lights if the stairs have at least (≥) 6 risers. This is the only requirement for multiple switches that control lights. Multiple switches for hallways and other rooms are often installed for occupant convenience and safety, but they are not required

Lights Required at Exterior Doors

1. Install at least (≥) 1 switch-controlled light outlet on the exterior side of every exterior door with grade level access. Exterior lights are not required at garage vehicle doors.

Lights Required in Attics, Crawl Spaces, and Basements

1. Install at least (≥) 1 light outlet in attics, crawl spaces, utility rooms, and basements if the area is used for storage or if it contains equipment that requires service. Locate the light outlet near any equipment that requires service.
2. Locate a switch for the light at the usual point of entry into the area. You may use a pull-chain controlled light if the light is located at the usual point of entry into the area. This means that if the light is not at the entrance to the area, the light must be switched at the entrance.

CONDUIT, TUBING, AND CABLE INSTALLATION (E3904)

Conduit and Tubing Installation

1. Install metallic conduit and tubing so that the conduit, tubing, junction boxes, fittings, and cabinets are both mechanically and electrically continuous over their entire length. This includes connections at junction boxes, fittings, and cabinets. Secure and continuous connections provide a path to clear ground faults that could occur in metallic conduit and tubing.
2. Install metal and nonmetallic conduit and tubing so that it is physically continuous over the entire length. Do not leave gaps in conduit or tubing that could expose wires to damage or contact.
3. Do not use conduit or tubing to support anything other than its own weight and the wires inside. You may support wires used to control the equipment served by the conduit or tubing. An example is thermostat cable.
4. Secure conduit, tubing, boxes, fittings, and cabinets firmly in place.
5. Make conduit bodies, junction boxes, and similar enclosures accessible. Accessible means not having to remove or damage permanent finish materials to access the enclosure.

Conduit and Tubing Wire Capacity

Most readers will not be pulling individual wires through conduit and tubing. For those who do, refer to the IRC Tables for limits on how many individual wires may be installed in various sizes and types of conduit and tubing. Note that these limits refer to individual insulated wires, not cable assemblies such as NM cable. Example: a 3 wire NM cable is not the same size and flexibility as the 3 individual wires contained in the NM cable. Thus, if the limit for a particular size of conduit or tubing is 3 wires, 3 wire NM cable would be too large for that conduit or tubing.

Wires in Stud Cavities used as HVAC Ducts

1. Install nonmetallic wiring methods perpendicular to the studs when the stud cavity is used as an HVAC duct. Do not run nonmetallic wiring methods parallel to the studs when the stud cavity is used as an HVAC duct. Avoid installing any nonmetallic wiring method through HVAC stud cavities, if possible.

JUNCTION BOXES AND DEVICE BOXES (E3905 AND E3906)

Wire Splices and Terminations

1. Enclose all wire splices and terminations, except splices approved for burial, in an approved enclosure. This enclosure is often a junction box or a conduit body. This enclosure may also be an approved enclosure inside of an appliance or fixture. Examples of enclosures inside appliances include electrical connection enclosures in furnaces, dishwashers, and in some light fixtures such as some fluorescent lights.
2. You may bury splices and taps in underground wires if the splices or taps are approved for burial. Buried splices and taps are usually not required to be accessible.
3. Make enclosures containing wire splices and terminations accessible. Accessible means not having to remove or damage permanent finish materials to access the enclosure.
4. Make or install enclosures containing wire splices and terminations moisture-proof when installed in damp or wet locations. Use only enclosures listed for wet locations in such locations.

Nonmetallic Box Installation

1. Use nonmetallic boxes only with NM type cable or with nonmetallic conduit or tubing. You may use nonmetallic boxes with metallic conduit or tubing if you maintain the electrical continuity of the metallic conduit or tubing by installing a bonding jumper through the box. In many situations it is easier to use a metallic box with metallic conduit or tubing.
2. Extend NM cable sheathing at least (≥) ¼ inch into a nonmetallic box knockout opening.
3. Secure NM cable, conduit, and tubing to each box. You may secure NM cable with cable clamps inside the box or with compression tabs provided where the cable enters the box. You do not need to secure NM cable to a standard single-gang box (2 ¼ by 4 inches) mounted in a wall or ceiling if you fasten the cable not more than (≤) 8 inches from the box and if the sheathing enters the box at least (≥) ¼ inch. Measure the 8 inches along the length of the sheathing, not from the outside of the box.

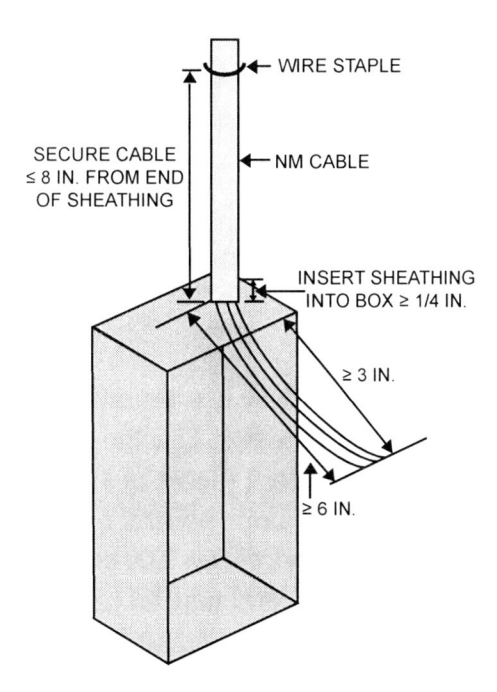

Rough-in Installation of NM Cable in Nonmetallic Box (E3905-0)
Figure 39-5

Light Fixture Box Installation

1. Use boxes designed for mounting light fixtures if a light fixture is to be mounted to the box. These boxes are usual 4 inch round or octagonal. You may use other boxes if the light fixture weighs not more than (≤) 6 pounds and is secured to the box using at least (≥) two #6 or larger screws.

2. Support light fixtures weighing more than (>) 50 pounds independently from the light fixture box. You may use the light fixture box to support light fixtures weighing at least (≤) 50 pounds. Note that ceiling fans are not light fixtures. Ceiling fans are addressed in Chapter 41.

Floor Box Type

1. Use only those boxes specifically listed to be mounted in floors as floor boxes.

Ceiling Fan Boxes

1. Use only those boxes specifically listed to support ceiling fans if the box provides the sole support for the fan. You may use any box if the box does not provide support for the fan; however, boxes usually provide the sole support for ceiling fans. See Chapter 41 for additional rules about ceiling fan installation.

Box Contents Limitations

1. Limit the number of wires, devices (such as switches and receptacles), and fittings in a box. This limitation is primarily based on the heat generated by the wires and devices in the box. The actual size of the box relative to its contents is a secondary consideration.

2. Use the cubic inch volume printed on the box or provided in the box manufacturer's instructions to determine a box's volume. Do not attempt to measure the box volume. Do not estimate box volume from the volume of similar size boxes. You will probably not get the same volume as provided by the manufacturer.
3. Use the wire volume table to determine the volume units required by wires, devices, and fittings in a box.
4. Calculate the volume units required by wires, devices, and fittings based on the following definitions:

Volume units for current-carrying wires Allow one volume unit for each individual hot (ungrounded) and neutral (grounded) wire in the box. Use the wire volume table to determine the volume units of common wire sizes. Example: 2 pieces of #14/2 NM are in a box. Each piece of this cable contains one hot (ungrounded) and one neutral (grounded) wire and one grounding wire. From the wire volume table, each #14 wire uses 2.00 cubic inches in the box. The total volume units required by the hot (ungrounded) and neutral (grounded) wires is 8 cubic inches.

Volume units for devices Allow two volume units for each device (switch or receptacle) in the box. Base the volume units on the largest hot (ungrounded) or neutral (grounded) wire in the box. Example: NM cable size #14 and #12 are in a box. From the wire volume table, #14 wire uses 2.00 cubic inches and #12 wire uses 2.25 cubic inches. Allow 4.5 cubic inches volume units (2 X 2.25 cubic inches) for each switch or receptacle in the box based on the volume of the larger #12 NM cable.

Volume units for grounding wires Allow one volume unit for all grounding wires in the box. Base the volume unit on the largest hot (ungrounded) or neutral (grounded) wire in the box.

Volume units for clamps Allow one volume unit for all internal cable clamps in the box, if any. Base the volume unit on the largest hot (ungrounded) or neutral (grounded) wire in the box.

Volume units for fittings Allow one volume for unit all fittings in the box, if any. Base the volume unit on the largest hot (ungrounded) or neutral (grounded) wire in the box.

TABLE E3905
Wire Volume Unit Table

wire size (AWG)	wire volume (cubic inches)
18	1.50
16	1.75
14	2.00
12	2.25
10	2.50
8	3.00
6	5.00

Box Contents Limitations Example

Example:

Question:
A two gang box has a marked volume of 30 cubic inches. The following will be placed in the box: 1 piece of #12/2 NM cable, 1 piece of #14/3 NM cable, 1 switch, 1 receptacle, no clamps or fittings. What is the total volume of all box contents and is the box large enough?

Answer:
1 #12 hot (ungrounded) plus 1 #12 neutral (grounded) wires times 2.25 cubic inches per wire equals 4.50 cubic inches

1 #12 grounding wire times 2.25 for all grounding wires in the box equals 2.25 cubic inches

2 #14 hot (ungrounded) plus 1 #14 neutral (grounded) wires times 2.00 cubic inches per wire equals 6.00 cubic inches

1 switch plus 1 receptacle times 4.50 cubic inches equals 9.00 cubic inches

4.50 + 2.25 + 6.00 + 9.00 = 21.75 cubic inches
The box is large enough for this application.

Box Opening Covers

1. Close all openings in boxes and conduit bodies with material that provides protection equal to the original opening cover. This means using plastic or metal knockout covers. Tape and cardboard do not provide equal protection.
2. Recess metal knockout covers in nonmetallic boxes and conduit bodies at least (≥) ¼ inch from the surface of the box or conduit body.
3. Cover open outlet boxes with a blank cover, a blank plate, or fixture canopy. Switch plates and receptacle plates do not provide complete closure for outlet boxes.
4. Ground metal covers and plates.

Box Installation Tolerances

1. Install boxes in noncombustible material, such as masonry, so that the front edge is set not more than (≤) ¼ inch back from the finished surface.
2. Install boxes in walls and ceilings made of wood or other combustible material so that the front edge is flush with the finished surface or projects from the finished surface.
3. Cut openings for boxes in drywall and plaster so that the opening is not more than (≤) ⅛ inch from the perimeter of the box.
4. You may use an extension device, such as an extension ring, that extends the box to the finished wall surface when a box is set back from the finished wall surface.

Box Support In Walls, Ceilings, and Floors

1. Provide support for boxes that rigidly and securely fastens them in place. You may use nails or screws to support these boxes.
2. Protect screws inside boxes so that the threads will not damage the wires.
3. Use wood braces that are at least (≥) 1 inch by 2 inches when using wood braces to support boxes.
4. Use "cut-in" or "old work" boxes that have approved clamps or anchors that are identified for the location where they are installed.

Box Support by Raceways

1. Do not support any junction or device boxes using only conduit or tubing if the box volume is larger than (>) 100 cubic inches.
2. Support boxes that do not contain switches, receptacles or light fixtures by using at least (≥) 2 conduits threaded wrench-tight into the box. Secure the conduit not more than (≤) 3 feet from the box if the conduit enters from different sides of the box. Secure the conduit not more than (≤) 18 inches from the box if the conduit enters from the same side of the box. Example: if the conduit enters the box from the top and bottom of the box, then secure the conduit not more than (≤) 3 feet from the box. Example: if the conduit enters the box from only the top or only from the bottom, then secure the conduit not more than (≤) 18 inches from the box.
3. Support boxes that contain switches or receptacles or light fixtures by using at least (≥) 2 conduits threaded wrench-tight into the box. Secure the conduit not more than (≤) 18 inches from the box.
4. You may use RMC or IMC metal conduit to support light fixtures under certain conditions. Refer to the IRC for the exceptions.

Combustible Material Under Fixture Canopy

1. Cover any combustible material between a box and a light fixture canopy with noncombustible material. This would occur, for example, when a light fixture is mounted on wood paneling. You must cover the wood paneling under the light fixture canopy with noncombustible material to avoid igniting the wood if arcing occurred under the light fixture canopy.

CABINETS AND PANELBOARDS (E3907)

Panelboard and Switch Cabinets as Junction Boxes

1. Do not use panelboard and switch cabinets as junction boxes or raceways unless there is sufficient room in the cabinet for the additional wires. This means that you may splice wires in or run wires through panelboard and switch cabinets only if the cabinet is large enough to accommodate the extra wires.

Panelboard Cabinets in Damp and Wet Locations

1. Install panelboard cabinets located in damp and wet locations so that water will not enter the cabinet. Use panelboard cabinets listed for damp or wet locations in damp locations and use panelboard cabinets listed for wet location in wet locations. Use fittings listed for wet locations when raceways or wires enter a panelboard cabinet from above in wet locations.
2. Provide at least (≥) a ¼ inch air space between a panelboard cabinet and the wall or other supporting surface.

Panelboard Cabinet Installation Tolerances

1. Install panelboard cabinets in noncombustible material so that the front edge projects not more than (≤) ¼ inch from the finished surface.
2. Install panelboard cabinets in walls and ceilings made of wood or other combustible material so that the front edge is flush with the finished surface or projects from the finished surface.
3. Cut openings for panelboard cabinets in drywall and plaster so that the opening is not more than (≤) ⅛ inch from the perimeter of the panelboard cabinet. Repair drywall and plaster around a panelboard cabinet so that there are no gaps greater than (>) ⅛ inch around the cabinet and cover.
4. Install panelboard cabinets vertically, unless vertical installation is not practical (NEC 240.33).

Panelboard Cabinet Opening Covers

1. Close all openings in panelboard cabinets and dead front covers with material that provides protection equal to the original opening cover. This means plastic or metal knockout covers. Tape and cardboard do not provide equal protection.
2. Recess metal knockout covers in nonmetallic cabinets at least (≥) ¼ inch from the surface of the cabinet.

Cables Secured to Cabinet

1. Secure each individual cable to panelboard cabinets and to similar enclosures, unless the exception applies.
2. You may run NM cable into the top of a surface mounted cabinet through an accessible rigid raceway under certain conditions. Refer to IRC Chapter 39 for the conditions.

EQUIPMENT GROUNDING (E3908)

When Equipment Grounding is Required

1. Ground metal parts in an electrical system including equipment cases, cabinets, boxes, conduit, tubing, light fixtures, and water pumps. Equipment cases include furnaces, air conditioning condensers, water heaters, dishwashers, and similar equipment.
2. You may ground metal parts in an electrical system by using any currently accepted wir-

ing method that provides a mechanically and electrically continuous path to the service grounding connection. These methods include:
   a) grounding wires contained in NM cable, and
   b) separate equipment grounding wires contained within the conduit serving equipment, and
   c) metal conduit and tubing when the fittings at terminations are listed for grounding.
3. Do not use a separate earth ground as the only means of grounding equipment. Example: do not install a separate driven ground rod to ground an air conditioning condenser.

Grounding to Neutral Wires (Bootleg Grounds)

1. Do not connect grounding and neutral (grounded) wires at any point past the service equipment. This includes not connecting grounding and neutral (grounded) wires at subpanels and at devices and equipment such as receptacles and metal motor and equipment cases. Grounding must be accomplished by a separate dedicated grounding wire or by metal conduit and tubing. Example: do not connect a receptacle grounding terminal to the neutral (grounded) terminal. This is sometimes called a "bootleg ground" and is a safety hazard.

Grounding with Flexible Metal Conduit

1. Use flexible metal conduit (FMC) and liquid-tight flexible metal conduit as the grounding conductor only if the length of the conduit is not more than ($\leq$) 6 feet and the circuit is not more than ($\leq$) 20 amps. Other limiting conditions exist that make using FMC as a grounding conductor impractical. Refer to the IRC for more information.

Equipment Grounding Wire Size

1. Use the following table to determine the correct wire size for an equipment grounding wire.
2. Size the equipment grounding wire based on the largest circuit ampacity rating when running multiple circuits in a raceway. You may use one equipment grounding wire to serve different equipment when one raceway contains all circuit wires. Example: if a raceway contains both #10 and #12 wires that serve different equipment, only one #10 grounding wire is required in the raceway.
3. In most residential wiring, the grounding wire is part of the NM cable and additional grounding wires are not necessary. This rule is used in residential wiring when separate wires are pulled in a raceway.

TABLE E3908
Equipment Grounding Wire Size Table

circuit rating (amps)	copper wire size (AWG)
15	14
20	12
30	10
40	10
60	10

Equipment Grounding Wires Installation in Boxes

1. Connect multiple equipment grounding wires together in boxes using a listed connector such as a wire nut. Do not rely only on twisting grounding wires together to make a permanent connection.
2. Do not rely on equipment or devices to maintain equipment grounding wire continuity. When multiple equipment grounding wires enter a box, connect the wires independently of the device and use a separate wire (pigtail) to connect the device to the connected wires.

Grounding Receptacles to Metal Boxes

1. Use a bonding jumper wire to connect a receptacle's grounding terminal to a grounded box or to a metal box unless the receptacle is listed for grounding by attaching the receptacle to the metal box using the receptacle's normal attachment screws.
2. You may use screws or nuts to attach the bonding wire to the box. Use screws with at least (≥) 2 threads connected to the box.

Paint on Grounding Connections

1. Clean paint and other nonconductive coatings from points where equipment grounding wires are connected together or are connected to equipment or devices.

FLEXIBLE CORDS (E3909)

Flexible Cord Permitted Uses

1. Use flexible cords only to connect an appliance to a receptacle and only if the appliance manufacturer's instructions allow connection by a flexible cord.
2. Do not run or conceal flexible cords in walls, ceilings, floors, or raceways.
3. Do not splice or tap flexible cords.
4. Provide power to flexible cords through an attachment plug. Do not hard-wire flexible cords directly to a power source.
5. Do not use flexible cords as a substitute for permanent wiring.
6. Refer to Chapter 41 for flexible cord lengths for specific appliances.

40

FINAL INSTALLATION OF SWITCHES, RECEPTACLES, AND LIGHTS

SWITCH INSTALLATION (E4001)

Switch Current Load Limitations

1. Do not use a switch in a circuit if the current load on the circuit exceeds the current rating of the switch. Example: a 15 amp snap switch may be overloaded if it switches ten 200 watt, 120 volt flood lights. Beware of overloads if the switch controls multiple high wattage flood lights or other high current draw equipment.
2. Use switches that are rated at least (≥) 80 percent of a motor's full load current rating.

Switches Connected to Aluminum Wire

1. Use 15 amp and 20 amp snap switches marked CO/ALR when connecting the switch to aluminum wires. You may use other snap switches if you splice a copper wire pigtail to the aluminum wire and connect the copper wire to the switch. Be sure to use an approved connector and/or anti-oxidant paste when splicing aluminum and copper wires.

Switch and Circuit Breaker Orientation

1. Install single-throw switches and circuit breakers so that ON is in the up position when the device is installed vertically. You may install single-throw switches and circuit breakers horizontally.
2. Use switches and circuit breakers that clearly indicate whether the switch is in the ON or OFF position. This does not apply to 3-way and 4-way switches. This requirement is frequently waived when rocker type switches are used.

Switch and Circuit Breaker Height

1. Locate switches not more than (≤) 79 inches above the finished floor or finished grade. Measure to the center of the handle when in the up position.
2. Locate switches in readily accessible places.

Timer Switches

1. Use timer switches with energized parts that are enclosed in the switch's case or enclose the timer switch in a cabinet or box.
2. Install a barrier to guard against contact with energized parts.

Timer Switch (PE4001-0)
Figure 40-1

Grounding of Switches, Boxes, and Faceplates

1. Ground metal boxes containing switches, and the switches themselves (including dimmers and similar devices), and metal faceplates covering switches. Ground the switch by mounting the switch to a grounded metal box using metal screws or by connecting an equipment grounding wire to the switch. Connect switches to the equipment grounding wire when using nonmetallic boxes.

Switches and Circuit Breakers in Wet Locations

1. Enclose switches and circuit breakers installed in wet locations in a weatherproof cabinet or enclosure or provide a weatherproof cover.
2. Do not locate switches in shower or tub spaces unless the switch is part of a listed tub or shower assembly.

Switching Neutral (Grounded) Wires

1. Switch only the hot (ungrounded) wire unless the switch simultaneously disconnects all wires in the circuit. Maintain required wire color coding throughout three-way and four-way circuits.

Switch Mounting in Boxes

1. Mount switches in boxes that are recessed from the wall by seating the switch's extension ears at the top and bottom of the switch against the wall surface.
2. Mount switches in boxes that are flush with the wall by seating the switch's mounting yoke or strap against the box.
3. Do not allow the switch to move when operated. This can, over time, cause wires to loosen, allow arcing, and cause a fire.

Switch Faceplate Installation

1. Install switch faceplates so that the plate completely covers the switch and so that the faceplate is flush against the wall. No gaps should exist between the switch handle and the faceplate and between the faceplate and the wall.

RECEPTACLE INSTALLATION (E4002)

Receptacle Current Rating

1. Install a receptacle with a current rating at least (≥) as large as the branch circuit <u>when circuit contains only one receptacle</u>. Example: use at least (≥) a 15 amp rated receptacle in a 15 amp branch circuit if the receptacle is the only one in the circuit.
2. Use the following table to determine the receptacle rating <u>when the circuit contains at least (≥) 2 receptacles or other outlets</u>. Note that a duplex receptacle counts as 2 receptacles.

TABLE E4002
Receptacle Ratings when used in Multiple Outlet Circuits

circuit rating (amps)	receptacle rating (amps)
15	15
20	15 or 20
30	30
40	40 or 50
50	50

Receptacle Grounding Type Use

1. Use only grounding type (3-prong) receptacles on 15 amp and 20 amp branch circuits.

Receptacles Connected to Aluminum Wire

1. Use 15 amp and 20 amp receptacles marked CO/ALR when connecting the receptacle to aluminum wires. You may use other receptacles if you splice a copper wire pigtail to the aluminum wire and connect the copper wire to the receptacle. Be sure to use an approved connector and/or anti-oxidant paste when splicing aluminum and copper wires.

Receptacle Mounting in Boxes

1. Mount receptacles in boxes that are recessed from the wall by seating the receptacle's extension ears at the top and bottom of the receptacle against the wall surface.
2. Mount receptacles in boxes that are flush with the wall by seating the receptacle's mounting yoke or strap against the box.
3. Do not allow the receptacle to move when a plug is inserted. This can, over time, cause wires to loosen, allow arcing, and cause a fire.

Receptacle Mounting on Box Covers

1. Attach receptacles mounted directly to box covers by using at least (≥) 2 screws attached to the box cover. This applies when the receptacle is supported only by a box cover and the cover is attached to and supported by a box.

Receptacle Faceplate Installation

1. Install receptacle faceplates so that the plate completely covers the receptacle and so that the faceplate is flush against the wall. No gaps should exist between the receptacle and the faceplate and between the faceplate and the wall.
2. Install receptacles so that the face of the receptacle is either flush with or projects out from a nonmetallic faceplate.
3. Install receptacles so that the face of the receptacle projects out from a metallic faceplate at least (≥) 1/64 inch.

Receptacles in Damp Locations

1. Install a receptacle cover that is weatherproof when the cover is closed and a plug is not inserted into a receptacle located in a damp location. This applies to 15 amp and 20 amp receptacles. A damp area is protected from direct contact with water. Refer to the definition of damp location. You may use a receptacle cover suitable for wet locations in a damp location.
2. Install a water-tight seal between a flush-mounted receptacle and its faceplate. This will require a gasket or sealant between the finished surface (such as stucco, brick, or siding) and the faceplate.

Damp Location Receptacle Cover Not Flush-Mounted (PE4002-1)
Figure 40-2

Receptacles in Wet Locations

1. Install a receptacle cover that is weatherproof when the cover is closed on any receptacle located in a wet location. This applies to 15 amp and 20 amp receptacles in any indoor or

outdoor wet location. This applies regardless of whether or not a plug is inserted into the receptacle. Refer to the definition of wet location.

2. Install a water-tight seal between a flush-mounted receptacle and its faceplate. This will require a gasket or sealant between the finished surface (such as stucco, brick, or siding) and the faceplate.

Wet Location Receptacle Cover Not Flush-Mounted (PE4002-2)
Figure 40-3

Receptacles Greater than Twenty Amps in Wet Locations

1. Install a damp location receptacle cover that is weatherproof when the cover is closed and a plug is not inserted into the receptacle. This applies when the receptacle is in a wet location and when the plug connected device should be attended when in use. An example of an attended device is a tool such as a welder. You may also use a receptacle cover suitable for wet locations.

2. Install a wet location receptacle cover that is weatherproof when the cover is closed and a plug is inserted into the receptacle. This applies when the receptacle is in a wet location and when the plug connected device may not be attended when in use. An example of an unattended device is a clothes dryer.

3. Install a water-tight seal between a flush-mounted receptacle and its faceplate. This will require a gasket or sealant between the finished surface (such as stucco, brick, or siding) and the faceplate.

Receptacles in Tubs and Showers

1. Do not install receptacles in and directly above tub and shower spaces.

Receptacle Terminal Physical Contact

1. Install receptacles so that the wiring terminals are not exposed to physical contact.

LIGHT FIXTURE INSTALLATION (E4003 AND E4004)

Light Fixture Definition

Light fixture The term light fixture includes incandescent and fluorescent lights that are flush-mounted, hanging, and recessed. The term also includes high intensity lights such as sodium and mercury-vapor lamps, and track lights. Note that ceiling fans are considered appliances (not light fixtures) and are covered in Chapter 41.

Light Fixture Support

1. You may use a securely attached box to support light fixtures weighing less than (<) 50 pounds. See also Section E3905. <u>Note that ceiling fans are not light fixtures.</u> Ceiling fans are addressed in Chapter 41.
2. Do not use the screw shell of a light fixture to support anything that weighs more than (>) 6 pounds or is more than (>) 16 inches in any dimension.

Protection of Energized Light Fixture Parts

1. Install light fixtures so that energized parts are not exposed and subject to contact.
2. Ground exposed metal parts of light fixtures.

Receptacle Inserts for Lamp Holders

1. Do not install receptacle inserts in lamp holders and do not use lamp holders as receptacles.

Recessed Lights Type and Installation

1. Use recessed lights that are labeled as being thermally protected. Thermal protection shuts off power to the light at high temperatures. Thermal protection is not required if the recessed light is made, labeled, and installed so that it functions as if it were thermally protected.
2. Use insulation contact (IC) rated recessed lights when the recessed parts are installed in an insulated attic. IC rated recessed lights may not require clearance to insulation or to combustible materials

High Density Discharge Lights

1. Use high density discharge lights that are labeled as being thermally protected. Thermal protection shuts off power to the light at high temperatures. Thermal protection is not required if the light is made, labeled, and installed so that it functions as if it were thermally protected. Examples of high density discharge lights include metal-halide, and sodium and mercury-vapor lights. These lights are not common in residential settings.

Lights in Wet and Damp Locations

1. Install lights in wet and damp locations so that water cannot enter or accumulate in the wiring or energized parts.
2. Use only lights labeled SUITABLE FOR WET LOCATIONS when installing lights that may be subject to direct contact with water. Refer to the definition of wet location.
3. Use lights labeled either SUITABLE FOR WET LOCATIONS or SUITABLE FOR DAMP LOCATIONS when installing lights in damp locations. Refer to the definition of damp location. Light fixtures, including ceiling fans, intended for indoors may not be installed in either wet or damp locations.

Ceiling Fans and Lights Near Tubs and Showers

1. Install ceiling fans, cord-connected lights, lights suspended by cords, chains, or cables, and track lights so that no part of the light or fan falls within an exclusion zone measuring 3 feet horizontally from the base of the tub or shower stall threshold and 8 feet vertically from the top of the tub rim or shower stall threshold. Parts include fan blades, bulb enclosures, hanging chains, and other part connected to or hanging from the light or fan.
2. Use light fixtures that are listed for damp locations if the fixture is: (a) located within the outside dimensions of the tub or shower, and (b) within (≤) 8 feet from the top of the tub rim or shower threshold.
3. Use light fixtures that are listed for wet locations if the fixture is: (a) located within the outside dimensions of the tub or shower, and (b) within (≤) 8 feet from the top of the tub rim or shower threshold, and (c) subject to shower spray.

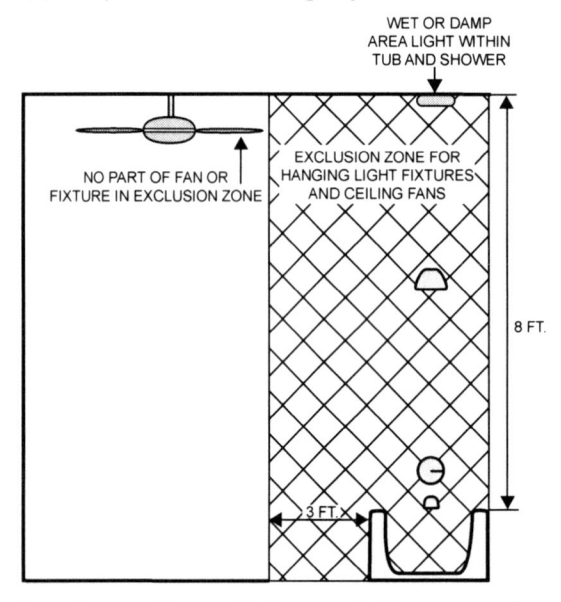

Exclusion Zone Near Tubs and Showers (E4003-0)
Figure 40-4

Light Fixtures Installed on Low-density Cellulose Fiberboard

1. Install fluorescent lights and lights with a ballast with at least (≥) 1 ½ inches clearance between the light case and low-density cellulose fiberboard. Clearance is not required if the light is listed and labeled for direct attachment to low-density cellulose fiberboard.

Light Fixtures Near Combustible Material

1. Install light fixtures so that combustible materials will not be subjected to temperatures greater than (>) 194° F. A light fixture includes any heat-generating parts such as the bulb, ballast, and transformer. Temperatures include normal operating temperatures and the higher temperatures that could occur if the fixture malfunctions. This situation may occur when the heat-generating parts of light fixtures are attached directly to materials such as wood paneling and wallpaper and may occur when the heat-generating parts are close to shelves storing combustible items.

Light Fixture Wiring

1. Connect wires to light fixtures so that the hot (ungrounded) wire is connected to the lamp holder center pin and so that the neutral (grounded) wire is connected to the lamp holder screw shell.
2. Protect light fixture wiring from physical damage and from damage by temperature exceeding the wire's temperature rating. Install any insulation that comes with the light fixture. This helps protect the wiring from high temperatures.

CLOTHES CLOSET LIGHT INSTALLATION (E4003.11)

Closet Storage Area Definition

Clothes closet A space intended for storage of clothing. A clothes closet usually contains a horizontal rod for hanging clothing. This definition implies that this section does not apply to storage areas such as linen closets and pantries. As with all codes, application of this section depends on interpretation by the local code official.

Closet storage area Clearances to light fixtures required by this IRC Section are between light fixtures and the <u>closet storage area</u>. The closet storage area is a space consisting of a hanging rod storage area and a shelf storage area. The required clearance applies to both areas. <u>The clearances to light fixtures apply whether or not shelves or hanging rods are currently installed in the closet.</u>

Hanging rod storage area Begin at the closet floor and end at 6 feet above the closet floor or at the highest hanging rod, whichever is higher. The hanging rod storage area includes all of the space within 24 inches horizontally from the back and sides of the closet walls.

Shelf storage area Begin at 6 feet above the closet floor or at the highest hanging rod, whichever is higher and end at the closet ceiling. The shelf storage area includes all of the space within 12 inches horizontally from the back and sides of the closet walls or within the width of the shelf, whichever is wider.

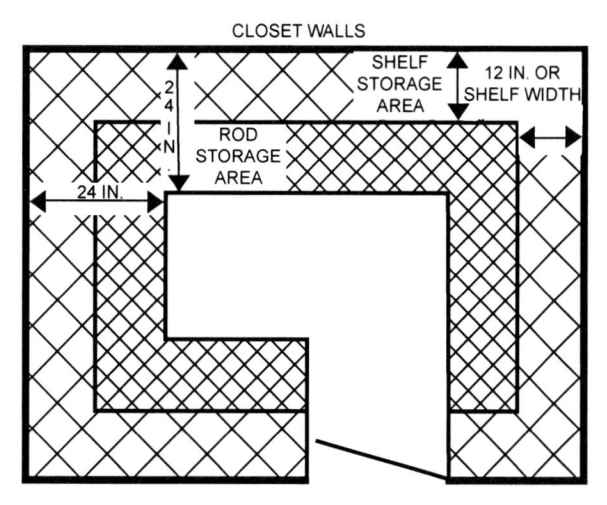

Clothes Closet Storage View from Above (E4003.11-2)
Figure 40-5

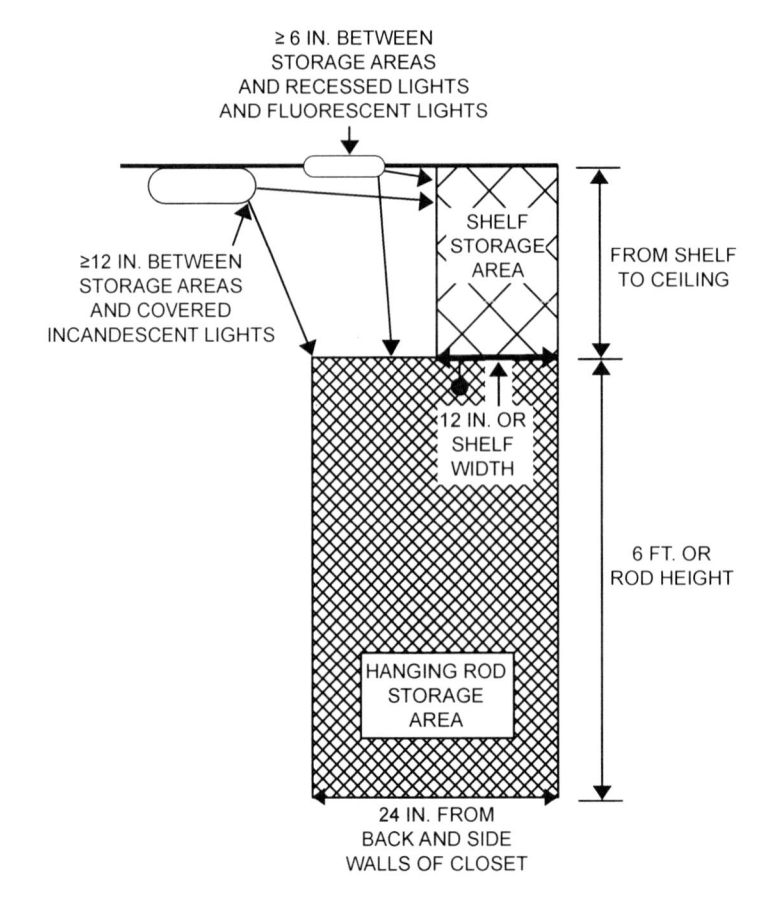

Clothes Closet Storage Area Side View (E4003.11-1)
Figure 40-6

Light Fixture Clearances in Clothes Closets

1. Do not install any incandescent light fixture in a clothes closet if any part of the lamp is exposed. This includes both surface mounted and recessed light fixtures. This includes incandescent light fixtures that have lamps such as compact fluorescent installed because the fluorescent lamp could be replaced with an incandescent lamp. This includes hanging light fixtures.

2. Provide at least (≥) 12 inches between surface mounted incandescent and LED light fixtures and the closest point of the closet storage area.

3. Provide at least (≥) 6 inches between recessed incandescent and LED light fixtures and the closest point of the closet storage area.

4. Provide at least (≥) 6 inches between fluorescent light fixtures and the closest point of the closet storage area.

5. You may install surface-mounted fluorescent and LED light fixtures within the closet storage area if the fixture is identified for use within the area.

TRACK LIGHTS (E4005)

Track Light Installation

1. Install track lights according to manufacturer's installation instructions using parts, hardware, and supports recommended by the track light manufacturer.
2. Do not install more lights or higher wattage lamps than specified by the track load rating.
3. Do not use track light components as receptacles.
4. Ground the track and maintain circuit continuity and polarity.

Track Light Prohibited Locations

1. Do not install track lights: (a) where likely to be subjected to physical damage, (b) in wet or damp locations, (c) where the track is concealed or extended through walls, ceilings, or partitions, (d) less than (<) 5 feet above finished floor unless the track operates at less than (<) 30 volts, (e) within the tub and shower exclusion area.

41
APPLIANCE INSTALLATION

APPLIANCE DEFINITION

Appliance The term appliance as used in this section includes portable small kitchen appliances, fixed appliances such as dishwashers, furnaces, and water heaters, and ceiling fans.

APPLIANCE INSTALLATION (E4101)

Appliance Installation Using Flexible Cords

1. Install appliances according to manufacturer's installation instructions.
2. Use the following table to determine the length of flexible cords that serve appliances listed for use with flexible cords.

TABLE E4101
Appliance Flexible Cord Length Table

appliance	minimum cord length (inches)	maximum cord length (inches)
disposal	18	36
dishwasher	36	48
trash compactor	36	48

Appliance Disconnecting Means

1. Provide a switch, circuit breaker, fuse, or other means to disconnect motors and heating and air conditioning condensers and air handlers from all hot (ungrounded) wires. Locate the disconnecting means within sight of the equipment. You may use the circuit breaker or fuse in the panelboard to disconnect small appliances that draw less than 300 watts and you may use the plug to disconnect plug-and-cord connected appliances.

Ceiling Fan Support

1. Support ceiling fans weighing not more than (≤) 70 pounds using boxes listed and labeled to support the fan's weight. Install the box according to the box and fan manufacturer's installation instructions. The fan's weight is measured with or without accessories such as light kits.
2. Support ceiling fans that weigh more than (>) 70 pounds independently from the box.

42

ELECTRICAL REQUIREMENTS FOR POOLS, SPAS, WHIRLPOOL TUBS, FOUNTAINS

APPLICATION OF THE MATERIAL IN THIS CHAPTER

This IRC chapter applies to electrical equipment near or associated with all swimming pools including above ground and below ground pools, indoor and outdoor pools, and permanent and temporary pools. This chapter also applies to spas, hot tubs, whirlpool bathtubs, decorative water fountains, and other bodies of water such as fish ponds and reflecting pools.

SWIMMING POOL AND SPA DEFINITIONS (E4201)

Bathtub (whirlpool) A whirlpool bathtub is a bathtub equipped with a pump and water circulation system and is designed to be filled and emptied with each use. These bathtubs are usually located in bathrooms. They are also called hydromassage tubs and are sometimes referred to by the brand name Jacuzzi®.

Fountain A fountain is an ornamental water feature including ornamental ponds and reflecting pools. Fountains more than (>) 18 inches deep may be subject to pool barrier and access requirements.

Light (dry-niche) A dry-niche light is installed in a wall below the water level and is sealed against water entry into the niche. Water does not surround the light inside the niche

Light (wet-niche) A wet-niche light is installed in a wall below the water level and is not sealed against water entry into the niche. Water surrounds the light inside the niche.

Light (no-niche) A no-niche light is installed above or below water level without a niche.

Niche A niche is an opening in a wall into which a light is installed. A niche is usually created by a forming shell.

Maximum water level The maximum water level is the highest level the water can reach before it spills out over the edge.

Spa and hot tub A spa or hot tub usually consists of a water-containing shell and a pump, heater, air blower, and other accessories. Spas and hot tubs may be located indoors or outdoors, but are not usually located in bathrooms. Spas and hot tubs are usually not drained after each use and are usually larger than whirlpool bath tubs.

Spa and hot tub (packaged or self-contained) A packaged or self-contained hot tub or spa is a factory-fabricated, free-standing system. The water-containing shell is usually fiberglass and is usually surrounded by a wood or fiberglass surround. These spas and hot tubs are usually located on the ground or raised on a deck or other suitable supporting structure. This contrasts with site-built spas and hot tubs which are usually in-ground concrete structures and are often built adjacent to a permanent swimming pool.

Swimming pool (permanent) A permanent swimming pool is any water-containing structure intended for recreational use that has a water depth greater than (>) 42 inches. All indoor swimming pools are defined as permanent swimming pools regardless of the water depth. Permanent swimming pools are usually fully or partially in-ground structures, but need not be so.

Swimming pool (temporary) A temporary or storable swimming pool is a water-containing structure intended for recreational use, constructed on or above ground, and has a water depth not more than (≤) 42 inches. This definition also includes water containing structures made using molded plastic or inflatable fabric walls.

SWIMMING POOL AND SPA WIRING METHODS (E4202)

Swimming Pool and Spa Common Wiring Methods

1. You may use Intermediate Metal Conduit, Rigid Metal Conduit and Rigid Nonmetallic Conduit in most swimming pool and spa applications. Refer to the IRC for a complete list of wiring methods and restrictions.
2. Include an equipment grounding wire with feeder wires between the pool equipment subpanel and the source of power for the subpanel. (E4205).

Flexible Cord Uses and Limitations Near Swimming Pools and Spas

1. You may use flexible cords to serve fixed or stationary swimming pool and spa equipment if all of the following apply:
    a) the circuit is rated not more than (≤) 20 amps, and if
    b) the flexible cord is not more than (≤) 3 feet long, and if
    c) the flexible cord has a copper grounding wire at least (≥) #12 AWG, and if
    d) the circuit does not serve underwater lights. These restrictions also apply to all flexible cord equipped lights on or near the pool deck within (≤) 16 feet from any point on the water surface. The 3 feet flexible cord length limitation does not apply to temporary swimming pools.
2. You may use a flexible cord between a listed underwater light and a junction box if there are no splices in the flexible cord and if the flexible cord has an insulated copper grounding wire at least (≥) #16 AWG.
3. You may use a flexible cord to serve an outdoor packaged spa or hot tub if the circuit is GFCI protected and if the flexible cord is not more than (≤) 15 feet long.
4. You may use a flexible cord to serve an indoor packaged spa or hot tub if the circuit is rated not more than (≤) 20 amps.
5. Connect the flexible cord equipment grounding wire to a fixed-in-place part of fixed or sta-

tionary equipment. Bond or mount the removable part of the equipment to the grounded fixed-in-place part of the equipment.

RECEPTACLES AND SWITCHES NEAR SWIMMING POOLS AND SPAS (E4203.1 – E4203.3)

Measuring Distance Between Receptacles and Pools and Spas

1. Measure the distance between a receptacle or a switch and the nearest inside wall of a pool or spa by using a straight line between the two points that does not penetrate a permanent barrier such as a door, window, wall, floor, or ceiling. Example: an interior receptacle that is 4 feet from the inside edge of an outdoor pool is acceptable because the receptacle and pool are separated by a wall.

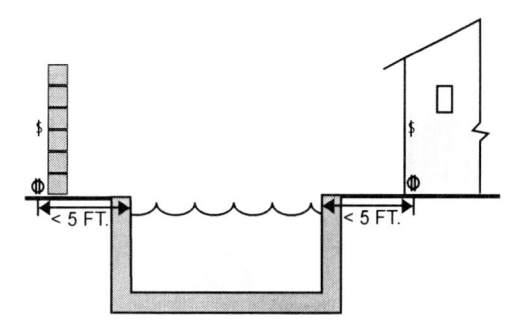

SWITCHES AND RECEPTACLES ARE OK WHEN INSIDE BUILDINGS OR BEHIND A PERMANENT BARRIER

Measuring Distances Between Pools, Receptacles, and Switches (E4203.1-1)
Figure 42-1

Receptacles Near Swimming Pools and Outdoor Spas and Hot Tubs

1. Do not locate any receptacles less than (<) 6 feet from the inside edge of all indoor and outdoor swimming pools and all outdoor spas and hot tubs. You may locate circulation system receptacles at least (≥) 6 feet and less than (<) 10 feet from the inside edge of any indoor or outdoor swimming pool and outdoor spa and hot tub if all of the following apply:
   a) the receptacle serves a pump motor or other load associated with the circulation system, and if
   b) the receptacle is a single locking type, and if
   c) the receptacle is GFCI protected.

3. Locate at least (≥) one 120 volt, 15 amp or 20 amp general purpose receptacle at least (≥) 6 feet and not more than (≤) 20 feet from the inside edge of all indoor and outdoor swimming pools and all outdoor spas and hot tubs. Locate this receptacle not more than (≤) 78 inches above the walking surface serving the swimming pool and outdoor spa and hot tub.

4. Place all receptacles located not more than (≤) 20 feet from the inside edge of all indoor and outdoor swimming pools and all outdoor spas and hot tubs on a GFCI protected circuit.

5. Place all 15 and 20 amp, 120 and 240 volt outlets serving pump motors, whether by receptacle or hard-wired connection, on a GFCI protected circuit.

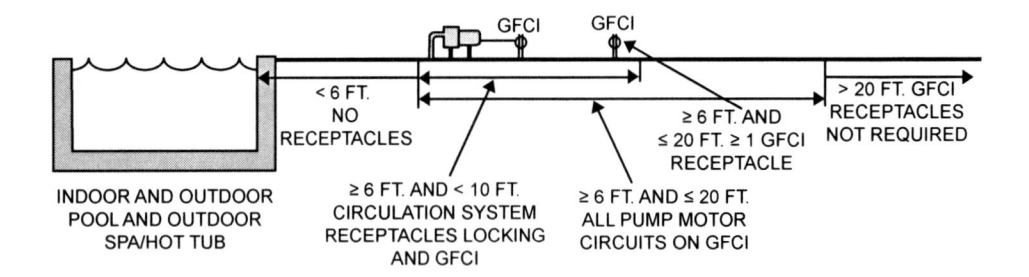

Receptacles Near Outdoor Pools and Spas (E4203.1-2)
Figure 42-2

Receptacles Near Indoor Spas and Hot Tubs

1. Do not locate receptacles less than (<) 6 feet from the inside edge of all indoor spas and hot tubs.
2. Locate at least (≥) one 120 volt, 15 amp or 20 amp receptacle between at least (≥) 6 feet and not more than (≤) 10 feet from the inside edge of all indoor spas and hot tubs.
3. Place all receptacles located within (≤) 10 feet from the inside edge of all indoor spas and hot tubs on a GFCI protected circuit.

Switches Near Swimming Pools and Spas

1. Locate switches at least (≥) 5 feet horizontally from the inside edge of indoor and outdoor swimming pools and spas and hot tubs. This restriction does not apply if: (a) a permanent barrier such as a solid fence or a wall is between the switch and the water's edge, or if (b) the switch is listed for use within 5 feet from a swimming pool or spa. This restriction does not apply to whirlpool bathtubs.

Electrical Disconnecting Means Near Swimming Pools and Spas

1. Install readily accessible equipment that will simultaneously disconnect power to all swimming pool and spa and hot tub related equipment, other than lights. Locate this equipment within sight of the equipment it serves and at least (≥) 5 feet from the inside edge of the swimming pool or spa. The equipment may be circuit breakers, fuses, or switches.

LIGHTS AND FANS NEAR SWIMMING POOLS AND SPAS (E4203.4)

Outdoor Pools, Spas, and Hot Tubs - New Lights and Fans

1. Do not install new or additional lights and ceiling fans in the following areas above and near <u>outdoor swimming pools, spas, and hot tubs</u>:
   a) directly above the pool, spa, or hot tub beginning at the maximum water level and extending 12 feet vertically, and
   b) beginning at the inside edge of the pool, spa, or hot tub and extending 5 feet horizontally and 12 feet vertically from the maximum water level.
2. Do not allow any part of the light or fan, including fan blades, within the restricted area. No exceptions exist for this limitation.

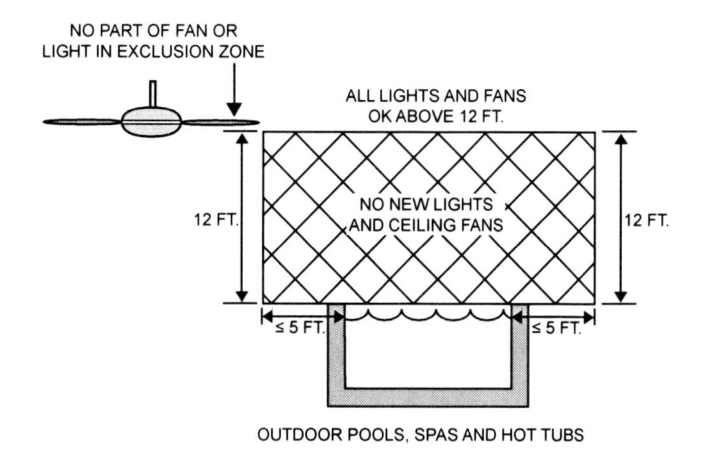

New Lights and Fans Near Outdoor Pools and Spas (E4203.4-1)
Figure 42-3

Indoor Pools, Spas, and Hot Tubs - New Lights and Fans

1. You may install new or additional lights and ceiling fans above and within (≤) 5 feet from the inside edge of <u>indoor swimming pools, spas and hot tubs</u> if all of the following are true:
   a) lights are completely enclosed (no exposed light bulbs), and if
   b) the circuit is GFCI protected, and if
   c) the vertical distance between the maximum water level and the lowest projection from the light or ceiling fan is at least (≥) 90 inches.

2. You may install surface mounted or recessed lights that are less than (<) 90 inches above <u>indoor spas and hot tubs</u> if all of the following are true:
   a) the circuit is GFCI protected, and if
   b) the light has a glass or plastic lens or globe or electrically isolated metal trim, and if
   c) the light is listed for damp locations.

3. You are not required to GFCI protect lights that have all parts more than (>) 12 feet above the maximum water level of indoor swimming pools, spas, and hot tubs.

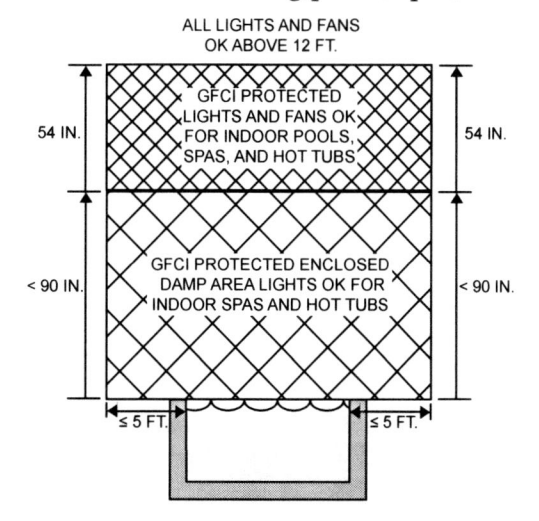

New Lights and Fans Near Indoor Pools and Spas (E4203.4-2)
Figure 42-4

Pools and Outdoor Spas, and Hot Tubs - Existing Lights

1. You may keep existing lights located within (≤) 5 feet from the inside edge of <u>indoor and outdoor swimming pools and outdoor spas and hot tubs</u> if all of the following are true:
   a) the light is at least (≥) 5 feet above the maximum water level, and if
   b) the light is securely fastened to the existing structure, and if
   c) the circuit is GFCI protected.

2. You <u>may not keep</u> existing lights located within (≤) 5 feet from the inside edge of <u>indoor and outdoor swimming pools and outdoor spas and hot tubs</u> if the existing lights are located less than (<) 5 feet above the maximum water level.

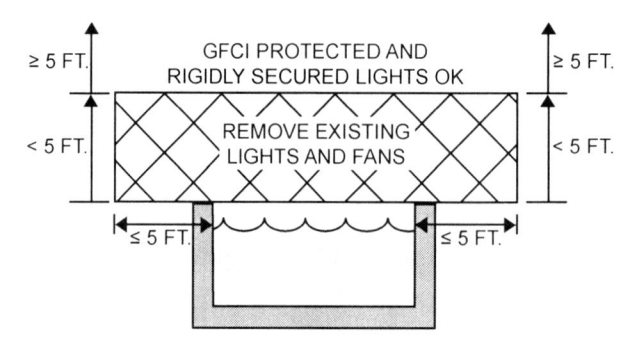

Existing Lights and Fans Near Indoor and Outdoor Pools and Outdoor Spas (E4203.4-3)
Figure 42-5

Pools, Spas, and Hot Tubs - Lights Between Five and Ten Feet from Water's Edge

1. Provide GFCI protection for lights installed between (≥) 5 feet and 10 feet from the inside edge of <u>indoor and outdoor swimming pools and outdoor spas and hot tubs</u> if the lights are less than (<) 5 feet above maximum water level or if the lights are not securely fastened to the structure. You are not required to provide GFCI protection for these lights if they are at least (≥) 5 feet above maximum water level and are securely fastened to the structure.

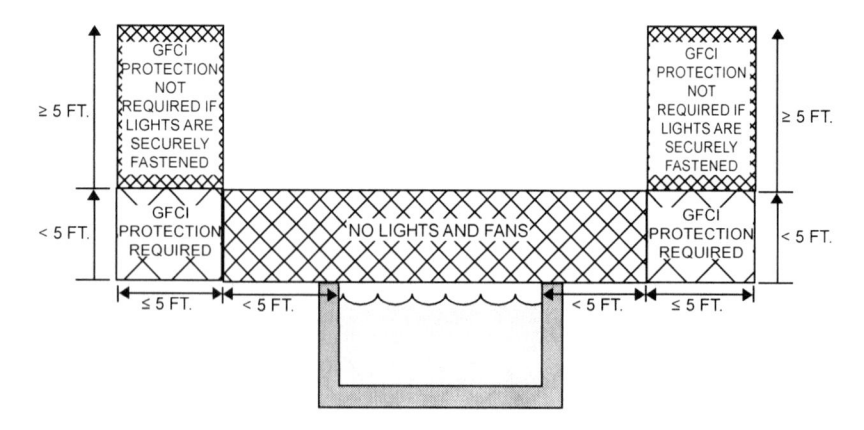

Lights and Fans Between Five and Ten Feet from Pools and Spas (E4203.4-4)
Figure 42-6

Communication, Telephone, and Other Outlets Clearances (E4203.5)

1. Locate outlets for cable TV, telephone, computer, remote control, door bells, and similar systems at least (≥) 10 feet from the inside edge of all indoor and outdoor swimming pools.

Overhead Wire Clearances (E4203.6)

1. Install telephone, cable TV, and satellite TV wires at least (≥) 10 feet vertically above and at least (≥) 10 feet horizontally from the inside edge of swimming pools, spas, and hot tubs, and any associated diving structures, observation stands, towers, and platforms. Note that broadband communication systems operate at higher voltages and are not the same as cable TV wires. Provide the same clearance to broadband communication system wires as to service drop wires operating at not more than (≤) 750 volts. See Section NEC Article 830.
2. Install electrical wires with the minimum vertical clearances from the following table. Maintain the vertical clearance for at least (≥) 10 feet horizontally from the structures listed in the table. Note that the (≤) 750 volt column applies to most residential overhead service drops.
3. Do not install new swimming pools, spas and hot tubs under existing telephone, cable TV, broadband communication, and electrical wires unless the required clearances are maintained.

TABLE E4203.6
Overhead Wire Clearance

structure requiring clearance (to any part of the structure)	≤ 750 volt wires supported by grounded messenger or neutral wire	≤15,000 volt wires not supported by grounded messenger or neutral wire	>15,000 and ≤50,000 volt wires not supported by grounded messenger or neutral wire
from water level at inside edge of pool/ spa, & from base of diving platform	22 feet	25 feet	27 feet
from top of diving platform	14 feet	17 feet	18 feet

532 Everybody's Building Code

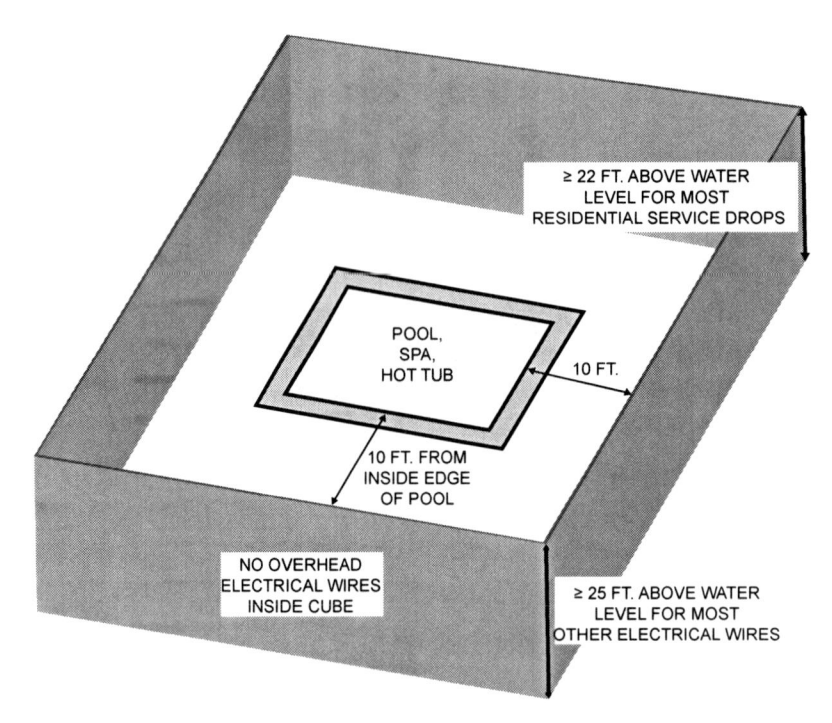

Pools and Spa Clearance to Residential Overhead Electrical Wires (E4203.6-1)
Figure 42-7

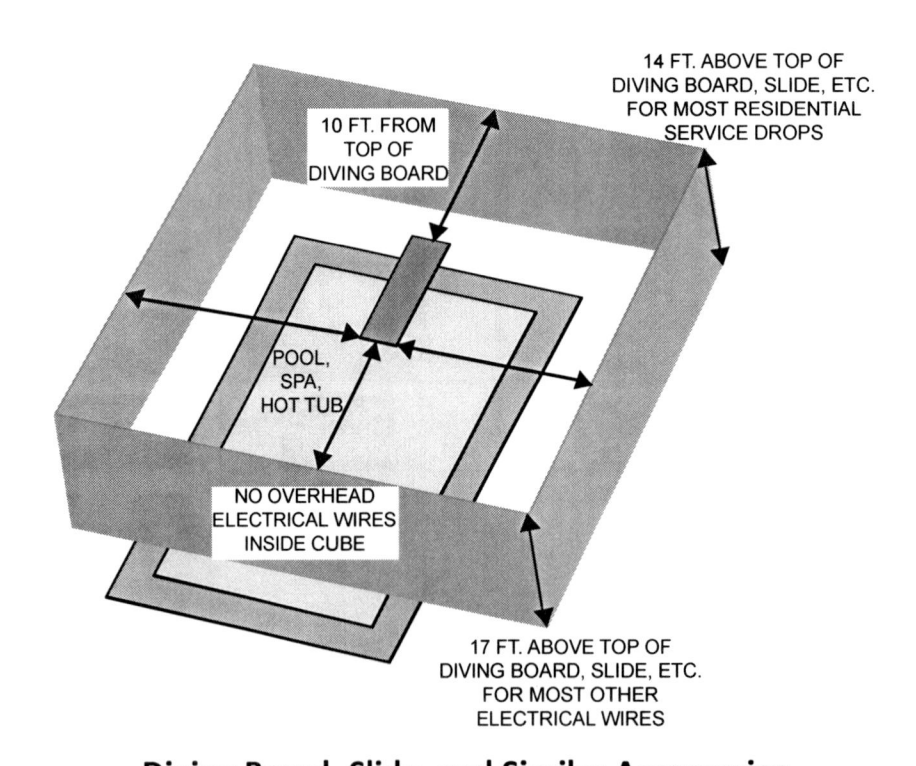

Diving Board, Slide, and Similar Accessories
Clearance to Residential Overhead Electrical Wires (E4203.6-2)
Figure 42-8

Underground Wire Clearances (E4203.7)

1. Do not install underground electrical wires within (≤) 5 feet horizontally from the inside walls of indoor and outdoor swimming pools and outdoor spas and hot tubs. This restriction does not apply to pool lights and other necessary pool equipment and it does not apply if space limits make the clearance impossible.
2. Use corrosion-resistant RMC or IMC or approved nonmetallic conduit or tubing to install underground electrical wires that are within (≤) 5 feet horizontally from the inside walls of indoor swimming pools and outdoor spas and hot tubs.
3. Bury RMC and IMC at least (≥) 6 inches deep and bury nonmetallic conduit or tubing at least (≥) 18 inches deep.

BONDING OF METAL NEAR SWIMMING POOLS AND SPAS (E4204)

Metal Parts Requiring Bonding - all Pools and Outdoor Spas and Hot Tubs

1. Connect together (bond) most metal near or associated with all indoor and outdoor swimming pools and outdoor spas, and hot tubs. This includes:
    a) All metal parts of the structure including reinforcing bars. The usual steel wire ties used to connect reinforcing bars are considered an adequate bonding connection when the ties are wound tight.
    b) All surfaces within (≤) 3 feet from the inside edge of conductive structures. Conductive structures include all forms of concrete and do not include vinyl liners and fiberglass shells. Surfaces include all unpaved, concrete, and other surfaces.
    c) Metal shells and mounting brackets of no-niche lights, except for listed low voltage lights.
    d) Metal parts and fittings inside or attached to the structure, except for isolated parts not more than (≤) 4 inches long that penetrate into the structure not more than (≤) 1 inch.
    e) Metal parts of electrical equipment associated with the water circulation system and any motorized pool covers. This includes pump motors, chemical injectors, water heating equipment, and motors for pool, spa, and hot tub covers.
    f) Metal wiring methods within (≤) 5 feet horizontally from the inside edge of the pool, spa, or hot tub and within (≤) 12 feet vertically from the maximum water level and from the top of any diving structure, viewing stand, and similar structures. Wiring methods include metal conduit, tubing, junction boxes, enclosures, lights, and fans.
    g) Water. Provide a conductive area of at least (≥) 9 square inches. Any combination of conductive surfaces from items (a) through (f) that are in conductive contact with the water satisfy this provision for bonding the water.
    h) Metal cases of water heating equipment. Follow manufacturer's instructions for grounding and bonding water heaters rated at more than (>) 50 amps.

Metal Parts Requiring Bonding - Indoor Spas and Hot Tubs

1. Connect together (bond) most metal near or associated with all indoor spas, and hot tubs. This includes:
    a) Metal parts and fittings inside or attached to the spa or hot tub. This does not include met-

al air and water jets, drain fitting, and similar parts if not connected to metal piping, and this does not include towel bars, mirror frames, and similar non-electrical equipment.

b) Metal parts of electrical equipment associated with the water circulation system. This includes pump motors and chemical injectors.

c) Metal exposed wiring methods and plumbing piping within (≤) 5 feet horizontally from the inside edge of the spa or hot tub. This includes metal conduit, tubing, junction boxes, enclosures, and plumbing pipes.

d) Metal within (≤) 5 feet from the inside edge of the spa or hot tub. This does not include metal separated by a wall, floor, or other permanent barrier.

Bonding Method

1. Install a solid copper bonding wire at least (≥) #8 AWG or install rigid brass or other corrosion-resistant metal conduit that connects all parts requiring bonding. Metal parts mean isolated pieces of metal that are not otherwise electrically connected. Example: the steel reinforcing shell of an in-ground concrete swimming pool is one metal part because all of the bars should be connected to each other by wire ties.

2. Use heat welds or approved pressure clamps made from stainless steel, brass, or copper to connect the bonding wire to bonded metal parts. Do not use solder or sheet metal screws.

3. You do not need to run the bonding wire to the electrical service equipment, panelboard, or grounding electrode.

4. Refer to IRC Section E4203 for bonding requirements when structural steel is encapsulated in a non-conducting material.

Bonding Discussion

The purpose of bonding is to connect metal parts together so that if one part becomes electrically energized its voltage will not be different from any nearby metal part. If metal parts are at different voltages, a person touching one part could become the electrical path to ground if he touches a nearby metal part. Bonding and grounding are not the same. Bonding connects metal parts to each other. Grounding connects electrical equipment to an earth grounding point.

Note that some metal parts, such as pool circulation equipment, must be both grounded and bonded. In this case, the grounding wire is usually contained in the electrical wires serving the equipment and the bonding wire is usually connected to the metal exterior of the equipment.

GROUNDING OF METAL NEAR SWIMMING POOLS AND SPAS (E4205)

Equipment Required to be Grounded

1. Ground the following equipment:
   a) all underwater lights except low-voltage lights listed for use without grounding, and
   b) all electrical equipment within (≤) 5 feet from the inside edge of an indoor or outdoor swimming pool, spa, or hot tub, and
   c) all electrical equipment associated with the circulating system of an indoor or outdoor swimming pool, spa, or hot tub, and
   d) junction boxes and transformer enclosures, and

e) ground-fault-circuit-interrupter (GFCI) receptacles and circuit breakers, and
f) subpanels (that are not part of the service equipment) that serve any electrical equipment associated with an indoor or outdoor swimming pool, spa, or hot tub.

Grounding Underwater Lights

1. Ground all underwater lights. Use an insulated copper equipment grounding wire at least (≥) #12 AWG for circuits not more than (≤) 20 amps. Do not splice the grounding wire. This grounding wire is in addition to the #8 AWG bonding wire required for a metal forming shell.
2. You may connect the underwater light's equipment grounding wire to the grounding terminal of equipment such as a junction box, transformer, GFCI, timer switch, or snap switch when the equipment is installed between the light and the panelboard. Connect the grounding terminal of the equipment directly (unspliced) to the grounding terminal at the panelboard.

Grounding Nonmetallic Conduit Serving Underwater Lights

1. Install an insulated copper grounding wire at least (≥) #8 AWG in any nonmetallic conduit installed between a wet-niche light and a junction box, transformer enclosure or other enclosure. Connect the wire at the junction box or enclosure and at the light's forming shell. Protect the forming shell connection with an approved potting compound that will resist the corrosive effects of the water. This grounding wire is in addition to any bonding wire required for a metal forming shell.

Grounding Underwater Lights Supplied by Flexible Cords

1. Use a flexible cord that contains an insulated copper grounding wire as part of the cord if using a flexible cord to supply a wet-niche or no-niche light. Use a grounding wire that is at least (≥) the same size as the supply wires and at least (≥) #16 AWG. Connect the grounding wire at the junction box or enclosure and at all exposed non-current-carrying metal parts of the light.

Grounding Motors

1. Install a copper equipment grounding wire between all motors associated with indoor and outdoor swimming pools, spas, and hot tubs and the grounding terminal at the panelboard. Use at least (≥) #12 AWG for motors on 15 amp and 20 amp circuits and at least (≥) #10 AWG for motors on circuits up to 60 amps. This grounding wire is in addition to the #8 AWG bonding wire required for the motor case.

Grounding Panelboards

1. Install an insulated copper grounding wire between a subpanel that supplies equipment for indoor and outdoor swimming pools, spas, and hot tubs and the grounding terminal at the service equipment or at the panelboard serving the pool panelboard. Use at least (≥) #12 AWG grounding wire for 15 amp and 20 amp panelboard feeders and at least (≥) #10 AWG grounding wire for panelboard feeders up to 60 amps.

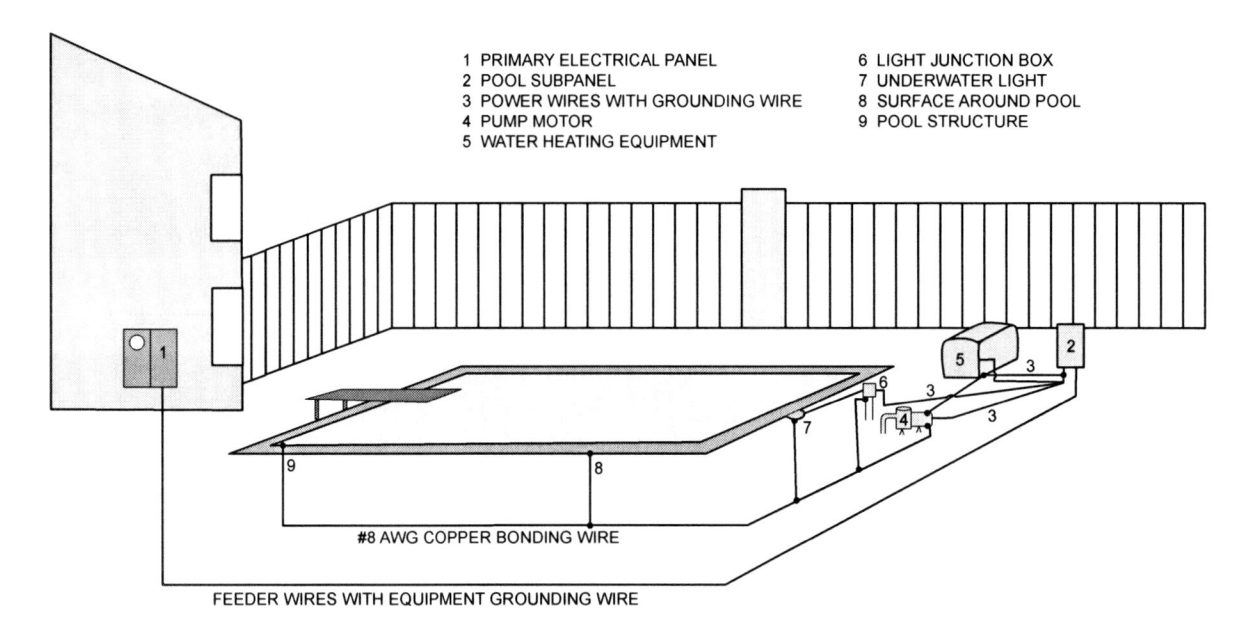

1 PRIMARY ELECTRICAL PANEL
2 POOL SUBPANEL
3 POWER WIRES WITH GROUNDING WIRE
4 PUMP MOTOR
5 WATER HEATING EQUIPMENT
6 LIGHT JUNCTION BOX
7 UNDERWATER LIGHT
8 SURFACE AROUND POOL
9 POOL STRUCTURE

Pool Bonding and Grounding (E4205-0)
Figure 42-9

INSTALLATION REQUIREMENTS FOR UNDERWATER LIGHTS, JUNCTION BOXES, AND OTHER EQUIPMENT NEAR POOLS AND SPAS (E4206)

Mixing GFCI Protected and Non-GFCI Protected Wires

1. Do not install GFCI protected wires in the same conduit, tubing, cable, raceway, or enclosure, with wires that are not GFCI protected. This restriction does not apply to equipment grounding wires and does not apply within panelboard cabinets.

Underwater Light GFCI Protection

1. Install GFCI protection for underwater lights operating at more than (>) 15 volts.
2. Do not install underwater lights on circuits operating at more than (>) 150 volts.

Underwater Light Depth

1. Install underwater lights so that the top of the light's lens is at least (≥) 18 inches below the normal water level. This restriction does not apply to lights listed for use at least (≥) 4 inches below normal water level.
2. Guard underwater lights with lenses facing other than vertical against human contact. Such a guard may include a substantial plastic cage covering the light's lens.

Wet-Niche Light Servicing

1. Install wet-niche lights so that they can be removed from the niche and placed on the pool deck to change lamps and for other maintenance and inspection. This means installing a cable that is long enough to reach the pool deck.

Underwater Light Junction Boxes

1. Use junction boxes listed and labeled for the intended use if using one to connect wires from underwater lights to wires from a panelboard. Size the box to comply with the box contents limitation in Section 3905.
2. Connect all metal conduit and grounding terminals to the junction box so that all metal is bonded together.
3. Locate junction boxes at least (≥) 4 inches above ground or pool deck level or at least (≥) 8 inches above maximum water level, whichever is higher, and at least (≥) 4 feet from the pool or spa inside wall. Do not locate junction boxes in walkways unless they are protected by a fixed structure such as a diving board or a fixed-in-place box.
4. You may use deck mounted junction boxes for lights operating at not more than (≤) 15 volts if an approved potting compound fills the box to prevent moisture entry and if the box is located at least (≥) 4 feet from the pool or spa inside wall.

Underwater Light Device Boxes

1. Use device boxes listed and labeled for the intended use if using one to connect wires from underwater lights to a transformer, GFCI, or other device such as a switch. Use a device box that has an air-tight seal between the conduit and the device box. Size the box to comply with the IRC box contents limitation.
2. Connect all metal conduit and grounding terminals to the device box so that all metal is bonded together.
3. Locate device boxes at least (≥) 4 inches above ground or pool deck level or at least (≥) 8 inches above maximum water level, whichever is higher, and at least (≥) 4 feet from the pool or spa inside wall. Do not locate device boxes in walkways unless they are protected by a fixed structure such as a diving board or a fixed-in-place box.

Strain Relief for Flexible Cords

1. Provide strain relief for flexible cords from underwater lights that enter junction and device boxes. This means providing a clamp or some other means to secure the cable and protect the electrical connections from movement.

Underwater Speakers

1. Use underwater speakers that are listed for the intended use.
2. Install underwater speakers in grounded and bonded forming shells in a manner similar to underwater lights.

Pool Cover Motors

1. Locate electric pool cover motors at least (≥) 5 feet from the pool inside edge unless the motor is covered or separated from the pool by a permanent barrier.
2. Locate the pool cover motor control so that the operator has full view of all parts of the pool.
3. Install pool motor covers on a GFCI protected circuit.

Electric Pool Area Heaters

1. Apply this section to electric heating units (such as radiant heaters) installed within (≤) 20 feet from the pool inside wall.
2. Install electric heating units at least (≥) 5 feet from the pool inside wall and not directly over the pool.
3. Fasten electric heating units securely to the structure.
4. Use electric unit heaters that are totally enclosed or guarded.
5. Use electric radiant heaters that are guarded. Install these heaters at least (≥) 12 feet vertically above the pool deck.

Storable Swimming Pool Pumps and Lights (E4207)

1. Use pumps and lights that are listed for the intended use with storable swimming pools. Install them according to manufacturer's instructions.
2. Install storable pool pumps and lights on a GFCI protected circuit.

Spa and Hot Tub GFCI Protection (E4208)

1. Install self-contained and packaged spas and hot tubs on a GFCI protected circuit if the heater load is not more than (≤) 50 amps. This does not apply if the self-contained or packaged spa or hot tub is listed and labeled as containing integral GFCI protection for all electrical parts within the unit.

Whirlpool Bathtubs (E4209)

1. Install whirlpool bathtub motors on a dedicated GFCI protected circuit.
2. Provide access to whirlpool bathtub motors and other electrical equipment. See access requirements in Chapter 27.
3. Install a copper bonding wire at least (≥) #8 AWG connecting all metal pipes, pump motors, and other electrical equipment associated with the whirlpool bathtub. Do not bond grounded double insulated whirlpool bathtub pump motors.

43

LOW VOLTAGE CIRCUITS

APPLICATION OF THE MATERIAL IN THIS CHAPTER

This IRC chapter applies to low voltage circuits such as door bells, thermostats and HVAC control circuits, security and fire alarm systems, intercom systems, and garage door opener controls. These circuits usually operate at not more than (≤) 30 volts. This chapter does not apply to communication circuits such as cable and satellite TV, broadband cable TV systems, and telephone systems.

Low Voltage Power Sources

1. Use transformers or power supplies listed as a Class 2 power source to run low voltage systems. Install the Class 2 power source according to manufacturer's instructions. An example of a Class 2 power source is a door bell transformer.
2. You may use a dry cell battery rated not more than (≤) 30 volts as a Class 2 power source.
3. Do not connect the output (load) side of a Class 2 power source to the output (load) side of other Class 2 power sources unless manufacturer's instructions allow the connection. Example: do not use two door bell transformers to supply the same door bell circuit unless the door bell manufacturer's instructions allow the use of multiple transformers in the circuit.

Doorbell Transformer (PE4300-0)
Figure 43-1

Low Voltage Wiring Methods

1. Limit the electric power circuit that supplies a Class 2 power source to not more than 120 volt, 20 amp.
2. Use at least (≥) #18 AWG wire to connect a Class 2 power source to the electric power supply

circuit. Limit the length of the Class 2 power supply connection wiring to not more than (≤) 12 inches if the connection wiring is smaller than (<) #14 AWG. Example: limit the length of the wires on the primary (line) side of a door bell transformer to not more than (≤) 12 inches if the primary side transformer wires are smaller than (<) #14 AWG.

3. Use cables listed as Class 2 cables to connect a Class 2 power supply to the low voltage device. Example: use cable listed for use with a door bell circuit between the door bell transformer and the door bell button and chime. Lamp cord or speaker wire may not have the same fire and smoke resistance rating as listed Class 2 cable.

Low Voltage and Electric Power Wire Separation

1. Do not run low voltage wires and electric power wires in the same conduit, tubing, raceway, junction and device box, or enclosure unless one of two exceptions exist. Example: do not run NM cable and door bell wires in the same conduit. Example: do not run door bell wires or security system wires in a panelboard cabinet or in a junction box with electric power wires.
2. You may have low voltage and electric power wires in the same raceway, box, and enclosure if the wires are separated by a physical barrier. Example: you may place a door bell transformer and Class 2 wires in the same cabinet with electric power wires if the door bell transformer and Class 2 wires are separated from the electric power wires by a physical barrier.
3. You may have low voltage and electric power wires in the same cabinet or box when the electric power wires are intended to supply power to the low voltage power source. Example: you may connect #14 AWG electric power wires and #18 AWG door bell transformer wires in the same junction box.
4. Separate low voltage and electric power wires by at least (≥) 2 inches. You may run low voltage and electric power wires near each other in a bundle and through the same bored holes in joists and studs if either all the low voltage wires or all the electric power wires are contained in metal or nonmetallic sheathing or raceways. Example: you may run sheathed NM cable and sheathed thermostat cable near each other in a bundle and through the same bored holes in joists and studs if the sheathing of the NM cable and thermostat cable remains intact over the entire length of the run.

Low Voltage Wire Installation and Support

1. Use building structural members such as joists and studs to support low voltage wires.
2. Do not use electrical conduit, tubing, raceways, or cables to support low voltage wires. This restriction does not apply if the raceway contains wires that supply power to the equipment associated with the Class 2 wires. Example: you may use a raceway containing electric power wires for a furnace or condenser to support the thermostat wires.
3. Install low voltage wires so that they will not be damaged by normal building use.
4. Install low voltage wires so they will not restrict access to service and maintenance panels including suspended ceiling panels. Example: do not run low voltage wires directly on top of suspended ceiling panels. Support the wires on the joists that support the suspended ceiling panels. Example: do not run thermostat wires so that they interfere with access to furnace maintenance panels.

Appendix E

MANUFACTURED HOMES

Manufactured Home Definition

Manufactured home A manufactured home (also called a mobile home) is a structure that is built in a factory and transported on wheels to its destination, usually in one or two sections. Work at the home site usually begins by providing a foundation to support the home and anchorage to secure it during high winds and seismic activity. Other work includes installing water supply and drainage pipes, installing HVAC ductwork that is not built into the structure, and connecting utilities such as electricity and gas.

Application of the Material in this Appendix

Design and construction of manufactured homes is governed by the Federal Department of Housing and Urban Development (HUD). The IRC does not govern components in and on the home such as the home's undercarriage, framing materials and methods, and plumbing, electrical, and HVAC fixtures and equipment within the home. The IRC governs the site work involved in placing the home on a lot and governs construction, repair, and alteration of connection to services such as water and sewer (or septic), gas, and electricity. This work includes the home's foundation, components of the plumbing, HVAC, and electrical, systems outside the home, connection of utility services to the home, and any accessory structures, such as stairs, ramps, porches, and storage buildings near the home. This appendix does not apply in a jurisdiction unless it is specifically adopted. Verify adoption of this appendix with the local building official.

Manufactured Home Use

1. Use a manufactured home as a single family dwelling. Using a manufactured home as a multiple family dwelling or commercial structure will usually require approval by the building official and may require zoning approval.

Manufactured Home Foundations

1. Provide a foundation for manufactured homes as specified by the home's manufacturer, or by an approved design professional, or by the HUD Permanent Foundations for Manufactured Housing (1996), or by prescriptive provisions of the IRC. Use the most stringent specifications if a conflict exists between different foundation specifications.
2. You may use the prescriptive foundation provisions of the IRC (E600) only if specifically approved by the building official.

Manufactured Home Footings and Piers (E600)

1. Place footings and piers on stable and undisturbed soil. Use engineered (compacted) fill of at least (≥) 1,000 psi if fill dirt is required.
2. Use one or more of the following as piers to support manufactured homes: (a) prefabricated load-bearing devices such as steel jacks, (b) concrete masonry units (concrete blocks) cemented using Type M, S, or N mortar, (c) at least (≥) 2,500 psi cast-in-place concrete.
3. Use concrete block piers at least (≥) 8 inch by 16 inch for piers not more than (≤) 36 inches tall. Place the cores of concrete block piers vertically. Cap concrete block piers with at least (≥) 4 inch solid cap blocks. Place the piers at right angles to the frame members they support.

Manufactured Home Anchors and Tie-Down Hardware

1. Install anchors and tie-down hardware according to the instructions from the home's manufacturer and the manufacturer of the anchoring or tie-down hardware.

Manufactured Home Accessory Structures

1. Do not attach accessory structures to a manufactured home unless approved by the building official. Accessory structures include porch and patio roofs, stairs, ramps, and storage sheds. Manufactured homes may not be designed to carry the additional load imposed by accessory structures. Waterproofing and flashing accessory structures is often an issue when attaching accessory structures.

Manufactured Home Crawl Spaces

1. Provide an access opening to the crawl space at least (≥) 18 inches by 18 inches and at least (≥) 3 square feet total area.
2. Locate the crawl space access so that water and sewer connections in the crawl space are accessible.
3. Provide at least (≥) 12 inches clearance between the ground and the lowest point of the home's floor framing system. Provide clearance to wood framing members as specified in Chapter 3.
4. Ventilate the crawl space as required in Chapter 4 and as required in Chapter 24 if combustion air is drawn from the crawl space.

Appendix F

RADON CONTROL

Radon Definition

Radon Radon is a naturally occurring radioactive gas that cannot be detected by any human senses. It is believed to be a cause of cancer, particularly lung cancer.

Application of the Material in this Appendix

Building officials in areas believed to be at high risk of Radon levels greater than (>) 4 picocurries per liter may require Radon control measures in new homes. While Radon can occur anywhere, it is more likely in the following states and metropolitan areas: Colorado, Idaho, Illinois, Indiana, Iowa, Kansas, Kentucky, Minnesota, Montana, Nebraska, New York, North Dakota, Ohio, Pennsylvania, South Dakota, Tennessee, Virginia, West Virginia, Wisconsin, Wyoming, Atlanta, Washington, DC. Verify with the local building official what, if any, Radon control measures are required in your area.

Radon Control General Discussion

Radon control involves two basic tactics: (1) seal all openings between the foundation and the living area, and (2) provide a means to collect and vent Radon gas from under the home. Radon control is relatively easy and inexpensive to install when a home is being built. It is far more difficult and expensive to install afterwards. Home buyers in Radon areas are now routinely requesting Radon tests. Homes that test high for Radon may be difficult to sell and may require expensive Radon control retrofitting. If you live in a Radon prone area, it may be wise to install Radon control measures even if not required by the local building official.

Radon Control Measures Under Concrete Slabs in Slab and Basement Foundations

1. Install at least (≥) 4 inches of clean stone between ¼ inch and 2 inches in size under basements and living areas. You may use other proven methods such as layers of sand and geotextile fabric.
2. Install 6-mil polyethylene sheeting over the stone. Lap joints in the sheeting at least (≥) 12 inches. Install the sheeting close around penetrations such as plumbing pipes. Seal all tears and punctures in the sheeting.
3. Install the stone and sheeting before pouring the concrete.
4. You are usually not required to install stone and sheeting under garages and exterior concrete slabs for carports, patios, walkways, and similar areas.

Sealing Penetrations of Slab and Basement Foundations

1. Seal penetrations of the concrete slab in slab-on-grade and basement foundations. Sealing

may consist of polyurethane caulk, gaskets, or other appropriate sealant applied according to manufacturer's instructions. Penetrations include: (a) plumbing pipes for water supply and drains, and (b) electrical raceways, and (c) joints between basement walls and the basement floor, and (d) control, isolation, and similar joints in concrete, and (e) condensate drains, and (f) sump pits.

Sealing Foundation Walls

1. Install a course of solid masonry or a course of hollow masonry grouted solid at or above finished grade level when using hollow masonry units for the foundation walls. This is usually done at the final masonry course. Install this solid masonry at the top course of any brick ledge made of hollow masonry. This prevents air movement from the foundation into living spaces.
2. Seal all penetrations of foundation walls such as water supply pipes and building sewer pipes.
3. Seal cracks in the foundation walls.

Sealing HVAC Equipment and Ducts in Crawl Spaces

1. Seal air handling units located in crawl spaces to prevent air from being drawn into the unit. Sealing may consist of foil tape or gaskets supplied by the air handling unit manufacturer.
2. Seal all ducts in the crawl space. Sealing the return ducts and plenum is particularly important.

Sealing Crawl Space Openings to Living Areas

1. Use caulk, approved weather stripping, or approved gaskets to seal openings between the crawl space and living areas. This includes penetrations for plumbing pipes and electrical cables and raceways and includes doors or hatches between crawl spaces and basements.

Crawl Space Ventilation System

1. Install a passive ventilation system in crawl spaces over living areas.
2. Install at least (≥) 6-mil polyethylene sheeting covering the entire crawl space area. Lap joints in the sheeting at least (≥) 12 inches. While not specifically required, it is good practice seal joints in the sheeting and to turn the sheeting up the crawl space walls and secure it to the walls.
3. Connect a 3 inch or 4 inch ABS or PVC pipe to a plumbing tee under the sheeting. Seal the sheeting tight around the tee and pipe. Run the pipe through the building to the roof. Terminate the pipe at least (≥) 12 inches above the roof and at least (≥) 10 feet from any window or other air intake opening of the building or of any nearby building. The 10 feet separation is not required if the window or opening is at least (≥) 2 feet below the pipe termination.

Concrete Slab Ventilation System

1. Install a passive ventilation system under the concrete slab of basements and slab-on-grade foundations.

Appendix F : Radon Control

2. Connect a 3 inch ABS or PVC pipe to one of the following:
   a) a plumbing tee inserted into the stone under the polyethylene sheeting, or
   b) an interior foundation drainage system, if one exists, or
   c) a sealed sump if the sump is connected to the sub-slab stone or to the interior foundation drainage system.
3. Do one of these before pouring the concrete. Seal around the pipe. Run the pipe through the building to the roof. Terminate the pipe at least (≥) 12 inches above the roof and at least (≥) 10 feet from any window or other air intake opening of the building or of any nearby building. The 10 feet separation is not required if the window or opening is at least (≥) 2 feet below the pipe termination.

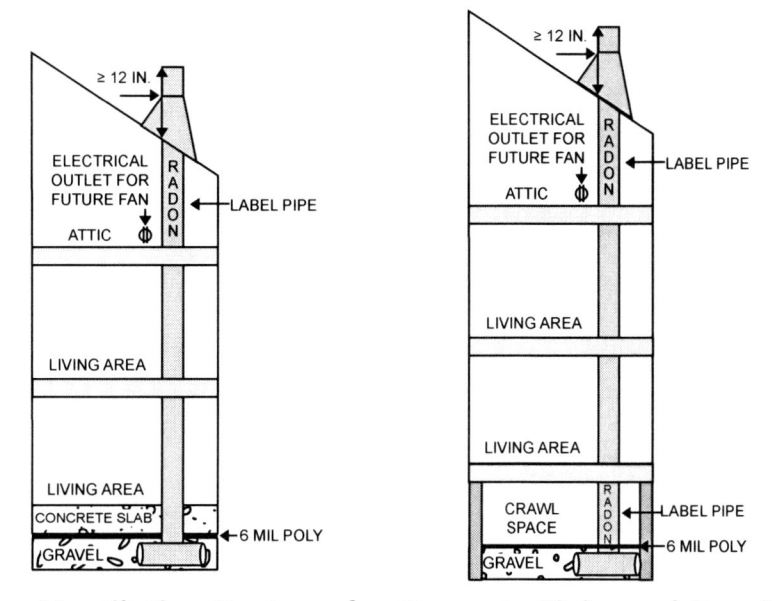

Passive Radon Ventilation Systems for Concrete Slabs and Crawl Spaces (F-0)
Figure F-1

Ventilation of Different Foundation Areas

1. Provide each foundation area with its own ventilation system when the foundation is separated by footings or other barriers or when the home has different foundation types. Example: an interior footing or thickened slab divides the area under a slab into two separate spaces. Provide each space with its own ventilation pipe system. Example: a split level home has a slab-on-grade foundation on the lower level and a crawl space under the upper levels. Provide a separate ventilation pipe system for each foundation type.
2. You may connect the different vent pipes together before they penetrate the roof or you may run each vent pipe separately through the roof.

Ventilation Pipe Requirements

1. Install ventilation pipes so that any water entering the pipe drains to the area under the polyethylene sheeting.
2. Leave the ventilation pipe accessible in the attic or at some other point for possible future installation of a ventilation fan.

3. Provide an accessible electrical connection at the ventilation pipe access for possible future installation of a ventilation fan.
4. Label accessible parts of the ventilation pipe with at least (≥) one label on each floor and attic that reads: "Radon Reduction System." This label is usually necessary only in the attic, basement, and crawl space. The Radon ventilation pipe is usually concealed in a chase through living areas.

Appendix G

SWIMMING POOL AND SPA BARRIERS AND ACCESS CONTROL

Application of the Material in this Appendix

This appendix applies to access barriers and entrapment provisions designed to reduce accidental drowning in swimming pools, spas, and hot tubs located at one and two family dwellings. States such as Arizona, California, Texas, and Florida and many cities have different requirements. Verify requirements with your local building official.

Swimming Pool Definition - Barrier and Access Control

For purposes of barrier and access control, a swimming pool is a body of water designed for recreational use that is more than (>) 24 inches deep. This includes swimming pools, spas, and hot tubs located indoors and outdoors. These structures may be in-ground, above-ground, temporary, or permanent. Note that some jurisdictions may place barrier and access controls on other bodies of water, such as fish ponds, reflecting pools, and fountains depending on their depth. Verify requirements with your local building official before beginning work on any water containing feature.

Outdoor Swimming Pool Barriers

1. Install a barrier around an outdoor swimming pool with the top of the barrier at least (≥) 48 inches above grade measured on the side facing away from the pool. Restrict the opening at the bottom of the barrier to not more than (≤) 2 inches measured on the side facing away from the pool. Restrict the size of any openings in the barrier so that a 4 inch sphere cannot pass.

2. Do not provide indentations or protrusions on solid barriers that could be used as hand or foot holds for climbing. Normal construction tolerances for the barrier material and tooled masonry joints are acceptable.

3. Place horizontal members of a barrier (such as a wood or iron fence) on the side facing the pool if the tops of the horizontal members are less than (<) 45 inches apart. Space the vertical members not more than (≤) 1 ¾ inches apart.

4. Place horizontal members of a barrier (such as a wood or iron fence) on either side of the pool if the tops of the horizontal members are at least (≥) 45 inches apart and if space between vertical members is not more than (≤) 4 inches.

5. You may use chain link fence as a barrier if the mesh openings are not more than (≤) 2 ¼ inches.

6. You may use lattice and similar diagonal material as a barrier if the openings are not more than (≤) 1 ¾ inches.
7. You may install the barrier for an above-ground pool on the ground around the pool or on the pool structure. You may use the walls of the pool itself as the barrier if the walls are at least (≥) 48 inches above grade at all points around the pool. Restrict the space between the bottom of the pool structure and the bottom of the barrier installed on the pool structure to not more than (≤) 4 inches.
8. Do not place objects near the barrier such as benches, planters, trees, or similar objects that could be used to help someone climb the barrier.

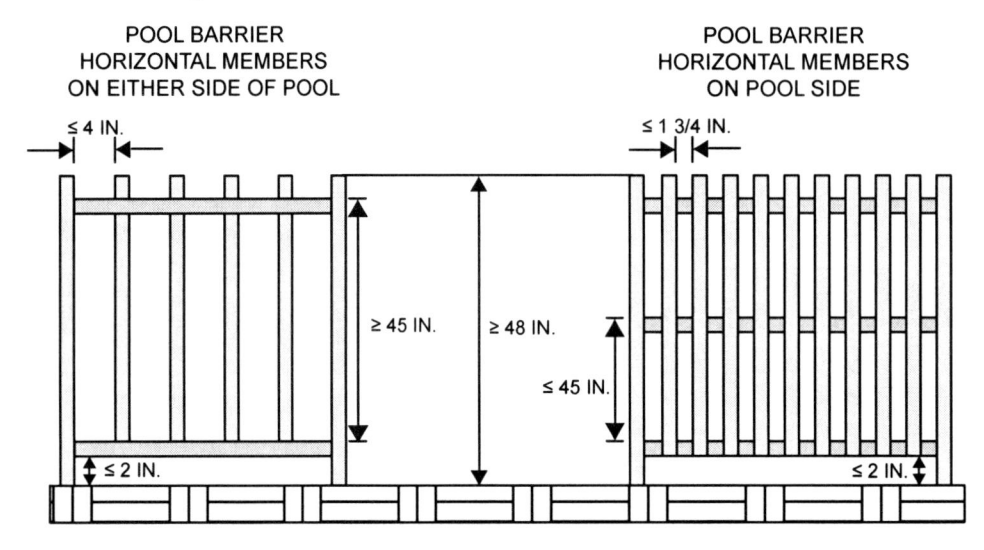

Pool Barriers (G-0)
Figure G-1

Gates in Pool Barriers

1. Install gates in pool barriers that comply with all pool barrier requirements for height and member spacing.
2. Install pedestrian access gates that swing away from the pool.
3. Equip pedestrian access gates with self-latching and self-closing devices.
4. Equip gates other than pedestrian access gates (such as double gates for vehicle access) with a self-latching device.
5. Locate the release mechanism of the self-latching device at least (≥) 54 inches from the bottom of the gate or locate the release mechanism at least (≥) 3 inches below the top of the gate and have no openings in the gate or barrier more than (>) ½ inch wide within at least (≥) 18 inches of the release mechanism.

House Door Barriers

1. Provide at least one of the following if doors from the house allow pool access: (a) a powered pool safety cover that complies with ASTM F 1346, or (b) an audible alarm that complies with UL 2017 on all doors that provide pool access, or (c) self-closing and self-latching devices approved by the building official all on doors that allow pool access.

House Barriers Best Practice

Open windows that provide direct access to a pool are also a hazard. While not required by the IRC barrier requirements, equipping windows with latches at least 54 inches above the floor or limiting the window opening to not more than 4 inches is a wise precaution and is required by some local jurisdictions. Beware of pet doors. Small children can crawl out these openings and into the pool area.

Above Ground Pool Barrier

1. Use one of the following methods to secure access to an above-ground pool if the pool itself is the barrier (height of the pool deck is at least (≥) 48 inches) or if the barrier is on the pool deck: (a) install the access ladder or steps so that it can be locked, secured, or removed to prevent access, or (b) surround the ladder or steps with one of the previously described barriers.

Indoor Swimming Pool Barriers

1. Equip all doors that allow access to an indoor swimming pool with one of the barriers listed in House Door Barriers.

Spa and Hot Tub Barrier Exception

1. You are not required to provide an access barrier for spas and hot tubs that have a safety cover than complies with ASTM F 1346.

Entrapment Protection

1. Provide entrapment protection on pool drains and other suction fittings that complies with ANSI/APSP 7.

Entrapment Protection Best Practice

Entrapment protection is not required for existing pool and spas; however, anti-entrapment drain covers are inexpensive and easy to install. It is wise to replace the flat drain covers in older pools with new anti-entrapment covers, particularly if children use the pool.

SATELLITE DISHES AND TELEVISION AND RADIO ANTENNAS (NEC ARTICLE 810)

Source of this Material

The material in this section is based on the National Electrical Code (NEC)®, 2005 Edition. Most local building officials use the NEC as a supplement to or in place of the IRC when dealing with residential electrical issues. The IRC does not address antennas, so the NEC is usually the appropriate source for rules regarding installation of antennas and the wires that connect them to the receiving equipment. Verify with the local building official which version, if any, of the NEC is adopted in your area.

Application of the Material in this Article

This article applies to receiving antennas such as satellite dishes, and traditional radio and television antennas. It does not apply to cable TV (see Article 820) system wiring and it does not apply to network powered broadband communication system wiring (see Article 830). This article also applies to radio transmission antennas and towers such as those used by amateur radio operators.

Antenna Wire and Coaxial Cable Description

Most wires used to connect receiving antennas and equipment are either coaxial cable or twin lead. Coaxial cable is usually round with a black or white outer jacket covering a braided shield (grounding conductor) and a white dielectric layer covering a copper center conductor. It is the most common wire used in modern television systems and broadband communication systems. Twin lead is a thin flat cable consisting of two small wires separated by a non-conducting material. It is usually some shade of brown in color. It is rarely used today and is most likely found on older television antennas.

Antenna Prohibited Installation Locations

1. Do not attach or install antennas on electric service entrance masts, or on poles that support electric power wires, or on plumbing vent pipes, or on furnace vent pipes.
2. Provide clearance between antennas and masts and electric power wires so that if the antenna falls, it is unlikely to fall on the electric power wires.

Antenna Wire and Cable Clearance to Electric Power Wires

1. Do not install outdoor, above-ground antenna wires and cables so that they cross over electric power wires. Avoid, if possible, installing outdoor, above ground antenna wires that

cross under electric power wires. Electric power wires include wires on overhead power poles, overhead service drop wires, and any electric power wires running between buildings.
2. Provide at least (≥) 2 feet clearance between outdoor, above-ground antenna wires and cables and electric power lines that can swing freely.
3. Provide at least (≥) 4 inches between outdoor antenna wires and cables and most residential electric power wires when both are secured so that they cannot move.
4. Provide at least (≥) 12 inches clearance between underground antenna wires and underground cables and electric power wires.
5. Provide at least (≥) 2 inches clearance between indoor antenna wires and cables and indoor electric power wires.

Lightning Arrestors

1. Install a lightning arrestor on each conductor of antenna twin lead. Ground the lightning arrestor as described below.
2. You are not required to install a lightning arrestor on coaxial cable if it is properly grounded.

Grounding Antennas, Masts, Wires, and Cables

1. Install a ground wire between metal antenna masts, towers, and support poles and an approved grounding point. Metal antenna masts include the short metal mast commonly found on satellite dishes.
2. Install a ground wire between the coaxial cable shield and an approved grounding point. <u>You must ground both the coaxial cable shield and any metal antenna mast</u>.
3. Use at least (≥) #10 AWG copper wire or #17 copper clad steel wire as the grounding wire. You may use a #8 AWG aluminum grounding wire if it is not in contact with masonry, and is not installed in a corrosive environment, and is installed at least (≥) 18 inches above the ground at all points including at the connection to the grounding point. Insulation is not required on the grounding wire. You may use solid or stranded grounding wire.
4. Run the grounding wire in as straight a line as possible from where the antenna wire or cable enters the building to an approved grounding point near where the antenna wire or cable enters the building.
5. Connect the grounding wire(s) to one of the following approved grounding points:
    a) the building electrical system grounding electrode, grounding electrode wire, or other metal part of the building electrical grounding electrode system such as a grounding electrode system metal enclosure, or
    b) a metal water service pipe not more than (≤) 5 feet from where the water service pipe enters the building, or
    c) the service equipment cabinet or metal service equipment raceway, or
    d) the other system bonding connection described in the IRC.
6. Do not connect the antenna mast or coaxial cable to its own ground rod unless both of the following are true: (a) none of the approved grounding points exists (extremely rare), and

552   Everybody's Building Code

(b) the separate ground rod is bonded to the building electrical system as described in the IRC.

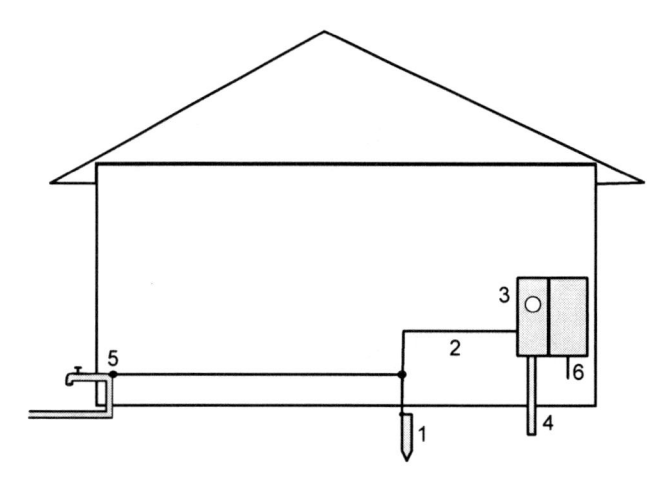

1 ROD GROUNDING ELECTRODE
2 GROUNDING ELECTRODE WIRE
3 METAL SERVICE EQUIPMENT CABINET
4 METAL SERVICE EQUIPMENT RACEWAY
5 MEAL WATER SERVICE PIPE GROUNDING ELECTRODE
6 EXPOSED BONDING WIRE

Approved Grounding Connection Points for Cable TV and Other Systems (NEC 810-1)
Figure NEC 810-1

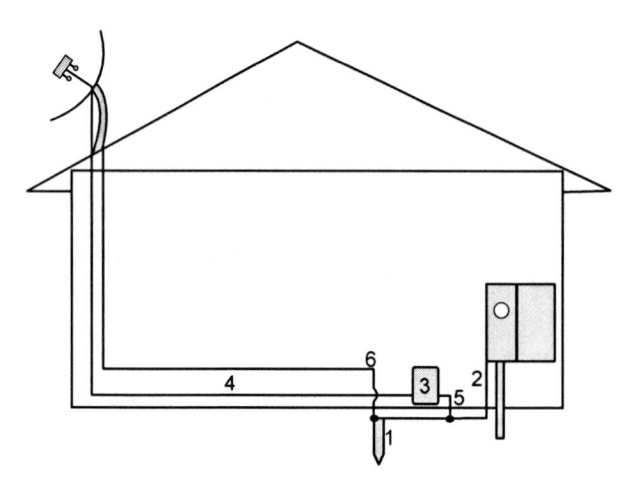

1 GROUNDING ELECTRODE
2 GROUNDING ELECTRODE WIRE
3 COAXIAL CABLE SPLITTER OR OTHER SATELLITE INTERFACE BOX
4 SATELLITE ANTENNA COAXIAL CABLE
5 COAXIAL CABLE GROUNDING WIRE
6 ANTENNA MAST GROUNDING WIRE

Typical Satellite Dish Antenna and Coaxial Cable Grounding (NEC 810-2)
Figure NEC 810-2

Grounding Wire Connection to the Grounding Point

1. Use a listed clamp, listed pressure connector, or other listed means to connect the grounding wire to the grounding point.

2. Install the listed connector so that it is both physically and electrically connected to the grounding point. This means removing paint, lacquer, rust, and other non-conductive material before attaching the listed connector to the grounding point.
3. Connect not more than one grounding wire to a listed connector unless the connector is listed to accept more than one wire.
4. Use a listed connector that is compatible with both the grounding point and the grounding wire material. Example: an iron or steel clamp is not compatible with a copper water pipe. Both materials will corrode over time.

CABLE TELEVISION SYSTEM WIRING – RESIDENTIAL (NEC ARTICLE 820)

Source of this Material

The material in this section is based on the National Electrical Code (NEC) ®, 2005 Edition. Most local building officials use the NEC as a supplement to or in place of the IRC when dealing with residential electrical issues. The IRC does not address cable television systems, so the NEC is usually the appropriate source for rules regarding wiring for these systems. Verify with the local building official which version, if any, of the NEC is adopted in your area.

Application of the Material in this Article

This article applies to cable television system wiring. These systems usually deliver only television services. They operate at up to 60 volts. This article does not apply to broadband communication system wiring (see Article 830) and it does not apply to satellite TV antenna wiring (see Article 810). Some very new communication systems use fiber-optic cables. This article does not apply to fiber-optic cables.

Coaxial Cable Description

Most cable television systems and equipment use coaxial cables. Coaxial cable is usually round with a black or white outer jacket covering a braided shield (grounding conductor) and a white dielectric layer covering a copper center conductor.

Television Cable Clearance to Electric Power Wires

1. Install outdoor, above-ground television cables above electric power wires whenever possible.
2. Avoid installing outdoor, above-ground television cables near electric power wires that can swing freely. Electric power wires include wires on overhead power poles, overhead service drop wires, and any electric power wires running between buildings. Provide at least (≥) 12 inches clearance between outdoor, above-ground television cables and electric power lines that can swing freely. Increase clearance to at least (≥) 40 inches at the power pole.
3. Provide at least (≥) 4 inches between outdoor television cables and most residential electric power wires when both are secured so that they cannot move.

Overhead Television Cable Clearance Above Roofs

1. Provide at least (≥) 8 feet vertical clearance between television cables and most low slope roofs.

2. Provide at least (≥) 18 inches vertical clearance between television cables and roof overhangs if not more than (≤) 4 feet of cable passes over the roof and if the cable terminates at a through-the-roof raceway or support. This is similar to clearances allowed for overhead service drop wires.
3. Provide at least (≥) 3 feet vertical clearance between television cables and roofs with a slope of at least (≥) 4 inches in 12 inches.

Grounding Television Cables

1. Install an insulated copper grounding wire at least (≥) #14 AWG between the coaxial cable shield and an approved grounding point.
2. Run the grounding wire in as straight a line as possible from where the television cable enters the building to an approved grounding point near where the television cable enters the building.
3. Limit the length of the grounding wire to not more than (≤) 20 feet. If where the television cable enters the building is more than (>) 20 feet from an approved grounding point, you may install at least (≥) an 8 feet long ground rod near where the television cable enters the building and bond the ground rod to the electrical service grounding system using at least (≥) #6 AWG copper wire.
4. Connect the copper grounding wire to one of the following approved grounding points:
    a) the building electrical system grounding electrode, grounding electrode wire, or other metal part of the building electrical grounding electrode system such as a grounding electrode system metal enclosure, or
    b) a metal water service pipe not more than (≤) 5 feet from where the water service pipe enters the building, or
    c) the service equipment cabinet or metal service equipment raceway, or
    d) the other system bonding connection described in the IRC.
5. Do not connect the television cable to its own ground rod unless both of the following are true: (a) no approved grounding point exists within (≤) 20 feet from where the coaxial cable enters the building (extremely rare), and (b) the separate ground rod is bonded to the building electrical system as described in the IRC.

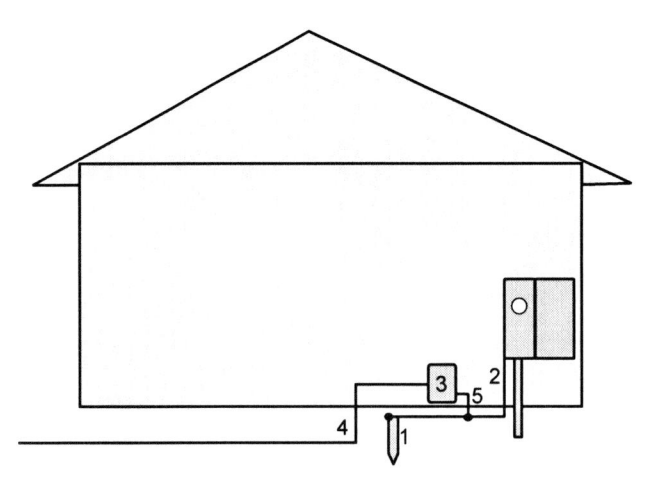

1 GROUNDING ELECTRODE
2 GROUNDING ELECTRODE WIRE
3 CABLE TV OR BROADBAND NETWORK INTERFACE BOX
4 CABLE TV OR BROADBAND COAXIAL CABLE
5 CABLE TV OR BROADBAND GROUNDING WIRE ≤ 20 FT. LONG

Typical Cable TV and Broadband Coaxial Cable Grounding (NEC 820-0)
Figure NEC 820-1

Grounding Wire Connection to the Grounding Point

1. Use a listed clamp, listed pressure connector, or other listed means to connect the grounding wire to the grounding point.
2. Install the listed connector so that it is both physically and electrically connected to the grounding point. This means that paint, lacquer, rust, and other non-conductive material must be removed before attaching the listed connector to the grounding point.
3. Connect not more than one grounding wire to a listed connector unless the connector is listed to accept more than one wire.
4. Use a listed connector that is compatible with both the grounding point and the grounding wire material. Example: an iron or steel clamp is not compatible with a copper water pipe. Both materials will corrode over time.

Television Cable and Electric Power Wire Separation

1. Do not run television cables in the same conduit, tubing, raceway, junction and device box, or enclosure with electric power wires unless one of two exceptions exist. Example: do not run NM cable and television cables in the same conduit.
2. You may have television cables and electric power wires in the same raceway, box, and enclosure if the wires are separated by a permanent physical barrier. Example: you may place television cables in the same cabinet with NM cables or wires if the television cables are separated from the NM cables or wires by a permanent physical barrier.
3. You may install television cables and electric power wires in the same cabinet or box when the electric power wires are intended to supply power to the television cable system.
4. Separate indoor television cables and electric power wires by at least (≥) 2 inches. You may run television cables and electric power wires near each other in a bundle and through the same bored holes in joists and studs if all the electric power wires are contained in metal or

nonmetallic sheathing or raceways. Example: you may run sheathed NM cable and television cables near each other in a bundle and through the same bored holes in joists and studs if the sheathing of the NM cable remains intact over the entire length of the run.

Television Cable Separation from Low Voltage and Communication Wires

1. You may run television cables in the same conduit, tubing, raceways, cabinets, and enclosures with low voltage cables, telephone and computer cables, fiber optic cables, and low power broadband cables if all cables are in their original jackets. Example: you may run television cable in the same conduit with door bell wires and thermostat wires, and telephone wires if all wires are in the factory-supplied jackets.

Television Cable Installation and Support

1. Use building structural members such as joists and studs to support television cables.
2. Use television cables approved for use in television systems. Verify with the television service provider the types of cable recommended for use with the television system. Refer to NEC Table 820.154 for approved cable types.

BROADBAND COMMUNICATION WIRING – RESIDENTIAL (NEC ARTICLE 830)

Source of this Material

The material in this section is based on the National Electrical Code (NEC) ®, 2005 Edition. Most local building officials use the NEC as a supplement to or in place of the IRC when dealing with residential electrical issues. The IRC does not address broadband communication systems, so the NEC is usually the appropriate source for rules regarding wiring for these systems. Verify with the local building official which version, if any, of the NEC is adopted in your area.

Application of the Material in this Article

This article applies to network powered broadband communication system wiring. These systems usually deliver television, telephone, internet, and similar services. They operate at up to 150 volts and 100 watts. This article does not apply to standard cable TV system wiring (see Article 820) and it does not apply to satellite TV antenna wiring (see Article 810). Some new communication systems use fiber-optic cables. This article does not apply to fiber-optic cables.

Broadband Cable Description

Most broadband communication systems and equipment use coaxial cables. Coaxial cable is usually round with a black or white outer jacket covering a braided shield (grounding conductor) and a white dielectric layer covering a copper center conductor.

Low and Medium Power Broadband System Definition

Low power broadband systems operate at not more than ($\leq$) 100 volts and medium power systems operate at not more than ($\leq$) 150 volts. Verify voltage rating and system classification with the broadband service provider. The operating voltage of the system affects how the cables are installed.

Overhead Broadband Cable Clearance to Electric Power Wires

1. Install outdoor, above-ground broadband communication cables above electric power wires whenever possible.
2. Avoid installing outdoor, above-ground broadband communication cables near electric power wires that can swing freely. Electric power wires include wires on overhead power poles, overhead service drop wires, and any electric power wires running between buildings. Provide at least ($\geq$) 12 inches clearance between outdoor, above-ground broadband communication cables and electric power lines that can swing freely. Increase clearance to at least ($\geq$) 40 inches at the power pole.

3. Provide at least (≥) 4 inches between outdoor broadband communication cables and most residential electric power wires when both are secured so that they cannot move.

Overhead Broadband Cable Clearance Above Ground

1. Measure the vertical clearance between overhead broadband cables and the ground, walkway, driveway, or street beginning at the lowest point hanging point of the cables and ending at the surface under the lowest point.
2. Provide at least (≥) 9.5 feet vertical clearance between broadband cables and finished grade, sidewalks, or platforms accessed by pedestrians only.
3. Provide at least (≥) 11.5 feet vertical clearance between overhead broadband cables and residential property and driveways.
4. Provide at least (≥) 15.5 feet vertical clearance between overhead broadband cables and public streets, alleys, roads, or parking areas subject to truck traffic.
5. Provide the same clearance between overhead broadband cables and swimming pools, spas, and hot tubs as for electrical wires.

Overhead Broadband Cable Clearance Above Roofs

1. Provide at least (≥) 8 feet vertical clearance between broadband cables and most low slope roofs.
2. Provide at least (≥) 18 inches vertical clearance between broadband cables and roof overhangs if not more than (≤) 4 feet of cable passes over the roof and if the cable terminates at a through-the-roof raceway or support. This is similar to clearances allowed for service drop wires.
3. Provide at least (≥) 3 feet vertical clearance between broadband cables and roofs with a slope of at least (≥) 4 inches in 12 inches.

Broadband Cable Burial Depth

1. Bury broadband cables at least (≥) 18 inches deep when the cables are not covered by concrete or enclosed in conduit or other raceways. You may reduce the depth to at least (≥) 12 inches when the cables are under concrete residential driveways, patios, and similar concrete slabs. Refer to the NEC for burial depths when the cables are enclosed in conduit or raceways.

Grounding Broadband Cables

1. Install an insulated copper grounding wire at least (≥) #14 AWG between the coaxial cable shield and an approved grounding point.
2. Run the grounding wire in as straight a line as possible from where the broadband cable enters the building to an approved grounding point near where the broadband cable enters the building.
3. Limit the length of the grounding wire to not more than (≤) 20 feet. If where the broadband cable enters the building is more than (>) 20 feet from an approved grounding point, you may install at least (≥) a 5 feet long ground rod near where the broadband cable enters the

building and bond the ground rod to the electrical service grounding system using at least (≥) #6 AWG copper wire.
4. Connect the copper grounding wire to one of the following approved grounding points:
    a) the building electrical system grounding electrode, grounding electrode wire, or other metal part of the building electrical grounding electrode system such as a grounding electrode system metal enclosure, or
    b) a metal water service pipe not more than (≤) 5 feet from where the water service pipe enters the building, or
    c) the service equipment cabinet or metal service equipment raceway, or
    d) the other system bonding connection described in the IRC.
5. Do not connect the broadband cable to its own ground rod unless both of the following are true: (a) no approved grounding point exists within (≤) 20 feet from where the coaxial cable enters the building (extremely rare), and (b) the separate ground rod is bonded to the building electrical system as described in the IRC.

Grounding Wire Connection to the Grounding Point

1. Use a listed clamp, listed pressure connector, or other listed means to connect the grounding wire to the grounding point.
2. Install the listed connector so that it is both physically and electrically connected to the grounding point. This means that paint, lacquer, rust, and other non-conductive material must be removed before attaching the listed connector to the grounding point.
3. Connect not more than one grounding wire to a listed connector unless the connector is listed to accept more than one wire.
4. Use a listed connector that is compatible with both the grounding point and the grounding wire material. Example: an iron or steel clamp is not compatible with a copper water pipe. Both materials will corrode over time.

Broadband Cable and Electric Power Wire Separation

1. Do not run low power or medium power broadband cables in the same conduit, tubing, raceway, junction and device box, or enclosure with electric power wires unless one of two exceptions exist. Example: do not run NM cable and any broadband cables in the same conduit.
2. You may have low power and medium power broadband cables and electric power wires in the same raceway, box, and enclosure if the wires are separated by a permanent physical barrier. Example: you may place broadband cables in the same cabinet with NM cables or wires if the broadband cables are separated from the NM cables or wires by a permanent physical barrier.
3. You may install low power and medium power broadband cables and electric power wires in the same cabinet or box when the electric power wires are intended to supply power to the broadband cable system.
4. Separate indoor broadband cables and electric power wires by at least (≥) 2 inches. You may run broadband cables and electric power wires near each other in a bundle and through the same bored holes in joists and studs if all the electric power wires are contained in metal or

nonmetallic sheathing or raceways. Example: you may run sheathed NM cable and broadband cables near each other in a bundle and through the same bored holes in joists and studs if the sheathing of the NM cable remains intact over the entire length of the run.

Low Power Broadband Cable Separation from Low Voltage and Communication Wires

1. You may run low power broadband cables in the same conduit, tubing, raceways, cabinets, and enclosures with low voltage cables, telephone and computer cables, fiber optic cables, and cable TV cables if all cables are in their original jackets. Example: you may run low power broadband cable in the same conduit with door bell wires and thermostat wires, and telephone wires if all wires are in the factory-supplied jackets.

Medium Power Broadband Cable Separation from Low Voltage and Communication Wires

1. You may NOT run medium power broadband cables in the same conduit, tubing, raceways, cabinets, and enclosures with low voltage cables, telephone and computer cables, fiber optic cables, and cable TV cables.

Broadband Cable Installation and Support

1. Use building structural members such as joists and studs to support broadband cables.
2. Use broadband cables approved for use in broadband systems. Verify the types of cable recommended for use with the broadband system with the broadband service provider. Refer to the NEC for approved cable types.

SOLAR PHOTOVOLTAIC SYSTEMS (NEC ARTICLE 690)

Source of this Material

The material in this section is based on the National Electrical Code (NEC) ®, 2005 Edition. Most local building officials use the NEC as a supplement to or in place of the IRC when dealing with residential electrical issues. The IRC does not address solar photovoltaic systems, so the NEC is usually the appropriate source for rules governing these systems. Verify with the local building official which version, if any, of the NEC is adopted in your area.

Limitations of the Material in this Chapter

This chapter contains the provisions that most readers will need when installing a stand-alone or grid tie solar photovoltaic (PV) system using commercially manufactured components that are intended for PV systems and installed by an experienced contractor. Readers who attempt to assemble a PV system using components purchased over the internet and from similar sources should review NEC Article 690 for possible additional requirements. Readers installing grid tie PV should also contact their electric utility for possible additional requirements.

Photovoltaic System Types

In its most basic form, a PV system is a collection of individual silicon-based solar cells that are assembled into modules that are in turn assembled into one or more arrays that produce direct current (DC) voltage when exposed to light. The PV system may use traditional stand-alone modules or it may use new thin film technology that is integrated into building materials, such as shingles. Thin film systems are not yet common. Using few other components, the array provides DC voltage to run DC compatible lights and equipment during the day and to charge batteries for use at night and on cloudy days. Obviously, this simple system is practical only for survivalists or for remote rustic buildings. Most PV systems are more complex.

The next level of complexity is a stand-alone PV system. In this system, most of the DC voltage from the array is passed through a device called an inverter that changes the DC voltage into alternating current (AC) voltage. The remaining DC voltage charges the batteries. A large enough system can power an average home that does not have high demand appliances like air conditioning and electric cooking. These systems are financially attractive when the building is located far from the electric grid.

The most common PV system is a grid tie system; also know as a utility-interactive system. Grid tie PV systems come in two forms. In one form, the PV system supplements power from the grid. If power from the PV system is greater than the power that building is using, the PV system may feed the power into the utility's grid. Utilities will usually pay for the power supplied to the grid, but the amount of the payment varies by utility.

It is important to note that a grid tie PV system automatically shuts down (in most configurations) when grid power is interrupted. This prevents a potentially dangerous power back feed condition that could injure workers who are trying to restore grid power. Thus, this form of grid tie PV system usually provides no power when grid power is down. The NEC allows a grid tie PV system to operate in stand-alone mode if it supplies circuits that are disconnected from the grid. A grid tie/stand-alone configuration requires sophisticated (read expensive) automatic relays and different building wiring and as such is not common in residential applications.

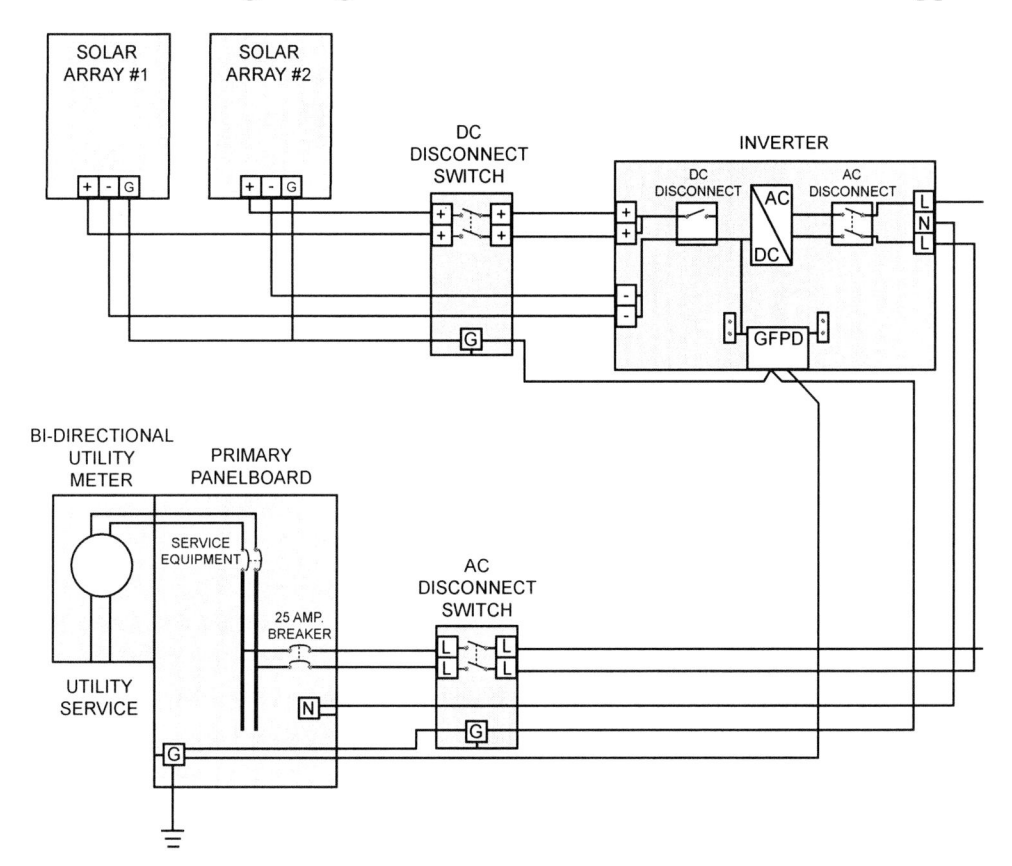

© 2009 Dream Home Consultants, LLC.

Typical Wiring Diagram of a 4kw PV (NEC 690-0)
Figure NEC 690-1

The other grid tie system form adds battery backup for power when grid power is interrupted. The PV still shuts down (in most configurations) when grid power is interrupted, but some power is available depending on the number and size of batteries. The additional cost of batteries and their storage and maintenance makes grid tie battery systems less popular than the regular grid tie system.

The most complex PV system is the hybrid system. This system uses other alternative energy sources in addition to the solar array to provide electricity for immediate use and to charge batteries. These other sources could include a fuel-powered generator, wind turbines, and/or a micro-hyrdo generator (a small water-powered generator). A hybrid system may be stand-alone or grid tie.

Common Photovoltaic System Components

A PV may contain the following components.

Solar modules (one or more) connected together to make an array. Modules may be connected in series or in parallel and arrays of modules may be connected in series or in parallel depending on the DC voltage input requirements of the inverter(s). Connection of modules in series produces a voltage equal to the sum of the voltages of the individual modules, similar to batteries in a flashlight.

Eight Modules in an Array (PNEC 690-1)
Figure NEC 690-2

Mounting brackets and hardware that are compatible with the solar modules and with roof covering on which the modules will be installed. Many roof-mounted modules will sit a few inches above the roof and at the same slope as the roof. Some roof-mounted modules, particularly on low slope roofs, may have supports that tilt the panels and improve the array tilt angle toward the sun.

Mounting Brackets with Bonding Jumpers Attached (PNEC 690-2)
Figure NEC 690-3

Conduit (tubing) and wires that are compatible with the mounting brackets and with the solar modules and that are large enough to handle the anticipated current generated by the PV system.

A DC disconnect switch that disconnects the output from the arrays and isolates the arrays from the rest of the system.

Inverters (one or more) that convert the DC voltage from the arrays into AC voltage. The required DC ground-fault protection device is usually contained in the inverter.

An AC disconnect switch that disconnects the output from the inverter and isolates the inverter from the building wiring and from the utility service.

Inverter and Disconnect Switches (PNEC 690-3)
Figure NEC 690-4

A circuit breaker (fuse) that connects the output from the inverter to the building wiring. This circuit breaker is usually installed in the primary panelboard, but it could be installed at any panelboard in the building wiring.

A tracker supporting one or more modules. A tracker is a motorized mounting device that moves the modules to follow the sun and maximize power output from the module(s).

Batteries to provide power at night and on cloudy days. PV system batteries are designed to last longer under the charging and discharging cycles common with PV systems.

Photovoltaic Component Grounding and Bonding

1. Bond (connect) metal parts of the arrays, mounting brackets, conduit, tubing, switches, cabinets, and inverters both physically and electrically to provide a path to ground for fault current.
2. Connect DC source(s) (such as arrays and batteries) and the AC output (inverters) to grounding electrode(s). Grounding usually occurs at the service equipment. Use grounding electrode wire(s) that are the same size as the service grounding electrode wires.
3. You may install separate grounding electrodes for the AC and DC circuits. If separate grounding electrodes are installed, bond the electrodes together using the same size wire as the service grounding electrode wire.

Photovoltaic Wire Protection

1. Protect individual wires by using conduit or tubing that is appropriate for the environment. Individual wires may run for short distances between modules if the wires are sunlight resistant.
2. You may use exterior cables such as UF and SE for the PV source (array) circuits.
3. Protect wires that run inside the building by using metal conduit or tubing.
4. Do not run PV system wires in the same conduit or tubing as other wires such as lighting and appliance branch circuit wires.
5. Install conduit and tubing as required in Chapter 39.

Photovoltaic Disconnecting Equipment

1. Install a disconnecting switch, circuit breaker, or fuse assembly between the array(s) and the inverter (or load if no inverter), and between any batteries and the inverter, and between the inverter and the AC load (panelboard). The equipment must disconnect only the hot (ungrounded) wires.
2. Make the disconnecting equipment readily accessible and permanently label the equipment to identify its function. The disconnecting equipment need not be readily accessible if is within sight of a grid tie inverter that is roof-mounted or otherwise not readily accessible.
3. Do not connect the output from an inverter to the load side of a GFCI circuit breaker. This type of connection is sometimes called back feeding. Do not back feed a GFCI circuit breaker.
4. Use disconnecting equipment that requires not more than ($\leq$) 6 hand movements in one location to disconnect power from each individual power source, such as the arrays or the batteries.

Labeled DC Disconnecting Switch (PNEC 690-4)
Figure PNEC 690-5

Photovoltaic Batteries

1. Connect batteries together so that they operate at not more than fifty volts.
2. Protect live parts of batteries and wires against accidental contact, dropped tools, and similar dangers.
3. Locate the top of metal racks that support batteries at least (≥) 6 inches above the tops of the battery cases.
4. Use deep cycle batteries that are made for PV systems. Automotive batteries do not work as well in PV systems and could be dangerous if improperly charged.

INDEX

A

Access
- attic 167
- crawl space 71
- electrical panels 436
- furnaces and air handlers 218
- gas valves 293
- handicap 60
- pool and spa barriers 547
- whirlpool bathtub pumps 361

Accessible, electrical, definition 441

Accessory structure
- definition 6
- electrical feeder circuit 453
- electrical grounding 461
- permit requirements 3

Address numbers, display requirements ... 60

Air admittance valve
- definition 353
- installation 428

Air conditioner water
See Condensate disposal

Air conditioner, room, branch
- circuit load 473

Air conditioning
- condenser branch circuit 473
- coolant access caps 234

Air gap
- definition and requirements 370
- reverse osmosis systems 386

Air handler branch circuits 474

Air intake opening
- damper requirement 215
- definition 6
- natural and mechanical 26
- prohibited locations, mechanical 246
- screens 27

Air-entrained concrete
- definition 6
- when required 62

Alarms, smoke and carbon monoxide 52
Aluminum siding installation 131
Ampere (amp) and ampacity, definition .. 441
Anchors, block wall 118
Angle iron, brick support 136
Angle stop valve requirements 381
Antenna, satellite and TV 550

Appliance
- access requirements 218
- definition of, electrical 524
- electrical, disconnecting requirements . 524
- electrical, installation 524
- elevation in garage 223
- flexible electrical cord connection 524
- fuel-burning, prohibited locations 267
- gas, vent not required 297
- physical protection 222

ARC fault circuit requirements 504
Artificial stone installation 133
Atmospheric vacuum breaker 372, 373

Attic
- access openings 167
- appliance access 219
- habitable, definition 6
- habitable, supporting walls 99
- lighting requirements 505
- receptacles 502
- sealing access openings 214
- storage, definition 148
- unventilated attics 165
- ventilation 164
- wire protection 493

Authority Having Jurisdiction liv

B

Backfill, plumbing pipes 350

Backflow prevention
- air gap 370
- boilers 373
- clothes washing machine 361
- definition 369
- dishwashing machine 360
- evaporative coolers 234
- fire sprinklers 373
- general installation requirements 372
- hose bibbs 372
- hydronic piping 261
- irrigation systems 373
- reverse osmosis systems 386
- solar heating 265
- testing of devices 347
- toilet 372

Backspan, definition 80
Backwater valve, requirements 409

Balcony
- cantilevered 81
- support posts and columns 59

Ballasts, fluorescent lights 471
Baluster, definition 6
Bar sink, GFCI receptacles 503
Barometric damper, gas 312

Basement
- ceiling height 29
- escape openings 39
- GFCI receptacles 503
- lighting requirements 505
- receptacles 501
- slabs, concrete strength 62

wall, energy efficiency definition 207
walls, wood attachment 58
Bathroom
   branch circuits 475
   ceiling height 29, 30
   fixtures, clearance to obstructions 30
   GFCI receptacles 502
   light, ventilation, fans 25
   receptacles 501
   safety glazing 31, 34
Bathtub
   lights nearby 520
   receptacles in bathtub 518
   temperature control valve 360
Batten
   definition 6
   panel siding 129
   tile roof 176
Beam, decay protection 57
Bedroom
   AFCI requirements 504
   entry from garage 19
   escape openings 39
Bend, plumbing definition 396
Bidet, installation 362
Block walls .... See Wall: block
Blocking
   definition 7
   floor joists 86
Boathouse, GFCI receptacles 503
Boiler
   backflow prevention 373
   installation requirements 258
Bollard 224
Bolts
   block wall 118
   deck ledger attachment 73
   foundation anchor 65
   treated wood 59
Bonding
   antenna 551
   cable TV 555
   conduit 505
   definition 441
   electrical service 465
   gas pipe 467
   phone and cable 466
   swimming pool 533
   water pipe 467
Bootleg ground 512
Bore
   ceiling joists and rafters 159
   floor joist 89
   stud 104
   trusses 89
Boxes, electrical .... See Electrical Boxes
Braced wall line, definition 7

Bracing, walls 106
Branch circuit
   air conditioning condensers 473
   ampacity reduction for temperature 483
   ampacity reduction for wire proximity 484
   amperage and voltage limits 470
   bathrooms 475
   central heating 474
   circuit breaker sizes 481
   cooking appliances, load calculation 471
   definition 442
   fluorescent lights 471
   kitchen 474
   laundry 474
   lighting and receptacles 475
   motors 471
   multiple outlet circuits 470
   multiwire 470
   NM cable ampacity table 481
   quantity of receptacles on circuit 475
   room air conditioner 473
   space heaters 473
   thirty amp 470
   water heaters 473
   wire ampacity table 481
   wiring methods allowed 489
Branch drain, definition 353
Branch vent
   definition 353
   vent sizing 427
Brick
   air space 135
   flashing 134
   height limits 136
   lintels 138
   roof framing support 137
   steel angle support 136
   wall ties 136
Bridging
   ceiling joist 148
   definition 7
   floor joist 87
Broadband communication system
   requirements 558
Building code, state and city codes liii
Building department liv
Building drain
   definition 353
   using existing pipes 346
Building occupancy, changes to 2
Building official liv
Building permit
   expiration 3
   inspections 4
   replacement roof covering 189
   when required 2

Building sewer
    definition 353
    using existing pipes 346
Built-up roof covering 188
Burial of wires 495
Buttress, definition 7
BW vent 304
Bypass valve, pool heater 260

C

Cabinets, electrical
    installation 510
    selection for environment 435
Cable TV wires
    requirements 554
    near swimming pools 531
Cable, electrical, definition 442
Cantilever floor joists, requirements 81
Carbon monoxide alarms, requirements 54
Carport
    definition 7
    floors, concrete strength 62
Cast-iron pipe joints 388
Caulk, siding installation 130
Ceiling fan
    near tubs and showers 520
    support 524
    support by box 507
    swimming pool, location 528
Ceiling height, minimum 29
Ceiling joist
    bridging 148
    hole size 159
    notch depth 159
    openings in 160
    span tables 150
    support 148
Cement lap siding installation 131
Cement panel siding installation 129
Certificate of occupancy 5
Chase, in block wall 116
Check valve, thermal expansion device
    requirement 374
Chimney
    add or remove appliances, liquid and
        solid-fuel 250
    add or remove gas appliances 299
    additional loads 203
    appliance venting 203
    cleanout 203, 251, 300
    clearance to combustibles 198
    corbelling 201
    cricket (saddle) 170, 196
    definition 7, 196
    factory-built 205
    fireblocking 21, 198

    flue liner 199
    flue size 199
    foundation 203
    gas vent 300
    height above roof 196, 300
    liner sizing, gas 317, 329
    offset 201
    seismic reinforcing 204
    size and shape change 201
    spark arrestor 197
    termination location 26
    used as vent, liquid and solid-fuel 249, 254
Cinder block walls .... *See* Wall: block
Circuit breaker
    connecting multiple wires 438
    identification of circuits 436, 487
    NM cable ampacity table 481
    orientation 514
    service entrance wires 454
    standard sizes 487
    wire ampacity tables 481
Circuit vent 422
Circuit, branch .... *See* Branch circuit
Class 2 power source, installation 539
Cleanout .... *See* Pipe, drain
Cleanout, masonry chimney 203, 251, 300
Clearance to combustible materials ....
    See Combustible materials
Closet bend, plumbing, definition 397
Closet doors, safety glazing 31
Closet flange
    connect to drain fitting 402
    definition 397
    installation 389
    toilet installation 358
Closet storage area, definition 521
Closet, water .... *See* Toilet
Clothes dryer
    exhaust ducts 235
    makeup air 237
Clothes washing machine, air gap 361
Code violations, inspections not a waiver 5
Code, building .... *See* Building code
Collar ties 147
Column, foundation 116
Column, wood, decay protection 59
Combination subflooring, definition 91
Combustible materials
    clearance to chimney 198
    clearance to cooktop 257
    clearance to gas appliances 277
    clearance to insulation 298
    clearance to liquid and solid-fuel
        appliances 220
    clearance to masonry fireplace 194
Combustion air
    air tight construction 296

Index

depletion by other systems 268
ducts 269
fireplace 204
from inside and outside home, gas 275
from inside home, gas 270
from outside home, gas 273
openings 269
prohibited sources 267
Common flue, solid-fuel appliances 250
Common vent
elbow, determining gas vent size 326
gas, definitions 313
liquid and solid-fuel 250
maximum size, gas 328
minimum size, gas 328
offset length limit, gas 326
reduction for manifold, gas 329
vent connector installation 311
Common vent, plumbing vent 417
Common wall
penetrations 19
townhouse 17
two-family dwellings 18
Compacted fill 94
Concrete
air-entrained 62
floors 94
strength 62
vapor retarders 94
Condensate
auxiliary cutoff switch 232
backup disposal systems 231
disposal 231
disposal, Category IV Appliance .. 2733 267
Condenser
branch circuits 473
coolant access caps 234
Conditioned attics 165
Conductor, definition 442
Conduit .... See also Wiring methods
electrical and mechanical continuity 505
gas pipe, installation in 287
installation and support 492
swimming pools 535
wires in 439
Connectors, gas pipe 295
Contractor selection iv
Cooking appliance circuit
branch circuit load calculation 471
feeder circuit load calculation 477
Cooking appliances
commercial 257
commercial, gas 344
Cooktop, clearance to combustibles 257
Coolant access caps 234
Coping
definition 7

on parapet walls 169
Corbel, chimney 201
Corrosion protection
gas pipe 288
plumbing pipe 349
Coupling, plumbing, definition 398
Crawl space
access opening 71
debris removal 72
equipment access 219
GFCI receptacles 503
lighting requirements 505
manufactured homes 542
radon control 544
receptacles 502
used as supply plenum 245
ventilated and unventilated 70
water drainage 72
wood framing in 57
Cricket, chimney 170, 196
Cripple wall, definition and
requirements 105
Cross-connection ...... See Backflow prevention
Crown venting 415
Cut glass, safety glazing 31

D

Damp location, definition 443
Damper
air intake and exhaust systems 215
definition 191
determining gas vent size 315, 324
fireplace, installation 193
gas, barometric 312
liquid and solid-fuel appliances 251
Dampproofing 68
Dead front cover, definition 442
Decay-resistant wood
decks 59
definition 56
support posts and columns 59
Deck
attachment to building 73
support posts and columns 59
Deflection, definition 13
Demolition, permit requirements 2
Direct-vent appliance definition 306
Dishwashing machine
directional fitting 358
installation 360
Disposal
directional fitting 358
dishwasher connection 360
Door
attaching to structure 123

egress door, definition
and requirements 41
exterior, landing requirements 42
fire separation 19
flashing 122
header span table 80
safety glazing 31
self-closing hinges 19
U-factor and SHGC requirements 210
Door bells 539
Downdraft exhaust fans 239
Downspout extensions, best practice 70
Draft hood
determining gas vent size 315
gas, general installation 312
liquid and solid-fuel, location 251
multiple hoods on single appliance 310
Draft inducer, definition 7
Draft regulator, oil appliance, chimney
venting 251
Draftstopping, definition and
requirements 23
Drain pan
auxiliary, air conditioner 232
auxiliary, separation from appliance 233
water heater 366
Drain pipe .... See Pipe, drain
Drainage fixture units description 390
Drainage, surface water 61
Drainage, wall 139
Drains, French 61, 433
Drip leg, gas pipe 291
Drip loops, electrical service 458
Drip pan, water heater 366
Driveway, permit requirements 3
Drop ceilings, fireblocking 21
Drop, electrical service .... See Service drop
Dryer, clothes .... See Clothes dryer
Drywall
adhesive 125
at tubs and showers 127
floating interior angles 124
installation 124
Duct
combustion air, gas 274
combustion air, materials and
installation 269
flexible, installation 240
framed 244
in garage 20
insulation and sealing 215
minimum size 247
prohibited return air locations 246
return locations with fuel-burning
appliances 247
size calculation 226
underground 245

Duplex .... See Two-family dwellings

E

Earthquake design areas 12
Eaves
distance from vents 26
fire separation distance 15
Edge spacing, fasteners, definition 95
Edge support
definition 91
roof sheathing 93
Egress openings 39
Elastomeric gasket, drain pipe joints 4
Elastomeric sealing sleeve 388
Elbow
common vent connector, gas 327
common vent offset, gas 326
vent reduction for elbow 316
Elbow, plumbing .... See Bend
Electric radiant heating
description 226
near swimming pools 538
Electrical boxes
ceiling fan support 507
content limits 507
covers 509
enclosing wire splices 506
floor 507
installation 509
light fixture support 507
opening protection 435
plastic box installation 506
support 510
wire length in box 438
Electrical circuit .... See Branch circuit
Electrical equipment
connection using flexible cords 513
grounding 511
Electrical panel
ampacity rating 487
cabinet and panelboard installation 510
circuit identification 487
clearances to obstructions 436
locations and access 437
multiple wires at terminals 438
overcurrent protection for panel 487
work light nearby 438
Electrical service
accessory structures 453
bonding 465
disconnect, main 448
grounding 459
grounding at accessory structure 461
grounding electrode 463
grounding electrode wire 467
grounding electrode wire protection 454

load calculation formula..........................449
minimum size..449
neutral wire size calculation 480
one service per dwelling..........................448
overcurrent protection 454
service definition......................................445
service drop definition 445
service drop installation 455
service entrance wires..............................458
service entrance wires definition...........445
service equipment definition 445
service mast installation..........................458
service point definition 445
wire size table...453
Electrical switches........................... See Switch
Electrical system, updating to
current code..434
Electrical terms, definitions 441
Electrical wire .... See Wire
Emergency escape openings.........................39
Emergency heating elements, heat pump 227
End nailing, fasteners, definition.................95
Energized, definition 442
Energy efficiency
application of IRC provisions 206
definitions...207
energy certificate requirements 206
insulation installation.............................206
Equipment
access in crawl space 219
access requirements................................218
elevation in garage...................................223
fixed electrical, definition 442
physical protection 222
sizing HVAC...226
Equipment grounding wire .....See Grounding
Evaporative coolers.......................................234
Exhaust
fans, damper requirement 215
fans, termination location.................26, 235
Expansion tank
boiler..259
solar...265
Exposure, definition...8
Exterior receptacles......................................501

F

Face nailing, fasteners, definition 95
Fall protection, windows 122
Fans
bathroom, ventilation................................25
damper requirement 215
kitchen exhaust 238
termination location 26, 235
Fastener
spacing in wood 95

treated wood...59
Faucet, hot/cold direction convention.......362
Feeder circuit
accessory structure grounding 461
accessory structures................................453
load calculation 476
neutral wire size calculation 480
Feeder, electrical, definition........................442
Felt ....See also Water-resistive paper
asphalt shingle underlayment 171
metal shingles...178
slate roof..181
tile roof..175
wood shakes 185
wood shingles...182
Fences
permit requirements....................................3
pool and spa barriers...............................547
Fenestration, definition 208
Fiber cement siding. See Cement panel siding
Fiber-optic cables..558
Fill valve, toilet, antisiphon 372
Fill, soil...94
Fire alarm wiring..539
Fire department connection.......................373
Fire escape openings......................................39
Fire separation
distance to building.................................14
garage..19
projections..15
Fire sprinkler
backflow prevention................................373
effective date..52
installation requirements........................382
Fireblocking
chimney...198
common walls 19
definition..21
fireplace...195
materials and installation 23
required locations 21
Firebox (hearth)
construction..192
definition...191
Fireclay liner 199
Fireplace
clearance to combustibles.......................194
combustion air..204
damper...193
definitions of parts...................................191
factory-built 205
fireblocking...195
foundation 195
gas...203
gas venting into chimney........................297
gaskets on doors 215
hearth (firebox) construction..................192

hearth extension construction 192
lintel installation 193
mantel and trim 194
smoke chamber 193
throat 193
Fire-resistive
common wall and floor 18
wall and ceiling penetrations 19
wall, penetrations 15
wall, separation distance 15
Firestopping .... *See* Fireblocking
Fittings, oil pipe 263
Fittings, plumbing .... *See* Pipe, drain
Fixture drain
definition 353
distance from trap 414
Fixture groups, water supply pipe sizing . 377
Fixture, plumbing
cutoff valve requirements 381
definition 353
general requirements 356
Flashing
asphalt shingles, sidewall 173
asphalt shingles, valley 173
brick and stone veneer 134
cement lap siding installation 131
definition 8
gas vent 302
general installation requirements 139
kick-out 140
metal shingles 179
plumbing pipe 352
plumbing vent 412
roof installation locations 169
slate roof 181
tile roof 177
window and door 122
wood shakes 187
wood shingles 184
Flat roof coverings 187
Flexible cords
connection to appliances 524
general requirements 513
swimming pools 526, 537
underwater lights 535
Flexible duct installation 240
Flexible metal hoses, oil pipes 263
Flight of stairs, definition 43
Float valve, toilet 358
Flood prone areas, plumbing installation 348
Flood-resistant construction 60
Floor
cantilevered 81
deflection under load 13
draftstopping 23
joist
attachment to beams 85

bearing on support 84
blocking 86
bridging 87
hole boring 89
lap at supports 85
notching 88
openings 90
span tables 76
under load-bearing walls 83
slab-on-grade 94
Floor drain, installation 361
Floor electrical boxes 507
Floor furnace 227
Flue liner
fireclay 199
use of space around 249
Flue size, chimney 199
Fluorescent lights, branch circuit loads 471
Flush valve, toilet 358
Flushometer tanks 358
Foam plastic insulation 55
Foam roof covering 188
Footing drains .... *See* Foundation drains
Footings
bolts and straps 65
concrete strength 62
definition 8
manufactured homes 542
steel reinforcing bars 64
thickness and slope 64
width 63
Foundation
bolts and straps 65
dampproofing and waterproofing 68
fireplace 195
height above street 67
insulation 56
walls 68
walls, concrete strength 62
Foundation drains, requirements 68
Fountain, definition 525
Framed walls, height and spacing 99
Framing
balloon, definition 6
platform, definition 9
Freezing, pipe 350
French drains 61, 43
Fresh air openings ...... *See* Air intake opening
Furnace
branch circuits 474
floor, vented 227
wall, vented 229
Furnace and air handler,
access requirements 218
Furnace ducts, flexible 240
Fuse .... *See* Circuit breaker

G

Garage
- appliance elevation 223
- appliance protection 224
- ceilings under habitable rooms 19
- definition 8
- door bracing 111
- fire separation 19
- floors
  - approved materials 20
  - concrete strength 62
- GFCI receptacles 503
- HVAC ducts 20
- receptacles 501

Garage door opener wiring 539
Garage, detached .... *See* Accessory structure
Gas appliance
- add or remove from chimney 299
- category I, II, III, IV definitions 312
- clearance to combustibles 277
- gas pipe connectors 295
- protection, seismic and weather 266
- replacement parts 266
- venting not required 297

Gas cooking appliances, commercial 344
Gas lights 344
Gas logs and log lighters 205
Gas pipe
- above ground 288
- adding new appliances or new pipe 281
- bonding, electrical 279, 467
- burial depth 289
- connection to appliances 295
- corrosion protection 285, 288
- drip tee 291
- extension past walls 289
- grounding 279
- in solid floors 286
- inspection and testing 289
- labeling 281
- leak testing 290
- outlet closure 289
- pipe types 284
- plastic 285
- pressure regulators 294
- prohibited locations and protection 286
- sediment trap 292
- shield plate 287
- size calculation 281
- strain by appliance 225
- support 290
- threads 285
- through foundations 287
- valves 293

Gas pressure regulator 294
Gas valves 293

Gas vent .... *See* Vent, gas
Gasket, elastomeric .... *See* Elastomeric gasket
Gauge
- boiler 258
- gas pressure 290
- oil tank 263

Geotechnical engineer 63
GFCI .... *See* Ground fault circuit interrupt
Girder
- bearing on support 84
- definition 79

Glass block walls .... *See* Wall, glass block
Glass, safety
- in and near doors 31
- in large windows 33
- labeling 31
- near pools, showers, and tubs 34
- near stairs 35

Glazing, definition 8
Glue, drywall 125
Goose neck, electrical service 458
Grade D paper .... *See* Water-resistive paper
Gray water recycling 348
Great Stuff® 55
Green board 127
Greenhouse, glazing 38
Ground fault circuit interrupt
- required circuits 502
- spa and hot tub 538
- swimming pool 536

Ground fault, definition 443
Ground ring electrodes 464
Grounded wire, connection in boxes 439
Grounded, definition 442
Grounding
- antenna 551
- at accessory structure 461
- broadband cables 559
- cable TV 555
- conduit, swimming pool 534
- equipment 511
- equipment grounding wire in feeders .. 476
- equipment grounding wire size 513
- metal boxes 513
- motors, swimming pool 535
- neutral and equipment grounding
  - connections 511
- receptalces 516
- service 459
- solar PV systems 565
- swimming pool 534
- swimming pool lights 535
- switches 515
- wire continuity 513

Grounding electrode
- bonding all electrodes 463
- concrete encased (ufer) 464

definition 443
gas pipe 279
installation 463
metal water pipe 463
Grounding electrode wire
    aluminum 467
    connection to electrode 468
    definition 443
    jumpers 468
    protection 454
Grounding wire, equipment
    connection in boxes 439
    definition 442
Guard, nail ... *See* Nail guard and shield plate
Guardrails .... *See* Guards
Guards
    definition and requirements 50
    safety glazing 35
Gutters
    best practice 70
    expansive or collapsible soils 61
    when required 143
Gypsum board .... *See* Drywall

H

Habitable room
    definition and requirements 24
    dimensions 29
Hallway
    dimensions 43
    receptacles 502
Handicap accessibility 50
Handrails
    ramps 50
    requirements 48
Hardboard lap siding installation 130
Hardboard panel siding installation 129
Hatch, sealing access openings 214
Head lap, definition 8
Header
    bearing on support 84
    definition 79
    joist openings 90
    span table 80
Hearth
    construction 192
    definition 192
Hearth extension, construction 192
Heat pump
    heating elements 227
    return duct size 247
Heat reclaimer, gas vent size 315, 324
Heat, required locations 25
Heater, room, gas vented 230
Heating and cooling equipment sizing 226

Heel-inlet
    drain fitting requirements 401
    plumbing, definition 398
High loop, dishwasher 360
Hills, setback from 66
Hinges, self-closing 19
Holes .... *See* Bore, stud and Floor joist, hole boring
Holes, in thermal envelope 214
Hose bibb
    stop-and-waste valve 381
    vacuum breaker 372
Hot tub .... *See* Swimming pool
Hot tub, safety glazing 34
Hot water heater .... *See* Water heater
House wrap
    stucco best practice 134
    stucco installation 132
Hub and spigot pipes 388
Hub, plumbing pipe, definition 354
Huricane design areas 12
HVAC
    equipment and duct sizing 226
    flexible duct installation 240
    grandfathering 217
    modifications per code 217
    underground ducts 245
Hydromassage tubs .... *See* Swimming pool
Hyronic piping 261

I

Ice dam
    asphalt shingles 172
    metal shingles 178
    roll roof covering 180
    slate roof 181
    wood shakes 185
    wood shingles 183
Ignition source elevation 223
Individual vent 416
Inlet, plumbing fitting .... *See* Pipe, drain
Inspections
    air sealing and insulation 214
    types of 4
    waiver of code violations 5
Insulation
    basement R-value 212
    blown and sprayed-in 213
    ceiling R-value 211
    clearance to heat source 24
    crawl space R-value 213
    ducts 215
    floor R-value 212
    hot water circulation pipes 215
    inspection 214
    installation 206

Index

pipes in mechanical systems 215
plastic foam and sheet 55
requirements table 209
shield from heat source 298
slab R-value 212
wall R-value 211
Intercom wiring 539
Intermediate spacing, fasteners, definition 95
Irrigation system, backflow prevention 373
Island fixture vent 425

J

J channels, aluminum and vinyl siding 131
Jack stud, definition 10
Jacuzzi® .... *See* Whirlpool bathtub
Jalousie, definition 8
Joints, plumbing pipe .... *See* Pipe, drain
Joist hanger
    attach joist to beam 85
    joist openings 91
Joist, ceiling .... *See* Ceiling joist
Joist, floor .... *See* Floor, joist
Junction boxes
    enclosing wire splices 506
    opening protection 435
    swimming pool 537

K

Kick-out flashing 140
King stud, definition 10
Kitchen
    branch circuits 474
    exhaust hood and duct 238
    GFCI receptacles 503
    receptacles, general requirements 498
Knob-and-tube wiring 488
Knockouts, opening protection 435

L

L vent
    as vent connector 309
    height above appliance 304
    oil appliance vent 255
Label, safety glass 31
Labeled
    definition 8
    electrical components 435
Labeling circuit breakers and fuses 436
Ladder, escape opening 40
Landing
    at exterior doors 42
    ramps 50
    stairway 46
    stairway, definition 43

Lateral
    electrical service, definition 445
    gas vent connector, definition 314
    vent reduction for elbow 316
Laundry branch circuits 474
Laundry chutes, fireblocking 21
Laundry receptacles 501, 503
Laundry sink .... *See* Laundry tray
Laundry tray
    definition 354
    standpipe connection 358
Lavatory *See also* Sink and Plumbing fixtures
Leak testing, gas pipes 290
Ledger
    attach joist to beam 85
    deck, attachment to building 73
    definition 8
    supporting floor joists 84
Light bulb energy requirements 216
Lighting branch circuits 475
Lightning arrestor 551
Lights
    closets 521
    definition 518
    exterior doors 505
    fixture wiring 521
    gas lights 344
    in attics, basements, crawl spaces 505
    locations required 504
    near tubs and showers 520
    receptacle inserts 519
    recessed 519
    stairway, locations 28
    support 519
    support by box 507
    swimming pool
        definition 525
        depth 536
        GFCI requirements 536
        grounding 535
        junction boxes 537
        location 528
    switch control 504
    track lights 523
    wet and damp locations 519
Lintel
    block wall 118
    block wall chase 116
    brick 138
    fireplace
        definition 191
        installation 193
Listed
    definition 9
    electrical components 435
Load center .... *See* Electrical panel
Load, structural, definition 13

Locations, damp and wet, definition.........443
Locks, egress door...41
Low voltage wiring..539
Low water cutoff, boiler 259

M

Macerating toilet 408
Maintenance, permit requirements 3
Makeup air
    clothes dryers 237
    kitchen exhaust 239
Manhole cover, backwater valve................409
Manifold, gas, multiple appliances
    using one vent connector........................310
Mantel, clearance to fireplace.....................194
Manual D..226
Manual J..226
Manufactured homes,
    general requirements 541
Manufacturer's instructions, when to use 1
Mass wall, definition.....................................208
Mechanical draft appliance definition 306
Metal hoses for oil piping 263
Metal panel roof covering............................188
Metal shingles..178
Mobile home ....See Manufactured homes
Modified bitumen roof covering................188
Monolithic (slab), definition 9
Mortar
    block wall 118
    glass block walls......................................122
Motor electrical circuits................................471
MP (medium pressure) regulator
    gas shutoff valve 294
    installation..295
Multiwire branch circuit
    grounded wire continuity 439
    requirements..470

N

Nail guard
    electrical cable 490
    gas pipe 287
    gas vent 298
    plumbing pipe...348
Nails
    asphalt shingles.......................................174
    deck ledger attachment............................73
    spacing in wood..95
    tile roof 177
Natural draft vents..249
Neutral load and wire size...........................480
Neutral wire............................. See Grounded
Niche, swimming pool light, definition....525
NM wire installation.....................................490

Nosing, stair tread
    definition..43
    requirements..45
Notch
    ceiling joist and rafter.............................159
    floor joist 88
    stud 104
    trusses..89

O

O ring, toilet 389
Occupancy
    certificate of 5
    changes to 2
Offset
    chimney..201
    common vent length limit, gas 326
    drain pipe...390
    plumbing, definition 354
Ohm's law, definition...................................443
Oil
    fill pipe...263
    pipes..263
    pressure..264
    pumps and valves...................................264
    storage tanks..262
    tank gauge..263
    tank vent...263
Openings
    air intake, mechanical 246
    air intake, natural and mechanical..........26
    floor joists..90
    rafters..160
OSB .... See Wood structural panels
Outlet, definition 443
Outlets..............................See also, Receptacles
Overcurrent protection......See Circuit breaker
Overflow pipe, toilet.....................................358

P

Panel, electrical .... See Electrical panel
Panel, wood, span ratings, definition..........91
Panelboard, electrical, definition 443
Parapet wall
    block construction...................................115
    coping...169
    definition..9
    townhouse 17
Penetrations, fire-resistive walls
    and ceilings..19
Permit, building............... See Building permit
Pet door, fire separation 19
Photovoltaic systems 562
Pier
    block..116
    definition..9

Pigtail 513
Pilaster, definition 9
Pipe, drain .. *See* also Pipe, plumbing, general
    cast-iron pipe joints 388
    cleanout, requirements 403
    closet flange 402
    connection to sewer 348
    connections and fittings 387
    definition 353
    double fittings 401
    drainage fixture units 390
    fittings
        definition 353
        descriptions of 396
        directional, dishwasher and disposal 358
        flow direction change 400
        general requirements 357
    fixture drain, distance from trap 414
    future fixtures 403
    heel and side-inlets 401
    joining different pipes to cast-iron 389
    offset 390
    pipe joints 388
    pipe materials 387
    size of pipe calculation 392
    size reduction 403
    slope 390
Pipe, gas ....*See* Gas pipe
Pipe, hot water and steam 261
Pipe, mechanical systems, insulation 215
Pipe, oil 263
Pipe, plumbing, general
    corrosion protection 349
    flashing exterior penetrations 352
    freezing protection 350
    protection through foundations 349
    puncture protection 348
    support 351
    trenches 350
Pipe, water supply
    bonding 467
    copper tube bending 386
    distribution pipe materials 384
    freezing protection 350
    grounding electrode 463
    insulation 215
    pipe size 377
    plastic pipe joints and fittings 385
    service pipe installation 384
    service pipe materials 383
    soldered joints and fittings 385
Plate, bottom, decay protection 57
Plate, top and bottom, requirements 103
Platform framing, definition 9
Plumbing definitions 353
Plumbing fixtures
    bidet 362
    clearance to obstructions 30
    clothes washing machine 361
    connection to sewer 348
    directional fittings 358
    dishwashing machine installation 360
    drain outlet size 360
    faucet, hot/cold direction convention ...362
    floor drain 361
    general requirements 357
    installation 357
    laundry tray 358
    required fixtures 30
    shower 362
    toilet 358
    waste receptors 358
    whirlpool bathtub 361
Plumbing vent
    air admittance valve 428
    branch vent, sizing 427
    circuit vent 422
    common vent 417
    crown vent 415
    developed length 427
    dry vent, definition 11
    flashing 412
    frost protection 412
    future fixtures 411
    height above fixture 411
    height above roof 412
    individual vent 416
    island fixture vent 425
    prohibited use 413
    sewage pump vents 427
    size of vent 427
    slope and support 410
    termination location 26, 413
    vent definition 356
    waste and vent 423
    waste stack vent 421
    wet vent 418
    when required 410
Plumbing, inspection and testing 346
Plywood ....*See* Wood Structural Panels
Plywood panel siding installation 129
Polarity identification, electrical devices ..440
Polyethylene sheeting
    foundation waterproofing 70
    in unventilated crawl space 71
Polystyrene insulation 55
Pool heaters 260
Pop-up stoppers 357
Porches, concrete strength 62
Positive pressure draft vents 249
Power exhauster 256, 298
Power, electrical, definition 445
Pressure gauge, boiler 258
Pressure regulator, gas 294, 345

Pressure relief valve, boiler 258
Pressure vacuum breaker 372
Pressure, water supply 374
Pressure-reducing valve
    thermal expansion device requirement 374
    when valve is required 374
Property line, fire separation distance 14
Protection
    gas pipe 287
    plumbing pipes 348
    wire in attics 493
PSI, definition 9
PSIG, definition 9
Pump, sewage
    installation 406
    vent 427
Pump, storm water 433
Purlin
    definition 9
    installation 145

Q

Quick-closing valve 375

R

Rabbet joint, definition 9
Raceway, definition 444
Radiant barrier 216
Radiant heating
    installation 226
    near swimming pools 538
Radon control 543
Rafter
    bridging 148
    collar ties 147
    hole size 159
    names of 144
    notch depth 159
    openings in 160
    purlin, installation 145
    span adjustment 158
    span tables 152
    support 148
Railings, safety glazing 35
Ramps, definition and requirements 49
Range
    branch circuit load 471
    clearance to combustibles 257
    definition 471
    feeder circuit load 477
Range exhaust hood .... *See* Kitchen exhaust hood and duct
Receptacle inserts 519
Receptacles
    AFCI requirements 504
    attic 502

    basement 501
    bathroom 501
    branch circuit requirements 474
    contact with terminals 518
    crawl space 502
    current rating 516
    damp locations 517
    definition 444
    exterior 501
    faceplate 517
    garage 501
    GFCI requirements 502
    hallway 502
    height above floor 497
    HVAC service 502
    installation 516
    kitchen
        branch circuits required 474, 498
            countertop spacing 498
            island and peninsula 499
    laundry 501
    location near appliances 500
    quantity on branch circuit 475
    spacing along walls 497
    spas, GFCI requirements 504
    swimming pool, location 527
    tub and shower spaces 518
    wet locations 517
    whirlpool tubs, GFC requirements 504
Receptor, waste
    definition 354
    general requirements 358
Recessed lights
    air leakage requirements 214
    installation 519
Recycle, gray water 348
Reduced pressure backflow preventer
    fire sprinkler 373
    irrigation 373
Refrigerant, condenser access caps 234
Repairs, permit requirements 2
Resistance, electrical, definition 444
Retaining walls
    definition 9
    general requirements 68
    permit requirements 3
Return air duct
    framed 244
    prohibited locations 246
Reverse osmosis systems,
    backflow prevention 386
Riser, stairway
    definition 43
    height 45
Rod and pipe electrodes 464
Roll roof covering 179

Romex®
    ampacity table 481
    installation 490
Roof
    drainage, low slope roofs 169
    flashing 169
    sheathing 93
Roof covering
    asphalt shingles 170
    low slope roofs 187
    metal panel 188
    metal shingles 178
    replacement 189
    roll mineral 179
    slate 180
    tile 174
    wood shake 185
    wood shingles 182
Room air conditioner branch circuit load . 473
Room heater
    gas, unvented 342
    gas, vented 230
Rooms, minimum size and ceiling height .. 29
R-value, definition 208

S

Saddle .... *See* Cricket
Saddle fitting, plumbing, definition 354
Safety glass .... *See* Glass, saftey
Sanitary tee, plumbing, definition 399
Satellite dish installation 550
Satellite TV wires, swimming pools 531
Sauna heater 257
Screens, at intake and exhaust
    terminations 27
Screws
    deck ledger attachment 73
    treated wood 59
Scuppers 169
Scuttle hole .... *See* Attic
Security system wiring 539
Sediment trap, gas pipe 292
Seismic design areas 12
Service .... *See* Electrical service
Service drop, electrical
    clearances 455
    definition 445
    support 458
Service entrance wires, electrical
    definition 445
    insulation 458
    protection 458
Service equipment, electrical, definition ... 445
Service head, electrical service 458
Service lateral, electrical, definition 445
Service mast, electrical service 458

Service point, electrical, definition 445
Service, electrical disconnect 448
Setback from slopes 66
Sewage ejector, installation 406
Sewer pipe .... *See* Pipe, drain
Shakes, wood 185
Sheetrock .... *See* Drywall
Shield plate
    electrical cable 490
    gas pipe 287
    gas vent 298
    plumbing pipe 348
Shingles
    asphalt (fiberglass) 170
    metal 178
    wood 182
Shiplap .... *See* Rabbet
Shower
    ceiling height 30
    clearance to obstructions 30
    compartment size 362
    drywall as wall covering 127
    entry opening size 362
    floor dimensions 364
    floor lining 365
    lights nearby 520
    receptacles in shower 518
    safety glazing 31
    temperature control valve 364
    wall coverings 31
    water supply riser 363
Shroud, gas vent 304
Shutoff valve, boiler 258
Side-inlet, drain fitting 401
Sidewalk, permit requirements 3
Siding
    aluminum and vinyl installation 131
    cement lap installation 131
    cement panel installation 129
    hardboard lap installation 130
    hardboard panel installation 129
    plywood and wood panel installation .. 129
    wood structural panel installation 129
    wood structural panel lap installation .. 130
Sill (sill plate), definition 10
Sill plate .... *See* Plate, bottom
Single-ply roof covering 188
Sink, clearance to obstructions 30
Skylight, definition and requirements 38
Slab-on-grade floor
    concrete strength 62
    general requirements 94
Slate roof covering 180
Sleeper, definition 10
Sliding glass patio doors 31

Slip joint
    access 357
    definition 354
Sloped ceilings, minimum height 29
Slopes, setback from 66
Smoke alarms
    remodeling update requirement 54
    requirements 52
Smoke chamber
    construction 193
    definition 191
Smoke detectors ....*See* Smoke alarms
Smoke shelf, definition 191
Soffits
    fire separation distance 15
    fireblocking 21
Soil
    expansive and collapsible 61, 143
    load bearing capacities 63
Soil, plumbing, definition 354
Solar energy systems, thermal 265
Solar heat gain coefficient (SHGC),
    definition 209
Solar photovoltaic systems 562
Soleplate, definition 10
Spa .... *See* Swimming pool
Span tables
    ceiling joists 150
    floor joists 76
    rafters 152
Span, definition 10
Span, wood panel span ratings 91
Spark arrestor
    definition 10
    general requirements 197
Speakers, underwater 537
Spiral stairs, requirements 47
Splash blocks 62
Splice, floor joist 85
Splice, wires 438
Sprinkler system ....*See* Fire sprinkler
Sprinkler, lawn .... *See* Irrigation system
Stack vent, definition 354
Stack, definition 354
Stained glass, safety glazing 31
Stairway
    definitions of parts 43
    fireblocking 21
    guards 50
    headroom height 44
    landing 46
    landing at door 42
    lights, locations and switching 28
    live loads 48
    riser height 45
    safety glazing 35
    spiral stairs 47

    tread requirements 45
    tread slope 46
    width 44
    winder tread 46
Standpipe
    definition 354
    general requirements 358
Staples, asphalt shingle fasteners 174
Steel reinforcing bars, footings 64
Step, stairway .... *See* Tread
Stone veneer .... *See* Brick
Stone, artificial installation 133
Stop-and-waste valve
    below ground installation 381
    definition 355
Storage shed .... *See* Accessory structure
Storm doors 31
Storm water drains 433
Strap
    foundation anchors 65
    top plate 105
Street address, display requirements 60
Street fitting, plumbing definition 399
Stucco
    curing 133
    installation 132
Stud
    hole boring 104
    jack, definition 10
    king, definition 10
    near ground 58
    notching 104
    spacing 99
Sub-drain .... *See* Building drain
Subfloor, definition 92
Sump pump, storm water pumps 433
Support
    ceiling fans 524
    decks and balconies 59
    gas pipes 290
    joists, headers, girders 84
    plumbing pipes 351
    wire and conduit 490
Surcharge, definition 10
Surface raceway, allowed uses 490
Swale
    definition 10
    drainage near home 61
Swamp coolers .... *See* Evaporative coolers
Sweep, plumbing, definition 399
Swimming pool
    barriers 547
    bonding 533
    communication outlet clearance 531
    cover for heated pools 215
    cover motors 537
    definition of terms 525

Index

electrical circuits near pools and spas ..527
electrical disconnects................................528
entrapment protection 549
fences 547
flexible cords..526
gates 548
GFCI requirements 536
grounding 534
heaters 260
lights, location 528
motors, grounding...................................535
receptacles location.................................527
safety glazing..34
space heaters..538
speakers..537
storable 538
switch, location 527, 528
timer switch 215
wire clearance..531
wiring methods..526
Switch
condensate cutoff....................................232
faceplate 516
grounding 515
height 514
installation 515
lights, locations required 504
orientation..514
stairway lights..28
swimming pool, location 527, 528
switching neutral wires 515
timer switches 515
wet locations..527

T

Tail piece
definition..355
disposal 358
general requirements 357
Tee, plumbing, definition.............................399
Telephone wires, swimming pools.............531
Temperature and pressure relief valve
general requirements 366
pool heaters 260
solar...265
Temperature gauge, boiler..........................258
Tempered glass..................... See Glass, safety
Terminal identification, electrical
devices 440
Termite protection..60
Thermal envelope
definition..207
sealing openings 214
Thermal expansion device,
when required 374
Thermal expansion tank, boiler 259

Thermal performance values table............209
Thermostat wiring 539
Thermostat, setback type requirement 215
Throat
definition..191
fireplace, installation 193
Tile roof covering 174
Timer switches..514
Tire stop..224
Toe nailing, fasteners, definition..................95
Toilet
backflow prevention................................372
clearance to obstructions 30
double sanitary tee 400
flange joint 389
installation requirements.......................358
macerating 408
O ring...389
plumbing fittings 395
Toilet room ventilation 25
Top plate
general requirements 103
notching...105
Townhouse
common wall 17
construction 17
definition..10
Track lights...523
Transformer, low voltage............................539
Trap
definition..355
floor drain traps 431
installation and requirements................431
multiple fixture outlets 432
prohibited types......................................432
Trap arm .... See Fixture drain
Tread
definition..44
stairway, requirements..............................45
Treated wood
cuts and holes..59
decks 59
definition..56
fasteners 59
Trench, plumbing pipes.............................350
Trim, foam plastic..55
Trimmers, joist openings..............................90
Truss, floor notch and bore.........................89
Truss, roof
bracing 162
changes and repairs................................164
connection to wall 164
installation 161
notch and bore..160
Two-family dwellings
electrical service 448
fire separation...18

U

UF wire installation 490
U-factor, definition 209
Ufer grounding electrode 464
Underground ducts 245
Underground gas pipe 289
Underground oil tanks 262
Underground storm drains 433
Underlayment
    asphalt shingles 171
    floors, wood structural panels 93
    metal shingles 178
    roof covering, definition 11
    slate roof 181
    tile roof 175
    wood shakes 185
    wood shingles 182
Underlayment, floors, definition 92
Ungrounded conductor, definition 446
Unventilated attics 165

V

Valley flashing
    asphalt shingles 173
    metal shingles 179
    slate roof 181
    tile roof 176
    wood shakes 187
    wood shingles 184
Valley, roof, definition 11
Valve
    backwater, requirements 409
    bathtub temperature control 360
    gas 293
    shower temperature control 364
    water supply valve requirments ... 381
    water, hot/cold direction convention 362
Vapor retarder
    attic 164
    concrete floors 94
    energy efficiency requirements 214
    in crawl space 71
    in framed walls 95
Vehicle impact protection, appliances 224
Vent
    add or remove appliances, liquid and solid-fuel 250
    draft inducer termination 256
    flashing 255
    height above roof, liquid and solid-fuel 255
    kitchen hood .... *See* Kitchen exhaust hood and duct
    liquid and solid-fuel 255
    masonry chimney used as 196
    power exhauster termination 256
    shrouds 255
    size, liquid and solid-fuel 256
    termination location 26
Vent connector, gas
    common vent connection 310
    connection into chimney 311
    connector larger than flue collar 318
    connector larger that flue 328
    connector smaller than vent 317
    definition and requirements 308
    length and rise definitions 314
    length limit common vent 324
    multiple appliance connectors 329
    single wall connector 311
    vent reduction for elbows 316
Vent connector, liquid and solid-fuel
    connection into fireplace and chimney . 253
    definition and requirements 252
Vent damper, gas 312
Vent stack, definition 356
Vent, clothes dryer .... *See* Clothes dryer exhaust ducts
Vent, common .... *See* Common vent
Vent, gas
    add or remove appliances 299
    altitude derating of appliance input 316
    chimney as vent 300
    chimney liner sizing 317, 329
    connection into chimney 297
    damper 312
    definition 314
    definitions of gas venting terms 312
    direct vent appliance definition 306
    direct vent appliance vent termination ... 307
    distance to sidewall 302
    draft hood 312
    elbow, determining vent size 327
    flashing 302
    flue liner 298, 302
    height above appliance 304
    height above roof 302
    height, definition 314
    insulation shields 298
    labeling in cold climates 298
    length limit, elbow 326
    length limit, offset 326
    mechanical draft appliance definition .. 306
    mechanical draft vent termination 306
    oil and gas appliance venting 301
    outdoor exposure 317
    positive pressure vent 297
    power exhauster 298
    reduction for elbows 316
    roof cap 302
    run along exterior walls 299
    shroud 304

single wall vent
    clearance to combustibles 305
    restrictions 305
    roof termination 305
size table
    common vent, B vent connector 331
    common vent, single wall connector 334
    masonry chimney, B vent connector . 337
    masonry chimney, single wall
        connector 340
    one appliance, B vent connector 320
    one appliance, single wall
        connector 322
size table interpolation and
    extrapolation 318
solid-fuel and gas appliance venting 301
termination location 26
venting not required 297
Vent, plumbing .... *See* Plumbing vent
Ventilation
    attic 164
    crawl space 70
    exhaust fan termination location 235
    kitchen 238
    mechanical air intake openings 246
    radon control 544
    required locations 25
Vinyl siding installation 131
Voltage, definition 446

W

Wall
    block 115
        chase 116
        multiple wythes 119
        parapet wall 115
        support 116
    bracing
        garage door walls 111
        general requirements 106
        large windows and doors 113
        let-in bracing 109
        siding 111
        wood panels 110
    concrete vertical exposed to weather 62
    dampproofing and waterproofing 69
    deflection under load 13
    exterior, concrete strength 62
    fire-resistive, penetrations 19
    fire-resistive, separation distance 15
    glass block 120
    height 199
    mass wall, definition 208
    non-load bearing, interior 103
    parapet 17
    retaining 68

stud spacing 99
top and bottom plates 103
Wall furnaces 229
Wall pocket 57
Wall ties, brick 136
Wall ties, in block walls 119
Waste and vent, plumbing 423
Waste receptor 358
Waste stack vent 421
Waste, plumbing, definition 357
Water circulating systems 215
Water closet .... *See* Toilet
Water control at foundation 62
Water cutoff device, boiler 259
Water distribution pipe 384
Water faucet, hot/cold
    direction convention 362
Water flow rate from fixtures 376
Water from air conditioners ....
    See Condensate disposal
Water heater
    branch circuit load 473
    cutoff valve 381
    drip pan 366
    prohibited locations 260
    relief valve 366
    seismic anchors 223
    thermal expansion device 374
Water meter, thermal expansion
    device requirement 374
Water pressure, minimum and maximum 374
Water service pipe 383
Water supply
    cutoff valves 381
    fixture units, pipe sizing 377
    flow rate 376
    hose bibb stop-and-waste valve 381
    outlets and valves below ground 381
    pipe size 377
    pressure 374
    thermal expansion devices 374
    water-hammer arrestor 375
Water supply pipe .... *See* also,
    Pipe, water supply
Water treatment, reverse osmosis 386
Water-hammer arrestor 375
Waterproofing 68
Water-resistive paper
    general installation requirements 128
    installation behind siding 129
    siding panels 129
    stucco installation 132
Weep holes, brick 135
Weep screed, stucco 133
Wet location
    definition 443
    NM wire installation 490

Wet vent 418
Whirlpool bathtub
    definition 525
    GFCI and bonding 538
    installation and pump access 361
Wind
    design areas 12
    exposure categories 12
Winder tread
    definition 44
    requirements 46
Window
    attaching to structure 123
    bathroom ventilation 25
    bracing walls with large windows 113
    distance from vents 26
    escape openings 39
    fall protection 122
    fire separation in garage 20
    flashing 122
    header span table 80
    replacement window, U-factor 211
    required locations 25
    safety glazing near doors 31
    safety glazing near stairs 35
    safety glazing, large windows 33
    U-factor and SHGC 210
Window air conditioner, branch
    circuit load 473
Window well 40
Wire
    aluminum, splice with copper 438
    ampacity reduction for temperature 483
    ampacity reduction for wire proximity 484
    ampacity table 481
    bending wire 494
    burial depth 495
    colors on insulation 439
    condensation exposure 495
    connection to terminals 438
    continuity, neutral and grounding
        wires 439
    damaged wire 438
    definition 447
    in conduit 439
    length in box 438
    parallel runs 439
    protection in attics and basements 493
    sheathing length in plastic boxes 506
    splices 438, 506
    sun exposure 495
    support 493
Wiring methods
    allowed uses 489
    conduit installation 492
    definition 488
    in HVAC ducts 506
    low voltage 539
    NM and UF wire installation 490
    pool and spa 526
    types 489
Wood
    attached to basement walls 58
    clearance to fireplace 194
    contact with masonry 57
    decay protection 56
    in crawl space 57
    near ground 58
    posts encased in concrete 59
Wood destroying organisms protection 60
Wood nailing
    definitions of terms 95
    nail spacing 95
Wood shakes 185
Wood shingles 182
Wood structural panel siding installation 130
Wood structural panels
    definition of terms 91
    floor sheathing 92
    roof sheathing 93
    subflooring 93
    wall bracing 110
Wood, treated .... *See* Treated wood
Wye, plumbing, definition 399
Wythe
    block wall 119
    definition 11

Y

Yard hydrant
    definition 355
    installation requirements 381

Z

Z-flashing, siding 129
Zoning
    change 2
    effect on building permit lv

2020

REDBOOKS™

Brands, Marketers, Agencies. Search less. Find More.

Powered by

winmo

Content Operations:
Business Manager: Peter Valli
Operations Manager: Himanshu P. Goodluck